THE GLOSSARY OF
NETWORKING

Compiled & Edited By:
Jatin Mishra

Rhythm

Independent
Publication

THE GLOSSARY OF NETWORKING

Compiled & Edited By:
Jatin Mishra

ISBN:9798862271485

9798862271485

Published by:

Rhythm Independent Publication,

Jinkethimmanahalli, Varanasi, Bengaluru, Karnataka, India - 560036

For all types of correspondence, send your mails to the provided address above.

The information presented herein has been collated from a diverse range of sources, comprehensive perspective on the subject matter.

3G Network Architecture

The 3G network architecture refers to the framework and organization of the third-generation mobile telecommunications technology. It defines the various components and their interactions in order to enable seamless communication between mobile devices, base stations, and other network elements. At the core of the 3G network architecture is the Radio Access Network (RAN), which consists of multiple base stations and their associated controllers. These base stations, also known as Node Bs, are responsible for transmitting and receiving data between mobile devices and the network. They are connected to the Core Network (CN) via the Radio Network Controllers (RNCs). The CN is the central part of the 3G network architecture and encompasses various functional entities. The main components of the CN include the Mobile Switching Center (MSC), the Serving GPRS Support Node (SGSN), and the Gateway GPRS Support Node (GGSN). The MSC is responsible for managing voice calls and establishing connections between different mobile devices. The SGSN and GGSN are responsible for managing packet-switched data transfer and interconnecting with external networks. In addition to these key elements, the 3G network architecture also includes various databases that store and manage subscriber information. These databases include the Home Location Register (HLR), the Visitor Location Register (VLR), and the Authentication Center (AuC). The HLR stores permanent user information, the VLR stores temporary user information, and the AuC performs authentication and encryption functions to ensure secure communication. The 3G network architecture supports multiple access technologies, including Universal Mobile Telecommunications System (UMTS) and Code Division Multiple Access (CDMA). UMTS is the most widely used access technology for 3G networks, providing high-speed data transfer and supporting multimedia applications. CDMA, on the other hand, utilizes a spread spectrum technique to allow multiple users to share the same frequency band simultaneously. In summary, the 3G network architecture defines the framework and components required for efficient and reliable communication in third-generation mobile networks. It encompasses the RAN, CN, and various databases, all working together to provide voice and data services to mobile users.

3G (Third Generation)

The term 3G, short for Third Generation, refers to the third generation of wireless communication technology used in mobile networks. It is an evolution of the previous 2G (Second Generation) technology, offering improved data transfer rates, higher capacity, and enhanced multimedia capabilities. 3G networks operate on various radio frequencies and use a technology called Code Division Multiple Access (CDMA) or Wideband Code Division Multiple Access (WCDMA) for data transmission. These networks provide users with faster and more efficient data transfers compared to their 2G counterparts. One of the significant advancements introduced by 3G networks is the ability to support broadband internet access on mobile devices. Users can access the internet, browse websites, and download files at relatively high speeds, making tasks such as email, web browsing, and video streaming more convenient and enjoyable. In addition to internet access, 3G networks also enable various multimedia services. Users can make video calls, participate in video conferences, and enjoy multimedia content such as music and video streaming. These services make use of the increased bandwidth offered by 3G networks, allowing for a richer and more immersive user experience. 3G technology also brought improvements in terms of network capacity and reliability. Compared to 2G networks, which had limitations in handling a high volume of users simultaneously, 3G networks could accommodate more users and offer more stable connections. This contributed to a more seamless communication experience and reduced congestion on the network. Furthermore, 3G networks played a significant role in the development and adoption of mobile applications. As data transfer rates increased, developers could create more sophisticated and feature-rich applications that utilized the capabilities of mobile devices to their full potential. This

1

led to the rapid growth of the mobile app industry and opened up new opportunities for businesses and individuals alike. In conclusion, 3G (Third Generation) technology revolutionized the mobile communication industry by significantly improving data transfer rates, enabling broadband internet access, supporting multimedia services, increasing network capacity, and fostering the growth of the mobile app ecosystem.

3G Vs. 4G Vs. 5G

3G, 4G, and 5G are different generations of wireless communication technologies used in mobile networks. These technologies provide faster and more reliable data transfer rates, allowing users to access the internet, make phone calls, and transmit other data wirelessly. 3G, or third-generation, introduced the concept of mobile broadband, enabling internet access on mobile devices at speeds up to 2 Mbps. It improved on the previous 2G technology by offering faster data rates, enhanced multimedia capabilities, and improved security features. With 3G, users were able to browse the internet, send and receive emails, and stream videos on their mobile devices. However, 3G had limitations in terms of coverage and capacity, leading to dropped calls and slower data speeds in crowded areas. 4G, or fourth-generation, was a significant advancement over 3G. It provided faster and more reliable internet connections, with download speeds up to 100 Mbps. 4G networks were designed to handle increasing data demands and enable seamless communication between devices. With 4G, users experienced improved call quality, reduced latency, and faster browsing and downloading speeds. Additionally, 4G brought enhanced multimedia capabilities, such as high-definition video streaming and online gaming. Overall, 4G provided a more efficient and seamless mobile experience compared to its predecessor. 5G, or fifth-generation, is the latest and most advanced wireless technology to date. It promises even faster data transfer rates, lower latency, and the ability to connect a massive number of devices simultaneously. With speeds up to 10 Gbps, 5G aims to revolutionize various industries, including healthcare, autonomous vehicles, and Internet of Things (IoT) applications. It will enable real-time communication and interconnectivity among devices, leading to advancements in areas like remote surgery, smart cities, and virtual reality. 5G networks will also have improved reliability and lower energy consumption, providing a more sustainable and connected future.

3GPP (3rd Generation Partnership Project)

The 3rd Generation Partnership Project (3GPP) is a global collaboration between telecommunications standards organizations that aims to develop a unified and standardized framework for third-generation (3G) mobile communications systems. It was established in December 1998 and has since become a crucial platform for coordinating the development and evolution of mobile communication technologies. 3GPP brings together various telecommunications standards development organizations, including regional standards bodies such as the European Telecommunications Standards Institute (ETSI), the Association of Radio Industries and Businesses (ARIB) in Japan, the Telecommunication Technology Committee (TTC) in Japan, and the China Communications Standards Association (CCSA) in China. Through this collaboration, 3GPP ensures that different regional and technological perspectives are taken into account during the development of mobile communication standards. The main objective of 3GPP is to define a set of technical specifications for mobile communication systems that enable global interoperability and compatibility. This includes specifying the radio access network (RAN) architecture, protocols, interfaces, and procedures for 3G and beyond systems, such as Long Term Evolution (LTE) and 5G. By providing a standardized framework, 3GPP facilitates the deployment of mobile communication networks that are capable of supporting a wide range of services and applications. One of the key features of 3GPP is its commitment to backward compatibility, which ensures that new generations of mobile communication technologies can coexist with older ones. This allows network operators to seamlessly upgrade their infrastructure and devices without causing disruptions to existing services. Additionally, 3GPP actively seeks input and feedback from various stakeholders, including network operators, device manufacturers, and service providers, to ensure that the standards meet their requirements and enable innovation in the industry. In summary, 3GPP is a collaborative project that brings together global telecommunications standards organizations to develop standardized specifications for 3G and beyond mobile communication systems. It plays a crucial role in enabling interoperability, compatibility, and backward compatibility, while also fostering innovation in the mobile communication industry.

3GPP LTE Standard

The 3rd Generation Partnership Project (3GPP) Long-Term Evolution (LTE) standard is a global standard for wireless communication networks, specifically designed for providing high-speed data transfer capabilities for mobile devices. It is used by mobile network operators worldwide to deliver faster and more reliable internet connectivity to their customers. LTE is the latest generation of wireless technology that surpasses its predecessors, such as 2G and 3G, in terms of data transfer speed, network capacity, and overall efficiency. The 3GPP LTE standard specifies a set of protocols and techniques that enable mobile devices to connect to the internet and communicate with each other seamlessly. In practical terms, the 3GPP LTE standard enables users to experience incredibly fast download and upload speeds on their mobile devices, allowing for smooth streaming of high-definition videos, quick file downloads, and faster web browsing. It also provides improved network capacity, allowing for more concurrent connections and better overall performance during periods of high network traffic. The 3GPP LTE standard achieves these advancements through various technical features, such as the use of Orthogonal Frequency Division Multiple Access (OFDMA) for efficient spectrum utilization, Multiple Input Multiple Output (MIMO) antenna systems for enhanced signal strength and coverage, and advanced modulation techniques for higher data transmission rates. Moreover, the 3GPP LTE standard includes support for Voice over LTE (VoLTE), which enables high-quality voice calls over the LTE network, as well as other services like video calling and messaging. It also encompasses security features to protect user data and privacy, ensuring secure and reliable communication over the network. Overall, the 3GPP LTE standard revolutionizes mobile networking by providing faster, more efficient, and reliable wireless communication for mobile devices. Its widespread adoption by mobile network operators around the world has led to the rapid expansion of LTE coverage, enabling users to enjoy high-speed internet connectivity wherever they go.

3GPP Release Versions Overview

3GPP is an international telecommunications organization responsible for defining standards for mobile communications systems. As technology evolves and new advancements are made, 3GPP periodically releases new versions of its specifications to keep up with the changing needs of the industry. These releases are collectively known as 3GPP Release Versions. Each release version brings about improvements and enhancements to the existing mobile network infrastructure, enabling new features and capabilities for mobile devices and networks. These releases typically involve updates to various aspects of the network, including radio access technology, core network architecture, protocols, and services.

3GPP Release Versions

3GPP (3rd Generation Partnership Project) is a collaboration between groups of telecommunications standards organizations that works on the development and maintenance of various mobile communication standards. One significant aspect of the 3GPP's work is the release versions that are periodically introduced to bring about advancements and improvements in mobile network technologies. Release versions in the context of networking refer to specific updates and additions to the existing mobile communication standards, which aim to enhance the functionality, performance, and capabilities of the networks. These releases are developed through a collaborative effort among multiple organizations and are based on extensive research, standardization, and testing. Each release version consists of a set of specifications that define the technical details and requirements for the implementation of new features and functionalities in mobile networks. These specifications cover a wide range of areas, including radio access technologies, core network architecture, protocols, security mechanisms, and services. The release versions follow a sequential numbering system, with each subsequent release building upon the foundation laid by the previous ones. The main objective of introducing new releases is to address the emerging needs and challenges faced by the mobile communication industry and to meet the ever-increasing demands for higher data rates, improved quality of service, and support for new applications and services. By introducing new release versions, 3GPP enables network operators and equipment manufacturers to upgrade their infrastructure and offer advanced services to their customers. It also facilitates interoperability between different network elements and ensures seamless connectivity across various mobile networks. In addition to the technical specifications, each release version also includes a set of testing and certification procedures to ensure compliance and conformance to the defined standards. This helps in promoting interoperability, reliability, and compatibility among different network equipment and ensures a consistent user experience across different devices and networks.

3GPP Standards Evolution

3GPP (3rd Generation Partnership Project) Standards Evolution refers to the ongoing development and enhancement of telecommunications standards for mobile networks. It is a collaboration between various telecommunications standards bodies, including the European Telecommunications Standards Institute (ETSI), the Association of Radio Industries and Businesses (ARIB) of Japan, the Alliance for Telecommunications Industry Solutions (ATIS) of the United States, the Telecommunications Technology Association (TTA) of South Korea, and the China Communications Standards Association (CCSA). The purpose of 3GPP Standards Evolution is to continually evolve and improve the technology and functionality of mobile networks to meet the ever-increasing demands of users and enable new services and applications. This evolution is driven by advancements in technology, changing market trends, and feedback from various stakeholders in the telecommunications industry. The evolution of 3GPP standards is carried out through a series of releases, with each release introducing new features, capabilities, and improvements to the existing standards. These releases are developed through a standardized process that involves multiple stages, including study and work item identification, technical specification development, approval, and finalization. Each release of 3GPP standards encompasses a wide range of areas, including radio access network (RAN) technologies, core network architecture, protocols, security, and performance requirements. The evolution of these standards enables the deployment of new technologies, such as 5G, and the continued optimization of existing ones to deliver better network performance, efficiency, and reliability. 3GPP Standards Evolution plays a crucial role in facilitating global interoperability and harmonization of mobile networks. It ensures that network equipment and devices from different vendors and operators can seamlessly work together, regardless of the geographical location. This interoperability fosters competition, drives innovation, and enables roaming services, allowing users to stay connected even when traveling abroad. In summary, 3GPP Standards Evolution is a continuous process of developing and refining telecommunications standards for mobile networks. It enables the adoption of new technologies, improves network performance, and ensures interoperability among different stakeholders in the telecommunications industry.

3GPP Standards

3GPP standards refer to the technical specifications developed by the Third Generation Partnership Project (3GPP) for mobile communication networks. 3GPP is a collaboration between various telecommunications standards organizations around the world, including the European Telecommunications Standards Institute (ETSI), Association of Radio Industries and Businesses (ARIB) in Japan, Telecommunications Technology Association (TTA) in Korea, and the Alliance for Telecommunications Industry Solutions (ATIS) in the United States. These standards are crucial in providing a common framework for the design and implementation of mobile communication networks, ensuring compatibility and interoperability across different vendors and operators. They define the protocols, interfaces, and procedures that enable mobile devices, such as smartphones and tablets, to connect to and communicate with cellular networks. Additionally, 3GPP standards cover a wide range of network technologies, including GSM, GPRS, EDGE, UMTS, LTE, and 5G.

4G (Fourth Generation)

4G (Fourth Generation) refers to a generation of wireless network technology that succeeded the third generation (3G) networks. It represents a significant leap in terms of speed, capacity, and overall performance. With 4G networks, users can experience faster data transfer rates, improved voice and video quality, and enhanced multimedia capabilities compared to previous generations. One of the key features of 4G is its ability to deliver high-speed internet connectivity, enabling users to download and upload data at much faster rates than before. This makes it possible to stream high-quality videos, download large files, and engage in real-time online activities without significant buffering or latency issues. Additionally, 4G networks support more simultaneous connections, allowing multiple devices to connect to the network and access high-speed internet simultaneously. Another important aspect of 4G networks is their ability to provide improved voice quality. Thanks to advancements in voice over internet protocol (VoIP) technology, 4G networks offer clearer and more reliable voice calls compared to previous generations. This enables users to have better quality conversations, particularly in noisy environments or areas with weak signal coverage. Furthermore, 4G networks have enhanced capabilities for multimedia applications. They enable high-definition video streaming and video conferencing, ensuring a smoother and more immersive experience for users. Additionally, the increased bandwidth and speed provided by 4G networks support the growing demand for data-intensive applications such as online gaming, virtual reality, and augmented reality. Overall, 4G networks have revolutionized the way we connect and communicate, offering faster speeds, improved voice quality, and enhanced multimedia capabilities. They have paved the way for mobile-centric lifestyles, enabling users to stay connected and access high-speed internet on the go. As technology continues to evolve, 4G networks serve as a foundation for future advancements, laying the groundwork for the development and deployment of newer network generations such as 5G.

4G LTE Technology

4G LTE (Fourth Generation Long Term Evolution) is a networking technology that provides high-speed and reliable wireless communication for mobile devices and data terminals. It is a digital cellular network technology that offers significant improvements in terms of speed, capacity, and performance compared to its predecessors. 4G LTE provides faster data transmission rates and lower latency compared to previous generations of mobile network technologies. It enables users to download and upload large files, stream high-definition videos, and engage in real-time online activities with minimal delays or interruption. This technology offers a more seamless and responsive user experience in various applications, such as video conferencing, online gaming, and media streaming. One of the key features of 4G LTE is its use of advanced radio access technologies, such as Orthogonal Frequency Division Multiplexing (OFDM) and Multiple Input Multiple Output (MIMO). OFDM divides the available frequency spectrum into multiple smaller subcarriers, allowing for efficient data transmission and improved signal quality. MIMO utilizes multiple antennas to transmit and receive data simultaneously, enhancing signal capacity and increasing network performance. 4G LTE also incorporates advanced network infrastructure and protocols, including IP Multimedia Subsystem (IMS), which enables seamless integration of voice, video, and data services over the IP-based network. This technology facilitates the convergence of various communication services, enabling operators to offer a wide range of innovative multimedia applications and services. Additionally, 4G LTE supports IP-based transport, allowing for seamless integration with the existing internet infrastructure. With its high data rates and low latency, 4G LTE serves as the foundation for various emerging technologies, such as Internet of Things (IoT), connected cars, and smart cities. It provides the necessary bandwidth and reliability to support the increasing number of connected devices and applications in today's digital age.

5G (Fifth Generation)

5G (Fifth Generation) is the newest standard of mobile network technology, designed to provide faster and more reliable communication compared to previous generations. It represents a significant advancement in wireless technology, offering an array of improvements and new capabilities that are set to revolutionize the way we connect and interact with devices. One of the key features of 5G is its ability to transmit data at extremely high speeds. With peak speeds reaching up to 10 gigabits per second, 5G enables lightning-fast downloads, seamless streaming of high-definition content, and real-time responsiveness. This opens up possibilities for a wide range of applications, including virtual reality, augmented reality, live streaming, and instant access to cloud-based services. 5G also boasts significantly lower latency compared to its predecessors. Latency refers to the delay in data transmission, and with 5G, it is expected to be as low as 1 millisecond. This near-instantaneous responsiveness is essential for applications that require real-time interaction, such as autonomous vehicles, remote surgeries, and immersive gaming experiences. Another major advantage of 5G is its ability to support a massive number of connected devices per area. While 4G networks can handle around 2,000 devices per square kilometer, 5G can support up to one million devices in the same area. This increased capacity paves the way for the Internet of Things (IoT) to flourish, allowing for seamless connectivity between various smart devices, smart cities, and smart infrastructure. Furthermore, 5G introduces network slicing, an innovative concept that enables the division of a single physical network infrastructure into multiple virtual networks. Each network slice can be tailored to specific requirements in terms of speed, capacity, and latency, allowing for efficient allocation of network resources and meeting the diverse needs of different applications.

5G NR (New Radio)

5G NR (New Radio) is a term used to describe the latest standard of wireless communication technology, specifically in the context of networking. It is the next generation of mobile network technology, designed to provide faster and more reliable connectivity for a wide range of devices and applications. 5G NR is an evolution of previous generations of wireless networks, such as 3G and 4G LTE. It introduces a range of new features and capabilities that aim to address the increasing demands for higher data speeds, lower latency, and improved network efficiency.

ARP (Address Resolution Protocol)

The Address Resolution Protocol (ARP) is a protocol used in computer networks to map an IP address to a Physical (MAC) address. It is primarily used in IPv4 networks, as IPv6 networks use a different protocol called Neighbor Discovery Protocol (NDP) for the same purpose. When a device wants to send data to another device on a network, it needs to know the MAC address of the destination device. However, devices communicate with each other using IP addresses. This is where ARP comes into play. The ARP protocol works in a simple two-step process. First, when a device wants to find the MAC address for a given IP address, it broadcasts an ARP request on the network. This request includes its own IP and MAC addresses and the IP address it wants to resolve. The request is broadcasted to all devices on the network. When a device receives the ARP request, it checks if the requested IP address matches its own. If it does, the device replies to the sender with its MAC address. This reply is called an ARP reply and is sent as a unicast message directly to the sender's MAC address. Once the device that initiated the ARP request receives the reply, it stores the MAC address in its ARP table. The ARP table is a cache that keeps track of IP-MAC address mappings for future reference. This allows the device to directly communicate with the destination device using its MAC address instead of having to send an ARP request every time. ARP is essential for the proper functioning of computer networks, as it enables devices to communicate with each other at the network layer by mapping IP addresses to MAC addresses. By maintaining an ARP table, devices can optimize network performance by reducing the need for frequent ARP requests.

ARP Poisoning

ARP poisoning, also known as ARP spoofing or ARP cache poisoning, is a type of network attack where an attacker sends falsified Address Resolution Protocol (ARP) messages over a local area network (LAN). ARP is a protocol used by computers to map an IP address to a physical or MAC address on a network. ARP poisoning attacks involve manipulating the ARP tables of targeted devices, leading them to send network traffic to the attacker's device instead of the intended destination. In a typical network, each device maintains an ARP table that maps IP addresses to MAC addresses. This table is used to determine the MAC address of a device when given its IP address. When a device wants to send data to another device on the network, it checks its ARP table and sends the data to the corresponding MAC address. ARP poisoning attacks exploit the inherent trust in ARP messages. During an attack, the attacker sends forged ARP messages to the targeted devices, claiming to be the owner of a particular IP address. The attacker's ARP messages contain their MAC address instead of the legitimate MAC address associated with that IP address. Once the targeted devices receive these forged ARP messages, they update their ARP tables with the spoofed MAC address. As a result, whenever the victim devices want to send data to the IP address associated with the attacker's ARP messages, they mistakenly send the data to the attacker's MAC address instead of the intended device. ARP poisoning attacks can have serious consequences. The attacker can intercept and manipulate network traffic, eavesdrop on sensitive information, or launch further attacks by redirecting or modifying the data sent by the victim devices. This type of attack is often used to perform Man-in-the-Middle (MitM) attacks, where the attacker secretly relays and alters communication between two parties without their knowledge.

6

ARP Spoofing

ARP Spoofing ARP Spoofing, also known as ARP poisoning or ARP cache poisoning, is a malicious technique used in computer networks to intercept and manipulate the Address Resolution Protocol (ARP) messages, allowing an attacker to redirect network traffic, steal sensitive information, or launch other types of cyber attacks. ARP is a protocol used in local area networks (LANs) to map an IP address to a physical MAC address. When a device wants to communicate with another device on the same network, it sends an ARP request to obtain the MAC address of the desired IP address. The ARP spoofing attack involves sending fake ARP replies, tricking the victim devices into associating their IP addresses with the attacker's MAC address instead of the legitimate MAC address. By successfully executing an ARP spoofing attack, an attacker can effectively become a "man-in-the-middle," intercepting and inspecting network traffic between two legitimate parties. This allows the attacker to eavesdrop on the communication, capture sensitive data such as passwords or credit card information, modify or inject new data into the communication, or even launch further attacks, such as denial-of-service attacks. ARP spoofing attacks can be particularly effective in switched LAN environments where devices are not configured to protect against such attacks. In these environments, the attacker can use ARP spoofing to redirect traffic intended for one device to another, allowing them to monitor and manipulate the communication without being detected. To protect against ARP spoofing attacks, network administrators can implement various security measures. These may include using ARP spoofing detection tools, enabling port security on network switches, implementing secure ARP protocol variants like ARP Secure, or using secure communication protocols such as SSL/TLS to encrypt sensitive data. In conclusion, ARP spoofing is a malicious technique used to intercept and manipulate ARP messages in computer networks. It allows attackers to gain unauthorized access to network traffic, steal sensitive information, or launch additional attacks. Organizations should implement proper security measures to protect against ARP spoofing and ensure the confidentiality and integrity of their network communications.

Access Control List (ACL)

An Access Control List (ACL) is a set of rules defined by a network administrator that determines what traffic is allowed to enter or leave a network based on a variety of factors. These factors can include the source and destination IP addresses, ports, protocols, and other characteristics of network traffic. ACLs are commonly used in network security to control access to resources and protect against unauthorized access or malicious activity. They are typically implemented in networking devices such as routers, switches, and firewalls, although they can also be applied at the host level on servers or other network endpoints.

Access Control

Access Control is a mechanism used in computer networks to regulate and manage the rights and permissions assigned to users, processes, or systems for accessing resources. It is a vital component of network security, ensuring that only authorized entities can gain access to sensitive information or perform specific actions within a network. Access Control primarily involves the establishment and enforcement of policies and rules that govern access privileges. These policies are implemented through various techniques and technologies, such as authentication, authorization, and auditing. Authentication is the process of verifying the identity of an entity attempting to access a network resource. It typically involves the use of credentials, such as usernames and passwords, biometrics, digital certificates, or token-based systems. By confirming the identity of users or systems, authentication helps ensure that only authorized personnel gain access to network resources. Authorization, on the other hand, deals with granting or denying specific privileges or rights to authenticated users or entities. It involves the use of access control lists (ACLs) or other methods to define what resources an entity can access and what actions it can perform. Authorization ensures that users have appropriate permissions based on their roles, responsibilities, and the security policies in place. Auditing plays a crucial role in access control by providing a means to monitor and track access attempts and activities within a network. It involves the generation and analysis of audit logs, which record important security-related events, such as successful or failed authentication attempts, changes to access permissions, and suspicious activities. Auditing helps detect potential security breaches, identify policy violations, and gather evidence for investigations. By implementing an effective access control system, organizations can minimize the risk of unauthorized access,

7

data breaches, and other security incidents. It helps maintain the confidentiality, integrity, and availability of network resources, ensuring that sensitive information remains secure and only accessible to authorized individuals or systems. Access Control is essential in protecting the valuable assets of a network and plays a critical role in overall network security.

Access Point Configuration

An access point configuration refers to the process of setting up and configuring a networking device known as an access point, which is used to connect wireless devices to a wired network. This configuration involves a series of steps that ensure the access point is properly functioning and secured, providing wireless connectivity to authorized users. Firstly, the access point needs to be physically installed in a suitable location, ideally in a central area within the network coverage range. Once installed, it requires a power source and is connected to the wired network through an Ethernet cable. The next step is to access the access point's configuration interface, which can usually be done through a web browser. This interface allows the administrator to make various settings and adjustments to customize the access point to the network's requirements. One of the primary configuration settings is the wireless network name, also known as the Service Set Identifier (SSID). The SSID is the name that appears when users search for available wireless networks. It should be unique and easily identifiable to avoid confusion. Additionally, security settings such as encryption and authentication methods need to be defined to ensure the network remains protected from unauthorized access. The access point configuration also involves setting the wireless channel, which determines the frequency at which the access point operates. Proper channel selection is crucial to avoid interference from other nearby wireless networks and devices. Another important aspect of access point configuration is managing the IP addressing. The access point should have a unique IP address assigned to it within the network, which allows it to communicate with other devices and access network resources. Lastly, the administrator should configure additional settings such as Quality of Service (QoS) to prioritize specific types of traffic, enable/disable certain features like guest access, and set up any necessary network protocols or firewall rules.

Access Point Installation

An access point installation is the process of setting up a device that allows wireless communication between devices on a local area network (LAN) and the internet. It acts as a central connection point for wireless devices, enabling them to connect to the network and access resources or services. During an access point installation, the location and configuration of the access point are carefully planned to ensure optimal coverage and performance. The access point is connected to the existing network infrastructure, such as a router or switch, using Ethernet cables. It is usually placed in a central location, away from physical obstructions, to provide maximum coverage to all devices within its range. The installation process involves several steps. Firstly, the installation site is surveyed to determine the best location for the access point. Factors such as signal strength, interference, and coverage area are taken into consideration. Once the location is determined, the access point is mounted securely on the wall or ceiling, using appropriate hardware. After the physical installation, the access point needs to be configured. This involves connecting to the access point using a computer or mobile device and accessing its web-based interface. The user will need to provide specific network settings, such as the network name (SSID) and security settings (WPA2, for example). These settings ensure that only authorized devices can connect to the network. After the access point is configured, it needs to be connected to the network infrastructure. This is done by connecting an Ethernet cable from the access point to a network switch or router. The access point will then broadcast the wireless network, allowing wireless devices to connect to it. An access point installation is crucial in establishing a reliable and secure wireless network. It provides a convenient and flexible way for devices to connect to the network without the need for physical cables. Proper installation and configuration ensure that the wireless network operates smoothly and efficiently, meeting the needs of the users.

Access Point Placement Strategies

Access Point Placement Strategies are methodologies and considerations used to determine the optimal positioning and deployment of access points in a network infrastructure. Access points are devices used to enable wireless communication by connecting wireless devices to a wired

8

network. The effectiveness and reliability of wireless network connectivity heavily depend on the placement and configuration of these access points. The goal of access point placement strategies is to provide seamless and consistent wireless coverage, ensuring that all devices within the network can connect and communicate effectively. Proper access point placement helps eliminate coverage gaps, reduce interference, and improve overall network performance.

Access Point Placement

Access Point Placement refers to the strategic positioning of access points in a network infrastructure to ensure optimal coverage and performance. An access point is a device that enables wireless devices to connect to a wired network. To provide seamless connectivity, access points must be strategically placed to maximize signal strength, minimize interference, and cater to the specific size and layout of the area to be covered. The placement of access points plays a crucial role in the overall network performance. It requires careful consideration of factors such as signal propagation, signal strength, and potential sources of interference. The goal is to achieve optimal coverage and ensure a reliable and high-speed connection for all wireless devices. When determining the placement of access points, several factors should be taken into account. The physical layout of the area, including walls, floors, and other obstacles, must be considered to ensure that the signal can penetrate through them effectively. The density of users and devices in a particular area also influences the number and positioning of access points. Signal strength is another critical factor to consider when placing access points. Access points should be positioned in a way that avoids signal degradation and interference. Thick walls, metal barriers, and other similar obstructions can weaken the signal, so access points should be positioned to minimize their impact. Furthermore, access points should be placed away from potential sources of interference, such as other electronic devices or wireless signals on the same frequency. Additionally, access point placement should aim for uniform coverage throughout the designated area. By strategically placing access points, network administrators can ensure that there are no dead zones or areas with weak connectivity. This is particularly important in larger areas where signal strength may vary, such as office buildings, campuses, or outdoor spaces. In conclusion, access point placement is a crucial aspect of network design and implementation. It involves carefully considering factors such as signal propagation, signal strength, and potential sources of interference to ensure optimal coverage and performance. By strategically placing access points, network administrators can provide reliable and efficient wireless connectivity for all users and devices within the network.

Access Point Security Best Practices

An access point is a device that enables wireless devices such as laptops, smartphones, and tablets to connect to a wired network. It acts as a bridge between the wireless and wired networks, allowing wireless devices to access resources and services available on the wired network. However, access points are vulnerable to security threats, and it is essential to implement best practices to secure them. Access point security best practices involve several measures to protect the access point from unauthorized access, data breaches, and other security risks. These practices include: 1. Change Default Settings: The default settings of an access point are often well-known and can be exploited by attackers. It is crucial to change the default administrator username and password to a strong, unique combination. Additionally, change the default SSID (network name) to something unrelated to the organization or location to avoid targeted attacks. 2. Enable Encryption: Encrypting wireless communications is essential to prevent eavesdropping and unauthorized access to network traffic. Implementing WPA2 (Wi-Fi Protected Access 2) or WPA3 encryption protocols ensures that data transmitted between devices and the access point is secure. 3. Use Strong Authentication: Implementing strong authentication methods, such as using WPA2-Enterprise with 802.1X authentication, ensures that only authorized devices can connect to the access point. This prevents unauthorized users from accessing the network and helps to mitigate the risk of insider attacks. 4. Disable Unnecessary Services: Access points often come with various services enabled by default that may not be necessary for the organization's requirements. It is essential to disable these unused services to minimize the attack surface and reduce the risk of exploitation. 5. Regularly Update Firmware: Access point manufacturers frequently release firmware updates that address security vulnerabilities and improve performance. It is crucial to regularly update the access point's firmware to ensure it has the latest security patches. Implementing these access point security best practices helps to protect the organization's network from unauthorized access and potential data breaches. By securing access points, organizations can ensure the confidentiality, integrity, and availability of their network resources, enhancing overall network security.

Access Point Security

An Access Point (AP) is a networking device that serves as a central point for wireless communication, allowing wireless devices such as laptops, smartphones, and tablets to connect to a wired network. Access Point Security refers to the measures taken to protect the access point and the wireless network from unauthorized access and potential security threats. Access Point Security involves various methods and protocols to ensure the privacy, confidentiality, and integrity of the wireless network. One of the primary security measures is the implementation of authentication and encryption protocols. Authentication ensures that only authorized devices can connect to the network, while encryption provides a secure means of transmitting data over the wireless network, making it difficult for potential attackers to intercept and decipher the information.

Access Point

An Access Point (AP) is a device that serves as a central point in a wireless network through which Wi-Fi capable devices can connect and communicate with each other. It acts as a bridge between wireless devices and a wired network, enabling wireless devices to access resources and services available on the network. The primary function of an AP is to provide a wireless signal coverage area and facilitate the exchange of data packets between connected devices. It operates within the radio frequency spectrum and uses antennas to transmit and receive wireless signals. When a Wi-Fi device, such as a laptop or smartphone, wants to connect to a network, it searches for nearby access points that are broadcasting their Service Set Identifier (SSID). Access points are commonly used in both home and business environments to create wireless networks. In homes, a single access point may be sufficient to provide coverage throughout the entire house. However, in larger areas or corporate settings, multiple access points may be deployed to ensure seamless connectivity and extend the wireless range. One of the key features of an access point is its ability to support multiple wireless devices simultaneously. It achieves this by dividing the available bandwidth into multiple channels, allowing several devices to communicate without interference. Access points also implement security measures, such as encryption and authentication, to protect the network from unauthorized access. In addition to connecting wireless devices to a wired network, access points can also be configured to operate in a wireless distribution system (WDS) mode. This allows multiple access points to be interconnected wirelessly, forming a mesh network where devices can roam between access points without losing connectivity. In summary, an access point is a fundamental component of wireless networks that acts as a central hub for connecting Wi-Fi capable devices to a wired network. It provides wireless coverage, facilitates the exchange of data packets, ensures multiple device support, and can be part of a larger mesh network.

Adaptive Forward Error Correction (FEC)

Adaptive Forward Error Correction (FEC) is a technique used in networking to improve the reliability and efficiency of data transmission over unreliable communication channels. It is a proactive error correction mechanism that adds redundancy to the transmitted data to enable the receiver to recover lost or corrupted packets. FEC operates by introducing additional bits, known as error correction codes, into the data stream at the sender's end. These codes are generated based on the original data and are designed to detect and correct errors that may occur during transmission. The sender then sends the data along with the error correction codes to the receiver. At the receiver's end, the error correction codes are used to check for errors in the received data. If errors are detected, the receiver can use the information provided by the error correction codes to correct the errors and reconstruct the original data. This allows the receiver to recover the lost or corrupted packets without the need for retransmissions from the sender. One of the key features of adaptive FEC is its ability to adapt to varying network conditions. It dynamically adjusts the amount of redundancy added to the data stream based on the perceived level of errors in the communication channel. This adaptivity helps optimize the utilization of network resources by balancing the trade-off between error correction and bandwidth efficiency. To achieve adaptivity, FEC algorithms monitor the error rate of the communication channel. If the error rate exceeds a predefined threshold, the FEC scheme increases the redundancy by

10

adding more error correction codes to the data stream. Conversely, if the error rate is below the threshold, the FEC scheme reduces the redundancy to conserve bandwidth. This adaptive behavior ensures that the error correction capability matches the current conditions of the network. In conclusion, adaptive FEC is a technique used in networking to improve the reliability and efficiency of data transmission over unreliable communication channels. By adding redundancy and error correction codes to the data stream, it enables the receiver to recover lost or corrupted packets without the need for retransmissions. Its adaptivity allows it to dynamically adjust the level of redundancy based on the error rate of the communication channel, optimizing the utilization of network resources.

Adaptive Routing Algorithms

Adaptive Routing Algorithms are a key component in computer networking that aim to dynamically select optimal paths for data packets to travel through a network. These algorithms adapt their routing decisions based on real-time network conditions, such as traffic congestion, link failures, and changing network topologies. Instead of relying on fixed routing tables, adaptive routing algorithms use sophisticated algorithms and techniques to make routing decisions on the fly. They continuously monitor the state of the network and adjust their routing decisions accordingly to ensure efficient and reliable data transmission.

Adaptive Routing Protocols

Adaptive routing protocols are a type of networking protocol that enables efficient and dynamic routing of data packets through a network. These protocols are designed to adapt and respond to changes in network topology and conditions, ensuring reliable and optimal delivery of data. Unlike static routing protocols, which use fixed routing tables that need to be manually configured, adaptive routing protocols use algorithms and metrics to dynamically determine the best path for each data packet as it traverses the network. This dynamic decision-making process allows adaptive routing protocols to quickly respond to changes in network conditions, such as link failures, congestion, or changes in network traffic.

Adaptive Routing In Networks

Adaptive routing in networks refers to the dynamic selection of the routing path for data packets in a network based on prevailing network conditions. It is a technique used to efficiently and effectively route information across a network, taking into account factors such as congestion, link failures, and traffic load. The main goal of adaptive routing is to optimize network performance by selecting the most suitable path for each data packet. This is achieved by continuously monitoring the network's state and dynamically adjusting the routing decisions to adapt to changing conditions.

Adaptive Routing

Adaptive routing, in the context of networking, refers to the ability of a network to dynamically select the most optimal path for routing data packets based on current network conditions and available resources. It is a crucial aspect of modern network architecture that aims to improve network performance, efficiency, and reliability. Traditional routing methods typically use static routing tables, which are predetermined and fixed paths for forwarding data packets. These routing tables are created based on factors such as the network topology, link costs, and administrative policies. However, these static routing tables may not always be optimal, especially in dynamic network environments where network conditions can vary rapidly. Adaptive routing overcomes the limitations of static routing by continuously monitoring network conditions and dynamically adapting routing decisions. This enables the network to intelligently reroute data packets in real-time, based on the current traffic load, link congestion, link failures, and other variables. One of the key advantages of adaptive routing is its ability to achieve load balancing across multiple paths. By actively monitoring network traffic, adaptive routers can distribute traffic across available paths in a manner that balances the load and prevents congestion. This leads to improved network performance and reduced latency. Furthermore, adaptive routing enhances network fault tolerance. In the event of a link failure, adaptive routers can quickly detect the failure and redirect the traffic through alternate paths, ensuring uninterrupted data flow. This resilience is particularly important in large-scale networks where a single link failure can cause significant disruptions. Adaptive routing algorithms can be classified into several categories, including distributed, centralized, and hybrid approaches. Distributed algorithms distribute the routing decision-making process across multiple routers, allowing each router to make local decisions based on its own information. Centralized algorithms, on the other hand, rely on a central controller to make global routing decisions for the entire network. Hybrid algorithms combine elements of both distributed and centralized approaches to achieve a balance between scalability and control.

Adaptive Security Appliance (ASA)

An Adaptive Security Appliance (ASA) is a networking device that provides firewall and Virtual Private Network (VPN) capabilities. It is typically used in large-scale enterprise networks to protect the network infrastructure from unauthorized access and malicious attacks. The ASA acts as a security gateway between the internal network (trusted network) and the external network (untrusted network, typically the Internet). It examines incoming and outgoing network traffic, filtering and inspecting packets based on set security policies and rules. This enables it to identify and block potential threats, such as malware, viruses, and intrusions, ensuring the integrity and confidentiality of data transmitted over the network. One of the key features of an ASA is its firewall functionality. It uses stateful packet inspection to analyze network traffic at the application layer, keeping track of the state of network connections. This allows the ASA to make informed decisions on whether to permit or deny traffic based on predefined security policies. It can also perform Network Address Translation (NAT), which hides the internal IP addresses of the network devices from the external network, further enhancing security. In addition to its firewall capabilities, the ASA also provides VPN services. It supports different VPN protocols, such as IPsec (Internet Protocol Security) and Secure Sockets Layer (SSL) VPN. These protocols allow remote users to securely access the internal network over the Internet, providing a secure and encrypted connection. This is particularly useful for remote or traveling employees who need to access company resources while maintaining data confidentiality. The ASA typically includes various features and modules to enhance network security. This may include Intrusion Prevention System (IPS) functionality, which actively monitors network traffic for known patterns of attacks and blocks them in real-time. It may also support advanced routing protocols, Quality of Service (QoS) mechanisms, and high availability features, ensuring reliable and optimized network connectivity. Overall, an ASA plays a critical role in securing enterprise networks by providing firewall and VPN capabilities. It helps protect sensitive data, prevents unauthorized access, and ensures the availability and integrity of network resources.

Adaptive Security Policy

An adaptive security policy is a dynamic set of rules and regulations implemented by a network to protect its resources and data from potential threats. This policy is flexible and responsive, allowing for continuous monitoring and adjustment based on the evolving nature of security threats. The purpose of an adaptive security policy is to ensure the confidentiality, integrity, and availability of a network's resources and data, while also promoting the efficient and effective use of those resources. It aims to strike a balance between the need for a secure network and the need for uninterrupted access to resources. Adaptive security policies are designed to address the constantly changing landscape of security threats. Traditional static security policies are often inadequate in dealing with new and emerging threats; they lack the flexibility and agility needed to respond quickly and effectively. In contrast, adaptive security policies are able to adapt to new threats by leveraging real-time intelligence, threat analytics, and automated responses. One key aspect of an adaptive security policy is the ability to detect and respond to anomalous behavior. By monitoring and analyzing network traffic and user behavior, an adaptive security policy can identify patterns that deviate from normal activity. This enables the policy to detect potential security breaches or unauthorized access attempts and take immediate action to neutralize the threat. Another important feature of an adaptive security policy is the ability to dynamically allocate resources based on changing security needs. For example, during periods of increased network traffic or heightened threat levels, the policy can allocate more resources to security measures to ensure the network remains protected. Overall, an adaptive security policy is essential in today's constantly evolving threat landscape. By continuously monitoring, analyzing, and adapting to new security threats, this policy helps to protect the integrity and availability of a network's resources and data while minimizing disruptions to legitimate users.

Adaptive Security Solutions

Adaptive Security Solutions refers to a set of measures and technologies implemented in a network to protect it from various security threats, vulnerabilities, and attacks. These solutions are designed to constantly adapt and respond to changing cyber threats, ensuring the network is protected from unauthorized access, data breaches, and other malicious activities. The main objective of Adaptive Security Solutions is to provide robust and dynamic security measures that can proactively identify, prevent, and respond to emerging threats in real-time. The solutions employ advanced techniques such as machine learning, behavioral analytics, and threat intelligence to continuously monitor network traffic, detect anomalies, and identify potential security risks. By utilizing adaptive security measures, networks can effectively defend against a wide range of threats, including malware, viruses, unauthorized access attempts, and denial-of-service attacks. These solutions enable network administrators to quickly detect and mitigate security incidents, minimizing the potential impact on organizational operations and data integrity. Adaptive Security Solutions typically consist of a combination of hardware and software components working together to create a multi-layered defense system. Firewalls, intrusion detection and prevention systems, antivirus software, and access control mechanisms are common elements of these solutions. In addition to proactive threat detection and prevention, Adaptive Security Solutions often include incident response capabilities. These enable organizations to effectively manage and remediate security incidents in a timely manner. Incident response processes and guidelines, as well as automated incident response tools, may be integrated into the overall security solution. Overall, Adaptive Security Solutions play a critical role in safeguarding networks and ensuring the confidentiality, integrity, and availability of data and resources. By constantly adapting to evolving threats and vulnerabilities, these solutions provide organizations with a comprehensive defense system that is capable of protecting against both known and unknown security risks.

Address Resolution Protocol (ARP) Cache Poisoning

Address Resolution Protocol (ARP) cache poisoning, also known as ARP spoofing or ARP poisoning, is a network security attack where an attacker alters the information in the ARP cache in order to redirect network traffic to their own device. The ARP protocol is responsible for mapping an IP address to a corresponding MAC address in a local network. By manipulating this mapping, an attacker can intercept and redirect network traffic to their own device, allowing them to perform various malicious activities such as eavesdropping, stealing sensitive information, or launching further attacks. The ARP cache, also known as the ARP table, is a collection of IP-to-MAC address mappings stored on a device within a local network. When a device needs to send data to another device within the same network, it consults its ARP cache to obtain the MAC address corresponding to the IP address of the destination device. If the mapping is not present in the cache, the device broadcasts an ARP request to the network, asking the device with the corresponding IP address to reply with its MAC address. In an ARP cache poisoning attack, the attacker relies on the lack of authentication or verification in the ARP protocol to modify the mappings in the target device's ARP cache. The attacker begins by sending spoofed ARP messages to the target device, claiming to be the device with a specific IP address, while providing their own MAC address. The target device updates its ARP cache with the manipulated mapping, associating the attacker's MAC address with the IP address in question. Once the attacker has successfully poisoned the target device's ARP cache, they can intercept and modify network traffic intended for other devices within the same network. For example, the attacker can redirect all network traffic intended for a specific IP address to their own device, allowing them to capture sensitive information or launch further attacks. ARP cache poisoning attacks can be mitigated through various security measures such as implementing ARP spoofing detection mechanisms, enabling port security features, and configuring static ARP entries. Additionally, the use of secure protocols such as DHCP snooping, IP source guard, or dynamic ARP inspection can help protect against these types of attacks.

Address Resolution Protocol (ARP)

Address Resolution Protocol (ARP) is a networking protocol used to map an IP address to a corresponding physical (MAC) address. It enables devices to communicate within a Local Area Network (LAN) by resolving the IP address of the destination device to its unique MAC address. ARP operates at the Internet Layer of the TCP/IP protocol suite and is essential for the proper functioning of LANs. When a device wants to send data to another device on the same network, it needs to know the MAC address of the destination device. ARP helps in this process by performing address resolution. The ARP protocol works by broadcasting a request message, called an ARP request, to all devices on the same network. This request contains the IP address of the device that the sender wants to communicate with. The devices on the network receive the request and check if the IP address matches their own. If a device recognizes the IP address as its own, it sends an ARP reply message back to the sender. This reply includes its MAC address. Once the sender receives the ARP reply, it can then map the IP address to the corresponding MAC address. This mapping is stored in the sender's ARP cache, which is a table that keeps track of IP-MAC address pairs. The sender can now use the MAC address obtained from the ARP reply to send data packets directly to the destination device. ARP is a stateless protocol, meaning it does not keep track of ongoing communications. Each ARP request and reply message is treated as an independent event. As a result, ARP messages are periodically broadcasted to update the ARP caches of the devices on the network, ensuring the accuracy of the IP-MAC address mappings. In conclusion, the Address Resolution Protocol (ARP) is a vital protocol in networking that facilitates the resolution of IP addresses to MAC addresses within a Local Area Network. It allows devices to communicate effectively by providing a mechanism to discover the MAC address associated with a given IP address.

Advanced Encryption Standard (AES)

The Advanced Encryption Standard (AES) is a symmetric encryption algorithm that is widely used in networking to secure data transmission and protect against unauthorized access. AES operates on blocks of data, encrypting or decrypting them using a secret key. It supports three key sizes: 128 bits, 192 bits, and 256 bits, providing different levels of cryptographic strength. The algorithm consists of a series of transformations, including substitution, permutation, and mixing operations, performed on the input data. The strength of AES lies in its ability to resist known attacks and its flexibility in supporting different key sizes. It is considered one of the most secure symmetric encryption algorithms currently available. AES has been adopted by various organizations and governments worldwide as a standard for securing sensitive information. When used in networking, AES ensures the confidentiality and integrity of data transmitted over a network. Before transmission, the sender encrypts the data using the AES algorithm and a secret key. The encrypted data is then sent over the network and received by the recipient. The recipient, with the corresponding secret key, decrypts the received data to recover the original message. AES is commonly used in Virtual Private Networks (VPNs), Secure Socket Layer (SSL), and Transport Layer Security (TLS) protocols to provide secure communication over the internet. It can be used to secure various network protocols, including email, web browsing, file transfer, and database access. In conclusion, the Advanced Encryption Standard (AES) is a widely used symmetric encryption algorithm in networking that ensures secure data transmission and protects against unauthorized access. Its strength lies in its resistance to attacks and its flexibility in supporting different key sizes, making it an ideal choice for securing sensitive information in various networking applications.

Advanced Persistent Threat (APT)

An Advanced Persistent Threat (APT) refers to a highly sophisticated and targeted cyberattack technique that is designed to infiltrate a network and remain undetected for an extended period. APTs are typically orchestrated by well-resourced and skilled threat actors, such as nation-states or organized cybercriminal groups, who possess advanced technical capabilities. The primary goal of an APT is to gain unauthorized access to sensitive information, such as intellectual property, classified data, or financial records. Unlike traditional cyberattacks that aim for immediate disruption or damage, APTs are characterized by their stealthy approach and long-term persistence within a compromised system or network. APTs involve a multi-stage attack strategy that begins with reconnaissance and initial network infiltration. The attackers employ advanced tactics like spear-phishing, social engineering, or zero-day exploits to gain a foothold in the target network. Once inside, they employ sophisticated tools and techniques to evade detection and establish a persistent presence. Once established, APTs utilize various methods to move laterally across the network, escalate privileges, and explore additional systems or resources. This lateral movement helps them to discover and access valuable data or systems that may be otherwise inaccessible. APTs often employ advanced techniques like privilege escalation, password cracking, or traffic manipulation to maneuver through the network

14

undetected. The key characteristic of APTs is their persistence. The attackers employ various strategies to maintain long-term access without being noticed by security safeguards. These strategies may involve backdoors, rootkits, or command-and-control (C2) infrastructure to maintain control of the compromised system and exfiltrate stolen data. They may also employ techniques to camouflage their activities and blend in with regular network traffic. Due to their advanced nature, APTs are challenging to detect and mitigate. Traditional security measures like firewalls, antivirus software, or intrusion detection systems may not be sufficient to defend against such threats. Protecting against APTs requires a comprehensive approach that includes robust security controls, threat intelligence, continuous monitoring, and proactive incident response strategies.

Air Gap

An air gap in the context of networking refers to a physical or logical isolation between two or more networks. It is designed to provide a layer of protection against unauthorized access and the spread of malware or other cyber threats. The concept of an air gap is based on the principle that connecting two networks increases the risk of data breaches and compromises. By implementing an air gap, organizations can create a secure barrier that prevents direct communication between networks, reducing the chances of cyber attacks and unauthorized data transfers.

Anomaly Detection

Anomaly detection in the context of networking refers to the process of identifying unusual or abnormal behavior within a network system that deviates from the expected or normal patterns. It involves analyzing network traffic, data, and activities to detect any suspicious or anomalous activities that may indicate potential security breaches, network malfunction, or performance issues. The goal of anomaly detection in networking is to detect and mitigate any abnormal behavior that could potentially compromise the security, integrity, availability, or performance of the network. By identifying and addressing anomalies promptly, network administrators can prevent or minimize the impact of potential threats, ensure the smooth operation of the network, and maintain the confidentiality, integrity, and availability of network resources.

Antivirus Software

Antivirus software is a network security application designed to detect, prevent, and remove malicious software, also known as malware, from computer systems. It is an essential tool in safeguarding the integrity, confidentiality, and availability of network resources, as well as protecting against potential threats that can compromise network security. Antivirus software operates by scanning files, email attachments, and various data streams for known patterns or signatures associated with malware. When a potential threat is detected, the antivirus software notifies the user and offers options to either quarantine, delete, or repair the infected files. It may also provide real-time protection by monitoring the system for malicious activities, such as unauthorized access attempts or suspicious network traffic.

Antivirus

An antivirus is a software program designed to detect, prevent, and remove malicious software, commonly known as malware, from computer systems and networks. It is an essential tool in network security, as it helps protect the integrity and confidentiality of data by identifying and eliminating potential threats. The primary function of an antivirus is to scan files, programs, and data stored on a network for any signs of malware. It uses various techniques and algorithms to compare the contents of files against a database of known malware signatures. If a match is found, the antivirus takes appropriate action, such as quarantining or deleting the infected file, to prevent further damage to the network. Antivirus software employs different methods to detect and combat malware, including signature-based detection, heuristic analysis, behavioral monitoring, and sandboxing. Signature-based detection involves comparing the data being scanned with a database of pre-defined malware signatures. Heuristic analysis, on the other hand, uses algorithms to identify suspicious patterns or behaviors that might indicate the presence of malware. Behavioral monitoring involves monitoring the activities of programs and processes running on the network to identify any abnormal or malicious behavior. Lastly, sandboxing creates an isolated environment where potentially harmful programs can be executed and analyzed without causing any harm to the network. Aside from scanning for malware, antivirus software also provides real-time protection by actively monitoring network activity. It scans incoming and outgoing data packets, email attachments, and website content to ensure they do not contain any malicious code. Additionally, antivirus software performs regular system scans to detect hidden or dormant malware that might have evaded detection during real-time monitoring. In conclusion, an antivirus is a software program that plays a vital role in network security by detecting, preventing, and removing malware from computer systems and networks. Its primary function is to protect the integrity and confidentiality of data by scanning for and eliminating potential threats. By employing various techniques and algorithms, an antivirus helps ensure the smooth and secure operation of a network.

Anycast IP Address Assignment

Anycast IP address assignment is a network routing technique that allows multiple devices to share the same IP address. In this technique, a single IP address is assigned to multiple devices located in different geographic locations. When a client sends a request to the anycast IP address, the request is automatically routed to the nearest device running the anycast service. The main purpose of using anycast IP address assignment is to improve the overall performance, reliability, and fault tolerance of network services. By distributing the load across multiple devices, anycast helps to reduce the response time for client requests and minimizes the risk of service downtime. In an anycast network, multiple devices are configured to advertise the same IP address using Border Gateway Protocol (BGP) or any other routing protocol. These devices are typically routers or servers that are located in different data centers or Points of Presence (PoPs) around the world. When a client wants to access a service provided by the anycast IP address, the client's request is first sent to the nearest routing device, which typically has the lowest latency based on network topology. The routing device examines the request and forwards it to the appropriate server or service based on factors such as network congestion, server load, or any other routing policies. The anycast IP address assignment technique relies on the underlying routing infrastructure to make routing decisions based on the shortest path or lowest latency. This means that the client is automatically connected to the most optimal server or service location without the need for any client-side configuration. Anycast IP address assignment is particularly useful for services that require high availability and low-latency responses, such as DNS resolution, content delivery networks (CDNs), or distributed databases. By distributing the load across multiple devices, anycast helps to improve the responsiveness of these services and ensures that clients are always connected to the nearest and most efficient server or service. Overall, anycast IP address assignment plays a crucial role in enhancing the performance, reliability, and fault tolerance of network services. By allowing multiple devices to share the same IP address and routing client requests to the nearest device, anycast helps to optimize network traffic, reduce response times, and improve the overall user experience.

Anycast IP Addressing

Anycast IP addressing is a network addressing technique that allows multiple devices to share the same IP address. Unlike unicast or multicast addressing, where a single IP address is assigned to a specific device or group of devices respectively, anycast addressing allows multiple devices to advertise the same IP address and route traffic to the closest or most suitable device based on routing protocols and metrics. In the context of networking, anycast IP addressing is particularly useful for improving the performance, efficiency, and redundancy of network services and applications. By allowing multiple devices to respond to the same IP address, anycast enables load balancing and traffic distribution across different network nodes, improving response times and reducing network congestion. Anycast IP addressing relies on routing protocols such as Border Gateway Protocol (BGP) to advertise the availability of a specific IP address from different locations or devices. When a client sends a request to an anycast IP address, routers in the network determine the closest device based on network metrics such as latency, hop count, or network congestion. The router then forwards the traffic to the determined device, which provides the requested service or content. One of the key advantages of anycast IP addressing is its inherent ability to provide fault tolerance and high availability. By distributing traffic across multiple devices sharing the same IP address, anycast ensures that even if one or a few devices become unavailable or experience issues, the network can still route traffic to other available devices offering the same services. Furthermore, anycast

16

IP addressing simplifies network management and reduces the complexity of DNS (Domain Name System) configuration. Instead of configuring multiple IP addresses for different servers or devices providing the same service, only one IP address needs to be assigned and advertised using anycast. This eliminates the need for complex load balancing techniques and allows for more straightforward management of network infrastructure. In summary, anycast IP addressing is a networking technique that allows multiple devices to share the same IP address. It improves network performance, offers fault tolerance, simplifies management, and enhances the high availability of network services and applications.

Anycast Routing Protocol

Anycast routing protocol is a network routing technique that enables multiple devices or locations to advertise the same IP address, allowing network traffic to be routed to the nearest or best-performing destination. Unlike unicast or multicast routing, which uses a one-to-one or one-to-many approach, anycast routing uses a one-to-nearest approach. This means that when multiple devices or locations are advertising the same IP address, the network will route traffic to the device or location that is closest in terms of network topology, latency, or other performance criteria. Typically, anycast routing protocols are used in distributed networks or systems where high availability, reliability, and performance are crucial. By allowing traffic to be directed to the nearest device or location, anycast routing can enhance overall network performance, reduce latency, and distribute network load more efficiently. To implement anycast routing, routers or network devices advertise the anycast IP address using a routing protocol such as Border Gateway Protocol (BGP) or Intermediate System to Intermediate System (IS-IS). When a router receives a packet destined for the anycast IP address, it selects the best path based on routing metrics and forwards the packet to the nearest device or location advertising that IP address. One of the main benefits of anycast routing is its ability to provide failover and fault tolerance. If one device or location becomes unavailable, the network will automatically route traffic to the next closest device or location advertising the anycast IP address. This ensures that services remain available even in the event of a failure. Anycast routing can be particularly useful in content delivery networks (CDNs), where multiple servers located in different locations can advertise the same IP address for improved performance and load balancing. It is also commonly used in distributed DNS systems, where multiple DNS servers advertise the same IP address to improve the availability and response time of DNS resolution. In summary, anycast routing protocol is a network routing technique that allows multiple devices or locations to advertise the same IP address, enabling network traffic to be routed to the closest device or location. It enhances network performance, provides fault tolerance, and is commonly used in distributed systems where high availability and reliability are critical.

Anycast Routing

Anycast routing is a method used in computer networking to efficiently distribute incoming traffic to the nearest available server or network node. It is a technique where multiple devices or servers share the same IP address and are geographically dispersed across different locations. This allows for load balancing and fault tolerance, as well as improved user experience and network performance. In an anycast network setup, all devices or servers share the same IP address and advertise it to the network using a common routing protocol. When a client sends a request to the anycast IP address, the routing infrastructure determines the nearest server based on network topology and chooses the best path to reach that server. The routing decision is made dynamically, considering various factors such as network latency, congestion, and server availability. One of the key advantages of anycast routing is its ability to reduce latency by directing traffic to the closest server. This is particularly useful for services that require low latency, such as content delivery networks (CDNs) or real-time communication applications. By distributing servers across multiple locations, anycast routing enables faster response times and a better user experience. Moreover, anycast routing provides built-in fault tolerance and high availability. If a server or network node becomes unreachable, the routing infrastructure automatically redirects traffic to the next closest server. This ensures that services remain accessible and minimizes the impact of hardware failures or network disruptions. Overall, anycast routing is a powerful technique in network engineering that improves performance, reliability, and scalability. It enables efficient load balancing, reduces latency, and provides fault-tolerant architectures. Anycast routing is commonly used in global CDNs, DNS servers, and other distributed systems where proximity and responsiveness are critical.

17

Anycast Service Providers

Anycast service providers are network operators that offer the ability to route traffic to multiple destinations using a single IP address. This is achieved by announcing the same IP address through multiple network locations, allowing the network to automatically route traffic to the closest or best-performing destination based on various factors such as network latency, congestion, or the number of hops.

Anycast Vs. Unicast

Anycast and unicast are two different methods of communication used in computer networking. Unicast is a one-to-one communication method where a single sender transmits data to a specific recipient. In this method, the data is addressed to the unique IP address of the intended recipient, ensuring that it reaches the correct destination. Unicast is commonly used in regular client-server interactions, where a client sends a request to a specific server and receives a response back. In contrast, anycast is a one-to-nearest communication method where a single sender transmits data to the nearest recipient among a group of potential recipients. In anycast, the same IP address is assigned to multiple devices or servers spread across different geographical locations. When a sender sends a packet with a destination address equal to the anycast address, the network automatically routes the packet to the nearest device/server based on network metrics such as latency or network congestion. This ensures efficient delivery of data by directing it to the closest possible recipient.

Anycast

Anycast is a networking technique that enables multiple servers to share the same IP address, allowing network traffic to be distributed to the closest or best-performing server based on routing protocols. It is extensively used to improve network performance, increase scalability, and enhance resilience and fault tolerance. In anycast, multiple servers are deployed at various locations and given the same IP address. When a client sends a request to the anycast IP address, the routing infrastructure determines the most suitable server to handle the request based on factors like network conditions, round-trip time, or network congestion. The client is unaware of this process and simply interacts with the anycast IP address as if it were a single server.

Application Delivery Controller (ADC)

An Application Delivery Controller (ADC) is a networking device that optimizes the delivery of applications over a network. It plays a crucial role in balancing the load across servers, accelerating application performance, and providing security for applications. ADCs act as intermediaries between clients and servers, ensuring that requests from clients are routed to the most appropriate server in order to achieve efficient load balancing. This is done by distributing incoming network traffic across multiple servers, thereby preventing any single server from becoming overwhelmed with requests. By evenly distributing the load, ADCs help to improve overall application performance and availability.

Application Layer Firewall

An application layer firewall, also known as a proxy firewall, is a network security device that operates at the application layer of the OSI model. It acts as an intermediary between the client and server applications to monitor and control communication traffic. The primary function of an application layer firewall is to examine the content of network packets at the application layer. It analyzes the data within the packets, including the headers and payload, to determine the nature of the traffic and enforce security policies. By doing so, it provides an additional layer of protection and enhances network security.

Application Security

Application Security refers to the measures and practices taken to protect the confidentiality, integrity, and availability of computer applications, software, and systems from potential threats and vulnerabilities. It involves implementing various security controls and techniques to ensure the protection of sensitive data, prevent unauthorized access, detect and mitigate potential

18

attacks, and ensure the overall reliability and safety of the application. Networking plays a crucial role in the context of application security as it encompasses the communication between different devices, systems, and applications. In a networked environment, applications rely on the underlying network infrastructure to transmit data, exchange information, and perform various operations. Therefore, network security is closely related to application security, as vulnerabilities or weaknesses in the network can impact the security posture of the applications running on that network.

Asymmetric Digital Subscriber Line (ADSL)

Asymmetric Digital Subscriber Line (ADSL) is a type of broadband communication technology that uses traditional copper telephone lines to transmit high-speed data over long distances. It is commonly used in residential and small business environments to provide internet access. ADSL operates on the principle of asymmetry, which means that the upload speed and the download speed are not the same. The download speed is typically higher than the upload speed, as most users consume more data from the internet than they send. This makes ADSL suitable for activities such as browsing websites, streaming videos, and downloading files.

Authentication Token

An authentication token in the context of networking is a numeric value or a string of characters that is used to verify the identity of a user or a network device when attempting to access a specific network resource or service. The authentication token serves as a form of digital credential, allowing the user or device to prove its authenticity to the network, typically during the login or connection process. The token is generated by the network system or acquired from a trusted authority and is then presented to the authentication system as evidence of the user or device's identity. The authentication token can take various forms depending on the authentication method being used. For example, in password-based authentication, the token could be the user's password itself. In token-based authentication, the token could be a physical smart card, a software-generated code, or a One-Time Password (OTP) sent to the user's mobile device. In certificate-based authentication, the token could be a digital certificate containing the user or device's public key. Once the authentication token is presented to the network, it is verified by the authentication system using a pre-established algorithm or protocol. The system checks if the token matches the expected value or if it can be decrypted using the appropriate cryptographic key. If the token is valid, the user or device is granted access to the requested network resource or service. If the token is invalid or expired, access is denied. Authentication tokens are crucial in ensuring the security and integrity of network resources. By requiring users or devices to present a valid token, unauthorized access and identity theft can be prevented. In addition, the use of authentication tokens allows for audit trails and logging, enabling network administrators to track and monitor user activities, detect suspicious behavior, and enforce access control policies. In summary, an authentication token in networking is a digital credential used to prove the identity of a user or device. It is presented to the network during the authentication process and, if valid, grants access to network resources. By utilizing authentication tokens, networks can enhance security and ensure only authorized individuals or devices can access sensitive information or services.

Authentication

Authentication is a process used in networking to verify the identity of a user, device, or system before granting access to resources or services. It is a critical aspect of network security, as it ensures that only authorized individuals or entities are granted access to sensitive information or functionalities. The authentication process involves the exchange of credentials between the user or device and the network. These credentials can be in the form of passwords, digital certificates, biometric data, or other authentication factors. The network compares the provided credentials with stored data to determine if they match, and grants or denies access accordingly. There are various authentication methods utilized in networking, each with its own strengths and weaknesses. The most common method is password-based authentication, where users provide a combination of username and password to verify their identity. However, passwords can be susceptible to theft, brute-force attacks, or social engineering techniques. Another widely used authentication method is the use of digital certificates. Digital certificates are issued by trusted Certificate Authorities and contain a digital signature that verifies the identity of the certificate holder. When a user presents a valid digital certificate, the network can trust the authenticity of the user's identity. Two-factor authentication (2FA) enhances security by requiring users to provide two separate authentication factors. This can include a combination of something the user knows (such as a password), something the user possesses (such as a physical token), or something the user biometrically is (such as a fingerprint). Authentication protocols play a crucial role in facilitating secure authentication processes. Common protocols include Remote Authentication Dial-In User Service (RADIUS) and Lightweight Directory Access Protocol (LDAP). These protocols enable centralized authentication and store user credentials in a secure and organized manner. Overall, authentication in networking is essential for ensuring the confidentiality, integrity, and availability of network resources. It helps prevent unauthorized access, protects sensitive data, and ensures that only authorized individuals or devices can interact with the network.

Authorization

Authorization in the context of networking refers to the process of granting or denying access to network resources based on the privileges and permissions assigned to an individual or entity. It is a crucial aspect of network security and plays a vital role in safeguarding the confidentiality, integrity, and availability of sensitive information and resources. When a user or device attempts to access a network, the authorization process validates their credentials and determines whether they have the necessary rights to perform the requested actions or access specific resources. This process typically involves multiple steps: The first step is authentication, where the user or device provides proof of their identity, often in the form of a username and password. This information is verified against a trusted source, such as a user database or directory service, to ensure the legitimacy of the user. Once the user's identity is confirmed, the second step is authorization. This step involves evaluating the user's rights and permissions, which are typically defined in an access control list (ACL) or a similar policy. The ACL specifies the specific resources, actions, or services that the user is allowed to utilize. Authorization can be based on various factors, such as the user's role, group membership, time of access, or the sensitivity of the resource. For example, an administrator may have complete access to all network resources, while a regular user may only have read-only access to certain directories. If the user's credentials and permissions match the access control policies, the authorization process grants them access to the requested resource. On the other hand, if their credentials or permissions are invalid or insufficient, access will be denied, and the user will be prevented from utilizing the resource. In addition to controlling individual access, authorization also helps in enforcing security policies and ensuring compliance with regulatory requirements. By carefully defining and managing user permissions, network administrators can mitigate the risk of unauthorized access, data breaches, and other security incidents.

Autonomous System (AS)

An Autonomous System (AS) in the context of networking refers to a set of connected IP networks managed and operated by a single administrative entity, known as an Internet Service Provider (ISP) or a large organization. It represents a collection of routers under a common administration, which adhere to a unique routing policy and share the same routing protocols. The primary purpose of an Autonomous System is to exchange routing information with other ASes to ensure efficient packet delivery across the Internet. Each AS is assigned a globally unique identifier, known as an Autonomous System Number (ASN), which is crucial for interconnecting and communicating with other ASes. The key characteristics of an AS include: 1. Autonomous System Number (ASN): Each AS is identified by a unique ASN, which is assigned by a Regional Internet Registry (RIR) or an National Internet Registry (NIR). The ASN is used to differentiate and identify the AS during routing updates and BGP (Border Gateway Protocol) peering. 2. Routing Policies: An AS has its own set of routing policies that determine how incoming and outgoing packets are handled. These policies include factors such as preferred routes, traffic engineering, and security measures. Routing policies play a crucial role in directing traffic flow within and between ASes. 3. Interior Gateway Protocol (IGP) vs. Exterior Gateway Protocol (EGP): Within an AS, routers use Interior Gateway Protocols (IGPs) such as OSPF (Open Shortest Path First) or IS-IS (Intermediate System to Intermediate System) to exchange routing information. However, when communicating between ASes, routers use Exterior Gateway Protocols (EGPs) such as BGP to exchange routing information. 4. Peering Relationships: ASes form peering relationships with each other to exchange routing information.

These relationships can be classified as transit, where one AS allows traffic from another AS to pass through, or as peering, where two ASes agree to exchange traffic with each other directly. 5. Internet Exchange Points (IXPs): IXPs serve as physical locations where multiple ASes connect their networks to exchange traffic efficiently. IXPs enable improved connectivity and reduced latency by providing a common meeting point for multiple ASes. In conclusion, an Autonomous System in networking refers to a collection of connected IP networks under a single administrative entity. With their own unique ASN, routing policies, and interconnection relationships, ASes play a fundamental role in the global routing infrastructure of the Internet.

Autonomous System Number (ASN)

An Autonomous System Number (ASN) is a unique identifier that is assigned to a group of IP networks under a central administrative authority. In the context of networking, an ASN is necessary to facilitate the routing of Internet traffic between different networks, ensuring efficient and reliable communication between autonomous systems. ASNs are primarily used in the Border Gateway Protocol (BGP), which is the protocol used to exchange routing information between autonomous systems on the Internet. Each ASN is associated with a set of IP prefixes that define the range of IP addresses controlled by that autonomous system.

BGP (Border Gateway Protocol)

BGP (Border Gateway Protocol) is a standardized exterior gateway protocol used in large-scale computer networks to facilitate the exchange of routing information between autonomous systems (AS). It is a crucial protocol that enables routers to communicate and make informed decisions about the most efficient paths for data traffic. BGP operates at the network layer of the Internet protocol suite and serves as one of the key building blocks of the Internet. Its primary function is to establish and maintain the paths through which data packets are transmitted across diverse networks, both within and between AS. BGP is what connects the various autonomous systems, which are individual networks managed by different organizations, effectively serving as the backbone of the Internet. Unlike interior gateway protocols (IGP) that handle routing within an autonomous system, BGP focuses on inter-autonomous system routing. Its main goal is to determine the best paths for data transmission by considering factors such as network policies, path availability, and network performance. BGP allows routers to exchange information about the availability and reachability of IP addresses, enabling them to build a comprehensive and dynamic map of network topology. BGP utilizes a complex system of attributes to make routing decisions. These attributes, such as AS path, next-hop, and local preference, assist routers in selecting the most optimal paths based on specific criteria set by network administrators. The protocol utilizes a path vector algorithm, where routers exchange routing information with their directly connected neighbors, and these updates propagate through the network until a stable routing table is achieved. One of the key advantages of BGP is its ability to support policy-based routing, allowing network administrators to exert control over how traffic flows through their network. This flexibility enables organizations to implement traffic engineering practices, load balancing strategies, and secure routing policies. BGP also incorporates mechanisms for loop prevention and mitigating network instability, ensuring reliable and efficient data transmission across the Internet.

Backbone Network

A backbone network refers to a high-speed network infrastructure that serves as the primary pathway for data communication within a larger network or organization. It connects various local area networks (LANs), wide area networks (WANs), and other network segments together, allowing them to communicate and share resources efficiently. The backbone network is designed to handle large volumes of data traffic and ensure fast and reliable transmission of information between different network components. It typically utilizes high-bandwidth transmission media, such as fiber optic cables, to support the demanding communication needs of interconnected networks.

Backdoor

A backdoor, in the context of networking, refers to a hidden and unauthorized method of access into a computer system or network infrastructure. It is typically created or exploited by attackers to gain unauthorized access to a system, bypassing normal security measures and controls. Backdoors can be implemented by malicious individuals or groups with malicious intent, such as hackers or cybercriminals, as well as by trusted insiders seeking to gain unauthorized access for their own personal or professional purposes. Once a backdoor is established, it allows the attacker to bypass authentication mechanisms and gain full or partial control over the compromised system or network. This unauthorized access provides the attacker with the ability to carry out various malicious activities, including but not limited to: 1. Gathering sensitive information: Backdoors can be used to extract valuable data from the compromised system or network, such as personal user data, financial information, or intellectual property. 2. Modifying or deleting data: Attackers may modify or delete files and data, disrupting normal operations and causing damage to the system or network. 3. Installing additional malware or malicious software: Backdoors often serve as entry points for attackers to install additional malware, such as keyloggers, ransomware, or spyware, expanding their control and capabilities within the compromised system or network. 4. Creating a launching pad: Attackers can utilize backdoors to pivot and launch further attacks from within the compromised environment, potentially targeting other systems or networks. Prevention and detection of backdoors are critical for maintaining the security and integrity of computer systems and networks. This involves implementing robust security measures, such as firewalls, intrusion detection systems, and regular security audits. Furthermore, keeping software and systems up to date with the latest patches and security updates can help mitigate vulnerabilities that backdoors often exploit. In conclusion, backdoors represent a serious threat to the confidentiality, integrity, and availability of computer systems and networks. Establishing and maintaining strong security measures is essential to mitigate the risk of unauthorized access and the potential harm that can result from backdoor exploitation.

Bandwidth Allocation Techniques

Bandwidth allocation techniques refer to the methods and strategies employed in networking to distribute available bandwidth among multiple users or applications. These techniques play a crucial role in managing network resources and optimizing the performance of the network. Different allocation techniques are used based on the specific requirements of the network and the nature of the traffic flow. One common technique for bandwidth allocation is fixed allocation, where a predetermined amount of bandwidth is allocated to each user or application. This method ensures that each user receives a fixed portion of the available bandwidth, regardless of the network conditions or the traffic demands. Fixed allocation is suitable for scenarios where the bandwidth requirements of the users or applications are known and do not fluctuate significantly. Another technique is dynamic allocation, which adjusts the bandwidth allocation based on the real-time network conditions and traffic demands. This approach optimizes the utilization of available bandwidth by dynamically allocating more or less bandwidth to users or applications as needed. Dynamic allocation techniques can include priority-based allocation, where higher priority users or applications receive a larger share of the bandwidth, or fair allocation, where bandwidth is distributed equally among users or applications. Contiguous allocation is another bandwidth allocation technique that involves allocating a continuous block of bandwidth to each user or application. This ensures that users or applications have dedicated bandwidth that is not shared with others. Contiguous allocation is often used in scenarios where each user requires a minimum guaranteed bandwidth for uninterrupted operation, such as in video streaming or real-time communication applications. Finally, statistical multiplexing is a technique where the available bandwidth is shared dynamically among multiple users or applications based on statistical analysis of their traffic patterns. This allows for efficient allocation of bandwidth by identifying periods of low traffic demand and allocating additional bandwidth to users or applications with higher demands. Statistical multiplexing is commonly used in scenarios where individual users or applications do not require a continuous dedicated bandwidth and can benefit from sharing the available resources efficiently.

Bandwidth Allocation

Bandwidth allocation in the context of networking refers to the distribution and management of available network resources between different users, applications, or devices. It is the process of assigning a specific amount of bandwidth or network capacity to each entity within a network to ensure efficient and fair utilization of resources. In a network, bandwidth represents the maximum amount of data that can be transmitted over a network connection in a given time period. It is measured in bits per second (bps) or a multiple thereof, such as kilobits per second

(Kbps) or megabits per second (Mbps). Bandwidth allocation involves dividing this finite resource among various network components to allow them to communicate and send/receive data. In practice, bandwidth allocation is crucial for maintaining a smooth and optimal network performance. Without proper allocation, network congestion and bottlenecks can occur, leading to degraded performance, increased latency, and slower data transfer speeds. Therefore, network administrators employ different techniques to allocate bandwidth effectively. One common method is Quality of Service (QoS) implementation, where administrators prioritize specific traffic types or applications over others based on pre-defined rules. For example, real-time applications such as VoIP or video conferencing may be given higher priority over non-real-time activities like web browsing or file downloads. Another technique is traffic shaping or traffic policing, which involves monitoring and controlling the flow of data packets to ensure they are within specified bandwidth limits. This allows administrators to prioritize critical traffic, limit bandwidth consumption for non-critical activities, or enforce policies based on user or application requirements. Overall, bandwidth allocation plays a vital role in managing network resources effectively and ensuring that all users, applications, and devices can access the necessary bandwidth without causing network congestion or performance issues. By carefully dividing the available bandwidth, network administrators can optimize network performance, enhance user experience, and maintain a stable and reliable network environment.

Bandwidth Control Tools

Bandwidth Control Tools refer to a set of software or hardware solutions that enable network administrators to manage and regulate the amount of data that can be transmitted over a network. These tools are primarily used to prevent network congestion, maintain quality of service, and ensure fair allocation of network resources to different users or applications. The main purpose of bandwidth control tools is to optimize the use of available bandwidth by implementing traffic shaping, traffic prioritization, and bandwidth allocation policies. By imposing restrictions on the amount of bandwidth that can be consumed by specific users, devices, or applications, these tools allow network administrators to prioritize critical traffic, such as business-critical applications, and restrict the bandwidth allocation for non-essential or bandwidth-intensive activities. Bandwidth control tools typically provide a range of features and functionalities, including: - Traffic monitoring: They allow network administrators to analyze network traffic patterns and identify bandwidth-consuming applications or users. This helps in understanding network utilization and making informed decisions regarding bandwidth allocation. - Traffic shaping: These tools enable administrators to regulate the flow of network traffic by setting rules and priorities. By prioritizing certain types of traffic over others, such as Voice over IP (VoIP) or video streaming traffic, administrators can ensure smooth and uninterrupted data transmission. - Quality of Service (QoS) management: Bandwidth control tools often include QoS management capabilities, which allow administrators to define and enforce service level agreements (SLAs) and quality parameters for different types of network traffic. This ensures that critical applications receive sufficient bandwidth and network resources to maintain smooth operation. - Bandwidth allocation: These tools enable administrators to allocate bandwidth resources based on predefined rules or policies. For example, they can limit the bandwidth usage for certain users or applications during peak hours, or allocate a higher bandwidth allocation to specific departments or teams within an organization. Overall, bandwidth control tools play a crucial role in maintaining network performance, preventing congestion, and maximizing the utilization of available bandwidth. By allowing network administrators to manage and regulate the flow of data, these tools ensure equitable distribution of network resources and enhance the overall efficiency and reliability of the network.

Bandwidth Management

Bandwidth management refers to the process of controlling and optimizing the utilization of available network bandwidth in order to ensure the efficient and fair distribution of network resources among users or applications. Bandwidth is the capacity of a network to transmit data, and it is typically measured in bits per second (bps) or a derivative unit such as kilobits per second (Kbps) or megabits per second (Mbps). In networking, bandwidth management plays a crucial role in maintaining network performance, preventing congestion, and prioritizing critical network traffic.

Bandwidth Monitoring

Bandwidth monitoring refers to the process of tracking and measuring the amount of data that is being transmitted over a network connection. It involves monitoring the speed and capacity of the network link in order to ensure optimal performance and identify any potential bottlenecks or issues that may arise. By monitoring the bandwidth, network administrators and IT professionals can gain valuable insights into the network's usage and performance. This information can help them make informed decisions about network capacity planning, troubleshooting, and optimization. Bandwidth monitoring allows organizations to effectively manage their network resources and ensure that the network operates at its full potential.

Bandwidth Speed Test

Bandwidth Speed Test is a method used to measure the speed and efficiency of data transfer between two or more network devices. It is an essential tool for network administrators and users to evaluate the performance and quality of their internet connections. The primary purpose of conducting a bandwidth speed test is to determine the rate at which data can be transmitted over a network connection. This measurement is usually expressed in bits per second (bps), kilobits per second (Kbps), megabits per second (Mbps), or gigabits per second (Gbps). The higher the bandwidth speed, the faster the data can be transferred. Typically, a bandwidth speed test involves sending a set amount of data from one device to another and measuring the time it takes to complete the transfer. The data is usually sent in the form of packets, which are small units of information. The test calculates the time it takes for the packets to travel from the source device to the destination device and back, and then divides the size of the data by the total time taken to determine the average transfer speed. Several factors can affect the results of a bandwidth speed test. These include network congestion, latency, packet loss, and the quality of the connection. Network congestion occurs when there is high traffic on the network, resulting in slower speeds. Latency refers to the delay in the transmission of data and can be caused by long distances between devices or inefficient routing. Packet loss occurs when packets are lost or dropped during transmission, leading to slower transfer speeds. The quality of the connection, including the type of network equipment and cables used, can also impact the results. Bandwidth speed tests are commonly used by individuals to determine if they are getting the internet speeds they are paying for from their internet service provider (ISP). It helps identify any performance issues or bottlenecks in the network. Network administrators also use bandwidth speed tests to identify potential problems and ensure optimal network performance. ISPs often provide their own speed testing tools for customers to use or recommend third-party speed testing websites. In conclusion, a bandwidth speed test is a valuable tool for assessing the speed and efficiency of data transfer over a network connection. It helps measure the rate at which data can be transmitted and identifies any performance issues or limitations in the network. By conducting regular speed tests, individuals and network administrators can ensure that they are getting the desired internet speeds and troubleshoot any connectivity problems.

Bandwidth Throttling

Bandwidth throttling, in the context of networking, refers to the intentional capping or slowing down of the internet connection speed by an Internet Service Provider (ISP) or network administrator. This technique is used to control the amount of data that can be transmitted or received by a device or network within a specific timeframe. The primary purpose of bandwidth throttling is to manage and regulate network traffic to ensure fair usage and prevent network congestion. By limiting the bandwidth available to each user or device, ISPs can prevent certain users or applications from monopolizing the network resources, which can negatively impact the overall network performance for other users.

Bandwidth Usage Monitoring

Bandwidth usage monitoring refers to the process of tracking and analyzing the amount of data being transmitted over a network connection within a specific period of time. It involves measuring the utilization of available bandwidth, typically expressed in bits per second (bps), to assess network performance, identify potential bottlenecks, and optimize network resources. By monitoring bandwidth usage, network administrators can gain valuable insights into how effectively the network resources are being utilized and detect any abnormal or excessive data traffic that may negatively impact network performance. This monitoring process involves capturing relevant data packets, analyzing them, and generating reports to provide a

24

comprehensive overview of network traffic patterns.

Bandwidth Utilization

Bandwidth Utilization refers to the measure of how much of a network's available bandwidth is being used at any given time. It represents the percentage of the total bandwidth that is actively being utilized by data transmission or communication activities. In networking, bandwidth refers to the maximum amount of data that can be transmitted over a network in a given time period. It is commonly measured in bits per second (bps) or its derivatives such as kilobits per second (kbps) or megabits per second (Mbps). Bandwidth utilization is important because it allows network administrators to understand how effectively the available network resources are being used. Bandwidth utilization can be influenced by various factors such as network congestion, the number of active users, the type of applications being used, and the size of the data being transferred. Higher bandwidth utilization indicates that a larger portion of the available network capacity is being utilized, while lower utilization implies that the network is underutilized and there is room for additional data transmission. Monitoring and managing bandwidth utilization is crucial for network performance optimization and efficient resource allocation. By analyzing bandwidth utilization patterns, network administrators can identify potential bottlenecks, optimize network configurations, and ensure that sufficient bandwidth is allocated to critical applications or services. Various tools and techniques are available to measure bandwidth utilization, including network monitoring software, traffic analysis tools, and quality of service (QoS) mechanisms. These tools can provide real-time and historical data on bandwidth utilization, enabling network administrators to identify peak usage periods, detect abnormal traffic patterns, and take proactive measures to maintain optimal network performance. In conclusion, bandwidth utilization is a key metric for assessing the efficiency and effectiveness of network usage. It helps network administrators make informed decisions regarding network capacity planning, troubleshooting, and resource allocation. By optimizing bandwidth utilization, organizations can ensure smooth data transmission, minimize latency, and deliver a satisfactory user experience.

Bandwidth

Bandwidth refers to the maximum data transfer rate of a network or internet connection. It is typically measured in bits per second (bps) or multiples of it, such as kilobits per second (Kbps), megabits per second (Mbps), or gigabits per second (Gbps). In the context of networking, bandwidth determines how much data can be transmitted within a given amount of time. It represents the capacity of a network to transmit and receive information from one point to another. Bandwidth is often used to describe the speed or capacity of an internet connection, indicating how quickly data can be sent and received.

Bastion Host

A bastion host, also known as a bastion server or a jump box, is a highly secured and hardened server that is strategically placed on a network to protect other systems from unauthorized access and potential vulnerabilities. It acts as a secure gateway between an external network, such as the internet, and an internal network, providing an additional layer of defense for critical systems and resources. The primary purpose of a bastion host is to control and manage access to sensitive resources within a network. It acts as a single point of entry for external users, allowing them limited and controlled access to specific services or systems. By restricting direct access to internal resources, the bastion host reduces the attack surface and enhances overall network security. Typically, a bastion host is configured with a set of stringent security measures to mitigate risks. It operates on a minimalistic software stack, only running essential services and applications. It is often equipped with advanced intrusion detection and prevention systems, strong authentication mechanisms, and robust access controls. When an external user wants to access internal resources, they have to connect to the bastion host first. The bastion host then authenticates the user, verifies their credentials, and grants them limited access based on predefined rules and policies. This access can include activities like tunneling, port forwarding, or remote administration. The bastion host acts as a buffer, filtering and inspecting incoming traffic to ensure only authorized connections are allowed through. Furthermore, bastion hosts are commonly implemented with additional security features, such as logging and auditing capabilities. They record and monitor all activities occurring on the host, capturing information about any attempted or successful breaches. This recorded data can be invaluable during incident response and forensic investigations, aiding in identifying the source and nature of a security incident. By using a bastion host, organizations can better protect their critical systems and sensitive data from potential threats. It strengthens network security by adding an extra layer of defense, controlling access, and reducing the attack surface. With its robust security measures and monitoring capabilities, the bastion host plays a crucial role in maintaining a secure network infrastructure.

Baud Rate

Baud Rate refers to the rate at which data is transferred over a communication channel in bits per second (bps). It is a fundamental parameter in networking that determines how fast data can be transmitted between devices. In the context of networking, Baud Rate plays a crucial role in ensuring the efficiency and reliability of data communication. It establishes the speed at which data can be sent and received, allowing devices to exchange information and communicate effectively. Baud Rate is typically expressed in units of bits per second (bps), indicating the number of binary digits (bits) that can be transmitted in one second.

Biometric Authentication

Biometric Authentication refers to the process of verifying an individual's identity based on their unique physical or behavioral characteristics. It utilizes biometric traits such as fingerprints, hand geometry, facial recognition, iris scans, voice patterns, or DNA to authenticate and grant access to secure systems or networks. This form of authentication has gained popularity in networking due to its high level of security and difficulty to replicate or fake. In a networking context, biometric authentication works by collecting and analyzing the biometric data of an individual and comparing it to pre-registered data stored in a database. When a user attempts to access a system or network, their biometric information is collected through specialized sensors or devices, which then convert the data into a digital format. This data is encrypted and compared with the stored biometric template to determine if there is a match. One of the key advantages of biometric authentication in networking is its inherent uniqueness and difficulty to forge. Unlike traditional methods like passwords or PINs, which can be easily forgotten, stolen, or guessed, biometric traits are specific to an individual and cannot be easily replicated or shared. This significantly enhances the security of network access, reducing the risk of unauthorized users gaining entry. Furthermore, biometric authentication provides a convenient and user-friendly approach to accessing networks. Instead of relying on memorizing complex passwords or carrying access cards, users can simply present themselves for biometric scanning. This streamlines the authentication process, saving time and effort for both users and system administrators. However, it is important to note that biometric authentication is not without limitations. Factors such as environmental conditions, injury, or aging can affect the accuracy and reliability of biometric systems. Additionally, concerns regarding privacy and data security arise due to the sensitive nature of biometric information, requiring robust protocols and safeguards to protect user data. In conclusion, biometric authentication in the context of networking involves verifying an individual's identity using their unique physical or behavioral traits. It offers enhanced security and convenience compared to traditional authentication methods, but it also presents challenges that need to be addressed effectively.

Biometric Data

Biometric data refers to any measurable physical or behavioral characteristics that can be used to uniquely identify individuals. These characteristics are used in the field of networking to authenticate and verify the identity of users, granting them access to authorized resources or services. In the realm of networking, biometric data can include various attributes such as fingerprints, facial features, iris or retina patterns, voice patterns, hand geometry, and even behavioral traits like typing rhythm or gait. These distinctive traits are captured using specialized devices such as fingerprint scanners, cameras, microphones, or sensors, and are then processed and stored in a secure manner.

Bit Error Rate (BER)

Bit Error Rate (BER) is a measure used in the field of networking to quantify the accuracy of data transmission over a network. It is defined as the ratio of the number of bits received

26

incorrectly to the total number of bits transmitted. The BER is typically expressed as a percentage or as a decimal value between 0 and 1. The BER is an important metric in networking as it provides valuable information about the quality of the network connection. A low BER indicates that the network is transmitting data with a high level of accuracy, while a high BER suggests that there are errors occurring during transmission.

Bit Rate

Bit Rate refers to the amount of data that can be transmitted over a network per unit of time. It measures the rate at which bits are transmitted or received from one device to another. In computer networks, data is transmitted in the form of binary bits, which can only have two possible values: 0 or 1. The Bit Rate measures how many of these bits can be transmitted or received in a given period of time, typically measured in seconds.

Bit

A bit, short for binary digit, is the most fundamental unit of information in computer systems and networking. It is a basic building block used to represent data and is the smallest unit of data that can be processed or transmitted in a network. A bit can have two possible values, either 0 or 1, representing the two states of a digital signal - off or on, false or true, low or high voltage. In computer networks, bits are used to transmit and store data. Networks transmit data in the form of packets, and each packet is divided into smaller units called bits. These bits are then sent over the network from the source to the destination. In this process, the bits travel through various network devices and communication channels, such as switches, routers, and cables, until they reach their intended destination. Bits play a crucial role in the transmission and storage of data in networking. By representing data as binary numbers composed of bits, computers and network devices can process, manipulate, and transmit information. A series of bits can be used to represent alphanumeric characters, images, sounds, videos, and any other form of digital data. When multiple bits are combined, they form larger units called bytes, where each byte consists of 8 bits. Bytes are used as a common unit of measurement for data storage and transmission in networking. Network speeds are often measured in bits per second (bps), indicating the number of bits transmitted or received in one second. In summary, a bit is the fundamental unit of information in computer systems and networks. It represents the smallest unit of data that can be processed and transmitted in a network. By combining bits, larger units such as bytes are formed, allowing for the representation and transmission of various forms of digital data.

BitTorrent

BitTorrent is a peer-to-peer file sharing protocol designed for efficient distribution of large files over the internet. It operates as a decentralized network, where users called "peers" contribute their upload bandwidth to assist in the transferring of files. Unlike traditional client-server models, BitTorrent relies on the swarm principle, where individuals download and upload files simultaneously. This approach allows for faster and more resilient file transfers, as downloading peers can obtain different parts of a file from multiple sources at the same time. BitTorrent works by breaking down files into smaller pieces, typically ranging from a few kilobytes to a few megabytes in size. These pieces are then distributed across the network, with each peer contributing to the overall distribution process. Peers can join or leave the network dynamically, making the system highly scalable and adaptable to network conditions. When a user wants to download a file through BitTorrent, they first obtain a .torrent file, which serves as a metadata container. This file contains information about the file to be downloaded and the network locations (IP addresses) of the peers currently hosting that file. The user then initiates a connection to the swarm, acquiring the desired pieces of the file from different peers until the entire file is reconstructed on their local machine. To ensure fairness and encourage optimal sharing, BitTorrent employs a tit-for-tat mechanism. This means that the more a user uploads to others, the faster their own download speed becomes. This incentive system helps distribute the burden of sharing and prevents any single peer from becoming overwhelmed with upload requests. BitTorrent offers several advantages over traditional downloading methods. It minimizes the strain on central servers by distributing bandwidth usage across multiple users. It also allows for resumable downloads, as individual pieces of a file can be obtained from any online peer at any given time. Furthermore, BitTorrent enables users to build communities around specific files, with dedicated trackers allowing the discovery of available peers and facilitating efficient distribution. In summary, BitTorrent is a decentralized file sharing protocol that leverages the collective power of its users to distribute files efficiently. By breaking down files into smaller pieces and enabling simultaneous downloading and uploading, it offers faster transfers and minimizes the load on centralized servers. Its peer-to-peer nature and incentive mechanisms foster resilient and scalable file sharing networks.

Bitrate

Bitrate, in the context of networking, refers to the rate at which bits are transmitted from one location to another in a network. It is a measure of the speed or capacity of a network connection, specifically in terms of the amount of data that can be transmitted over the network per unit of time. The bitrate is usually expressed in bits per second (bps) and is a fundamental metric used in network communications. It quantifies the efficiency and performance of a network by determining how quickly data can be sent and received between devices connected to the network.

Black Hat Hacker

A black hat hacker is an individual who engages in hacking activities with malicious intent, often for personal gain or to cause harm. This term is used in the context of computer networking to describe a person who uses their technical skills to exploit vulnerabilities in computer systems and networks. Black hat hackers use various methods to compromise network security, such as seeking out weaknesses in software or hardware, exploiting security loopholes, or using social engineering techniques to gain unauthorized access. Once they gain access to a network, they may conduct various illegal activities, including stealing sensitive data, launching distributed denial-of-service (DDoS) attacks, defacing websites, or even distributing malware. Unlike white hat hackers, who work to improve network security and often help organizations identify and fix vulnerabilities, black hat hackers operate outside the boundaries of ethical hacking. Their actions are typically illegal and done without permission from the network or system owners. Black hat hackers can pose significant threats to individuals, businesses, and governments. Their activities can result in financial loss, reputational damage, or even compromise national security. Organizations must constantly stay vigilant, implementing robust security measures and staying updated on the latest threats and vulnerabilities. Employing skilled cybersecurity professionals and conducting regular security audits can help minimize the risk of being targeted by black hat hackers.

Black Hat Hacking

Black Hat Hacking refers to the malicious act of breaking into computer networks or systems with the intention of exploiting or causing harm. It is considered illegal and unethical, as it involves bypassing security measures and unauthorized access to private information. Black Hat Hackers, also known as crackers or cybercriminals, possess extensive knowledge of computer systems, networks, and software vulnerabilities. Their primary objective is to gain unauthorized access to sensitive data, disrupt system operations, and exploit weaknesses for personal gain.

Blacklist

Blacklist, in the context of networking, refers to a list of IP addresses, domains, or email addresses that are deemed malicious, suspicious, or undesirable. These blacklists are created and maintained by various organizations, such as internet service providers (ISPs), cybersecurity companies, and spam filtering services, to prevent unwanted network traffic or communications. When an IP address, domain, or email address is blacklisted, it means that it has been identified as involved in malicious activities, such as sending spam emails, distributing malware, participating in DDoS attacks, or engaging in other types of cybercrime. The purpose of blacklisting is to protect networks, systems, and users from potential threats and disruptions. Blacklists can be created using different methods. Some organizations compile blacklists based on reports from users or their own analysis of network traffic and behavior. Others may rely on reputation data from trusted sources or use advanced algorithms to identify patterns indicative of malicious activity. Network administrators and service providers often utilize blacklists as a part of their network security measures. By implementing blacklists, they can block or filter incoming network traffic or communications from blacklisted sources. This helps to minimize the risk of cyberattacks, reduce spam or unwanted emails, and maintain the overall network integrity. It is important to note that blacklists are not infallible and can sometimes include legitimate IP addresses or domains by mistake. These false positives can lead to unintended consequences, such as blocking genuine emails or preventing access to legitimate websites. Therefore, regular monitoring, evaluation, and updates are necessary to ensure the accuracy and effectiveness of blacklists.

Blue Team

A Blue Team refers to a group of cybersecurity professionals tasked with defending and securing a network against potential cyber threats and attacks. Complementing the Red Team, which plays the role of an attacker, the Blue Team takes on the defensive side of cybersecurity. The main responsibility of the Blue Team is to identify vulnerabilities, detect and respond to incidents, and implement measures to mitigate and prevent future security breaches. They work proactively to strengthen the network's security posture and ensure the confidentiality, integrity, and availability of sensitive information and resources.

Bluetooth PAN (Personal Area Network)

Bluetooth PAN (Personal Area Network) is a type of wireless network technology that allows multiple devices to connect and communicate with each other within a limited area, typically within a range of about 30 feet. It operates using short-range radio waves in the 2.4 GHz frequency band. This network enables the creation of ad-hoc connections between devices such as smartphones, tablets, laptops, and peripherals like printers, keyboards, or headsets. Bluetooth PAN can be used to transmit data, share internet connections, or stream audio between these devices without the need for any physical connections.

Bluetooth Range

Bluetooth range is the maximum distance over which Bluetooth devices can communicate with each other. Bluetooth is a wireless technology used for short-range communication between devices, typically within a range of about 10 meters (30 feet). It operates in the 2.4 GHz frequency band and uses radio waves to send and receive data. The range of Bluetooth depends on several factors, including the power class of the devices and the surrounding environment. Bluetooth devices are typically classified into three power classes: Class 1, Class 2, and Class 3. Class 1 devices have the longest range, with a maximum distance of around 100 meters (300 feet). Class 2 devices have a range of about 10 meters, while Class 3 devices have a range of about 1 meter. The range of Bluetooth can also be affected by obstacles such as walls, furniture, and other electronic devices. The signal may be weakened or blocked by these obstacles, reducing the effective range of the Bluetooth connection. The range may also be affected by interference from other wireless devices operating in the same frequency band, such as Wi-Fi routers or microwave ovens. To maximize the range of a Bluetooth connection, it is important to ensure that the devices are within range of each other and that there are no major obstacles or sources of interference. It is also recommended to keep the devices' firmware and drivers up to date, as these updates often include improvements to the Bluetooth range and performance. In summary, Bluetooth range refers to the maximum distance over which Bluetooth devices can communicate with each other. It depends on factors such as the power class of the devices, the surrounding environment, and the presence of obstacles or sources of interference. By taking these factors into account, users can optimize the range and performance of their Bluetooth connections.

Bluetooth Security Protocols

Bluetooth security protocols refer to the set of procedures and measures implemented in Bluetooth technology to ensure the confidentiality, integrity, and availability of transmitted data. These protocols play a crucial role in protecting Bluetooth-enabled devices against various security threats and vulnerabilities. One of the primary Bluetooth security protocols is the Bluetooth Secure Simple Pairing (SSP) protocol. This protocol is responsible for establishing a secure connection between two devices by authenticating and encrypting the communication. It uses various cryptographic algorithms, such as Elliptic Curve Diffie-Hellman (ECDH) for key

29

exchange and AES-CCM for encryption. The SSP protocol also includes features like device authentication, which verifies the identity of the devices before establishing a connection. Another important protocol is the Bluetooth Secure Connections (SC) protocol. It enhances the security of Bluetooth connections by improving the key exchange process. The SC protocol introduces an additional level of security by using out-of-band (OOB) authentication methods, such as Near Field Communication (NFC) or QR codes. These methods provide a reliable way to exchange the encryption keys without the risk of interception or tampering. Furthermore, the Bluetooth Core Specification also incorporates the Bluetooth Security Manager (SM) protocol. This protocol defines the procedures for link key generation, encryption, pairing, and authentication. It establishes a trust relationship between devices and ensures that the data transmitted over the Bluetooth connection remains secure. The Bluetooth security protocols also include measures to prevent unauthorized access and eavesdropping. For instance, Bluetooth devices utilize frequency hopping spread spectrum (FHSS) technique, which changes the frequency channel multiple times per second. This technique makes it difficult for attackers to intercept and decipher the transmitted data. Additionally, Bluetooth devices implement user-friendly security features, such as PIN codes and passkeys, to prevent unauthorized pairing and access.

Bluetooth Security

Bluetooth security refers to the measures and protocols in place to protect the confidentiality, integrity, and availability of data transmitted over a Bluetooth network. Bluetooth is a wireless technology that allows devices to communicate and exchange data over short distances without the need for physical connections. Security is a critical aspect of Bluetooth networking due to the potential risks associated with unauthorized access, data interception, and tampering. Several security mechanisms are implemented to mitigate these risks and ensure the safe transmission of data over Bluetooth. One of the primary security measures in Bluetooth is authentication. This process verifies the identity of devices attempting to connect to each other. Authentication typically involves the exchange of passwords, PINs, or digital certificates to establish trust between devices. By ensuring only trusted devices can connect, authentication prevents unauthorized access to the network. Encryption is another crucial security aspect of Bluetooth. It involves encoding the transmitted data in such a way that it can only be decoded by the receiving device with the correct decryption key. Encryption protects against eavesdropping and interception of sensitive information, ensuring that it remains confidential even if intercepted. To further safeguard Bluetooth connections, devices also use pairing to establish a secure connection. Pairing involves the exchange of encryption keys and other security parameters between two devices, creating a trusted relationship. Once paired, the devices can securely communicate without the risk of other devices intercepting the information. In addition to authentication, encryption, and pairing, Bluetooth security protocols also include mechanisms to protect against threats such as man-in-the-middle attacks, bluesnarfing, and bluejacking. These threats exploit vulnerabilities in Bluetooth devices or connections to gain unauthorized access, steal data, or manipulate devices. Overall, Bluetooth security is essential for safeguarding wireless communication and ensuring the privacy and integrity of data transmitted over Bluetooth networks. Through authentication, encryption, pairing, and other security measures, Bluetooth technology can be used with confidence in a wide range of applications, including wireless headsets, keyboards, IoT devices, and more.

Bluetooth

Bluetooth is a wireless technology that enables communication between devices over short distances. It operates in the 2.4 GHz frequency range and uses radio waves to transmit data between devices such as smartphones, tablets, laptops, and peripherals like keyboards, mice, and headphones. Bluetooth technology was first introduced in 1994 by Ericsson, a Swedish telecommunications company. It was intended to provide a simple and secure way to connect devices without the need for cables or manual configuration. The name "Bluetooth" was inspired by Harald Bluetooth, a Danish king who united Denmark and Norway in the 10th century. Bluetooth utilizes a technique called frequency hopping spread spectrum (FHSS) to minimize interference from other wireless devices operating in the same frequency range. The data transmission in Bluetooth is divided into packets, which are transmitted over multiple frequencies within the frequency range. This hopping technique allows for reliable and robust communication even in the presence of interference. One of the key features of Bluetooth is its ability to create a personal area network (PAN) known as a piconet. In a piconet, one device acts as the master, while other devices act as slaves. The master device controls the communication and can connect with up to seven active slave devices simultaneously. Each piconet has a unique hopping pattern, which ensures that devices in separate piconets do not interfere with each other. Bluetooth supports various profiles that define specific functions and capabilities, such as audio streaming, file transfer, and wireless printing. These profiles enable different Bluetooth-enabled devices to communicate and provide standardized functionalities across different manufacturers. Bluetooth devices can automatically discover and pair with each other, making it convenient for users to establish connections without manual intervention. Overall, Bluetooth technology has become widely adopted and is used in a wide range of devices, including smartphones, tablets, laptops, headphones, speakers, and smart home devices. Its versatility, simplicity, and low power consumption make it a popular choice for short-range wireless communication and connectivity between devices.

Border Gateway Protocol (BGP) Route Reflector

Border Gateway Protocol (BGP) is a protocol used in computer networking to facilitate the exchange of routing information between different autonomous systems (AS). It is commonly used in large-scale networks, such as the Internet, where multiple ASs need to communicate with each other. A BGP Route Reflector is a type of BGP device that assists in the distribution of routing information within an AS. In a typical BGP setup, all routers within an AS maintain full routing tables and exchange routing information with each other. This can lead to scalability issues as the number of routers and the size of the routing tables increase. A Route Reflector is introduced to address this scalability challenge. It acts as a central point within the AS and allows for the reduction of the number of BGP sessions required between routers. Instead of each router maintaining a full mesh of BGP sessions with all other routers, they only establish BGP sessions with the Route Reflector(s). A Route Reflector receives routing updates from its clients (the routers in the AS) and reflects these updates to other clients. It maintains a list of the best routes received from each client and propagates these routes to other clients. This allows for the dissemination of routing information across the AS without the need for every router to establish direct BGP sessions with each other. The use of a Route Reflector simplifies the BGP configuration within an AS and reduces the memory and processing power requirements on individual routers. Additionally, it improves convergence time in the network by decreasing the number of BGP update messages exchanged between routers. However, it is important to design the Route Reflector hierarchy carefully to ensure scalability and minimize the impact of single points of failure.

Border Gateway Protocol (BGP)

Border Gateway Protocol (BGP) is a routing protocol used in computer networks to exchange routing information and facilitate the exchange of data packets across different networks or autonomous systems (AS). BGP is designed to provide a scalable and reliable method for routing between ASs, which are individual networks managed by a single organization, such as an internet service provider (ISP). It enables the exchange of routing information between routers in different ASs, allowing them to determine the most efficient path for transmitting data between networks.

Botmaster

A network is a collection of interconnected devices, such as computers, servers, routers, switches, and other network-enabled devices, that can communicate with each other to share data, resources, and information. Networks provide a means of communication and collaboration between devices, allowing users to access and share data securely, efficiently, and reliably.

Botnet Detection

A botnet, in the context of networking, refers to a collection of compromised computers or devices that are controlled by a central command and control (C&C) system. These computers or devices, commonly referred to as "bots" or "zombies," are usually infected with malware without the knowledge or consent of their owners. This network of compromised devices is typically used for malicious purposes, such as launching coordinated attacks, spreading malware, stealing information, or engaging in spamming activities. Botnets are a significant threat to the security and stability of computer networks, as they have the ability to carry out large-scale attacks that can cause considerable damage. Detecting botnets is a crucial step in network security, as it allows for the identification and mitigation of these malicious networks. Botnet detection techniques involve analyzing network traffic and identifying patterns or behaviors that are indicative of botnet activities. These techniques rely on various methods, such as anomaly detection, signature-based detection, and traffic analysis, to uncover the presence of botnets within a network. Anomaly detection involves monitoring network traffic and identifying abnormal patterns or behaviors that deviate from the expected norms. This can be achieved by analyzing metrics like network traffic volume, protocol usage, or communication patterns. Any significant deviation from the normal behavior can indicate the presence of a botnet. Signature-based detection, on the other hand, relies on predefined signatures or patterns that are associated with known botnet activity. These signatures can be based on known characteristics or behaviors of specific botnet families or malware variants. By comparing network traffic against these signatures, it is possible to identify and classify network traffic associated with botnet activities. Traffic analysis techniques involve examining the flow of network traffic to identify communication patterns or activities that are commonly associated with botnets. This can include analyzing communication protocols, ports, or suspicious IP addresses. By detecting these patterns, it becomes possible to pinpoint potential botnet command and control servers or infected devices within a network. Overall, botnet detection plays a vital role in network security by enabling the identification and prevention of botnet activities. This allows network administrators to take appropriate measures to protect their networks and devices from the harmful effects of botnets, thereby ensuring the integrity and availability of network resources.

Botnet

A botnet refers to a network of compromised computers or devices that are under the control of a central command and control (C&C) server, typically operated by a malicious actor or a cybercriminal. These compromised computers, often referred to as "bots" or "zombies," are typically infected with malware, allowing the attacker to remotely control and manipulate them. Botnets are commonly created by exploiting vulnerabilities in computer systems or by tricking users into downloading malware through various means, such as malicious email attachments, drive-by downloads, or social engineering techniques. Once a botnet is established, the infected computers can be instructed to perform various malicious activities, including but not limited to: - Sending spam emails: Botnets are frequently used to send large volumes of spam emails, often promoting scams, phishing attempts, or the distribution of other malware. - Distributed Denial of Service (DDoS) attacks: Botnets can be harnessed to launch DDoS attacks, where the compromised computers collectively inundate a target website or network with an overwhelming amount of traffic, causing it to become inaccessible. - Mining cryptocurrencies: Botmasters may opt to use their botnets to mine cryptocurrencies, such as Bitcoin or Monero, by using the computational power of the infected machines to perform the resource-intensive calculations required for mining. - Stealing sensitive information: Botnets can be used for stealing personal information, such as login credentials, financial details, or any other data that can be exploited for financial gain or further cyber attacks. Botnets pose significant threats to the security and integrity of networks and systems worldwide. The widespread distribution of bots makes it challenging to detect and mitigate such attacks effectively. Countermeasures against botnets involve proactive security measures, such as installing and regularly updating antivirus software, keeping systems patched, and educating users about safe internet practices.

Bottleneck

A bottleneck in networking refers to a situation where there is a point in a network's infrastructure or design that acts as a constraint or limitation, causing a decrease in performance and efficiency. It is a concept often used to describe the phenomenon of congested or overloaded network resources. When a bottleneck occurs, it hinders the flow of data within the network, leading to delays, slower network speeds, and decreased overall capacity. This can significantly impact the performance of applications and services that rely on the network, causing latency issues, dropped connections, and reduced user experience.

Bridge Protocol Data Units (BPDU)

Bridge Protocol Data Units (BPDU) are messages used in networking to exchange information between bridges in a network. BPDU messages are typically sent using the Spanning Tree Protocol (STP) to determine the network topology and prevent loops from occurring. When a bridge is powered on or connected to a network, it starts sending out BPDUs to all other bridges in the network. These BPDUs contain information about the bridge itself, such as its MAC address and bridge ID. They also contain information about the network, including the root bridge and the path cost to reach the root bridge.

Bridge

A bridge is a networking device that operates at the data link layer of the OSI model. It connects two or more network segments together, allowing them to communicate with each other. A bridge helps in extending a LAN (Local Area Network) by interconnecting multiple network segments or LANs. The primary function of a bridge is to forward network traffic between the connected segments using MAC (Media Access Control) addresses. It examines the source MAC address of each incoming frame, learns the MAC address and the associated port on which it arrives, and then maintains a forwarding table or MAC address table. This table keeps track of the MAC addresses of devices connected to each port of the bridge. When a frame arrives at a bridge, it checks the destination MAC address in the forwarding table. If the destination MAC address is listed in the table, the frame is forwarded only to the corresponding port. This process is known as filtering. If the destination MAC address is not found in the table, the bridge floods the frame to all ports except the one it arrived on. This ensures that the frame reaches the destination device even if its address is not known. Bridges are typically used to break large networks into smaller segments, reducing the overall amount of network traffic and improving performance. They are also used to extend the reach of a network by connecting remote network segments over a long distance using bridges equipped with wireless or wired connections. In more advanced network architectures, bridges are often replaced by switches. Switches offer similar functionality to bridges but have additional features like full-duplex communication, VLAN (Virtual Local Area Network) support, and higher port densities. However, bridges are still used in certain scenarios, such as connecting different types of networks or when a simpler and more cost-effective solution is required.

Bridging Protocol

A bridging protocol is a networking protocol that enables devices to communicate with each other and forwards data packets between them in a local area network (LAN) or a wide area network (WAN) environment. It operates at the data link layer of the OSI model, providing a method for devices to share information and exchange data. The primary function of a bridging protocol is to connect different network segments together, creating a single logical network. It achieves this by learning the MAC (Media Access Control) addresses of devices connected to each network segment and building a forwarding table based on this information. This table is used to determine the destination of incoming data packets and forward them to the appropriate network segment. By doing so, the bridging protocol ensures that data reaches its intended destination and allows devices in different segments to communicate with each other seamlessly.

Broadband

Broadband is a type of high-speed internet connection that provides users with the ability to transmit and receive data at a faster rate compared to traditional dial-up connections. It is characterized by its ability to support the simultaneous transmission of multiple signals or channels over a single medium. Unlike dial-up connections, broadband utilizes a wide range of frequencies to transmit data, allowing for faster and more efficient communication. It can be delivered using various technologies, including Digital Subscriber Line (DSL), cable, fiber optic, or wireless connections.

Broadcast Domain

A broadcast domain is a logical division of a computer network, where all devices within the division can directly communicate with each other at the data link layer. In simpler terms, it is an area within a network where broadcast traffic is contained. When a device sends a broadcast message, it is intended for all devices within the same broadcast domain. This message is sent to a special broadcast address that is understood by all devices in the domain. The devices within the broadcast domain receive the message and process it accordingly.

Broadcast Storm Prevention

Broadcast storm prevention is a crucial concept in the field of networking that aims to mitigate the adverse effects of excessive or redundant broadcast traffic within a network. A broadcast storm occurs when there is a continuous loop of broadcast packets being transmitted and retransmitted throughout the network, creating a state of network congestion and impeding normal network operation. The prevention of a broadcast storm involves implementing various techniques and protocols to detect and control broadcast traffic, preventing it from overwhelming the network. These techniques can be classified into two main categories: hardware-based prevention and software-based prevention. In hardware-based prevention, network switches and routers play a significant role. These devices use mechanisms such as spanning tree protocol (STP) and rapid spanning tree protocol (RSTP) to eliminate redundant paths and prevent loops within the network. By actively blocking certain ports or redundant links, switches can effectively reduce the chance of a broadcast storm occurring due to looping broadcasts. Software-based prevention, on the other hand, relies on the configuration and management of network protocols and settings. One common approach is to implement broadcast domain segmentation, where the network is divided into smaller, isolated broadcast domains using techniques such as virtual LANs (VLANs). This helps to control and limit the propagation of broadcast traffic, as well as provide better network performance and security. In addition, network administrators can also configure network devices to use broadcast storm control mechanisms. This involves setting thresholds for acceptable levels of broadcast traffic, beyond which the devices will temporarily block or restrict further broadcasts. This prevents broadcast storms from occurring by proactively managing and regulating the amount of broadcast traffic allowed on the network. Overall, broadcast storm prevention is crucial for maintaining a stable and efficient network environment. By implementing a combination of hardware-based and software-based prevention techniques, network administrators can effectively minimize the impact of broadcast storms, reduce network congestion, and ensure smooth and uninterrupted network operation.

Broadcast Storm

A broadcast storm in the context of networking refers to a situation where network broadcast packets are continuously transmitted and forwarded across a network, resulting in excessive network traffic and causing performance degradation or even network failure. It occurs when a network device receives a broadcast packet and broadcasts it back out on all ports, causing other devices to receive and rebroadcast the same packet, creating a cycle of continuous broadcasts. A broadcast storm can be triggered by various factors, such as network loops, misconfigured network devices, or malicious activities. Network loops occur when there are multiple paths between network devices, creating a loop in the network topology. When a broadcast packet enters the loop, it circulates endlessly, being broadcasted on all connected ports of each device in the loop. This can consume network resources, overwhelm network devices, and lead to network congestion. Misconfigured network devices can also contribute to a broadcast storm. For example, if a switch is wrongly configured to flood broadcast packets to all ports instead of forwarding them intelligently, it can result in unnecessary broadcasts and subsequent storms. In addition, rogue network devices or compromised devices within a network can deliberately initiate broadcast storms as part of a malicious attack, causing disruption or denial of service for legitimate network traffic. To mitigate and prevent broadcast storms, network administrators employ several techniques. The most common method is implementing spanning tree protocols (STP) or other loop prevention mechanisms that detect and block network loops, preventing the propagation of broadcast storms. Network administrators also configure switches to intelligently handle broadcast packets, allowing them to be forwarded only to the necessary ports instead of flooding the entire network. Proper network segmentation and design, along with the use of VLANs (Virtual LANs), can also help contain broadcast traffic. In conclusion, a broadcast storm is a phenomenon in networking where continuous broadcasting and forwarding of broadcast packets result in excessive network traffic, causing network performance degradation or failure. It can be triggered by network loops, misconfigured devices, or malicious activities. By implementing loop prevention mechanisms, intelligent packet forwarding, and network segmentation, network administrators can effectively mitigate and prevent broadcast storms, ensuring stable and efficient network operation.

Broadcast Traffic Analysis

Broadcast traffic analysis is a process of monitoring and analyzing network traffic that is broadcasted to multiple recipients within a network. In the context of networking, a broadcast is a data packet that is sent from one device to all other devices within a network segment. This type of communication is often used for network discovery, service announcements, and other general-purpose communication. During broadcast traffic analysis, various techniques are employed to capture and analyze the broadcast traffic. This analysis provides valuable insights into the overall network performance, potential security threats, and identification of network anomalies. It helps network administrators and analysts to understand the behavior of the network and take necessary actions to optimize its performance and security. Broadcast traffic analysis involves the examination of different aspects of the broadcast traffic, including the source and destination addresses, protocol types, packet sizes, and content. By analyzing these attributes, network administrators can identify potential issues such as excessive broadcast storms, network congestion, and misconfigured network devices. One of the main objectives of broadcast traffic analysis is to identify unnecessary or excessive broadcast traffic, as it can consume valuable network resources and impact the performance of the entire network. By monitoring and analyzing the broadcast traffic, network administrators can determine the root causes of excessive broadcasts and take appropriate actions to minimize their impact. Furthermore, broadcast traffic analysis is also crucial for ensuring network security. By analyzing the content and structure of broadcast packets, network administrators can detect potential security threats and intrusions. This analysis helps in identifying abnormal network behavior, such as unauthorized network scans or suspicious traffic patterns, which can indicate the presence of malicious activities. In summary, broadcast traffic analysis is the systematic monitoring and analysis of network traffic that is sent from one device to all other devices within a particular network segment. It helps in optimizing network performance, identifying potential network issues, and ensuring network security. By examining various attributes of the broadcast traffic, network administrators can gain valuable insights into the overall network behavior and make informed decisions regarding the network infrastructure and security measures.

Broadcast Traffic Filtering

Broadcast Traffic Filtering is a network management technique that involves the identification and control of broadcast traffic within a network. Broadcast traffic refers to the data packets that are sent by a device to all other devices on the same network segment. Network devices, such as switches and routers, use broadcast traffic to communicate essential information, such as address resolution and network updates, to all devices within their broadcast domain. While broadcast traffic is necessary for network operation, excessive broadcast traffic can cause network congestion, increased latency, and reduced network performance. The primary purpose of broadcast traffic filtering is to manage and control the amount of broadcast traffic within a network. By implementing broadcast traffic filtering mechanisms, network administrators can minimize the negative impact that excessive broadcasts can have on network performance. There are several techniques that can be used for broadcast traffic filtering. One commonly used technique is the use of network segmentation, where the network is divided into smaller subnets or VLANs. This helps to limit the scope of broadcast traffic, as broadcasts are only sent to devices within the same subnet or VLAN. Another technique is the use of access control lists (ACLs) or firewall rules. These rules can be configured to allow or deny certain types of broadcast traffic based on specific criteria, such as source IP address, destination IP address, or protocol type. Furthermore, network administrators can also employ traffic shaping or traffic policing mechanisms to limit the amount of broadcast traffic that is allowed within the network. This involves setting bandwidth limits or prioritizing certain types of traffic, effectively reducing the impact of broadcast traffic on other network activities. In conclusion, broadcast traffic filtering is a network management technique that aims to control and minimize the impact of excessive broadcast traffic within a network. By implementing mechanisms such as network segmentation, ACLs, and traffic shaping, network administrators can ensure optimal network performance and reduce the potential for network congestion.

Broadcast Traffic

Broadcast traffic, in the context of networking, refers to the transmission of data packets from one device to all devices on a local network. It is a form of communication where a single source sends information to all other devices on the network, regardless of whether they are the intended recipients or not.Broadcast traffic is a fundamental aspect of network communication, as it allows for the dissemination of important information, such as network announcements, address resolution, and service discovery. However, it can also introduce inefficiencies and potential security risks if not properly managed.

Broadcasting Technology

Broadcasting technology refers to the transmission of data, information, or content to a wide audience via a network. It allows for the simultaneous distribution of data to multiple recipients, making it an efficient and cost-effective method for reaching a large number of individuals or devices. In the context of networking, broadcasting technology plays a crucial role in disseminating information across a network. It ensures that data or messages are delivered to all connected devices within a network, regardless of their location or individual address. This makes broadcasting essential for various network applications, including television, radio, internet streaming, and multicast communication.

Brute Force Attack

A brute force attack is a method used by hackers to gain access to a system or network by systematically trying all possible combinations of usernames and passwords until the correct combination is found. This type of attack is often used when the attacker does not have any specific information about the target system or the user accounts. During a brute force attack, the attacker uses automated tools that generate and test millions of different combinations of usernames and passwords in rapid succession. These tools apply different patterns and variations to common passwords, such as dictionary words, dates, keyboard patterns, and even commonly used character substitutions (e.g., replacing "e" with "3" or "o" with "0"). The purpose is to exploit weak or easily guessable credentials. Brute force attacks can be highly effective if proper security measures are not in place. They rely on the assumption that a user's password is weak, predictable, or easily discoverable. In many cases, people tend to use simple and easily guessable passwords, such as "123456" or "password." The attacker leverages this human tendency and systematically tests these common passwords, along with their variations, until access is gained. Network administrators need to implement several measures to mitigate the risk of brute force attacks. The first step is establishing a strong password policy that requires users to create complex and unique passwords. Passwords should include a combination of uppercase and lowercase letters, numbers, and special characters. Additionally, enforcing regular password changes and preventing the reuse of old passwords can also help protect against brute force attacks. Another effective measure is implementing account lockout policies. This means that after a certain number of failed login attempts, an account will be temporarily or permanently locked. This prevents the attacker from making an unlimited number of attempts and slows down the brute force attack process significantly. Finally, network administrators can also implement network and system monitoring tools that can detect and block unusual login attempts. These tools can analyze patterns and detect excessive login failures from a single IP address, signaling a potential brute force attack. Once detected, the system can automatically block or flag the IP address, preventing further access attempts.

Buffer Overflow

A buffer overflow refers to a coding vulnerability that occurs when a program tries to write more data to a buffer (a temporary storage area) than it can handle, resulting in the excess data overflowing into neighboring memory locations. In the context of networking, buffer overflows can pose significant security risks. When data is sent over a network, it is typically divided into smaller units called packets. These packets are temporarily stored in buffers at various points within the network devices, such as routers or switches, before being forwarded to their destination. If a buffer is not correctly sized or if a program does not have proper checks in place, it can be susceptible to buffer overflow attacks.

Business Continuity Planning (BCP)

36

Business Continuity Planning (BCP) refers to the process of creating and implementing strategies and measures to ensure the uninterrupted operation of a network or system in the event of a disruption or disaster. It involves identifying potential risks and vulnerabilities, developing contingency plans, and establishing protocols and procedures to mitigate the impact of any disruptions. The purpose of BCP is to minimize downtime, reduce financial losses, and maintain essential functions and services during unexpected events such as natural disasters, cyber-attacks, hardware or software failures, or human error. It aims to ensure that critical network infrastructure and services remain available and functional, allowing businesses to continue their operations with minimal disruption. BCP typically involves several key components and steps: 1. Risk Assessment: This involves identifying and evaluating potential risks and vulnerabilities that could pose a threat to the network or system. It includes analyzing the likelihood and impact of each risk to prioritize them accordingly. 2. Business Impact Analysis (BIA): BIA assesses the potential consequences and impacts of disruptions on various aspects of the business, such as operations, finances, reputation, and customer service. It helps determine the critical functions and resources that need to be protected and prioritized. 3. Development of Recovery Strategies: Based on the risk assessment and BIA, organizations develop strategies and plans to recover from disruptions. These strategies may include redundancy, backup systems, data recovery procedures, and alternative communication channels. 4. Plan Implementation: This involves putting the BCP strategies and measures into action. It includes training employees, establishing communication protocols, implementing backup and recovery procedures, and regularly testing and updating the plan to ensure its effectiveness. 5. Testing and Maintenance: BCP should be regularly tested and reviewed to identify any gaps or weaknesses in the plans. Testing may involve simulated exercises or tabletop drills to evaluate the response and effectiveness of the BCP. Regular maintenance ensures that the plan remains up-to-date and relevant to changing technologies, risks, and business requirements. In conclusion, Business Continuity Planning is a critical aspect of network management that aims to ensure the resilience and availability of essential functions and services in the face of disruptions. Adopting effective BCP measures can help organizations minimize the impact of unforeseen events and ensure business continuity.

CISO (Chief Information Security Officer)

A CISO, or Chief Information Security Officer, is a senior executive in an organization who is responsible for overseeing and managing the information security program. The main objective of a CISO is to protect the organization's sensitive information from unauthorized access, use, disclosure, disruption, modification, or destruction. The CISO is responsible for developing and implementing the organization's information security strategies, policies, and procedures. This includes assessing the current security posture, identifying vulnerabilities and threats, and developing appropriate controls and measures to mitigate risks. The CISO is also responsible for ensuring compliance with applicable laws, regulations, and industry standards. The CISO works closely with other stakeholders within the organization, such as the executive team, IT department, legal and compliance teams, and business units, to ensure that information security is integrated into all aspects of the organization's operations and activities. The CISO is responsible for raising awareness and promoting a culture of security within the organization, including providing training and education to employees. In addition, the CISO is responsible for managing the organization's incident response and recovery processes. This includes developing and maintaining an incident response plan, conducting regular drills and exercises, and coordinating with relevant stakeholders to handle security incidents in a timely and effective manner. Furthermore, the CISO is responsible for staying up-to-date with the latest trends, technologies, and best practices in information security. This includes monitoring the threat landscape, participating in industry forums and conferences, and collaborating with external organizations and experts to exchange knowledge and understand emerging threats and risks. In summary, the CISO plays a crucial role in protecting the organization's information and ensuring its confidentiality, integrity, and availability. By implementing a comprehensive information security program, the CISO helps to minimize the impact of security incidents and breaches, safeguard the organization's reputation and assets, and maintain the trust and confidence of customers, partners, and stakeholders.

Cable Modem

A cable modem is a networking device that allows for the transmission of digital data over a cable television network. It serves as the interface between the user's computer or network and the cable provider's network. The cable modem connects to the user's computer or network through an Ethernet or USB connection. It also connects to the cable provider's network through a coaxial cable connection. This allows the user to access the internet and other online services through their cable television connection.

Cable Tester

A cable tester is a device used in networking to determine the functionality and quality of network cables. It is designed to assist network administrators and technicians in identifying and resolving connectivity issues in networks. The role of a cable tester is to evaluate the performance of various types of network cables, including Ethernet cables (such as Cat5, Cat5e, Cat6, and Cat6a) and coaxial cables. It helps validate the installation process and ensure that the cables are properly terminated and wired according to industry standards.

Carrier Ethernet

Carrier Ethernet is a high-speed networking technology designed for use by telecommunications providers and enterprises to transmit data over wide area networks (WANs). It is based on Ethernet, a widely used local area network (LAN) technology, but with enhancements and additional features that make it suitable for long-distance and high-capacity data transmission. Carrier Ethernet provides a scalable and flexible solution for connecting multiple locations or offices within an organization, as well as for connecting multiple organizations or customers to a service provider network. It offers high bandwidth, low latency, and high reliability, making it ideal for applications that require real-time or high-performance data transmission, such as voice and video communications, cloud computing, and data storage. One of the key features of Carrier Ethernet is its ability to support multiple service types, including point-to-point, point-to-multipoint, and multipoint-to-multipoint connections. This allows service providers to offer a variety of services to their customers, such as dedicated internet access, virtual private networks, and Ethernet virtual private lines. Carrier Ethernet networks are typically built using a combination of fiber optic and copper cables, along with Ethernet switches and routers. These networks are highly scalable, allowing for easy expansion and adding new services or subscribers without significant infrastructure changes. Carrier Ethernet also includes a set of standardized protocols and technologies, such as the Metro Ethernet Forum (MEF) specifications, which ensure interoperability between different network equipment vendors and service providers. This promotes competition and innovation in the market, as customers are not locked into a single vendor or service provider. In summary, Carrier Ethernet is a networking technology that enables high-speed, reliable, and scalable data transmission over wide area networks. It offers a wide range of services and is widely used by telecommunications providers and enterprises for connecting multiple locations and delivering various data services to customers.

Carrier Sense Multiple Access (CSMA)

Carrier Sense Multiple Access (CSMA) is a medium access control protocol used in computer networking to regulate the transmission of data over a shared communication medium. It is designed to avoid or minimize collisions between multiple devices attempting to transmit data simultaneously. In CSMA, devices connected to a network listen for signals before transmitting data. They utilize a carrier sense mechanism to detect if the medium (e.g., the Ethernet cable) is busy or idle. If the medium is busy, the device will wait until it becomes idle. This helps prevent collisions between multiple devices transmitting data at the same time, which could result in data corruption and loss. When a device identifies the medium as idle, it initiates the transmission of its data. However, since other devices may also detect the medium as idle simultaneously, the possibility of a collision still exists. To further decrease the chances of collisions, CSMA utilizes a "multiple access" strategy that incorporates a "sense" mechanism, where devices continue to monitor the medium while transmitting data. If a device detects another transmission while it is still transmitting, it will abort its transmission and wait for a random time period before attempting to transmit again. This random backoff period helps ensure fairness and gives each device an equal chance to retransmit its data. CSMA is commonly implemented in Ethernet networks, where multiple devices share the same physical layer. Ethernet uses CSMA/CD (Carrier Sense Multiple Access with Collision Detection), which adds collision detection capabilities. In

CSMA/CD, devices listen for signals even while transmitting, allowing them to detect collisions. Detected collisions result in a "jam signal," indicating to all devices on the network that a collision has occurred. The devices then initiate their random backoff periods before attempting to transmit again, reducing the chance of further collisions. Overall, CSMA plays a vital role in managing access to a shared communication medium in computer networks. By utilizing carrier sense and multiple access strategies, it helps prevent or minimize collisions, ensuring efficient and reliable data transmission.

Carrier Sense Multiple Access With Collision Detection (CSMA/CD)

Carrier Sense Multiple Access with Collision Detection (CSMA/CD) is a network protocol used for sharing a single transmission medium among multiple network devices. It is primarily used in Ethernet networks to prevent collisions and efficiently utilize the available bandwidth. In CSMA/CD, each network device listens or "senses" the transmission medium before attempting to send data. If the medium is idle, the device starts transmitting its data. However, if another device is already transmitting, the device waits until the medium is free before transmitting. While a device is transmitting data, it continues to listen to the medium for any indications of collisions. Collisions occur when multiple devices attempt to transmit data simultaneously, causing a disruption in the network. CSMA/CD uses a mechanism called collision detection to identify these collisions. If a device detects a collision, it immediately stops transmitting and sends a jam signal to inform all other devices on the network to halt their transmission. After a random backoff period, the device that caused the collision will attempt to retransmit its data. This randomization reduces the likelihood of collisions reoccurring. CSMA/CD requires the network devices to be capable of receiving and transmitting data simultaneously. This is achieved using a technique called full-duplex, where separate channels are used for sending and receiving data. Without full-duplex capability, CSMA/CD would be unable to detect and handle collisions effectively. CSMA/CD is a contention-based protocol, meaning that devices compete for the right to transmit data. While it provides a relatively simple and efficient way to share a network medium, it is vulnerable to high collision rates as the number of devices on the network increases or the network becomes congested. To mitigate these limitations, technologies like switch-based Ethernet have been developed, which use collision-free methods like Carrier Sense Multiple Access with Collision Avoidance (CSMA/CA) or point-to-point links. However, CSMA/CD continues to be an important protocol in traditional Ethernet networks.

Cat5e Cable

Cat5e cable, also known as Category 5 Enhanced cable, is a type of Ethernet network cable that is widely used for transmitting data within a network. It is an improved version of the original Cat5 cable, providing enhanced performance and reliability. Designed to support Fast Ethernet and Gigabit Ethernet, Cat5e cable is capable of transmitting data at speeds of up to 1000 megabits per second (Mbps) over distances of up to 100 meters. It consists of four pairs of twisted copper wires, enclosed in a durable outer sheath.

Certificate Authority (CA)

A Certificate Authority (CA) is an entity within a network infrastructure that plays a crucial role in the security and authentication of digital certificates. Its primary function is to verify the identity of entities, such as individuals, organizations, or devices, and issue digital certificates to prove their authenticity. In a network environment, digital certificates serve as electronic passports or identification documents. They are used to validate the identity of participants in secure communications, such as websites, email servers, virtual private networks (VPNs), and more. Digital certificates consist of a public key, which is used for encryption and authentication, and additional information about the certificate holder.

Certificate Revocation List (CRL)

A Certificate Revocation List (CRL) is a crucial component of network security that serves as a repository of revoked certificates. It provides a mechanism for verifying the validity of digital certificates used in public key infrastructure (PKI) systems. A CRL is typically created and published by a Certificate Authority (CA) responsible for issuing digital certificates. The CRL contains a list of revoked certificates that have been deemed compromised, expired, or invalidated for any other reason. When a certificate is revoked, it is important to communicate this information to entities relying on the certificate to ensure the security and integrity of network communications. The CRL is structured as a digitally signed document, which enhances its trustworthiness and ensures its integrity. It includes information such as the certificate serial numbers that have been revoked, the date of revocation, and the reason for revocation. Additionally, the CRL may contain information about the CA itself, including its public key, to verify the authenticity of the CRL. Network entities, such as clients and relying parties, can check the validity of a digital certificate by consulting the associated CRL. They can obtain the CRL through various methods, such as downloading it from the CA's website or querying a network service specifically designed for distributing CRLs. To validate a certificate, the client or relying party fetches the CRL and verifies its integrity using the CA's public key. The client then checks if the certificate in question appears on the CRL and if it has been revoked. If a match is found, the client knows the certificate is no longer valid and should not be trusted for secure communications. Regularly updating and checking the CRL is essential to ensure the timely identification of revoked certificates. Outdated or incomplete CRLs can lead to the acceptance of compromised certificates, compromising the security of the network. In summary, a Certificate Revocation List (CRL) is a signed document maintained by a CA that contains a list of revoked certificates. It enables network entities to verify the validity of digital certificates and ensures the integrity of secure communications in a PKI infrastructure.

Cipher Suite

A cipher suite is a set of encryption algorithms and protocols used in networking to establish secure communication between two parties. It is an important component of Transport Layer Security (TLS) and Secure Sockets Layer (SSL) protocols. The cipher suite contains a combination of cryptographic algorithms, key exchange methods, and message authentication codes. It determines the level of security for the data transmission and ensures the confidentiality, integrity, and authenticity of the information exchanged over a network. When two parties, such as a client and a server, initiate a secure communication session, they negotiate a cipher suite that they both support. The negotiation process, known as the handshake, is crucial for establishing a secure and reliable connection. The cipher suite includes the following elements: 1. Key Exchange Algorithm: This algorithm is used to securely exchange cryptographic keys between the client and the server. It ensures that the keys are not intercepted or tampered with during transmission. 2. Encryption Algorithm: This algorithm encrypts the data using the shared keys to protect it from unauthorized access. It ensures that the information is scrambled and only decipherable by the intended recipient. 3. Message Authentication Code (MAC) Algorithm: This algorithm verifies the integrity of the transmitted data by generating a unique code, known as a MAC, using a secret key. The receiver can verify the authenticity of the data by comparing the MAC received with the calculated MAC. 4. Secure Hash Algorithm (SHA): This algorithm generates hash values that ensure the integrity of the data by creating unique digital fingerprints. It allows the receiver to verify if the data has been altered during transmission. By using a cipher suite, network communications can be protected against eavesdropping, tampering, and other security threats. The choice of cipher suite depends on the level of security required and the compatibility between the communicating parties. In conclusion, a cipher suite is a combination of encryption algorithms, key exchange methods, and message authentication codes used to establish secure communication in networking. It ensures the confidentiality, integrity, and authenticity of the transmitted data, providing a secure and reliable connection.

Ciphertext

A ciphertext refers to the output of an encryption algorithm, which is the result of transforming plaintext into an encoded form of data that is unintelligible without the use of a secret key or password. It is an essential concept in the field of networking, as it plays a crucial role in ensuring the security and confidentiality of data transmission over networks. When data is transmitted over a network, it is vulnerable to interception and unauthorized access. To protect sensitive information from being intercepted and understood by unauthorized parties, encryption is used. Encryption is the process of converting plaintext into ciphertext, making it unreadable to anyone without the proper decryption key. The ciphertext is created through the use of encryption algorithms, which are complex mathematical functions designed to transform data in a way that is difficult to reverse without the proper key. These algorithms take the plaintext as

40

input and use the encryption key to perform a series of mathematical operations, resulting in the ciphertext. The encryption key is essentially a secret code that is needed to convert the ciphertext back into its original plaintext form. One common encryption algorithm used in networking is the Advanced Encryption Standard (AES), which is widely used in various network security protocols. AES uses a symmetric key, meaning that the same key is used for both encryption and decryption. Other encryption algorithms, such as the Rivest Cipher (RC4) and Data Encryption Standard (DES), may also be used depending on the specific requirements of the network. Once the ciphertext is generated, it can be safely transmitted over the network. If an unauthorized party intercepts the ciphertext, they will not be able to understand its contents without the decryption key. Upon reaching the intended recipient, the ciphertext can be decrypted using the appropriate decryption key, and the original plaintext can be retrieved. In summary, a ciphertext is the encrypted form of data that is generated through the use of encryption algorithms. It ensures the security and confidentiality of data transmission over networks by making the information unintelligible to unauthorized parties. The ciphertext can only be decrypted and understood with the proper decryption key, which serves as the secret code for reversing the encryption process and retrieving the original plaintext form.

Circuit Switching

Circuit Switching is a networking technology that establishes a dedicated communication path between two nodes for the duration of a connection. It was a widely used method for transmitting voice and data before the advent of packet switching.In circuit-switched networks, a physical connection is established between the source and destination before any data transmission occurs. This connection, also known as a circuit, remains active for the entire duration of the communication. The dedicated nature of the circuit ensures a consistent quality of service and guarantees the availability of bandwidth throughout the connection.The process of establishing a circuit involves three main phases: circuit establishment, data transfer, and circuit termination.In the circuit establishment phase, the network resources required for the communication are reserved. This typically involves allocating bandwidth and configuring switches and routers along the path. Once the circuit is successfully established, the source node can start sending data to the destination.During the data transfer phase, the source node transmits the data continuously over the dedicated circuit. This allows for real-time, uninterrupted communication between the sender and receiver. However, since the circuit is dedicated, it cannot be used by any other communication until the connection is terminated.The circuit termination phase occurs when the communication is complete or explicitly ended by either the source or destination node. The network resources allocated for the circuit are released, allowing them to be utilized by other connections.Circuit switching offers several advantages, such as guaranteed bandwidth and constant latency, making it suitable for applications that require real-time communication, like voice and video calls. However, it is inefficient for bursty data traffic and can result in wasted resources when the circuit is idle.Packet switching, which is widely used in modern networks, replaced circuit switching as it allows for more efficient use of network resources by dividing data into small packets. These packets are independently routed across the network, resulting in better scalability and flexibility.In conclusion, circuit switching is a networking technology that establishes a dedicated communication path between two nodes for the entire duration of a connection. While it has advantages in terms of guaranteed bandwidth and constant latency, it has been largely superseded by packet switching in modern networks.

Cisco ACI (Application Centric Infrastructure)

Cisco ACI (Application Centric Infrastructure) is a software-defined networking (SDN) solution that provides centralized management and automation of network infrastructure in data centers. It is designed to streamline network operations and improve application performance by integrating physical and virtual networking elements into a single cohesive system. ACI follows a policy-driven approach, where network administrators define and enforce policies that dictate how applications should be treated in the network. These policies are based on the specific requirements of each application, including performance, security, and scalability. ACI enables the translation of these policies into network configurations, allowing applications to receive the appropriate level of service. The key components of Cisco ACI include the Application Policy Infrastructure Controller (APIC), the Nexus 9000 series switches, and the Cisco Application Virtual Switch (AVS). The APIC serves as the centralized management and policy engine of the ACI fabric, providing a single point of control for the entire network infrastructure. It allows network administrators to define policies, automate network provisioning, and monitor the performance of the network. The Nexus 9000 series switches are the building blocks of the ACI fabric. These switches support both traditional networking protocols and the ACI-specific protocols required for policy enforcement and operation. They provide high-performance connectivity between servers, storage systems, and other network devices, ensuring low-latency and high-bandwidth communication within the data center. The Cisco AVS is a virtual switch that integrates with ACI, extending the benefits of the policy-driven approach to virtualized environments. It allows network administrators to define and enforce policies on virtual machines, ensuring consistent performance and security across both physical and virtual infrastructure. In summary, Cisco ACI is a comprehensive SDN solution that simplifies network management, enhances application performance, and improves agility in data center environments. By adopting a policy-driven approach and integrating physical and virtual networking elements, ACI enables organizations to leverage the full potential of their applications while reducing operational complexity.

Cisco ACL (Access Control List)

An Access Control List (ACL) is a network security feature that controls the traffic flow between network devices based on predefined rules. It acts as a filter that permits or denies network packets from passing through a router, switch, or firewall. ACLs are commonly used to enhance network security by controlling access to network resources and protecting against unauthorized access or denial-of-service (DoS) attacks. ACLs operate by evaluating packets against a set of rules or conditions defined by the network administrator. These rules contain specific criteria, such as source IP address, destination IP address, protocol, port number, and other packet attributes. Based on the conditions defined in the ACL rules, packets are either allowed to pass through or dropped, ensuring that only legitimate and authorized network traffic is permitted.

Cisco AMP (Advanced Malware Protection)

Cisco AMP (Advanced Malware Protection) is a comprehensive security solution that is designed to protect networks against various types of advanced malware attacks. It provides proactive threat detection, continuous monitoring, and advanced analytics to enhance the overall security posture of network infrastructures. AMP combines several key features to offer robust protection against malware. One of its primary functionalities is malware detection, which involves the use of advanced algorithms and machine learning techniques to identify and analyze potential threats. By examining the behavioral patterns and characteristics of files and applications, AMP can identify and block malware before it can cause any harm. Another important aspect of Cisco AMP is its real-time threat intelligence capability. This feature allows the solution to receive updated information from multiple sources, such as global threat intelligence feeds and security research centers. By leveraging this collective knowledge, AMP can quickly identify emerging threats and provide timely protection to networks. In addition to detection and threat intelligence, Cisco AMP also offers advanced analytics and retrospective security. These features aim to provide deeper insights into potential security incidents and enable organizations to respond effectively. AMP's analytics capabilities allow organizations to analyze and correlate various security events, helping them understand the root causes and potential impact of these incidents. Furthermore, Cisco AMP supports retrospective security, which means it can continuously analyze and monitor file activity even after it has been deemed safe. This feature is valuable for identifying any potential threats that may have been dormant or undetectable initially. Cisco AMP can be deployed as a standalone solution or integrated into existing network security infrastructures. It is compatible with a wide range of Cisco products, including firewalls, routers, and switches, enabling organizations to have a unified security management platform. In conclusion, Cisco AMP is an advanced malware protection solution that helps organizations defend their networks against evolving threats. By combining proactive detection, real-time threat intelligence, and advanced analytics, AMP provides comprehensive security coverage and enhances the overall resilience of network infrastructures.

Cisco AMP For Endpoints

Cisco AMP for Endpoints is a comprehensive cybersecurity solution that provides advanced threat protection for network devices and endpoints within an organization's network. It leverages the power of cloud computing and artificial intelligence to detect, analyze, and respond to cyber threats in real time. AMP, short for Advanced Malware Protection, is designed to defend against a wide range of cyber threats, including viruses, malware, ransomware, and phishing attacks. It offers multiple layers of protection, ensuring that potential threats are identified and neutralized before they can cause harm to the network or compromise sensitive data. One of the key features of Cisco AMP for Endpoints is its ability to analyze file behavior. Every file entering the network or being accessed by an endpoint is thoroughly examined, looking for any suspicious or malicious activities. This allows the solution to identify and block potential threats, even if they have not been explicitly identified in threat intelligence databases. Additionally, Cisco AMP for Endpoints utilizes machine learning algorithms to identify patterns and anomalies that may indicate an ongoing or imminent attack. The solution continuously learns from new data and adapts its threat detection capabilities to stay ahead of emerging threats. Furthermore, Cisco AMP for Endpoints provides extensive visibility into the network's security posture. It provides detailed reports and analytics that allow network administrators to identify vulnerabilities, track trends, and make informed decisions to enhance their organization's overall security posture. The solution also offers automated response capabilities, allowing it to take immediate action to contain and mitigate threats. This can include isolating compromised devices from the network, quarantining malicious files, and initiating remediation processes to restore affected endpoints to a secure state. In summary, Cisco AMP for Endpoints is a powerful cybersecurity solution that combines advanced threat detection, analysis, and response capabilities. It helps organizations protect their network and endpoints from a wide range of cyber threats, ensuring the integrity and confidentiality of critical data.

Cisco AMP For Networks

Cisco AMP for Networks is a comprehensive network security solution that provides advanced malware protection for all network traffic. It uses a combination of behavioral analytics, continuous monitoring, and global threat intelligence to detect and block known and unknown threats in real-time. With Cisco AMP for Networks, organizations can enhance their network security posture by gaining visibility and control over all network traffic. It can protect both physical and virtual network environments, providing a scalable solution for small businesses to large enterprises.

Cisco ASA (Adaptive Security Appliance)

The Cisco ASA (Adaptive Security Appliance) is a multifunctional network security device that provides firewall, virtual private network (VPN), and intrusion prevention system (IPS) capabilities. It is designed to protect computer networks from unauthorized access, threats, and attacks, ensuring the confidentiality, integrity, and availability of network resources. The ASA combines various security features into a single integrated platform, making it an essential component of network infrastructure in many organizations. It acts as a first line of defense by inspecting incoming and outgoing traffic and enforcing security policies to mitigate risks and vulnerabilities. As a firewall, the ASA employs stateful packet inspection to analyze network traffic at the application layer and make decisions based on contextual information. It examines packets to determine their source, destination, and protocol, allowing or blocking them based on predefined access control rules. By enforcing access controls, the ASA prevents unauthorized access and protects against denial-of-service (DoS) attacks. In addition to firewall capabilities, the ASA also provides VPN functionality. It enables secure remote access to corporate networks over public networks such as the internet, allowing employees to connect from remote locations while maintaining the confidentiality of data transmitted. The ASA supports different VPN protocols, including IPsec and SSL, and implements encryption, authentication, and data integrity mechanisms to create secure tunnels between remote users and the corporate network. Furthermore, the ASA incorporates an intrusion prevention system (IPS) to detect and prevent network attacks. It analyzes network traffic for known or suspected threats, including malware, viruses, and intrusion attempts, and takes immediate action to block or mitigate them. By continuously monitoring and analyzing network traffic, the ASA provides real-time threat prevention and helps protect against emerging threats. In summary, the Cisco ASA is a versatile network security device that combines firewall, VPN, and IPS functionalities. It plays a critical role in safeguarding networks against unauthorized access, threats, and attacks, ensuring the secure and reliable operation of network infrastructures.

Cisco ASA VPN

A Cisco ASA VPN (Virtual Private Network) is a network security solution provided by Cisco Systems, specifically designed to ensure secure remote access to corporate networks over the internet. It allows authorized users to securely connect to and communicate with a private network, such as a corporate intranet, from a remote location outside the organization's physical premises. The Cisco ASA VPN creates a secure tunnel between the user's device and the private network, encrypting the traffic to protect it from unauthorized access or interception.

Cisco ASAv (Adaptive Security Virtual Appliance)

The Cisco ASAv (Adaptive Security Virtual Appliance) is a virtualized network security solution provided by Cisco Systems. It is designed to protect virtual and cloud environments, offering the same security features as Cisco's physical security appliances but with the flexibility and scalability of virtualization technology. As a virtual appliance, the Cisco ASAv can be deployed on various hypervisors such as VMware ESXi, Microsoft Hyper-V, or in cloud environments like Amazon Web Services (AWS) and Google Cloud Platform (GCP). It functions as a firewall, providing essential network security functions such as access control, threat prevention, and VPN capabilities. The ASAv offers a range of security features, including stateful packet inspection (SPI), network address translation (NAT), virtual private network (VPN) encryption, and intrusion prevention system (IPS) capabilities. It supports advanced security protocols like IPsec VPN, SSL VPN, and Secure Shell (SSH) for secure remote access to the network. With the Cisco ASAv, administrators have full visibility and control over network traffic flowing through the virtualized environment. It allows for the application of granular security policies based on user and application awareness, ensuring that network resources are protected from unauthorized access and potential threats. In addition to its security capabilities, the ASAv offers high availability features such as active-active and active-standby failover configurations, ensuring uninterrupted network connectivity even in the event of hardware or software failures. The Cisco ASAv can be managed and monitored through a web-based user interface (UI) or command-line interface (CLI), providing flexible options for network administrators to configure, update, and troubleshoot the virtual appliance. It can also integrate seamlessly with other Cisco security products and management platforms, facilitating centralized control and consolidated security management. In summary, the Cisco ASAv is a virtualized network security solution that provides essential firewall and security features to protect virtual and cloud environments. With its flexible deployment options, comprehensive security capabilities, and ease of management, the ASAv helps organizations ensure the integrity, confidentiality, and availability of their network resources in virtualized and cloud-based infrastructures.

Cisco ASR (Aggregation Services Router)

A Cisco ASR (Aggregation Services Router) is a high-performance, modular router designed for service providers and enterprise networks. It is specifically built to handle large-scale WAN aggregation, edge routing, and broadband services, offering superior reliability, scalability, and security. The Cisco ASR series routers are characterized by their robust architecture, using a distributed software architecture that separates control and forwarding functionality. This design allows for high-performance packet forwarding, while providing flexibility and scalability to accommodate future network growth and evolving service requirements. One of the key features of the Cisco ASR is its ability to aggregate and route diverse types of traffic. It supports a wide range of interfaces, including Ethernet, TDM, and optical interfaces, enabling the consolidation of multiple services over a single platform. With its integrated service modules, such as firewalls, VPNs, load balancers, and IPsec acceleration, the ASR can provide comprehensive service offerings to meet the needs of both provider and enterprise networks. Another important aspect of the Cisco ASR routers is their support for advanced IP Services, including IP/MPLS (Multi-Protocol Label Switching), which allows for efficient traffic engineering, quality of service (QoS) mechanisms, and fast reroute capabilities. These features enable service providers to meet stringent service level agreements (SLAs) and ensure optimal performance for critical applications. In terms of scalability, the Cisco ASR routers are designed to support high-speed connectivity with high port densities and high throughput capabilities. They can handle the increasing demands of today's data-intensive applications and the exponential growth of network traffic. Furthermore, the ASR series offers hardware redundancy and resiliency features, ensuring uninterrupted service even in the event of component failures. In conclusion, the Cisco ASR (Aggregation Services Router) is a versatile and powerful router that provides service providers and enterprise networks with a highly scalable, reliable, and secure solution for WAN aggregation, edge routing, and broadband services. Its advanced features, modular design, and support for a wide range of interfaces make it an ideal choice for network deployments requiring high performance, flexibility, and future-proofing.

Cisco Aironet

Cisco Aironet is a brand of wireless access points and wireless LAN controllers that are designed and manufactured by Cisco Systems. It is a popular solution for creating reliable and high-performance wireless networks in various environments, including enterprise businesses, educational institutions, and public spaces. Aironet access points are the key building blocks of a wireless network, providing connectivity and access to network resources for wireless devices such as laptops, smartphones, and tablets. They are designed to support the latest wireless standards, such as IEEE 802.11ac, and offer advanced features to enhance security, scalability, and overall network performance.

Cisco AnyConnect NAM (Network Access Manager)

Cisco AnyConnect NAM (Network Access Manager) is a software application developed by Cisco Systems that provides secure network connectivity and access control for users in a network environment. When deployed in a network, Cisco AnyConnect NAM ensures that users can securely connect to the network and access resources based on their authentication and authorization levels. This software application acts as a virtual private network (VPN) client, enabling users to establish encrypted connections to the network, regardless of their location. Cisco AnyConnect NAM offers various features that enhance network security and access control. It provides support for multiple authentication methods, including username and password, digital certificates, and two-factor authentication. This ensures that only authorized users can access the network and its resources. In addition, Cisco AnyConnect NAM allows network administrators to enforce granular access policies based on user roles, group memberships, time of day, and location. These policies can be configured to restrict access to certain resources, limit network bandwidth, or apply other security measures as required. The software application also includes built-in endpoint assessment capabilities, which enable network administrators to ensure that connecting devices meet certain security requirements before granting access to the network. This prevents compromised or vulnerable devices from accessing sensitive resources, protecting the network from potential threats. Cisco AnyConnect NAM is compatible with a wide range of operating systems, including Windows, macOS, and Linux. It can be deployed in a centralized manner, allowing network administrators to manage and configure the application across multiple devices from a single management console. Overall, Cisco AnyConnect NAM is a powerful network access management solution that provides secure connectivity and access control for users in a network environment. It enhances network security, simplifies management, and ensures that only authorized users can access network resources.

Cisco AnyConnect Secure Mobility Client

Cisco AnyConnect Secure Mobility Client is a software application developed by Cisco Systems that provides remote access to enterprise networks securely. It is particularly designed to allow users to connect to an organization's network resources from anywhere, at any time, using any device, while ensuring the security and privacy of data transmission. With the increasing trend of remote work and the rise of mobile devices, the need for secure remote access to corporate networks has become crucial for organizations. The Cisco AnyConnect Secure Mobility Client serves as a key solution to this demand by establishing a secure VPN (Virtual Private Network) connection between the user's device and the designated network. The primary function of the Cisco AnyConnect Secure Mobility Client is to encrypt the communication between the user's device and the network, ensuring confidentiality and preventing unauthorized access or interception of data. By creating a secure tunnel, it extends the network's security policies and protocols to the user's remote location, allowing them to access shared files, applications, and resources as if they were physically present in the office. Beyond secure connectivity, this client software offers additional features to enhance the user experience and network management. It supports multi-factor authentication methods, such as certificates, RSA SecurID, or even biometrics, to ensure stronger authentication and prevent unauthorized access. It also includes advanced endpoint assessment capabilities, which enable network administrators to enforce security policies and verify the compliance of connecting devices before granting access to network resources. The Cisco AnyConnect Secure Mobility Client is compatible with various operating systems, including Windows, macOS, Linux, iOS, and Android, providing flexibility for users across different devices. It can be deployed and managed centrally by network administrators using Cisco's management platforms, simplifying the administration and configuration of remote access policies and security settings.

Cisco AnyConnect VPN

Cisco AnyConnect VPN is a virtual private network (VPN) solution provided by Cisco Systems, Inc. It enables secure remote access to network resources for users, allowing them to connect to a private network over the public internet. The Cisco AnyConnect VPN solution offers a secure way for users to connect to their organization's network from any location, using any device, such as laptops, smartphones, or tablets. It establishes an encrypted tunnel between the user's device and the organization's network, ensuring that all data transmitted between them remains confidential and protected from unauthorized access.

Cisco AnyConnect

Cisco AnyConnect is a secure and reliable virtual private network (VPN) solution developed by Cisco for remote access to networks. It provides secure and encrypted connections between remote users and the corporate network, ensuring that data transmitted between them remains confidential and protected. With Cisco AnyConnect, users can securely access resources, such as files, applications, and internal websites, from anywhere in the world, as long as they have an internet connection. It establishes a secure tunnel between the user's device and the corporate network, allowing them to securely access internal resources as if they were physically present within the network.

Cisco BGP (Border Gateway Protocol)

Border Gateway Protocol (BGP) is a standardized exterior gateway protocol used in computer networking to enable the exchange of routing information among autonomous systems (AS). It is designed to allow the efficient and scalable routing of traffic on the Internet. BGP is responsible for establishing and maintaining communication between individual routers, called BGP speakers, within an AS or between different ASs. It enables routers to exchange information about the network paths and choose the most optimal route for forwarding traffic. Unlike interior gateway protocols like Routing Information Protocol (RIP) or Open Shortest Path First (OSPF), which are used within a single AS, BGP is an exterior gateway protocol used to connect different ASs. ASs are unique networks under the control of a single administrative entity, such as an internet service provider (ISP) or a large enterprise. The primary goal of BGP is to ensure reliable and efficient packet routing across the Internet. It achieves this by utilizing a path-vector routing algorithm, which takes into account multiple factors when selecting the best path for forwarding traffic. These factors may include network policies, link quality, and available bandwidth. One of the key features of BGP is its ability to support rich policy-based routing. Network administrators can define policies and specify conditions under which traffic should be routed or filtered. This level of control allows organizations to optimize their network performance and prioritize specific types of traffic. BGP operates through the exchange of routing updates, known as BGP messages, between neighboring routers. These updates contain information about reachable network prefixes and associated attributes. BGP speakers use this information to build a comprehensive routing table, which is used to make forwarding decisions. By utilizing BGP, network engineers and administrators can establish highly resilient and scalable networks through the efficient exchange of routing information between ASs. It plays a critical role in facilitating the global connectivity of the Internet and ensures the reliable and secure delivery of data packets across diverse networks.

Cisco CME (CallManager Express)

Cisco CME (CallManager Express) is a feature of Cisco IOS software that provides a solution for small to medium-sized businesses to establish and manage their own telephony system. It is a cost-effective and flexible option for organizations that require a comprehensive communication network but do not have the resources for a full-scale enterprise telephony solution. Cisco CME includes a variety of features and functions that enable businesses to efficiently handle phone calls and manage their communication infrastructure. It supports various IP telephony features such as call forwarding, call transfer, call waiting, and conferencing, allowing users to handle their calls in a professional and seamless manner. One of the key advantages of Cisco CME is its integration with Cisco Unified Communications Manager (CUCM), which is the main call processing component of Cisco's enterprise telephony solution. This integration enables businesses to establish a scalable and highly reliable voice network that can seamlessly connect multiple locations and support various communication devices, such as IP phones, analog devices, and softphones. Cisco CME also offers advanced features such as unified messaging, which allows users to access their voicemail and email messages in a single inbox, improving productivity and simplifying communication management. It also supports enhanced security features, including secure voice communication using encryption protocols like Secure Real-Time Transport Protocol (SRTP) and Transport Layer Security (TLS). The management and administration of Cisco CME is done through a web-based interface, Cisco Configuration Professional (CCP), which provides an intuitive and user-friendly platform for configuring and monitoring the telephony system. Administrators can easily manage users, phone lines, call routing, and other system settings, simplifying the overall management of the communication network. In conclusion, Cisco CME is a powerful telephony solution that enables small to medium-sized businesses to establish and manage their own communication network. It offers a wide range of features and functions, seamless integration with Cisco Unified Communications Manager, and simplified management through Cisco Configuration Professional. With Cisco CME, organizations can enhance their communication capabilities and improve overall productivity.

Cisco CUBE (Cisco Unified Border Element)

Cisco CUBE (Cisco Unified Border Element) is a feature-rich network device that performs the functions of a border gateway router in a Cisco Unified Communications system. It acts as a border element between two different IP networks, providing secure and reliable connectivity for voice and video communication over IP. CUBE plays a crucial role in enabling communication between an organization's IP-based telephony system and the outside world. It acts as an interface between the organization's IP network and the public network, ensuring seamless connectivity and efficient routing of voice and video traffic. CUBE performs a variety of functions that are essential for successful voice and video communication over IP: 1. Session Border Controller (SBC): CUBE acts as a session border controller, providing secure connectivity and managing multiple sessions simultaneously. It ensures that communication sessions are established and maintained correctly, performing tasks such as protocol mediation, call admission control, and media termination. 2. Interoperability: CUBE supports a wide range of protocols and codecs, enabling interoperability between different IP-based communication platforms. It ensures that voice and video traffic can be efficiently transported between systems using different protocols and codecs, allowing organizations to integrate diverse communication technologies seamlessly. 3. Transcoding: CUBE has the capability to perform transcoding, converting media streams between different audio and video codecs. This allows for smooth communication between systems that use different codecs, ensuring compatibility and optimal media quality. 4. Security: CUBE provides advanced security features to protect the organization's voice and video communication. It supports encryption protocols, such as Transport Layer Security (TLS) and Secure Real-Time Transport Protocol (SRTP), ensuring confidentiality and integrity of media streams. CUBE also includes firewall functionality, protecting the organization's network from unauthorized access and malicious attacks. Cisco CUBE is a powerful and versatile device that plays a critical role in enabling secure and efficient voice and video communication over IP networks. Its feature set and capabilities make it an essential component of Cisco Unified Communications systems, providing organizations with the tools they need to connect and communicate effectively.

Cisco CUC (Cisco Unity Connection)

Cisco Unity Connection (CUC) is a component of the Cisco Unified Communications Manager (CUCM) suite that provides voicemail and unified messaging services for Cisco IP telephony environments. It is designed to enhance communication and collaboration within organizations by allowing users to access and manage their voicemail messages from multiple devices and platforms. CUC integrates with the Cisco IP telephony infrastructure to provide a comprehensive

47

voicemail solution that supports a range of features and functions. It allows users to receive, send, and store voicemail messages, as well as access them through various methods such as email, phone, web browser, or mobile applications. CUC also offers advanced features like message synchronization, voice recognition, speech-to-text transcription, and automated attendants. One of the key benefits of CUC is its ability to unify different communication channels, enabling users to access and manage their voicemail messages alongside other forms of communication such as email and instant messaging. This integration helps streamline workflows and improve productivity by centralizing message management and reducing the need for multiple platforms or applications. Furthermore, CUC provides administrators with a range of tools for managing and configuring voicemail services. They can set up user mailboxes, define voicemail policies, customize greetings, and perform other administrative tasks through a web-based interface. CUC also supports integration with Active Directory and LDAP directories, simplifying user provisioning and authentication processes. In terms of scalability and redundancy, CUC offers a highly available architecture that can be deployed in a distributed manner across multiple servers, ensuring business continuity even in the event of hardware or network failures. It supports clustering, load balancing, and mirroring techniques to provide high availability and fault tolerance. In summary, Cisco Unity Connection is a robust voicemail and unified messaging solution that enhances communication and collaboration within organizations. It allows users to access and manage voicemail messages from multiple devices and platforms, while providing advanced features and administrative tools for efficient message management. With its integration capabilities and scalability, CUC is a valuable component of the Cisco Unified Communications Manager suite.

Cisco Catalyst 9000 Series

The Cisco Catalyst 9000 Series is a family of network switches designed to deliver high-performance, secure, and reliable connectivity for modern networking environments. These switches are built with advanced technology and features that enable organizations to optimize their network infrastructure and adapt to changing business requirements. With the Catalyst 9000 Series, Cisco aims to address the ever-increasing demands of digital transformation and the rising complexity of network operations. The series offers a range of switches, including the Catalyst 9200, Catalyst 9300, Catalyst 9400, Catalyst 9500, and Catalyst 9600, each tailored to meet specific deployment needs. One of the key features of the Catalyst 9000 Series is its support for Cisco's Software-Defined Access (SD-Access) architecture. This architecture simplifies network design and deployment by automating the provisioning and management of network policies across wired and wireless devices. It allows organizations to segment and secure their networks at scale, ensuring that each user and device only has access to the appropriate resources. Another notable feature of the series is its enhanced security capabilities, including integrated threat defense and encrypted traffic analytics. By integrating security directly into the network infrastructure, the Catalyst 9000 Series provides end-to-end protection against advanced threats and helps organizations detect and respond to security incidents more effectively. Furthermore, the Catalyst 9000 Series incorporates Cisco's Intent-Based Networking (IBN) technology, which enables network administrators to define business intents and automatically translate them into network configurations. This approach simplifies network management, improves operational efficiency, and enhances the overall network performance. In summary, the Cisco Catalyst 9000 Series is a comprehensive portfolio of network switches that offers advanced technologies and features to enable organizations to build agile, secure, and intelligent networks. By leveraging SD-Access, integrated security, and IBN capabilities, the series helps businesses adapt to evolving networking demands and deliver an improved user experience.

Cisco Catalyst Switches

A Cisco Catalyst Switch is a type of networking device that is designed to connect multiple devices, such as computers, servers, and printers, within a local area network (LAN). It operates at the data link layer of the OSI model and provides advanced switching capabilities to ensure efficient data transfer and network management. Cisco Catalyst Switches are known for their high performance, scalability, and flexibility. They are widely used in enterprise networks, data centers, and service provider environments to support a variety of applications and services. These switches offer a range of features and capabilities that enable organizations to build reliable and secure networks.

Cisco Cloud Services Router (CSR)

The Cisco Cloud Services Router (CSR) is a virtual router designed by Cisco Systems to enable enterprises to extend their network to the cloud infrastructure. It offers the same features and functions as a physical router, but it runs on a virtual machine in a cloud environment. The CSR acts as a bridge between the on-premises network and the cloud infrastructure, allowing organizations to connect and manage their network resources securely and efficiently. It provides a flexible and scalable solution for network connectivity in a cloud environment, enabling seamless communication between various cloud services, data centers, and branch offices.

Cisco Collaboration Edge

The Cisco Collaboration Edge is a networking solution that enables secure and seamless communication and collaboration between remote users and the organization's internal network. It allows users outside the company's premises to connect and access the collaboration tools and services offered by Cisco, such as voice and video conferencing, instant messaging, presence, and file sharing. With the Cisco Collaboration Edge, remote users can enjoy the same communication experience as if they were physically present in the office. They can connect to the network using various devices, including laptops, smartphones, and tablets, regardless of their location or network provider. This flexibility empowers employees to work remotely, increasing productivity and efficiency.

Cisco DHCP (Dynamic Host Configuration Protocol)

The Cisco DHCP (Dynamic Host Configuration Protocol) is a network protocol used to automatically assign IP addresses and other network configuration parameters to devices on a network. It simplifies network administration by reducing the need for manual IP address configurations. DHCP operates on a client-server model, where a DHCP server is responsible for assigning IP addresses and other network settings, while DHCP clients are devices that request and receive these parameters. The server maintains a pool of available IP addresses and dynamically assigns them to clients when they connect to the network.

Cisco DNA Analytics And Assurance

Cisco DNA Analytics and Assurance is a comprehensive network management solution that combines advanced analytics and proactive monitoring to deliver insights and ensure optimal network performance. Cisco DNA Analytics uses machine learning algorithms to analyze vast amounts of network data and identify patterns, trends, and anomalies. This allows network administrators to detect and troubleshoot issues proactively, reducing downtime and improving network reliability. With its ability to analyze historical data, Cisco DNA Analytics also enables predictive modeling and capacity planning, helping organizations make informed decisions about network investments. Cisco DNA Assurance complements the analytics capabilities by providing real-time monitoring and visibility into the network infrastructure. It continuously collects data from network devices, applications, and users to assess the overall health and performance of the network. This includes monitoring key performance indicators such as latency, packet loss, and device availability. By leveraging AI and machine learning, Cisco DNA Assurance can quickly identify and diagnose network issues, enabling fast resolution and minimizing impact on users. One of the key features of Cisco DNA Analytics and Assurance is its intuitive dashboard and reporting interface. It provides a consolidated view of network performance metrics, alert notifications, and recommended actions. This allows network administrators to quickly identify and prioritize issues, streamline troubleshooting, and make data-driven decisions. Furthermore, Cisco DNA Analytics and Assurance offers automation capabilities, allowing administrators to automate routine tasks such as device configuration, software updates, and policy enforcement. This reduces the complexity and time required to manage the network, while also minimizing the risk of human errors. In summary, Cisco DNA Analytics and Assurance is a powerful network management solution that leverages advanced analytics, proactive monitoring, and automation to optimize network performance, detect issues before they impact users, and enhance overall network reliability.

Cisco DNA Assurance

Cisco DNA Assurance is a comprehensive network management solution that leverages data analytics and machine learning to provide real-time insights and ensure optimal network performance. It is designed to simplify network operations, enhance productivity, and improve the overall network experience for users. With Cisco DNA Assurance, network administrators can gain visibility into the entire network infrastructure, including devices, applications, and users. This enables them to proactively detect and resolve network issues before they impact the end user experience. The solution collects and analyzes data from various sources, including network devices, telemetry, and user behavior, to identify patterns, anomalies, and trends that could indicate potential problems or opportunities for optimization. Cisco DNA Assurance offers a range of features and capabilities to support network troubleshooting and performance optimization. It provides a centralized dashboard that displays real-time insights and alerts, allowing administrators to quickly identify and address network issues. The solution also offers automated problem diagnosis and resolution, leveraging machine learning algorithms to analyze data and recommend appropriate actions. This helps reduce manual intervention and speeds up the troubleshooting process. Another key aspect of Cisco DNA Assurance is its ability to provide detailed visibility and analytics into application performance. Administrators can track application usage, monitor performance metrics, and identify bottlenecks or performance degradations. This allows them to prioritize critical applications, allocate network resources efficiently, and ensure a high-quality user experience. Furthermore, Cisco DNA Assurance supports policy-based automation, enabling administrators to define and enforce network policies. This ensures consistent compliance with security and operational guidelines, as well as facilitates the deployment of new services or applications across the network. The solution also provides predictive analytics capabilities, allowing administrators to forecast network capacity requirements and plan for future growth. In summary, Cisco DNA Assurance is a comprehensive network management solution that combines data analytics, machine learning, and automation to ensure optimal network performance. It provides administrators with real-time insights, automates problem diagnosis and resolution, and offers detailed visibility into application performance. By simplifying network operations and enhancing network efficiency, Cisco DNA Assurance helps organizations maximize their network investments and deliver a superior user experience.

Cisco DNA Center

Cisco DNA Center is a software-defined networking (SDN) platform that enables network administrators to centralize and automate the management of their network infrastructure. It provides a single console for network provisioning, policy definition, and network monitoring, simplifying the processes involved in managing a network.With Cisco DNA Center, administrators can design, deploy, and configure their network infrastructure more efficiently. They can use the intuitive graphical interface to create network profiles, define policies, and apply them to different devices or groups of devices, eliminating the need for manual configuration on each device.Moreover, Cisco DNA Center offers advanced analytics capabilities that enable administrators to gain insights into network performance, security threats, and user behavior. It collects and analyzes network data, providing actionable intelligence that can help administrators optimize network performance, detect and mitigate security threats, and identify and resolve issues more proactively.In addition, Cisco DNA Center provides automation features that streamline operational tasks and reduce human error. It supports network automation through APIs, allowing administrators to integrate the platform with other software or tools to automate workflows and eliminate manual intervention. This improves efficiency, reduces downtime, and enhances overall network reliability.Cisco DNA Center also plays a crucial role in implementing network segmentation and security policies. It allows administrators to create virtual networks, enforce access control policies, and segment network traffic based on different criteria such as user roles, device types, or applications. This helps organizations improve network security, prevent unauthorized access, and protect critical resources from potential breaches.In summary, Cisco DNA Center is a comprehensive SDN platform that empowers network administrators to simplify and automate network management. It offers centralized provisioning, policy definition, and network monitoring capabilities, enabling administrators to design, deploy, and manage network infrastructure more efficiently. With advanced analytics and automation features, Cisco DNA Center helps optimize network performance, enhance security, and streamline operational processes.

Cisco DNS (Domain Name System)

The Cisco DNS (Domain Name System) is a critical component of networking that translates domain names into IP addresses. It serves as a decentralized system that stores records of domain names and their associated IP addresses to enable efficient and reliable communication across the internet. When a user enters a domain name into a web browser, the browser communicates with a DNS resolver to obtain the corresponding IP address. The DNS resolver is typically provided by the user's internet service provider (ISP) or by a third party, such as Google or Cisco. The Cisco DNS operates as a hierarchical system that consists of multiple DNS servers. At the top of the hierarchy are the root DNS servers, which are responsible for managing the top-level domains (TLDs), such as .com, .org, and .net. These root servers maintain a directory of authoritative name servers for each TLD. When a DNS resolver receives a domain name query, it contacts one of the root DNS servers to obtain the IP address of the authoritative name server for the appropriate TLD. The resolver then contacts the authoritative name server, which holds the DNS records for the specific domain name. The authoritative name server retrieves the requested IP address and sends it back to the resolver, which in turn provides it to the user's web browser. In addition to translating domain names into IP addresses, the Cisco DNS also supports reverse DNS lookup. This process involves translating an IP address back into a domain name. Reverse DNS lookup is commonly used for security purposes, such as identifying the sender of an email or preventing spam. Cisco DNS plays a vital role in ensuring the smooth functioning of the internet by providing a scalable and reliable method for resolving domain names into IP addresses. Its hierarchical structure and distributed architecture contribute to the overall efficiency and stability of the DNS system, making it an essential component of modern networking.

Cisco DUO Security

Cisco DUO Security is a comprehensive network security solution that provides multi-factor authentication (MFA) and secure access controls to protect against unauthorized access and mitigate potential security threats in network environments. With Cisco DUO Security, organizations can enhance their network security by implementing MFA, which involves verifying the identity of users through multiple factors such as passwords, secure tokens, biometrics, or push notifications on mobile devices. This additional layer of authentication helps prevent unauthorized access even if passwords are compromised. Furthermore, Cisco DUO Security enables organizations to enforce access controls based on user and device attributes. It allows administrators to define policies that restrict access to specific applications or resources based on factors such as user roles, device health, location, and time of access. This granular control over access helps prevent unauthorized users or compromised devices from gaining access to sensitive data or systems. In addition to MFA and access controls, Cisco DUO Security also offers endpoint visibility and security analytics. It provides administrators with real-time visibility into the security posture of devices attempting to access the network, allowing for quick identification and remediation of potential threats. The solution also generates detailed security reports and analytics, providing insights into user behavior and potential security risks. Overall, Cisco DUO Security is a powerful network security solution that combines multi-factor authentication, access controls, endpoint visibility, and security analytics. It helps organizations strengthen their network security, protect against unauthorized access, and mitigate the risk of data breaches or other security incidents.

Cisco EIGRP (Enhanced Interior Gateway Routing Protocol)

Cisco EIGRP (Enhanced Interior Gateway Routing Protocol) is a dynamic routing protocol used in computer networking to efficiently exchange information and route data packets across interconnected networks. It is specifically designed for use within an autonomous system (AS) and operates at the OSI (Open Systems Interconnection) layer 3, which is the network layer. EIGRP is an advanced version of the traditional Interior Gateway Routing Protocol (IGRP) with added enhancements and features. EIGRP utilizes a proprietary routing algorithm that calculates the best and fastest path for routing data traffic from the source to the destination. It takes into account various factors such as network bandwidth, delay, reliability, and load balancing to determine the optimal route. This ensures that data packets are transmitted efficiently and the network performance is optimized. One of the key benefits of EIGRP is its ability to support a variety of network protocols, including Internet Protocol (IP), Internet Protocol version 6 (IPv6), AppleTalk, and Novell Internetwork Packet Exchange (IPX). It can seamlessly handle different types of network traffic and ensure smooth communication between diverse network devices. EIGRP operates in a loop-free manner by using a Diffusing Update Algorithm (DUAL) to prevent routing loops and ensure the stability of the network. DUAL also allows for fast convergence, which means that EIGRP can quickly adapt to network changes and update its routing tables accordingly. This enables efficient use of network resources and improves the overall network performance. Another key feature of EIGRP is its support for load balancing, which distributes network traffic across multiple paths to avoid congestion and optimize the use of available bandwidth. By intelligently redistributing data packets, EIGRP avoids bottlenecks and ensures reliable and efficient data transmission. In summary, Cisco EIGRP is a versatile and advanced routing protocol used in computer networks to exchange routing information and efficiently route data packets. Its features such as dynamic routing, loop prevention, fast convergence, and load balancing contribute to improved network performance and reliability.

Cisco Email Security

Cisco Email Security is a comprehensive network solution designed to protect organizations from email-based threats and safeguard their communication systems. It offers a range of robust security features that mitigate risks associated with email-based attacks, such as phishing, malware, and spam. As an integral part of Cisco's networking portfolio, Email Security leverages advanced technologies and algorithms to identify and block malicious emails, ensuring the integrity, availability, and confidentiality of email communication within an organization. By actively scanning incoming and outgoing emails, it prevents sensitive information from being compromised and helps maintain regulatory compliance.

Cisco EtherChannel

EtherChannel is a networking technology developed by Cisco that allows the bundling of multiple physical Ethernet links between two switches into a single logical link. This logical link increases the available bandwidth and provides redundancy in case of link failure. The creation of an EtherChannel involves combining up to eight physical links into a single logical link. These physical links can be of different speeds or even different types, such as copper or fiber optic. Once combined, they act as a single high-capacity link with aggregated bandwidth, making it ideal for situations where a single link is insufficient to meet the demands of a network.

Cisco Expressway

Cisco Expressway is a networking solution that provides secure remote access for users outside of the corporate network. It acts as a gateway between external users and internal network resources, allowing them to securely communicate and collaborate with other users and access corporate services. Expressway works by establishing a secure connection between external users and the corporate network, ensuring that data transmitted over the internet is protected from unauthorized access. It serves as a middleman between the user's device and the internal resources, performing tasks such as authentication, encryption, and traffic control.

Cisco FMC (Firepower Management Center)

Cisco FMC (Firepower Management Center) is a networking solution that provides centralized management and control of Cisco Firepower security appliances. It offers advanced security features and streamlined administration, allowing organizations to efficiently monitor and secure their network infrastructure. With Cisco FMC, network administrators can easily deploy and configure Cisco Firepower appliances, such as Next-Generation Firewalls (NGFWs), Intrusion Prevention Systems (IPS), and Advanced Malware Protection (AMP) devices. It provides a unified interface for managing all these security components, simplifying the overall administration process. One of the key features of Cisco FMC is its ability to collect and analyze network traffic data in real-time. It captures network packets, performs deep packet inspection, and records important information about traffic patterns, sources, and destinations. This visibility enables administrators to quickly identify and mitigate potential security threats. Moreover, Cisco FMC integrates with Cisco Talos, a global threat intelligence organization, to provide up-to-date information on emerging threats and malware signatures. This collaboration enables the FMC to automatically detect and block known malicious activities across the network. Another significant capability of Cisco FMC is its centralized policy management. It allows administrators to define and enforce network security policies that are automatically applied to all connected Firepower devices. This ensures consistent security measures are in place throughout the network, reducing the risk of misconfigurations or security gaps. Cisco FMC also offers powerful reporting and analytics features. It generates detailed reports on network activities, security events, and overall system performance. These reports provide valuable insights for monitoring network health, identifying security vulnerabilities, and demonstrating compliance with regulatory standards. In summary, Cisco FMC provides a comprehensive solution for managing and securing network infrastructure. With its centralized management, real-time monitoring, threat intelligence integration, and policy enforcement capabilities, it enables organizations to maintain a strong security posture and effectively safeguard their critical assets.

Cisco FTD (Firepower Threat Defense)

Cisco FTD, or Firepower Threat Defense, is a network security solution provided by Cisco Systems. It is a software-based firewall system that combines multiple security features to protect networks from various threats. FTD integrates traditional firewall functionality with advanced threat prevention capabilities to provide comprehensive network security. It offers features such as stateful firewall, intrusion prevention system (IPS), application control, advanced malware protection (AMP), and virtual private network (VPN) support. One of the key benefits of Cisco FTD is its ability to identify and stop threats in real-time. It uses a combination of signature-based and behavior-based monitoring to detect and block malicious activities. The IPS feature analyzes network traffic for known attack signatures, while the advanced malware protection feature uses heuristics and machine learning algorithms to identify and block unknown threats. In addition to threat prevention, Cisco FTD also provides visibility and control over network traffic. It allows administrators to define policies and rules to govern network access and application usage. This granular control helps in preventing unauthorized access and ensuring regulatory compliance. Another important feature of Cisco FTD is its integration with the Cisco Firepower Management Center (FMC). FMC is a centralized management platform that allows administrators to configure and monitor multiple Firepower devices from a single interface. It provides a holistic view of the network security posture and simplifies the management of security policies and rules. Cisco FTD can be deployed in various network environments, ranging from small businesses to large enterprise networks. It is available as a physical appliance or a virtual appliance, allowing flexibility in deployment options. The software is regularly updated with the latest threat intelligence to ensure effective protection against emerging threats. In conclusion, Cisco FTD is a comprehensive network security solution that combines firewall, IPS, application control, advanced malware protection, and VPN support. It provides real-time threat prevention, granular visibility and control, and centralized management capabilities to protect networks from various cyber threats.

Cisco Firepower Device Manager (FDM)

Cisco Firepower Device Manager (FDM) is a network security management tool provided by Cisco Systems. It is designed to simplify the configuration, monitoring, and troubleshooting of Cisco Firepower Threat Defense (FTD) devices. FDM allows network administrators to manage FTD devices through a web-based interface, providing a user-friendly and intuitive way to configure and monitor network security policies. With FDM, administrators can easily create and modify access control policies, configure firewall and intrusion prevention system (IPS) rules, and manage VPN configurations.

Cisco Firepower Management Center

Cisco Firepower Management Center is a centralized security management solution that provides organizations with comprehensive visibility and control over their network security infrastructure. It is designed to streamline and simplify the management of Cisco Firepower Next-Generation Firewall (NGFW) appliances, Intrusion Prevention Systems (IPS), Advanced Malware Protection (AMP), and other security products. With Cisco Firepower Management Center, network administrators can efficiently configure, monitor, and troubleshoot security policies across multiple devices from a single centralized dashboard. It offers a rich set of features, including advanced threat intelligence, real-time event monitoring, and powerful analytics capabilities to detect and mitigate potential security threats proactively. The platform enables organizations to define and enforce security policies consistently across the network infrastructure, ensuring consistent protection against emerging threats. It also provides granular control over network traffic by allowing administrators to create and manage access control policies based on application type, user identity, device type, and other parameters. Cisco Firepower Management Center empowers network administrators with actionable intelligence by providing detailed visibility into network traffic patterns, user behavior, and security events. It generates comprehensive reports and alerts, enabling organizations to quickly identify and respond to security incidents. The solution integrates with Cisco Talos, one of the largest threat intelligence organizations globally, to provide up-to-date information on the latest threats and vulnerabilities. This enables organizations to stay ahead of evolving threats and make informed decisions when it comes to network security. In summary, Cisco Firepower Management Center is a centralized security management solution that helps organizations streamline the management of their network security infrastructure. It offers comprehensive visibility, granular control, and advanced threat intelligence to detect and mitigate potential security threats effectively.

Cisco Firepower NGFW (Next-Generation Firewall)

Cisco Firepower NGFW (Next-Generation Firewall) is a network security device that provides advanced protection against modern threats and enhances network visibility and control. It combines traditional firewall capabilities with next-generation intrusion prevention systems (IPS), advanced malware protection (AMP), and application visibility and control (AVC) to deliver comprehensive and effective network security. Cisco Firepower NGFW offers a robust and scalable solution for businesses of all sizes, from small to large enterprises. It is designed to protect networks and data from unauthorized access, malicious activities, and malicious software, while also allowing organizations to securely enable critical applications and services. Key features of Cisco Firepower NGFW include: - Firewall: The device acts as a traditional firewall, implementing rules and policies to control network traffic and protect against unauthorized access. - Intrusion Prevention System (IPS): Cisco Firepower NGFW proactively monitors and blocks network traffic that matches known attack signatures or exhibits suspicious behaviors, providing real-time protection against cyber threats. - Advanced Malware Protection (AMP): Leveraging advanced detection techniques, Cisco Firepower NGFW identifies and blocks known and unknown malware, including viruses, worms, Trojans, and ransomware. - Application Visibility and Control (AVC): Cisco Firepower NGFW offers deep visibility into network traffic, allowing administrators to identify and control applications and users, ensuring proper usage and bandwidth management. - VPN Connectivity: Cisco Firepower NGFW supports secure remote access and site-to-site virtual private network (VPN) connectivity, enabling employees to securely connect to the network from remote locations. - Centralized Management: The device can be centrally managed through Cisco's Firepower Management Center, providing a unified interface for configuring policies, monitoring network activities, and generating reports. Overall, Cisco Firepower NGFW is an essential component of a comprehensive network security strategy, protecting organizations from a wide range of threats and enabling secure and efficient business operations.

Cisco Firepower NGIPS (Next-Generation Intrusion Prevention System)

Cisco Firepower NGIPS (Next-Generation Intrusion Prevention System) is a comprehensive network security solution that combines advanced threat detection and prevention capabilities with real-time intelligence, rapid response, and centralized management. It is specifically designed to protect networks from unauthorized access, malicious activities, and potential security breaches. Firepower NGIPS leverages a combination of advanced technologies, including deep packet inspection, application control, intrusion detection and prevention, and malware protection, to provide multiple layers of defense against various types of threats. By analyzing network traffic in real-time, it can identify and block known and unknown threats before they can cause any harm to the network. One of the key features of Firepower NGIPS is its advanced threat intelligence. It continuously receives updates from Cisco Talos, a renowned threat intelligence organization, which ensures that it is always up-to-date with the latest threat information and can effectively detect and prevent emerging and evolving threats. The centralized management capabilities of Firepower NGIPS make it easy to deploy, manage, and monitor the security policies across the network. It provides a unified interface for configuring and monitoring the security appliances, as well as generating comprehensive reports and alerts for potential security incidents. Firepower NGIPS also supports integration with other Cisco security solutions, such as Cisco Umbrella and Cisco Threat Grid, to provide enhanced protection and visibility across the entire network infrastructure. This integration allows for a more coordinated and effective response to security incidents, minimizing the impact and reducing the time to remediation. In conclusion, Cisco Firepower NGIPS is a powerful network security solution that provides advanced threat detection and prevention capabilities, real-time intelligence, rapid response, and centralized management. It helps organizations to proactively protect their networks from a wide range of threats and ensure the security and integrity of their network infrastructure.

Cisco Firepower Services

Cisco Firepower Services is a comprehensive network security platform designed to protect organizations from cyber threats. It combines industry-leading firewall capabilities, advanced threat detection and prevention, and secure remote access into a single solution. At its core, Cisco Firepower Services consists of a next-generation firewall (NGFW) that provides advanced firewall features such as stateful inspection, application-aware control, and intrusion prevention system (IPS) capabilities. These features allow organizations to establish robust network security policies to control access and protect their network infrastructure from unauthorized access and malicious activities. In addition to the NGFW capabilities, Cisco Firepower Services also integrates advanced threat detection and prevention technologies to identify and block emerging and sophisticated cyber threats. This includes real-time malware detection, sandboxing for analyzing suspicious files, and deep visibility into network traffic to identify anomalies and potential security breaches. Cisco Firepower Services also offers secure remote access capabilities through its Virtual Private Network (VPN) functionality. This allows authorized users outside the organization's network to securely connect to the network infrastructure, ensuring seamless access to resources while maintaining a high level of security. Furthermore, Cisco Firepower Services provides centralized management and reporting capabilities, allowing administrators to efficiently configure, monitor, and analyze security policies across the entire network. This centralized approach simplifies the management of security infrastructure and enables organizations to quickly respond to security incidents and make informed decisions based on real-time insights. Overall, Cisco Firepower Services is a comprehensive and integrated network security platform that helps organizations defend against a wide range of cyber threats. It combines firewall, advanced threat detection and prevention, secure remote access, and centralized management capabilities to provide a robust and scalable security solution.

Cisco Firepower Threat Defense (FTD)

Cisco Firepower Threat Defense (FTD) is a networking solution designed to provide advanced threat detection and prevention capabilities for organizations. It combines the features and functionalities of Cisco ASA (Adaptive Security Appliance) with additional benefits and enhanced security capabilities. FTD offers a comprehensive approach to network security by integrating firewall, intrusion prevention system (IPS), and advanced threat protection (ATP) functionalities into a single solution. It leverages a combination of signature-based and behavior-based analysis techniques to detect and mitigate various types of cyber threats. One of the key features of FTD is its Next-Generation Firewall (NGFW) capability. It provides granular control over network traffic, allowing administrators to define detailed security policies based on application, user, and content. This helps in preventing unauthorized access and ensuring secure communication within the network. Additionally, FTD incorporates an Intrusion Prevention System (IPS) that continuously monitors network traffic for known attack patterns and malicious activities. It uses a vast signature database to identify and block known threats in real-time, preventing potential network breaches. Furthermore, FTD offers Advanced Malware Protection (AMP) which helps in detecting and preventing the spread of malware across the network. It utilizes sophisticated malware analysis techniques to identify and block both known and unknown malware threats, providing proactive defense against emerging threats. In terms of management and visibility, FTD provides a centralized management console that enables administrators to configure, monitor, and troubleshoot the network security infrastructure. It offers detailed reporting and analytics capabilities, allowing organizations to gain insights into their network traffic and security posture. In summary, Cisco Firepower Threat Defense (FTD) is a powerful networking solution that combines firewall, intrusion prevention, and advanced threat protection functionalities. It provides organizations with the ability to secure their network infrastructure against various cyber threats, ensuring a high level of protection and visibility.

Cisco Firepower Threat Defense Virtual (FTDv)

Cisco Firepower Threat Defense Virtual (FTDv) is a network security solution that combines firewall capabilities with advanced threat protection features. It is a virtualized security platform that helps organizations protect their networks from various cyber threats. FTDv is designed to be used in virtualized environments, allowing organizations to create and deploy multiple virtual instances of the solution to protect their networks. This virtualized approach offers flexibility and scalability, as organizations can easily add or remove instances based on their network security needs. FTDv provides robust firewall capabilities, including stateful inspection, access control, and network address translation. These features allow organizations to define and enforce security policies to control network traffic and protect against unauthorized access. In addition to traditional firewall capabilities, FTDv incorporates advanced threat protection features to combat modern cyber threats. It utilizes Cisco's next-generation Intrusion Prevention System (NGIPS) and Advanced Malware Protection (AMP) technologies to detect and prevent a wide range of threats, including malware, exploits, and vulnerabilities. FTDv also includes a comprehensive management interface that allows organizations to centrally manage and monitor their network security. This interface provides visibility into network traffic, security events, and policy enforcement, enabling organizations to quickly respond to potential security incidents. Overall, Cisco Firepower Threat Defense Virtual (FTDv) is a powerful network security solution that combines firewall capabilities with advanced threat protection features. It helps organizations protect their networks from a wide range of cyber threats, providing flexibility, scalability, and centralized management.

Cisco GLBP (Gateway Load Balancing Protocol)

Cisco GLBP (Gateway Load Balancing Protocol) is a network protocol that enables the load balancing and redundancy of multiple routers serving as default gateways for hosts on a LAN (Local Area Network). It combines the advantages of load balancing and redundancy to improve network efficiency and reliability. GLBP operates by allowing multiple routers to share the same virtual IP address as a default gateway. These routers form a GLBP group, and one of the routers is elected as the active virtual gateway (AVG), responsible for forwarding packets to the virtual IP address. The other routers in the group act as backup virtual gateways (BVGs) and assume the AVG role if the current AVG fails. This shared responsibility allows for load balancing and fault tolerance.

Cisco HSRP (Hot Standby Router Protocol)

Cisco HSRP, or Hot Standby Router Protocol, is a redundancy protocol used in computer networks to ensure high availability and reliable communications. It is specifically designed for networks that use multiple routers connected in parallel, providing a backup mechanism that allows for automatic failover in case of router failure. HSRP works by designating one router as the active router and the others as standby routers. The active router performs all network operations, while the standby routers constantly monitor the active router's operation and synchronously update their configuration to match that of the active router. This synchronization ensures that the standby routers are ready to take over instantly in the event of a failure.

Cisco HyperFlex Connect

Cisco HyperFlex Connect is a software-defined, hyperconverged infrastructure solution designed for networking environments. It enables organizations to efficiently manage and scale their network systems by consolidating compute, storage, and networking functions into a single integrated platform. Cisco HyperFlex Connect leverages virtualization technology to create a unified pool of computing, storage, and networking resources. By virtualizing these components, it simplifies network management, improves resource utilization, and enhances overall system performance. The solution eliminates the need for separate infrastructure silos and enables seamless integration between hardware and software components. The key features of Cisco HyperFlex Connect include: - **Scalability**: The solution allows organizations to scale their network systems by adding or removing resources as needed. It enables seamless expansion without disrupting ongoing operations and ensures high availability and reliability. - **Simplified Management**: Cisco HyperFlex Connect provides a centralized management interface that allows administrators to easily configure, monitor, and control network resources. It offers an intuitive graphical user interface (GUI) that simplifies administrative tasks and reduces the learning curve. - **Data Efficiency**: The solution incorporates data reduction techniques such as deduplication and compression to optimize storage utilization and minimize data footprint. It helps organizations to effectively manage their data and improve storage efficiency. - **High Performance**: Cisco HyperFlex Connect delivers high performance by leveraging cutting-edge technologies such as solid-state drives (SSDs) and software-defined networking (SDN). It ensures low latency, high throughput, and rapid data access for demanding networking applications. - **Data Protection**: The solution includes advanced data protection features such as replication, snapshots, and backup to safeguard critical data. It helps organizations to minimize the risk of data loss and ensure business continuity. - **Flexibility**: Cisco HyperFlex Connect offers flexibility in terms of deployment options. It can be deployed on-premises or in a hybrid cloud environment, allowing organizations to choose the deployment model that best suits their needs.

Cisco HyperFlex Edge

Cisco HyperFlex Edge is a technology solution that combines computing, networking, and storage resources in a single integrated system. It is designed to bring the power and capabilities of a data center to the network edge, where it can be deployed in remote locations or branch offices. The main objective of Cisco HyperFlex Edge is to provide a reliable, scalable, and efficient infrastructure for running applications and services at the edge of the network. It offers a compact and all-in-one solution that eliminates the need for separate servers, storage arrays, and networking equipment, thereby reducing complexity and simplifying management.

Cisco HyperFlex HX-Series

Cisco HyperFlex HX-Series is a networking solution designed to provide high performance, scalability, and flexibility for virtualized environments. It combines computing, networking, and storage resources into a single system, thereby simplifying data center operations and reducing costs. The HX-Series leverages the power of software-defined networking (SDN) and hyperconverged infrastructure (HCI) to deliver a unified platform that integrates compute, storage, and networking services. This enables organizations to easily deploy, manage, and scale their infrastructure, while also benefiting from increased agility and improved operational efficiency.

Cisco HyperFlex

Cisco HyperFlex is a comprehensive and cutting-edge networking solution that combines computing, storage, and networking resources into a single infrastructure. It is designed to provide organizations with the flexibility, scalability, and performance required to meet the demands of modern data centers. HyperFlex utilizes software-defined technology to simplify the management and operation of data center resources. It leverages a hyperconverged architecture, which means that all components, including servers, storage, and networking, are integrated into a single platform. By consolidating these resources, HyperFlex eliminates the need for separate management and provisioning tools, reducing complexity and streamlining operations.

Cisco IOS (Internetwork Operating System)

Cisco IOS (Internetwork Operating System) is a software used in Cisco networking devices such as routers and switches. It is a proprietary operating system developed by Cisco Systems specifically for their network devices. Cisco IOS provides the foundation for routing, switching, and security features of Cisco devices. It allows network administrators to manage and configure various aspects of the network, including routing protocols, access control lists, virtual private networks (VPNs), and quality of service (QoS). With Cisco IOS, network administrators can create and manage networks, control traffic flow, and ensure secure communication between devices. It is designed to be scalable, reliable, and secure, making it suitable for both small and large-scale networks. The key features of Cisco IOS include: 1. Routing: Cisco IOS supports various routing protocols such as RIP (Routing Information Protocol), OSPF (Open Shortest Path First), and BGP (Border Gateway Protocol), allowing devices to exchange routing information and dynamically update routing tables. 2. Switching: Cisco IOS enables layer 2 switching, allowing devices to forward traffic based on MAC addresses. It supports VLANs (Virtual Local Area Networks) and can perform VLAN tagging and trunking. 3. Security: Cisco IOS provides a range of security features to protect the network and its resources. It supports features such as access control lists (ACLs), firewalls, VPNs, and encryption protocols. 4. Quality of Service: Cisco IOS allows administrators to prioritize network traffic and allocate bandwidth based on specific criteria. This ensures that critical applications receive sufficient bandwidth and network resources, improving overall network performance. 5. Management: Cisco IOS provides various management tools and protocols to monitor and control network devices. It supports SNMP (Simple Network Management Protocol), Telnet, SSH (Secure Shell), and web-based management interfaces. In summary, Cisco IOS is the operating system that powers Cisco networking devices. It offers a range of features and functionalities to manage and control networks, making it an essential component for network administrators in configuring and maintaining Cisco devices.

Cisco IP Phone

A Cisco IP Phone is a type of technology device used for communication within a network infrastructure. Specifically designed for Voice over Internet Protocol (VoIP) communication, these phones allow users to make and receive calls over an internet connection rather than traditional analog phone lines. With its integration into the network, a Cisco IP Phone becomes a functional endpoint within a larger communication system, such as a unified communications network or a private branch exchange (PBX). These phones are typically connected to a local area network (LAN) or a wide area network (WAN), allowing users to connect and communicate with other IP phones, as well as traditional telephone lines when configured appropriately.

Cisco IP SLA (Service Level Agreement)

Cisco IP SLA (Service Level Agreement) is a feature provided by Cisco networking devices that allows for the measurement of performance metrics, such as network delay, packet loss, and jitter, to ensure the delivery of high-quality services over IP networks. IP SLA operates by generating synthetic network traffic, known as probes or test packets, that are sent between two devices in the network. These probes can be configured to mimic real network traffic, such as VoIP calls or video streaming, allowing network administrators to accurately monitor performance from end to end.

Cisco IPSec VPN

Cisco IPSec VPN, short for Cisco Internet Protocol Security Virtual Private Network, is a secure networking technology that enables remote users to securely connect to a private network over the internet. It provides a secure and encrypted tunnel for data transmission, ensuring confidentiality, integrity, and authenticity of the data being transmitted. Cisco IPSec VPN is based on the IPSec protocol suite, which is a framework of protocols and algorithms used for securing IP communications. IPSec stands for Internet Protocol Security and is widely used in virtual private networks, particularly in enterprise environments where remote access is required. The main purpose of Cisco IPSec VPN is to create a secure connection between a remote user and a private network, such as a corporate network or a branch office network. It allows remote users to access network resources and applications as if they were directly connected to the private network, regardless of their physical location. The security provided by Cisco IPSec VPN is achieved through the use of various components, including authentication, encryption, and key management. Authentication ensures that the remote user is authorized to access the private network by verifying their identity through credentials such as usernames and passwords. Encryption is used to protect the confidentiality and integrity of the data transmitted over the VPN by transforming it into an unreadable form that can only be deciphered by the intended recipient. Key management is responsible for generating and distributing encryption keys used for securing the VPN connection. Overall, Cisco IPSec VPN offers a reliable and secure solution for remote access to private networks. It allows organizations to extend their network infrastructure to remote employees, partners, or customers, providing them with secure access to resources and applications. This technology plays a crucial role in ensuring the privacy and security of data transmitted over public networks, allowing organizations to maintain a high level of confidentiality and protect against unauthorized access.

Cisco ISE (Identity Services Engine)

The Cisco ISE (Identity Services Engine) is a comprehensive network access control solution that provides visibility, control, and security enforcement for enterprise network infrastructures. It serves as a centralized policy engine that securely authenticates and authorizes devices and users attempting to connect to a network. ISE works by integrating with various network elements, such as switches, routers, wireless access points, and security appliances, to enforce policies based on user, device, and context information. It leverages various authentication methods, including 802.1X, MAC authentication bypass, web authentication, and guest access, to ensure that only authorized users and devices gain network access.

Cisco ISE Posture Assessment

The Cisco ISE Posture Assessment is a feature of Cisco Identity Services Engine (ISE) that checks the health and compliance of network devices and endpoints connected to a network. It ensures that devices meet the defined security policies and posture requirements before granting access to network resources. When a device or endpoint connects to the network, Cisco ISE Posture Assessment examines its security posture to determine if it meets the specified standards and policies. It checks for the presence of antivirus software, firewall settings, operating system patches, secure configurations, and other security measures that are critical for a device's compliance. The assessment process involves several components: 1. Endpoint Security Software: Cisco ISE communicates with endpoint security software installed on devices, such as antivirus software, to collect information about the device's security status. 2. Posture Policies: Network administrators define posture policies based on organizational security standards and compliance requirements. These policies define the specific security checks and requirements that devices must meet to be considered compliant. 3. Agent and Agentless Assessments: Cisco ISE supports both agent and agentless posture assessments. Agents are software installed on endpoints, while agentless assessments use built-in capabilities of network devices to perform security checks. Both methods collect data about the device's security posture and compare it against the defined policies. 4. Remediation and Enforcement: If a device fails to meet the posture requirements, Cisco ISE can initiate remediation actions to bring the device into compliance. These actions may include updating software, applying patches, or configuring security settings. Once the device becomes compliant, it is granted access to the network resources. The Cisco ISE Posture Assessment plays a crucial role in network security by ensuring that only devices that meet the security standards can access the network. It helps prevent the spread of malware, enforce security policies, and protect sensitive information from unauthorized access. By continuously monitoring and assessing devices' posture, organizations can maintain a secure and compliant network environment.

Cisco ISE Profiling

Cisco ISE Profiling is a feature of the Cisco Identity Services Engine (ISE) that is utilized in network management to classify and identify devices connecting to a network based on their characteristics and behavior. Profiling allows network administrators to gain a deeper understanding of the devices on their network, enabling them to enforce appropriate network policies and security measures. Using various methods, Cisco ISE Profiling collects information about devices by examining factors such as their device type, operating system, MAC address, and network traffic patterns. This data is then used to create device profiles, which consist of a set of attributes that define specific characteristics of a device. Device profiling is essential in network management as it allows administrators to differentiate between authorized and unauthorized devices, ensuring that only trusted devices are granted network access. By accurately identifying devices, network administrators can implement appropriate access policies, such as enforcing security measures or providing specific network services based on the device profile. Cisco ISE Profiling employs a combination of active and passive profiling techniques to gather information. Active profiling involves actively probing devices on the network to collect data, such as device banners or responses to specific queries. Passive profiling, on the other hand, involves analyzing network traffic to determine device characteristics based on patterns and behavior. Once a device profile is created, Cisco ISE

59

Profiling continuously monitors the network to update and maintain the profiles. This ensures that devices are accurately classified and identified even when they undergo changes or updates. In summary, Cisco ISE Profiling is a feature within the Cisco Identity Services Engine that enables network administrators to classify and identify devices connecting to a network based on their characteristics and behavior. By creating device profiles and continuously updating them, network administrators can enforce appropriate network policies and security measures to protect their network from unauthorized access and potential threats.

Cisco ISR (Integrated Services Router)

The Cisco ISR, or Integrated Services Router, is a networking device specifically designed to provide a wide range of IT services within a single platform. It combines the capabilities of multiple devices, such as routers, switches, firewalls, and virtual private network (VPN) appliances, into one integrated solution. The Cisco ISR offers comprehensive networking services for both small and large enterprise networks. It serves as a primary gateway between local area networks (LANs) and wide area networks (WANs), allowing for secure and efficient data transmission between different network segments. With its integrated services, the Cisco ISR enables businesses to simplify their network infrastructure, reduce complexity, and save costs by consolidating multiple devices into a single platform. It provides various features and functionalities that are essential for building, managing, and securing modern networks. One of the key features of the Cisco ISR is its routing capabilities. It is equipped with advanced routing protocols, such as Border Gateway Protocol (BGP) and Open Shortest Path First (OSPF), which enable efficient traffic routing and load balancing across multiple network paths. In addition to routing, the Cisco ISR offers a wide range of services, including advanced security features to protect the network from external threats. It includes built-in firewall and intrusion prevention system (IPS) functionalities, which help safeguard the network from unauthorized access, data breaches, and malicious attacks. The Cisco ISR also supports virtual private network (VPN) technologies, allowing for secure remote access and site-to-site connectivity. It enables businesses to establish secure connections between different locations over the internet, ensuring data confidentiality and integrity. Furthermore, the Cisco ISR provides quality of service (QoS) capabilities, which prioritize network traffic and ensure optimal performance for critical applications. It supports features like traffic shaping, bandwidth allocation, and congestion management, allowing businesses to prioritize real-time applications, such as voice and video, over less critical traffic. Overall, the Cisco ISR is a versatile networking solution that offers a range of integrated services, including routing, security, VPN, and QoS. It simplifies network management, enhances security, and improves efficiency, making it an ideal choice for businesses of all sizes.

Cisco IWAN (Intelligent WAN)

Cisco IWAN (Intelligent WAN) is a network solution designed to optimize and enhance Wide Area Network (WAN) performance, reduce costs, and improve overall network efficiency. It seamlessly integrates multiple WAN sources, such as MPLS, broadband, and cellular, to deliver reliable and scalable connectivity to remote sites. The key features of Cisco IWAN include: Traffic Optimization: Cisco IWAN utilizes advanced routing and traffic management techniques to prioritize critical applications and ensure optimal performance. It employs dynamic path selection to intelligently route traffic over the most appropriate path based on real-time network conditions, reducing congestion and providing a consistent and reliable user experience. Application Visibility and Control: With deep packet inspection and application recognition capabilities, Cisco IWAN enables granular visibility into network traffic. This allows network administrators to identify and prioritize specific applications or application categories, ensuring that critical applications receive the necessary bandwidth and resources to function optimally. Secure Connectivity: Cisco IWAN integrates robust security features, including stateful firewall, intrusion prevention, and virtual private network (VPN) technologies. It provides secure connectivity for remote sites, protecting sensitive data and ensuring compliance with industry regulations. Additionally, it offers end-to-end security for all traffic, regardless of the underlying transport mechanism. Intelligent Path Control: Cisco IWAN leverages multiple WAN sources, such as MPLS, broadband, and cellular, to create a resilient and flexible network infrastructure. It dynamically selects the best path for each application or user session, taking into account factors such as latency, packet loss, and bandwidth availability. This enables efficient utilization of available network resources and improves application performance. Centralized Management and Orchestration: Cisco IWAN provides a centralized management platform that simplifies network administration and troubleshooting. Network policies and configurations can be easily deployed and managed from a single interface, reducing operational complexity and minimizing the risk of errors. Furthermore, it enables network administrators to monitor and analyze network performance in real-time, facilitating proactive troubleshooting and capacity planning.

Cisco Identity Services Engine (ISE)

The Cisco Identity Services Engine (ISE) is a network security and policy management platform that allows organizations to centrally manage and enforce policies for user authentication, network access, and device security. ISE provides a highly secure network infrastructure by controlling access to the network based on user identity, device type, and location. It helps organizations ensure that only authorized users and devices have access to network resources, while also providing visibility and control over network traffic and security threats.

Cisco IronPort

The Cisco IronPort is a secure email gateway appliance that provides advanced threat protection, email security, and data loss prevention for organizations. It is designed to address the challenges associated with email security, including spam, viruses, phishing attacks, and other malicious content. As a networking device, the Cisco IronPort sits at the network perimeter and acts as a gateway for inbound and outbound email traffic. It examines incoming emails for potential threats and applies various security measures to ensure the delivery of clean emails to recipients. The Cisco IronPort uses a multi-layered approach to email security, including anti-spam filtering, antivirus protection, and content filtering. It leverages advanced technologies such as reputation filtering, heuristics, and machine learning algorithms to identify and block spam emails, viruses, and other types of harmful content. One of the key features of the Cisco IronPort is its ability to detect and prevent phishing attacks. Phishing is a common method used by cybercriminals to trick users into providing sensitive information such as usernames, passwords, and credit card details. The Cisco IronPort analyzes email content, URLs, and attachments to identify phishing attempts and blocks them before they reach users' inboxes. In addition to its security capabilities, the Cisco IronPort also provides data loss prevention (DLP) functionality. DLP helps organizations protect sensitive data by monitoring outgoing emails for confidential information such as credit card numbers, social security numbers, and intellectual property. It can enforce policies to prevent unauthorized disclosure and ensure regulatory compliance. In summary, the Cisco IronPort is a networking appliance that offers comprehensive email security and data loss prevention for organizations. It protects against spam, viruses, phishing attacks, and other threats, while also helping organizations safeguard sensitive information and maintain regulatory compliance.

Cisco Jabber Guest

Cisco Jabber Guest is a software application that enables external users to securely communicate with internal users within a network. It is designed to provide a simple and secure way for guests, clients, or partners to connect and collaborate with the internal network without requiring a separate VPN connection or compromising network security. This application acts as a bridge between external users and the internal communication infrastructure, allowing them to participate in voice and video calls, send messages, share files, and join meetings, just like internal users do. It offers real-time communication capabilities through a web browser, making it easily accessible for guests without the need to install any additional software.

Cisco Jabber SDK

The Cisco Jabber SDK provides a set of tools and resources for developing applications that leverage the Jabber communication platform within a network environment. Designed for network administrators and developers, the SDK enables the integration of real-time communication capabilities, such as instant messaging, presence, voice, and video, into existing network infrastructure and applications. The primary purpose of the Cisco Jabber SDK is to facilitate the creation of custom communication applications that seamlessly interact with the Cisco Jabber platform. By using the SDK, developers can leverage the robust features and functionality of Jabber to enhance the communication capabilities of their applications. The

Cisco Jabber SDK offers a comprehensive set of application programming interfaces (APIs) that allow developers to access and manipulate the various communication services provided by Jabber. These APIs provide methods for initiating and terminating voice and video calls, sending and receiving instant messages, managing contacts and presence information, and accessing other communication-related features. Through the Jabber SDK, developers can integrate these communication services into their applications, extending their functionality and empowering users to communicate in real time. This can improve collaboration and productivity within an organization, as users can easily connect and communicate with colleagues, partners, and customers. Moreover, the Cisco Jabber SDK supports various platforms and programming languages, enabling developers to build cross-platform applications that are compatible with different operating systems and devices. This flexibility allows for the creation of unified communication solutions that seamlessly work across multiple platforms, including desktop computers, laptops, tablets, and mobile devices. In conclusion, the Cisco Jabber SDK provides the necessary tools and resources for developers to integrate real-time communication capabilities into their network applications. By leveraging the Jabber platform, developers can extend the functionality of their applications, enable seamless communication, and enhance collaboration within an organization.

Cisco Jabber

Cisco Jabber is a unified communications application that enables real-time collaboration and messaging within a networking environment. It provides various communication tools such as instant messaging, voice and video calling, presence information, and desktop sharing. Designed for businesses and organizations, Cisco Jabber offers a secure and scalable solution to enhance teamwork and productivity. It allows users to connect with their colleagues, partners, and clients, regardless of their location or device.

Cisco MSE (Mobility Services Engine)

The Cisco MSE (Mobility Services Engine) is a networking device that provides location-based services and analytics for wireless networks. It offers a comprehensive set of features and capabilities to optimize the performance, security, and user experience of wireless networks. The Cisco MSE acts as a centralized platform that integrates with wireless access points and collects data about the devices and clients connected to the network. It uses various location-tracking technologies such as Wi-Fi triangulation and BLE (Bluetooth Low Energy) to determine the real-time location of wireless devices within the coverage area. One of the primary functions of the Cisco MSE is to provide accurate location information for wireless devices. It uses a combination of techniques to determine the location, including signal strength, time difference of arrival (TDOA), and angle of arrival (AOA). This information can be used for various purposes, such as asset tracking, security monitoring, and proximity-based marketing. In addition to location services, the Cisco MSE also offers advanced analytics capabilities. It collects and analyzes data about user behavior, network performance, and application usage to provide valuable insights for network administrators. This information can help identify areas of improvement, troubleshoot network issues, and optimize the performance of wireless networks. The Cisco MSE is designed to be scalable and flexible, allowing it to adapt to the needs of different organizations and environments. It can support a large number of wireless access points and can be seamlessly integrated into existing network infrastructures. It also supports integration with other Cisco products and solutions, such as wireless controllers and security appliances. In summary, the Cisco MSE is a powerful networking device that provides location-based services and analytics for wireless networks. It offers accurate location information, advanced analytics capabilities, and seamless integration with other Cisco products, enabling organizations to optimize the performance and user experience of their wireless networks.

Cisco Meeting Server

Cisco Meeting Server is a collaboration solution that enables seamless video, audio, and web conferencing for organizations. It provides an integrated platform for virtual meetings, allowing participants to connect from any location and device. With Cisco Meeting Server, organizations can host secure and productive meetings, regardless of the participants' physical location. It supports both scheduled and ad-hoc meetings, ensuring flexibility and convenience for users. The main components of Cisco Meeting Server include the Meeting Server itself, which acts as a central hub for managing conferences, the Web Proxy, which enables web-based access to meetings, and the Multipoint Control Unit (MCU), which handles the mixing and routing of audio and video streams. One of the key features of Cisco Meeting Server is its interoperability. It is designed to work with a wide range of communication devices and systems, including Cisco and non-Cisco endpoints. This allows organizations to leverage their existing infrastructure and investments, ensuring a smooth transition to the Cisco Meeting Server platform. Cisco Meeting Server also offers advanced collaboration features, such as screen sharing, content sharing, and real-time document editing. These features enable participants to collaborate effectively and share information during meetings, enhancing productivity and decision-making. Security is a top priority for Cisco Meeting Server. It provides encryption for audio, video, and data streams, ensuring that confidential information remains protected. Additionally, it offers authentication and access control mechanisms to prevent unauthorized access to meetings. In summary, Cisco Meeting Server is a comprehensive collaboration solution that brings together video, audio, and web conferencing capabilities. It offers flexibility, interoperability, advanced collaboration features, and robust security, making it an ideal choice for organizations seeking to enhance their communication and collaboration capabilities.

Cisco Meraki MX Security Appliances

The Cisco Meraki MX Security Appliances are networking devices designed to provide comprehensive security and networking capabilities to organizations. These appliances combine various security features, such as firewall, VPN, intrusion prevention, content filtering, and advanced malware protection, in a single, integrated solution. The MX Security Appliances are part of the Cisco Meraki cloud-managed networking portfolio, which means that they can be centrally managed through a cloud-based dashboard. This simplifies deployment and management, allowing IT administrators to easily configure and monitor the security appliances from anywhere, without the need for on-site hardware or software. With the MX Security Appliances, organizations can establish secure site-to-site and client VPN connections, ensuring that data transmitted over the network is encrypted and protected from unauthorized access. The appliances also include advanced intrusion prevention capabilities, which help identify and block malicious traffic or attacks before they can reach the internal network. In addition, the MX Security Appliances offer content filtering capabilities, allowing organizations to control access to websites and applications based on predefined policies. This helps enforce acceptable use policies, protect against malware and phishing attacks, and improve overall network performance by preventing bandwidth-intensive applications from consuming too much network resources. The appliances also integrate with Cisco's Advanced Malware Protection (AMP) technology, which helps detect and block advanced malware threats in real-time. AMP uses cloud-based threat intelligence and machine learning algorithms to analyze file behavior and identify potential threats, providing an additional layer of protection against known and unknown malware. In summary, the Cisco Meraki MX Security Appliances provide organizations with a comprehensive and centrally managed solution for network security. By combining multiple security features in a single device and leveraging cloud-based management, these appliances offer simplified deployment, increased visibility, and enhanced protection against various cyber threats.

Cisco Meraki

Cisco Meraki is a cloud-managed networking solution that provides centralized control and visibility over an organization's network infrastructure. It offers a wide range of networking devices, including routers, switches, wireless access points, and security appliances, all managed through a single web-based dashboard. With Cisco Meraki, network administrators can easily deploy, configure, and manage their network devices without the need for complex command-line configurations or dedicated on-site appliances. The cloud-based architecture of Cisco Meraki allows for seamless scalability and remote management, making it an ideal solution for organizations of all sizes. One of the key features of Cisco Meraki is its intuitive and user-friendly dashboard. The dashboard provides a centralized view of the entire network, allowing administrators to monitor network performance, manage devices, and troubleshoot issues from anywhere. This eliminates the need for physical access to network equipment and provides greater flexibility in managing the network. Another important aspect of Cisco Meraki is its security capabilities. It includes built-in security features such as firewall, intrusion prevention system (IPS), and content filtering, which helps protect the network from unauthorized access and potential threats. These security features can be easily configured and managed through the dashboard, ensuring a comprehensive and robust security posture for the network. Additionally, Cisco Meraki offers advanced network analytics and reporting tools. Administrators can access real-time and historical data on network usage, client behavior, and application performance. This insight allows for better network optimization, capacity planning, and troubleshooting. In summary, Cisco Meraki is a cloud-managed networking solution that provides centralized control, visibility, and security for an organization's network infrastructure. It offers an intuitive dashboard, seamless scalability, and remote management capabilities. With its comprehensive security features and advanced analytics tools, Cisco Meraki is a valuable solution for organizations looking to simplify their network management and enhance overall network performance.

Cisco Mobility Express

Cisco Mobility Express is a feature within the Cisco WLAN solution that allows for easy management and deployment of wireless networks. It provides a simplified way to set up and manage a Wi-Fi network in small to medium-sized businesses, without the need for a dedicated controller. This solution is designed to be cost-effective and easy to deploy, making it an ideal choice for organizations that have limited IT resources. With Cisco Mobility Express, businesses can quickly deploy and manage access points using a web-based interface, eliminating the need for complex configurations or additional hardware.

Cisco NAT (Network Address Translation)

Cisco Network Address Translation (NAT) is a process used in networking that allows multiple devices on a private network to share a single public IP address. It involves the translation of IP addresses and port numbers between the private network and the public network, enabling communication between devices on different networks. NAT plays a crucial role in conserving public IP addresses and securing the private network by hiding its internal IP structure from the external network. NAT operates at the network layer of the TCP/IP protocol stack and is commonly used in scenarios where a network needs to connect to the internet through a limited number of public IP addresses. It can be implemented through various methods, including static NAT, dynamic NAT, and port address translation (PAT), each with its own specific use cases and configurations.

Cisco NTP (Network Time Protocol)

The Cisco NTP (Network Time Protocol) is a protocol used in networking to synchronize the time between devices on a network. It is designed to ensure that all devices on the network have the same time, allowing for accurate and consistent timekeeping. The NTP protocol works by using a hierarchical system of servers to distribute time information. At the top of the hierarchy are a group of primary reference time servers, which obtain the time from highly accurate sources, such as atomic clocks. These primary servers then share their time information with secondary servers, which in turn share their time with other devices on the network. Each device on the network can be configured to act as a client, requesting time information from one or more NTP servers. The client sends a request packet to the server, which includes a timestamp. The server responds with a reply packet that includes its own timestamp, allowing the client to calculate the round-trip delay and adjust its clock accordingly. There are several benefits to using NTP in a network environment. One of the most important is the ability to accurately timestamp events and log files. This is essential for troubleshooting, auditing, and ensuring the integrity of data. Additionally, NTP can be used to coordinate tasks that require precise timing, such as coordinating distributed systems or synchronizing time-sensitive applications. Cisco offers a variety of NTP solutions, including both hardware and software options. These solutions can be integrated into existing Cisco network infrastructure, allowing for easy deployment and management. Cisco NTP also includes features such as authentication and access control, which enhance security and ensure the accuracy of time information.

Cisco NetFlow

Cisco NetFlow is a network protocol developed by Cisco Systems that allows network administrators to collect and analyze traffic data on their networks. It provides visibility into the flow of network traffic, helping administrators identify network anomalies, monitor network performance, and troubleshoot network issues. NetFlow operates by capturing metadata about network traffic, such as source and destination IP addresses, port numbers, traffic volumes, and timestamps. This metadata is then exported in the form of flow records to a NetFlow collector or analyzer. The flow records are stored and processed to generate network traffic reports, which can be used for various purposes, including capacity planning, security analysis, and billing. The key benefits of Cisco NetFlow include: 1. Network Visibility: NetFlow provides detailed visibility into network traffic by collecting and analyzing information about the source, destination, and volume of traffic flows. This helps administrators understand how network resources are being utilized and identify potential bottlenecks or security threats. 2. Network Performance Monitoring: By monitoring traffic flows, NetFlow allows administrators to track network performance metrics such as bandwidth utilization, response times, and packet loss. This information can be used to optimize network resources, identify performance issues, and ensure quality of service. 3. Security Analysis: NetFlow can be a valuable tool for detecting and investigating security incidents. By analyzing flow records, administrators can identify abnormal traffic patterns, potential security breaches, or suspicious activities on the network. This enables them to take proactive measures to protect the network and mitigate potential risks. 4. Capacity Planning: By understanding network traffic patterns and trends, administrators can estimate future capacity requirements and plan network upgrades or expansions accordingly. NetFlow reports can provide insights into peak usage times, traffic patterns, and applications consuming the most bandwidth, helping administrators optimize network resources and ensure smooth network operations. Overall, Cisco NetFlow is a powerful network monitoring and analysis tool that provides granular visibility into network traffic, enabling administrators to optimize network performance, enhance security, and plan for future network needs.

Cisco Nexus 1000V

The Cisco Nexus 1000V is a software-based virtual switching solution that extends the functionality of Cisco's Nexus switch family into virtualized environments. Designed specifically for virtualization deployments, the Nexus 1000V is integrated with VMware vSphere, providing advanced networking capabilities and bringing enterprise-class networking features to virtualized environments. With the Nexus 1000V, virtual machines (VMs) can be connected to virtual networks with the same level of control and management as physical networks. It acts as a virtual distributed switch that provides advanced networking features such as VLANs, Quality of Service (QoS), access control lists (ACLs), and link aggregation, enabling seamless integration with existing network infrastructures. The Nexus 1000V introduces the concept of Virtual Ethernet Modules (VEMs) and Virtual Supervisor Modules (VSMs). VEMs are the data plane components residing in each VMware ESXi hypervisor and handle the networking functions required by the VMs running on that host. VSMs, on the other hand, are the control plane components that manage the VEMs and provide centralized configuration and monitoring of the virtual switches. By separating the control plane from the data plane, the Nexus 1000V decouples the network management and policies from the underlying physical infrastructure, allowing for more flexibility and agility in virtualized environments. This enables network administrators to apply consistent network policies across both physical and virtual networks, simplifying network management and improving operational efficiency. In addition to the advanced networking capabilities, the Nexus 1000V also integrates with Cisco's Data Center Network Manager (DCNM) for centralized management and monitoring of the virtual switches. This provides a single pane of glass for managing both the physical and virtual networks, enhancing visibility and simplifying troubleshooting. In summary, the Cisco Nexus 1000V is a software-based virtual switching solution that extends the capabilities of Cisco's Nexus switch family to virtualized environments. It provides advanced networking features, integrates with VMware vSphere, and allows for centralized management and control of virtual switches, bringing enterprise-class networking to virtualized infrastructures.

Cisco Nexus Switches

Cisco Nexus switches are a series of high-performance Ethernet switches designed for data center networks. These switches are specifically built to meet the demanding requirements of virtualization, cloud computing, and high-bandwidth applications. The Cisco Nexus switch family offers a variety of models that range from entry-level switches to high-density, high-performance switches. These switches provide a scalable solution for enterprise and service provider

65

environments, offering flexibility, reliability, and advanced features.

Cisco OSPF (Open Shortest Path First)

OSPF, which stands for Open Shortest Path First, is a networking protocol that is widely used for routing and forwarding internet protocol (IP) packets. It was developed by Cisco Systems as an open standard protocol for interior gateway routing within autonomous systems (AS) in an IP network. OSPF is based on the shortest path first (SPF) algorithm, which calculates the best path for routing traffic based on various metrics. OSPF operates within an autonomous system, which is a collection of routers and networks under a single administrative domain. It enables routers within the same AS to exchange information about network topology, link costs, and other metrics. This allows OSPF to dynamically calculate the shortest path to a destination and update the routing table accordingly. Key features of OSPF include its ability to support variable-length subnet masking (VLSM), which allows for more efficient addressing and routing, and its support for Classless Inter-Domain Routing (CIDR), which enables the aggregation of IP addresses for more efficient routing. OSPF also supports multiple areas within an AS, which allows for better scalability by reducing the size of the link-state database. The OSPF routing protocol utilizes a hierarchical structure with routers organized into areas. Each area has a designated router (DR) and a backup designated router (BDR) to manage communication within that area. These routers exchange link-state advertisements (LSAs) to build and maintain a consistent view of the network topology. OSPF uses several types of LSAs, including router LSAs, network LSAs, and summary LSAs, to describe the connectivity and metrics of the various routers and networks within the AS. OSPF also incorporates mechanisms for load balancing and failover, allowing for efficient distribution of traffic across multiple paths and automatic rerouting in the event of network failures. It supports authentication to ensure the security and integrity of routing information exchanged between routers. In summary, OSPF is a dynamic routing protocol that utilizes the SPF algorithm to calculate the best path for routing IP packets within an autonomous system. It provides efficient and scalable routing by maintaining a consistent view of the network topology and dynamically updating the routing table based on changing conditions.

Cisco PIX Firewall

A Cisco PIX Firewall is a network security device that provides protection and control for computer networks. It acts as a barrier between trusted internal networks and untrusted external networks, preventing unauthorized access and protecting the network from various threats. The main purpose of a Cisco PIX Firewall is to inspect incoming and outgoing network traffic based on predefined security policies. It does this by examining the contents of each packet and making decisions on whether to allow or deny the traffic based on these policies. The firewall can also perform Network Address Translation (NAT) to hide internal IP addresses from external networks, enhancing network security. Cisco PIX Firewalls are commonly used in corporate environments to secure connections between internal networks and the Internet, as well as to establish secure virtual private networks (VPNs) between remote locations. They can handle high traffic loads and provide reliable security services, making them suitable for organizations with large and complex networks. Key features of Cisco PIX Firewalls include stateful packet inspection, which keeps track of the state of network connections and only allows legitimate traffic to pass through; application layer inspection, which analyzes the content of application protocols to detect and block potential attacks; and VPN support, which enables secure remote access and site-to-site connectivity. To configure a Cisco PIX Firewall, network administrators use the command-line interface (CLI) or a graphical user interface (GUI) provided by Cisco. They define access control lists (ACLs) that specify which types of traffic are allowed or denied, set up policies for NAT, and configure VPN parameters. Ongoing management and monitoring of the firewall are critical to ensure its effectiveness in protecting the network.

Cisco Port Security

Cisco Port Security is a network security feature used to restrict access to a switch port based on the MAC address of the devices connected to that port. It is an essential mechanism to prevent unauthorized access and enhance the overall security of the network infrastructure. The primary purpose of Cisco Port Security is to ensure that only authorized devices are allowed to connect to the network through a specific switch port. It works by associating the MAC address of the allowed devices with the respective port, creating a binding between the two. Any attempt to connect an unauthorized device to that port will trigger a security violation and take appropriate action to mitigate the security breach.

Cisco Prime Infrastructure

Cisco Prime Infrastructure is a network management platform that provides a centralized solution for configuring, monitoring, and troubleshooting a wide range of network devices. It offers a comprehensive set of tools and services that help network administrators streamline their operations and ensure the efficient performance of their network infrastructure. Cisco Prime Infrastructure allows administrators to manage and control their entire network through a single interface, eliminating the need for multiple management systems. It supports a variety of network devices, including routers, switches, wireless access points, and security appliances, allowing administrators to easily configure and monitor all aspects of their network infrastructure. With Cisco Prime Infrastructure, administrators can quickly and efficiently deploy new devices and services, saving time and reducing the risk of errors. It simplifies the configuration process by providing templates and wizards that guide administrators through the necessary steps. It also provides real-time monitoring and troubleshooting capabilities, allowing administrators to identify and resolve network issues before they impact the performance and availability of the network. Cisco Prime Infrastructure offers comprehensive visibility into network performance and utilization. It provides detailed reports and analytics that help administrators optimize their network resources and identify potential bottlenecks. It also offers advanced security features, such as threat detection and mitigation, to protect the network from malicious activities. Overall, Cisco Prime Infrastructure is a powerful network management platform that helps administrators streamline their operations, improve network performance, and ensure the security and availability of their network infrastructure. It is a reliable and scalable solution that can support networks of all sizes, from small businesses to large enterprises. With its intuitive interface and robust features, it enables administrators to easily configure, monitor, and troubleshoot their network devices, allowing them to focus on more strategic tasks and drive business innovation.

Cisco QoS (Quality Of Service)

Quality of Service (QoS) in the context of networking refers to the ability to prioritize and control network resources in order to meet specific requirements for different types of data traffic. QoS ensures that network devices can treat different types of data with varying levels of importance, so that critical data, such as real-time voice or video, can be delivered with minimal delay, while non-critical data can be given lower priority. By implementing QoS mechanisms, networks can optimize their performance, improve user experience, and efficiently utilize available bandwidth. QoS mechanisms, which operate at different layers of the network stack, enable network administrators to classify, prioritize, and manage traffic flows based on defined policies. Here are some key components of QoS: Classification: Traffic is classified into separate categories or classes based on defined criteria such as protocol, source/destination IP address, port numbers, or DiffServ (Differentiated Services) Code Point (DSCP). This classification enables network devices to recognize and differentiate between various types of traffic. Marking: Once traffic is classified, QoS mechanisms mark packets by assigning unique labels or values to indicate their priority. Common marking methods include setting Differentiated Services Code Points (DSCP) within the IP packet header or assigning a CoS (Class of Service) value within the Layer 2 Ethernet frame header. Policing: QoS mechanisms implement policies to enforce traffic limits and prevent data streams from overwhelming the network. Traffic policing involves rate-limiting incoming or outgoing traffic to conform to predefined thresholds. Policing mechanisms can drop or remark packets that exceed these thresholds. Queuing and Scheduling: QoS mechanisms use queuing and scheduling algorithms to manage how packets are processed and transmitted. Priority Queuing (PQ), Weighted Fair Queuing (WFQ), and Class-Based Queuing (CBQ) are examples of algorithms that determine the order and priority in which packets are sent. Congestion Avoidance and Control: Congestion can occur when the volume of traffic exceeds the network's capacity. QoS mechanisms employ techniques such as Random Early Detection (RED) and Weighted Random Early Detection (WRED) to identify and manage congestion before it degrades network performance. By implementing QoS, networks can provide different levels of service to different applications or types of traffic, ensuring that critical data is given priority and enjoys the necessary resources for optimal delivery. This results in improved network performance, reduced latency, and better overall user experience.

Cisco RADIUS

Cisco RADIUS, also known as Remote Authentication Dial-In User Service, is a networking protocol that provides authentication, authorization, and accounting services for users who request access to a network. It is commonly used in enterprise networks, ISPs, and other large-scale network environments to ensure secure and controlled access for users. The Cisco RADIUS server acts as a central authentication server, receiving authentication requests from clients such as routers, switches, wireless access points, and VPN concentrators. These clients send user credentials, typically in the form of a username and password, to the RADIUS server for verification. Upon receiving an authentication request, the RADIUS server performs a series of checks to validate the user's credentials. It connects to an identity store, such as a database or directory service, to retrieve the user's information and compare it with the supplied credentials. If the credentials match, the RADIUS server sends an acknowledgment to the client, granting the user access to the network. In addition to authentication, Cisco RADIUS also provides authorization services. Once a user is authenticated, the RADIUS server can govern their authorized access rights based on predefined policies. These policies can restrict or allow access to specific resources, networks, or services, depending on the user's role, group, or other attributes. Another crucial feature of Cisco RADIUS is accounting, which enables the collection and tracking of network usage information. The RADIUS server keeps a record of user sessions, including start and end times, data transferred, and other relevant details. This information is valuable for billing purposes, network management, and auditing. Overall, Cisco RADIUS plays an integral role in network security and management. It provides a centralized authentication mechanism, helps enforce access controls, and maintains visibility into user activities. By implementing Cisco RADIUS, organizations can enhance the security, reliability, and efficiency of their networks while ensuring that authorized users can access the resources they need.

Cisco RTP (Real-Time Transport Protocol)

The Real-time Transport Protocol (RTP) is a network protocol that is primarily designed to deliver real-time audio and video data over IP networks. It is widely used in communication systems, such as Voice over IP (VoIP) and video conferencing, to transmit media streams between participants. RTP provides a set of mechanisms to ensure the timely delivery of audio and video data while maintaining synchronization between the sender and receiver. It operates on top of the User Datagram Protocol (UDP) in the transport layer of the Internet Protocol Suite. One of the key features of RTP is its ability to handle real-time multimedia streams. It supports the transmission of continuous media, such as audio and video, by breaking them into manageable data packets. These packets include a sequence number and a timestamp, allowing the receiver to reconstruct the media stream and maintain synchronization. RTP also offers mechanisms to handle network congestion and packet loss. It utilizes a feedback system called Real-time Transport Control Protocol (RTCP) to monitor the quality of the media stream and provide feedback to the sender. This feedback includes information about packet loss, round-trip time, and jitter, which helps the sender adjust the transmission rate and improve the overall quality of the stream. Furthermore, RTP supports the transmission of multiple media streams within a single session. It allows participants to send and receive audio, video, and other types of media concurrently, providing a foundation for multi-stream applications such as video conferencing and multimedia streaming. In conclusion, RTP is a network protocol that enables the reliable and efficient transmission of real-time audio and video data over IP networks. It provides mechanisms for synchronization, congestion control, and multi-stream support, making it an essential component in various communication systems and applications.

Cisco Room Kit

The Cisco Room Kit is a video conferencing solution that offers an immersive and collaborative meeting experience for users. It is designed for modern workplaces and conference rooms, providing high-quality audio and video performance with advanced features. The Room Kit includes a codec, camera, speakers, and a touch control panel. The codec serves as the central hub, connecting all the components and enabling communication with other video endpoints or devices. The camera captures high-definition video, ensuring clear and lifelike visuals during meetings. The Room Kit's audio system consists of integrated speakers and microphones, delivering crystal-clear sound quality for both remote and local participants. The speakers provide rich and immersive audio, while the microphones capture voices from all directions, ensuring everyone can be heard clearly. The touch control panel is used to initiate and control video conferences. It offers a user-friendly interface, allowing users to easily adjust settings, join meetings, and share content. The panel is intuitive and responsive, enhancing the overall user experience and simplifying collaboration in meeting rooms. In addition to its hardware components, the Cisco Room Kit also includes advanced software features. It supports Cisco's collaboration platform, allowing users to connect and collaborate seamlessly with other Cisco video endpoints and devices. The platform enables features such as screen sharing, content annotation, and document collaboration. Overall, the Cisco Room Kit is a comprehensive video conferencing solution that combines high-quality hardware and advanced software features. It provides a seamless and immersive meeting experience, enabling users to collaborate effectively regardless of their location. With its user-friendly interface and reliable performance, the Room Kit enhances productivity and communication in modern workplaces.

Cisco Router

A Cisco router is a networking device that is designed to forward data packets between different computer networks. It is an essential component of a computer network infrastructure as it acts as a central hub through which all network traffic passes, allowing devices on the network to communicate with each other and with other networks. Specifically, a router is responsible for determining the best path for data packets to travel from one network to another based on the destination IP address. It uses routing tables, which contain information about the different network addresses and their corresponding paths, to make these decisions. By continuously assessing and updating these routing tables, a Cisco router ensures efficient and reliable data transmission.

Cisco SD-Access (Software-Defined Access)

Cisco SD-Access (Software-Defined Access) is a network architecture and solution that enables the automation and simplification of network provisioning, management, and security. It leverages the principles of software-defined networking (SDN) to provide a more agile, scalable, and secure network infrastructure. SD-Access is designed to address the growing demands and complexities of modern networks, where traditional manual configuration and management methods are no longer sufficient. By decoupling the network control plane from the underlying hardware and centralizing network policies, SD-Access enables organizations to take advantage of advanced automation, analytics, and security capabilities. At the core of SD-Access is a centralized controller called the Cisco DNA Center, which provides a single point of control for network operations. This controller uses Intent-Based Networking (IBN) concepts to translate high-level business policies into actionable network configurations, drastically reducing the time and effort required for provisioning and change management. SD-Access utilizes a network fabric based on Cisco's Digital Network Architecture (DNA) to simplify network design and deployment. It combines the power of virtualization, segmentation, and automation to create a fabric that is secure, scalable, and highly resilient. By abstracting the network services from the underlying infrastructure, SD-Access allows for simplified management and dynamic policy enforcement. One of the key benefits of SD-Access is the ability to provide consistent policy enforcement and security across the entire network, regardless of the underlying transport technology or device type. By segmenting the network into virtual networks or "trust domains," organizations can enforce granular access policies based on user, device, or application context, reducing the risk of unauthorized access or lateral movement within the network. In summary, Cisco SD-Access is a software-defined networking solution that brings automation, simplicity, and security to network operations. By decoupling the control plane from the underlying hardware and centralizing network policies, it enables organizations to build and manage networks more effectively, resulting in increased agility, scalability, and resilience.

Cisco SD-WAN (Software-Defined WAN)

Software-Defined WAN (SD-WAN) is a networking solution that enables organizations to securely connect their branch offices, data centers, and cloud environments through a centralized control plane. Unlike traditional Wide Area Networks (WANs), which relied on dedicated MPLS circuits, SD-WAN utilizes software-defined networking (SDN) principles to virtualize and optimize network functions. SD-WAN offers a software-based approach to network connectivity, allowing businesses to leverage multiple transport technologies, such as broadband internet, 4G/5G wireless, and MPLS, to establish secure and reliable connections between their distributed locations. It replaces complex static routing with intelligent routing algorithms that dynamically determine the most efficient path for data traffic based on application, network conditions, and security requirements. By decoupling the control plane from the underlying hardware, SD-WAN simplifies network management and provides centralized visibility and control over distributed networks. This centralized control is typically achieved through a cloud-based management interface or a dedicated controller, which enables administrators to configure, monitor, and secure the entire network from a single point of management. One of the key advantages of SD-WAN is its ability to improve network performance and user experience. It achieves this by applying application-aware routing policies that prioritize critical applications and data traffic, while optimizing bandwidth utilization and minimizing latency. SD-WAN also incorporates Quality of Service (QoS) functionality to ensure consistent performance for real-time applications like voice and video conferencing. Moreover, SD-WAN enhances network security by integrating advanced encryption and authentication mechanisms. It enables organizations to segment their network traffic and implement granular security policies, thereby reducing the attack surface and mitigating the risk of unauthorized access or data breaches. In summary, Cisco SD-WAN is a software-defined networking solution that transforms traditional WANs into agile, scalable, and secure networks. It provides centralized control, intelligent routing, improved performance, and enhanced security for organizations with distributed network environments.

Cisco SD-WAN

Cisco SD-WAN, also known as Cisco Software-Defined Wide Area Networking, is a networking technology that provides a scalable, secure, and efficient way to connect distributed branch locations to the wide area network (WAN). It utilizes software-defined networking (SDN) principles to optimize the performance and reliability of the WAN infrastructure. With Cisco SD-WAN, organizations can intelligently route traffic across multiple WAN links, including MPLS, broadband, and cellular connections. It uses centralized management and policy enforcement to dynamically determine the best path for each application, based on factors such as bandwidth requirements, network conditions, and security policies. One of the key benefits of Cisco SD-WAN is its ability to provide application-aware routing. By analyzing the traffic patterns and characteristics of different applications, it can prioritize critical applications and ensure they receive the necessary bandwidth and quality of service (QoS). This improves the overall user experience and productivity, particularly for cloud-based applications that require reliable and low-latency connections. Cisco SD-WAN also enhances network security by leveraging integrated security features. It provides end-to-end encryption for data transmitted over the WAN, ensuring secure communication between branch locations and data centers. Additionally, it can integrate with other security solutions, such as firewalls and threat intelligence platforms, to detect and mitigate potential threats. The centralized management capabilities of Cisco SD-WAN allow administrators to configure and monitor the entire WAN infrastructure from a single interface. They can easily deploy new branch locations, update policies, and troubleshoot network issues without the need for on-site IT personnel. This reduces operational complexity and streamlines network management processes. In summary, Cisco SD-WAN is a networking technology that combines software-defined networking, application-aware routing, and integrated security to deliver a scalable, secure, and efficient wide area network solution for distributed organizations. It enables organizations to optimize their WAN infrastructure, improve application performance, enhance network security, and simplify network management.

Cisco SIP (Session Initiation Protocol)

SIP, also known as Session Initiation Protocol, is a communication protocol that enables the control and management of multimedia communication sessions in networking environments. It is an application layer protocol widely used in Voice over IP (VoIP) systems to initiate, modify, and terminate multimedia sessions involving voice, video, and messaging. SIP operates in a client-server architecture similar to HTTP, where one device, known as the User Agent Client (UAC), initiates a session by sending a request to another device, called the User Agent Server (UAS). These requests and responses are sent over the IP network using the UDP or TCP transport protocol. The main purpose of SIP is to establish and tear down communication sessions between two or more devices. It handles tasks such as call setup, termination, user availability detection, and feature negotiation. SIP utilizes a text-based format for messages, making it human-readable and easy to troubleshoot. One key feature of SIP is its ability to handle user mobility and presence. With SIP, a user can be reached on any device, whether it's a desk phone, a softphone application on a computer, or a mobile device. This flexibility allows for seamless communication regardless of the user's location or chosen device. SIP also supports various advanced features, including call transfer, call forwarding, call waiting, and conference calling. It can integrate with other protocols such as RTP (Real-time Transport Protocol) for the transmission of voice and video data, and it can interact with other communication protocols like H.323, which is commonly used in video conferencing systems. In summary, SIP is a protocol used in networking to establish, modify, and terminate multimedia communication sessions. It provides a versatile and flexible mechanism for initiating VoIP calls, supporting user mobility, and enabling advanced features in communication systems.

Cisco SIP Trunking

Cisco SIP Trunking is a technology that facilitates the transmission of voice and multimedia communications over the internet using the Session Initiation Protocol (SIP) protocol. It enables businesses to connect their on-premises Private Branch Exchange (PBX) phone systems with the Public Switched Telephone Network (PSTN) through an IP network, eliminating the need for traditional phone lines. SIP Trunking leverages the power of IP-based networks to provide a cost-effective and efficient solution for communication needs. It allows businesses to consolidate their voice and data traffic onto a single network, simplifying management and reducing costs. By utilizing the internet for communication, SIP Trunking offers scalability, flexibility, and global connectivity, enabling businesses to connect with customers, partners, and branches anywhere in the world.

Cisco SNMP (Simple Network Management Protocol)

SNMP, which stands for Simple Network Management Protocol, is a widely used protocol in networking that allows network administrators to manage and monitor network devices. It is an application layer protocol that operates on the Internet Protocol (IP) suite. SNMP is designed to facilitate the management and monitoring of network devices such as routers, switches, servers, and printers. It provides a standardized framework for collecting information about these devices, configuring their settings, and receiving notifications about any events or issues that occur.

Cisco SSH (Secure Shell)

SSH (Secure Shell) is a cryptographic network protocol that provides a secure method for remote access and control of network devices. It is primarily used by network administrators to securely manage remote devices and perform administrative tasks on them. SSH operates at the application layer of the OSI model and utilizes encryption techniques to ensure the confidentiality, integrity, and authenticity of data transmitted over a network. It replaces the insecure and plaintext-based protocols such as Telnet with a secure and encrypted communication channel. One of the key features of SSH is its ability to establish secure and authenticated connections between remote devices. It uses public-key cryptography to authenticate the client and the server, ensuring that the remote device is not impersonated or compromised. The server and client exchange encryption keys during the initial handshake process, which are then used to encrypt and decrypt data sent over the network. Additionally, SSH provides a variety of encryption algorithms, such as AES, 3DES, and Blowfish, to secure the data transmission. It also supports compression, allowing efficient bandwidth utilization for slower connections. SSH also has built-in support for forwarding ports, allowing remote access to services running on a secured network. SSH is widely used in networking environments to manage routers, switches, firewalls, and other network devices remotely. It offers a secure alternative to traditional remote management methods, ensuring that sensitive information, such as login credentials and command outputs, are protected from eavesdropping and tampering.

Cisco SSL VPN

Cisco SSL VPN, also known as Cisco Secure Socket Layer Virtual Private Network, is a technology that allows remote users to securely access a private network or internal resources over the internet using the Secure Sockets Layer (SSL) protocol. SSL VPN provides a secure

71

and encrypted connection between the remote user's device, such as a laptop or smartphone, and the corporate network, ensuring confidentiality, integrity, and authentication of the transmitted data. By leveraging SSL, an industry-standard encryption protocol, Cisco SSL VPN ensures that all data transmitted between the user's device and the corporate network is encrypted and cannot be intercepted or tampered with by unauthorized individuals. This encryption takes place before the data is sent over the public internet, providing end-to-end protection for sensitive information.

Cisco STP (Spanning Tree Protocol)

The Spanning Tree Protocol (STP) is a network protocol used to prevent loops in Ethernet networks. It ensures that only one path is active between any two network devices at a time, while the other redundant paths are blocked. This prevents the occurrence of broadcast storms and avoids the wastage of network resources due to multiple frame copies. STP operates by electing a root bridge within the network, which becomes the central reference point for all other network devices. Each device participates in the process of electing the root bridge by exchanging Bridge Protocol Data Units (BPDUs), which contain information about the device's identity, priorities, and costs. The root bridge is chosen based on the lowest Bridge ID, which consists of a device's Bridge Priority and MAC address. Once the root bridge is elected, each network device determines its role in the network based on its proximity to the root bridge. The device with the lowest cost path to the root bridge becomes the designated bridge for that particular segment. All other devices are designated as non-root bridges. Each network device maintains a forwarding table storing information about the active and blocked ports. This table is continuously updated based on the reception of BPDUs and changes in the network topology. The designated bridge communicates with neighboring devices to exchange BPDUs, which contain information about the root bridge and path costs. The information from BPDUs is used to identify and activate the shortest path to the root bridge, while blocking redundant paths to avoid loops. In the event of a network change or failure, STP recalculates the shortest path and adjusts the forwarding table accordingly. It can reconfigure the network within seconds to adapt to changes and prevent disruptions. This makes STP a crucial protocol for ensuring the reliability and stability of Ethernet networks.

Cisco Security Appliances

Cisco Security Appliances are network devices designed to provide advanced security features and protect against potential threats to a network. These appliances are specifically designed by Cisco Systems, a renowned networking hardware company, to ensure the confidentiality, integrity, and availability of network resources. These security appliances are equipped with various security features and technologies such as firewalls, intrusion prevention systems (IPS), virtual private network (VPN) capabilities, content filtering, and advanced threat detection. Firewalls act as the first line of defense by monitoring and controlling the traffic between different networks, allowing only authorized and legitimate communication. The IPS functionality detects and prevents malicious activities by monitoring network traffic and identifying potential threats, such as malware or unauthorized access attempts. The VPN capabilities of Cisco Security Appliances provide secure and encrypted connections between remote networks or users, ensuring that sensitive data transmitted over the network remains protected and confidential. Content filtering allows administrators to control and restrict access to certain websites or types of content, helping to prevent users from accessing potentially harmful or inappropriate material. In addition to these core security features, Cisco Security Appliances often come integrated with advanced threat detection technologies. These technologies use machine learning algorithms and behavior analysis to identify and block emerging threats or suspicious activities on the network. This proactive approach helps to minimize the risk of successful cyber attacks and provides organizations with enhanced security. Cisco Security Appliances are commonly used in enterprise environments, where large-scale networks require robust security measures. They can be deployed at various points within the network architecture, such as perimeter protection at the network edge, securing internal network segments, or protecting individual devices or endpoints. Their central management capabilities allow administrators to easily configure, monitor, and update the security policies and settings across multiple appliances, simplifying the management and maintenance of network security.

Cisco Spark Board

Cisco Spark Board is an all-in-one collaboration tool that combines video conferencing, digital whiteboarding, and wireless screen sharing into a single device for teams to collaborate and communicate seamlessly in real-time. Designed specifically for businesses, Cisco Spark Board revolutionizes the way teams work together by providing a digital workspace for brainstorming, idea sharing, and decision making. Equipped with a high-definition camera, microphones, and speakers, the Spark Board enables teams to conduct face-to-face meetings with remote members, ensuring effective communication and collaboration regardless of geographical location. The digital whiteboard feature of the Spark Board allows teams to draw, write, and annotate on a shared canvas in real-time. With its touch-enabled display and pen-like stylus, users can easily collaborate on documents, diagrams, and presentations, making it easier to share ideas and make updates on the fly. Additionally, the whiteboard content can be saved and shared with team members for reference or future use. Furthermore, the wireless screen sharing capability of the Spark Board eliminates the need for additional cables or adapters. Users can effortlessly share their screens from laptops, tablets, or smartphones, enabling seamless transition between different devices during presentations or collaborations. From a networking perspective, Cisco Spark Board operates on the Cisco Spark cloud platform, ensuring secure and reliable connectivity for teams to collaborate. It leverages Cisco's industry-leading networking technologies, such as Cisco Unified Communications Manager (CUCM), to deliver high-quality audio and video communication experiences. In conclusion, Cisco Spark Board is a versatile collaboration tool that combines video conferencing, digital whiteboarding, and wireless screen sharing to enhance teamwork and productivity in business environments. With its intuitive interface and seamless integration with the Cisco Spark cloud platform, teams can collaborate effectively and efficiently, regardless of their physical location.

Cisco Spark Hybrid Services

Cisco Spark Hybrid Services is a networking solution that combines the capabilities of on-premises infrastructure with cloud-based services to address the needs of businesses seeking a flexible and secure communication and collaboration platform. With Cisco Spark Hybrid Services, organizations can leverage their existing on-premises infrastructure, such as Cisco Unified Communications Manager (CUCM) or Cisco TelePresence Video Communication Server (VCS), while also taking advantage of the innovative features and scalability offered by Cisco Spark, a cloud-based platform. This hybrid approach allows businesses to maintain control over their network and data while benefiting from the agility and cost-effectiveness of cloud services. By integrating with on-premises infrastructure, Cisco Spark Hybrid Services enables businesses to extend the reach of their collaboration tools, enabling employees to connect and collaborate seamlessly with colleagues, partners, and customers anywhere, anytime, and on any device. Key features of Cisco Spark Hybrid Services include: 1. Hybrid Call Service: This feature allows businesses to connect their on-premises phone systems to the Cisco Spark cloud, enabling users to make and receive calls from Cisco Spark clients on desktops, laptops, and mobile devices. 2. Hybrid Calendar Service: With this feature, organizations can integrate their on-premises calendar systems, such as Microsoft Exchange or Office 365, with Cisco Spark, enabling users to schedule and join meetings directly from Cisco Spark clients. 3. Hybrid Directory Service: This service allows businesses to sync their on-premises directory, such as Microsoft Active Directory, with Cisco Spark, ensuring that users have access to up-to-date contact information. 4. Hybrid Media Service: This feature enables organizations to use their existing on-premises video infrastructure, such as Cisco TelePresence, in conjunction with Cisco Spark, providing a seamless video collaboration experience. By leveraging the power of both on-premises infrastructure and cloud-based services, Cisco Spark Hybrid Services provides businesses with a flexible, secure, and scalable solution for communication and collaboration. This enables organizations to enhance productivity, streamline workflows, and drive innovation across their entire network infrastructure.

Cisco Spark Room Kit

The Cisco Spark Room Kit is a powerful collaboration device designed specifically for networked environments. It combines audio, video, and content sharing capabilities to create a seamless communication experience for teams and individuals. At its core, the Cisco Spark Room Kit is a video conferencing system that integrates with existing Cisco network infrastructure. It allows users to join meetings from anywhere, using any device, and interact with participants in real-time. The Room Kit supports high-definition video and audio, ensuring a clear and immersive communication experience. In addition to video conferencing, the Cisco Spark Room Kit also supports content sharing. Users can easily share presentations, documents, and other files during meetings, enabling collaborative work and enhancing productivity. The Room Kit's advanced content sharing features allow participants to mark up shared content, making it easy to highlight and annotate information. The Cisco Spark Room Kit is designed to be easy to deploy and manage. It seamlessly integrates with Cisco network infrastructure, making it a scalable and efficient solution for large organizations. The Room Kit can be centrally managed, allowing IT teams to easily monitor and update multiple devices from a single interface. Overall, the Cisco Spark Room Kit is a versatile collaboration device that brings teams together in a networked environment. It provides a seamless communication experience, combining high-quality audio and video with advanced content sharing capabilities. With its easy deployment and management features, the Room Kit is a reliable solution for organizations looking to enhance their collaborative work.

Cisco Spark

Cisco Spark is a cloud-based collaboration platform designed for teams to connect and work together seamlessly regardless of physical location. It provides a secure and integrated messaging, meeting, and calling experience to facilitate communication and collaboration among team members. With Cisco Spark, users can send instant messages, start video conferences, and make voice calls from any device, including desktop computers, laptops, tablets, and smartphones. The platform offers real-time messaging capabilities where team members can chat individually or in group conversations, making it easy to share ideas, ask questions, and collaborate on projects. The platform also provides video conferencing features, allowing users to schedule and host meetings with team members or external participants. These meetings can be joined from any device, enabling remote or dispersed teams to connect face-to-face and have productive discussions. Cisco Spark's video conferencing capabilities include screen sharing, file sharing, and virtual whiteboarding, enhancing collaboration during meetings. In addition to messaging and meetings, Cisco Spark offers calling features that enable users to make voice calls to individual team members or external phone numbers. These calls can be made using either the desktop or mobile application, providing flexibility and convenience for users who are on the go. One of the key benefits of Cisco Spark is its seamless integration with other Cisco collaboration tools and platforms, such as Webex and Cisco Unified Communications Manager. This integration allows users to access and use multiple collaboration tools within a single interface, streamlining their workflow and improving productivity. Overall, Cisco Spark provides teams with a comprehensive and secure collaboration solution that facilitates communication, enhances teamwork, and improves productivity. Its cloud-based nature ensures easy access and scalability, making it an ideal choice for organizations of all sizes looking to boost collaboration among team members.

Cisco StackWise

Cisco StackWise is a technology used in networking that allows multiple switches to be connected together to form a single logical unit. It provides a unified and scalable solution for network management, enhancing performance, reliability, and manageability. With Cisco StackWise, switches are interconnected using high-speed stacking cables, creating a single switching unit with a shared management and data plane. This allows for simplified network management, as the stack can be managed as a single entity, with a single IP address and a single configuration file. This eliminates the need to individually manage each switch in the stack, reducing complexity and saving time. StackWise also provides enhanced redundancy and resiliency to the network. In the event of switch failure, the stack can continue to function seamlessly, with traffic automatically being rerouted through the remaining switches in the stack. This ensures uninterrupted network connectivity and minimizes downtime. Additionally, StackWise supports hot-swappable components, allowing for easy replacement of faulty switches without disrupting network operations. Another key feature of Cisco StackWise is its scalability. Up to nine switches can be stacked together, forming a single logical unit with shared resources. This allows for increased network capacity and performance, as traffic can be distributed across multiple switches in the stack. In addition, StackWise supports virtual stacking, which enables the creation of multiple logical stacks within a physical stack. This provides flexibility in network design and allows for easy management of different network segments. In summary, Cisco StackWise is a technology that enables the creation of a unified and scalable network infrastructure. It simplifies network management, provides enhanced redundancy and resiliency, and allows for increased network capacity. By utilizing StackWise, organizations can achieve improved network performance, reliability, and efficiency.

Cisco Stealthwatch

Cisco Stealthwatch is a comprehensive network security solution that provides real-time visibility and threat detection for organizations of all sizes. It leverages advanced analytics and machine learning techniques to monitor network traffic and identify potential threats, including malware, unauthorized access attempts, and data exfiltration. With Stealthwatch, organizations can gain a deeper understanding of their network infrastructure, identify anomalies, and respond quickly to mitigate potential risks. It collects and analyzes network flow data from various sources, including routers, switches, and firewalls, to create a holistic view of network activity.

Cisco Systems

Cisco Systems is a multinational technology company that specializes in networking solutions and services. Founded in 1984, Cisco has become a leading provider of networking hardware, software, and related services, playing a vital role in the growth and development of the internet. With a comprehensive portfolio of networking products and solutions, Cisco helps businesses and organizations connect, communicate, and collaborate effectively. Their offerings include routers, switches, wireless systems, security products, collaboration tools, and cloud-based services. Cisco's networking solutions enable the creation and management of robust and secure networks that facilitate the seamless transfer of data, voice, and video information. These networks form the backbone of the internet, connecting devices, systems, and users across different locations, whether local or global. The company's network infrastructure products, such as routers and switches, form the core components of a network, ensuring reliable connectivity and efficient data transmission. These devices enable data packets to be routed and switched between various points within a network, allowing for smooth communication between connected devices. Cisco also offers a range of security products that safeguard networks from potential threats and cyber-attacks. These security solutions help protect sensitive data, prevent unauthorized access, and ensure network integrity, providing a reliable and secure environment for communication and information exchange. Additionally, Cisco provides collaboration tools that facilitate effective communication and teamwork within organizations. These tools include web conferencing, video conferencing, instant messaging, and other unified communication solutions, enhancing productivity and efficiency in today's interconnected business world. Furthermore, Cisco's cloud-based services offer scalable and flexible solutions for network management, storage, and computing needs. This cloud infrastructure allows organizations to leverage the power of virtualization and easily adapt to changing business requirements. In summary, Cisco Systems is a prominent technology company specializing in networking solutions and services. Through its comprehensive product portfolio, Cisco enables the creation of reliable, secure, and efficient networks, playing a crucial role in connecting and empowering organizations in the digital age.

Cisco TACACS+

TACACS+ is a networking protocol used for authentication, authorization, and accounting (AAA) services. It stands for Terminal Access Controller Access Control System Plus. TACACS+ provides a secure and centralized method for network administrators to control access to network devices and services. In the context of networking, TACACS+ is primarily used for controlling access to routers, switches, and other network devices. It allows network administrators to define policies and rules for user authentication and authorization, as well as monitor and record accounting information for auditing and billing purposes. Authentication is the process of verifying the identity of a user or device requesting access to the network. TACACS+ uses a username and password combination, which is encrypted and transmitted securely to the TACACS+ server for verification. This ensures that only authorized users are granted access to the network. Authorization is the process of determining what actions or operations a user or device is allowed to perform once authenticated. With TACACS+, network administrators can define granular access control policies based on user roles, privilege levels, or specific commands. This helps ensure that users are only granted the necessary privileges to perform their tasks, reducing the risk of unauthorized access or misuse of network resources. Accounting involves the monitoring and recording of network resource usage. TACACS+ can collect and log accounting information such as user login/logout times, executed commands, and data transfer statistics. This data can be used for audits, troubleshooting, or billing purposes. TACACS+ operates using a client-server model. Network devices act as TACACS+ clients and communicate with a central TACACS+ server. The server stores user credentials and access control policies, and performs the authentication, authorization, and accounting functions. This centralized approach provides a scalable and manageable solution for large networks with many devices and users. In summary, TACACS+ is a networking protocol that offers authentication, authorization, and accounting services to control access to network devices. It ensures secure user verification, allows granular access control, and provides monitoring and recording of network activity.

Cisco TelePresence Codec

The Cisco TelePresence Codec is a network device that enables high-quality video and audio communication between remote locations. It is designed to provide a lifelike and immersive meeting experience, allowing participants to interact as if they were in the same room. As a vital component of Cisco TelePresence systems, the Codec compresses, decompresses, and transmits audio and video signals in real-time. It leverages advanced networking technologies to facilitate seamless communication over IP networks, ensuring smooth and reliable transmission of multimedia data. The Codec incorporates various features and functionalities that enhance the overall video conferencing experience. It supports multiple video resolutions, including high-definition (HD), to deliver crystal-clear visuals. It also includes stereo audio capabilities, enabling participants to hear the conversation with exceptional clarity. Furthermore, the Cisco TelePresence Codec incorporates sophisticated algorithms to optimize bandwidth usage without compromising on the quality of the communication. This allows organizations to establish video conferencing connections even over limited network resources while still maintaining a high level of performance. With its interoperability, the Codec can seamlessly integrate with other Cisco TelePresence devices and third-party video conferencing systems. It supports various signaling protocols, including SIP and H.323, ensuring compatibility and enabling communication across different platforms and vendors. The Cisco TelePresence Codec is designed to be user-friendly, featuring an intuitive interface and straightforward controls. It enables participants to easily initiate and manage video calls, adjust settings, and share content during meetings. It also supports advanced features such as screen layouts, dual-stream capabilities, and the ability to record meetings for future reference. In addition, the Codec offers enhanced security measures to protect sensitive information during video conferencing sessions. It supports encryption protocols and authentication mechanisms, ensuring that only authorized participants can access the communication and that the data remains secure and confidential. Overall, the Cisco TelePresence Codec is a crucial component in enabling immersive and effective communication between geographically dispersed individuals or teams. It empowers organizations to achieve collaborative decision-making, increase productivity, and reduce travel expenses through lifelike virtual meetings.

Cisco TelePresence MCU (Multipoint Control Unit)

A Cisco TelePresence MCU (Multipoint Control Unit) is a device used in networking to facilitate multi-party video conferences. It serves as the central point for managing and controlling the audio and video connections between participants in a telepresence session. The Cisco TelePresence MCU acts as a bridge, enabling multiple endpoints or participants to connect and communicate with each other during a video conference. It is designed to provide a seamless and immersive experience by ensuring that all participants can see and hear each other clearly, as if they were in the same room. The MCU works by receiving and processing audio and video streams from different endpoints, and then routing them to the appropriate destinations. It supports various video codecs and resolutions to accommodate different network conditions and endpoint capabilities. The audio streams are mixed to ensure all participants can hear each other, while the video streams are displayed on the respective endpoints' screens. In addition to audio and video management, the Cisco TelePresence MCU also handles other essential functions, such as encryption and decryption of the communication streams to ensure security and privacy. It also offers advanced features like screen layout customization, allowing participants to view the video feeds in different arrangements, such as side-by-side or in a grid. The Cisco TelePresence MCU is a crucial component in large-scale video conferencing deployments, as it enables organizations to connect and collaborate with multiple participants, regardless of their physical location. It provides a cost-effective solution for businesses to conduct virtual meetings, training sessions, and presentations, as it eliminates the need for travel and allows real-time communication across different locations. In summary, the Cisco TelePresence MCU is a networking device that enables multi-party video conferences by managing and controlling the audio and video connections between participants. It acts as a bridge, processing and routing the audio and video streams to ensure a seamless experience for all participants.

Cisco TelePresence Management Suite

The Cisco TelePresence Management Suite (TMS) is a comprehensive solution designed for managing Cisco TelePresence endpoints and infrastructure within a network environment. It provides organizations with the necessary tools and features to efficiently control, monitor, and troubleshoot their TelePresence systems, ensuring optimal performance and user experience. TMS offers centralized management capabilities, allowing administrators to easily configure and maintain multiple TelePresence devices from a single interface. This includes scheduling meetings, managing users and endpoints, and allocating resources such as bandwidth and conferencing resources. By streamlining these tasks, TMS helps reduce the complexity and time required for managing a TelePresence network. One of the key features of Cisco TMS is its scheduling functionality. It enables users to schedule TelePresence meetings and conferences, integrating with common calendar applications such as Microsoft Outlook. This simplifies the process of setting up and organizing virtual meetings, making it more convenient for participants and increasing overall productivity. Additionally, TMS provides comprehensive monitoring and reporting capabilities. It allows administrators to monitor the health and performance of TelePresence endpoints in real-time, ensuring that any issues or faults are quickly identified and resolved. The reporting feature provides detailed analytics and usage statistics, enabling organizations to gain valuable insights into the utilization and effectiveness of their TelePresence infrastructure. Furthermore, TMS supports integration with other network management systems and protocols, enabling seamless integration into existing network environments. This enhances interoperability and facilitates the integration of TelePresence systems with other network services and applications. Overall, the Cisco TelePresence Management Suite plays a critical role in the effective management and operation of Cisco TelePresence networks. Its centralized management capabilities, scheduling functionality, monitoring and reporting features, and integration capabilities make it an essential tool for organizations seeking to optimize their TelePresence deployment.

Cisco TelePresence Server

The Cisco TelePresence Server is a networking device that enables high-quality video conferencing and collaboration experiences across different locations. It allows users to connect and share information in real-time, as if they were in the same room, enhancing communication and productivity in business environments. The TelePresence Server acts as a bridge between multiple video endpoints, such as Cisco TelePresence systems, third-party video conferencing systems, and software applications running on PCs or mobile devices. It provides a centralized platform for hosting and managing video conferences, ensuring seamless connectivity and interoperability between different devices and networks. The main function of the TelePresence Server is to process and distribute video and audio streams in real-time, maintaining high-definition quality and low latency. It uses advanced video compression and network optimization techniques to deliver smooth and immersive video conferencing experiences, even over low-bandwidth networks. Users can see and hear each other with exceptional clarity, allowing for natural and productive meetings. The TelePresence Server supports various video conferencing features, such as video layouts, to control the positioning and size of participants' video feeds on the screen. It enables content sharing by allowing presenters to share documents, presentations, or multimedia files during a conference. The server also supports multi-point conferencing, enabling users to connect with multiple participants simultaneously, fostering collaboration and teamwork. Furthermore, the TelePresence Server offers security features to protect video conferences and sensitive information. It supports encryption protocols to secure video and audio streams, preventing unauthorized access or eavesdropping. The server can integrate with existing enterprise security infrastructure, allowing administrators to apply policies and restrictions to video conferences. In summary, the Cisco TelePresence Server is a networking device that facilitates high-quality video conferencing and collaboration experiences. It serves as a central hub for connecting various video endpoints and facilitates real-time communication between participants, promoting efficient collaboration, and reducing the need for travel. The server's advanced features and security measures make it a reliable and effective solution for businesses of all sizes seeking to enhance communication and productivity.

Cisco TelePresence Touch Panel

The Cisco TelePresence Touch Panel is a user interface device designed to provide easy and intuitive control of Cisco TelePresence video conferencing systems. It is a touch-enabled control panel that allows users to interact with the various features and functions of the TelePresence system. The Touch Panel serves as the primary input device for users to control and navigate through the user interface of the TelePresence system. It is equipped with a high-resolution touch screen display, which enables users to select options, input commands, and make adjustments using their fingertips. The Touch Panel offers a range of functions and capabilities to facilitate efficient and seamless operation of Cisco TelePresence video conferencing solutions. Users can use the Touch Panel to initiate or join video conference calls, control camera movements and angles, adjust audio and video settings, share content or presentations, and collaborate with remote participants. In addition to its intuitive touch interface, the Touch Panel also provides physical buttons for quick access to commonly used functions and commands. These buttons are strategically placed for easy reach and enable users to perform tasks with minimal effort and without distracting from the conferencing experience. The Touch Panel is designed to seamlessly integrate with other components of the Cisco TelePresence system, such as cameras, screens, microphones, and speakers. It connects to these devices using standard networking protocols and interfaces, allowing for easy and seamless communication and control. Overall, the Cisco TelePresence Touch Panel plays a crucial role in enhancing the usability and effectiveness of Cisco TelePresence video conferencing systems. It provides a user-friendly interface that enables users to control and manage various aspects of the TelePresence system, resulting in a smooth and productive conferencing experience.

Cisco TelePresence

Cisco TelePresence is a high-definition video conferencing technology developed by Cisco Systems, designed to provide immersive and lifelike video collaboration experiences over a network. It enables participants in different locations to communicate and collaborate as if they were in the same room, making meetings more productive and efficient. Cisco TelePresence leverages advanced networking technologies to deliver a seamless experience, with crisp audio and high-definition video quality. It utilizes a combination of codec, camera, and display technology to transmit and display lifelike images, enabling participants to see each other clearly and capture subtle visual cues that are essential for effective communication. With Cisco TelePresence, users can establish point-to-point or multipoint video calls, allowing multiple participants to join the meeting from different locations. The technology supports various collaboration features, such as content sharing, whiteboarding, and document annotation, to enhance productivity and facilitate effective decision-making. One of the key advantages of Cisco TelePresence is its simplicity. The technology is straightforward to deploy and use, requiring minimal technical expertise. Participants can join a TelePresence session with just a few clicks, without the need for complex setup or configuration. Furthermore, Cisco TelePresence is highly secure, with built-in encryption and authentication mechanisms to protect sensitive data during transmission. It also supports integration with existing collaboration tools and infrastructure, allowing organizations to leverage their existing investments and streamline their communication workflows. In summary, Cisco TelePresence is a video conferencing technology that enables immersive and lifelike communication experiences over a network. It combines advanced networking, audiovisual, and collaboration capabilities to create a seamless and productive meeting environment for participants in different locations. References: https://www.cisco.com/c/en/us/solutions/collaboration/video-conferencing/index.html

Cisco Telnet

Cisco Telnet is a network communication protocol that enables remote command-line access to Cisco devices, such as routers or switches. It allows network administrators to connect to these devices from a remote location and manage them using a text-based interface. Telnet acts as a

78

virtual terminal, providing a means to access and control the connected device remotely, as if the administrator were physically present. The remote administrator can execute various commands to configure, monitor, and troubleshoot network devices. When establishing a Telnet session, the remote administrator must provide the IP address or hostname of the Cisco device they wish to connect to, as well as appropriate login credentials. Once the connection is established, the administrator can navigate through the device's command-line interface (CLI) and issue commands. Telnet operates using the Transmission Control Protocol (TCP) and typically communicates over port 23. It uses a client-server model, where the Cisco device acts as the server, listening for incoming Telnet connections, and the remote administrator's computer acts as the client. The Telnet client on the administrator's computer initiates the connection and sends commands to the server, which then executes them and sends back the output. One key advantage of using Cisco Telnet is its ability to manage network devices remotely, which can significantly simplify network administration tasks. This remote accessibility is particularly useful in cases where the devices are geographically dispersed or located in inaccessible areas. It allows administrators to configure and troubleshoot devices from a centralized location, saving time and resources. However, it is worth mentioning that Cisco Telnet has some security concerns, as the entire communication, including login credentials, is transmitted in plaintext format. This makes it vulnerable to eavesdropping or unauthorized access. To mitigate these risks, it is recommended to use a more secure alternative to Telnet, such as Secure Shell (SSH), which encrypts the communication between the client and the server.

Cisco Threat Grid

Cisco Threat Grid is a comprehensive network security solution designed to identify and protect against a wide range of cyber threats. It provides advanced threat intelligence and analysis capabilities to help organizations proactively defend their networks and respond to emerging security risks. At its core, Cisco Threat Grid is a powerful malware analysis platform that allows security teams to efficiently analyze and identify malicious files and activities. It leverages advanced, cloud-based sandboxing technology to execute suspicious files in a controlled environment, providing deep visibility into their behavior and capabilities. By submitting suspicious files to Cisco Threat Grid, security analysts can quickly determine whether these files are malware, and if so, gain valuable insight into its functionality and potential impact. This analysis helps organizations understand the tactics, techniques, and procedures employed by cybercriminals, enabling them to better defend against future attacks. In addition to its malware analysis capabilities, Cisco Threat Grid also aggregates threat intelligence from a wide range of sources, including global sensors, research teams, and customer contributions. This wealth of information allows security teams to stay informed about the latest threats and trends, ensuring they are well-prepared to detect and respond to emerging cyber attacks. Cisco Threat Grid integrates seamlessly with other Cisco security products, such as firewalls, intrusion prevention systems, and security information and event management (SIEM) platforms. This integration enables organizations to automate threat detection and response, reducing the time and effort required to mitigate security incidents. In summary, Cisco Threat Grid is a comprehensive network security solution that combines advanced malware analysis capabilities with extensive threat intelligence. By leveraging cloud-based sandboxing technology and aggregating information from multiple sources, it enables organizations to proactively defend their networks against a wide range of cyber threats.

Cisco Trust Agent

The Cisco Trust Agent is a software application developed by Cisco Systems that enables network administrators to enforce security policies and ensure the integrity of endpoint devices connecting to the network. As part of Cisco's Network Admission Control (NAC) architecture, the Trust Agent serves as an endpoint assessment and remediation tool. It is installed on client devices such as computers, laptops, and mobile devices and works in conjunction with other Cisco security products, such as Cisco Secure Access Control Server (ACS) and Cisco Security Agent, to provide a comprehensive network security solution.

Cisco TrustSec

Cisco TrustSec is a comprehensive security solution that is specifically designed for computer networks, providing authentication, encryption, and access control features. It aims to securely connect users, devices, and applications within a network, ensuring data confidentiality, integrity, and availability. TrustSec offers a flexible and scalable network architecture that enables policy-based access control throughout the network infrastructure. It uses the concept of security groups to classify and enforce policies based on logical groupings of network endpoints. These security groups can be defined based on location, department, role, or any other organizational attribute.

Cisco UCS Central

Cisco UCS Central is a software application that provides centralized management and control for Cisco Unified Computing System (UCS) environments. It serves as a central point of control for managing multiple UCS domains, enabling administrators to easily and efficiently manage a large-scale UCS deployment. With Cisco UCS Central, network administrators can efficiently manage and orchestrate policies and configurations across multiple UCS domains in a simplified and streamlined manner. It provides a unified view of the entire UCS infrastructure, allowing administrators to monitor and troubleshoot any issues, quickly identify and resolve problems, and scale the infrastructure as needed.

Cisco UCS Director

Cisco UCS Director is a comprehensive software solution that enables simplified management and orchestration of computing, networking, and storage resources in a data center environment.By providing a single pane of glass for managing and automating various infrastructure components, UCS Director streamlines operations, enhances agility, and optimizes resource utilization.

Cisco UCS (Unified Computing System)

Cisco UCS (Unified Computing System) is a data center networking solution that integrates computing, networking, storage access, and virtualization resources into a single cohesive system. It combines Cisco's networking expertise with industry-standard server hardware to provide a flexible, scalable, and efficient infrastructure for managing and delivering IT services. The main components of the Cisco UCS are the Fabric Interconnects, UCS Manager, and the UCS servers. The Fabric Interconnects are the core networking devices that provide connectivity to the rest of the data center infrastructure. They serve as the central point for managing and controlling all traffic within the UCS system. The UCS Manager is a software application that provides a single unified interface for managing all aspects of the Cisco UCS. It allows administrators to configure, monitor, and troubleshoot the entire system from a single, centralized location. The UCS Manager also includes a robust set of management features, including service profiles, which allow administrators to define the hardware, firmware, and BIOS settings for each server in the system. The UCS servers are the physical hardware that run the applications and services in the data center. Cisco offers a wide range of UCS server models, ranging from blade servers to rack servers. These servers are designed to provide high performance, reliability, and scalability, making them suitable for a variety of workloads, from virtualization to high-performance computing. One of the key benefits of Cisco UCS is its ability to streamline and simplify data center operations. By integrating computing, networking, and storage resources into a single system, it eliminates the need for separate devices and reduces the complexity and cost associated with managing multiple systems. It also allows for more efficient use of resources, as administrators can easily allocate and reallocate computing and storage capacity as needed. In addition, Cisco UCS provides a highly flexible and scalable platform for virtualization. It supports a wide range of hypervisors and virtualization technologies, allowing organizations to consolidate their IT infrastructure and improve resource utilization. The UCS Manager's service profiles further enhance the virtualization capabilities by enabling the rapid deployment and provisioning of virtualized workloads. Overall, Cisco UCS is a comprehensive data center networking solution that offers seamless integration of computing, networking, storage, and virtualization resources. Its flexible and scalable architecture, combined with its simplified management and high performance, makes it an ideal choice for organizations looking to modernize their data center infrastructure and optimize their IT operations.

Cisco Umbrella

Cisco Umbrella, formerly known as OpenDNS, is a cloud-based security platform that provides a first line of defense against threats on the internet. It acts as a secure DNS resolver, filtering and blocking malicious websites and applications before they can reach the network. With Cisco Umbrella, organizations can protect their network devices and users from accessing harmful or inappropriate content, preventing malware infections, data breaches, and other cyberattacks. It offers advanced threat intelligence and real-time updates to identify and block threats, even those that use encryption to bypass traditional security measures.

Cisco Unified Communications Manager (CUCM)

Cisco Unified Communications Manager (CUCM) is an enterprise call control and session management platform that is used to provision, control, and manage voice and video communications within an organization's network. It is a critical component of Cisco's Unified Communications suite of products. CUCM provides a robust and scalable solution for businesses of all sizes, allowing them to consolidate their communication infrastructure into a single platform. It offers advanced telephony features, such as call routing, call queuing, call forwarding, call park, and call pickup, as well as video and multimedia services, including video conferencing and streaming media. Using CUCM, organizations can establish and manage their own private voice and video networks, reducing the reliance on traditional telephony services and enabling the integration of voice and video communication with other applications and services, such as email, instant messaging, and customer relationship management (CRM) systems. CUCM operates on an IP-based network and leverages the Session Initiation Protocol (SIP) as its primary signaling protocol. It can integrate with various Cisco and third-party devices, such as IP phones, softphones, video endpoints, gateways, and telepresence systems, enabling seamless communication across different devices and locations. Administrators can use CUCM's web-based interface to configure and manage the system, including user accounts, devices, dial plans, call routing rules, and security settings. The platform offers robust security features, such as encryption, authentication, access control, and secure connectivity options, ensuring the confidentiality and integrity of communication data. CUCM also provides advanced management and monitoring capabilities, allowing administrators to monitor system performance, track call quality metrics, generate reports, and troubleshoot issues. It offers high availability and redundancy features, such as clustering, load balancing, and failover mechanisms, to ensure business continuity and minimize downtime. In summary, Cisco Unified Communications Manager (CUCM) is a comprehensive call control and session management platform that brings together voice, video, and multimedia communication services into a single, scalable solution. It enables organizations to enhance collaboration, improve productivity, and streamline their communication infrastructure.

Cisco Unified Computing System (UCS) Manager

The Cisco Unified Computing System (UCS) Manager is a management platform used for managing and administering Cisco's Unified Computing System. It is a critical component of Cisco's unified data center architecture. The UCS Manager provides a unified and centralized interface for managing all aspects of the UCS infrastructure. It enables administrators to configure and monitor the physical resources, such as servers, networking components, and storage devices, as well as the virtualized environments and applications running on the UCS platform. The UCS Manager simplifies the management of complex data center environments by abstracting the underlying infrastructure and presenting it as a logical and easily manageable system. It provides a comprehensive set of tools and features, including service profiles, templates, policies, and automation capabilities, to streamline administrative tasks and improve operational efficiency. The core functionality of the UCS Manager includes the ability to create and manage service profiles. A service profile encapsulates the required configuration settings for a server, including its identity, boot options, firmware versions, and network connectivity. By using service profiles, administrators can easily provision and deploy new servers, clone existing configurations, and perform server migrations without the need to manually configure each individual server. Furthermore, the UCS Manager integrates with other Cisco management tools and platforms, such as the Cisco Application Policy Infrastructure Controller (APIC) and Cisco UCS Director, to provide end-to-end management and automation capabilities. It supports standard APIs and protocols, allowing for seamless integration with third-party tools and systems. In summary, the Cisco UCS Manager is a powerful and comprehensive management platform for Cisco's Unified Computing System. It enables administrators to efficiently provision, configure, and monitor the entire UCS infrastructure, resulting in improved scalability, flexibility, and operational agility in the data center environment.

Cisco Unified Contact Center

Cisco Unified Contact Center (CUCC) is an integrated networking solution designed to manage and optimize customer interactions across multiple communication channels. It combines various technologies, including voice, video, email, web chat, and social media, to enable efficient and personalized customer service experiences. At its core, CUCC consists of a network infrastructure that connects various components, such as contact center agents, customers, and supporting systems, in a seamless manner. The main aim of CUCC is to improve customer satisfaction, increase operational efficiency, and drive business outcomes.

Cisco VLAN (Virtual Local Area Network)

Cisco VLAN (Virtual Local Area Network) is a technology that allows network administrators to segment a physical network into smaller logical networks. Each VLAN operates as if it were a separate physical network, even though it shares the same physical infrastructure. With VLANs, a network administrator can create different groups of users or devices, regardless of their physical location, and assign them to a specific VLAN. This segmentation provides several benefits, such as improved network performance, increased security, and simplified network management.

Cisco VPN Client

The Cisco VPN Client is a software application that allows users to establish a secure, encrypted connection between their devices and a remote network over a public network, such as the internet. It is a virtual private network (VPN) solution developed by Cisco Systems, a leading provider of networking equipment and services. The primary purpose of the Cisco VPN Client is to provide users with a secure method of accessing resources on a remote network. This is especially useful for individuals or organizations that need to connect to their office network while working remotely or for connecting branch offices of an organization to a central network. The Cisco VPN Client uses encryption and authentication protocols to ensure the confidentiality, integrity, and authenticity of data transmitted over the network. When a user initiates a connection with the Cisco VPN Client, their device establishes a secure tunnel with a VPN server located on the remote network. This tunnel is created using industry-standard protocols, such as IPsec (Internet Protocol Security) or SSL/TLS (Secure Sockets Layer/Transport Layer Security). These protocols ensure that data transmitted between the user's device and the VPN server is encrypted and cannot be intercepted by unauthorized individuals or entities. Additionally, the Cisco VPN Client provides a mechanism for remote users to authenticate themselves before accessing network resources. This can be done through various methods, such as passwords, digital certificates, or two-factor authentication. By verifying the user's identity, the VPN client ensures that only authorized individuals can establish a connection to the remote network. In summary, the Cisco VPN Client is a software application that enables users to establish secure, encrypted connections to remote networks. It provides a reliable and secure method of accessing resources on a remote network while ensuring the confidentiality, integrity, and authenticity of transmitted data. Organizations and individuals can use the Cisco VPN Client to securely connect to their office networks or establish connections between branch offices, promoting productivity and data security.

Cisco VPN Concentrator

A Cisco VPN Concentrator is a networking device that provides secure remote access to a private network over the internet. It acts as a central point for managing and controlling VPN (Virtual Private Network) connections from remote clients, such as laptops, smartphones, or tablets. With a VPN Concentrator, organizations can establish a secure connection between a remote user and the corporate network, allowing them to access resources and services as if they were physically present in the office. This is especially useful for employees who work remotely or for businesses with multiple branch offices.

Cisco VPN (Virtual Private Network)

A Virtual Private Network (VPN) is a secure and private connection established between two or more networks over a public network, such as the internet. It allows organizations to extend their private network resources securely over a public network, enabling remote users or branches to access resources as if they were directly connected to the private network. VPN technology leverages encryption and authentication to ensure confidentiality, integrity, and authenticity of transmitted data. Encryption scrambles the data into an unreadable form, preventing unauthorized access or eavesdropping. Authentication verifies the identities of the communicating parties, ensuring that only authorized users can access the network.

Cisco VRRP (Virtual Router Redundancy Protocol)

Cisco VRRP (Virtual Router Redundancy Protocol) is a networking protocol designed to provide a redundant and highly available default gateway to hosts on a LAN (Local Area Network). It works by allowing multiple routers to work together and appear as a single virtual router, providing a seamless failover mechanism in case of a primary router failure. VRRP operates by designating one router as the virtual router master and the other routers as backups. The master router is responsible for forwarding traffic and answering ARP (Address Resolution Protocol) requests for the shared virtual IP address. The backup routers continuously monitor the master router and take over its responsibilities if it becomes unavailable. This ensures that the virtual IP address remains active and reachable even if the master router fails. When multiple routers are configured with VRRP, they communicate with each other using multicast IP addresses. They exchange VRRP advertisement messages over a LAN to determine the state of the virtual router and the priority of each router. The router with the highest priority becomes the master router, while the others become backups. VRRP utilizes a preemptive mechanism, where a backup router with a higher priority can preempt the master router and become the new master if it becomes available. This helps to ensure that the most capable router is always serving as the master, providing optimal network performance and reliability. In addition to redundancy, VRRP also supports load balancing among multiple routers by distributing traffic among them. This load balancing feature can enhance network performance by utilizing the resources of multiple routers simultaneously. By implementing VRRP, network administrators can effectively eliminate single points of failure in their LANs, ensuring uninterrupted network connectivity and minimizing downtime. VRRP is widely used in environments with critical network infrastructures, such as data centers, enterprise networks, and service provider networks. In conclusion, Cisco VRRP is a networking protocol that enables multiple routers to function as a single virtual router, providing redundancy and high availability for the default gateway. It uses a master-backup model, where the master router handles traffic and ARP requests, with backup routers taking over in case of failures. VRRP supports load balancing and has a preemptive mechanism to ensure optimal performance. It is a crucial tool for network administrators to achieve reliable and fault-tolerant LAN environments.

Cisco VSS (Virtual Switching System)

A Virtual Switching System (VSS) is a network technology introduced by Cisco Systems that enables the combination of two physical Cisco Catalyst switches into a single logical switch, thereby providing simplified network management and increased network scalability. The main purpose of implementing VSS is to create a unified system with enhanced resiliency and high availability. By combining two physical switches into one logical entity, VSS eliminates the need for the traditional use of spanning tree protocol (STP) to prevent network loops. Instead, VSS uses Cisco's proprietary technology called Virtual Switching System Link (VSL) to connect the two physical switches and provide a redundant and non-blocking interconnect. This allows for active-active access to both switches and optimizes network performance. VSS provides several advantages for network administrators. Firstly, it simplifies network management by treating the two physical switches as a single logical device. This means that configurations, monitoring, and troubleshooting can be performed on the VSS as a whole, rather than on individual switches. Additionally, software upgrades and maintenance activities can be performed without any impact on network connectivity, as VSS provides continuous operation during such activities. Another benefit of VSS is increased network scalability. With VSS, the ports on the two physical switches are combined to create a larger port channel, resulting in greater bandwidth capacity for network traffic. The logical switch also allows for the creation of larger Layer 2 domains, enabling the extension of VLANs across multiple physical switches. This flexibility is particularly useful in data centers or enterprise networks where high traffic loads and scalability are critical. In summary, a Virtual Switching System (VSS) is a network technology that combines two physical Cisco Catalyst switches into a single logical switch. It simplifies network management, provides high availability and resilience, and offers increased network scalability. By eliminating the need for spanning tree protocol and utilizing a redundant interconnect, VSS optimizes network performance and enables a more efficient and scalable network infrastructure.

Cisco Video Conferencing

Cisco Video Conferencing refers to the technology and infrastructure provided by Cisco Systems for conducting remote meetings and collaboration through audiovisual communication. It enables real-time, face-to-face interactions between individuals or groups located in different geographic locations, using high-quality audio and video streams. Cisco Video Conferencing is a key networking solution that empowers organizations to connect and collaborate efficiently, regardless of physical barriers. It leverages the capabilities of IP networks to transmit audio and video data securely and reliably, ensuring clear and seamless communication. This technology facilitates virtual meetings that mimic in-person interactions, with participants able to see and hear each other in real-time. It makes use of video cameras, microphones, and speakers to capture and transmit audiovisual data between endpoints. Cisco Video Conferencing systems include purpose-built hardware, such as room-based telepresence systems, as well as software-based solutions that can be deployed on personal computers, smartphones, and tablets. Video conferencing offers numerous benefits to organizations, including increased productivity, reduced travel expenses, and enhanced collaboration. It allows remote employees, customers, and partners to join meetings from anywhere with an internet connection, overcoming the limitations of time and distance. Participants can share content, such as presentations and documents, in real-time, further enhancing collaboration and decision-making. Cisco Video Conferencing also supports advanced features and functionalities to enhance the meeting experience. This includes support for multipoint conferences, where multiple participants can join the same meeting from different locations. It also enables integration with other collaboration tools, such as instant messaging and file sharing, for a more comprehensive communication experience. In addition to its networking capabilities, Cisco Video Conferencing provides robust security measures to protect sensitive information exchanged during remote meetings. This includes encryption of audio and video data, authentication mechanisms to verify participant identities, and secure transmission protocols to prevent unauthorized access. In summary, Cisco Video Conferencing is a networking solution that enables organizations to conduct real-time remote meetings and collaboration through audiovisual communication. It leverages IP networks to transmit high-quality audio and video streams, enhancing productivity, reducing costs, and fostering seamless collaboration.

Cisco Viptela

Cisco Viptela, also known as Cisco SD-WAN, is a software-defined wide area network (SD-WAN) solution provided by Cisco Systems. SD-WAN is an evolution of traditional wide area networking that enables organizations to connect and manage multiple branch offices and remote locations through a centralized control plane.Cisco Viptela simplifies the management and operation of wide area networks by decoupling the network hardware from the control plane, making it highly scalable and flexible. It uses a cloud-based management platform that provides a single pane of glass for administrators to configure, monitor, and troubleshoot the network.

Cisco VoIP (Voice Over IP)

Cisco VoIP, commonly known as Voice over IP, is a networking technology that enables the transmission of voice communications over an IP network, such as the internet or a private local area network (LAN). VoIP converts analog voice signals into digital data packets, which are then transmitted using Internet Protocol (IP) packets. This technology allows for the integration of voice and data services onto a single network, eliminating the need for separate voice and data networks. With Cisco VoIP, businesses can take advantage of cost savings, increased flexibility, and enhanced productivity.

Cisco Voicemail

Cisco Voicemail is a network-based service that allows users to receive, store, and manage voice messages. It is an integral part of Cisco's Unified Communications solutions, providing a reliable and scalable voicemail system for organizations. The primary purpose of Cisco Voicemail is to provide users with a centralized location to store and access voice messages. Instead of using traditional answering machines or physical voicemail boxes, Cisco Voicemail leverages the power of the network to deliver voice messages directly to the user's email or computer. This allows for more flexibility and convenience, as users can listen to their voicemail messages from anywhere with an internet connection. With Cisco Voicemail, users can receive notifications of new messages via email or text message, ensuring that they are alerted promptly. They can then access their voicemail messages through various devices, such as IP phones, computers, or smartphones. This versatility allows for seamless integration into the user's existing communication infrastructure. One of the key features of Cisco Voicemail is its ability to support multiple mailboxes. This means that organizations can set up individual voicemail accounts for each employee, enabling personalized greetings and voice messages. Users can also customize their voicemail settings, such as the length of time before a call goes to voicemail or the order in which messages are played. Cisco Voicemail also offers advanced capabilities, such as voicemail-to-text transcription. This feature automatically converts voicemail messages into text format, allowing users to read their messages instead of listening to them. This is particularly useful in situations where it may be inconvenient or impossible to play a voicemail message out loud. In summary, Cisco Voicemail is a network-based voicemail service that enables users to receive, store, and manage voice messages. It offers features such as email notifications, multiple mailboxes, and voicemail-to-text transcription, enhancing the user's communication experience and providing greater flexibility and convenience.

Cisco WIPS (Wireless Intrusion Prevention System)

Cisco WIPS (Wireless Intrusion Prevention System) is a network security solution specifically designed to detect and prevent unauthorized access and malicious activities on wireless networks. It provides continuous monitoring, analysis, and protection against potential threats and attacks that target wireless infrastructure. WIPS functions by examining the radio frequencies used by wireless devices to identify and respond to any abnormal or suspicious behavior in the network. It actively scans the airwaves to detect rogue or unauthorized access points, client devices, and other potential security risks. Once identified, WIPS takes appropriate actions to mitigate the risks and prevent any further compromise of the network. Some key features of Cisco WIPS include: 1. Intrusion Detection: WIPS constantly monitors the wireless network for any signs of intrusion or unauthorized activities. It detects and alerts administrators about any unusual or suspicious behavior, such as the presence of rogue access points, unauthorized device connections, or abnormal traffic patterns. 2. Intrusion Prevention: In addition to detecting threats, WIPS actively prevents them from causing harm to the network. It can automatically block or contain rogue access points, devices, or clients, preventing them from accessing the network or causing any potential damage. 3. Rogue Access Point Detection: WIPS scans the radio spectrum to identify any rogue access points that may have been deployed within the vicinity of the network. It helps administrators locate and eliminate these unauthorized access points, ensuring that only authorized wireless infrastructure is used within the network. 4. Policy Enforcement: WIPS enforces security policies and compliance regulations for wireless networks. It ensures that only approved devices and clients can connect to the network, and it can enforce encryption standards, authentication protocols, and other security measures to maintain a secure wireless environment. In conclusion, Cisco WIPS is a powerful network security solution that helps organizations protect their wireless networks from unauthorized access, intrusions, and other potential security threats. By providing continuous monitoring, detection, and prevention capabilities, WIPS ensures the integrity and security of wireless infrastructure while maintaining compliance with security policies and regulations.

Cisco WLC Configuration

Cisco WLC Configuration refers to the process of setting up and managing a Cisco Wireless LAN Controller (WLC) device for the purpose of controlling and managing wireless access points (APs) in a network. The WLC acts as a central controller for the APs, providing centralized management, security, and configuration capabilities. With Cisco WLC Configuration, network administrators can efficiently configure and manage wireless networks, ensuring seamless connectivity, security, and optimal performance. The configuration process involves various steps and settings that need to be properly configured to meet the specific requirements of the network.

Cisco WLC (Wireless LAN Controller)

A Cisco WLC, or Wireless LAN Controller, is a networking device that is designed to manage and control multiple access points (APs) in a wireless local area network (WLAN). It serves as a centralized platform for configuring, monitoring, and optimizing the WLAN infrastructure, providing a unified management interface for the entire wireless network. The Cisco WLC acts as a bridge between the wireless clients and the wired network, ensuring seamless connectivity and efficient data transmission. It plays a critical role in managing the various aspects of the WLAN, including authentication, security, quality of service (QoS), and mobility. By centralizing these functions, the WLC simplifies network management and enhances the overall performance and reliability of the wireless network. One of the key advantages of using a Cisco WLC is its ability to provide centralized control and visibility over the entire wireless network. It allows network administrators to configure and manage all the APs from a single interface, making it easier to enforce consistent security policies, manage user access, and troubleshoot network issues. Furthermore, the Cisco WLC supports various authentication methods to ensure secure access to the wireless network. It can integrate with external authentication servers, such as RADIUS or Active Directory, to authenticate users and enforce access controls based on their credentials. This helps prevent unauthorized access and protects sensitive data transmitted over the WLAN. In terms of mobility, the Cisco WLC enables seamless roaming for wireless clients as they move between different APs within the network. It ensures uninterrupted connectivity by dynamically transferring client sessions from one AP to another without interruption. This smooth handoff between APs enhances the user experience and reduces the likelihood of dropped connections. In summary, a Cisco WLC is a vital component of a WLAN infrastructure, providing centralized management, security, and mobility capabilities. It simplifies network administration, enhances security, and improves the overall performance and user experience of the wireless network.

Cisco Webex Board

The Cisco Webex Board is a cutting-edge networking device that enables seamless collaboration and communication for teams, regardless of their physical location. It combines the functionalities of a digital whiteboard, video conferencing system, and collaboration tool into a single platform. With the Cisco Webex Board, teams can engage in real-time interactions, allowing them to brainstorm, share ideas, and make decisions efficiently. The device boasts a high-resolution touch screen display, which provides a responsive and intuitive interface for users to interact with. Additionally, it supports multi-touch gestures, such as pinch-to-zoom and swipe, enhancing the users' ability to collaborate effectively. One of the key features of the Cisco Webex Board is its seamless integration with Cisco Webex Meetings, a powerful video conferencing platform. Users can initiate video conferences directly from the board, enabling face-to-face interactions with remote team members. The board's wide-angle camera and high-quality microphones ensure crystal-clear audio and video, creating an immersive conferencing experience. Beyond video conferencing, the Cisco Webex Board also allows teams to share and annotate documents, images, and presentations in real-time. Multiple users can contribute simultaneously, fostering a collaborative environment that encourages active participation and engagement. The board's built-in whiteboarding capabilities enable users to draw, write, and erase directly on the screen, mimicking the experience of using a traditional whiteboard. In terms of connectivity, the Cisco Webex Board supports both wired and wireless connections, ensuring flexibility and versatility. It can connect to the corporate network via Ethernet, providing reliable and secure internet access. Additionally, it supports Wi-Fi connectivity, allowing users to connect their laptops, smartphones, or tablets to the board wirelessly, further enhancing collaboration possibilities. In conclusion, the Cisco Webex Board is a comprehensive networking device that revolutionizes team collaboration and communication. It combines the features of a digital whiteboard, video conferencing system, and collaboration tool, enabling seamless interactions for teams working remotely. With its intuitive interface, high-resolution display, and integration with Cisco Webex Meetings, the Webex Board empowers teams to work together efficiently and effectively.

Cisco Webex Cloud

Cisco Webex Cloud is a collaboration platform provided by Cisco Systems specifically designed to facilitate web conferencing, video meetings, and team collaboration in a corporate network environment. It is a cloud-based solution that offers a variety of communication and collaboration tools to enhance productivity and efficiency in business operations. Webex Cloud enables organizations to connect employees, partners, and customers from different locations in real-time, allowing them to collaborate seamlessly through audio and video conferencing, screen sharing, document sharing, and instant messaging. The platform supports both one-on-one and group meetings, making it suitable for small teams as well as large-scale conferences.

Cisco Webex Meetings Server

Cisco Webex Meetings Server is a communication and collaboration solution specifically designed for networking environments. It allows individuals and teams to conduct virtual meetings, presentations, and webinars, facilitating real-time interactions and content sharing. Utilizing Webex Meetings Server, users can connect with colleagues, partners, customers, or clients from any location, enabling effective communication and collaboration regardless of physical distance. The platform supports both audio and video conferencing, allowing participants to have face-to-face interactions, while also offering audio-only options for participants who may not have access to video capabilities.

Cisco Webex Meetings

Cisco Webex Meetings is a networking solution that allows individuals to collaborate and communicate through virtual meetings. It provides a platform for remote participants to interact in real-time using audio, video, and chat features. With Cisco Webex Meetings, users can host meetings or join meetings organized by others. The platform offers a variety of tools and features that enhance the meeting experience, such as screen sharing, document sharing, and whiteboarding capabilities. These features enable participants to share and collaborate on content, making it easier to present ideas, discuss projects, or conduct training sessions remotely.

Cisco Webex Teams

Cisco Webex Teams is a collaboration platform designed for networking professionals to communicate and collaborate effectively. It offers a wide range of features and tools that enable users to connect with colleagues, share information, and work together on projects in real-time. One of the main features of Cisco Webex Teams is the messaging function, which allows users to send instant messages to individuals or groups. This feature is essential for networking professionals as it enables them to quickly and efficiently communicate with team members, clients, and other stakeholders. The messaging function also supports the sharing of files, making it easy to exchange important documents, presentations, and other resources. In addition to messaging, Cisco Webex Teams also provides audio and video conferencing capabilities. These features allow users to have face-to-face conversations with colleagues or clients, no matter their physical location. This is particularly beneficial for networking professionals who may need to collaborate with team members or conduct meetings with clients across different regions or time zones. Furthermore, Cisco Webex Teams offers project management tools that aid in organizing and tracking tasks. Users can create virtual spaces called teams, where they can collaborate, share updates, and assign tasks. This feature streamlines project management processes and ensures that all team members are on the same page regarding project progress and deadlines. In terms of security, Cisco Webex Teams prioritizes data protection and privacy. It offers end-to-end encryption, meaning that all messages, files, and calls are secure and cannot be intercepted by unauthorized individuals. This level of security is crucial for networking professionals who handle sensitive information, such as client data or confidential project details. In conclusion, Cisco Webex Teams is a powerful collaboration platform that facilitates effective communication, collaboration, and project management for networking professionals. Its messaging, audio and video conferencing, and project management features enable teams to work together seamlessly, regardless of their geographical location. With its emphasis on security, Cisco Webex Teams ensures the protection of sensitive data, making it a reliable choice for networking professionals.

Cisco Webex

Cisco Webex is a networking solution that enables teams to collaborate and communicate seamlessly. It offers a range of tools and features that facilitate virtual meetings, file sharing, real-time messaging, and more. With Cisco Webex, users can join meetings from anywhere, using any device with an internet connection. The platform supports video conferencing, allowing participants to see and hear each other, enhancing communication and fostering a sense of connectedness. Additionally, it provides screen sharing capabilities, enabling users to share presentations, documents, or applications to facilitate discussions and collaborations. The real-time messaging feature of Cisco Webex allows teams to communicate instantly, whether through one-on-one chats or group conversations. This fosters efficient and effective collaboration, as team members can easily ask questions, provide updates, or share ideas. The platform also supports file sharing, allowing users to exchange documents, images, or other files seamlessly. Cisco Webex is not limited to internal team collaboration but also caters to external interactions. It enables organizations to conduct webinars, online training sessions, or virtual events, reaching a wider audience and facilitating knowledge sharing. It also offers the option for attendees to join meetings via phone, ensuring accessibility for participants with limited internet connectivity. In terms of security, Cisco Webex provides several measures to safeguard confidentiality and privacy. It utilizes encryption to protect data transmission between participants, ensuring that sensitive information remains secure. The platform also supports authentication mechanisms, such as password protection and meeting lock, to prevent unauthorized access to meetings. Overall, Cisco Webex is a comprehensive networking solution that empowers teams to collaborate effectively regardless of their location. By offering a range of communication and collaboration tools, it enhances productivity, facilitates knowledge sharing, and enables seamless virtual interactions.

Cisco Wireless Access Points (APs)

Cisco Wireless Access Points (APs) are network devices used to provide wireless connectivity to devices such as laptops, smartphones, and tablets. They are an essential component of wireless networks, allowing devices to connect to the network without the need for physical cables. APs are typically connected to a wired network infrastructure, such as a switch or router, and are responsible for transmitting and receiving wireless signals. They receive data from wireless devices, such as user requests or network traffic, and forward it to the back-end network infrastructure.

Cisco Wireless Access Points

Cisco Wireless Access Points are network devices that provide wireless connectivity to devices such as laptops, smartphones, and tablets within a specified area. They act as central hubs for wireless communication, enabling users to connect to a network and access resources without the need for physical cables. These access points work on the principle of radio frequency (RF) technology, transmitting and receiving data through the airwaves using Wi-Fi protocols. They are designed with antennas that emit radio signals, allowing wireless devices to communicate with the access point and establish a connection to the network. Cisco Wireless Access Points offer several key features and functionalities that enhance network connectivity and security. They provide high-speed wireless connectivity, enabling users to access network resources and the internet with fast data transfer rates. These access points support various Wi-Fi standards, such as 802.11n, 802.11ac, and 802.11ax, ensuring compatibility with a wide range of devices. One of the significant advantages of Cisco Wireless Access Points is their ability to create multiple wireless networks or SSIDs (Service Set Identifiers). This feature allows network administrators to separate different types of devices or user groups onto different networks, providing enhanced security and improved bandwidth management. For example, a company can have a separate network for employees and guests, ensuring that sensitive data remains secure. Moreover, Cisco access points support advanced security protocols, such as Wi-Fi Protected Access (WPA) and WPA2, to encrypt data transmitted over the wireless network. They also incorporate features like rogue access point detection, preventing unauthorized devices from accessing the network. Additionally, they offer Quality of Service (QoS) capabilities, enabling administrators to prioritize network traffic for applications that require higher bandwidth or lower latency. Deployment of Cisco Wireless Access Points can be done individually or in a coordinated manner to form a wireless network infrastructure. When multiple access points are strategically placed, they create a wireless coverage area called a wireless LAN (Local Area Network). This allows users to roam seamlessly between access points without losing connectivity, providing consistent and reliable network connection across a larger area. In conclusion, Cisco Wireless Access Points are integral components of modern networking, delivering wireless connectivity to devices and enabling efficient communication within a network. By providing fast and secure wireless access, these access points enhance productivity and convenience for users while offering robust management and control for network administrators.

Cisco Wireless LAN Controller (WLC)

A Cisco Wireless LAN Controller (WLC) is a networking device that is responsible for managing and controlling wireless access points (APs) within a wireless network. It acts as a central point of control for all the APs, providing a unified management interface and coordinating their actions to ensure seamless and efficient operation of the wireless network. The WLC serves as the brain of the wireless network, handling tasks such as AP configuration, control, and monitoring. It provides a wide range of features and functionalities to optimize the performance, security, and overall user experience of the wireless network. The primary function of the WLC is to authenticate and authorize wireless clients, such as laptops, smartphones, or tablets, to connect to the wireless network. It ensures that only authorized devices can access the network and applies security policies to protect against unauthorized access or malicious activities. The WLC also manages the allocation of radio frequencies to different APs, preventing interference and optimizing network performance. Additionally, the WLC enables centralized management of the entire wireless network infrastructure. It allows network administrators to configure and control multiple APs from a single management interface, simplifying network management and reducing operational overhead. The WLC also provides comprehensive monitoring and reporting capabilities, allowing administrators to track the performance, analyze the traffic, and troubleshoot issues in the wireless network. Furthermore, the WLC supports various advanced features to enhance the functionality and efficiency of the wireless network. These include features like load balancing, seamless roaming, quality of service (QoS), and guest access control. Load balancing ensures that wireless clients are evenly distributed among the APs to avoid congestion and optimize performance. Seamless roaming allows clients to maintain a continuous connection when moving between APs without any noticeable interruption. QoS ensures that critical applications and services receive the necessary network resources for optimal performance. Guest access control enables the creation of separate guest networks with limited access privileges. In summary, a Cisco Wireless LAN Controller (WLC) is a vital component of a wireless network infrastructure. It provides centralized management, control, and optimization of the network, ensuring secure and efficient wireless connectivity for users.

Cisco Wireless LAN

The Cisco Wireless LAN (WLAN) is a networking technology that enables wireless connectivity between devices in a local area network (LAN). It allows users to connect their devices, such as laptops, smartphones, and tablets, to the LAN without the need for physical cables. Cisco WLAN utilizes radio waves to transmit and receive data between the devices and the LAN infrastructure. It operates in the 2.4 GHz and 5 GHz frequency bands, providing fast and reliable wireless connectivity with high data transfer rates. One of the key components of a Cisco WLAN is the access point (AP). The AP acts as a bridge between the wireless devices and the LAN, enabling them to communicate with each other and access network resources. It serves as a central point for managing and controlling the wireless network. Another important component of Cisco WLAN is the wireless controller. The controller is responsible for managing and coordinating the activities of the APs, ensuring seamless connectivity and optimal performance. It provides advanced features such as authentication, encryption, and quality of service (QoS) to enhance the security and reliability of the wireless network. In addition to the access points and controllers, Cisco WLAN also includes other supporting devices such as antennas, switches, and routers. These devices work together to provide a complete wireless networking solution that can be easily deployed and managed. Cisco WLAN offers several benefits to organizations and individuals alike. It provides flexibility and mobility, allowing users to access the network and resources from anywhere within the coverage area. It also simplifies network installation and scalability, as new devices can be easily added to the network without the need for additional cabling. Furthermore, Cisco WLAN offers enhanced security features to protect the network from unauthorized access and data breaches. It supports various encryption protocols such as WPA2 and 802.1X authentication, ensuring that only authorized users can connect to the network. In conclusion, the Cisco Wireless LAN is a wireless networking technology that enables wireless connectivity between devices in a LAN. It utilizes radio waves and consists of access points, controllers, and other supporting devices. With its flexibility, scalability, and security features, Cisco WLAN is a reliable solution for organizations and individuals seeking wireless connectivity.

Cisco Wireless Mesh

Cisco Wireless Mesh refers to a networking technology that allows the creation of a wireless network infrastructure using a series of interconnected access points. These access points, also known as mesh nodes, establish a self-configuring and self-healing network without the need for additional wired connections. The fundamental principle of Cisco Wireless Mesh networking is the use of multiple access points that work together to form a meshed network. Instead of relying on a single access point as in traditional wireless networks, a wireless mesh network leverages the capabilities of multiple access points to provide a seamless and robust network coverage. In a Cisco Wireless Mesh network, each access point acts as a potential point of connection for other access points within its range. These points are interconnected through wireless links, forming a dynamic and flexible network topology. This allows for greater coverage and enables the network to adapt to changes in the environment or network conditions. A key advantage of Cisco Wireless Mesh is its ability to self-configure and self-heal. This means that if a node fails or a new node is added, the network can automatically adjust to maintain connectivity. The self-healing aspect ensures that if one path in the network fails, alternate paths are dynamically established to ensure continuous communication. Another essential feature of Cisco Wireless Mesh is the ability to dynamically route traffic. Each node in the mesh network determines the most optimal path for forwarding data packets based on factors such as signal strength, network congestion, and available bandwidth. This enables efficient utilization of network resources and ensures that data is delivered in the most efficient manner. Cisco Wireless Mesh networks also provide enhanced security features to protect the network and its users. These include encryption, authentication mechanisms, and the ability to isolate different user groups or services within the network. In summary, Cisco Wireless Mesh is a networking technology that establishes a self-configuring and self-healing wireless network infrastructure using multiple interconnected access points. It offers extensive coverage, adaptability, dynamic routing capabilities, and enhanced security features.

Cisco PxGrid

Cisco pxGrid, or Platform Exchange Grid, is a framework that enables the integration and exchange of contextual information between different security platforms within a network infrastructure. It provides a standardized and secure way for various network security services to share information and work together in real time. With pxGrid, different security systems, such as firewalls, intrusion prevention systems, identity services engines, and vulnerability assessment tools, can share information about security events, policies, and user identities. This information exchange allows for a more coordinated and efficient response to threats and improves overall network security.

Classless Inter-Domain Routing (CIDR)

Classless Inter-Domain Routing (CIDR) is a method used in computer networking to allocate and manage IP addresses more efficiently. CIDR is an extension of the original IP addressing scheme, which used fixed-length prefixes to divide the IP address space into different address classes. In CIDR, IP addresses are represented by a combination of the network address and the network prefix length. The network address specifies the network to which the IP address belongs, while the network prefix length indicates the number of bits in the network address that are used for identifying the network. This approach allows for more flexible allocation of IP addresses, as it removes the strict division between distinct classes of addresses. Instead, CIDR enables the allocation of variable-sized address blocks, called CIDR blocks, based on the specific needs of an organization or network. These CIDR blocks can range in size from a single address to a large block containing thousands or millions of addresses. CIDR also introduces the concept of route aggregation, which reduces the size of routing tables by combining multiple smaller routes into a single larger route. This helps to conserve routing table memory and improves the efficiency of routing protocols. By aggregating routes, network administrators can achieve more efficient use of network resources and improve overall network performance. To specify a CIDR block, the network address is followed by a slash (/) and a number indicating the length of the network prefix. For example, 192.168.0.0/16 represents a CIDR block that includes all IP addresses from 192.168.0.0 to 192.168.255.255, with the first 16 bits (or the first two octets) indicating the network address. In conclusion, CIDR is a method used in networking to allocate and manage IP addresses more efficiently. It allows for flexible allocation of variable-sized address blocks and introduces route aggregation to optimize routing tables. CIDR has become the standard addressing scheme in modern networks and has greatly contributed to the scalability and efficiency of the internet.

Click Fraud

Click Fraud is a term used in the context of networking to refer to a fraudulent practice characterized by the deliberate and deceptive clicking of online advertisements. It involves the false generation of clicks on online ads with the intention of inflating website traffic or generating revenue through pay-per-click advertising programs. The primary purpose of click fraud is to deceive advertisers, search engines, and ad networks, ultimately leading to financial gain for the fraudster. Click fraud can be perpetrated in various ways, often utilizing automated software programs known as "click bots" or by employing human click farms. Click bots are computer programs that are designed to mimic legitimate user behavior, such as clicking on ads or visiting websites. These bots may be controlled by fraudsters remotely or operate autonomously, continuously clicking on ads without any human interaction. Click farms, on the other hand, involve individuals or groups hired to manually click on ads, usually across multiple devices and IP addresses, to create the illusion of genuine user engagement. Click fraud can have severe consequences for both advertisers and advertising networks. Advertisers who fall victim to click fraud may suffer financial losses as they are billed for ad clicks that hold no real value in terms of genuine user interest or engagement. Additionally, their advertising campaigns may become less effective as a result of inaccurate data and engagement metrics. Advertising networks, such as Google AdWords or Facebook Ads, bear the responsibility of identifying and mitigating click fraud to maintain the integrity of their platforms. They employ various methods and algorithms to detect suspicious click patterns, such as analyzing IP addresses, device types, and user behavior. When click fraud is suspected, these networks typically refund advertisers for fraudulent clicks and may even ban or suspend accounts associated with fraudulent activity. In conclusion, click fraud is a fraudulent practice in the context of networking that involves the deliberate and deceptive generation of clicks on online advertisements. It aims to deceive advertisers, search engines, and ad networks for financial gain. The use of click bots and click farms are common methods employed to perpetrate click fraud. Advertisers and advertising networks must remain vigilant in detecting and mitigating this fraudulent activity to protect their finances and maintain the effectiveness of online advertising campaigns.

Clickjacking

Clickjacking, also known as a UI redress attack, is a malicious technique that tricks users into clicking on a webpage element without their knowledge or intent. This attack is exploited by overlaying or transparently embedding legitimate content or UI elements within a webpage, thereby deceiving users into interacting with unintended content. Clickjacking allows attackers to carry out unauthorized actions, such as executing JavaScript code, capturing sensitive data, or performing operations on behalf of the victim. Clickjacking exploits the vulnerability in web browser security models that do not adequately prevent hidden elements from being triggered by unintended clicks. The attack can be performed by manipulating the HTML code of a webpage, or by using iframes, framesets, or CSS techniques to position hidden elements above clickable buttons or links.

Client-Server Model

The client-server model is a networking architecture that describes the relationship between two types of computers: the client and the server. In this model, the client is the computer or device that initiates a request for a service, while the server is the computer or device that provides the requested service. The client-server model operates on a request-response pattern. The client sends a request to the server, specifying the type of service it requires. The server, upon receiving the request, processes it and sends back a response containing the requested information or service. This communication between the client and server is facilitated through a network connection.

Client-Side Attack

A client-side attack refers to a type of cyber attack that targets vulnerabilities in the client-side components of a network, such as web browsers, email clients, and other applications installed on the end-user's computer or device. This attack aims to exploit weaknesses in these client-side components to gain unauthorized access, deliver malicious payloads, or perform other malicious activities. In a client-side attack, the attacker typically takes advantage of security vulnerabilities, misconfigurations, or weak user behaviors to compromise the client-side component. This can include exploiting known software vulnerabilities, tricking users into downloading and executing malicious files or scripts, or manipulating user inputs to bypass security controls.

Cloud Access Security Broker (CASB)

A Cloud Access Security Broker (CASB) is a networking solution that provides organizations with visibility, control, and security over their cloud-based applications and services. It acts as an intermediary between users and cloud service providers, enforcing security policies and monitoring access to ensure the safety and compliance of data stored in the cloud. CASBs offer several key features that enhance network security in cloud environments. Firstly, they provide visibility into cloud usage, giving organizations an understanding of which applications are being used, by whom, and for what purposes. This visibility allows businesses to identify any potential security risks and take proactive measures to mitigate them. Secondly, CASBs offer data loss prevention capabilities. They monitor and analyze data flows between users and cloud services, looking for sensitive data that may be at risk of being leaked or stolen. CASBs can implement policies to prevent unauthorized access, enforce encryption, and even block or quarantine certain types of data to prevent data breaches. Thirdly, CASBs enable organizations to enforce security policies consistently across multiple cloud platforms. With the increasing adoption of Software-as-a-Service (SaaS) applications and Infrastructure-as-a-Service (IaaS) platforms, it becomes crucial to have a centralized solution that can monitor and control access to these diverse cloud environments. CASBs provide a unified approach to security, enabling organizations to apply policies consistently and efficiently. Additionally, CASBs offer threat protection capabilities. They leverage machine learning and artificial intelligence to detect and prevent various types of cyber threats, such as malware, phishing attempts, and account hijacking. By analyzing user behavior and identifying anomalous activities, CASBs can help protect sensitive data and prevent security incidents. In summary, a Cloud Access Security Broker plays a critical role in networking by providing organizations with visibility, control, and security over their cloud-based applications and services. It offers features like visibility into cloud usage, data loss prevention, consistent policy enforcement, and threat protection. With the increasing adoption of cloud technologies, CASBs have become essential tools to ensure the safety and compliance of data stored in the cloud.

Cloud Computing Models

Cloud computing models refer to the different ways in which cloud services are delivered to users over a network, typically the internet. These models can be categorized into three main types: Infrastructure as a Service (IaaS), Platform as a Service (PaaS), and Software as a Service (SaaS). IaaS is the most basic cloud computing model, providing virtualized computing resources such as virtual machines, storage, and networks. It allows users to deploy and manage their own applications on the cloud infrastructure, giving them greater control and flexibility. Users can scale resources up or down based on their needs and only pay for what they use. This model is particularly attractive for businesses that want to avoid the maintenance and costs associated with managing physical infrastructure. PaaS, on the other hand, goes a step further by providing a platform for developers to build, deploy, and manage applications without having to worry about the underlying infrastructure. It includes tools, frameworks, and runtime environments that enable developers to focus on developing the application code rather than managing the underlying infrastructure. PaaS offers a more streamlined and efficient development process, allowing teams to collaborate and rapidly iterate on their applications. SaaS is the most user-focused cloud computing model, providing ready-to-use applications that are accessed over the internet. Users can access these applications through web browsers or thin client applications without the need for installation or maintenance on their local devices. SaaS applications are typically subscription-based, allowing users to pay for the software on a per-user or per-use basis. This model offers great convenience and accessibility, making it popular for software such as office productivity suites, customer relationship management (CRM) software, and enterprise resource planning (ERP) systems.

Cloud Computing Networking

Cloud computing networking refers to the practice of utilizing remote servers hosted on the internet to store, manage, and process data rather than using a local server or personal computer. This allows for the efficient delivery of various computing resources and services, such as data storage, applications, and networking capabilities, through a network connection. In a cloud computing network, multiple servers are connected together using various networking technologies to form a larger infrastructure, commonly known as a cloud. These servers are typically housed in data centers owned and operated by cloud service providers. Users or organizations can then access these resources and services over the internet using a variety of devices, such as computers, smartphones, or tablets. The primary advantage of cloud computing networking is its scalability and flexibility. With traditional local server setups, organizations often face limitations in terms of storage capacity, processing power, and network bandwidth. In contrast, cloud computing networking allows for the easy scaling up or down of resources based on demand. This means that organizations can quickly adapt to changing needs without having to invest in additional hardware or infrastructure. Another key benefit of cloud computing networking is its cost-effectiveness. Rather than purchasing and maintaining expensive hardware and software, organizations can leverage the resources and services offered by cloud service providers on a pay-as-you-go basis. This not only reduces upfront costs but also eliminates the need for ongoing maintenance and upgrades. Furthermore, cloud computing networking enables improved collaboration and accessibility. By storing data and applications in the cloud, users can easily access and collaborate on files and projects from anywhere with an internet connection. This enhances productivity and enables remote or distributed teams to work together seamlessly. In summary, cloud computing networking allows for the efficient delivery of computing resources and services over the internet. By leveraging the scalability, cost-effectiveness, and accessibility offered by cloud service providers, organizations can optimize their IT infrastructure and enhance their overall productivity and efficiency.

Cloud Networking Infrastructure

Cloud Networking Infrastructure refers to the underlying set of hardware, software, and network resources that are required to support the exchange of data and information between cloud-based services, applications, and users. Cloud computing has revolutionized the way businesses operate by allowing them to access and utilize computing resources from anywhere at any time. However, in order to provide seamless access to these resources, a robust and reliable networking infrastructure is essential. This infrastructure is responsible for connecting various components of the cloud ecosystem, including data centers, servers, storage devices, and end-user devices. The hardware component of cloud networking infrastructure includes routers, switches, and other network devices that facilitate the transfer of data packets across the network. These devices are responsible for directing network traffic, ensuring efficient data transmission, and maintaining network security. Additionally, the hardware infrastructure also includes servers and storage devices that store and process data within the cloud environment. The software component of cloud networking infrastructure includes various networking protocols and algorithms that govern the flow of data across the network. These protocols, such as Transmission Control Protocol/Internet Protocol (TCP/IP), ensure reliable and secure data transfer between different entities in the cloud ecosystem. Additionally, network management software is used to monitor and manage the network infrastructure, enabling administrators to optimize network performance, detect and resolve network issues, and allocate network resources efficiently. Cloud networking infrastructure also includes the network resources that connect the cloud environment with external networks, such as the internet or private networks. These resources may include virtual private networks (VPNs), firewalls, and load balancers, which help secure the network and manage incoming and outgoing traffic. In conclusion, cloud networking infrastructure plays a crucial role in enabling the efficient operation of cloud-based services and applications. It provides the necessary connectivity and resources for data exchange, ensuring seamless access and reliable communication within the cloud ecosystem.

Cloud Networking Models

Cloud networking models refer to the different architectures and approaches used to connect and manage network resources in a cloud environment. These models aim to optimize network performance, improve scalability, and enhance security in cloud-based infrastructures. One of the most commonly used cloud networking models is the Virtual Private Cloud (VPC) model. In this model, cloud service providers (CSPs) offer customers isolated and logically separate virtual networks within the public cloud infrastructure. VPCs allow organizations to maintain control over their networking environment, define subnets, set up access control policies, and establish secure connections to other networks or on-premises infrastructure. By leveraging the VPC model, organizations can ensure the privacy and security of their data while benefiting from the scalability and flexibility of the cloud. Another popular cloud networking model is the Software-Defined Networking (SDN) model. SDN decouples the control plane from the data plane, allowing network administrators to centrally manage and configure network resources programmatically. By separating network intelligence from the physical infrastructure, SDN simplifies network management, improves agility, and enables the automation of network provisioning and configuration tasks. SDN also facilitates the implementation of network policies and enables the efficient utilization of network resources. In addition to VPCs and SDN, cloud networking models also include options such as multi-cloud networking and cloud-native networking. Multi-cloud networking refers to the process of connecting and managing resources across multiple cloud environments from different CSPs. It allows organizations to leverage different cloud providers based on their specific needs and gain redundancy and high availability. Cloud-native networking, on the other hand, focuses on enabling the seamless integration of networking capabilities with cloud-native applications. It leverages container orchestration platforms like Kubernetes to provide networking services that are specifically designed for highly dynamic and scalable cloud-native applications. Overall, cloud networking models play a crucial role in enabling organizations to harness the full potential of cloud computing. Whether through VPCs, SDN, multi-cloud networking, or cloud-native networking, these models provide the necessary foundations for building, managing, and securing network resources in the cloud.

Cloud Networking Platforms

Cloud networking platforms refer to the tools, services, and infrastructure that enable networking functionalities and capabilities to be provisioned and managed in a virtualized cloud environment. These platforms bring together the benefits of cloud computing and networking to provide more flexible, scalable, and cost-effective networking solutions for businesses and organizations. In cloud networking platforms, networking resources such as routers, switches, firewalls, and load balancers are virtualized and delivered as software-defined services, rather than being tied to physical hardware. This decoupling of network functionalities from the underlying hardware allows for more agility and ease of management, as well as efficient resource utilization. Cloud networking platforms offer a wide range of features and capabilities that enhance the networking experience in the cloud. These may include: 1. Infrastructure as a Service (IaaS) capabilities: The platforms provide the necessary infrastructure components for networking, such as virtual machines, storage, and compute resources, which can be provisioned and managed according to the specific needs of the network. 2. Virtual Private Clouds (VPCs): VPCs offer isolated and secure networking environments within the cloud, allowing organizations to set up their own virtual networks with defined subnets, IP address ranges, and connectivity options. 3. Software-defined Networking (SDN): SDN enables the centralized management and control of network infrastructure through software, providing a more programmable and automated approach to configuring and managing networks. 4. Network Function Virtualization (NFV): NFV allows for the virtualization of network functions, such as firewalls, load balancers, and intrusion detection systems, making them deployable as software instances and easily scalable. 5. Routing and Switching: Cloud networking platforms provide routing and switching functionalities that enable the efficient transfer of data packets between different network components and endpoints. By leveraging cloud networking platforms, organizations can benefit from improved scalability, flexibility, and cost-efficiency in managing their networks. These platforms enable the deployment of networking services on-demand and allow for rapid provisioning, scaling, and reconfiguration of network resources to meet changing business requirements. Furthermore, the virtualized nature of cloud networking platforms reduces the reliance on physical infrastructure, leading to cost savings in terms of hardware procurement, maintenance, and operational expenses. Overall, cloud networking platforms play a pivotal role in enabling the seamless integration of cloud computing and networking, empowering organizations with enhanced networking capabilities in the dynamic and ever-evolving cloud environment.

Cloud Networking Services

Cloud networking services refer to the use of networking technologies and resources provided by cloud service providers to connect and manage networks and devices over the internet. These services leverage the infrastructure, scalability, and flexibility of cloud computing to enable organizations to create, deploy, and manage their networking infrastructure without the need for physical hardware or on-premises resources. Cloud networking services typically consist of a combination of virtualized networking components, software-defined networking (SDN) technologies, and network management tools. They allow organizations to build and operate their networks in a more agile, cost-effective, and scalable manner compared to traditional networking approaches. The key components of cloud networking services include: - Virtual Private Cloud (VPC): It provides organizations with isolated virtual networks within a shared cloud infrastructure. VPCs enable organizations to define their own network topology, subnets, and IP address ranges, providing greater control and security. - Virtual Private Network (VPN): It allows organizations to create secure connections between their on-premises networks and cloud resources or between different cloud regions. VPNs ensure the confidentiality and integrity of data transmitted over the network. - Load Balancing: Cloud networking services offer load balancing capabilities that distribute incoming network traffic across multiple servers or instances to improve performance, availability, and scalability. Load balancing ensures that no single server or resource is overwhelmed with excessive traffic. - Network Security: Cloud networking services include a range of security features such as firewalls, intrusion detection systems, and encryption protocols to protect networks and data from unauthorized access, cyber threats, and data breaches. - Network Monitoring and Analytics: Cloud networking services provide tools and capabilities to monitor network performance, troubleshoot issues, and analyze network traffic. These services enable organizations to gain insights into network behavior, identify bottlenecks, and optimize network performance. Overall, cloud networking services offer organizations a flexible and scalable approach to network management, enabling them to leverage the benefits of cloud computing while ensuring security, performance, and reliability for their networks and applications.

Cloud Networking Solutions

Cloud networking solutions refer to the use of virtualized networking resources that are delivered via the cloud. This approach allows organizations to access and manage their networking infrastructure remotely, without the need for physical hardware or on-premises setups. With cloud networking solutions, businesses can leverage the scalability and flexibility of the cloud to easily provision and deploy network services. These solutions typically involve the use of software-defined networking (SDN) technologies, which separate the network control plane from the data plane. This separation enables organizations to programmatically control and automate their network infrastructure, making it more agile and responsive to changing business needs.

Cloud Networking

Cloud Networking refers to the practice of connecting and managing different resources, such as servers, storage devices, and applications, within a cloud computing environment. It involves the use of virtualization technologies to create virtual networks that allow organizations to efficiently utilize and manage their resources over the internet. In cloud networking, the physical infrastructure is abstracted and replaced by virtualized components, providing a flexible and scalable solution for network management and connectivity. It enables organizations to leverage the benefits of cloud computing, such as on-demand access to resources, cost savings, and increased agility.

Cloud Security

Cloud security refers to the set of measures and protocols designed to protect cloud-based

95

systems, applications, and data from unauthorized access, data breaches, and other cyber threats. It encompasses the various strategies, technologies, and best practices used to safeguard cloud environments, applications, and the sensitive data stored within them. Cloud security plays a critical role in ensuring the confidentiality, integrity, and availability of cloud-based resources. It involves implementing a combination of technical controls and administrative policies to mitigate risks and protect against unauthorized access, data leaks, and other security incidents.

Cloud Storage

Cloud storage refers to the online storage of data on remote servers that can be accessed through the internet. It is a technology that allows individuals, businesses, and organizations to store and manage their data in a secure and flexible manner. The main purpose of cloud storage is to provide a reliable and scalable solution for storing, backing up, and sharing data. Instead of relying on physical storage devices like hard drives or servers, cloud storage utilizes a network of remote servers to store and manage data. These servers are typically owned and maintained by a cloud storage provider. Cloud storage offers several advantages compared to traditional forms of data storage. Firstly, it provides virtually unlimited storage capacity, allowing users to store large amounts of data without worrying about running out of space. Additionally, cloud storage offers high availability, ensuring that data is accessible at all times, even in the event of hardware failures or natural disasters. Another key advantage of cloud storage is its ease of use. Users can access their stored data from any device with an internet connection, making it convenient for remote work and collaboration. Moreover, cloud storage services often provide synchronization capabilities, allowing users to automatically sync their data across multiple devices. Security is a critical aspect of cloud storage. Data stored in the cloud is encrypted to protect it from unauthorized access. The use of encryption ensures that even if someone gains access to the server, they will not be able to decipher the data without the encryption key. Cloud storage providers also implement robust security measures, such as firewalls and access controls, to prevent breaches and data loss. Overall, cloud storage offers a flexible, scalable, and secure solution for storing and managing data. Its advantages, including unlimited storage capacity, high availability, accessibility, synchronization, and security, make it an essential technology for individuals, businesses, and organizations in the modern digital age.

Cloud-Based Network Management

Cloud-Based Network Management refers to the process of managing and monitoring a computer network using cloud-based technologies and services. It involves utilizing remote servers, hosted on the internet, to collect and analyze network data, as well as to manage network devices and services. This approach offers numerous advantages over traditional on-premises network management techniques. Firstly, it eliminates the need for organizations to maintain and update costly hardware and software on their premises. Instead, network management tasks are offloaded to cloud service providers who handle the infrastructure and software requirements. This not only reduces upfront investment costs but also frees up internal IT resources, allowing them to focus on core business activities. Cloud-Based Network Management provides remarkable scalability and flexibility. As the network grows, organizations can easily scale up their network management capabilities by simply requesting additional resources from the cloud service provider. This eliminates the complexity and time-consuming process of procuring and deploying new hardware or software. Likewise, organizations can also downscale their network management resources during periods of low network activity, thus optimizing cost-efficiency. Furthermore, cloud-based network management offers improved accessibility and ease of use. Network administrators can remotely access the management system from any location with an internet connection, using any device with a compatible web browser. This enables administrators to monitor and control the network anytime and anywhere, enhancing efficiency and reducing response times in case of network issues or troubleshooting needs. The cloud-based approach also provides robust security features. Cloud service providers typically employ sophisticated security protocols, including encryption and multi-factor authentication, to protect network data and prevent unauthorized access. These security measures often exceed the capabilities of individual organizations, making cloud-based network management a more secure option than traditional on-premises solutions. In conclusion, Cloud-Based Network Management revolutionizes the way organizations manage and monitor their computer networks. By leveraging cloud technologies, organizations can reduce costs, improve scalability and flexibility, enhance accessibility and ease of use, and benefit from robust security features.

Coaxial Cable Connectors Types

Coaxial cable connectors are types of connectors used in networking to connect coaxial cables. A coaxial cable is a type of cable used for transmitting electrical signals, commonly used for television and internet connections. It consists of a central conductor wire surrounded by insulating material, a metal shield, and an outer cover or sheath. The connectors are used to connect the cable to various components and devices, allowing for the transmission of signals. There are several types of coaxial cable connectors commonly used in networking. BNC connectors, which stands for Bayonet Neill–Concelman, are commonly used in television and video applications. They are typically used to connect coaxial cables to video equipment and are known for their quick-connect and disconnect capabilities. BNC connectors feature a bayonet-style coupling mechanism that allows for easy and secure connections. F-type connectors are another common type of coaxial cable connector used in networking. They are most commonly used in television and cable TV applications. F-type connectors have a threaded interface that provides a secure connection and helps to prevent signal loss. These connectors are typically used to connect coaxial cables to devices such as TVs, cable boxes, and satellite receivers. N-type connectors, also known as Type N connectors, are commonly used in wireless and communication applications. They are designed to provide a reliable and secure connection for higher frequency signals. N-type connectors have a threaded coupling mechanism and are commonly used in outdoor networking equipment such as antennas and access points. SMA connectors, or SubMiniature version A connectors, are another type of coaxial cable connector commonly used in networking. They are commonly used in wireless and communication applications and feature a threaded coupling mechanism. SMA connectors are known for their high performance and are often used in applications that require precise and accurate signal transmission. These are just a few examples of the types of coaxial cable connectors commonly used in networking. Each type of connector has its own unique features and characteristics, making them suitable for different applications. The choice of connector depends on the specific networking requirements and the equipment being used.

Coaxial Cable Connectors

A coaxial cable connector is a type of electrical connector that is used to attach a coaxial cable to a network device or equipment. It is designed to provide a secure and reliable connection between the cable and the device, ensuring efficient transmission of data or signals. Coaxial cable connectors are commonly used in networking applications, particularly in the field of telecommunications and data communications. They are used to connect various network devices, such as routers, switches, modems, and antennas, to the coaxial cables that carry the data or signals.

Coaxial Cable Installation

Coaxial Cable Installation refers to the process of setting up and connecting coaxial cables for networking purposes. Coaxial cables are a type of transmission medium commonly used in networking to transfer data between devices. The installation process involves several steps that ensure the proper connection and functionality of the coaxial cables. Firstly, the coaxial cable needs to be selected based on the specific networking requirements. The cable should have the necessary specifications, such as the appropriate bandwidth and impedance, to support the intended network speed and ensure reliable data transmission. Once the suitable cable is chosen, it needs to be properly prepared for installation. The next step in coaxial cable installation is to run the cable along the desired pathway. This may involve drilling holes, utilizing conduits, or using cable trays to ensure neat and organized cable management. It is essential to consider factors such as cable length, signal attenuation, and protection against interference during the cable routing process. After routing the cable, the connectors at each end of the coaxial cable need to be properly installed. The connectors ensure a secure and reliable connection between the cable and the networking devices. Different types of connectors exist, such as BNC connectors and F-type connectors, and the appropriate connector should be used based on the networking equipment being utilized. Once the connectors are in place, the coaxial cable can be connected to the networking devices, such as routers, switches, or modems. The connections should be made securely and snugly to prevent signal loss or interference. It is also important to verify the correct connection of the cable to the appropriate ports on the networking devices. After completing the physical installation of the coaxial cable, the network setup should be tested to ensure proper functionality and data transmission. This may involve testing the signal quality, measuring the network speed, and ensuring that there is no interference or loss of signal. Any issues or faults discovered during the testing phase should be addressed and rectified to guarantee optimal network performance. In conclusion, coaxial cable installation is a crucial process in networking that involves the selection, routing, connector installation, and connection of coaxial cables. By following the proper procedures and considering important factors, the installation ensures reliable and efficient data transfer between networking devices.

Coaxial Cable Types

Coaxial cables are a type of transmission medium commonly used in networking to carry high-frequency electrical signals from one device to another. They consist of a central conductor, which is surrounded by an insulating layer, a metallic shield, and an outer protective covering. The coaxial cable design provides several advantages for networking applications, such as high bandwidth capabilities, resistance to signal interference, and long-distance transmission capabilities. There are different types of coaxial cables used in networking, each with its own specific characteristics and applications: 1. RG-6: This type of coaxial cable is commonly used for cable television (CATV) distribution systems and high-speed internet connections. Its low attenuation and high bandwidth make it ideal for transmitting large amounts of data over long distances. 2. RG-58: RG-58 coaxial cables are widely used for Ethernet connections in computer networks. They have a smaller diameter compared to RG-6 cables, making them more flexible and easier to install in tight spaces. 3. RG-11: RG-11 coaxial cables are ideal for long-distance networking applications. They have a larger diameter and lower attenuation compared to RG-6 and RG-58 cables, allowing for better signal transmission over greater distances. 4. RG-59: This type of coaxial cable is commonly used for video surveillance systems and CCTV applications. It has a higher impedance compared to RG-6 and RG-58 cables, which helps maintain signal quality over longer cable runs. Overall, coaxial cables play a crucial role in networking by providing a reliable and efficient means of transmitting high-frequency signals. Their various types and characteristics allow for optimized performance in different networking applications, whether it be for internet connectivity, data transmission, or video surveillance.

Coaxial Cable

Coaxial cable is a type of cable that is widely used in networking to transmit high-frequency signals with low loss and interference. It consists of a central conductor, an insulating layer, a metallic shield, and an outer insulating layer. The central conductor is typically made of copper and is responsible for carrying the actual signal. It is surrounded by an insulating layer, usually made of plastic, which prevents any electrical leakage and interference between the central conductor and the metallic shield. The metallic shield, which is made of a conductive material like braided or foil copper, surrounds the insulating layer and provides protection against external electromagnetic interference. This shield also ensures that the signal remains confined within the cable, reducing the chances of crosstalk or signal loss. The outer insulating layer, similar to the inner insulating layer, is made of a durable plastic material. It provides additional protection to the cable from physical damage and moisture, ensuring its longevity and stability. Coaxial cable is characterized by its impedance, which is the ratio of voltage to current in an electrical circuit. Most commonly used coaxial cables in networking have an impedance of 50 or 75 ohms. The choice of impedance depends on the specific networking application and the equipment being used. One of the significant advantages of using coaxial cable in networking is its ability to transmit signals over longer distances without significant loss. It is also highly resistant to interference, making it ideal for carrying high-speed data and video signals. Coaxial cable is widely used in various networking applications, including cable television (CATV), local area networks (LANs), and telecommunications. In conclusion, coaxial cable plays a vital role in networking as it provides a reliable and efficient medium for transmitting high-frequency signals. Its design, including the central conductor, insulating layers, metallic shield, and outer insulation, ensures minimal loss and interference, making it a preferred choice for many networking professionals.

Coaxial Connector

Coaxial connectors are commonly used in networking to transmit signals between devices. They consist of a central conductor surrounded by an insulating layer, a metal shield, and an outer insulating layer. Coaxial connectors are designed to provide a reliable and secure connection for the transmission of data and signals. The central conductor of a coaxial connector carries the electrical signal, while the metal shield provides protection against interference and signal loss. The outer insulating layer provides insulation and prevents short circuits. Coaxial connectors are typically used for high-frequency signals, such as those used in networking environments.

Coaxial Splitter

A coaxial splitter, in the context of networking, is a device that allows a single coaxial cable to be split into multiple connections. It is commonly used in cable television (CATV) systems and in Ethernet networks. Coaxial splitters are designed to divide the incoming signal from the main cable into two or more separate signals. This allows multiple devices to be connected to the same cable, enabling them to receive and transmit data simultaneously without interfering with one another.

Coaxial Termination

A coaxial termination, in the context of networking, refers to a device used to terminate the end of a coaxial cable. It is primarily used to absorb or dissipate the excess energy or signal reflections that occur when a coaxial cable is not properly terminated. When a coaxial cable is not terminated correctly, signal reflections can occur, resulting in reduced signal quality, increased noise, and potential data errors. These reflections happen when the signal encounters an impedance mismatch at the end of the cable, causing a portion of the signal to bounce back along the cable.

Collision Avoidance

Collision Avoidance in the context of Networking refers to the measures and techniques implemented to prevent or minimize collisions in a network. A collision occurs when two or more devices attempt to transmit data over a shared medium, such as an Ethernet network, at the same time. Collisions can result in data loss, reduced network efficiency, and increased latency. To avoid collisions, various mechanisms are used, including: 1. Carrier Sense Multiple Access with Collision Detection (CSMA/CD): This protocol is commonly used in Ethernet networks. It ensures that devices listen to the medium before transmitting, and if they detect another transmission, they wait a random time before trying again. CSMA/CD helps to prevent multiple devices from transmitting simultaneously, reducing the chances of collisions. 2. Switching: Ethernet switches create dedicated connections between devices, known as microsegments or VLANs, avoiding the need for devices to share a single collision domain. By dividing the network into smaller segments, switches significantly reduce the likelihood of collisions. 3. Full-duplex communication: Full-duplex communication allows devices to transmit and receive data simultaneously, eliminating the possibility of collisions. This is commonly achieved through the use of switches or modern network interface cards (NICs) that support full-duplex operation. 4. Token Ring: In a token ring network, devices pass a special token around to gain access to the medium. Only the device holding the token can transmit, minimizing the chances of collisions. This approach is less common today but was popular in the past. By implementing collision avoidance techniques, networks can ensure efficient and reliable data transmission. These methods help to reduce the occurrence of collisions, improving network performance and minimizing the chances of data loss or corruption. Collision avoidance is a fundamental aspect of network design and is vital for supporting high-speed and reliable communication.

Collision Detection

Collision detection in networking refers to the process of identifying when two or more data packets collide on a shared network medium. A collision occurs when multiple devices or nodes attempt to transmit data simultaneously, resulting in a loss of data or corrupted data. This collision detection mechanism is crucial for network protocols that operate in a shared medium environment, such as Ethernet. In a shared medium network, multiple devices are connected to the same physical medium, such as a coaxial cable or an Ethernet cable. These devices use a technique called Carrier Sense Multiple Access with Collision Detection (CSMA/CD) to share the network medium and avoid collisions as much as possible.

Collision Domain

A collision domain is a network segment in which network devices share the same communication medium, such as a hub or a shared Ethernet cable. In this domain, multiple devices contend for the use of the medium and can potentially collide with each other when trying to transmit data simultaneously. When a device wants to transmit data, it listens to the medium to ensure there is no ongoing transmission. If it detects that the medium is idle, the device starts transmitting. However, if another device starts transmitting at the same time, a collision occurs, resulting in a jumbled message that neither device can understand. In a collision domain, collision detection mechanisms are employed to detect these collisions and handle them. When a collision is detected, a device stops transmitting, waits for a random amount of time, and then retries the transmission. This backoff and retry process helps to minimize the likelihood of subsequent collisions. Older Ethernet networks that used hubs created large collision domains because all devices connected to the hub shared the same bandwidth and could potentially collide with each other. However, the introduction of switches revolutionized network design by creating smaller collision domains. A switch divides a network into multiple collision domains by creating a separate communication path for each connected device. This way, only the devices involved in a particular communication share a collision domain, reducing the possibility of collisions and improving network performance.

Common Vulnerabilities And Exposures (CVE)

A Common Vulnerabilities and Exposures (CVE) is a standardized identifier for a unique security vulnerability or exposure found in software or hardware products. It is a comprehensive list of publicly-known vulnerabilities that have been assigned a unique CVE identification number. The purpose of the CVE is to provide a unified way of identifying and tracking vulnerabilities across different systems and organizations. Each CVE entry contains a brief description of the vulnerability, its impact, and relevant details such as affected versions and mitigation steps. These entries are maintained and published by the MITRE Corporation, a nonprofit organization that operates the CVE program.

Computer Emergency Response Team (CERT)

A Computer Emergency Response Team (CERT) is a group of experts responsible for detecting, preventing, and responding to computer security incidents and vulnerabilities within a network or an organization. In the context of networking, a CERT is typically established to protect and secure information systems, networks, and digital assets. They play a crucial role in managing and mitigating the risks associated with cybersecurity threats and attacks. CERTs are often comprised of individuals with diverse expertise in the areas of network security, incident response, system administration, cryptography, and vulnerability analysis. They work collaboratively to develop strategies, policies, and procedures to ensure the security, integrity, and availability of network resources. The primary responsibilities of a CERT include: Detection: CERTs are responsible for monitoring network traffic, logs, and systems to identify any abnormal or suspicious activities that may indicate a potential security incident. They use various software tools and techniques to detect and analyze security breaches in real-time. Prevention: CERTs play a proactive role in preventing security incidents by implementing and maintaining security controls, such as firewalls, intrusion detection systems, antivirus software, and access controls. They continuously evaluate and update security measures to adapt to evolving threats and vulnerabilities. Response: When a security incident occurs, a CERT is responsible for initiating and coordinating an effective response. They work swiftly to contain, mitigate, and resolve the incident, minimizing the impact on the network and the organization's operations. CERTs follow established incident response procedures and collaborate with relevant stakeholders, including law enforcement and external security organizations. Reporting and Communication: CERTs ensure timely and accurate reporting of security incidents to appropriate parties, both within the organization and to external entities if needed. They maintain clear and concise communication channels to keep stakeholders informed about the incident response efforts and provide guidance on security best practices. Coordination and Collaboration: CERTs often collaborate with other CERTs, security organizations, and industry peers to share information, intelligence, and best practices. They participate in forums and communities to stay updated on emerging threats, vulnerabilities, and countermeasures, fostering a collective effort to enhance network security. In conclusion, a Computer Emergency Response Team (CERT) is a specialized group of experts that play a crucial role in ensuring the security and resilience of networks. They detect, prevent, and respond to security incidents, while also promoting collaboration and communication within the cybersecurity community.

Computer Network Defense (CND)

Computer Network Defense (CND) is a comprehensive strategy that involves measures and procedures designed to protect computer networks from unauthorized access, exploitation, disruption, or damage. It encompasses a range of tactics, techniques, and procedures aimed at identifying and mitigating threats, vulnerabilities, and risks. CND focuses on securing network infrastructure, systems, and data by implementing a layered defense approach. This approach involves the use of multiple security measures to protect the network from potential attacks. These measures include firewalls, intrusion detection systems (IDS), intrusion prevention systems (IPS), antivirus software, and encryption protocols. The primary goal of CND is to ensure the confidentiality, integrity, and availability of network resources and information. Confidentiality refers to the protection of sensitive data and ensuring that it is accessible only to authorized individuals or systems. Integrity ensures that data remains unaltered and trustworthy by detecting and preventing unauthorized modifications. Availability means that network resources are accessible and usable by authorized users when needed. CND involves continuous monitoring and analysis of network traffic, system logs, and security events to detect and respond to potential threats. This proactive approach allows for the identification of suspicious activities, vulnerabilities, or indicators of compromise. Timely detection and response are crucial for minimizing the impact of security incidents and preventing further exploitation. Another important aspect of CND is incident response. This involves the systematic and coordinated efforts to address and mitigate security incidents. It includes steps such as incident detection, containment, eradication, and recovery. Incident response procedures ensure that security incidents are handled effectively, minimizing the impact on the network and allowing for the restoration of normal operations. CND also involves user awareness and training programs to educate individuals about safe computing practices and potential security risks. These programs help to promote a security-conscious culture within an organization and empower users to recognize and report suspicious activities. In summary, Computer Network Defense is a comprehensive approach that aims to protect network resources and information from unauthorized access, exploitation, and damage. It involves the implementation of multiple security measures, continuous monitoring, incident response procedures, and user awareness programs. Through these proactive measures, CND helps to safeguard network infrastructure, systems, and data, ensuring the confidentiality, integrity, and availability of network resources.

Content Delivery Network (CDN)

A Content Delivery Network (CDN) is a distributed network of servers or nodes that are strategically placed in multiple data centers across different geographical locations. The main purpose of a CDN is to efficiently deliver web content to users by reducing latency and improving website performance. When a user requests a piece of content, such as a webpage, image, or video, the CDN automatically identifies the server closest to the user's location and delivers the content from that server. This helps minimize the distance the content needs to travel, reducing the time it takes for the content to reach the user's device.

Content Delivery Service

A Content Delivery Service (CDS) is a networking solution that efficiently delivers media content, such as videos, images, and web pages, to end-users through a distributed network of servers and data centers. It improves the speed, scalability, and reliability of content delivery by reducing the distance between the content and the users. CDS works by strategically storing copies of the content in multiple locations, often referred to as points of presence (PoPs), across different geographies. These PoPs are typically located closer to the end-users, minimizing the latency and reducing the time it takes for the content to reach them. When a user requests content, the CDS automatically determines the most optimal PoP based on factors like the user's location, network conditions, and server availability.

Content Distribution Network (CDN) Architecture

A Content Distribution Network (CDN) architecture is a network design that is specifically designed to deliver content efficiently and reliably over the Internet. It is a system of interconnected servers strategically placed in multiple geographic locations to improve the performance, availability, and scalability of content delivery to users. The architecture of a CDN typically consists of three main components: origin servers, edge servers, and a distributed network infrastructure. At the core of the CDN architecture are the origin servers, which are responsible for hosting the original content. These servers store the master copies of the content, such as images, videos, web pages, and other static or dynamic files. The edge servers are located in various locations across the globe and act as caches for the content. They are strategically placed closer to the end users to minimize latency and improve the user experience. When a user requests content, the CDN system automatically determines the closest edge server and delivers the content from that server. This reduces the distance between the user and the server, resulting in faster content delivery. The distributed network infrastructure of a CDN is responsible for managing and directing the traffic flow across the network. It ensures that the content is delivered efficiently by routing requests to the most appropriate edge server. This infrastructure employs various techniques, such as load balancing and traffic optimization, to distribute the workload evenly and avoid overloading any single server. Additionally, CDN architectures often include features like content replication and caching to further improve performance and availability. Content replication involves duplicating content across multiple edge servers, allowing for faster delivery and increased redundancy. Caching, on the other hand, involves storing frequently accessed content in the edge servers' caches, reducing the need to fetch content from the origin server each time it is requested. In summary, a Content Distribution Network (CDN) architecture is a system of interconnected servers that work together to efficiently deliver content to users across the Internet. By leveraging the strategic placement of edge servers and employing various optimization techniques, CDNs aim to provide faster, more reliable, and scalable content delivery.

Content Filtering Solutions

Content filtering solutions refer to the mechanisms and technologies implemented within a computer network to monitor and control the flow of information passing through it. These solutions are designed to enforce policies and restrictions on internet access, ensuring that users adhere to acceptable use guidelines and preventing unauthorized or inappropriate content from being accessed or distributed. Content filtering solutions typically work by analyzing network traffic and examining the content of data packets to determine if they contain restricted or undesirable material. This analysis can involve filtering based on criteria such as keywords, file types, URLs, or even specific phrases. When a packet is identified as potentially violating the filtering rules, it may be blocked, modified, or redirected according to predefined policies set by network administrators.

Content Filtering

Content Filtering, in the context of networking, refers to the process of controlling and restricting the access to certain types of content or websites on a network. It is a mechanism utilized by network administrators to ensure that users accessing the network are only able to view and interact with appropriate and authorized content, while blocking or limiting access to undesirable or malicious content. Content filtering is typically implemented using specialized software or hardware devices known as content filters or web filters. These filters work by examining incoming network traffic, such as web requests, and comparing it against a set of predefined rules or policies. These rules can be configured by the network administrator to determine what types of content or websites should be allowed, blocked, or limited. The rules can be based on various criteria, such as website categories, keywords, file types, or even specific URLs.

Content Inspection

Content inspection in the context of networking refers to the process of analyzing network traffic to identify and filter specific types of content. It involves examining the data packets that flow through a network, inspecting their headers and payload, and determining if they comply with certain predefined criteria or policies. During content inspection, various techniques are employed to examine the content of network traffic. These techniques can include pattern matching, deep packet inspection, and protocol analysis. Pattern matching involves searching for specific patterns or signatures in the data packets to identify content that matches certain criteria. Deep packet inspection goes beyond simple pattern matching and involves a more detailed analysis of the content, including the application layer protocols and data structures. Protocol analysis focuses on analyzing the specific protocols used in the network traffic to identify any anomalies or suspicious behavior.

Content Management Systems (CMS)

A Content Management System (CMS) is a software application that allows users to create, manage, and publish digital content on the internet. It provides a centralized platform for organizing, editing, and storing various types of content such as text, images, videos, and documents. CMSs are widely used in the context of networking as they enable multiple users to collaborate on content creation and management. With a CMS, different individuals or teams can access and work on the same content simultaneously, increasing efficiency and productivity in organizations.

Content Security Policies (CSP)

Content Security Policies (CSP) are a set of directives that are used to define and enforce a set of security rules within a web application. CSP helps to protect a website from various types of attacks by specifying the types of content that a browser should and should not load. These policies can help mitigate the risks associated with cross-site scripting (XSS) attacks, clickjacking, and other web vulnerabilities. CSP works by allowing website administrators to define a whitelist of trusted sources from which their website can load content. This whitelist can include trusted domains for scripts, stylesheets, images, fonts, and other types of resources that a website may need to load. By restricting the source domains from which a website can load content, CSP helps to prevent malicious code from being executed on the user's browser. The directives provided by CSP can be specified through HTTP headers or meta tags within an HTML document. The policies defined in CSP are applied by the user's browser when loading the web page, allowing the browser to enforce the security rules specified by the website. CSP uses a directive-based approach, where each directive defines a specific type of content and the allowed or trusted sources from which that content can be loaded. For example, the "script-src" directive is used to specify the trusted sources from which scripts can be loaded. Similarly, the "style-src" directive is used to specify the trusted sources for stylesheets. In addition to specifying trusted sources, CSP also provides other directives to control various aspects of content loading and execution. These directives include "default-src" to specify the default sources for all types of content, "referrer" to control how the browser sends referrer information, and "report-uri" to specify a URL where the browser can report security violations. By implementing a content security policy, website administrators can greatly enhance the security of their web applications. CSP helps to prevent various types of attacks by limiting the sources from which content can be loaded, thereby reducing the risk of malicious code execution in the user's browser. It is an important tool in the defense against web vulnerabilities and should be considered as an essential part of any website's security strategy.

Content Security Policy (CSP)

Content Security Policy (CSP) is a network security mechanism that helps protect web applications against various types of attacks, such as cross-site scripting (XSS) and code injection. It is implemented using HTTP headers and provides a way for website administrators to specify the types of content that are allowed to be loaded and executed on their web pages. CSP works by allowing website administrators to define a set of policies that dictate which external resources can be loaded and executed by the web page. These policies are defined in a "Content-Security-Policy" HTTP header, which is sent by the server to the client's browser along with the web page. The CSP policies specify the domains or sources from which various types of content can be loaded, such as scripts, stylesheets, images, fonts, and media files. For example, a policy might specify that scripts can only be loaded from the same origin as the web page, or from a trusted domain. This helps prevent malicious scripts from being injected into a web page and executed in the user's browser. CSP also provides protection against XSS attacks by allowing website administrators to specify a "script-src" policy that restricts the types of scripts that can be executed. This helps prevent attackers from injecting malicious scripts into a web page and stealing sensitive user information. In addition to specifying allowed content sources, CSP also supports various directives that enable fine-grained control over the behavior of web pages. For example, the "default-src" directive specifies the default policy for all types of content, while the "report-uri" directive specifies a URL to which violation reports should be sent. CSP is an effective security mechanism because it helps minimize the impact of security vulnerabilities in web applications. By restricting the types of content that can be loaded and executed, CSP reduces the attack surface and makes it more difficult for attackers to exploit vulnerabilities. Overall, Content Security Policy is a crucial network security mechanism that provides website administrators with a powerful tool to protect their web applications against a wide range of attacks. By enforcing a set of policies that control the loading and execution of content, CSP helps ensure the integrity and security of web pages for users.

Converged Network

A converged network, in the context of networking, refers to a unified infrastructure that carries voice, data, and video traffic over a single network. This convergence allows for the integration and sharing of resources, such as cabling and equipment, resulting in cost savings, increased efficiency, and simplified management.Traditionally, voice, data, and video traffic were transmitted over separate networks using dedicated lines and equipment. This approach required maintaining multiple networks, which can be expensive and complex to manage.In a converged network, all forms of communication are transmitted using the same network infrastructure, often based on Internet Protocol (IP). This infrastructure includes switches, routers, and other networking devices that support the transmission and routing of different types of traffic.The convergence of voice, data, and video allows for the integration of various communication systems, including traditional telephony, video conferencing, email, instant messaging, and data transfer. This integration enables users to access and communicate using multiple platforms and devices, such as IP phones, computers, smartphones, and tablets.From a technical standpoint, the convergence of different types of traffic requires mechanisms to prioritize and manage traffic based on its nature and requirements. Quality of Service (QoS) protocols and techniques, such as traffic shaping and prioritization, are used to ensure real-time applications, like voice and video, receive sufficient network resources and are not adversely affected by other types of traffic.A converged network offers several benefits. It simplifies network management by reducing the number of networks and associated equipment that need to be maintained. It also allows for more efficient use of network resources, as traffic can be dynamically prioritized and allocated based on demand and requirements. Additionally, a converged network enables greater flexibility and scalability, as new services and applications can be easily added and integrated into the existing infrastructure.

Credential Stuffing

Credential Stuffing refers to a cyber attack technique that involves the automated injection of a large number of stolen credentials, such as usernames and passwords, into a target system. This technique relies on the fact that many individuals reuse the same credentials (or slight variations of them) across multiple online services or platforms. By leveraging credential stuffing, attackers attempt to gain unauthorized access to user accounts by systematically testing a large number of stolen credentials against a target application or network. The goal is to exploit the common practice of password reuse and potentially gain access to valuable information or services.

Cross-Site Request Forgery (CSRF)

Cross-Site Request Forgery (CSRF) refers to a type of network attack that leverages the trust relationships established between a user's web browser and a targeted website. In a CSRF attack, the attacker tricks a victim into unknowingly performing unwanted actions on a particular website. The attack is typically carried out by enticing the victim to click on a malicious link or visit a compromised website. Upon visiting the attacker-controlled page, the victim's browser automatically executes a request (typically a form submission) to a targeted website that the victim has a valid session with. Since the request is originating from the victim's browser, the targeted website trusts it and processes it accordingly.

Cross-Site Scripting (XSS)

Cross-Site Scripting (XSS) refers to a type of security vulnerability in networking wherein an attacker injects malicious scripts into trusted websites viewed by users. This allows the attacker to execute their arbitrary code within the victims' web browser, compromising their privacy, stealing sensitive information, or even taking control over their accounts. XSS attacks occur when a website fails to properly validate or sanitize user input before displaying it on web pages. Attackers exploit this vulnerability by injecting malicious code, typically in the form of JavaScript, into the website's input fields, comments sections, or other user-generated content. When unsuspecting users view the compromised webpage, their browsers execute the attacker's script, without their knowledge or consent. This attack can take different forms, including: - Stored XSS: The malicious code is permanently embedded in a website's database and displayed to all visitors who access that page. - Reflected XSS: The injected code only appears in the website's server response to specific user requests, such as a search query or a URL parameter. The attacker must lure victims into clicking a manipulated link to initiate the attack. - DOM-based XSS: The attacker exploits vulnerabilities in client-side scripting by manipulating the Document Object Model (DOM) of a web page, causing the browser to execute malicious code. The consequences of an XSS attack can be severe. Attackers may gain unauthorized access to sensitive information, such as login credentials, session tokens, or personal data. They can manipulate the compromised website to display false or misleading content, tricking users into disclosing confidential information or executing unwanted actions. Additionally, XSS attacks pave the way for further exploitation, enabling attackers to spread malware, launch phishing campaigns, or perform session hijacking. To prevent XSS attacks, web developers should implement proper input validation and output encoding. Input validation ensures that user-entered data matches the expected format, while output encoding converts special characters into their harmless equivalents. Additionally, using Content Security Policy (CSP) headers help enforce browser-side security policies and restrict the execution of external scripts. In conclusion, XSS is a serious security vulnerability that allows attackers to inject malicious scripts into trusted websites, compromising the integrity and privacy of users. Implementing effective security measures is crucial to prevent XSS attacks and protect users from the potential harm they can cause.

Cryptography

Cryptography is a field in networking that encompasses techniques for securing communication and data transmission by converting plain text into unintelligible cipher text and vice versa. It involves the use of mathematical algorithms and secret keys to encrypt and decrypt data, ensuring confidentiality, integrity, and authenticity in network communication. The primary goal of cryptography in networking is to protect sensitive information from unauthorized access or modification during transmission. By employing various cryptographic algorithms and protocols, it enables secure communication between different entities over a network. This ensures that data remains confidential, meaning only authorized individuals can access the content of the message. Confidentiality is achieved through encryption, where the original data is transformed into an unreadable format using an encryption algorithm and a secret key. Only the intended recipient possessing the corresponding decryption key can revert the cipher text back to its original form. Cryptography also plays a significant role in ensuring the integrity of data transmitted across a network. Integrity refers to the assurance that the data remains unaltered during transmission. Cryptographic techniques such as message authentication codes (MACs) and digital signatures are used to detect any unauthorized modification or tampering of the data. MACs generate a unique tag that is appended to the message, allowing the receiver to verify the integrity of the content. Digital signatures involve the use of asymmetric cryptography, where the sender signs the content with their private key, and the recipient can verify the authenticity and integrity of the message using the sender's public key. Authentication is another crucial aspect of cryptography in networking. It involves verifying the identity of the communicating parties to ensure that the information is being transmitted between trusted entities. Cryptographic protocols such as Transport Layer Security (TLS) and Secure Shell (SSH) utilize different techniques like symmetric and asymmetric encryption, certificates, and digital signatures to authenticate entities in a network. This prevents attackers from impersonating legitimate users or devices and gaining unauthorized access to sensitive information. In conclusion, cryptography is a fundamental concept in networking that ensures secure communication by providing confidentiality, integrity, and authentication. It employs mathematical algorithms, secret keys, and cryptographic protocols to convert plaintext into cipher text, verify the integrity of data, and authenticate communicating entities. By implementing cryptography, organizations can protect sensitive information and maintain the security of their network communication.

Cyber Attack Mitigation

Cyber Attack Mitigation refers to the efforts taken to prevent, detect, and respond to cyber attacks in the context of networking. It involves implementing various strategies, practices, and technologies to minimize the potential impact of cyber threats on network systems and infrastructure. The goal of cyber attack mitigation is to safeguard the confidentiality, integrity, and availability of network resources, including data, applications, and services. This is accomplished through a multi-layered approach that combines preventive measures, proactive monitoring, threat intelligence, incident response, and continuous improvement.

Cyber Attack Vector

A cyber attack vector in the context of networking refers to a method or pathway through which an attacker gains unauthorized access to a network system or compromises its security. It typically involves exploiting vulnerabilities in the network infrastructure, devices, or applications to gain control or steal sensitive information. Cyber attackers constantly evolve their tactics to exploit weaknesses in networks, making it crucial for network administrators to be aware of potential attack vectors and take appropriate measures to mitigate risks. Some common types of cyber attack vectors include: 1. Phishing: Attackers send deceptive emails or messages, pretending to be from a trusted source, in order to trick users into revealing sensitive information like usernames, passwords, or credit card details. 2. Malware: Malicious software such as viruses, worms, trojans, or ransomware is used to gain unauthorized access to a network. Users unknowingly download or execute the malware, which then exploits vulnerabilities to perform its intended actions. 3. Denial of Service (DoS) or Distributed Denial of Service (DDoS): Attackers overwhelm a network or system with a flood of traffic or requests, rendering the network or system unable to respond to legitimate user requests. 4. Man-in-the-Middle (MitM) Attacks: Attackers intercept and manipulate communication between network users, allowing them to eavesdrop, steal sensitive information, or modify data without detection. 5. SQL Injection: Attackers exploit vulnerabilities in web applications that use a database backend by injecting malicious SQL code. This allows them to retrieve, modify, or delete database records, potentially gaining unauthorized access to sensitive information. 6. Social Engineering: Attackers manipulate human psychology to trick individuals into revealing sensitive information or performing actions that compromise network security. These are just a few examples of the numerous cyber attack vectors that can be exploited. Network administrators must remain vigilant in implementing security measures such as firewall configurations, intrusion detection systems, regular security patches, and user awareness training to protect against these attack vectors.

Cyber Attack

A cyber attack refers to a malicious attempt to breach the security of a network, computer system, or device with the intent to disrupt normal operations, steal sensitive information, or cause damage. These attacks are carried out by individuals or groups, often referred to as hackers, who exploit vulnerabilities in the target network or system. Cyber attacks can take various forms, including but not limited to: 1. Malware Attacks: These involve the use of malicious software to gain unauthorized access to a network or system. Common types of malware include viruses, worms, spyware, and ransomware. 2. Phishing: Phishing attacks typically involve sending deceptive emails or messages to individuals, tricking them into revealing sensitive information such as passwords or credit card details. These attacks often mimic legitimate organizations or individuals. 3. Denial of Service (DoS) Attacks: In a DoS attack, the attacker overwhelms a targeted network or system with a flood of fake traffic, rendering it unable to handle legitimate requests. This disrupts the availability of services and can lead to significant downtime. 4. Man-in-the-Middle (MitM) Attacks: In a MitM attack, the attacker intercepts communication between two parties without their knowledge. This allows the attacker to eavesdrop, modify, or manipulate the data being transmitted, potentially leading to unauthorized access or data theft. 5. SQL Injection: SQL injection attacks exploit vulnerabilities in web applications that interact with databases. By inserting malicious SQL code into user inputs, attackers can manipulate the database and gain unauthorized access to sensitive data. Cyber attacks pose a significant threat to individuals, organizations, and even nations, as the potential damage can range from financial losses to compromised national security. Therefore, it is crucial for network administrators and system users to implement effective security measures, such as firewalls, encryption, and regular updates, to mitigate the risk of cyber attacks and protect sensitive information.

Cyber Resilience

Cyber resilience, in the context of networking, refers to the ability of a network or system to withstand and recover from cyber threats and attacks while maintaining the essential functionality and integrity of its operations. It encompasses a range of proactive and reactive measures that organizations employ to protect their networks and data from potential threats and to ensure continuity of operations even in the face of cyber incidents. A cyber resilient network is designed to anticipate, prevent, detect, and respond to cyber threats effectively. It combines various security measures and practices, including but not limited to, secure configuration management, threat intelligence and analysis, network segmentation, access controls, vulnerability management, incident response planning, backup and recovery procedures, and continuous monitoring. The concept of cyber resilience acknowledges that no security system is impenetrable, and that organizations must assume that they will face cyber threats at some point. As such, a cyber resilient network is not solely focused on preventing attacks but also on how quickly an organization can identify, contain, and recover from an incident. Proactive measures taken to enhance cyber resilience include regularly updating and patching software, implementing strong access controls, educating employees about cybersecurity best practices, and conducting vulnerability assessments and penetration testing. These measures aim to reduce the attack surface and increase the network's ability to withstand attacks. Reactive measures, on the other hand, involve incident response planning and implementation of procedures to minimize the impact of an attack or breach. This includes isolating affected systems, restoring services from backups, conducting forensic investigations, and learning from the incident to improve future resilience. Overall, cyber resilience is a crucial aspect of networking as it enables organizations to maintain operational continuity, protect sensitive data, and adapt to an ever-evolving threat landscape. It requires a holistic approach that combines technical controls, policies and procedures, and a culture of cybersecurity awareness and vigilance.

Cyber Threat Intelligence

Cyber Threat Intelligence, in the context of networking, refers to the process of collecting and analyzing information about potential cyber threats that could harm an organization's network infrastructure, systems, or data. It involves gathering and evaluating data from various sources, such as security logs, threat intelligence feeds, and open-source intelligence, to identify and understand potential cyber threats. The goal of Cyber Threat Intelligence is to provide organizations with actionable insights and knowledge about potential threats, enabling them to proactively defend against cyber attacks and mitigate risks. By staying proactive and well-informed, organizations can better protect their network assets, prevent data breaches, and maintain operational continuity in the face of evolving cyber threats.

Cybersecurity Framework

A Cybersecurity Framework is an integrated set of guidelines, best practices, and processes designed to protect the integrity, confidentiality, and availability of data and information within a networked environment. This framework serves as a blueprint for organizations to establish and maintain a robust and effective cybersecurity posture. Networking, in the context of cybersecurity, refers to the interconnectedness of devices, systems, and users within a network infrastructure. It encompasses the communication and exchange of data between these entities, both internally and externally. The Cybersecurity Framework provides organizations with a structured approach to managing and safeguarding their networked environments. It encompasses various aspects of cybersecurity, including risk assessment, vulnerability management, incident response, and security awareness. By implementing this framework, organizations can establish a comprehensive and proactive approach to protecting their network assets from cybersecurity threats. The framework consists of several key components and stages. Firstly, organizations need to conduct a thorough risk assessment to identify potential vulnerabilities and threats specific to their network environment. This involves evaluating the assets, network infrastructure, and potential attack vectors that could be exploited. Based on the findings of the risk assessment, organizations can then develop and implement appropriate security controls and measures to mitigate identified risks. This may include implementing firewalls, intrusion detection systems, access controls, and encryption protocols, among others. Additionally, the framework emphasizes the importance of continuous monitoring and proactive threat intelligence. Organizations should establish mechanisms to detect and respond to cybersecurity incidents in real-time, ensuring prompt and effective incident response and recovery. Furthermore, the Cybersecurity Framework emphasizes the need for ongoing education and training for employees. By promoting security awareness and best practices, organizations can reduce the likelihood of successful cyberattacks and ensure that employees are equipped to identify and report potential threats. In conclusion, a Cybersecurity Framework provides organizations with a structured approach to ensure the protection of their networked environments. It encompasses various components and stages, including risk assessment, security controls implementation, continuous monitoring, incident response, and security awareness. Through the implementation of this framework, organizations can establish and maintain an effective cybersecurity posture in the ever-evolving threat landscape.

Cybersecurity Frameworks

A cybersecurity framework in the context of networking refers to a structure or guideline that organizations can use to manage and protect their network infrastructure from cyber threats. It provides a set of best practices, standards, and guidelines to help organizations identify, detect, protect, respond to, and recover from cyberattacks. The main purpose of a cybersecurity framework is to help organizations establish a strong cybersecurity posture by implementing effective security controls and measures. It enables organizations to assess their current security posture, identify vulnerabilities and areas of improvement, and develop a comprehensive cybersecurity strategy to mitigate risks and protect their network infrastructure. A cybersecurity framework typically consists of several components, including risk assessment, vulnerability management, incident response, access control, data protection, and security awareness training. These components work together to ensure that the organization's network infrastructure is secure and resilient against cyber threats. One commonly used cybersecurity framework is the NIST Cybersecurity Framework (CSF), developed by the National Institute of Standards and Technology (NIST) in the United States. The NIST CSF provides a flexible and adaptable framework that organizations can use to manage cybersecurity risk based on their specific needs and requirements. It consists of five core functions: identify, protect, detect, respond, and recover. These functions help organizations to establish a strong cybersecurity foundation by identifying assets and vulnerabilities, implementing appropriate security measures, detecting and responding to threats, and recovering from incidents. Another popular cybersecurity framework is the ISO/IEC 27001, which provides a systematic approach to manage information security risks. It includes a comprehensive set of controls and measures that organizations can implement to protect their information assets, including network infrastructure. In conclusion, a cybersecurity framework in the context of networking is a structured approach that organizations can use to manage and protect their network infrastructure from cyber threats. It provides a set of best practices, standards, and guidelines to help organizations establish a strong cybersecurity posture and mitigate risks effectively.

Cybersecurity Policies

Cybersecurity policies in the context of networking refer to a set of guidelines and practices that are implemented to protect computer systems, networks, and data from unauthorized access, attacks, and other digital threats. These policies outline the procedures, rules, and measures that organizations should adopt to ensure the confidentiality, integrity, and availability of their information assets.Cybersecurity policies are crucial for maintaining a secure network infrastructure and mitigating potential risks. They serve as a framework for organizations to establish a strong security posture and facilitate the implementation of appropriate security controls and technologies.Cybersecurity policies encompass various aspects of network security, including but not limited to:• Access Control: Policies that govern the granting and revocation of user access privileges to network resources.• Authentication and Authorization:

Policies that determine the procedures and methods used to verify the identity of network users and grant them access based on their privileges.• Data Encryption: Policies that prescribe the use of encryption techniques to protect sensitive data from unauthorized disclosure or modification.• Network Monitoring: Policies that define the methods and tools used to monitor network traffic, detect potential security incidents, and investigate suspicious activities.• Incident Response: Policies that outline the steps to be taken in the event of a cybersecurity incident, including reporting, containment, eradication, and recovery procedures.• Security Awareness and Training: Policies that focus on educating employees about cybersecurity best practices, promoting a culture of security, and reducing the likelihood of human errors that could lead to security breaches.By implementing and enforcing cybersecurity policies, organizations can enhance their overall security posture, minimize the potential impact of cyber threats, and ensure the continuity of their networking operations. These policies should be regularly reviewed, updated, and communicated to all relevant stakeholders to address emerging threats and adapt to evolving technologies.

Cybersecurity Posture

A cybersecurity posture, in the context of networking, refers to an organization's overall approach and strategy in protecting its computer systems, networks, and data from unauthorized access, use, disclosure, disruption, modification, or destruction. It involves implementing a broad range of security measures and practices to prevent, detect, and respond to cyber threats effectively. The goal of a strong cybersecurity posture is to minimize the risk and potential impact of cyber attacks and to safeguard the confidentiality, integrity, and availability of digital information. It encompasses various aspects, including technology, people, processes, and policies, and requires a comprehensive and proactive approach to security.

Cybersecurity Risk Assessment

A cybersecurity risk assessment is a formal evaluation conducted to identify and analyze potential risks and vulnerabilities that could lead to unauthorized access, damage, or disruption of network systems and data. By assessing these risks, organizations can develop strategies and systems to mitigate and manage the threats effectively, ensuring the protection of confidential information, system integrity, and continuity of network operations.

Cybersecurity Threat Modeling

Cybersecurity threat modeling is the systematic process of identifying potential threats and vulnerabilities in a networked system. It involves assessing the risks associated with these threats and prioritizing them based on their potential impact on the confidentiality, integrity, and availability of the network. The purpose of cybersecurity threat modeling is to ensure that appropriate measures are taken to protect the network from potential attacks. By identifying and understanding the threats and vulnerabilities, network administrators can design and implement effective security controls to mitigate these risks. Threat modeling typically involves several steps. Firstly, the network architecture is analyzed to identify potential entry points or weak links where an attacker could gain unauthorized access. This includes examining the network infrastructure, hardware, software, and configurations. Next, potential threats are identified based on known attack vectors, vulnerabilities, and emerging risks. This can include threats from malicious actors such as hackers, malware, or internal threats such as insider attacks. Threats may also arise from human error, software bugs, or natural disasters. Once the threats are identified, their impact on the network is assessed. This involves determining the potential consequences of a successful attack, such as data breaches, service disruption, or financial loss. Threats are prioritized based on their likelihood of occurrence and the impact they would have on the network. The final step is to develop and implement security controls to mitigate the identified threats. This may include measures such as firewalls, intrusion detection systems, access controls, encryption, and regular security updates. The effectiveness of these controls should be periodically evaluated and adjusted as needed. Cybersecurity threat modeling plays a crucial role in network security by proactively identifying and addressing potential risks. By understanding the threats and vulnerabilities, network administrators can take the necessary steps to protect the network and safeguard sensitive information.

Cybersecurity Threats

Cybersecurity threats in the context of networking refer to potential risks and vulnerabilities that can compromise the confidentiality, integrity, and availability of data and systems within a network. These threats encompass a wide range of malicious activities that exploit vulnerabilities in network devices, software applications, and human behavior. One common form of cybersecurity threat is a network attack, which involves unauthorized access to a network or its resources. Attackers may exploit weak passwords, software vulnerabilities, or social engineering techniques to gain access to sensitive data or disrupt network operations.

Cybersecurity

Cybersecurity, in the context of networking, refers to the process of protecting computers, servers, networks, and data from unauthorized access, attacks, and damage. It involves implementing measures and practices to ensure the confidentiality, integrity, and availability of network resources and information. The goal of cybersecurity is to safeguard the networking infrastructure and systems from various threats, such as malware, viruses, hackers, and social engineering. By establishing robust security measures, organizations can prevent unauthorized access to sensitive data, maintain the integrity of their network, and minimize the risk of network downtime and data breaches.

DDoS Attack Detection

A Distributed Denial of Service (DDoS) attack is a malicious attempt to disrupt the normal functioning of a network, service, or website by overwhelming it with a flood of internet traffic from multiple sources. The goal of a DDoS attack is to exhaust the target's resources, such as bandwidth, processing power, or memory, rendering it unable to provide its intended services to legitimate users. In a DDoS attack, the attacker typically utilizes a network of compromised computers, known as a botnet, to carry out the attack. These compromised computers, often referred to as "zombies" or "bots," are under the control of the attacker and are used to send a massive amount of traffic to the target simultaneously, creating a distributed and coordinated effort to overwhelm the target's resources. DDoS attacks can vary in size and complexity, with some attacks reaching terabits per second in traffic volume. The attack traffic can be generated using various techniques, including sending a flood of legitimate-looking requests, exploiting vulnerabilities in network protocols, or using amplification techniques to multiply the attack traffic by reflecting or amplifying it from other vulnerable systems. Detecting and mitigating DDoS attacks is a critical task for network administrators and security professionals. Several techniques and tools are employed to identify and respond to DDoS attacks promptly. These include traffic analysis, anomaly detection, and rate limiting, among others. Monitoring network traffic patterns and identifying sudden spikes or abnormal patterns can help identify potential DDoS traffic. Intrusion detection and prevention systems (IDS/IPS) can also be used to detect and mitigate the attacks in real-time. Additionally, network service providers often deploy specialized equipment and services that leverage traffic profiling, filtering, and rate limiting capabilities to mitigate the impact of DDoS attacks.

DDoS Attack Prevention Measures

A DDoS (Distributed Denial of Service) attack is a type of cyber attack where multiple compromised devices are used to flood a targeted system or network with a large amount of traffic, overwhelming its resources and causing it to become inaccessible to legitimate users. This attack aims to disrupt the normal functioning of the target system or network and exploit vulnerabilities in its infrastructure. DDoS attack prevention measures are strategies and techniques implemented to mitigate the impact of such attacks and ensure the availability and integrity of the targeted system or network. These measures can be categorized into three main areas: 1. Network Infrastructure Protection: This involves the implementation of security measures at the network level to detect and filter malicious traffic. This can include the use of firewalls, intrusion detection systems (IDS), and load balancers. Firewalls act as a barrier between the internal network and external traffic, allowing only authorized traffic to pass through. IDS monitors network traffic for signs of suspicious activity and can trigger alerts or block traffic from identified malicious sources. Load balancers distribute traffic evenly across multiple servers, reducing the impact of a DDoS attack by preventing a single server from being overwhelmed. 2. Traffic Analysis and Anomaly Detection: This involves monitoring network traffic patterns and identifying any abnormal or suspicious behavior that may indicate a DDoS

110

attack. Traffic analysis tools can identify unusual spikes in traffic volume or patterns that deviate from normal behavior. Anomaly detection techniques use machine learning algorithms to establish baseline behavior and detect deviations from it. Early detection of DDoS attacks allows for timely response and mitigation efforts. 3. Scalable and Redundant Infrastructure: The implementation of a scalable and redundant infrastructure can help mitigate DDoS attacks by distributing the attack traffic across multiple servers or data centers. This involves setting up redundant hardware, such as servers and routers, as well as employing load balancing and failover mechanisms. By spreading the attack traffic, the impact on any single component or system is minimized, allowing the network to continue to operate and serve legitimate users.

DDoS Attack Prevention

A Distributed Denial of Service (DDoS) attack prevention is a set of measures and strategies implemented to protect a network or an online service from being overwhelmed by an excessive amount of illegitimate traffic, rendering it unavailable to legitimate users. A DDoS attack occurs when a large number of compromised devices, often part of a botnet, are orchestrated to flood a target network or service with an overwhelming volume of traffic. This flood of traffic consumes the network's resources, such as bandwidth, processing power, or memory, leading to a degradation or complete disruption of the targeted service. DDoS attack prevention mechanisms aim to detect and mitigate these attacks to ensure the availability and integrity of the targeted network or service. These measures can be broadly categorized into three main areas: network layer, application layer, and security protocols. At the network layer, various techniques are employed to differentiate legitimate traffic from malicious traffic. This includes traffic profiling and filtering, where traffic patterns and characteristics are analyzed to identify anomalies or suspicious behavior. Additionally, network administrators may implement rate limiting or traffic shaping techniques to ensure traffic flows within acceptable thresholds, preventing overload situations. At the application layer, DDoS attack prevention mechanisms focus on protecting specific applications or services hosted on the network. This can be achieved through traffic inspection and filtering, which detects and blocks malicious requests or patterns targeting specific applications or vulnerable areas. Content Delivery Networks (CDNs) can also be employed to distribute traffic across multiple servers, increasing the network's capacity to withstand DDoS attacks. Security protocols, such as the Border Gateway Protocol (BGP) and the Domain Name System Security Extensions (DNSSEC), play a crucial role in DDoS attack prevention. BGP allows network administrators to implement filtering and routing policies to mitigate or contain DDoS traffic. DNSSEC provides authentication and integrity verification mechanisms for DNS responses, preventing DNS-based DDoS attacks. Overall, DDoS attack prevention is a proactive approach to protect networks and services from becoming victims of disruptive DDoS attacks. By implementing a combination of network, application, and security protocol-based strategies, organizations can reduce the risk of downtime, financial losses, and reputational damage associated with these malicious attacks.

DDoS Attack Vectors

A DDoS attack, also known as a Distributed Denial of Service attack, is a malicious attempt to disrupt the normal functioning of a network, service, or website by overwhelming it with a flood of internet traffic. In a DDoS attack, multiple compromised computers, often referred to as "botnets," are used to send an excessive amount of data packets or requests to the target network, service, or website simultaneously. These botnets are typically formed by infecting numerous computers with malware, turning them into zombies under the control of the attacker. The primary goal of a DDoS attack is to render the targeted network, service, or website unavailable to its intended users. By overwhelming the target with an overwhelming amount of traffic, the attacker can exhaust its resources, such as bandwidth, processing power, or memory, leading to severe performance degradation or complete unavailability. DDoS attacks can utilize various attack vectors or methods to achieve their objective. The most common DDoS attack vectors include: Syn Flood Attack: This attack exploits the TCP three-way handshake process by overwhelming the target with numerous SYN requests, exhausting its resources and preventing it from establishing legitimate connections. UDP Flood Attack: In this attack, the attacker floods the target network with UDP packets, consuming its resources and causing network congestion. HTTP Flood Attack: This attack targets web servers by sending a massive amount of legitimate-looking HTTP requests, thereby overwhelming the server's resources and making it unable to respond to legitimate requests. ICMP Flood Attack: In an ICMP flood attack,

111

the attacker floods the target with a large number of ICMP Echo Request packets, saturating the network and preventing legitimate packets from reaching their destination. Slowloris Attack: This attack involves sending HTTP GET or POST requests to the target web server at an extremely slow rate, gradually consuming its available resources and causing a denial of service. These are just a few examples of DDoS attack vectors; attackers can use a combination of these methods or employ more sophisticated techniques to achieve their objectives. The increasing availability of DDoS-for-hire services and easily accessible tools makes it important for organizations to implement robust DDoS mitigation strategies to protect their networks, services, and websites from such attacks.

DDoS (Distributed Denial Of Service)

A Distributed Denial of Service (DDoS) attack is a malicious attempt to disrupt the normal functioning or availability of a computer network, service, or website by overwhelming it with a flood of internet traffic from multiple sources. The term "distributed" refers to the fact that the attack is orchestrated using multiple compromised devices or computers that have been infected with malware, creating a network of bots or zombies under the control of the attacker. The goal of a DDoS attack is to exhaust the resources of the targeted network, rendering it unable to respond to legitimate users or shutting it down completely. By flooding the targeted network with a high volume of incoming traffic, the attackers overwhelm the system's capacity to handle the requests, causing a denial of service for legitimate users. DDoS attacks exploit vulnerabilities in network infrastructure or application layers, targeting weaknesses in firewalls, routers, or servers. They can utilize various techniques to amplify the attack, such as reflective amplification, which involves bouncing traffic off other servers or devices to increase the volume of data sent to the target. There are different types of DDoS attacks, including volumetric, TCP state-exhaustion, and application layer attacks. Volumetric attacks aim to consume the available bandwidth of the target's network by flooding it with massive amounts of data. TCP state-exhaustion attacks target the network's resources, such as its firewalls or load balancers, by initiating multiple incomplete connections or exhausting their state tables. Application layer attacks focus on overwhelming a specific application or service, such as a web server, by exploiting vulnerabilities at the application layer. DDoS attacks have become increasingly sophisticated and can have severe consequences for targeted organizations, including financial losses, reputational damage, and disruption of critical services. Mitigating and defending against DDoS attacks requires a combination of proactive measures, such as network monitoring, traffic filtering, and rate limiting, as well as reactive strategies, including incident response and coordination with internet service providers to block or filter malicious traffic.

DDoS Mitigation Strategies

DDoS mitigation strategies refer to the proactive measures implemented by network administrators to defend against distributed denial of service (DDoS) attacks. DDoS attacks occur when multiple compromised devices, often part of a botnet, flood a targeted network or website with an overwhelming amount of traffic, rendering it inaccessible to legitimate users. These attacks exploit vulnerabilities in the network's infrastructure or application layer and can lead to significant financial losses, reputational damage, and disruptions to normal business operations. The primary goal of DDoS mitigation strategies is to ensure network availability and protect the targeted network or website from being overwhelmed by malicious traffic. These strategies involve a combination of preventative measures, early detection techniques, and responsive actions to minimize the impact of DDoS attacks. By implementing robust mitigation strategies, network administrators can effectively mitigate the risk and potential damage caused by DDoS attacks.

DDoS Mitigation

DDoS mitigation refers to the process of preventing and mitigating Distributed Denial of Service (DDoS) attacks in a networking environment. DDoS attacks involve overwhelming a target system or network with a flood of internet traffic from multiple sources. This flood of traffic can be in the form of requests, packets, or connections, and is aimed at overwhelming the target's resources, causing them to become unreachable or severely degraded in terms of performance.

DDoS Protection Services

DDoS Protection Services refer to a set of security measures implemented to detect and mitigate Distributed Denial of Service (DDoS) attacks in a computer network. DDoS attacks are designed to overwhelm network resources, rendering the targeted system or service inoperable. These attacks involve flooding the network with a high volume of traffic or requests from multiple sources simultaneously. The goal is to exhaust the system's capacity to handle legitimate traffic and disrupt its normal operations. DDoS Protection Services aim to prevent and minimize the impact of such attacks by employing various techniques and technologies. One common method is traffic filtering, where incoming network traffic is scrutinized and malicious traffic is identified and blocked. This filtering is often performed at different levels, such as the network layer or application layer, depending on the nature of the attack. Another approach is traffic diversion, where incoming traffic is redirected to specialized servers or content delivery networks (CDNs) capable of handling large volumes of requests. This helps distribute the load and prevent the targeted system from being overwhelmed. Additionally, rate-limiting techniques can be applied to control the number of incoming requests from individual sources, preventing the system from being flooded. DDoS Protection Services also involve real-time monitoring and detection mechanisms to identify potential attacks before they cause significant damage. This includes analyzing network traffic patterns, monitoring for anomalies, and detecting common DDoS attack signatures. Once an attack is detected, appropriate measures are taken to mitigate its impact, such as blocking traffic from specific sources or applying traffic prioritization rules. Furthermore, DDoS Protection Services often include advanced reporting and analytics capabilities to provide insights into attack trends, patterns, and vulnerabilities. This enables network administrators to strengthen their defenses and proactively enhance the overall security posture of the network.

DHCP (Dynamic Host Configuration Protocol)

DHCP, which stands for Dynamic Host Configuration Protocol, is a networking protocol that enables the automatic assignment of IP addresses, subnet masks, default gateways, and other network configuration parameters to network devices. It operates in a client-server model, where DHCP servers are responsible for managing and assigning these network parameters, and DHCP clients obtain this information from the server. The main purpose of DHCP is to simplify the process of IP address management within a network. Instead of manually assigning unique IP addresses to each device, DHCP allows for the automatic allocation and management of these addresses. This dynamic allocation ensures that devices receive the necessary network configurations without requiring manual intervention, making it efficient and scalable for large networks. When a DHCP client device joins a network, it sends out a DHCP discovery message to locate a DHCP server. The server responds with a DHCP offer, which includes the available IP address and other network configuration parameters. The client then sends a DHCP request to confirm its intent to use the offered IP address. Finally, the server acknowledges this request with a DHCP acknowledgement, and the client is allowed to use the provided information to configure its network settings. In addition to IP address assignment, DHCP also supports IP address lease management. IP addresses can be leased to clients for a specific period, after which they must be renewed or released back to the DHCP server. This allows for efficient use of available IP addresses, preventing address exhaustion while ensuring that devices have appropriate network configurations. DHCP is widely used in both small and large networks, including home networks, corporate networks, and internet service providers. It simplifies network administration, reduces errors, and supports scalability by automating the process of IP address assignment and management. DHCP plays a crucial role in enabling seamless network connectivity and efficient resource utilization within modern computer networks.

DHCP Lease

A DHCP lease is a temporary assignment of an IP address by a DHCP server to a client device on a network. The Dynamic Host Configuration Protocol (DHCP) is a network protocol that enables automatic assignment of IP addresses, as well as other network configuration information, to devices on a network. When a client device is connected to a network, it sends out a DHCP broadcast requesting an IP address. The DHCP server receives this request and checks its pool of available addresses. If an IP address is available, the server assigns it to the client device and sends a DHCP lease offer. The client device can then accept the offer and send a DHCP lease request to the server to confirm the assignment. The DHCP lease has a specific duration or lease time, which is negotiated between the DHCP client and server. Once the client device is assigned an IP address, it can use this address to communicate on the

113

network for the duration of the lease. The lease time is typically a few hours or days but can be configured to be longer or shorter. During the lease period, the client device can renew the lease by sending a DHCP lease renewal request to the server. If the server approves the renewal, it extends the lease time. If the client device does not renew the lease before it expires, the IP address is returned to the DHCP server's pool of available addresses and can be reassigned to another client device. Additionally, DHCP leases can include other configuration information such as subnet mask, default gateway, DNS servers, and other network settings. This allows client devices to automatically obtain all necessary network parameters without manual configuration.

DHCP Relay Agent

DHCP Relay Agent is a networking device or software that facilitates communication between DHCP clients and DHCP servers on different subnets. It acts as an intermediary, forwarding DHCP messages between these two entities, enabling DHCP lease allocation and configuration in a multi-subnet network environment. When a DHCP client sends a DHCP discover message to obtain an IP address, it broadcasts the message on its local subnet. However, if the DHCP server is located on a different subnet, the DHCP discover message will not reach it. This is where the DHCP Relay Agent comes into play. It intercepts the DHCP discover message and forwards it to the appropriate DHCP server on the client's behalf. The process works as follows: 1. The DHCP client sends a DHCP discover message to obtain an IP address. 2. The DHCP Relay Agent, installed on a router or switch, intercepts the DHCP discover message. 3. The DHCP Relay Agent adds its own IP address and the source IP address of the DHCP client to the DHCP discover message. 4. The DHCP Relay Agent unicasts the modified DHCP discover message to one or more DHCP servers it is configured to work with. 5. The DHCP server receives the DHCP discover message from the DHCP Relay Agent, allocates an IP address, and sends a DHCP offer back to the Relay Agent. 6. The DHCP Relay Agent forwards the DHCP offer back to the DHCP client by adding the client's IP address as the destination IP address. 7. The DHCP client receives the DHCP offer, and if it accepts it, it sends a DHCP request to the DHCP server via the DHCP Relay Agent. 8. The DHCP server acknowledges the DHCP request and sends a DHCP acknowledgement message to the DHCP Relay Agent. 9. The DHCP Relay Agent forwards the DHCP acknowledgement message to the DHCP client. In summary, the DHCP Relay Agent bridges the gap between DHCP clients and DHCP servers on different subnets, allowing for the allocation and configuration of IP addresses in a network with multiple subnets. It acts as a middleman, forwarding DHCP messages between clients and servers to ensure successful communication and IP address assignment within the network.

DHCP Relay Configuration

DHCP Relay is a networking configuration that allows for the communication between DHCP clients and DHCP servers located on different network segments. It involves the use of a relay agent that forwards DHCP messages between the client and the server, allowing the client to obtain an IP address and other network configuration information. When a DHCP client requests an IP address, it broadcasts a DHCPDISCOVER message. In a local network, the DHCP server would directly receive and respond to this message. However, in a network that has multiple subnets or VLANs, the client's broadcast message cannot reach the DHCP server as it is limited to the local network segment. This is where the DHCP relay agent comes into play. The DHCP relay agent is responsible for receiving the DHCPDISCOVER message from the client and relaying it to the DHCP server. It accomplishes this task by encapsulating the original DHCP message as a unicast packet, which can be routed to the server. The relay agent adds its own IP address and the source IP address of the client to the encapsulated packet before forwarding it. This allows the DHCP server to identify the client's network segment and allocate an appropriate IP address from the correct IP pool. Once the DHCP server receives the relayed DHCPDISCOVER message, it sends a DHCPOFFER message back to the relay agent. The DHCP relay then forwards the DHCPOFFER back to the client, encapsulating it as a broadcast message. This broadcast reaches the client, and it can now choose to accept the offered IP address by sending a DHCPREQUEST message. The request is again relayed by the DHCP relay agent to the server, which sends a DHCPACK message to confirm the allocation of the IP address to the client. In summary, DHCP Relay is a network configuration that enables DHCP clients and servers to communicate across different network segments. It involves the use of a relay agent that receives DHCP messages from clients, encapsulates them, and forwards them

114

to the DHCP server. This allows DHCP clients to obtain IP addresses and other network configuration information even when the DHCP server is located on a different network segment.

DHCP Server Configuration Tools

A DHCP (Dynamic Host Configuration Protocol) server is a network server that automatically assigns IP addresses and other network configuration settings to devices on a network. DHCP allows for efficient management of IP addresses and eliminates the need for manual IP address configuration. DHCP server configuration tools are software or utilities that are used to configure and manage DHCP servers. These tools provide a user-friendly interface to configure various DHCP server settings and perform tasks such as assigning IP address ranges, specifying lease durations, and configuring DNS (Domain Name System) settings.

DHCP Server Configuration

DHCP Server Configuration refers to the process of setting up the Dynamic Host Configuration Protocol (DHCP) server to assign IP addresses, subnet masks, default gateways, and other network configuration parameters to the client devices on a network. DHCP is a network protocol that allows network administrators to automate the process of IP address assignment and network configuration management. It simplifies the administration of IP addresses on a network by eliminating the need to manually assign static IP addresses to individual devices. Instead, the DHCP server dynamically assigns IP addresses to devices as they connect to the network. To configure a DHCP server, the network administrator needs to perform several steps: 1. IP Address Pool: The administrator defines a range of IP addresses, subnet masks, and other network configuration parameters that the DHCP server can assign to client devices. This range is also known as the DHCP address pool. 2. Lease Duration: The administrator sets the lease duration for the IP addresses assigned by the DHCP server. Lease duration refers to the amount of time a client device can use an assigned IP address before it needs to renew the lease. 3. Static IP Address Assignment: The administrator can assign specific IP addresses to devices based on their MAC addresses. These IP addresses are known as static IP addresses and are typically used for devices that require a fixed IP address, such as servers. 4. Subnet Configuration: The administrator configures the subnet mask, default gateway, and other network parameters to ensure proper communication between the DHCP server and the client devices. 5. Other Configuration Options: The administrator can configure additional options such as DNS server addresses, domain names, time servers, and other network parameters that the DHCP server can provide to the client devices. Once the DHCP server is configured, it listens for DHCP requests from client devices and responds with the appropriate network configuration parameters. Client devices that are configured to use DHCP will automatically request IP addresses from the DHCP server during the network initialization process. In summary, DHCP Server Configuration is the process of setting up the DHCP server to automatically assign IP addresses and network configuration parameters to client devices, simplifying the administration of IP addresses on a network.

DHCP Server Management

DHCP Server Management refers to the process of configuring and maintaining a Dynamic Host Configuration Protocol (DHCP) server within a network infrastructure. DHCP is a network protocol that allows devices to easily obtain IP addresses and other network configuration information automatically. In DHCP server management, an administrator is responsible for setting up and maintaining the DHCP server to ensure proper allocation of IP addresses to devices within the network. This involves defining IP address ranges, configuring lease durations, and specifying other optional parameters such as default gateway, domain name servers, and subnet masks. The primary task in DHCP server management is to define the IP address pool. The administrator specifies a pool of available IP addresses from which the DHCP server can dynamically assign addresses to devices that join the network. By defining appropriate address ranges, the administrator ensures that there are enough IP addresses to accommodate all the devices in the network. Once the IP address pool is set up, the administrator can configure other parameters, such as lease durations. Lease durations determine how long a device can hold a specific IP address before it needs to renew its lease. This helps in managing address allocation effectively and prevents IP address exhaustion within the network. In addition to managing IP address allocation, DHCP server management also

115

involves specifying optional parameters that are provided to clients during the address assignment process. These parameters include default gateway, domain name servers, and subnet masks. By configuring these parameters appropriately, the administrator ensures that devices on the network can communicate smoothly with each other and with external networks. Monitoring the DHCP server is another important aspect of DHCP server management. The administrator should regularly check the server logs and statistics to ensure its proper functioning. This helps in identifying any potential issues, such as address conflicts or server overload, and allows timely troubleshooting to maintain uninterrupted network connectivity.

DHCP Server

A DHCP server, also known as Dynamic Host Configuration Protocol server, is a network service that automatically assigns IP (Internet Protocol) addresses and other network configuration information to devices on a network. It functions as a central point of control in a local area network (LAN), providing a convenient and automated method for managing IP addresses and network settings. The primary purpose of a DHCP server is to simplify network administration and eliminate the need for manual IP address configuration. Instead of manually assigning individual IP addresses to each device, the DHCP server dynamically assigns and manages IP addresses within a defined range, known as a DHCP pool. This allows for efficient allocation of IP addresses and avoids conflicts or duplication of addresses. When a device, such as a computer or smartphone, connects to a network that is DHCP-enabled, it broadcasts a DHCP discovery message seeking an IP address lease. The DHCP server receives this message and responds with a DHCP offer, providing the device with an available IP address. If the device accepts the offer, it sends a DHCP request to the server, confirming the assignment of the IP address. The server then sends a DHCP acknowledgement to the device, finalizing the lease of the IP address and completing the network configuration process. In addition to IP address assignment, a DHCP server can also provide other essential network information to devices, such as subnet masks, default gateways, DNS (Domain Name System) server addresses, and lease duration. These configurations are automatically delivered to the devices during the DHCP process, enabling them to connect to the network and communicate with other devices and services. Overall, a DHCP server plays a crucial role in network management and connectivity by simplifying the assignment and management of IP addresses. It saves time and effort for network administrators, ensuring efficient utilization of IP addresses and seamless integration of devices into the network.

DHCP Snooping

DHCP Snooping is a network security feature that allows network administrators to mitigate certain types of network attacks by monitoring and filtering DHCP traffic. With DHCP Snooping, network devices such as switches are configured to actively inspect DHCP packets and prevent any unauthorized or rogue DHCP servers from distributing IP addresses to client devices on the network. The process involves selectively allowing DHCP server messages to pass through, while dropping or rate-limiting any DHCP messages from unknown or untrusted sources. The main purpose of DHCP Snooping is to prevent DHCP-related attacks such as DHCP spoofing or DHCP starvation attacks. DHCP spoofing occurs when an attacker sets up a rogue DHCP server on the network, with the intention to provide false IP addresses and other network settings to legitimate clients. This can lead to various forms of network disruptions, data breaches, or unauthorized access to systems. To prevent such attacks, DHCP Snooping maintains a trusted binding table that stores details about authorized DHCP servers, known as trusted sources, along with the MAC addresses of the client devices that have obtained IP addresses from these trusted servers. Any DHCP messages received from untrusted or unknown sources are analyzed against this trusted binding table. If the message is found to be unauthorized, it is dropped or limited based on predefined configuration rules. DHCP Snooping is a crucial aspect of overall network security, as it adds an additional layer of protection against unauthorized DHCP servers and potential network attacks. By filtering and monitoring DHCP traffic, it helps ensure that clients on the network receive legitimate IP addresses and network parameters from trusted sources, effectively preventing malicious activities and maintaining network integrity.

DMZ (Demilitarized Zone)

116

A Demilitarized Zone (DMZ) in the context of networking refers to a physical or logical network segment that sits between an internal network and an external network like the internet. It acts as a buffer zone that provides an additional layer of security to protect the internal network from unauthorized access.The primary purpose of a DMZ is to host public-facing servers or services that need to be accessible from the internet, such as web servers, email servers, or DNS servers. By placing these servers in the DMZ, organizations can isolate them from the internal network, reducing the risk of an attacker gaining direct access to sensitive resources or data.

DNS Cache Poisoning

DNS cache poisoning is a network security attack that involves corrupting the DNS cache of a DNS resolver, resulting in the insertion of fraudulent DNS records. These fraudulent records are then used to redirect users to malicious websites or to intercept sensitive information. In a typical DNS lookup process, when a user tries to access a website by its domain name, the DNS resolver takes the responsibility of translating that domain name into the corresponding IP address. To speed up the translation process, DNS resolvers maintain a cache that stores previously resolved domain names and their corresponding IP addresses. This cache is called the DNS cache. DNS cache poisoning occurs when an attacker manages to inject or manipulate the DNS cache, causing it to store incorrect or malicious IP address mappings. This attack can be executed in various ways, but the most common method involves exploiting vulnerabilities in the DNS protocol or leveraging DNS spoofing techniques. By poisoning the DNS cache, the attacker can control the IP address resolution process, leading users to unintended destinations. The consequences of DNS cache poisoning can be severe. Once the cache is corrupted, legitimate requests for a specific domain name will be resolved to the attacker's IP address instead of the actual IP address associated with the domain. This allows the attacker to redirect users to fraudulent websites that may mimic legitimate ones, tricking them into entering sensitive information such as login credentials or financial details. Moreover, attackers can use DNS cache poisoning to launch other attacks, such as man-in-the-middle attacks, where they intercept and manipulate communications between users and legitimate servers. To mitigate the risk of DNS cache poisoning, various measures can be implemented. Implementing DNSSEC (Domain Name System Security Extensions) can enhance the security of DNS by adding cryptographic signatures to DNS responses, ensuring their authenticity. Regularly updating DNS software and applying patches is also crucial, as it helps protect against known vulnerabilities. Additionally, network administrators should monitor DNS traffic for any suspicious activities, and DNS resolvers should be configured to only accept responses from authorized DNS servers.

DNS (Domain Name System)

The Domain Name System (DNS) is a decentralized naming system used to translate human-readable domain names into the numerical IP addresses needed for locating and identifying devices and services on a network. It serves as a sort of "phone book" for the internet, enabling users to access websites, send emails, and interact with other online services by using recognizable domain names instead of complex IP addresses. When a user enters a domain name into a web browser or a network request is made, the DNS is queried to obtain the corresponding IP address for that domain. This lookup process involves a hierarchical structure of DNS servers called the DNS hierarchy. The hierarchy is organized in a tree-like structure, with the root server(s) at the top, followed by top-level domain (TLD) servers, authoritative name servers, and finally, caching resolver servers that are typically provided by internet service providers (ISPs). During a DNS lookup, if the requested domain name is not already cached by a resolver server, the lookup starts at the root server. The root server then directs the query to the appropriate TLD server based on the domain's extension (such as .com or .org). The TLD server further directs the query to the authoritative name server responsible for the specific domain being looked up, which holds the necessary information about that domain's IP address(es). The DNS uses various protocols and record types to store and distribute this information across the network. One key record type is the "A" record, which maps a domain name to its corresponding IPv4 address. Another record type is the "AAAA" record, which maps a domain name to its corresponding IPv6 address. There are also other record types for different purposes, including storing mail server information (MX records) and nameserver information (NS records).

DNS Hijacking

117

DNS hijacking refers to the act of redirecting DNS queries to a malicious or unauthorized DNS server. It involves compromising the Domain Name System (DNS) infrastructure, which is responsible for translating domain names into IP addresses. This unauthorized redirection allows attackers to control and manipulate the flow of network traffic, potentially leading to various malicious activities such as phishing, data exfiltration, and distributing malware. By exploiting vulnerabilities in DNS protocols, attackers can modify the DNS records that associate domain names with IP addresses. They can achieve this by compromising DNS servers, routers, or the target's network infrastructure. Once the DNS records are changed, users attempting to access a particular website are redirected to a fraudulent website or an attacker-controlled server, which can be designed to mimic the legitimate site in order to deceive users.

DNS Load Balancing

DNS Load Balancing is a technique used in computer networking that distributes incoming client requests across multiple servers to ensure efficient utilization of resources and improve the overall performance and availability of a network service. This process involves the use of a Domain Name System (DNS) server to redirect client traffic to different servers based on factors like server load, proximity, or defined algorithms. When a client initiates a request to access a particular network service, such as a website, the first step is establishing a connection with the DNS server. The DNS server then maps the client's request to the corresponding IP address of the server hosting the service. In a traditional setup, the DNS server would simply provide a single IP address in response to the client's request. However, in a DNS load balancing scenario, the DNS server returns multiple IP addresses, each corresponding to a different server that hosts the same network service. These IP addresses are typically arranged in a round-robin fashion or based on predefined load balancing algorithms. The client's device will select one of the IP addresses and initiate a connection with the corresponding server. This technique allows the distribution of client requests across multiple servers, ensuring that no single server becomes overwhelmed with traffic. By distributing the workload evenly, DNS load balancing improves the overall performance and response times of the network service, as each server handles a smaller portion of the total requests. Additionally, if one of the servers becomes unavailable, the DNS server can easily remove its IP address from the list, preventing client requests from being directed to an unresponsive or overloaded server. In summary, DNS load balancing is a fundamental mechanism used in networking to enhance the performance, availability, and scalability of network services. By intelligently distributing client requests across multiple servers, it helps to achieve a more efficient utilization of resources and ensure a reliable and responsive user experience.

DNS Protocol Types

The Domain Name System (DNS) is a protocol used in computer networks to translate domain names into IP addresses and vice versa. It is responsible for resolving human-friendly domain names like www.example.com to their corresponding IP addresses like 192.0.2.1. The DNS protocol operates using different types of messages and records to perform these translations and maintain the integrity of the DNS infrastructure. Here are three main types of DNS protocols: 1. Recursive DNS (RDNS): Also known as a DNS resolver, this type of protocol is used by client devices to resolve domain names. When a client initiates a DNS query for a domain name, the recursive DNS server assists in finding the IP address for that domain name. It does this by querying other DNS servers in a recursive manner until it obtains the desired IP address. The recursive server caches the result, improving future response times for subsequent queries. 2. Authoritative DNS (ADNS): This protocol refers to the DNS servers that are responsible for storing and providing authoritative information about specific domains. When a recursive DNS server cannot find the IP address for a domain name in its cache, it sends a query to an authoritative DNS server. The authoritative DNS server houses the correct and up-to-date records for the given domain and responds with the requested IP address. These servers are typically managed by domain owners or their designated DNS hosting providers. 3. Caching DNS (CDNS): As the name suggests, caching DNS servers store previously resolved DNS records in their cache. When a client device makes a DNS query, the caching DNS server will check its cache first to see if it has the required IP address. If present, it retrieves the IP address from the cache, without needing to query the recursive or authoritative DNS servers. This caching mechanism helps reduce network latency and improves the overall efficiency of DNS resolution. In summary, recursive DNS servers handle the DNS resolution process for client devices, authoritative DNS servers store and provide domain-related information, and caching DNS servers store previously resolved DNS records to improve efficiency. These three types of DNS protocols work together to ensure smooth and accurate domain name to IP address translations in computer networks.

DNS Record Types

DNS (Domain Name System) is a hierarchical decentralized naming system that converts domain names (e.g., www.example.com) into corresponding IP addresses (e.g., 192.0.2.1) necessary for locating and identifying computer services and devices on a network. DNS records are used to store various types of information associated with a domain name. In networking, there are several types of DNS records, each serving a specific purpose. A NS (Name Server) record specifies the authoritative DNS server for a domain. It associates a domain name with a list of name servers responsible for that domain. When a user tries to access a website, the NS record helps in identifying the name servers that can provide the corresponding IP address. A A (Address) record maps a domain name to an IPv4 address. It is used to translate a domain name into an IP address that machines on a network can understand. When a user enters a website address, the A record allows the network to find the matching IP address associated with that domain name. A AAAA (IPv6 Address) record performs a similar function to the A record but maps a domain name to an IPv6 address. It is used when a website is hosted on a server that supports IPv6 connectivity. The AAAA record enables communication between IPv6-enabled devices on the network. A CNAME (Canonical Name) record creates an alias or nickname for a domain name. It allows multiple domain names to be associated with the same IP address. The CNAME record is commonly used when creating subdomains or setting up vanity URLs. A MX (Mail Exchange) record specifies the mail server responsible for accepting incoming email for a particular domain. When someone sends an email to an address under a specific domain, the MX record helps deliver the email to the correct mail server. A TXT (Text) record allows domain owners to store arbitrary textual information associated with a domain. It is commonly used for adding SPF (Sender Policy Framework) records to specify authorized email servers or for domain verification purposes, such as when setting up various online services. A SRV (Service) record is used to define the location of a specific service on a network. It provides information about the hostname, port number, and other details required to locate and access a particular service associated with a domain. DNS records play a crucial role in facilitating communication and connectivity across networks by providing essential information for the proper functioning of various internet services.

DNS Resolution Process

The DNS (Domain Name System) resolution process is a fundamental aspect of networking that allows users to access websites and resources on the internet using domain names instead of IP addresses. When a user enters a domain name in their web browser, such as www.example.com, the DNS resolution process is initiated to translate this human-readable domain name into a numerical IP address that is used to locate the requested website or resource on the internet. The DNS resolution process involves several steps: Step 1: Querying the Local DNS Cache The first step in the DNS resolution process is to query the local DNS cache. DNS caching is used to store previously resolved domain names and their corresponding IP addresses for a certain period of time. If the domain name is found in the local DNS cache and is still valid, the corresponding IP address is retrieved, and the resolution process is complete. Step 2: Querying the Recursive DNS Servers If the domain name is not found in the local DNS cache or the cache entry has expired, the next step is to query the recursive DNS servers. These servers have the ability to recursively resolve domain names by querying other DNS servers, if needed. Recursive DNS servers follow a hierarchical structure, where they start by querying the root DNS servers, then the top-level domain (TLD) servers, and finally the authoritative DNS servers for the specific domain. Step 3: Querying the Root DNS Servers If the recursive DNS server does not have the IP address for the requested domain name in its cache, it will query the root DNS servers. These servers maintain a complete and authoritative database of the IP addresses for all top-level domains (TLDs). The root DNS servers respond to the query with the IP address of the TLD server responsible for the requested domain. Step 4: Querying the TLD DNS Servers The recursive DNS server then queries the TLD DNS servers, which are responsible for specific TLDs such as .com, .org, or .net. The TLD DNS servers respond with the IP address of the authoritative DNS server for the requested domain. Step 5: Querying the Authoritative DNS Servers Finally, the recursive DNS server queries the authoritative DNS servers for the requested domain. These servers are directly managed by the organization or entity that owns the domain and have the most up-to-date information about the IP address of the domain name. The authoritative DNS servers respond to the query with the IP address of the requested domain name. Once the IP address is obtained from the authoritative DNS server, it is stored in the local DNS cache for future use and is used to establish a connection to the requested website or resource on the internet.

DNS Resolver

A DNS resolver is a networking component that is responsible for converting domain names into their corresponding IP addresses. It is an essential part of the DNS (Domain Name System) infrastructure, which is used to facilitate the communication between devices on a computer network. When a user enters a domain name (e.g., www.example.com) into a web browser, the DNS resolver plays a crucial role in the process of resolving and retrieving the IP address associated with that domain name. The resolver operates by sending queries to DNS servers to obtain the necessary information. The DNS resolver can be configured in two ways: as a recursive resolver or as an iterative resolver. A recursive resolver is designed to handle the entire resolution process, starting from the initial request until the final response is obtained. It sends queries to DNS servers, receives the responses, and provides the IP address back to the user's device. In contrast, an iterative resolver is responsible for sending queries to DNS servers but does not handle the entire resolution process. Instead, it receives partial information from the DNS server and continues to query other DNS servers until the IP address is obtained. Iterative resolvers are commonly used by DNS servers to resolve queries from recursive resolvers. The DNS resolver plays a crucial role in network performance, as it can cache the results of previous queries. This caching mechanism helps to reduce the response time for subsequent requests for the same domain name. By storing the IP address locally, the resolver can avoid the need for additional queries, improving the overall efficiency and speed of the resolution process. In summary, a DNS resolver is a vital component in the DNS infrastructure that converts domain names into IP addresses. It can be configured as a recursive resolver or an iterative resolver and plays a significant role in improving network performance through its caching mechanism.

DNS Security Measures

DNS security measures refer to the tactics and strategies implemented to protect the Domain Name System (DNS) from various threats and vulnerabilities. DNS is an integral part of the internet infrastructure, responsible for translating user-friendly domain names into their corresponding IP addresses, enabling users to access websites and other online services. One of the fundamental security measures for DNS is DNSSEC (Domain Name System Security Extensions). DNSSEC is a set of protocols and cryptographic techniques that add an extra layer of security to DNS, ensuring the authenticity and integrity of DNS responses. It prevents DNS spoofing, cache poisoning, and other forms of DNS attacks by enabling the verification of DNS data through digital signatures. Another important measure is the implementation of firewalls and access control lists (ACLs) to restrict unauthorized access to DNS servers. Firewalls act as a barrier between the internal DNS infrastructure and external networks, filtering traffic based on predetermined rules. ACLs, on the other hand, allow network administrators to define specific access rules, allowing only trusted entities to communicate with DNS servers. Regular software updates and patch management are crucial in maintaining DNS security. DNS software vendors release updates frequently to address newly discovered vulnerabilities and security weaknesses. By keeping DNS servers up to date with the latest patches, organizations can minimize the risk of known vulnerabilities being exploited by malicious actors. Implementing secure configurations and following security best practices are also vital in enhancing DNS security. This includes disabling unnecessary DNS services, enforcing strong password policies, practicing least privilege access control, and regularly auditing DNS server configurations for any potential security gaps. Network monitoring and logging play a significant role in DNS security. By monitoring DNS traffic and logging DNS activities, potential attacks and anomalies can be detected and investigated in a timely manner. This enables network administrators to take appropriate actions to mitigate threats and prevent unauthorized access to DNS servers. Lastly, conducting regular security assessments, such as DNS vulnerability scanning and penetration testing, can help identify any weaknesses or vulnerabilities in the DNS infrastructure.

These assessments allow organizations to proactively address potential security risks and implement necessary control measures.

DNS Server

A DNS server, short for Domain Name System server, is a central component in networking that translates human-readable domain names into their corresponding numerical IP addresses. It functions as a distributed database, storing and managing a vast number of domain names and their associated IP addresses, allowing users to access websites and other network resources by using easily memorable names instead of complex numerical addresses. The DNS server plays a critical role in the internet infrastructure by resolving the domain names requested by clients into IP addresses that computers can understand. When a user types a domain name into a web browser, the browser sends a request to the DNS server, asking for the IP address associated with that domain name. Upon receiving the request, the DNS server consults its database, which consists of various records known as DNS resource records (RRs), such as A, AAAA, CNAME, MX, and NS records. These RRs hold information about domain names, IP addresses, mail servers, and other crucial details. The DNS server searches for the requested domain name within its database and returns the corresponding IP address back to the requesting client. In cases where the DNS server does not have the requested domain name in its cache or database, it acts as a resolver and communicates with other DNS servers in a hierarchical manner. This process, known as DNS resolution, involves multiple levels of DNS servers, starting from the root DNS servers, then moving to the top-level domain (TLD) servers, and finally reaching the authoritative DNS servers responsible for the requested domain name. The DNS server operates on the principle of caching, meaning it stores the responses it receives for a certain period of time. This caching mechanism helps to improve the efficiency of DNS resolution and reduce the load on the DNS infrastructure by preventing the repetitive querying of the same domain names. In summary, the DNS server acts as a crucial intermediary in the network by translating human-readable domain names into their corresponding IP addresses, allowing users to access resources on the internet using easily remembered names. Through its distributed database and hierarchical resolution process, the DNS server plays a key role in ensuring smooth and efficient communication in the interconnected world of networking.

Dark Fiber

Dark fiber refers to unused or unlit fiber optic cables that have been laid but are not currently being utilized for data transmission. These fiber optic cables are typically installed by telecommunication companies or internet service providers, often in anticipation of future need or as part of network expansion plans. Dark fiber allows for the potential of high-speed data transmission since it offers virtually unlimited bandwidth. Unlike traditional lit fiber, which is actively used to transmit data, dark fiber is "dark" because it is not carrying any data signals. It is essentially a blank canvas waiting to be activated.

Darknet

Darknet refers to a private network that is intentionally isolated from the public internet and is designed to provide anonymity and privacy to its users. It is a subset of the deep web, which consists of all the web pages that are not indexed by search engines. Darknet is accessed using special software and configurations that allow users to remain anonymous by encrypting their communications and obfuscating their IP addresses. The primary objective of the darknet is to create a hidden and secure environment where individuals can share information and engage in activities without being monitored or traced by government agencies, internet service providers, or other potential adversaries. It serves as a haven for users who seek privacy, including whistleblowers, activists, journalists, and individuals engaged in illegal or controversial activities.

Data Breach

A data breach is a security incident where sensitive, protected, or confidential data is accessed, viewed, or stolen without authorization. It involves the unauthorized access to data stored on various digital platforms or networks, leading to its potential misuse, exposure, or compromise. Data breaches typically occur when attackers exploit vulnerabilities in a network's security infrastructure, allowing them to gain unauthorized access to the data. This can happen through various means, such as hacking, social engineering, or the accidental disclosure of information. Once the attackers gain access, they can extract or copy sensitive data, including personal information, financial records, or intellectual property. The stolen data can be used for various malicious purposes, including identity theft, financial fraud, blackmail, or even corporate espionage. Data breaches pose significant risks to individuals, businesses, and organizations. They can result in financial losses, reputational damage, legal consequences, and an erosion of trust. The impacts of a data breach can be far-reaching, affecting not only the targeted entity but also its customers, partners, and stakeholders. To mitigate the risk of data breaches, organizations must implement robust security measures. These may include regular vulnerability assessments and penetration testing, the use of strong encryption techniques, multi-factor authentication, limiting access privileges, and continuous monitoring of network activity. In the event of a data breach, organizations must respond promptly and effectively. This typically involves identifying the breach, containing the incident to prevent further damage, conducting a thorough investigation, notifying affected individuals or entities, and taking appropriate measures to prevent similar incidents in the future. In conclusion, a data breach refers to the unauthorized access, viewing, or theft of sensitive data, often resulting from security vulnerabilities in a network. It can have severe consequences for individuals, businesses, and organizations, emphasizing the importance of robust security measures and proper incident response protocols.

Data Center Cooling

Data center cooling refers to the process of maintaining the optimal temperature and humidity levels within a data center environment to ensure that the networking equipment and servers operate efficiently and avoid any overheating issues. Cooling in a data center is crucial as the networking equipment generates heat during its normal operation. The heat generated can cause damage to the equipment and result in system failures and downtime if not properly controlled. Therefore, effective cooling strategies are implemented to remove the heat and maintain a suitable environment.

Data Center Design

A data center design refers to the strategic and systematic planning of a physical infrastructure that houses and supports a network's computing and storage resources. It involves the careful consideration of various factors, such as layout, power supply, cooling, security, scalability, and redundancy, to ensure optimal performance, reliability, and efficiency of the network operations. A well-designed data center provides a centralized location for the management, storage, and processing of data, applications, and services. It serves as the nerve center of a network, encompassing all the necessary hardware, software, and networking components that facilitate the smooth functioning of an organization's IT infrastructure.

Data Center Efficiency

Data center efficiency refers to the measure of how effectively and efficiently a data center is able to use its resources to deliver computing services while minimizing energy consumption and costs. In the context of networking, data center efficiency focuses on optimizing the performance and energy usage of the networking infrastructure within the data center. In order to achieve high levels of efficiency, data centers must implement various strategies and technologies. These may include: 1. Virtualization: By virtualizing the network infrastructure, data centers can consolidate network resources, reduce the number of physical devices, and optimize the utilization of available bandwidth. 2. Traffic engineering: Through the use of sophisticated routing algorithms, data centers can intelligently distribute network traffic, ensuring that the network resources are utilized in an efficient manner. This helps to avoid congestion and minimizes the energy consumption of the network devices. 3. Power management: Data centers can employ power management techniques such as dynamic voltage scaling and frequency scaling to optimize the energy usage of networking equipment. By dynamically adjusting the power consumption based on the current network load, unnecessary energy wastage can be avoided. 4. Cooling and ventilation: Efficient cooling and ventilation systems are crucial for maintaining optimal operating conditions within the data center. By implementing advanced cooling techniques and airflow management strategies, data centers can minimize energy consumption and ensure the proper functioning of networking equipment. Ultimately, data center efficiency in networking is about finding the right balance between performance, resource utilization, and energy consumption. By employing the aforementioned strategies, data centers can enhance their networking infrastructure's efficiency, reduce costs, and minimize their environmental footprint.

Data Center Interconnect (DCI)

Data Center Interconnect (DCI) refers to the networking technology and architecture used to connect multiple data centers, allowing them to function as a unified and scalable infrastructure. DCI enables data centers to exchange information, share resources, and provide high-performance services to end-users. In the context of networking, DCI involves the establishment of reliable and secure connections between data centers, typically over long distances. This enables seamless data transfer and communication between geographically dispersed data centers, allowing them to act as a single entity rather than isolated entities.

Data Center Migration

Data Center Migration refers to the process of transferring an existing data center infrastructure, including servers, storage devices, and networking equipment, from one location to another. This relocation is usually done to improve efficiency, enhance security, or accommodate business growth. During a data center migration, several tasks need to be carefully planned and executed to ensure minimal disruption to the business operations. These tasks include: 1. Assessment and Planning: This involves conducting a comprehensive analysis of the current data center infrastructure, identifying any gaps or inefficiencies, and developing a detailed migration plan. The plan should include a timeline, budget, and resources required for the migration. 2. Network Design and Configuration: Before moving the data center, the new location needs to be prepared with appropriate networking infrastructure. This may involve configuring routers, switches, firewalls, and other network devices to support the anticipated workload and ensure seamless connectivity. 3. Data Migration: This is one of the critical steps in the process, which involves transferring all the data and applications from the old data center to the new one. The data migration can be a complex and time-consuming task, requiring careful planning to ensure data integrity and minimal downtime. 4. Testing and Validation: Once the data migration is complete, thorough testing and validation should be conducted to ensure that all systems are functioning correctly in the new environment. This includes testing the network connectivity, application performance, and security measures. 5. Decommissioning the old data center: After the successful migration and validation, the old data center infrastructure needs to be decommissioned properly. This involves shutting down the servers, removing the networking equipment, and disposing of any obsolete or redundant hardware. In summary, data center migration is a complex process that involves the relocation of an existing data center infrastructure. Proper planning, network configuration, data migration, testing, and decommissioning are essential to ensure a smooth and successful migration with minimal disruptions to business operations.

Data Center Network Fabric

Data Center Network Fabric refers to the underlying infrastructure that connects computing resources, such as servers, storage devices, and networking devices, in a data center. It is a high-performance, reliable, and scalable network architecture designed to meet the demands of modern data centers. The fabric is built using a combination of switches, routers, and other network devices interconnected through high-speed links. It provides a fully meshed, non-blocking, and low-latency network environment, enabling efficient communication between various components within the data center. The main objective of a data center network fabric is to ensure seamless and uninterrupted connectivity between servers and storage devices, facilitating rapid data transfer and access. It creates a unified and flexible network, facilitating the movement and sharing of data across the data center. Data traffic is efficiently routed within the fabric, avoiding congestion and optimizing performance. Data center network fabrics are typically built using a hierarchical architecture, comprising three layers: the access layer, the aggregation layer, and the core layer. The access layer connects servers and storage devices, providing access to the fabric. The aggregation layer aggregates traffic from multiple access layer switches and provides connectivity to the core layer. The core layer is responsible for high-speed data transfer and interconnection between different segments of the data center. In addition to hierarchical architecture, data center network fabrics often incorporate advanced features such as virtualization, software-defined networking (SDN), and automation. These features enable greater agility, scalability, and manageability of the network fabric, as well as support for emerging technologies like cloud computing and virtualization. In conclusion, a data center network fabric is the foundational network infrastructure in a data center, providing high-performance, reliable, and scalable connectivity between computing resources. It is an essential component in modern data centers, enabling efficient data transfer, seamless communication, and optimal utilization of resources.

Data Center Networking

Data Center Networking refers to the network infrastructure and architecture that connects various computing resources within a data center facility. It involves the design, implementation, and management of a robust and reliable network to support the operations and communications requirements of the data center. Typically, a data center comprises a large number of servers, storage devices, switches, routers, and other networking equipment, all interconnected through a complex network. The primary goal of data center networking is to provide high-performance, low-latency, and scalable connectivity between these components to ensure efficient data transfer and communication. Data center networking involves several key components and technologies. Firstly, switches and routers are used to connect different devices within the data center and form the backbone of the network infrastructure. These devices facilitate the flow of data packets and enable communication between servers, storage systems, and other network devices. In addition to switches and routers, data center networking can also utilize load balancers, which distribute network traffic across multiple servers to ensure optimal performance and prevent overload on any single server. Firewalls and security devices are implemented to protect the data center network from unauthorized access and cyber threats. Virtualization technologies are another crucial aspect of data center networking. By virtualizing network resources, such as virtual switches and virtual LANs, data centers can achieve better resource utilization, improved scalability, and enhanced flexibility in managing network configurations. Furthermore, data center networking often incorporates high-speed interconnect technologies, such as InfiniBand or Ethernet, to enable fast and efficient data transfer between servers and storage systems. These technologies enhance overall performance and reduce latency, particularly in scenarios involving high-volume data processing and storage operations. Overall, data center networking plays a vital role in ensuring the smooth operation and connectivity of computing resources within a data center facility. It enables efficient data transfer, communication, and resource sharing, ultimately contributing to the overall performance and reliability of the data center infrastructure.

Data Center Redundancy

Data center redundancy refers to the practice of building multiple physical infrastructure components within a network to ensure high availability and reliability of critical services. The redundancy measures are put in place to minimize the risk of system failure and to guarantee continued operation even in the event of a failure in one or more components. A redundant data center design typically includes redundant power sources, network connections, servers, storage devices, and cooling systems. These redundant components are interconnected and configured in such a way that if one component fails, another component automatically takes over without any disruption to the services provided by the data center.

Data Center Virtualization

Data center virtualization refers to the process of creating multiple virtual instances of data center resources, such as servers, storage, and networking components, using software technologies. It aims to optimize resource utilization, increase flexibility, and improve scalability in data center environments.In the context of networking, data center virtualization involves the abstraction and virtualization of network components, such as switches, routers, firewalls, and load balancers. These virtualized network elements are created and controlled by software-defined networking (SDN) technologies, enabling the creation of virtual networks that are decoupled from the physical network infrastructure.

Data Classification

Data Classification refers to the process of categorizing and organizing data based on certain predefined criteria in the context of networking. It involves assigning different labels or tags to data based on their characteristics or attributes, allowing for efficient storage, retrieval, and transmission of information within a network. Data classification plays a crucial role in networking as it enables the efficient management and control of data flow within and between networks. By classifying data, network administrators are able to prioritize traffic, allocate resources, and ensure appropriate access control mechanisms are in place. One common method of data classification in networking is based on the type of data being transmitted. This can include classifying data as text, images, audio, video, or any other multimedia format. By identifying the type of data, network devices can employ specific protocols and algorithms to optimize the transmission and storage. Another important aspect of data classification is based on the sensitivity or criticality of the information. This involves categorizing data as public, confidential, internal, or strictly private. By applying appropriate security measures and encryption algorithms, network administrators can protect sensitive data from unauthorized access or tampering. Furthermore, data classification allows for the implementation of Quality of Service (QoS) mechanisms within a network. By categorizing data based on priorities or importance, network devices can allocate resources accordingly, ensuring that critical applications or services receive higher bandwidth or lower latency. This ensures a smooth and uninterrupted experience for end users. In conclusion, data classification is an essential process in networking that involves categorizing data based on specific criteria such as type and sensitivity. By classifying data, network administrators can optimize resource allocation, implement security measures, and improve the overall efficiency of data transmission and storage within a network.

Data Encryption

Data encryption is a fundamental concept in networking that involves the conversion of plain, readable data into an encoded form known as ciphertext. This process aims to secure the confidentiality and integrity of information transmitted over a network, protecting it from unauthorized access or interception. Encryption algorithms leverage mathematical functions to perform cryptographic operations on data. These algorithms use a cryptographic key as a parameter to determine how the encryption and decryption processes are carried out. The key can be a string of characters or a long binary sequence, and its length directly impacts the strength of the encryption.

Data Exfiltration

Data Exfiltration, in the context of Networking, refers to the unauthorized removal or extraction of data from a network or a system. It involves the deliberate transfer of sensitive or valuable information to an external location by bypassing security measures and controls. Data exfiltration can occur through various methods, exploiting vulnerabilities and weaknesses in the network infrastructure. One common method is through the use of malware or malicious software. Attackers can inject malware into a system, allowing them to gain unauthorized access and subsequently extract data from the network. This can be done through various techniques, such as keylogging, where keystrokes are recorded and transmitted to the attacker, or through the use of spyware, which secretly collects and sends sensitive information. Another method of data exfiltration is through network protocols and communication channels. Attackers can exploit weaknesses in protocols and communication channels to intercept and capture data during transmission. For example, they may perform a man-in-the-middle attack, where they position themselves between the sender and receiver, intercepting and capturing the data being exchanged. Furthermore, data exfiltration can also occur through physical means. Attackers may physically gain access to a network or system and extract data directly through storage devices or by bypassing security measures. Additionally, insiders with authorized access can also facilitate data exfiltration by intentionally leaking or transferring sensitive information without proper authorization. Data exfiltration poses significant risks to organizations and individuals, as it can result in the exposure of sensitive information, such as personal data, financial information, or intellectual property. The consequences of data exfiltration can include financial loss, reputational damage, legal implications, and the compromise of individuals' privacy. To mitigate the risk of data exfiltration, organizations should implement robust security measures, such as firewalls, intrusion detection systems, and encryption protocols. Regular security audits and vulnerability assessments should be conducted to identify and address potential weaknesses in the network infrastructure. Additionally, employee awareness and training programs can help educate individuals about the risks of data exfiltration and promote responsible online behavior. In conclusion, data exfiltration refers to the unauthorized extraction of data from a network or system. It can occur through various methods, including malware, network protocols, physical access, and insider threats. Organizations should take proactive measures to protect against data exfiltration and minimize the potential impact of these security breaches.

Data Leakage Prevention (DLP)

Data Leakage Prevention (DLP) is a network security measure that aims to prevent unauthorized access, transmission, or storage of sensitive data within an organization's network. It is designed to detect and prevent the accidental or intentional leakage of data, such as confidential information, intellectual property, customer data, and financial records. By implementing DLP mechanisms, organizations can proactively monitor and control data flow across their network infrastructure. This helps in mitigating the risks associated with data breaches, compliance violations, and financial losses that can result from the unauthorized exposure of sensitive information.

Data Link Layer

The data link layer is a layer of the networking protocol stack that is responsible for the reliable transfer of data between two network nodes connected by a physical link. It ensures that data frames are transmitted error-free and in the order they were sent. At the data link layer, data is organized into frames, which consist of a header and a trailer. The header contains control information such as source and destination addresses, sequencing information, and error detection codes. The trailer contains error checking information, such as a cyclic redundancy check (CRC) or a checksum, that allows the receiving node to detect any transmission errors. The data link layer provides several key functions to ensure reliable data transfer. These functions include: 1. Framing: The data link layer encapsulates network layer packets into frames by adding a header and a trailer. This allows the receiving node to correctly identify the start and end of each data frame. 2. Error detection and correction: The data link layer includes error detection codes in the frame trailer, which allow the receiving node to detect and sometimes correct errors in the transmitted data. This ensures data integrity and reliability during transmission. 3. Flow control: The data link layer manages the flow of data between the sender and receiver to prevent data overload. It uses techniques such as stop-and-wait or sliding window protocols to control the rate of data transmission. 4. Access control: The data link layer is responsible for resolving conflicts that may arise when multiple nodes share the same physical link. It uses techniques such as carrier sense multiple access (CSMA) or token passing to ensure fair and efficient access to the network. Overall, the data link layer plays a crucial role in ensuring the smooth and reliable transfer of data over a physical link in a network. It establishes a logical communication channel between two network nodes and provides mechanisms for error detection, flow control, and access control. Without the data link layer, reliable communication between network devices would not be possible.

Data Loss

Data Loss refers to the unintentional or accidental loss of information or data stored in a computer system or transmitted over a network. It occurs when data becomes inaccessible, corrupted, or deleted due to various factors such as hardware failure, software issues, human error, or network disruptions. Hardware failures can lead to data loss when storage devices, such as hard drives or solid-state drives, malfunction or crash. Power outages, voltage surges, or physical damage to the hardware can result in the permanent loss of data. On the other hand, software issues like bugs, crashes, or software conflicts may cause data corruption or accidental deletion. Human error plays a significant role in data loss incidents. Accidentally formatting the wrong drive, deleting important files unintentionally, or mishandling storage media can result in irreversible data loss. Moreover, human actions can also introduce malware or viruses into a system, potentially causing data loss or damage. Network disruptions are another common cause of data loss. Interruptions in network connectivity, such as sudden disconnections or network failures, can lead to data packets being lost in transit. Incomplete data transfers or corrupted data packets can result in data loss, particularly in scenarios such as file downloads, cloud storage syncs, or database replication. Data loss prevention is crucial in networking to ensure the integrity, availability, and confidentiality of data. Implementing robust backup and recovery strategies, both locally and on remote servers or cloud platforms, helps mitigate the impact of data loss incidents. Regularly updating software and hardware, utilizing strong security measures, and training users on best practices for data handling are essential to reduce the risk of data loss.

Data Masking

Data masking is a technique used in networking to protect sensitive information from unauthorized access by obfuscating or replacing it with fake or partially anonymized data. It is primarily employed in data transmission over computer networks, where the risk of interception or unauthorized access is high. The purpose of data masking is to ensure the confidentiality and integrity of sensitive data while allowing it to be shared or transmitted over networks. By masking the original data, organizations can prevent unauthorized individuals or malicious software from accessing and exploiting sensitive information such as personally identifiable information (PII), financial data, or intellectual property.

Data Packet

A data packet is a unit of data that is transmitted over a network. It is the basic building block of network communication and encapsulates a piece of information along with control information required for transmission. The data packet consists of two main parts: the header and the payload. The header contains information about the packet itself, while the payload carries the actual data being transmitted. The header typically includes details such as the source and destination addresses, sequence number, and error-checking information. When data is sent over a network, it is divided into smaller, fixed-size packets to enable efficient transmission. These packets are then transmitted individually and reassembled at the receiving end to reconstruct the original data. This segmentation of data allows for improved reliability, as each packet can take its own route through the network and is less likely to be affected by network congestion or errors. Data packets are transmitted using various network protocols, such as Internet Protocol (IP) for communication over the internet. These protocols define the rules for how packets are formatted, addressed, transmitted, and routed in a network. Through these protocols, data packets can be exchanged between different devices, regardless of their underlying hardware or operating systems. As data packets travel through a network, they may pass through multiple intermediate devices such as routers, switches, and gateways. These devices examine the headers of the packets to determine the best path for forwarding them towards their destination. The process of packet switching ensures efficient and reliable transmission of data across the network.

Data Protection Officer (DPO)

A Data Protection Officer (DPO) is a designated person responsible for overseeing and ensuring the implementation of data protection policies and practices within an organization. The role of a DPO is central to ensuring compliance with data protection laws, regulations, and best practices. The primary responsibility of a DPO is to protect the rights and privacy of individuals by ensuring that their personal data is processed in a lawful and transparent manner. This involves providing guidance and advice to the organization's management and staff on data protection issues, as well as monitoring and auditing data processing activities to ensure compliance with applicable laws and regulations. In the context of networking, a DPO plays a crucial role in safeguarding the confidentiality, integrity, and availability of data transmitted and stored across networks. They are responsible for overseeing the implementation of technical and organizational measures to protect sensitive data from unauthorized access, disclosure, alteration, or destruction during transmission or storage. The DPO works closely with network administrators and security teams to identify potential vulnerabilities and threats to data security within the network infrastructure. They provide guidance on the implementation of appropriate security controls, such as encryption protocols, access controls, and intrusion detection systems, to mitigate these risks and ensure the confidentiality and integrity of data exchanged over the network. Furthermore, the DPO ensures that data protection principles, such as the minimization of data collection, purpose limitation, and data retention, are adhered to in the context of network operations. They also play a vital role in ensuring that individuals' rights, such as the right to be informed, right of access, and right to erasure, are respected and upheld within the network environment. In summary, a Data Protection Officer in the context of networking is a designated individual responsible for ensuring compliance with data protection laws and regulations, as well as safeguarding the security and privacy of data transmitted and stored across networks. They work closely with network administrators and security teams to implement and enforce data protection measures, as well as provide guidance and advice on data protection issues within the network infrastructure.

Data Retention Policy

A data retention policy in the context of networking refers to a formal set of guidelines and procedures implemented by an organization to govern the storage and management of data generated by network activities. It outlines the duration for which different types of data should be retained, as well as the methods and systems used for storing and disposing of data once it is no longer required. This policy is crucial for maintaining data integrity, preserving crucial information, and ensuring compliance with legal and regulatory requirements. By defining clear rules on data retention, organizations can minimize the risk of data loss, unauthorized access, and data breaches. Furthermore, it provides a framework for efficient data management, as it helps in identifying and discarding outdated or irrelevant data. The data retention policy typically categorizes data based on its sensitivity, legal obligations, and business needs. For instance, it may differentiate between personal identifiable information, financial records, and general operational data. Each category may have specific retention periods determined by factors such as applicable laws, industry regulations, and internal policies. Additionally, the policy may specify the formats in which data should be retained, whether in physical form or electronic records. Implementing a data retention policy involves various considerations. Organizations need to allocate appropriate storage resources to accommodate the required data volumes for the specified retention periods. They must also establish secure data backup and restoration processes to ensure data continuity and protection against loss or corruption. Ongoing monitoring and periodic audits should be conducted to verify compliance and identify any deviations or deficiencies in the retention process. Lastly, the data retention policy should include guidelines on data disposal, specifying methods for securely erasing or destroying data that has exceeded its retention period. This may involve utilizing data sanitization tools, physical destruction methods, or outsourcing data destruction services.

Data Retention

Data retention in the context of networking refers to the practice of storing and preserving data for a specified period of time. It involves capturing and maintaining data packets, logs, and various network-related information to meet regulatory requirements, ensure network security, and facilitate troubleshooting and analysis. Data retention is essential for many reasons. Firstly, it enables organizations to comply with legal and regulatory obligations. Certain industries, such as finance and healthcare, have specific guidelines and regulations that necessitate the retention of data for a specific duration. By retaining data, organizations can ensure they are prepared for potential audits and legal inquiries. Additionally, data retention plays a crucial role in network security. Storing data allows network administrators to identify and investigate security incidents, detect and prevent unauthorized access, and track any suspicious activities. It provides a historical record that can be utilized to analyze patterns, identify vulnerabilities, and enhance the overall security posture of the network. Furthermore, data retention assists in troubleshooting and diagnosing network issues. By preserving network-related data, administrators can analyze the captured information to identify the root causes of problems, resolve issues, and improve network performance. It enables them to trace network traffic, monitor the behavior of devices, and determine the sequence of events leading to a specific incident. While data retention is crucial, it also presents challenges. Storing large amounts of data requires significant storage capacity and resources. Organizations must carefully manage and prioritize the data they retain to ensure cost-effectiveness and compliance. Implementing robust backup and archival systems is essential to maintain data integrity and accessibility over time. In conclusion, data retention in networking refers to the practice of storing and preserving network-related data for regulatory compliance, security purposes, and troubleshooting. It enables organizations to meet legal requirements, enhance network security, and facilitate effective network management and analysis.

128

Data Security

Data security in the context of networking refers to the protection of digital information from unauthorized access, use, disclosure, alteration, or destruction during transmission and storage across interconnected devices and systems. It involves implementing measures to ensure the confidentiality, integrity, and availability of data to authorized individuals, while preventing unauthorized individuals from gaining access to or manipulating the data. Data security encompasses various techniques and protocols designed to safeguard data in diverse networking environments, such as local area networks (LANs), wide area networks (WANs), and the internet. These techniques aim to mitigate the risks and vulnerabilities associated with data breaches, hacking, malware, and other cyber threats that can compromise the sensitive information stored or transmitted over networks. Confidentiality is a crucial aspect of data security, as it ensures that only authorized individuals or entities can access specific information. Encryption plays a significant role in maintaining confidentiality by encoding data using cryptographic algorithms, making it unreadable to anyone without the decryption key. This technique is commonly employed in virtual private networks (VPNs) and secure socket layer/transport layer security (SSL/TLS) protocols to protect sensitive data transmitted over public networks. Data integrity involves maintaining the accuracy and consistency of data throughout its lifecycle. Various mechanisms, such as checksums and hash functions, are utilized to detect and prevent unauthorized modifications or tampering of data. These mechanisms enable the verification of data integrity by comparing calculated hashes or checksums with the original values. Availability ensures that authorized individuals can access the required data when needed. Measures like redundancy, fault tolerance, and backup systems are implemented to ensure uninterrupted access to data, even in the event of hardware failures, natural disasters, or malicious activities. Data security also involves implementing access control mechanisms, such as user authentication, authorization, and accountability, to regulate and monitor individuals' access to data. This includes the use of strong passwords, two-factor authentication, and implementing role-based access control (RBAC) policies. In conclusion, data security in networking refers to the protection of digital information from unauthorized access, use, disclosure, alteration, or destruction during transmission and storage across interconnected devices and systems. Its main objectives are to maintain confidentiality, integrity, and availability of data, while implementing access control mechanisms to ensure authorized access and prevent data breaches.

Data Sovereignty

Data sovereignty refers to the concept that data is subject to the laws and regulations of the country where it is collected, processed, or stored, and that control over that data resides with the country or organization that owns it. It emphasizes the rights and responsibilities of individuals, businesses, and governments in regards to the data they generate and handle. In the context of networking, data sovereignty encompasses the control and ownership of data as it flows across networks and is accessed by various devices and applications. It asserts that data should be protected, secured, and governed in accordance with the laws and regulations of the country or region where it originates or resides. Data sovereignty is an important consideration in today's interconnected world where information is consistently transmitted across international borders. It impacts businesses, governments, and individuals who rely on networks to communicate and access data. The concept recognizes the need for the preservation of privacy, security, and intellectual property rights. Governments around the world have implemented various laws and regulations to ensure data sovereignty. These laws can include requirements for local data storage, restrictions on data transfers outside of the country, and regulations governing the access and use of personal data. These measures are put in place to protect national security, individuals' rights, and the economic interests of the country. Data sovereignty also plays a crucial role in data protection. It allows countries and organizations to define their data protection standards and ensure that the data remains within their control. This is particularly important when dealing with sensitive and confidential information, such as personal or financial data. In summary, data sovereignty in the context of networking refers to the control, ownership, and protection of data as it traverses networks and is accessed by various devices and applications. It entails ensuring that data is subject to the laws and regulations of the country or region where it originates or resides, and that individuals, businesses, and governments maintain their rights and responsibilities regarding their data. This concept aims to protect privacy, security, and intellectual property rights, and to foster trust and accountability in the digital world.

Data Theft

Data theft refers to the unauthorized obtaining, copying, or storage of sensitive or confidential data from a computer or network without the consent or knowledge of the owner. In the context of networking, data theft occurs when an individual or entity gains unauthorized access to a network, system, or device and retrieves or manipulates sensitive information. This can include personal identifiable information (PII), financial data, intellectual property, trade secrets, or any other valuable data stored within the network. Data theft can be carried out through various methods, such as hacking, phishing, or social engineering. Hacking involves exploiting vulnerabilities in network security systems to gain access to data. Phishing involves tricking individuals into revealing their sensitive information by masquerading as a legitimate entity. Social engineering refers to manipulating individuals into providing access to their data through deceit or manipulation. The consequences of data theft can be severe and wide-ranging. By gaining unauthorized access to sensitive information, perpetrators can use the stolen data for financial gain, identity theft, corporate espionage, or other malicious activities. This can result in financial losses, reputational damage, loss of customer trust, legal implications, and regulatory non-compliance. To mitigate the risk of data theft, various security measures and best practices should be implemented. These may include strong authentication methods, encryption of sensitive data, regular security audits and updates, employee training on data security protocols, and robust firewall and network monitoring systems. Data theft is a constant threat in today's interconnected world. The increasing reliance on digital networks and the growing sophistication of cybercriminals make it essential for organizations and individuals to prioritize data security. By taking proactive steps to protect sensitive information and staying vigilant against evolving threats, the risk of data theft can be minimized, and the integrity of networks and systems can be preserved.

Data Wiping

Data wiping in the context of networking refers to the process of permanently erasing data from a storage device or media, rendering it unrecoverable. This process ensures that sensitive or confidential information cannot be accessed or retrieved, thereby protecting the privacy and security of both individuals and organizations. Data wiping involves overwriting the existing data on a storage device with zeros or random characters, making it extremely difficult or virtually impossible to recover the original data. This method is preferred over simply deleting files or formatting the storage device, as those methods only remove references to the data, rather than actually erasing it. The need for data wiping arises when a storage device is no longer needed or is being repurposed. This can include hard drives, solid-state drives (SSDs), USB flash drives, and other media. By securely wiping the data, organizations can comply with data privacy regulations and prevent unauthorized access to sensitive information. Data wiping can be performed using specialized software tools that overwrite the entire storage device multiple times. Government and data security standards often specify the number of times the data should be overwritten to ensure complete eradication. These tools usually provide different algorithms for overwriting data, each with varying levels of security and speed. The chosen algorithm should balance security requirements with practical considerations. Additionally, organizations may choose to physically destroy storage devices if data wiping is not sufficient. This entails physically shredding or incinerating the device to ensure that the data cannot be recovered. Overall, data wiping is a critical process in maintaining the confidentiality and privacy of data within a networking environment. By permanently erasing data from storage devices, organizations can protect sensitive information and prevent unauthorized access, thereby maintaining compliance with data privacy regulations and safeguarding the security of individuals and organizations alike.

Deep Packet Inspection (DPI)

Deep Packet Inspection (DPI) is a method of analyzing and examining the content and data of network packets at the application layer of the network protocol stack. It involves scrutinizing the entire packet, including both the header and payload, to gain insight into the type, source, and destination of the data being transmitted. By implementing DPI, network administrators and security analysts are able to inspect packet-level information and identify specific patterns or signatures within the data. This enables them to understand network traffic patterns, detect anomalies, and apply appropriate policies or actions to ensure network efficiency and security. DPI goes beyond traditional packet inspection techniques by employing advanced algorithms and deep analysis methods to understand the context and purpose of the data being transmitted. It allows for more granular visibility into network traffic, such as application-specific information, user behavior, and content characteristics. One of the primary benefits of DPI is its ability to facilitate network management and optimization. By inspecting and classifying packets based on their content, network administrators can gain valuable insights into the types of applications running on the network, the amount of bandwidth they consume, and the quality of service they require. This information can then be used to prioritize network resources, allocate bandwidth effectively, and ensure optimal performance for critical applications. In terms of security, DPI plays a crucial role in identifying and mitigating potential threats or malicious activities. By examining the content of packets, DPI can detect various forms of network attacks, such as intrusion attempts, malware propagation, and data exfiltration. It can also enforce security policies by filtering or blocking packets that violate predefined rules or signatures. However, the use of DPI has raised concerns over privacy and data protection, as it allows for deep inspection of sensitive user information. To address these concerns, organizations implementing DPI should ensure they have appropriate safeguards and policies in place to protect user privacy and comply with relevant laws and regulations.

Default Gateway

The default gateway is a fundamental concept in computer networking that refers to the IP address of the router or gateway device that connects a host computer or network to the internet or another network segment. In a computer network, devices such as computers, servers, printers, and other network-enabled devices communicate with each other using IP addresses. An IP address is a unique identifier assigned to each device on a network, allowing data to be sent and received between devices. However, when devices on a local network want to communicate with devices outside of their local network, such as accessing the internet or connecting to remote networks, they rely on a default gateway. The default gateway serves as the access point for traffic that needs to leave a local network. It acts as an intermediary between the local network and other networks. When a device on a local network wants to communicate with a device outside of its network, it sends the data packets to the default gateway. The default gateway then routes the packets to the appropriate destination, either within the same network or beyond, based on the destination IP address. For example, if a computer on a local network wants to access a website on the internet, it will send the request to the default gateway. The default gateway will examine the destination IP address of the website and determine the appropriate path for the request to be routed. It will pass the request to the next network device, such as an ISP's router, which will continue to route the request until it reaches its destination. Without a properly configured default gateway, devices on a local network would not be able to communicate with devices outside of their network. The default gateway plays a crucial role in enabling connectivity between multiple networks, allowing devices to access resources and services located beyond their immediate network.

Default Route

A default route, also known as the gateway of last resort, is a network route used by a router to forward traffic to an unspecified destination. It is typically used as a fallback option when no specific route is available for a given destination. In a computer network, routers are responsible for routing packets of data across different networks. They use routing tables to determine the most appropriate path for forwarding the packets. A routing table consists of a list of known destinations and the corresponding next hops or gateways through which the packets should be sent. When a router receives a packet, it first checks its routing table to find a matching specific route for the packet's destination. If a specific route is found, the router forwards the packet to the corresponding next hop. However, if no specific route is found, the router uses the default route to forward the packet. The default route is often represented by the IP address 0.0.0.0/0, which essentially means any destination. It acts as a catch-all route when the router has no other specific routes available. The default route is usually configured on the router connected to an Internet service provider (ISP), allowing it to handle traffic for any destination not explicitly defined in its routing table. By using a default route, routers can efficiently handle large numbers of packets without having to check each packet for a specific route. This simplifies and speeds up the routing process, particularly in situations where there are numerous possible destinations with no defined routes. It's worth noting that the use of a default route introduces some security risks. Since it forwards traffic to any destination, it can potentially be exploited by malicious actors to intercept or manipulate network traffic. Proper security measures, such as access control lists (ACLs) and firewalls, should be implemented to mitigate these risks.

Demilitarized Zone (DMZ)

A Demilitarized Zone (DMZ) is a segregated network zone that acts as a buffer between an organization's internal network and an external network, usually the internet. It is designed to enhance the security of an organization's network infrastructure by isolating potentially vulnerable systems from direct exposure to external threats. A DMZ is typically implemented using a combination of firewalls, routers, and various security mechanisms to create a secure and controlled environment. It is often used to host internet-facing services, such as web servers, email servers, or public-facing applications, while keeping the internal network protected from potential attacks.

Denial Of Inventory (DoI) Attack

A Denial of Inventory (DoI) attack refers to a type of cybersecurity attack that targets the availability and reliability of network resources by exploiting vulnerabilities in an organization's inventory management system. This attack aims to disrupt the normal functioning of a network by depleting or exhausting the inventory resources, rendering the system unavailable to legitimate users. In the context of networking, inventory management systems play a crucial role in tracking and maintaining the availability of network resources such as IP addresses, domain names, server capacity, and other critical infrastructure components. These systems help organizations effectively allocate, monitor, and control the utilization of network resources to ensure smooth network operations. A DoI attack involves malicious actors intentionally targeting an organization's inventory management system to disrupt network operations. By exploiting vulnerabilities in the system, attackers can manipulate or exhaust the available inventory, leading to widespread network service outages and denying access to legitimate users. One common method used in a DoI attack is to flood the inventory management system with a high volume of requests or transactions, overwhelming the system's capacity to handle the load. This flood of requests leads to resource depletion and may cause system delays, timeouts, or crashes, effectively rendering the network resources temporarily or permanently unavailable. Another approach in a DoI attack is to exploit vulnerabilities within the inventory management system itself. Attackers may target weaknesses such as insecure authentication mechanisms, insufficient access controls, or lack of input validation. By exploiting these vulnerabilities, attackers can gain unauthorized access to the inventory management system, manipulate inventory data, or disrupt its normal operation. The consequences of a successful DoI attack can be severe for organizations relying on highly available network resources. These attacks can lead to significant financial losses, disrupt business operations, damage reputation, and result in customer dissatisfaction. Additionally, a successful DoI attack can serve as a diversion for other malicious activities, allowing attackers to exploit the resulting chaos and compromise other parts of the network infrastructure.

Denial Of Inventory (DoI)

Denial of Inventory (DoI) refers to a type of attack in the context of networking where an attacker aims to disrupt the availability and functionality of inventory systems within a network. Inventory systems are crucial components of a network as they track and manage various resources, such as hardware, software, and equipment. In a DoI attack, the attacker targets the inventory system by overwhelming it with an excessive amount of data or requests, causing it to become unresponsive or crash. This denies legitimate users or network administrators access to crucial information about the inventory, hindering their ability to effectively manage and utilize network resources.

Denial Of Service (DoS) Attack

A Denial of Service (DoS) attack is a malicious attempt to disrupt the normal functioning of a

132

network, service, or website by overwhelming it with a flood of illegitimate requests. The aim of a DoS attack is to render the targeted network or service incapable of providing its intended functionality to legitimate users. During a DoS attack, the attacker uses various techniques to consume the target's vital resources such as bandwidth, processing power, or memory, causing it to become overloaded and unable to handle legitimate user requests. This results in degradation or complete unavailability of the targeted network, service, or website.

Denial Of Service (DoS)

A Denial of Service (DoS) attack is a type of cyber attack that aims to disrupt or limit the availability of network resources, services, or devices to legitimate users. This attack typically involves overwhelming the target system or network with an excessive amount of traffic or requests, rendering it incapable of handling legitimate traffic and causing services to become unavailable. In a DoS attack, the attacker exploits vulnerabilities in the target network or system to flood it with malicious traffic or requests. This flood of traffic consumes the available network bandwidth, processing power, or memory, thereby exhausting the resources and making it impossible for legitimate users to access the services. The primary goal of a DoS attack is to disrupt the functioning of the targeted network or system and prevent it from serving its intended purpose.

Denial-Of-Service (DoS) Attack

A Denial-of-Service (DoS) attack refers to the deliberate and malicious attempt to disrupt the normal functioning of a computer network, service, or website by overwhelming it with a flood of illegitimate network traffic or resource requests. The goal of a DoS attack is to render the targeted network or service unavailable to its intended users temporarily or indefinitely. In a DoS attack, the attacker typically exploits vulnerabilities in the target's network infrastructure or applications in order to flood the network with an excessive amount of data or resource requests. This flood of traffic overwhelms the target's resources such as bandwidth, processing power, or memory, making it unable to respond to legitimate user requests effectively. As a result, the targeted network or service becomes slow, unresponsive, or completely inaccessible. There are different types of DoS attacks that can be employed, including: - Ping flood attack: The attacker sends a large number of ICMP echo requests (pings) to the target, overwhelming its network and causing it to become unresponsive. - SYN flood attack: The attacker exploits the three-way handshake process of the Transmission Control Protocol (TCP) to flood the target with a high volume of TCP SYN requests, exhausting its available network resources. - UDP flood attack: The attacker sends a flood of User Datagram Protocol (UDP) packets to the target, consuming its network bandwidth and rendering it incapable of handling legitimate traffic. - HTTP flood attack: The attacker sends a massive number of HTTP requests to a web server, saturating its resources and making the website inaccessible to legitimate users. DoS attacks can have severe consequences for businesses and organizations, leading to financial losses, damaged reputation, and disruption of critical services. To mitigate the impact of DoS attacks, network administrators can employ various defense mechanisms such as firewalls, intrusion detection systems, load balancing, and traffic filtering to identify and block malicious traffic before it reaches the target. In summary, a Denial-of-Service (DoS) attack is a deliberate assault on a computer network or service that aims to overwhelm its resources and render it inaccessible to legitimate users. Such attacks exploit vulnerabilities in network infrastructure or applications, flooding the target with excessive traffic or requests and causing disruption to normal operations.

DiffServ (Differential Services)

DiffServ (Differential Services) is a network architecture that provides quality of service (QoS) differentiation for different types of network traffic. It is designed to prioritize and manage different types of network traffic based on their requirements and importance, ensuring optimal performance and resource utilization. In the traditional best-effort internet, all packets are treated equally and given the same priority, resulting in a lack of prioritization for different types of traffic. This can lead to congestion, delays, and packet loss, particularly for real-time or high-priority applications such as voice and video streaming. DiffServ addresses these issues by classifying network traffic into different classes, each with its own set of rules and priorities. These classes are defined based on the perceived importance and requirements of the traffic, such as real-time

133

applications, interactive applications, and bulk data transfers. DiffServ employs the use of Differentiated Services Code Point (DSCP) values in the IP header to mark packets belonging to different classes. This marking allows network devices, such as routers and switches, to identify and prioritize packets accordingly. Based on the defined classes and DSCP values, network devices can implement various QoS mechanisms to ensure the desired level of service for each class. These mechanisms include traffic shaping, traffic policing, and queuing algorithms. With DiffServ, network administrators have the flexibility to define and enforce policies that align with their network requirements and bandwidth availability. Different types of traffic can be given different levels of priority, guaranteeing the necessary bandwidth and resources for critical applications while efficiently utilizing network resources. Overall, DiffServ provides a scalable and efficient solution for managing network traffic, allowing for the differentiation and prioritization of different types of traffic based on their specific requirements and importance. By prioritizing critical applications and managing network congestion, DiffServ helps ensure optimal performance and user experience in modern networks.

Digital Certificate

A digital certificate, in the context of networking, is a cryptographic document that is used to verify the authenticity and integrity of data transmitted over a network. It serves as a form of identification for individuals, organizations, or devices that are communicating with each other in a secure manner. A digital certificate is issued by a trusted third party, known as a Certificate Authority (CA). The CA acts as a trusted intermediary that vouches for the identity of the entity to whom the certificate is issued. It ensures that the information contained in the certificate is accurate and reliable. The digital certificate contains several important pieces of information. Firstly, it includes the identity of the entity to whom the certificate is issued, which is typically represented by a unique domain name or an IP address. Secondly, it includes the public key of the entity, which is used for encryption and verification purposes. Lastly, it includes the digital signature of the CA, which ensures the integrity of the certificate itself. When two entities communicate over a network, they can use digital certificates to establish a secure connection. During the connection establishment process, the server presents its digital certificate to the client. The client then validates the certificate by checking its digital signature and verifying it against the CA's public key. If the certificate is valid, the client can trust the identity of the server and proceed with the secure communication. Digital certificates play a crucial role in ensuring the security of online transactions, such as e-commerce and online banking. They provide a means of verifying the authenticity of websites and protecting sensitive information, such as credit card numbers and personal data, from unauthorized access or tampering.

Digital Forensics

Digital forensics, in the context of networking, refers to the process of collecting, analyzing, and preserving digital evidence to investigate and prevent cybercrime or network security incidents. It involves the application of forensic techniques and tools to extract and interpret data from various digital devices and network sources. The main objective of digital forensics is to reconstruct the events that occurred in a networked environment, identify the individuals or entities involved, and provide evidence that can be used in legal and administrative proceedings. This field is crucial in today's digital age, as cybercrimes continue to rise and pose significant threats to individuals, organizations, and even national security. The process of digital forensics typically involves several stages. The first stage is the identification and preservation of evidence, where network administrators or forensic experts ensure that relevant data and network logs are collected and protected from alteration or destruction. This step is critical to maintain the integrity and admissibility of the evidence in court. The next stage is the examination and analysis of the collected data. This involves using specialized tools and techniques to retrieve and interpret information from network logs, system files, databases, and other digital evidence sources. The goal is to uncover any malicious activities, unauthorized access attempts, or security breaches that may have occurred in the network. Once the analysis is complete, the findings are documented in a report that summarizes the evidence, methodology, and conclusions. This report can be used by law enforcement agencies, legal professionals, or internal security teams to support investigations, legal proceedings, or network security improvement efforts. Digital forensics also plays a significant role in incident response and network security management. By analyzing digital evidence, organizations can determine the root causes of security incidents, identify vulnerabilities, and develop effective countermeasures to prevent future attacks. In conclusion, digital forensics in the context of networking is a multidisciplinary field that combines elements of computer science, law enforcement, and legal expertise. It is essential for investigating cybercrimes, preserving evidence, and enhancing network security. By following a systematic and rigorous approach, digital forensic experts can provide valuable insights and support to protect networks from malicious activities and ensure a safe online environment.

Digital Identity

A digital identity refers to the unique information associated with an individual or entity on the internet or in a computer network. It is used to authenticate and verify the identity of users and establish their online presence. Digital identities are created and managed through the use of personal data, such as usernames, passwords, biometric information, and various electronic identification tokens. In networking, digital identities play a crucial role in ensuring secure and authorized access to network resources. They enable individuals to establish a verifiable identity within a network and grant or restrict access privileges based on their assigned digital identity. Digital identities also facilitate the exchange of information, transactions, and interactions between network participants, such as users, applications, and systems.

Digital Signature

A digital signature is a cryptographic technique used in networking to verify the authenticity and integrity of digital data. It provides a way to ensure that the transmitted data is unaltered and came from the expected source. When data is sent over a network, there is a risk that it may be intercepted or tampered with by unauthorized individuals. A digital signature helps mitigate this risk by adding a unique identifier to the data packet. This identifier, known as the digital signature, can be used to verify that the data has not been modified during transmission. A digital signature is created using a private key and a hashing algorithm. The private key is a secret key known only to the sender, while the hashing algorithm is a mathematical function that produces a fixed-size string of characters from the input data. The hashing algorithm ensures that even a small change in the input data will result in a completely different output. To create a digital signature, the sender first calculates the hash value of the data using the hashing algorithm. The sender then encrypts this hash value using their private key. The resulting encrypted hash value, along with the original data, is sent to the receiver. Upon receiving the data and digital signature, the receiver can verify the authenticity and integrity of the data by performing the following steps: 1. Decrypt the digital signature using the sender's public key, which is freely available to anyone. 2. Calculate the hash value of the received data using the same hashing algorithm used by the sender. 3. Compare the decrypted digital signature with the calculated hash value. If they match, it means that the data has not been tampered with during transmission, and it originated from the expected sender. In summary, a digital signature provides a way to verify the authenticity and integrity of digital data in networking. It ensures that the transmitted data has not been modified and comes from the expected source, helping to maintain data security and trust in online communications.

Directory Traversal Attack

A directory traversal attack, also known as path traversal or directory climbing, is a type of web application vulnerability that allows an attacker to access files and directories that are stored outside the web server's defined root directory. This attack takes advantage of improper handling of user input by the server, usually by not properly sanitizing user-supplied data. The attack begins when an attacker submits input that includes characters that have special meaning within web URLs, such as ".." or "../". These characters are used to traverse directories and access files that are placed in parent directories or arbitrary locations outside the root directory. By exploiting this vulnerability, the attacker gains unauthorized access to sensitive information, including configuration files, code, and even system files. For example, consider a vulnerable web application that allows users to download files by specifying the file name in the URL. The server-side code might concatenate the user-supplied file name with a base directory path to construct the complete file path. However, if the application does not properly validate and sanitize the file name, an attacker can manipulate the input and include "../" sequences to traverse directories. By repeatedly adding "../" and specifying file names, an attacker could eventually reach directories and files that should not be accessible. This might include access to password files, customer databases, or other sensitive information. The attacker can then download, modify, or delete these files, potentially leading to further compromise of the system or unauthorized access to valuable data.

Distributed Computing

Distributed computing refers to the use of multiple computers or servers, connected through a network, to solve complex computational problems or perform tasks that would be difficult or impossible for a single computer to handle. It involves the distribution of workload, data, and resources across these connected computers to improve efficiency, speed, and reliability. In a distributed computing system, each computer or server is referred to as a node, and each node has its own processing power, memory, and storage capabilities. These nodes communicate with each other using network protocols, allowing them to work together in a coordinated manner. One of the key advantages of distributed computing is parallelism. By dividing a task into smaller sub-tasks and distributing them across multiple nodes, parallel processing can be achieved, leading to faster execution and increased productivity. This is particularly beneficial for computationally intensive tasks, such as scientific simulations, big data processing, or rendering graphics in video games. Another important aspect of distributed computing is fault tolerance. Since the workload and data are distributed across multiple nodes, the failure of one or a few nodes does not cause a complete system failure. The system can continue to function using the remaining nodes, ensuring high availability and reliability. Distributed computing also allows for scalability. As the workload or data size increases, new nodes can be added to the system to handle the additional load. This scalability feature makes distributed computing suitable for handling large-scale projects or accommodating fluctuating workloads. Various techniques and algorithms are used to coordinate and manage the distributed computing system. These include task scheduling algorithms, load balancing techniques, data replication strategies, and fault detection and recovery mechanisms. Additionally, distributed file systems and distributed databases are commonly used to efficiently store and access data across the distributed system. Overall, distributed computing plays a crucial role in modern networked environments, enabling the efficient utilization of resources, improved performance, fault tolerance, and scalability. It has become an essential paradigm in the field of networking, supporting a wide range of applications and services, from cloud computing and distributed artificial intelligence to distributed data processing and scientific research.

Distributed Denial-Of-Service (DDoS) Attack

A Distributed Denial-of-Service (DDoS) Attack is a type of cyber attack that disrupts and hinders the availability of a targeted computer network or service by overwhelming it with a flood of illegitimate requests or excessive traffic. Unlike a regular Denial-of-Service (DoS) attack, a DDoS attack is carried out using multiple sources, often a large number of compromised computers, known as "bots" or "zombies." These sources are typically part of a botnet, a network of compromised computers controlled remotely by an attacker. The motive behind a DDoS attack can vary, ranging from vandalism and revenge to financial gain or political activism. The attack is executed by sending an enormous volume of traffic to a target, such as a website or online service, with the aim to consume all available resources or exhaust the network infrastructure's capacity. By doing so, the legitimate users are denied access to the intended service, causing significant disruption and potential financial losses for the targeted organization. DDoS attacks can utilize various techniques to flood the targeted network or service. Some common methods include: - SYN Flood: An attacker exploits the TCP three-way handshake by sending a high volume of SYN requests, overwhelming the target's capacity to respond. - UDP Flood: The attacker sends a large number of User Datagram Protocol (UDP) packets to a specific port on the target, saturating the network and consuming server resources. - ICMP Flood: The attacker exploits the Internet Control Message Protocol (ICMP) by flooding the target with "ping" requests, causing network congestion or device performance degradation. Preventing and mitigating DDoS attacks pose significant challenges due to their distributed nature. This requires implementing effective network security measures, such as firewall rules, intrusion prevention systems (IPS), and anomaly detection mechanisms. Additionally, organizations may employ traffic analysis tools and content delivery networks (CDNs) to absorb and filter malicious traffic, effectively reducing the impact of DDoS attacks. Overall, DDoS attacks are a persistent threat to network availability and can cause severe disruptions. Implementing robust security measures and staying vigilant against emerging attack techniques are crucial to defend against these malicious activities.

Distributed Firewall

A distributed firewall is a network security solution that is implemented across multiple network devices to protect the entire network infrastructure from unauthorized access and malicious activities. It consists of a distributed set of firewall instances that are deployed at various points within the network, effectively creating a security perimeter. The primary function of a distributed firewall is to enforce access control policies by examining and filtering network traffic. It inspects incoming and outgoing packets at the network layer and applies predefined rules or policies to determine whether to block or allow the traffic. By implementing a distributed firewall, organizations can establish a consistent and unified security policy across the network, ensuring that all traffic is subjected to the same level of scrutiny. One of the key advantages of a distributed firewall is its ability to handle high volumes of network traffic while maintaining performance and scalability. By distributing the firewall functionality across multiple devices, it can effectively handle the increased load without becoming a bottleneck. This is particularly important in large-scale networks where the volume of traffic can be substantial. Another benefit of a distributed firewall is its ability to provide granular control over network traffic. It allows organizations to define specific rules and policies based on various parameters such as source IP addresses, destination IP addresses, port numbers, protocols, and application signatures. This level of granularity enables organizations to tailor their security policies to meet their specific needs and mitigate risks effectively. Furthermore, a distributed firewall enhances network resilience by providing redundancy and fault tolerance. In the event of a failure or outage in one device, the traffic can be automatically rerouted through alternate paths, ensuring that network connectivity and security are not compromised. In conclusion, a distributed firewall is a robust network security solution that utilizes multiple instances of firewalls deployed across the network to protect against unauthorized access and malicious activities. It offers high performance, scalability, granular control, and network resilience, making it a crucial component of a comprehensive network security strategy.

Domain Name Registrar

A Domain Name Registrar is a type of organization that manages the reservation of internet domain names. It is responsible for maintaining a central database of registered domain names and their associated information. The main function of a registrar is to facilitate the registration process for individuals or businesses who want to acquire a domain name for their website or online presence. When someone wants to register a domain name, they typically go through a domain name registrar. The registrar acts as an intermediary between the domain name registrant (the person or organization registering the domain) and the central authority responsible for managing domain names, usually a domain name registry or a domain name system (DNS) operator. During the registration process, the registrar collects the necessary information from the registrant, such as their name, contact details, and the desired domain name. The registrar then submits this information to the domain name registry for verification and inclusion in the central database. If the domain name is available and meets the necessary requirements, it is registered and becomes active for the registrant to use. In addition to registration, domain name registrars also offer services such as domain name transfer, renewal, and management. They may provide tools and interfaces for registrants to modify their registered domain's DNS settings, update contact information, or set up additional services like email forwarding or domain redirects. Domain name registrars play a crucial role in the functioning of the internet by ensuring the uniqueness and accessibility of domain names. They help individuals and businesses establish their online presence by providing a straightforward and streamlined process for acquiring and managing domain names. By maintaining the central database of domain names, registrars enable the proper functioning of the DNS, allowing internet users to access websites using their memorable and recognizable domain names.

Domain Name System (DNS)

The Domain Name System (DNS) is a decentralized naming system for computers, services, or any resource connected to the internet or a private network. It translates domain names, which are easily recognizable and memorable strings like "example.com," into the numerical IP addresses that computers use to identify and communicate with each other. DNS plays a crucial role in networking by providing a hierarchical structure that allows for the efficient and organized management of domain names. The system is designed to be distributed, meaning there is no centralized authority responsible for maintaining the entire DNS database. Instead, multiple DNS servers across the internet work together to resolve domain name queries. When a user enters a domain name into their web browser or other network application, the DNS acts as a translator between human-readable domain names and machine-readable IP addresses. It starts with the user's device sending a DNS query to their configured DNS resolver, which can be either provided by their internet service provider or a third-party DNS resolver. The resolver then forwards the query to a series of DNS servers, starting from the root DNS servers. These root servers have information about the top-level domains like .com, .org, etc., and they direct the resolver to the authoritative DNS servers responsible for the specific domain being queried. The authoritative servers then return the IP address associated with the requested domain name back to the resolver, which, in turn, returns it to the user's device. DNS not only translates domain names to IP addresses but also supports other types of records called Resource Records (RRs), such as mail exchange (MX) records for email routing, name server (NS) records for indicating the authoritative servers for a domain, and more. These records provide additional information related to the domain and its services. In summary, the Domain Name System is a critical component of networking that translates domain names to IP addresses and enables users to access resources on the internet in a more user-friendly and convenient manner.

Domain Name System Security Extensions (DNSSEC)

Domain Name System Security Extensions (DNSSEC) is a set of security protocols that aim to enhance the security and integrity of the Domain Name System (DNS). DNSSEC adds an extra layer of protection by digitally signing DNS data to verify its authenticity, preventing unauthorized modifications and unauthorized access to DNS information. Traditionally, DNS has been vulnerable to various threats, such as DNS cache poisoning, man-in-the-middle attacks, and DNS spoofing. These attacks can lead to the rerouting of internet traffic, redirection to malicious websites, or interception of sensitive information. DNSSEC mitigates these risks by using cryptographic signatures to provide a trustworthy way to verify DNS data.

Domain Name

A domain name is a unique alphanumeric string that is used to identify a specific network or website on the internet. It serves as the address or location where users can access the network or website. Domain names are an essential component of the Domain Name System (DNS), which enables the translation of domain names into IP addresses. Instead of remembering complex IP addresses, users can simply enter a domain name, and the DNS will map it to the corresponding IP address.

Dynamic Host Configuration Protocol (DHCP)

Dynamic Host Configuration Protocol (DHCP) is a networking protocol that enables network administrators to centrally manage and automate the assignment of IP addresses and other related network configuration parameters to devices on a network. It provides a standardized way for devices to obtain IP addresses, subnet masks, default gateways, and other network configuration information necessary for communication within a network. With DHCP, network administrators can ensure that devices on a network are assigned unique IP addresses without the need for manual assignment. This eliminates the possibility of IP address conflicts and simplifies the management of IP address assignments. DHCP operates on a client-server model, where DHCP servers are responsible for assigning and managing IP addresses, and DHCP clients request and receive address configuration information. When a device connects to a network, it sends out a DHCP Discover message to discover available DHCP servers on the network. DHCP servers then respond with a DHCP Offer, providing the device with an available IP address and other network configuration options. The device then selects one of the offered configurations and sends a DHCP Request message to the chosen DHCP server. The DHCP server receives the DHCP Request and sends a DHCP Acknowledge message to confirm the assignment of the IP address and other configuration parameters to the device. The device can now use the assigned IP address to communicate within the network. DHCP also supports the renewal and release of IP address leases, allowing devices to obtain new configurations or release previously assigned IP addresses. DHCP simplifies network administration by providing automatic and centralized management of IP address assignments. It eliminates the need for manual configuration of network parameters on each device, making it more efficient and less error-prone. DHCP also supports the dynamic allocation of IP addresses, where IP addresses are only assigned to devices when needed, reducing IP address wastage. In summary, DHCP is a networking protocol that automates and simplifies the assignment of IP addresses and network configuration parameters to devices on a network. It enables network administrators to efficiently manage IP address assignments and ensures seamless communication within the network.

Edge Computing

Edge computing refers to a decentralized computing infrastructure that brings computation and data storage closer to the location where it is needed. This architecture aims to reduce latency, network congestion, and bandwidth usage by processing data and running services at the network edge. In traditional networking, data generated by devices, such as sensors, cameras, or smartphones, is typically sent to a centralized data center or cloud for processing and analysis. However, this approach can result in delays due to the distance between the devices and the data center, especially when dealing with large volumes of real-time data. Edge computing addresses these challenges by distributing the computing tasks and bringing them closer to the source of the data. This is achieved by deploying edge servers or devices at the edge of the network, closer to the devices generating the data. These edge devices can include routers, gateways, or specialized edge servers. By processing data at the edge, edge computing reduces latency and improves real-time decision-making. It enables faster response times, making it suitable for applications that require real-time analytics, such as autonomous vehicles, industrial IoT, or augmented reality. Furthermore, edge computing can alleviate network congestion and bandwidth usage since the data is processed locally before being sent to the central data center or cloud. This reduces the need to transfer massive amounts of raw data over the network, leading to cost savings and more efficient network utilization. Edge computing also enhances data privacy and security by keeping sensitive data closer to the source and minimizing exposure to potential threats in transit. It enables local data processing and storage, which can be useful for compliance with data protection regulations and maintaining data sovereignty. In conclusion, edge computing is a decentralized computing model that brings computation and data storage closer to the source of data generation. It reduces latency, network congestion, and bandwidth usage while improving real-time decision-making, data privacy, and security.

Egress Filtering

Egress Filtering in the context of networking refers to the practice of controlling and monitoring outgoing network traffic from a network or system. It involves implementing and enforcing security policies and rules to filter and restrict the flow of data leaving a network or system. The main purpose of egress filtering is to protect the network and its users from various security threats and potential malicious activities. By filtering outgoing traffic, organizations can prevent unauthorized data leakage, limit the spread of malware or viruses, and reduce the risk of sensitive information being accessed or transmitted outside the network.

Email Security

Email Security refers to the set of measures and protocols implemented to protect email communication from unauthorized access, interception, and malicious attacks. It is essential in the networking domain to ensure the confidentiality, integrity, and availability of email messages exchanged between users or organizations. One of the main components of email security is authentication. This involves verifying the identity of both the sender and the recipient to ensure that only authorized users can access the email system. Authentication methods commonly used in email security include username and password authentication, digital certificates, and two-factor authentication. Another crucial aspect of email security is encryption. Encryption transforms the content of an email message into an unreadable format using complex algorithms. This ensures that even if the message is intercepted during transmission or stored on a server, it remains protected from unauthorized access. Encryption can be applied to both the email message itself and the attachments, providing end-to-end security. To mitigate the risk of spam and phishing emails, email security solutions employ various filtering techniques. Spam filters analyze incoming messages and determine whether they are genuine or unwanted based on predefined criteria. Phishing filters, on the other hand, identify fraudulent emails attempting to deceive recipients into revealing sensitive information, such as passwords or financial details. By filtering out these malicious emails, email security helps prevent users from falling victim to scams or other cyber-attacks. Furthermore, email security also addresses the issue of malware and viruses. Attachments and embedded links in emails can carry harmful code that can infect devices and compromise their security. Email security solutions employ antivirus software and threat detection techniques to scan incoming emails and block any attachments or links that contain malicious content. In addition to these measures, email security encompasses measures such as data loss prevention, email archiving, and secure protocols for email transmission. Data loss prevention aims to prevent accidental or intentional leakage of sensitive information through emails, while email archiving ensures proper storage and retrieval of email records for compliance and legal purposes. Secure protocols, such as Transport Layer Security (TLS), are used to encrypt the connection between the email server and the recipient's device, further enhancing the security of email transmission. Overall, email security is of paramount importance in networking to safeguard the confidentiality, integrity, and availability of email communication. It encompasses a range of measures and protocols, including authentication, encryption, filtering, malware protection, data loss prevention, archiving, and secure protocols, to ensure the secure exchange of emails between users and organizations.

Encryption Key

An encryption key, in the context of networking, refers to a specific string of characters or code that is used to encrypt and decrypt data during transmission over a network. Encryption is the process of converting plain, readable information into an unreadable format known as ciphertext, which can only be accessed and understood by authorized recipients with the correct encryption key. The primary purpose of encryption keys in networking is to ensure the security and privacy of data being transmitted across various network devices and protocols. In order to prevent unauthorized access and eavesdropping, encryption techniques such as the Advanced Encryption Standard (AES) or the Rivest Cipher (RC4) are commonly employed.

Endpoint Detection And Response (EDR)

Endpoint Detection and Response (EDR) is a cybersecurity approach that focuses on the detection, investigation, and response to advanced threats and malicious activities specifically targeting endpoints within a network. Endpoints refer to individual devices such as desktops, laptops, servers, and mobile devices that connect to a network. EDR solutions are designed to continuously monitor and collect endpoint data, using various methods such as log files, system behavior analysis, and real-time threat intelligence. This data is then analyzed using advanced algorithms and machine learning techniques to identify any suspicious or malicious activities that may indicate a potential security breach or attack.

Endpoint Protection Platform (EPP)

An Endpoint Protection Platform (EPP) is a network security solution that provides comprehensive protection for endpoints, including desktops, laptops, servers, and mobile devices, within an organization's network. It aims to secure these endpoints from various threats such as malware, ransomware, exploits, and phishing attacks. EPP solutions typically include a range of security features that work together to detect, prevent, and respond to potential threats. These features can include: 1. Antivirus/Antimalware: EPP solutions employ antivirus and antimalware technologies to scan for and block malicious software or files that may be present on endpoints. They use signature-based detection, as well as behavioral analysis and machine learning algorithms, to identify and eliminate known and unknown malware. 2. Firewall: EPP solutions often include a built-in firewall to monitor and control incoming and outgoing network traffic on endpoints. Firewalls help prevent unauthorized access and can block malicious network activity, such as network-based attacks or the communication between a compromised endpoint and a command-and-control server. 3. Intrusion Detection and Prevention: EPP solutions may have intrusion detection and prevention capabilities that can monitor for and block suspicious activities or patterns that may indicate an ongoing attack. These features can analyze network traffic, system logs, and behavior to identify potential threats and take appropriate

140

action to mitigate them. 4. Endpoint Detection and Response (EDR): EPP platforms often include EDR capabilities, which enable organizations to monitor and investigate endpoint activities in real-time. EDR allows security teams to identify and respond to advanced threats, detect system vulnerabilities, conduct forensic analysis, and apply incident response measures. 5. Data Loss Prevention (DLP): EPP solutions may offer DLP features to prevent the unauthorized transfer or disclosure of sensitive data from endpoints. DLP functionalities can monitor and control data transfers, prevent data leakage through various channels, and enforce encryption and access control policies. Overall, an Endpoint Protection Platform plays a crucial role in securing the network by protecting endpoints from a wide array of cyber threats. By combining multiple security features, it provides a layered defense strategy that helps ensure the confidentiality, integrity, and availability of an organization's network and data.

Endpoint Security

Endpoint security is a crucial aspect of network security that focuses on protecting individual devices or endpoints, such as laptops, desktops, mobile phones, and servers, from unauthorized access, malicious attacks, and data breaches. It involves implementing a range of security measures and policies to safeguard the endpoints, as they are the gateway to accessing the network and its resources. The main objective of endpoint security is to ensure the confidentiality, integrity, and availability of the data stored and processed on these endpoints. It aims to prevent unauthorized users or malware from gaining access and compromising the devices or the network they are connected to. By protecting the endpoints, organizations can mitigate the risks associated with cyber threats, minimize the potential damage of a security breach, and maintain the overall security posture of their network infrastructure. Endpoint security solutions typically include a combination of technologies and practices, including antivirus and antimalware software, firewalls, intrusion detection and prevention systems, data encryption, vulnerability management, and user authentication mechanisms. These tools work together to defend against various types of threats, such as malware infections, network intrusions, phishing attacks, and data exfiltration. In addition to proactive security measures, endpoint security also involves monitoring and managing the endpoints to detect and respond to security incidents effectively. This may include continuous monitoring of endpoint activities, regular security assessments and audits, incident response plans, and timely patching and updating of software and firmware. Endpoint security teams often rely on centralized management platforms or security information and event management (SIEM) systems to streamline these tasks and gain visibility into the security status and events across all endpoints.

Ethernet Cable Types

Ethernet cables are essential components in networking that facilitate the transmission of data between devices. These cables are commonly used to connect computers, routers, switches, and other network devices to establish a wired network connection. There are several types of Ethernet cables with varying capabilities and characteristics. The main types include: 1. Cat5e: Cat5e cables are an improved version of the Cat5 cables and are widely used for Ethernet networking. They support data transfer speeds up to 1,000 Mbps (1 Gigabit per second) and operate at frequencies of up to 100 MHz. These cables consist of four twisted pairs of copper wires and are backward compatible with Cat5 cables. 2. Cat6: Cat6 cables offer higher performance compared to Cat5e cables. They support data transfer speeds up to 10,000 Mbps (10 Gigabit per second) and operate at frequencies of up to 250 MHz. Cat6 cables also have improved insulation to reduce crosstalk and enhance performance. They are backward compatible with Cat5e and Cat5 cables. 3. Cat6a: Cat6a cables are an enhanced version of Cat6 cables. They support data transfer speeds up to 10,000 Mbps (10 Gigabit per second) and operate at frequencies of up to 500 MHz. These cables have improved shielding and insulation to minimize alien crosstalk and ensure reliable performance. Cat6a cables are backward compatible with Cat6, Cat5e, and Cat5 cables. 4. Cat7: Cat7 cables are designed to meet the requirements of more demanding networks. They support data transfer speeds up to 10,000 Mbps (10 Gigabit per second) and operate at frequencies of up to 600 MHz. Cat7 cables feature individually shielded twisted pairs and additional shielding overall, offering superior protection against external electromagnetic interference. They are backward compatible with previous Ethernet cable types. Ethernet cables are typically terminated with RJ-45 connectors that enable easy connectivity to network devices. The choice of Ethernet cable type depends on the specific networking requirements, such as the desired data transfer speeds, network distance, and susceptibility to interference. Using the appropriate Ethernet cable ensures reliable and efficient data transmission in networks.

Ethernet Cable

Ethernet Cable is a type of high-speed networking cable commonly used in Local Area Networks (LANs) to connect devices such as computers, routers, switches, and servers. It is designed to transmit signals between devices to facilitate communication and data transfer within a network. Ethernet Cable consists of multiple pairs of twisted wires that are protected by an outer jacket. The most common type of Ethernet Cable used today is known as Category 5e or Cat5e, which supports data transmission speeds of up to 1,000 Mbps (1 Gigabit per second).

Ethernet Cabling Standards (E.G., Cat6)

Ethernet cabling standards, such as Cat6, refer to the specifications and requirements that govern the physical properties of the cables used in networking. These standards are developed and maintained by various organizations, including the Institute of Electrical and Electronics Engineers (IEEE) and the Telecommunications Industry Association (TIA). Cat6, short for Category 6, is a type of Ethernet cable that supports higher data transfer rates and provides better performance compared to previous generations, such as Cat5e. It is designed to operate at frequencies up to 250 MHz and can support data transmission speeds of up to 10 gigabits per second (Gbps).

Ethernet Frame Format

The Ethernet frame format refers to the structure or organization of data within a data link layer frame used in Ethernet networks. It defines how the information is encapsulated and transmitted from one device to another over a physical medium, such as copper or fiber optic cables. Ethernet is a widely used technology for local area networks (LANs) and serves as the foundation for internet connections. The Ethernet frame format allows for the reliable transfer of data between devices by providing a standardized structure that all devices within a network can understand and interpret.

Ethernet Frame Structure

The Ethernet Frame Structure is a standardized format used in networking to transmit data packets between devices over an Ethernet network. It is designed to provide reliable and efficient communication by organizing data in a specific layout within a frame. The Ethernet Frame Structure consists of various fields that contain essential information for successful transmission and reception of data. These fields are arranged in a specific order, starting with the Preamble, Destination MAC Address, Source MAC Address, EtherType or Length, Data, and Frame Check Sequence (FCS). The Preamble is a sequence of alternating 1s and 0s used to synchronize the receiving device's clock with the sender's clock. It also helps the receiving device identify the start of a frame. The Destination MAC Address field contains the MAC address of the intended recipient device, while the Source MAC Address field contains the MAC address of the sending device. The EtherType or Length field determines the type or length of the data being transmitted. This field specifies whether the data is an Ethernet II frame (using EtherType) or IEEE 802.3 frame (using Length). The Data field carries the actual payload, which can be a combination of network layer packets, control information, or user data. It has a minimum length of 46 bytes and a maximum length of 1500 bytes. The Frame Check Sequence (FCS) field is used for error detection. It contains a cyclic redundancy check (CRC) value that is computed based on the contents of the frame. The receiving device calculates its own CRC value and compares it with the FCS to check for any transmission errors or data corruption. The Ethernet Frame Structure provides a reliable means of transmitting data over an Ethernet network. Its standardized format allows devices from different manufacturers to communicate effectively. By organizing data within frames and including necessary information such as MAC addresses and error detection, the Ethernet Frame Structure enables efficient and error-free data transmission.

Ethernet Frame

An Ethernet frame is a data packet that is used in computer networks to transmit information

142

between devices. It is the basic unit of data transmission in an Ethernet network and is responsible for the reliable transfer of data from one device to another. The Ethernet frame consists of several components, each serving a specific purpose in the transmission process. These components include the preamble, start frame delimiter, destination and source MAC addresses, type or length field, data payload, and the frame check sequence. The preamble is a series of alternating 1s and 0s that informs the receiving device about the incoming transmission. It helps the device synchronize with the sender and identify the start of the frame. Following the preamble is the start frame delimiter, which marks the end of the preamble and the beginning of the frame. It consists of a special bit pattern that indicates the start of the actual data transmission. The destination and source MAC addresses are essential parts of the Ethernet frame. The destination MAC address specifies the intended recipient of the frame, while the source MAC address identifies the sender. These addresses enable devices to determine whether the frame is meant for them or if it should be ignored. The type or length field indicates the type of data being transmitted or the length of the frame. It helps the receiving device correctly interpret and process the data payload. The data payload contains the actual information being transmitted, such as a file, email, or web page. It can vary in size depending on the needs of the network. Finally, the frame check sequence is a mathematical calculation that allows the recipient device to verify the integrity of the received frame. It helps detect and correct any errors that may have occurred during transmission. If the frame check sequence does not match the calculated value, the frame is considered corrupt, and the recipient requests retransmission. In summary, an Ethernet frame is a structured data packet used in computer networks for transmitting information. It includes various components that ensure reliable transmission, such as the preamble, start frame delimiter, MAC addresses, type or length field, data payload, and frame check sequence. These components work together to facilitate the efficient and error-free transfer of data between devices in an Ethernet network.

Ethernet Hub

An Ethernet hub is a networking device that connects multiple devices within a local area network (LAN). It operates at the physical layer of the OSI model, which is responsible for transmitting raw binary data across the network. When data is transmitted from one device to another, it is first converted into electrical signals and then sent through a network cable. An Ethernet hub receives these signals and broadcasts them to all connected devices. Each device on the network examines the signals and determines if they are intended for them. If not, the devices discard the signals, preventing them from affecting the performance of the network.

Ethernet Speed Standards

Ethernet speed standards refer to the various specifications and capabilities of Ethernet networks in terms of data transfer rates. Ethernet is a widely used networking technology that allows computers and other devices to communicate with each other over a wired connection. The speed of an Ethernet network is determined by the maximum amount of data that can be transferred in a given amount of time. This is typically measured in bits per second (bps) or its derivatives such as kilobits per second (Kbps), megabits per second (Mbps), or gigabits per second (Gbps). Over the years, Ethernet speed standards have evolved and improved to keep up with the increasing demands for faster and more efficient networks. The original Ethernet standard, known as 10BASE-T, supported a maximum data transfer rate of 10 Mbps. This was sufficient for many early networking applications but became inadequate as the need for higher speeds emerged. Subsequent Ethernet speed standards were introduced to address the need for faster networks. Some of the notable standards include Fast Ethernet (100BASE-TX), which provided a data transfer rate of 100 Mbps, and Gigabit Ethernet (1000BASE-T), which increased the speed to 1 Gbps. As network requirements continued to grow, even faster Ethernet speed standards were developed. These included 10 Gigabit Ethernet (10GBASE-T), which provided speeds of up to 10 Gbps, and 40 Gigabit Ethernet (40GBASE-T) and 100 Gigabit Ethernet (100GBASE-T), which further increased the speed to 40 Gbps and 100 Gbps, respectively. The latest Ethernet speed standard is 400 Gigabit Ethernet (400GBASE-T), which offers blazing fast speeds of up to 400 Gbps. These ultra-high speeds are particularly important for data centers, cloud computing, and other bandwidth-intensive applications that require rapid data transfer. In summary, Ethernet speed standards define the maximum data transfer rates that can be achieved over Ethernet networks. These standards have evolved over time to keep up with the increasing demands for faster and more efficient networking. From the original 10 Mbps

Ethernet to the latest 400 Gbps Ethernet, these speed standards have revolutionized the way we communicate and share information over wired networks.

Ethernet Switching

Ethernet switching is a networking technology that allows for the efficient and orderly exchange of data packets between multiple devices within a local area network (LAN). It operates at the data link layer of the Open Systems Interconnection (OSI) model, which deals with the addressing and routing of data between network devices. At its core, an Ethernet switch functions as a central hub for connecting multiple devices, such as computers, printers, and servers, within a LAN. It receives incoming data packets from one device and selectively forwards the packets to the appropriate destination device based on their destination MAC addresses. This process is known as filtering or forwarding. When a data packet arrives at an Ethernet switch, it reads the destination MAC address in the packet's header to determine which port it should be sent out. The switch maintains a MAC address table, also known as a forwarding table or content addressable memory (CAM) table, which maps MAC addresses to specific switch ports. By referencing this table, the switch can quickly and efficiently route packets to their intended recipients. One of the key advantages of Ethernet switching is its ability to isolate traffic within a LAN. Unlike older hub-based networks, where all devices shared the same bandwidth and any data sent by one device was received by all other devices, an Ethernet switch only sends packets to their intended recipients. This minimizes network congestion and allows for increased network performance. Additionally, Ethernet switching supports full-duplex communication, which means that devices can send and receive data simultaneously. This enhances the overall efficiency and speed of data transmission within a network. In summary, Ethernet switching is a fundamental networking technology that enables the efficient and targeted exchange of data packets within a LAN. It utilizes MAC addresses to forward packets to their intended destinations, isolating traffic and improving network performance. By facilitating full-duplex communication, Ethernet switching enhances the overall efficiency and speed of data transmission within a network.

Ethernet

Ethernet is a widely used networking technology that enables devices to communicate with each other over a local area network (LAN). It is a physical and data link layer protocol, which means that it defines how devices are physically connected and how they communicate with each other. Ethernet uses a system of wired connections, typically using copper or fiber optic cables, to transmit data between devices. This physical layer is responsible for ensuring that the signals are properly transmitted and received. At the data link layer, Ethernet defines the format and structure of data packets and the rules for how devices communicate on the network. It specifies the method of accessing the network and how devices can send data to each other without interfering with other devices. Ethernet uses a shared medium, where multiple devices can transmit data concurrently, but it employs a collision detection mechanism to avoid data collisions. Ethernet operates using the Carrier Sense Multiple Access with Collision Detection (CSMA/CD) algorithm. Devices on the network listen for other devices transmitting before sending their own data to ensure that they do not cause a collision. If a collision does occur, devices follow a backoff and retransmission process to ensure successful delivery of the data. This collision detection and resolution method allows for efficient communication on the network. Ethernet has evolved over time, with various iterations offering faster speeds and improved performance. The most common types of Ethernet networks today include Fast Ethernet (100 Mbps), Gigabit Ethernet (1 Gbps), and 10 Gigabit Ethernet (10 Gbps). These faster speeds have allowed for more bandwidth-intensive applications and increased network performance. Ethernet is a reliable, scalable, and cost-effective solution for local area networks. It provides a standardized framework for devices to communicate and has become the de facto standard for wired LAN connections in both residential and business settings. Ethernet has also been an integral component of the internet, as it is used in network routers and switches to transmit data between networks. In conclusion, Ethernet is a foundational technology in computer networking that allows devices to connect and communicate over a local area network. It provides the physical and data link layers of the networking stack and has been instrumental in the development of the modern internet.

Ethical Hacker

An ethical hacker, also known as a white-hat hacker, is an individual or a professional who is hired by an organization to assess the security of computer systems, networks, and software applications. The primary goal of an ethical hacker is to identify vulnerabilities in the network infrastructure and recommend appropriate security measures to mitigate the risk of potential cyber attacks. Unlike malicious hackers or black-hat hackers, ethical hackers perform their activities with the consent and knowledge of the organization, and they abide by a strict code of ethics. Ethical hackers use a variety of techniques and tools to simulate cyber attacks and exploit vulnerabilities. They employ their technical skills and knowledge to identify weaknesses in the network, such as misconfigurations, weak passwords, software vulnerabilities, or social engineering techniques that could be exploited by malicious individuals. By conducting these tests, ethical hackers can provide valuable insights into the organization's security posture and help protect sensitive data from unauthorized access. One of the key roles of an ethical hacker is to perform network reconnaissance, which involves gathering information about the target network, such as IP addresses, server versions, network topology, and other relevant details. This information allows them to understand the potential attack surface and focus their efforts on areas that are more susceptible to exploitation. Another important aspect of ethical hacking is vulnerability assessment and penetration testing. This involves actively probing the network infrastructure for vulnerabilities and attempting to exploit them to gain unauthorized access or perform other malicious activities. These tests help identify weak points in the network infrastructure before they can be exploited by malicious actors. Upon identifying vulnerabilities, ethical hackers document their findings and provide detailed reports to the organization. These reports typically include a description of the vulnerabilities, the risk they pose, and recommendations for remediation. Ethical hackers work closely with the organization's IT team to ensure that the necessary security measures are implemented to address the identified issues. In summary, an ethical hacker is a skilled professional who is hired to proactively identify and address security weaknesses in computer systems, networks, and software applications. Their main objective is to help organizations improve their security posture and defend against potential cyber threats.

Evil Twin Attack

An Evil Twin Attack is a type of network security attack that involves the creation of a fraudulent Wi-Fi access point (AP) that imitates a legitimate AP. This attack is carried out by an attacker who sets up a rogue wireless AP with the same SSID (Service Set Identifier) as the legitimate AP and utilizes other methods to deceive users into connecting to the malicious AP instead of the legitimate one. The purpose of an Evil Twin Attack is to trick users into unknowingly connecting to the attacker's AP, which gives the attacker the ability to eavesdrop on their network activity, steal sensitive information such as login credentials or credit card numbers, and even inject malicious code or conduct further attacks. This type of attack takes advantage of the trust that users typically have in the legitimacy of Wi-Fi networks. One of the common methods used in an Evil Twin Attack is to create a rogue AP in a public location such as a coffee shop, airport, or hotel, where users regularly connect to Wi-Fi networks. The attacker typically gives their fake network a name that is similar or identical to the legitimate network, making it more difficult for users to distinguish between the two. When users attempt to connect, they may be prompted to enter a password or other credentials, which the attacker can use to gain unauthorized access to their accounts. Another technique used in Evil Twin Attacks is to dynamically clone the MAC address of the legitimate AP, further increasing the deception. This makes it even harder for users to differentiate between the two networks, as the MAC address is a unique identifier associated with the hardware of the AP. To protect against Evil Twin Attacks, it is important to be cautious when connecting to public Wi-Fi networks. Users should verify the authenticity of the network by checking with the establishment or using alternative methods of authentication, such as using a VPN (Virtual Private Network) or connecting through a trusted network instead. Additionally, keeping devices updated with the latest security patches and using strong, unique passwords can help mitigate the risk of falling victim to an Evil Twin Attack.

Exploit Kit

An Exploit Kit is a type of malicious software toolkit that is used by cyber attackers to take advantage of vulnerabilities in computer systems or software applications. It is essentially a collection of tools, scripts, and software that are packaged together to automate the process of finding and exploiting weaknesses in a target system. Exploit Kits typically consist of several components, including an exploit payload, an exploit framework, and a command and control (C&C) server. The exploit payload is the actual malicious code that takes advantage of a specific vulnerability in the target system. The exploit framework provides the necessary infrastructure and framework for running the exploit payload, while the C&C server is responsible for managing the communication between the attacker and the compromised system. When a user visits a website that is infected with an exploit kit, the kit automatically scans the visitor's system for known vulnerabilities. If it identifies a vulnerability that matches the capabilities of its exploit payload, the kit delivers the payload to the target system, potentially allowing the attacker to gain unauthorized access or install malware. Exploit Kits are often distributed through various channels including compromised websites, malvertising (malicious advertising), and spam emails. They have been used to deliver a wide range of malware, including ransomware, banking trojans, and keyloggers. To protect against exploit kits, it is important to keep computer systems and applications up to date with the latest security patches and updates. It is also recommended to use a reputable antivirus or antimalware software, as well as implement network security measures such as firewalls and intrusion detection systems.

Exploit

An exploit in the context of networking refers to a specific technique or method used to take advantage of vulnerabilities within a computer system, network, or software application. It involves the unauthorized use of these vulnerabilities to gain access to confidential information, disrupt normal network operations, or execute malicious activities. Exploits can target various layers of the network stack, including physical, data link, network, transport, and application layers. These vulnerabilities may exist due to poorly designed or implemented network protocols, misconfigurations, or unpatched software. The goal of an exploit is to bypass the security measures in place and gain unauthorized control or access to a system or network. One common type of exploit is the use of a buffer overflow attack, where an attacker overwhelms a system by inputting more data than it can handle. This overflow can overwrite critical memory areas, leading to the execution of arbitrary code. Another type of exploit is a denial-of-service (DoS) attack, where an attacker floods a network or system with excessive requests or data, causing it to become overwhelmed and unresponsive. Exploits can also target specific software vulnerabilities, such as those found in popular operating systems, web applications, or network devices. Attackers may utilize exploit kits, which are pre-packaged software tools that automate the process of identifying and exploiting vulnerabilities in target systems. To mitigate the risk of exploits, network administrators and system operators need to regularly update their software and apply security patches. They should also implement intrusion detection and prevention systems, firewalls, and access controls to prevent unauthorized access or malicious activities.

FTP (File Transfer Protocol)

File Transfer Protocol (FTP) is a standard network protocol used for transferring files between a client and a server on a computer network. It is a simple and efficient way to share files over a network, allowing users to upload and download files from a remote server. FTP operates on the client-server model, where a client initiates a connection with a server to transfer files. The client is typically a personal computer or workstation, while the server is a computer hosting the FTP service. The client sends commands to the server to perform various file operations, such as listing directories, uploading files, downloading files, and deleting files. FTP uses TCP/IP as its underlying transport protocol, providing reliable and ordered delivery of data packets. It utilizes two separate channels for communication: the control channel and the data channel. The control channel is used for sending commands and receiving responses between the client and server. It handles tasks such as authentication, establishing the data channel, and managing file transfers. When a file transfer is initiated, the control channel is used to negotiate and establish a separate data channel for transferring the actual file contents. This separation allows for efficient concurrent transfers and prevents the control channel from being occupied solely by transfer data. The data channel can be established using two modes: active mode or passive mode depending on network configurations. FTP supports various file operations, including uploading files from the client to the server (put), downloading files from the server to the client (get), renaming files, deleting files, creating directories, and navigating through the directory structure. It also provides a range of file transfer modes to optimize performance and compatibility, such as ASCII mode for text files and binary mode for non-text files. FTP provides basic authentication mechanisms for securing file transfers. Users typically authenticate themselves with a username and password, although anonymous FTP allows users to connect without providing credentials. However, FTP does not encrypt data during transfer, making it vulnerable to interception. Therefore, it is recommended to use additional security measures, such as Secure FTP (SFTP) or FTP over SSL/TLS, to protect sensitive information during transmission.

FTP Server

An FTP (File Transfer Protocol) server, in the context of networking, refers to a network device or software application that allows the transfer of files between client devices and the server. It is a fundamental component of the client-server model where the server is responsible for hosting the files and the client devices can access and retrieve them as needed. FTP servers operate on the Transmission Control Protocol/Internet Protocol (TCP/IP) network architecture, which is the standard protocol suite used for data transmission over the internet. They utilize a client-server setup where the server runs FTP server software, and clients connect to it using FTP client software. FTP servers provide a secure and reliable means of file exchange between devices within a network or over the internet. Users can upload or download files, create directories, delete files, and perform other file management tasks using FTP client software. When a client connects to an FTP server, it establishes a control connection through TCP port 21 for sending commands and receiving responses. This control connection authenticates the client and sets up the necessary parameters for the data transfer. The actual file transfer occurs over a separate data connection, typically initiated by the server using TCP port 20. The data connection facilitates the transfer of files, ensuring the integrity and efficient transmission of data. An important feature of FTP servers is the ability to define different access privileges for different users or user groups. This allows for fine-grained control over who can access or modify specific files and directories. The server administrator can define user accounts, assign passwords, and set permissions to restrict or grant access as necessary. FTP servers also support various data transfer modes, such as active and passive mode, to accommodate different network configurations and security requirements. Active mode requires the client to open a port for data transfer, while passive mode allows the client to request the server to open a port. Overall, FTP servers are essential components of network infrastructures, enabling efficient and secure file transfer between clients and servers. They play a crucial role in facilitating collaboration, data sharing, and resource management in various industries and organizations.

Fast Ethernet

Fast Ethernet is a technology used in computer networking that provides a higher data transfer rate compared to traditional Ethernet. It operates at a speed of 100 megabits per second (Mbps), which is ten times faster than the original Ethernet standard. This higher speed allows for faster transmission of data over a network, resulting in improved performance and efficiency. Fast Ethernet is based on the same principles as Ethernet, utilizing the same media access control (MAC) protocol and frame format. It uses twisted-pair copper cables or fiber-optic cables to transmit data between network devices. This technology is commonly used in local area networks (LANs) to connect computers, servers, printers, and other devices.

Fiber Optic Cable

A fiber optic cable is a high-speed data transmission medium that consists of thin strands of glass or plastic fibers, through which modulated light signals are transmitted. These fibers are designed to carry large amounts of data over long distances at extremely high speeds. The concept is based on the principle of total internal reflection, where light is transmitted through the fiber by continuously bouncing off the walls of the fiber due to a difference in refractive index between the core and the cladding. Fiber optic cables offer several advantages over traditional copper cables. Firstly, they have a much higher bandwidth capacity, allowing for the transmission of large amounts of data in a shorter amount of time. This makes them ideal for applications that require high-speed data transfer, such as internet connectivity, video streaming, and cloud computing. Secondly, fiber optic cables are not affected by electromagnetic interference, unlike copper cables. This means that they can carry data over longer distances without signal degradation or loss. Additionally, fiber optic cables are more secure as they do not emit any electromagnetic signals that can be intercepted or tapped into.

Another key advantage of fiber optic cables is their smaller size and lighter weight compared to copper cables. This makes them easier to install, maintain, and transport, especially in areas with limited space or difficult terrains. They are also more resistant to environmental factors such as temperature changes, moisture, and corrosion. Despite their advantages, fiber optic cables also have some limitations. They require specialized equipment and expertise for installation and maintenance, which can be costly. Additionally, fiber optic cables are fragile and can be damaged if bent or twisted excessively. In conclusion, fiber optic cables are a crucial component of modern networking systems. Their high-speed and high-capacity capabilities make them essential for transmitting data over long distances quickly and efficiently. They offer increased security, resistance to interference, and are more lightweight and compact compared to traditional copper cables. However, they also require specialized knowledge and care during installation and maintenance.

Firewall Configuration Tools

A firewall configuration tool is a software application or utility that is used to manage and configure firewall settings and policies in a computer network. Firewalls are a critical component of network security, as they act as a barrier between a trusted internal network and an untrusted external network, such as the internet. They monitor and control inbound and outbound network traffic based on predefined security rules and policies. Firewall configuration tools simplify the process of setting up, managing, and updating these rules and policies.

Firewall Configuration

A firewall configuration refers to the set of rules and parameters that govern the operation and behavior of a firewall within a network environment. A firewall acts as a barrier between a trusted internal network and an untrusted external network, such as the internet. Its primary purpose is to monitor and control network traffic, allowing or blocking specific types of communication based on predefined rules. The configuration of a firewall involves specifying various settings and policies to ensure that it functions effectively and securely. These settings determine how the firewall filters and handles incoming and outgoing network traffic, as well as how it protects the internal network from unauthorized access and external threats. In a firewall configuration, administrators define rules that determine which packets are allowed to pass through the firewall and which ones are blocked. These rules are based on factors such as source and destination IP addresses, port numbers, protocol types, and specific application or service requirements. By carefully crafting these rules, administrators can create a strong defense against potential security vulnerabilities. Firewall configurations may also involve configuring various security features, such as intrusion detection and prevention systems (IDPS), virtual private network (VPN) support, and logging and monitoring capabilities. These additional features enhance the overall security posture of the network and provide valuable insights into potential security incidents or policy violations. Regular updates and maintenance are crucial for firewall configurations to remain effective. As network environments evolve and new threats emerge, administrators need to review and update firewall rules to adapt to the changing landscape. This may involve implementing new rules, removing obsolete ones, or modifying existing rules to reflect updated security policies. In summary, a firewall configuration encompasses the rules, settings, and parameters that govern the operation of a firewall in a network environment. It plays a critical role in securing the network by controlling and monitoring network traffic, blocking unauthorized access, and protecting against various external threats.

Firewall Management Software

A firewall management software is a network security tool that allows organizations to centrally manage and configure their firewalls. It provides administrators with a graphical interface or command-line interface to configure and monitor firewall settings, rules, and policies across multiple devices. Firewalls act as a barrier between an organization's internal network and the external network, such as the internet. They monitor and control incoming and outgoing network traffic based on predetermined security rules. By doing so, firewalls help protect the organization's network from unauthorized access, data breaches, malware, and other cyber threats.

Firewall Rule Optimization

Firewall rule optimization is a process in the field of networking that aims to enhance the efficiency and effectiveness of firewall rules. Firewalls act as a first line of defense by monitoring and controlling network traffic, allowing or blocking connections based on predefined rules. These rules are crucial for maintaining network security and preventing unauthorized access to the network. However, as networks grow in complexity and traffic volume increases, managing firewall rules becomes challenging. Firewall rule optimization involves analyzing and fine-tuning the existing firewall rules to achieve optimal performance and security. This process helps identify redundant, ineffective, or conflicting rules and eliminates them. By removing unnecessary rules, firewall performance can be improved, resulting in faster processing speed for network traffic. Additionally, it reduces the risk of rule conflicts that may lead to security vulnerabilities.

Firewall Rule

A firewall rule is a predefined set of conditions and actions that determine how network traffic is allowed or blocked based on specific criteria. Firewall rules act as a crucial line of defense to protect networks from unauthorized access, potential threats, and malicious activities. Each firewall rule consists of two main components: the conditions and the actions. The conditions define the criteria that the network traffic must meet in order to be evaluated by the firewall rule. These conditions can include factors such as IP addresses, port numbers, protocols, or specific keywords. The actions, on the other hand, specify what should happen to the network traffic that matches the defined conditions. Firewall rules are typically configured and managed by network administrators to enforce security policies and control the flow of network traffic. They are essential in ensuring that only authorized and legitimate traffic is allowed into and out of the network, while blocking or mitigating potential threats or unauthorized accesses. Firewall rules are often organized in a hierarchical structure, which allows for more granular control over network traffic. Rules are evaluated in a sequential manner, and the actions specified in matched rules are applied accordingly. This allows for prioritization of certain types of traffic or specific security measures to be implemented. By defining firewall rules, network administrators are able to customize network security policies to meet the specific needs of their organization. This includes controlling access to certain resources, defining trusted sources or networks, and identifying and blocking suspicious or malicious activities. Overall, firewall rules play a critical role in maintaining the security and integrity of a network. They provide the necessary means to filter and control network traffic, protecting the network from potential threats, unauthorized access, and ensuring the confidentiality, availability, and integrity of its resources.

Firewall Rulebase

A firewall rulebase is a set of policies or rules that are defined within a network firewall to control the flow of network traffic. It acts as a security mechanism, allowing or denying specific types of traffic based on predetermined criteria. These rules are defined by the network administrator and are implemented within the firewall to protect the network from unauthorized access and potential security threats. The rulebase serves as a decision-making tool for the firewall, determining which types of traffic are permitted or denied.

Firewall Rules

A firewall is a network security device that monitors incoming and outgoing network traffic based on predetermined security rules. These rules define what types of traffic are allowed or blocked based on various criteria such as the source and destination IP addresses, port numbers, protocol types, and other specific attributes of the network packets. Firewall rules act as a barrier between trusted and untrusted networks, allowing or denying access to certain resources to prevent malicious or unauthorized activities. By examining network packets, firewalls can enforce security policies by either allowing or blocking traffic based on the defined rules.

Firewall Ruleset

A firewall ruleset is a set of instructions or guidelines that determines how a firewall should filter network traffic. It defines the criteria and conditions for allowing or blocking communication between different network zones or devices within a network. Each rule in a firewall ruleset specifies a combination of source and destination IP addresses, ports, protocols, and other parameters to determine how traffic should be handled. The ruleset is typically configured by network administrators to enforce security policies and protect the network from unauthorized access or malicious activities.

Firewall Security Policies

A firewall security policy refers to a set of guidelines and rules that govern the operation and usage of a firewall within a network environment. It outlines the specific actions and actions that the firewall should take to ensure the network's security and protect it from unauthorized access, malicious activities, and potential threats. The firewall security policy serves as a critical component of network security management, as it helps to define and enforce the security measures that need to be respected by both the users and the network administrators. It provides a framework that helps in identifying and controlling the types of network traffic that are allowed to pass through the firewall, as well as those that should be blocked or restricted. Typically, a firewall security policy includes the following elements: 1. Access control rules: These rules define the criteria and conditions that determine whether a network communication should be allowed or denied. Access control rules are based on factors such as source IP addresses, destination IP addresses, specific ports, and protocols. 2. Authentication and authorization policies: These policies determine how users are authenticated and authorized to access the network resources. They include guidelines for password management, user account provisioning, and defining user roles and privileges. 3. Logging and auditing requirements: These requirements specify the type and level of logging that should be performed by the firewall to track and monitor network activity. It includes the storage and retention of log data for future analysis and forensic investigations. 4. Network segmentation: This refers to dividing the network into different security zones or segments and applying different security policies to each of them. This helps to limit the impact of potential security breaches by isolating sensitive resources or assets. 5. Software and firmware updates: This policy outlines the procedures and timelines for installing updates and patches to keep the firewall software and firmware up to date, addressing any identified vulnerabilities and ensuring continued protection. In conclusion, a firewall security policy is a crucial element of network security, as it establishes the rules and guidelines for protecting the network from threats and unauthorized access. It helps to ensure that only legitimate and authorized network traffic is allowed to pass through the firewall, providing a secure network environment for organizations.

Firewall Security

A firewall is a network security device that monitors and filters incoming and outgoing network traffic based on predetermined security rules. It acts as a barrier between a trusted internal network and an untrusted external network (such as the internet) to protect the internal network from unauthorized access and potential security threats. A firewall operates at the network level, examining packets of data that pass through it to determine if they should be allowed or blocked. It uses a set of predefined rules or policies to analyze the data packets and make decisions on whether to permit or deny their passage. These rules can be based on various factors such as the source and destination IP addresses, port numbers, protocol type, and specific keywords or patterns in the data. Inbound traffic filtering is a key function of a firewall, as it prevents unauthorized access from external sources. It checks incoming data packets against the established rules and if they meet the criteria, it allows them to enter the network. If a packet does not comply with the rules, it is discarded or blocked. By controlling access to the network, a firewall helps to defend against common cyber-attacks, such as unauthorized access attempts or malicious code injections. Outbound traffic filtering is another essential aspect of firewall security. It monitors and controls the data leaving the internal network, ensuring that only authorized communication occurs. This helps to prevent the loss of sensitive data and the transmission of malware from within the network. Firewalls also provide additional security features such as Network Address Translation (NAT) and Virtual Private Network (VPN) support. NAT allows multiple devices on a network to share a single public IP address, which adds an extra layer of anonymity and protection against external threats. VPN support enables secure remote access to the network, allowing users to establish encrypted connections over public networks. Overall, firewalls are an integral part of network security, serving as a first line of defense against unauthorized access and potential threats. They play a crucial role in safeguarding the confidentiality, integrity, and availability of network resources and data.

Firewall Types

A firewall is a network security device or software that monitors and controls incoming and outgoing network traffic based on predetermined security rules. It acts as the first line of defense against unauthorized access and potential threats from the internet or other networks. There are several types of firewalls that can be implemented in a network, each with its own specific characteristics and functionality. The main types of firewalls include packet-filtering firewalls, stateful inspection firewalls, proxy firewalls, and next-generation firewalls. Packet-filtering firewalls are the most basic type of firewall and operate at the network layer (Layer 3) of the OSI model. They examine packets and filter them based on specific criteria, including source and destination IP addresses, ports, and protocols. These firewalls can block or allow packets based on these criteria, providing a basic level of network security. Stateful inspection firewalls, also known as dynamic packet-filtering firewalls, operate at both the network and transport layers (Layer 4) of the OSI model. In addition to filtering packets based on specific criteria, they also maintain a record of the connection state to ensure that only valid packets are allowed through. This type of firewall provides enhanced security by analyzing the context of the connections. Proxy firewalls, also known as application-level gateways, operate at the application layer (Layer 7) of the OSI model. They act as intermediaries between clients and servers, forwarding requests and responses while enforcing security policies. Proxy firewalls can provide deep inspection of application-layer protocols, offering advanced security features such as content filtering and application-specific controls. Next-generation firewalls (NGFWs) incorporate the capabilities of the previous firewall types and introduce additional advanced security features. They are designed to provide granular application and user-level visibility and control, threat intelligence, intrusion prevention, VPN connectivity, and other security services. NGFWs often include advanced technologies like deep packet inspection, intrusion detection and prevention systems, and reputation-based filtering. In summary, firewalls are essential components of network security, protecting networks from unauthorized access and potential threats. They come in different types, each offering various levels of security features and functionalities. By implementing the appropriate type of firewall, organizations can safeguard their network infrastructure and data from malicious activities.

Firewall

A firewall is a network security device that monitors incoming and outgoing network traffic and decides whether to allow or block certain traffic based on predefined security rules. It acts as a barrier between internal trusted networks and external untrusted networks, such as the internet. The main purpose of a firewall is to protect a network and its resources from unauthorized access, threats, and potential attacks. It filters and inspects all network packets passing through it, analyzing various attributes of the traffic, including the source and destination IP addresses, protocols, ports, packet size, and content. Based on these attributes and the configured rules, the firewall makes decisions on how to handle each packet. Firewalls can be implemented at different layers of the network, including the network layer, transport layer, and application layer. Network layer firewalls, also known as packet filters, examine the header information of each packet to determine whether to allow or discard it. They can enforce policies based on source and destination IP addresses, ports, and other fields in the packet header. Transport layer firewalls, such as stateful inspection firewalls, maintain a state table to track the state of network connections. They inspect not only packet headers but also the content and context of the communication to make more intelligent decisions. Application layer firewalls, also known as proxy firewalls, go even further by examining the actual application data being transmitted and applying security policies specific to the application protocols. Firewalls can be deployed in various forms, including hardware appliances, software applications, or a combination of both. They can be configured to allow or deny traffic based on specific IP addresses, port numbers, protocols, and other criteria. Additionally, firewalls can provide other security features, such as Network Address Translation (NAT), Virtual Private Network (VPN) support, and logging and reporting capabilities. Overall, firewalls are essential components in network security architectures, forming the first line of defense against potential threats and unauthorized access attempts. They help organizations maintain confidentiality, integrity, and availability of their networks and data by enforcing security policies and preventing malicious activities from reaching trusted resources.

Firmware Development Tools

151

Firmware development tools refer to the software programs and utilities used in the process of creating, testing, and debugging firmware for networking devices. Firmware, in the context of networking, refers to the software code that is stored and executed on the hardware components of networking devices, such as routers, switches, and wireless access points. These tools are specifically designed to facilitate the development and deployment of firmware for networking devices. They provide a range of features and capabilities that allow firmware developers to efficiently write, test, and optimize firmware code for networking devices.

Firmware Development

Firmware development in the context of networking refers to the process of creating and updating the software instructions stored in the firmware of network devices. Firmware is a type of software that is permanently stored in read-only memory (ROM) or flash memory and is essential for the operation and control of the hardware components of a network device. Network devices, such as routers, switches, and wireless access points, rely on firmware to provide the necessary functionality for communication and network management. Firmware developers work on designing, coding, and testing the software instructions that define the behavior and capabilities of these devices. Firmware development involves several stages, including specification, design, implementation, and testing. At the specification stage, the requirements for the firmware are defined, taking into account factors such as the device's intended functionality, performance, and security. The design stage involves creating the architecture and structure of the firmware, deciding how different components and modules will interact with each other. The implementation phase is where the actual coding takes place. Firmware developers write the software instructions using programming languages and tools specific to the target hardware. They ensure that the firmware is optimized for resource usage and can efficiently handle network traffic and various protocols. Testing is a critical part of firmware development to ensure that the software instructions work as intended and meet the specified requirements. Testers conduct various types of testing, including unit testing, integration testing, and system testing, to identify and fix any bugs or issues in the firmware. Overall, firmware development in networking plays a crucial role in enabling network devices to perform their intended functions. It ensures the efficient and reliable operation of these devices, as well as facilitates the implementation of new features or enhancements through firmware updates.

Firmware Recovery

Firmware recovery, in the context of networking, refers to the process of restoring or updating the firmware of a networking device to its original or updated version. Firmware is a type of software that is embedded in hardware devices to control their behavior and functionality. It is typically stored in read-only memory (ROM) or flash memory within the device. There are various reasons why firmware recovery may be necessary. This may include software bugs or glitches that cause the device to malfunction, security vulnerabilities that need to be patched, or the need to update the device with new features or enhancements. In some cases, the firmware may become corrupted or damaged, rendering the device inoperable or unstable. Firmware recovery allows network administrators or users to resolve these issues by restoring the firmware to a known good state. The process of firmware recovery often involves some level of user intervention and requires specific tools or software provided by the device manufacturer. These tools may be in the form of a firmware recovery utility or a firmware update package. The user typically connects the device to a computer or network, runs the designated software or utility, and initiates the firmware recovery process. During the recovery process, the device may enter a special mode that allows the firmware to be updated or restored. This mode is often referred to as recovery mode or bootloader mode. Once the device is in this mode, the recovery software communicates with the device and transfers the new or updated firmware to the device's memory. The firmware is then programmed onto the device, replacing the previous firmware version. It is essential to follow the manufacturer's instructions carefully when performing firmware recovery to avoid any potential issues or complications. This may include ensuring a stable power source, using the correct firmware version, and verifying the integrity of the firmware file before initiating the recovery process.

Firmware Security Updates

A firmware security update is a software update that addresses vulnerabilities and improves the security of a networking device's firmware. Firmware is a type of software that is embedded in hardware devices, and it provides the low-level control and functionality of the device. Networking devices, such as routers, switches, and access points, have firmware that controls their operation and allows them to communicate and transfer data over a network. However, just like any software, firmware can have vulnerabilities that could be exploited by attackers to gain unauthorized access to the device or compromise its security. Firmware security updates are released by the device manufacturers to address these vulnerabilities and enhance the security of the device. These updates may fix known security flaws, patch vulnerabilities, or introduce additional security features to protect against emerging threats. Updating the firmware of networking devices is crucial for maintaining a secure network environment. It helps to ensure that the devices can withstand attacks and operate with the latest security measures. Typically, firmware security updates are distributed by the manufacturers through official channels, such as their websites or software update utilities. Users are encouraged to regularly check for updates and apply them as soon as they become available to minimize the risk of security breaches.

Firmware Security

Firmware security refers to the measures and practices put in place to protect the firmware of networking devices and systems from unauthorized access, tampering, and exploitation. Firmware, in the context of networking, refers to the permanent software programmed into hardware devices such as routers, switches, and firewalls, which allows them to perform their specific functions. The security of firmware is crucial for maintaining the integrity, confidentiality, and availability of networking systems. It impacts the overall security posture of a network, as compromised firmware can lead to various malicious activities, including unauthorized access, data breaches, and network disruptions. There are several key aspects to consider when securing firmware in a networking environment: Firstly, secure firmware involves ensuring that only authorized and authenticated individuals or entities can access and modify the firmware of networking devices. This can be achieved by implementing strong access control mechanisms, such as unique usernames and strong passwords, as well as multifactor authentication techniques. Secondly, firmware security includes protecting firmware from malicious modification or tampering. Firmware updates should be obtained from trusted sources and authenticated before installation. Additionally, firmware should be digitally signed and verified to ensure its integrity and authenticity. Thirdly, continuous monitoring and vulnerability management are essential for maintaining firmware security. Regularly scanning firmware for vulnerabilities and applying patches or updates promptly can help prevent potential security breaches and exploit attempts. Lastly, secure firmware also involves maintaining a secure supply chain for networking devices. This includes ensuring that firmware is not compromised during the manufacturing and distribution processes, as well as regularly reviewing and auditing the security practices of vendors and suppliers. In conclusion, firmware security is a critical aspect of network security, as it directly impacts the overall security and reliability of networking systems. By implementing robust access control mechanisms, protecting against tampering, maintaining secure supply chains, and regularly monitoring for vulnerabilities, organizations can mitigate the risks associated with firmware security and enhance the overall security posture of their networks.

Firmware Update Procedures

Firmware update procedures in the context of networking refer to the specific steps and protocols that are followed to update the firmware of network devices, such as routers, switches, or access points. Firmware is a type of software that is embedded in the hardware of these devices and governs their operation and functionality. Periodic firmware updates are necessary to ensure the security, stability, and performance of the network. The firmware update process typically involves the following steps: 1. Preparing for the update: Before initiating the firmware update, it is important to gather all the necessary information, such as the latest firmware version available for the device, release notes, and any specific instructions or requirements provided by the manufacturer. It is also advisable to take a backup of the device's current configuration to minimize the risk of data loss or downtime. 2. Verifying compatibility: It is crucial to verify the compatibility of the new firmware version with the network device and the existing network infrastructure. This may involve checking for hardware specifications, feature support, and interoperability with other devices or software on the network. 3. Uploading the firmware:

Once the necessary preparations are made, the new firmware version needs to be uploaded to the network device. This is typically done using a dedicated firmware update tool or utility provided by the manufacturer. The update may be performed through a direct wired connection to the device or through a management interface, such as a web-based administration console. 4. Installing and testing the firmware: After uploading the firmware, the device needs to install and apply the update. This may involve a reboot or temporary disruption of service. Once the update is applied, it is important to thoroughly test the device to ensure that it functions correctly and that all desired features and settings are preserved. 5. Verifying and monitoring: After completing the firmware update, it is crucial to verify that the device is running the expected firmware version. This can be done by checking the device's firmware information or by using management tools or software that provide visibility into the network. Additionally, ongoing monitoring and maintenance are necessary to ensure that the device remains up-to-date with the latest firmware updates and patches that are released by the manufacturer.

Firmware Update

A firmware update, in the context of networking, refers to the process of updating the firmware or software that controls the operation and functionality of networking devices such as routers, switches, and modems. Firmware is a type of software that is installed on hardware devices to provide the necessary instructions for their proper functioning. Networking devices, like any other electronic devices, may require firmware updates to fix bugs, improve performance, add new features, or enhance security. These updates are typically provided by the manufacturer of the device and can be downloaded and installed either manually or automatically.

Firmware Upgrade

Firmware upgrade refers to the process of updating the software embedded in networking devices, such as routers, switches, and access points, to a newer version or revision. This upgrade is typically performed to resolve known bugs and security vulnerabilities, introduce new features, or improve the overall performance and stability of the device. During a firmware upgrade, the existing firmware is overwritten with the newer version. This can be done manually through a user interface provided by the device manufacturer or through an automated process, in which the device connects to a server and downloads the updated firmware. The upgrade process may vary depending on the device and the specific firmware version being upgraded.

Firmware

Firmware, in the context of networking, refers to the software programming that is permanently stored on a network device's read-only memory (ROM) or non-volatile memory. It serves as the operating system for the network device, providing instructions for its functioning and controlling its hardware components. Firmware is specific to the make and model of a device and is typically developed and provided by the manufacturer.

First Hop Redundancy Protocol (FHRP)

First Hop Redundancy Protocol (FHRP) is a networking protocol designed to provide redundant paths for data packets on a local area network (LAN). It ensures the availability and reliability of network resources by allowing multiple routers to act as a single virtual gateway. FHRP is commonly used in environments where uninterrupted network connectivity is critical, such as in enterprise networks, data centers, and service provider networks. There are several FHRP protocols available, including Hot Standby Router Protocol (HSRP), Virtual Router Redundancy Protocol (VRRP), and Gateway Load Balancing Protocol (GLBP). These protocols operate at the network layer and enable a group of routers to work together to provide fault tolerance and load balancing. HSRP is one of the most widely used FHRP protocols. It allows multiple routers to function as a virtual standby gateway, with one router acting as the active gateway and the others as standby gateways. The active gateway forwards packets on behalf of the virtual gateway, and if the active gateway fails, one of the standby gateways takes over the role of the active gateway automatically. This seamless failover ensures that network traffic is not interrupted in the event of a failure. VRRP is another FHRP protocol that provides similar functionality to HSRP. It also allows multiple routers to act as a virtual gateway, with one router as the master and the others as backups. The master router forwards packets on behalf of the virtual gateway, and if it fails, another router takes over the role of the master router. VRRP uses a virtual IP address that is shared among the routers, ensuring that clients on the LAN continue to have access to the network resources even if the master router fails. GLBP is a more advanced FHRP protocol that not only provides redundancy but also distributes the traffic load across multiple routers. It allows multiple routers to act as a virtual gateway, similar to HSRP and VRRP, but it also balances the traffic load by assigning different virtual MAC addresses to different clients. This load balancing capability enables efficient utilization of network resources and greater scalability. In summary, FHRP is a network protocol that enables multiple routers to work together to provide redundant paths and seamless failover in case of a failure. It ensures high availability and reliability of network resources and is commonly used in enterprise networks, data centers, and service provider networks.

Form Grabber

A form grabber is a type of malware that is designed to intercept data entered into online forms, primarily for the purpose of stealing sensitive information. This form of cyber attack poses a significant threat to network security, as it allows attackers to capture valuable data such as login credentials, credit card details, and personal information. Form grabbers typically operate by infecting a user's device, often through a malicious email attachment or a compromised website. Once installed, the malware works silently in the background, monitoring internet traffic and capturing any data entered into online forms. The captured data is then sent back to the attacker's server, where it can be used for various malicious purposes. This may include identity theft, financial fraud, or unauthorized access to online accounts. One of the key characteristics of a form grabber is its ability to bypass encryption measures in order to intercept data. This means that even if a website has implemented security measures such as SSL/TLS encryption, the malware can still capture the data before it is encrypted and sent over the network. To protect against form grabber attacks, it is essential to have robust network security measures in place. This includes using up-to-date antivirus software, regularly patching and updating software and operating systems, and implementing strong access controls and authentication mechanisms. Additionally, user education and awareness play a crucial role in preventing form grabber attacks. Users should be trained to recognize and avoid suspicious emails and websites, and they should always exercise caution when entering sensitive information online.

Formjacking

Formjacking refers to a cyber attack technique used by malicious actors to steal sensitive information, particularly payment card details, entered by users on online forms. This form of attack specifically targets e-commerce websites and other online platforms that require users to submit personal information through forms. During a formjacking attack, the attacker embeds malicious code into a legitimate website's payment processing page or form, typically through a compromised third-party script. When a user enters their payment card details or other sensitive information into the form, the malicious code intercepts and captures the data without the user's knowledge. The stolen information is then sent to the attacker or a remote server, where it can be sold on the dark web or used for fraudulent purposes.

Forward Error Correction (FEC)

Forward Error Correction (FEC) is a technique used in networking to improve data reliability by adding redundant information to the transmitted data. The additional information is used to detect and correct errors that may occur during transmission, ensuring accurate data delivery. In a network communication system, data is divided into packets for transmission. These packets are susceptible to errors due to various factors such as noise, interference, or distortion in the communication channel. FEC is designed to address these issues by adding redundancy to the packets. When transmitting data, FEC algorithms generate and append error correction codes (ECC) to the original packets. These codes are calculated based on the content of the packets using mathematical formulas. The ECC, also known as parity bits, contain information that can be used to detect and correct errors. At the receiver's end, the FEC mechanism analyzes the received packets and uses the ECC to identify and correct any errors. If errors are detected, the receiver uses the redundant information provided by the ECC to reconstruct the original data accurately. This process helps to ensure the integrity and reliability of the transmitted data. FEC offers several benefits in networking: 1. Improved Reliability: By detecting and correcting errors,

FEC ensures that the data received at the destination is an accurate representation of the original data. 2. Reduced Latency: Since errors can be corrected at the receiver's end, there is no need for retransmission of corrupted packets, leading to reduced latency in data transmission. 3. Bandwidth Efficiency: By adding redundant information to the packets, FEC reduces the need for retransmissions, optimizing the utilization of available network bandwidth. 4. Error Recovery: FEC can recover lost or corrupted packets by reconstructing the missing data using the redundant information. However, FEC also has certain limitations. It can introduce additional overhead due to the inclusion of redundant data, which may reduce the overall data throughput. Additionally, FEC has a limited ability to correct errors beyond a certain threshold, and for severe error conditions, alternative error recovery mechanisms may be required. In conclusion, FEC is a valuable technique in networking that increases data reliability by adding redundant information to transmitted packets. It helps to detect and correct errors, ensuring the accuracy and integrity of the received data.

Fragment Offset

The fragment offset is a key component of the IPv4 header that is used in networking to handle the fragmentation and reassembly of data packets. In order to transmit data over a network, it is divided into smaller blocks called packets. These packets carry the necessary information to route them to their destination. In some cases, the size of the data being transmitted may exceed the maximum packet size that can be handled by the network infrastructure. When this happens, the data must be fragmented into smaller packets that can be transmitted individually. The fragment offset is a field within the IPv4 header that specifies the position of a particular fragment within the original data packet. It is measured in units of 8-byte blocks, also known as octets. The value of the fragment offset field indicates the position of the fragment relative to the start of the original data packet. When a data packet is fragmented, each fragment includes a header that contains the fragment offset field. This field allows the receiving device to properly reassemble the fragments back into the original data packet. By using the fragment offset, the receiving device can determine the correct order of the fragments and reconstruct the original data packet. The fragment offset field is crucial for ensuring the reliable delivery of data packets. It allows network devices to handle the fragmentation and reassembly process efficiently, even when transmitting data that exceeds the maximum packet size. By properly ordering and reassembling the fragments, the receiving device can successfully reconstruct the original data packet and deliver it to the intended destination.

Fragmentation

Fragmentation in the context of networking refers to the division of data packets into smaller units to allow for their efficient transmission across a network. When data is transmitted over a network, it is broken down into smaller segments called packets. Fragmentation occurs when these packets are further divided into smaller fragments to accommodate the maximum transmission unit (MTU) size supported by the network. The need for fragmentation arises when the size of the data packet exceeds the maximum size that can be transmitted over the network. This can occur due to various factors such as network limitations, different network devices having varying MTU sizes, or when data is sent from a network with a larger MTU to a network with a smaller MTU.

Frame Check Sequence (FCS)

A Frame Check Sequence (FCS) is a field in the data link layer of a network packet that is used to detect errors during transmission. FCS provides a mechanism to verify the integrity of the received data and ensure that it has not been corrupted or altered in transit. When a network device sends a packet, it calculates the FCS by performing a mathematical algorithm on the packet data and attaching the result as a fixed-length sequence of bits at the end of the packet. The FCS is calculated using a checksum or a cyclic redundancy check (CRC) algorithm, which generates a unique sequence based on the data in the packet. Upon receiving a packet, the receiving device recalculates the FCS using the same algorithm and compares it to the FCS that was transmitted with the packet. If the calculated FCS matches the received FCS, it means that the packet has been received without any errors. However, if the calculated FCS does not match the received FCS, it indicates that the packet has been corrupted during transmission or has been tampered with. The comparison of the FCS values allows the receiving device to detect errors such as bit flips, noise, or interference that may have occurred while the packet was being transmitted. If an error is detected, the receiving device can request the sender to retransmit the packet to ensure the accuracy and reliability of the data transmission. By including the FCS in each packet, networks can achieve a higher level of data integrity and accuracy. The FCS acts as a means of error detection, allowing network devices to identify and correct any errors that may have occurred during transmission. Without the FCS, errors in the received data would go unnoticed, leading to potential data corruption and loss.

Frame Relay

Frame Relay is a network protocol used in telecommunications to efficiently transmit data between devices across a wide area network (WAN). It operates at the data link layer of the Open Systems Interconnection (OSI) model and facilitates the efficient and reliable delivery of data packets. Frame Relay works by dividing data into smaller units called frames, which are then transmitted between network devices. These frames contain address information, control information, and the actual data payload. The frames are forwarded through virtual circuits, which are logical connections established between devices in the network.

Fuzz Testing

Fuzz Testing, also known as fuzzing, is a technique used in network testing to detect software vulnerabilities by providing unexpected or invalid inputs to target systems. It aims to discover faults, crashes, or unexpected behavior in network protocols, applications, or services. The process involves sending a large number of random or mutated inputs, typically generated by automated tools, to the target system. These inputs can be traffic packets, messages, or data inputs that are designed to test various aspects of the system's behavior. Fuzzing is often used to identify and exploit vulnerabilities in network protocols or the implementation of network services.

Gateway Configuration Best Practices

Gateway Configuration Best Practices refers to the set of guidelines and procedures that should be followed in order to effectively and efficiently configure gateways in a networking environment. A gateway is a device or software component that acts as an entrance or exit point between two networks, allowing for communication and data transfer. By configuring gateways properly, organizations can ensure optimal network performance, security, and compatibility. There are several key aspects to consider when implementing gateway configuration best practices. One important aspect is security. Gateways should be configured with appropriate security measures, such as firewalls, intrusion detection systems, and virtual private networks (VPNs), to protect against unauthorized access, malware, and other cyber threats. Additionally, strong authentication mechanisms, such as two-factor authentication, should be employed to ensure that only authorized individuals can access the gateway. Another aspect to consider is network performance. Gateways should be configured to prioritize traffic and allocate bandwidth appropriately. Quality of Service (QoS) settings can be used to prioritize certain types of traffic, such as voice or video data, over less time-sensitive data. Additionally, network Address Translation (NAT) can be utilized to efficiently manage IP address allocation and ensure smooth communication between different networks. Compatibility is also a key consideration in gateway configuration. Gateways should be configured to support the protocols and technologies used in the network environment. For example, if a network uses IPv6, the gateways should be configured to support IPv6 addressing and routing. Configuring gateways to be compatible with the specific networking equipment and systems deployed in the network can help avoid compatibility issues and ensure seamless communication.

Gateway Configuration

A gateway configuration, in the context of networking, refers to the process of setting up and managing the settings related to a gateway device. A gateway serves as an entry and exit point for network traffic between different networks or network segments. To configure a gateway, various parameters and settings need to be specified depending on the requirements of the network. These settings may include the IP address, subnet mask, default gateway, DNS server, security configurations, and routing protocols.

Gateway Device Configuration

A gateway device configuration refers to the process of setting up and customizing a network device that acts as a gateway between different networks. It involves configuring various parameters and settings to enable the device to efficiently route network traffic between networks, apply security measures, and provide additional network services. Gateway devices, also known as routers or gateways, play a crucial role in networking by connecting separate networks and enabling communication between them. They are responsible for directing incoming and outgoing data packets, ensuring that they reach their intended destinations. To perform these tasks effectively, gateway devices must be properly configured.

Gateway Device

A gateway device, in the context of networking, refers to a hardware or software component that acts as an intermediary between two or more different networks. It facilitates communication and data transfer between these networks, which may use different protocols or have differing network architectures. Gateway devices operate at the network layer of the OSI model and are responsible for routing network traffic, performing protocol conversions, and providing network security capabilities. They play a critical role in connecting networks of different types, such as local area networks (LANs) and wide area networks (WANs), or different network technologies like Ethernet and Wi-Fi.

Gateway IP

A gateway IP, in the context of networking, refers to the IP address of a device or server that acts as an entry point or exit point for data traffic within a network. It serves as a link or bridge between different networks, allowing communication and the transfer of data between them. Gateways play a crucial role in the transmission of data packets by directing them to their respective destinations, whether that be within the same network or to an external network, such as the internet. They act as a sort of translator, converting the protocols used within one network into a format that can be understood by another network.

Gateway Router

A gateway router is a networking device that serves as a central point for connecting multiple networks together. It is designed to facilitate the communication between different networks, allowing data to be transferred smoothly and efficiently. Essentially, a gateway router acts as an intermediary between two or more networks, ensuring that data packets are directed to the appropriate destination. It performs various functions to enable this process, such as routing, network address translation (NAT), and firewall protection.

Gateway Security

Gateway security refers to the measures implemented at the gateway interface of a network to protect it from unauthorized access and to ensure the confidentiality, integrity, and availability of data transmitted through the network. It involves a combination of hardware, software, and protocols that are designed to identify and mitigate potential security threats before they can penetrate the network. One of the primary purposes of gateway security is to act as a barrier between the internal network and the external environment, such as the internet. It acts as a gateway or a bridge that controls the traffic flowing in and out of the network, allowing authorized traffic to pass through while blocking or inspecting potentially malicious traffic. This helps in minimizing the risk of unauthorized access, data breaches, and other security incidents. Gateway security solutions typically include firewalls, intrusion detection and prevention systems (IDS/IPS), virtual private networks (VPNs), and secure email gateways. These components work together to enforce various security policies and measures to protect the network. Firewalls are a fundamental component of gateway security that monitor and filter incoming and outgoing network traffic based on predefined rules. They examine packet headers and apply access control lists to determine whether to allow or block specific traffic. IDS/IPS systems are designed to detect and prevent unauthorized access and malicious activities within the network by analyzing network traffic patterns and behavior. They can identify and respond to various types of attacks, such as DDoS attacks, port scans, and intrusion attempts. A VPN is a secure and encrypted connection that allows users to access the network remotely over the internet. It provides confidentiality and integrity for data transmission, ensuring that sensitive information remains protected from eavesdropping and tampering. Secure email gateways play a crucial role in protecting against email-based threats, such as phishing attacks and malware. They analyze incoming and outgoing emails, filter out malicious content, and block suspicious attachments or URLs. In conclusion, gateway security plays a vital role in protecting networks from potential security threats. By implementing robust gateway security measures, organizations can ensure the confidentiality, integrity, and availability of their network resources, safeguard sensitive information, and prevent unauthorized access or data breaches.

Gateway Subnet

A gateway subnet is a subnet within a network that is specifically reserved to host gateway devices. It is a vital component in network infrastructure, serving as the entry point between different networks or systems. The purpose of a gateway subnet is to facilitate communication and enable data transfer between networks that use different protocols or technologies. A gateway subnet is typically used in a virtual network environment, where different virtual machines or resources require access to the external network or internet. In this scenario, the gateway subnet acts as a bridge or interface that connects the virtual network to the broader network, ensuring seamless connectivity and secure data transmission.

Gateway

A gateway, in the context of networking, refers to a network device or a software program that acts as an entry or exit point between two different networks. It is responsible for connecting different networks that use different protocols, enabling communication and data transfer between them. Gateways serve as an interface between networks that use different communication protocols, such as Ethernet, TCP/IP, or Token Ring. They provide a translation layer, converting data from one format or protocol to another, ensuring compatibility and successful communication between networks.

Global System For Mobile Communications (GSM)

The Global System for Mobile Communications (GSM) is a standard developed for the digital cellular networks used for voice and data communication services. It is one of the most widely used mobile network technologies globally, providing seamless and interoperable communication capabilities. GSM is based on a combination of technologies, including time division multiple access (TDMA) and frequency division multiple access (FDMA), which enable multiple users to share the same frequency band simultaneously. This allows for efficient utilization of scarce radio spectrum resources, enabling high-capacity mobile network deployments. GSM networks consist of three main components: mobile stations (MS), base transceiver stations (BTS), and mobile switching centers (MSC). The MS refers to the end-user devices, such as mobile phones or tablets, which communicate with the network. BTSs are responsible for transmitting and receiving signals between MSs and the network, while MSCs handle call routing and switching functionalities. GSM networks operate on different frequency bands, which vary between different geographical regions and network operators. This allows for seamless global roaming capabilities, as mobile devices can connect to different networks while travelling without the need for complex network reconfiguration. One of the key advantages of GSM is its ability to provide secure and reliable communication through various encryption techniques. This ensures the confidentiality and integrity of voice and data transmissions over the network, protecting users' privacy and sensitive information. In addition to voice calls, GSM networks support a range of data services, including short message service (SMS), multimedia messaging service (MMS), and mobile internet access. This enables users to exchange text messages, multimedia content, and access the internet from their mobile devices. GSM has been continuously evolving to meet the increasing demand for higher data speeds and capacity. Enhanced versions of GSM, such as Enhanced Data rates for GSM Evolution (EDGE), have been deployed to provide improved data transmission rates, paving the way for the transition to third-generation (3G) and fourth-generation (4G) mobile networks. In summary, GSM is a standardized digital cellular network technology that enables seamless voice and data communication services worldwide. Its efficient spectrum utilization, secure transmission, and support for various data services have made it the foundation for mobile communication networks across the globe.

Google Cloud Networking

Google Cloud Networking refers to the networking capabilities and services provided by Google Cloud Platform (GCP) for connecting and managing resources within the cloud environment. With Google Cloud Networking, users can create and configure virtual networks, subnets, and firewall rules to ensure secure and efficient communication between different cloud resources such as virtual machines, storage buckets, and databases. It provides the necessary infrastructure and tools to establish connectivity, manage traffic, and maintain a reliable network environment.

Google Cloud Platform (GCP) Networking

Google Cloud Platform (GCP) Networking refers to the set of technologies, services, and configuration options provided by Google Cloud Platform for establishing and managing network connectivity within and between GCP resources and external networks. GCP Networking encompasses various key components and features that enable reliable and secure communication between different resources and environments within the GCP infrastructure. These components include Virtual Private Cloud (VPC), subnets, routes, firewalls, load balancers, and Virtual Private Network (VPN) gateways. At the core of GCP Networking is the Virtual Private Cloud (VPC), which acts as a logical private network segment within GCP. VPCs provide isolation and segmentation of resources, allowing users to create their own virtual networks with customizable IP address ranges. Within a VPC, users can create multiple subnets to further segregate resources and control access using firewall rules. To enable communication between resources located in different VPCs or between GCP and external networks, GCP Networking provides routing capabilities. Routing allows users to define and manage how network traffic is directed between subnets, VPCs, and external networks. This ensures that network traffic reaches its intended destination efficiently and securely. GCP Networking also includes various load balancing options to distribute incoming network traffic across multiple resources, ensuring high availability and scalability. Load balancers can be used to balance traffic between virtual machines (VMs) within a VPC, across multiple regions, or even between on-premises infrastructure and GCP resources. To enhance security and control access to resources, GCP Networking offers powerful firewall capabilities. Users can define firewall rules to allow or deny specific types of traffic based on source and destination IP addresses, protocols, and ports. This helps protect resources from unauthorized access and ensures that network traffic complies with predefined security policies. In addition, GCP Networking provides Virtual Private Network (VPN) gateways, which allow secure and encrypted connections between GCP VPCs and on-premises networks. This enables users to extend their on-premises infrastructure to GCP or establish secure connections with partners or remote offices. Overall, GCP Networking offers a comprehensive set of features and tools to establish and manage network connectivity within and across GCP resources. By leveraging these networking capabilities, users can create reliable, scalable, and secure network architectures for their applications and services hosted on the Google Cloud Platform.

Gray Hat Hacking

Gray Hat Hacking refers to the practice of individuals who engage in hacking activities with both ethical and unethical intentions. These individuals possess knowledge and skills in various networking technologies and exploit vulnerabilities within computer networks to gain unauthorized access, manipulate data, or compromise security. Gray Hat Hackers differ from White Hat Hackers, who hack with ethical intentions, and Black Hat Hackers, who engage in hacking activities solely for malicious purposes. Gray Hat Hackers often act as a sort of "middle ground," as they may initially exploit vulnerabilities in computer networks without permission but then inform the network administrator of these vulnerabilities, allowing them to be fixed.

Graylist

A graylist, in the context of networking, refers to a type of security measure implemented by network administrators to control access to a network or its resources. Unlike a blacklist, which completely denies access to specific entities, or a whitelist, which allows access only to specified entities, a graylist is a middle ground that grants limited access initially and then assesses and adjusts the access level based on certain criteria. When an entity, such as an IP address, domain, or user, tries to access a network or its resources, it is initially placed on the graylist, which means that it is neither completely allowed nor denied access. During this time, the network administrator can observe the entity's behavior and collect information on its intentions, activities, and potential threats. The graylist period allows the administrator to make informed decisions about whether to grant full access, deny access, or continue with limited access. The criteria used to assess the entity's access level during the graylist period can vary depending on the network's security policies and requirements. These criteria may include factors such as the entity's reputation, previous interactions with the network, compliance with security protocols, and any suspicious activities detected. Monitoring tools, such as intrusion detection systems and log analyzers, are often used to gather relevant data and support decision-making in this process. Graylisting can serve various purposes within a networking context. It can be used to protect against potential threats from malicious entities, such as hackers or spammers, by subjecting them to closer examination before granting full access. It can also be employed for legitimate entities that may have exhibited unusual behavior, allowing the administrator to verify their intentions and take appropriate actions. Additionally, graylisting can be useful for managing network resources efficiently by allowing limited access initially and adjusting it based on actual resource usage. Overall, graylisting provides network administrators with a flexible and dynamic approach to control access, combining the benefits of both blacklisting and whitelisting. By granting limited access initially and then evaluating the entity's trustworthiness, a graylist ensures a higher level of security and helps to maintain the integrity and availability of network resources.

Grey Hat Hacker

A Grey Hat Hacker is an individual who engages in hacking activities with mixed motivations and intentions. They generally fall in between the categories of Black Hat Hackers and White Hat Hackers. Unlike Black Hat Hackers who conduct hacking activities with malicious intent, and White Hat Hackers who use their skills to identify and fix vulnerabilities for ethical purposes, Grey Hat Hackers operate in a grey area, where the line between ethical and unethical hacking is blurred. Grey Hat Hackers often discover vulnerabilities in computer systems, networks, or software applications without permission. However, their intentions may not be purely malicious or destructive. They may exploit these vulnerabilities to gain unauthorized access to networks or systems, retrieve sensitive information, or disrupt services, but without malicious intent. Instead, they usually aim to raise awareness about the vulnerabilities and encourage organizations to address them.

HTTP (Hypertext Transfer Protocol)

HTTP (Hypertext Transfer Protocol) is a networking protocol that enables the transfer of structured documents over the internet. It is an application layer protocol that allows the communication between clients and servers. The protocol follows a client-server model, where the client initiates a request to the server, and the server responds with the requested data. HTTP operates on top of the TCP/IP protocol suite and uses TCP as its transport protocol. It uses a textual format to define the structure of the messages exchanged between the client and server. HTTP messages consist of a request or a response, each containing a request line or status line, headers, and a message body (when necessary).

HTTP Request

An HTTP request is a message sent by a client to a server requesting a particular action or resource. It is a key component of the Hypertext Transfer Protocol (HTTP), which is the foundation of data communication on the World Wide Web. A client, usually a web browser, initiates an HTTP request by specifying the desired action or resource using a Uniform Resource Locator (URL). The URL contains the protocol (HTTP), the server name or IP address, and optionally, the path to the specific resource. The client then sends the request to the server using a TCP/IP connection. The HTTP request consists of several parts. The first part is the request line, which specifies the HTTP method, the target URL, and the HTTP protocol version. The most common HTTP methods are GET and POST. GET requests retrieve information from the server, while POST requests submit data to the server. After the request line, there are optional request headers, which provide additional information about the client or the desired resource. These headers can include information like the user agent (the client's software and

161

version), cookies, accepted languages, and more. The server uses these headers to determine how to handle the request or to provide specific responses. Following the headers, there can be an optional message body, which contains data sent by the client. This is typically used in POST requests to submit form data, but it can also be used in other scenarios where the client needs to send data to the server. Once the HTTP request is complete, the client sends it to the server. The server processes the request, performs the requested action, and sends back an HTTP response, which contains the requested resource or information about the action performed. Overall, HTTP requests play a crucial role in networking and web communication. They enable clients to interact with servers, retrieve resources, submit data, and accomplish various tasks on the World Wide Web.

HTTPS (Hypertext Transfer Protocol Secure)

HTTPS (Hypertext Transfer Protocol Secure) is a secure version of HTTP that provides encrypted communication between a client and a server over a computer network. It is used to ensure the integrity and confidentiality of data transmitted between the client (such as a web browser) and the server (such as a website). HTTPS uses the SSL/TLS (Secure Sockets Layer/Transport Layer Security) protocols to encrypt data before transmitting it. This encryption process involves the use of cryptographic keys to scramble the data into an unreadable format, making it difficult for unauthorized parties to intercept and understand the information being transmitted. When a client requests a secure connection to a server, the server responds by sending its SSL/TLS certificate. This certificate contains a public key that the client can use to establish a secure connection. The client then generates a session key, encrypts it with the server's public key, and sends it back to the server. Both the client and the server now possess the same session key, which they use to encrypt and decrypt the data being transmitted between them. HTTPS not only provides data encryption but also ensures data integrity. This means that any data sent over HTTPS cannot be tampered with during transmission. To achieve data integrity, HTTPS uses digital signatures. These signatures are created by generating a unique hash value for the data, encrypting it with the private key associated with the SSL/TLS certificate, and attaching it to the data being transmitted. Upon receiving the data, the recipient can verify the integrity of the data by decrypting the signature using the public key associated with the sender's certificate. By utilizing HTTPS, websites can protect sensitive information such as login credentials, credit card numbers, and personal details from unauthorized access and eavesdropping. It ensures that the communication between the client and server remains confidential and secure. This is especially important when handling sensitive data on websites that require user authentication or involve financial transactions. In summary, HTTPS is a secure version of HTTP that uses SSL/TLS protocols to encrypt and protect data transmission between a client and a server. It provides data confidentiality, integrity, and ensures secure communication over a computer network.

Hacker Group

Hacker Group refers to a collection of individuals who collaborate and work together to conduct unauthorized activities within computer networks, with the intention of gaining unlawful access to sensitive information, manipulating system configurations, or disrupting network services. These groups, often referred to as black hat hackers, engage in a variety of malicious activities, including but not limited to, stealing personal data, launching cyber attacks, distributing malware, and defacing websites. The members of a hacker group possess advanced technical skills and knowledge of computer systems, networks, and software vulnerabilities, which they exploit to achieve their illicit objectives. Hacker groups are typically organized hierarchically, with different members having varied roles and responsibilities within the group. These roles may include leading the group, overseeing technical aspects, managing communication and recruitment, or executing specific attack techniques. This division of labor allows hacker groups to operate efficiently and effectively, maximizing their impact while minimizing the risk of detection and apprehension. Hacker groups often establish their presence on online forums and underground communities, where they share tools, techniques, and insights with like-minded individuals. These platforms serve as a means for collaboration, knowledge exchange, and recruitment. By leveraging collective expertise, hacker groups gain an advantage in discovering and exploiting vulnerabilities in computer networks and systems. The motivations behind the activities of hacker groups can vary widely. Some groups may pursue financial gain by stealing credit card information, extorting individuals or organizations, or conducting fraudulent activities. Others

162

may be driven by ideological beliefs, seeking to disrupt governmental or corporate entities as a form of protest. Additionally, hacker groups may engage in state-sponsored cyber espionage, focused on gathering intelligence or disrupting rival nations. Due to the illegal and malicious nature of their activities, hacker groups are subject to prosecution and face severe legal consequences if identified and apprehended. To counter their actions, organizations employ various security measures, including network monitoring, intrusion detection systems, encryption, and vulnerability assessments. Collaboration between law enforcement agencies, cybersecurity firms, and international organizations also plays a crucial role in combating the activities of hacker groups and mitigating the risks they pose to network security and privacy.

Hacker Toolkit

A Hacker Toolkit in the context of networking refers to a collection of software tools and utilities that are commonly used by hackers or cybersecurity professionals to conduct various network-related activities. These tools are often utilized to identify vulnerabilities, exploit weaknesses, test network security measures, and assess the overall resilience of a network infrastructure. The Hacker Toolkit encompasses a wide range of applications, scripts, scanners, and protocols that can be employed to carry out different network hacking techniques. This toolkit usually includes tools for network mapping and reconnaissance, vulnerability assessment, network scanning, packet sniffing, password cracking, traffic analysis, and network exploitation. Network mapping and reconnaissance tools assist in gathering information about the target network, such as IP addresses, open ports, and system configurations. This information aids in identifying potential entry points and vulnerabilities within the network infrastructure. Vulnerability assessment tools, on the other hand, evaluate the security posture of a network by scanning for known vulnerabilities within network devices, systems, and applications. These tools help in uncovering weaknesses that can be exploited by an attacker. Network scanning tools are designed to discover hosts, services, and devices within a network. They facilitate the identification of accessible systems and open ports that can be targeted for further exploitation. Packet sniffing tools, also known as network analyzers, capture and analyze network traffic to gather sensitive information, such as usernames, passwords, and other confidential data. These tools are commonly used to intercept and analyze network packets for security analysis or malicious purposes. Password cracking tools focus on breaking password or encryption protocols to gain unauthorized access to network resources. They employ techniques like brute force, dictionary attacks, or rainbow table lookup to decrypt passwords or encryption keys. Traffic analysis tools help in examining network traffic patterns and can unveil suspicious activities, network bottlenecks, or malicious behaviors. Network exploitation tools are used to take advantage of identified vulnerabilities within the network. For instance, these tools can be deployed to escalate privileges, gain unauthorized access, breach firewalls, or launch denial-of-service (DoS) attacks. They enable hackers to exploit weaknesses and compromise network security.

Hacker

A hacker is an individual who possesses advanced technical skills and knowledge in the field of computer networking. They are proficient in exploiting vulnerabilities in computer systems and networks with the intention of gaining unauthorized access, manipulating data, or causing disruption. Hackers can be categorized into different types based on their motivations, techniques, and legality of their activities. The term "hacker" can have both positive and negative connotations. In a positive sense, it refers to individuals who use their expertise to identify and fix security weaknesses in systems, known as ethical hackers or security professionals. They work to strengthen the security of networks and protect them from malicious attacks by understanding the mindset and methods of potential attackers. On the other hand, hackers also include individuals engaging in illegal activities, often referred to as "black hat" hackers. These individuals exploit vulnerabilities in computer networks for personal gain, financial profit, or simply to cause chaos and disruption. They may engage in activities such as unauthorized access, data theft, financial fraud, or spreading malware. There is also a gray area in the hacking realm known as "gray hat" hackers. These individuals may operate in ethically ambiguous situations, where their motives or methods are not clearly defined as black or white. They may access systems without permission but disclose vulnerabilities to the system owner, often with the intention of helping to improve security. Hackers use a variety of techniques and tools to gain unauthorized access to networks. These techniques include social engineering, password cracking, network scanning, and exploiting software vulnerabilities. Once inside a network, a hacker can engage in various activities such as eavesdropping on communications, altering or deleting data, disrupting services, or gaining control over critical systems. To combat hacking activities, organizations employ various security measures, including firewalls, intrusion detection systems, encryption, and regular security audits. Additionally, hacker communities have formed worldwide to share knowledge, collaborate on research, and develop defensive strategies against potential threats. In conclusion, a hacker is a technically skilled individual who possesses the expertise to exploit weaknesses in computer networks for both good and malicious purposes. Their activities can range from identifying and fixing vulnerabilities to engaging in illegal activities such as unauthorized access and data theft. The constant evolution of hacking techniques and the continuous efforts to enhance network security contribute to an ongoing battle between hackers and security professionals.

Hash Function

A hash function is a mathematical function that takes an input (or "message") and produces a fixed-size string of characters, which is typically a hexadecimal or binary representation. In the context of networking, hash functions are primarily used for data integrity checking and data retrieval optimization. Data integrity checking is essential in networking to ensure that the data being transmitted or stored remains unchanged and is not tampered with during transit. Hash functions play a vital role in this process by producing a unique hash value or checksum from the input data. This hash value acts as a digital fingerprint for the data, enabling detection of any alterations or corruption. When transmitting data over a network, the sender can calculate the hash value of the data using a hash function. This hash value is then included with the data being sent. Upon receiving the data, the receiver can recalculate the hash value using the same hash function. If the calculated hash value matches the received hash value, it indicates that the data was not modified during transmission. Any changes in the data would result in a different hash value, alerting the receiver to potential tampering. Hash functions also play a significant role in data retrieval optimization in networking. In large-scale networks, efficient data retrieval is crucial to minimize latency and ensure optimal performance. Hash functions are used to map data to specific locations within a network, such as caching servers or distributed storage systems. For example, in content delivery networks (CDNs), hash functions are used to map requested content (e.g., web pages, images) to specific CDN servers. This mapping is based on the hash value generated from the content's identifier. By consistently mapping the same content to the same server, hash functions help optimize content retrieval and distribution across the network, reducing network congestion and improving overall performance.

Heuristic Analysis

Heuristic Analysis is a technique used in the field of networking to evaluate the efficiency and performance of communication protocols and algorithms. It involves the evaluation and measurement of a system based on experience and practical knowledge instead of relying solely on formal mathematical proofs or rigorous testing. During heuristic analysis, various aspects of a network are assessed, including its design, architecture, routing algorithms, flow control mechanisms, and error handling protocols. The goal is to identify potential weaknesses or areas of improvement in order to enhance the overall functionality and efficiency of the network.

Honeynet

A honeynet is a network infrastructure that is specifically designed to be the target of cyber attacks. It is a tool used by cybersecurity professionals to study and analyze the behavior of hackers, malware, and other malicious activities. The honeynet consists of various interconnected honeypots, which are decoy systems or applications that simulate real network elements to attract hackers. These honeypots are intentionally vulnerable and contain simulated valuable data or services to lure attackers.

Honeypot Network

Honeypot

A honeypot in the context of networking refers to a security technique that involves the creation of an attractive target or resource with the purpose of drawing in and detecting hackers, potential intruders, or malicious software. It is essentially a decoy system or network that is intended to be compromised, enabling security professionals to gather valuable information about cyber threats and attackers. The primary function of a honeypot is to deceive and divert attackers away from critical or sensitive systems, while simultaneously allowing security experts to monitor and analyze the techniques, tactics, and motives of potential attackers. By analyzing the activities and behaviors of malicious actors within the honeypot environment, security professionals can gain insights into new attack vectors, emerging threats, and vulnerabilities that can be leveraged to strengthen overall network security.

Host-Based Firewall

A host-based firewall is a security mechanism that is installed and configured on an individual computer or host to protect it from unauthorized access and malicious activities. It operates at the network layer of the TCP/IP protocol stack, analyzing inbound and outbound network traffic based on predetermined rules and policies. The main purpose of a host-based firewall is to control the flow of network packets to and from a specific host, thereby preventing unauthorized access and ensuring the security and integrity of the host and its data. By filtering network traffic, it acts as a barrier between the host and the external network, allowing only authorized communication and blocking or alerting on any suspicious or malicious activities.

Host-Based Intrusion Detection System (IDS)

A Host-Based Intrusion Detection System (IDS) is a network security technology that monitors the activities and behavior of a single host or device on a network in order to detect and respond to unauthorized or malicious activities. The primary function of a Host-Based IDS is to analyze events and data generated by a single host, such as a server or workstation, in order to identify any suspicious or abnormal patterns that may indicate a security breach or compromise. By examining various system logs, network traffic, and user activity, the IDS can alert network administrators or security personnel of potential threats in real-time, allowing for immediate investigation and response. Unlike Network-Based IDS (NIDS) which monitor network traffic at a global level, a Host-Based IDS focuses on the individual host level, providing detailed information and analysis specific to that particular device. This makes it particularly effective in detecting insider threats, targeted attacks, and other malicious activities that may be missed by a NIDS. A Host-Based IDS typically operates by collecting and analyzing system logs, event logs, file integrity data, and other relevant information from the host being monitored. It uses various detection methods and techniques, such as signature-based detection, anomaly detection, and behavior-based analysis, to identify potential threats or malicious activities. These detection methods are often supplemented with rule sets or policies that define specific criteria for identifying suspicious behavior. Once a potential security threat or intrusion is detected, the Host-Based IDS can take various response actions, such as generating alerts, blocking network connections, initiating system backups, or even quarantining or isolating the affected host from the network. These actions are typically defined by the network administrators or security policies and are designed to mitigate the impact of the security incident and prevent further damage or compromise. In summary, a Host-Based Intrusion Detection System is a network security technology that focuses on monitoring and analyzing the activities of a single host or device to detect and respond to unauthorized or malicious activities. It plays a crucial role in protecting the integrity and security of individual hosts within a network by providing real-time threat detection and response capabilities.

Host-Based Intrusion Detection

Host-Based Intrusion Detection (HIDS) refers to a network security system that aims to detect and prevent unauthorized access or malicious activities on individual computer systems within a network. It operates by monitoring and analyzing the behavior and configuration of an individual host to identify any signs of intrusion or suspicious activities. HIDS focuses on the security of a single host or endpoint, such as a server, workstation, or any other network-connected device. It works by examining the internal activities and log files of the host to identify and alert any malicious or anomalous behavior. This includes monitoring system files, registry entries, network connections, and user activities.

Host-Based Intrusion Prevention System (IPS)

A Host-Based Intrusion Prevention System (IPS) is a network security technology that is deployed on individual computers or servers to monitor and detect unauthorized access attempts and stop them before they can cause damage. It functions as an additional layer of defense alongside traditional firewalls, antivirus software, and other security measures. The primary purpose of a Host-Based IPS is to prevent or mitigate attacks that specifically target the host system it is installed on. It does this by analyzing network traffic and system behavior in real-time, looking for suspicious or malicious activities. When such activities are detected, the IPS can take immediate action to block or quarantine the traffic, terminate malicious processes, or alert the system administrator for further investigation. The key features and capabilities of a Host-Based IPS typically include: 1. Signature-based detection: The IPS relies on a database of known attack signatures to identify and block known threats. These signatures are regularly updated to keep up with the evolving threat landscape. 2. Anomaly-based detection: The IPS uses behavioral analysis to identify abnormal network traffic or system behavior that may indicate a potential attack. It can learn the normal behavior patterns of the host system and raise alarms when deviations occur. 3. Real-time monitoring: The IPS continuously monitors network traffic and system events, providing real-time protection against intrusions. It can actively block or deny suspicious traffic or system activities before they can compromise the security of the host. 4. Event logging and reporting: The IPS keeps a detailed log of security events, including detected threats, blocked traffic, and system alerts. These logs are crucial for post-incident analysis, forensic investigations, and compliance auditing. 5. Integration with centralized management systems: The IPS can be centrally managed and configured, allowing system administrators to have a unified view of the security posture of all the host systems within the network. Overall, a Host-Based IPS provides an essential layer of protection for individual computers and servers against various forms of network attacks. By actively monitoring and responding to security threats, it helps to safeguard the integrity, confidentiality, and availability of the host system and the network it is connected to.

Host-Based Security Measures

Host-Based Security Measures refers to a set of techniques and practices implemented to protect the individual systems (hosts) within a network from security threats, vulnerabilities, and attacks. These measures are designed to defend the integrity, confidentiality, and availability of the host's resources and data, ensuring that unauthorized access or malicious activities are prevented or mitigated. One commonly used host-based security measure is the implementation of antivirus software. Antivirus programs are designed to detect, prevent, and remove malicious software, such as viruses, worms, and Trojan horses, from infecting a host system. These programs typically scan files and processes, comparing them against a vast database of known malware signatures, patterns, and behaviors to identify and neutralize potential threats. Another important host-based security measure is the use of firewalls. Firewalls operate as a protective barrier between a host system and the external network, monitoring and controlling incoming and outgoing network traffic based on predefined security rules. By analyzing the communication packets, firewalls can filter out potentially harmful or unauthorized connections, preventing malicious actors from exploiting vulnerabilities or gaining unauthorized access to the host system. Intrusion detection and prevention systems (IDS/IPS) are also common host-based security measures. IDS continuously monitor network activities, looking for abnormal or suspicious behavior that could indicate a security breach or attack. When such activities are detected, IDS generate alerts or take automated actions to prevent or mitigate the potential threat. IPS, on the other hand, not only detect but also actively block or prevent unauthorized activities or attacks, adding an extra layer of security to the host system. In addition to these measures, host-based security also involves regular patching and updating of operating systems and software applications. Patch management helps to fix known vulnerabilities and weaknesses in the host system, reducing the risk of exploitation by attackers. It is crucial to keep the system up to date with the latest security patches, as vulnerabilities are often discovered and addressed by software vendors. Overall, host-based security measures play a crucial role in safeguarding individual systems within a network from various security threats. By implementing these measures, network administrators can ensure the protection of their host systems, maintaining the overall security and stability of the network infrastructure.

Host-Based Security Software

166

Host-Based Security Software refers to a type of software application or tool that is installed and operates on individual computer systems or hosts. It is designed to protect these hosts from various security threats and risks that may arise from network connections, user interactions, or external attacks. This software includes a range of security features and capabilities that are specifically tailored to the host operating system and its local environment. It can be seen as an essential component in securing networked systems, as it focuses on protecting the individual hosts themselves rather than the overall network infrastructure.

Hosted Domain Name System (DNS)

A Hosted Domain Name System (DNS) refers to a system that offers domain name service capabilities to clients, with the entire DNS infrastructure being managed and maintained by a third-party service provider. In this setup, the responsibility of managing DNS records, resolving domain names to IP addresses, and handling the overall DNS infrastructure lies with the hosting provider, relieving the client of these tasks. In a hosted DNS, clients delegate their DNS management to the service provider by configuring their domain names to use the DNS servers provided by the hosting company. This delegation is usually done by updating the domain's DNS settings at the registrar, specifying the DNS server addresses provided by the hosting provider. Once the DNS delegation is complete, the hosting company takes responsibility for the following tasks: - Maintaining the DNS servers: The hosting provider manages the servers that host the DNS records for the client's domain. This involves ensuring the servers are properly configured, regularly updated, and running optimally to provide seamless DNS resolution. - Managing DNS records: The hosting provider handles the creation, modification, and deletion of DNS records for the client's domain. This includes records such as A (address) records, MX (mail exchange) records, CNAME (canonical name) records, and others. The client typically interacts with the hosting provider's DNS management interface to make changes or additions to these records. - Resolving DNS queries: When a user tries to access a website or service associated with the client's domain, their device sends a DNS query to the hosting provider's DNS servers. The hosting provider's DNS infrastructure then resolves the domain name to the corresponding IP address and returns it to the user's device, enabling the connection to be established. A hosted DNS offers several benefits to clients, including simplified DNS management, improved reliability and performance, and access to advanced DNS features and configurations. By outsourcing DNS management to a reliable hosting provider, clients can focus on their core activities without worrying about the complexities of DNS infrastructure maintenance.

Hostname

A hostname is a label assigned to a device connected to a computer network. It is used to identify and locate the device within the network. Hostnames are typically alphanumeric names assigned to network devices such as computers, servers, routers, or IoT devices. In a networking context, a hostname plays a vital role in network communication. It serves as an easy-to-remember and meaningful identifier for both humans and software applications. Instead of relying solely on numeric addresses (IP addresses) to access a device, hostnames provide a more user-friendly way to refer to devices within the network.

Hot Standby Router Protocol (HSRP)

Hot Standby Router Protocol (HSRP) is a network protocol used for providing redundancy and high availability in a computer network. It is an industry-standard protocol that allows multiple routers to work together as a virtual router, providing failover capabilities in case of router failure. HSRP provides a way to create a redundant path for data traffic, ensuring uninterrupted network connectivity. HSRP works by allowing routers to elect a primary router, which is responsible for forwarding network traffic. The primary router actively participates in the network and responds to network traffic. In addition to the primary router, one or more standby routers are elected as backups. These backup routers are in a standby mode, monitoring the primary router's status and ready to take over in case of failure. When a router fails, the standby router with the highest priority takes over the role of the primary router. The transition from the primary router to the standby router is seamless, ensuring no disruption in network connectivity. HSRP also supports load balancing, allowing multiple routers to distribute network traffic and share the workload. HSRP operates at the network layer (Layer 3) of the OSI model and uses IP multicast messages to communicate between routers. Each router participating in HSRP is assigned a virtual IP address, which is used as the default gateway for devices connected to the network. This virtual IP address is shared between the routers, providing a single point of entry into the network. HSRP is commonly used in enterprise networks, data centers, and other critical networking environments to ensure high availability and redundancy. It provides a straightforward and reliable solution for network failover, allowing organizations to maintain uninterrupted connectivity and minimize network downtime. By implementing HSRP, organizations can improve their network's reliability and ensure continuous access to network resources.

Hybrid WAN

A Hybrid WAN is a network infrastructure that combines multiple types of connections, such as MPLS, internet, and cellular, to provide organizations with a more flexible and cost-effective wide area networking solution. This approach allows businesses to leverage the strengths of different connection types to meet their specific needs. MPLS connections, known for their reliability and security, can be used for critical applications and sensitive data transmission, while internet connections can be utilized for non-critical traffic, such as web browsing or email. By using a combination of connection types, a Hybrid WAN offers improved bandwidth, scalability, and flexibility compared to a traditional WAN that relies solely on MPLS or internet connections. With the ability to prioritize traffic based on application requirements, businesses can ensure optimal performance for critical applications and avoid congestion or performance degradation. One of the major benefits of a Hybrid WAN is its cost-effectiveness. Traditional MPLS connections can be costly, especially for organizations with multiple branch locations. By incorporating internet connections, businesses can offload non-critical traffic from expensive MPLS links, resulting in significant cost savings. Additionally, a Hybrid WAN provides increased resiliency and redundancy. If one connection type fails, the traffic can automatically be rerouted through another available connection, minimizing downtime and ensuring continuous network connectivity. Furthermore, a Hybrid WAN enables organizations to easily adapt and scale their network infrastructure as their needs evolve. As new branch locations are added or existing ones are relocated, businesses can easily deploy new connections using available internet or cellular options, significantly reducing deployment time and costs. In summary, a Hybrid WAN combines multiple connection types to create a more flexible, cost-effective, and scalable wide area networking solution. By leveraging the strengths of different connection types, businesses can optimize performance, reduce costs, and improve network resiliency.

Hypertext Transfer Protocol (HTTP)

Hypertext Transfer Protocol (HTTP) is a networking protocol that allows for the communication and transfer of data on the World Wide Web (WWW). It serves as the foundation for the transmission of hypertext documents, which are formatted text documents that contain hyperlinks to other resources on the web. HTTP operates on the client-server model, where a client, typically a web browser, initiates a request to a server, and the server responds with the requested data. HTTP is a stateless protocol, meaning that each request from the client is treated as an independent transaction without any knowledge of previous requests. When a client wants to retrieve a web resource, it sends an HTTP request message to the server, specifying the desired resource using a Uniform Resource Identifier (URI). The request message consists of a request line, which includes the HTTP method (e.g., GET, POST, PUT), the URI, and the version of HTTP being used. Upon receiving the request, the server processes it and sends an HTTP response message back to the client. The response includes a status line indicating the outcome of the request (e.g., 200 OK, 404 Not Found) and the requested data, which is often in the form of an HTML document. The client then interprets the response and renders the web page for the user to view. HTTP utilizes various methods or verbs to define the actions that can be performed on web resources. The most commonly used methods include: - GET: Retrieves a representation of the specified resource. - POST: Submits data to be processed by the server. - PUT: Updates or replaces a resource at a specific URI. - DELETE: Removes the specified resource. HTTP also supports the concept of headers, which are additional pieces of information that can be included in both requests and responses. Headers provide metadata about the request or response, such as the content type, encoding, and authentication credentials. They allow for more control and customization of the communication between the client and the server. In summary, HTTP is a protocol that facilitates the transfer of data and communication between clients and servers on the web. It provides a standardized method for requesting and delivering hypertext documents, enabling users to access and

168

interact with web resources seamlessly.

Hypertext Transfer Protocol Secure (HTTPS)

Hypertext Transfer Protocol Secure (HTTPS) is a secure version of the Hypertext Transfer Protocol (HTTP) that is used for secure communication over a computer network. It is widely used on the internet to provide a secure channel between the client (such as a web browser) and the server (such as a web server). HTTPS utilizes cryptographic protocols, such as Transport Layer Security (TLS) or Secure Sockets Layer (SSL), to ensure the confidentiality and integrity of the data exchanged between the client and the server. These protocols use encryption algorithms to encrypt the data, making it unreadable to any eavesdroppers or attackers who might intercept the communication. When a client wants to establish a secure connection with a server using HTTPS, the following steps are generally followed: 1. The client sends a request to the server, indicating that it wants to establish a secure connection using HTTPS. 2. The server responds by sending its digital certificate, which contains its public key and is issued by a trusted certificate authority. This certificate is used to verify the authenticity of the server. 3. The client verifies the authenticity of the server's certificate by checking its digital signature and ensuring that it is issued by a trusted certificate authority. 4. If the certificate is deemed valid, the client generates a random symmetric encryption key and encrypts it using the server's public key. This encrypted key is then sent to the server. 5. Both the client and the server now have the same symmetric encryption key, which they can use to encrypt and decrypt the data exchanged between them. By using HTTPS, sensitive information such as passwords, financial transactions, and personal data can be securely transmitted over the network without being compromised. The use of encryption ensures that even if the communication is intercepted, the data remains confidential and cannot be deciphered by unauthorized parties.

ICMP Echo Request

An ICMP Echo Request is a message used in networking to test the reachability and responsiveness of a network device or host. It is also known as a ping request, as it is commonly used with the ping utility to diagnose network connectivity issues. The ICMP (Internet Control Message Protocol) is a network layer protocol that serves various functions, including error reporting, network congestion control, and network troubleshooting. The ICMP Echo Request is a specific type of ICMP message that is sent from one device to another to request an echo reply.

ICMP Error Codes

ICMP Error Codes, also known as Internet Control Message Protocol Error Codes, are a set of standardized error codes used in networking to communicate error messages between network devices. ICMP is a network protocol that operates at the internet layer of the OSI model and is responsible for providing feedback about network conditions, error reporting, and diagnostic information. When a network device encounters an error or an exceptional condition, it generates an ICMP error message to inform the sender about the issue. These error messages contain specific error codes that indicate the type and nature of the encountered problem.

ICMP Error Messages

ICMP error messages refer to specific notifications sent by Internet Control Message Protocol (ICMP) to indicate network-related errors or issues. ICMP is an integral part of the Internet Protocol Suite and is designed to assist in diagnosing network problems and facilitating communication between network devices. ICMP error messages are generated by network devices such as routers, switches, and hosts to report errors encountered during the transmission and processing of IP packets. These messages are sent to the original sender of the problematic IP packet, informing them about the encountered error and potentially helping them identify and resolve the issue. ICMP error messages serve crucial functions within networking protocols. They allow network devices to notify the sender about various issues that may occur during packet delivery, such as unreachable destinations, time exceeded limits, or packet fragmentation problems. Additionally, ICMP error messages also play a role in determining network connectivity and measuring network performance through protocols like Ping or Traceroute. Examples of ICMP error messages include: 1. Destination Unreachable:

169

This message is sent by a router or host to notify the sender that the destination IP address is unreachable or not recognized. 2. Time Exceeded: This message is sent by a router to indicate that the Time-to-Live (TTL) value of the IP packet has reached zero, resulting in the packet being discarded. This message is often used by diagnostic tools like Traceroute to determine the route taken by packets to reach their destination. 3. Source Quench: This message is sent by a router to inform the sender that the network is congested and requests them to reduce their transmission rate. 4. Redirect Message: This message is sent by a router to inform the sender that a better route to the destination exists and advises them to update their routing table accordingly. It is essential for network administrators and technicians to understand and interpret ICMP error messages accurately. By analyzing these messages, they can identify and troubleshoot network issues, optimize routing, and ensure efficient communication within the network.

ICMP (Internet Control Message Protocol)

ICMP (Internet Control Message Protocol) is a network-layer protocol, used for sending error messages and operational information between network devices. It is an essential part of the internet protocol suite and is primarily used for troubleshooting network connectivity issues, reporting errors, and managing network congestion. ICMP operates by sending control messages, known as ICMP messages, to different devices within a network. These messages are encapsulated within IP packets and are used to report errors, exchange network management information, and diagnose network problems. ICMP messages are sent by network devices, such as routers, to communicate important information about the status of the network. These messages can include error messages, such as "destination unreachable" or "time exceeded," which indicate that a packet could not be delivered to its destination or has exceeded its time-to-live (TTL) value. In addition to error messages, ICMP also supports various types of messages for network management purposes. For example, the "echo request" and "echo reply" messages, commonly known as pings, are used to test network connectivity by sending a request from one device to another and receiving a reply. ICMP is crucial for troubleshooting network connectivity issues as it provides valuable information about network errors. Network administrators can use ICMP to identify and diagnose issues, such as unreachable hosts, network congestion, or misconfigured routers. By analyzing ICMP messages, administrators can pinpoint the cause of network problems and take necessary actions to resolve them. Furthermore, ICMP plays a significant role in the internet's ability to control network congestion. When network devices detect congestion, they can send ICMP messages to notify other devices, which can then adjust their transmission rates to alleviate the congestion. This helps in maintaining the overall performance and stability of the network. In summary, ICMP is a network-layer protocol that enables the exchange of error messages and vital network information between devices. It is critical for troubleshooting network issues and plays a key role in managing network congestion. By using ICMP, network administrators can diagnose problems and optimize network performance.

ICMP Messages

ICMP (Internet Control Message Protocol) is a network protocol used in the Internet Protocol (IP) suite to report errors and provide diagnostic information within networks. It operates at the network layer of the TCP/IP model and allows devices to communicate important messages to each other for network management purposes. ICMP messages provide feedback and control functionality in a network, ensuring effective communication and troubleshooting. ICMP messages are typically generated by network devices, such as routers and hosts, in response to events or errors encountered during data transmission. These messages are encapsulated within IP packets and sent to the source IP address specified in the original packet. ICMP messages can be classified into different types, each serving a specific purpose in network communication. One common type of ICMP message is the "Echo Request" (Type 8) and its corresponding "Echo Reply" (Type 0). These messages are commonly referred to as "ping" and are used to test the reachability and response time of a remote host. When a device sends an Echo Request message to a destination host, the host should respond with an Echo Reply message, indicating that it is reachable and operational. This functionality is widely used for network troubleshooting and monitoring. Other ICMP message types include "Destination Unreachable" (Type 3), which indicates that the requested destination is not reachable or that a specific service is unavailable, and "Time Exceeded" (Type 11), which indicates that a packet has exceeded its time-to-live (TTL) value and was discarded. ICMP messages also facilitate the fragmentation of IP packets when they exceed a network's maximum transmission unit (MTU), ensuring successful reassembly at the destination. In addition to error reporting and troubleshooting, ICMP messages can also be used for important network management functions such as Path MTU Discovery. This allows devices to identify the maximum MTU size along a network path, ensuring efficient data transmission without fragmentation. Overall, ICMP messages play a critical role in network communication by providing error reporting, diagnostic information, and control functionality. They enable devices to effectively communicate important messages to maintain network integrity and troubleshoot issues in a timely manner.

ICMP Packet Types

The Internet Control Message Protocol (ICMP) is a network protocol that operates at the network layer of the OSI model. It is used by network devices, such as routers, to send error messages and operational information to hosts and other network devices. ICMP packets are classified into several types, each serving a specific purpose in networking. These types include: 1. Echo Request (Ping) - Type 8: This type of ICMP packet is used to check the reachability and latency of a particular host on the network. A host sends an Echo Request packet to another host, and if the receiving host is available and reachable, it responds with an Echo Reply packet. Ping is a common utility that uses ICMP Echo Request packets to measure round-trip times and network connectivity. 2. Echo Reply (Ping) - Type 0: This type of ICMP packet is the response to an Echo Request packet. When a host receives an Echo Request packet, it replies with an Echo Reply packet, indicating that it is available and reachable. 3. Destination Unreachable - Type 3: When a router or firewall encounters a problem while forwarding IP packets, it sends a Destination Unreachable packet to the source host to inform it of the issue. This ICMP packet type contains different codes to indicate the specific reason for the destination being unreachable, such as network unreachable, host unreachable, protocol unreachable, port unreachable, fragmentation needed, etc. 4. Source Quench - Type 4: Source Quench packets are used by routers to request a sender to reduce the rate of sending packets. They are sent when the router's buffers are congested, indicating that the network is experiencing high traffic or congestion. Upon receiving a Source Quench packet, the sender slows down its packet transmission to alleviate the congestion. 5. Time Exceeded - Type 11: This ICMP packet type is generated by routers when the Time To Live (TTL) value in an IP packet reaches zero or expires. It helps identify network loops or routing issues. The Time Exceeded packet is sent back to the source host to notify it that the packet could not reach its destination within the allocated TTL. There are two subtypes within this type: Time To Live Exceeded in Transit and Fragment Reassembly Time Exceeded. These are just a few examples of the ICMP packet types used in networking. Each type serves a different purpose in providing error reporting, troubleshooting, and maintaining network efficiency.

ICMP Redirect Messages

ICMP Redirect Messages are network control messages that are sent by routers to inform hosts about a better next-hop router for a particular destination IP address. These messages are part of the Internet Control Message Protocol (ICMP) and are used in network communication to optimize the routing of IP packets. When a router receives an IP packet destined for another network, it examines its routing table to determine the appropriate next-hop router. However, in certain situations, a router may identify a better next-hop router for the destination network than the original router specified in the packet. In such cases, the router sends an ICMP Redirect Message to the source host, indicating the new next-hop router that should be used for future communication with the destination network.

ICMP Redirect

ICMP redirect is a communication protocol used in networking to inform a host that a better route is available for a particular destination. It is a message exchange between routers and hosts, where a router notifies a host that it could reach a destination more efficiently through a different router. This notification enables the host to update its routing table and use the new route for subsequent communications. When a host sends a packet to a destination, it first consults its routing table to determine the appropriate router to forward the packet. However, if the host's routing table indicates that the next-hop router is not the optimal choice, the router can use ICMP redirect to inform the host about the better route. The router sends an ICMP redirect message to the host, specifying the new router that should be used.

IP Address Conflict

An IP Address Conflict refers to a situation in computer networking when two or more devices on the same network are assigned the same IP address. An IP address is a unique identifier that is assigned to each device connected to a network, allowing them to communicate with each other. In a typical network setup, devices are automatically assigned IP addresses by a DHCP (Dynamic Host Configuration Protocol) server. However, conflicts can occur when two devices are assigned the same IP address, which can lead to communication issues and network disruptions.

IP Address Resolution Protocol (ARP)

IP Address Resolution Protocol (ARP) is a network protocol used for resolving an IP address to its corresponding MAC address in a Local Area Network (LAN) environment. ARP is a crucial component of the Internet Protocol (IP) suite and plays a significant role in facilitating communication between devices at the data link layer. When a device wants to send data to another device within the same network, it uses the IP address of the destination device. However, at the data link layer, which deals with MAC addresses, the destination MAC address is required. This is where ARP comes into play. The ARP protocol enables devices to map IP addresses to their corresponding MAC addresses, ensuring accurate delivery of data packets across the network. ARP operates through broadcast messages, allowing a requesting device to send an ARP request message to all devices on the LAN. The ARP request contains the IP address of the destination device, and it asks for the MAC address associated with that IP address. The device that holds the corresponding IP-MAC mapping will respond with an ARP reply message. This reply contains the MAC address requested by the originating device. Once the ARP reply is received, the device that initiated the ARP request can now communicate with the destination device. It stores the IP-MAC mapping in its ARP cache, which is a temporary memory where ARP tables are maintained. By doing this, subsequent communication between the two devices becomes more efficient, as the MAC address translation is no longer required. In summary, ARP is a protocol used for obtaining the MAC address corresponding to an IP address within a LAN. It enables devices to communicate by associating IP addresses with their respective MAC addresses. ARP requests are broadcasted, and the device that holds the requested IP-MAC mapping responds with an ARP reply. The requesting device then updates its ARP cache for future reference, improving communication efficiency.

IP Address

An IP address, short for Internet Protocol address, is a numerical label assigned to every device connected to a computer network that uses the Internet Protocol for communication. It serves two main functions: identifying the host or network interface, and providing the location of the host in the network. IP addresses are essential for the functioning of the internet as they enable devices to communicate with each other. They are composed of a series of numbers separated by periods, such as 192.168.0.1. This format, known as IPv4, is the most widely used version. In networking, an IP address can be divided into two main types: private and public. Private IP addresses are used within a local area network (LAN) and are not directly accessible from the internet. They are reserved for internal use and are typically assigned by the router or network administrator. Public IP addresses, on the other hand, are unique to each device and are used to access the internet. They are assigned by internet service providers (ISPs) and can change over time. IP addresses are hierarchical, with each section representing a different level of network. The first section, known as the network address, identifies the network itself. The remaining sections, called the host address, identify the specific device within that network. In addition to IPv4, there is another version called IPv6, which uses a different addressing scheme to accommodate a larger number of devices. IPv6 addresses are written in a different format and provide a significantly larger number of unique addresses compared to IPv4.

IP Filtering

IP filtering, also known as packet filtering, is a networking technique used to control the flow of

172

data packets based on their source or destination IP addresses. It involves analyzing the IP header of each packet and making decisions on whether to forward, block, or modify the packet based on predefined rules and policies. IP filtering works by comparing the source and destination IP addresses of a packet with a set of filtering rules. These rules are typically defined by network administrators and can be configured on routers, firewalls, or other network devices. Each rule consists of one or more conditions that must be met for the filtering action to be applied. When a packet arrives at a network device, it is inspected by the IP filtering mechanism. The device checks if the packet matches any of the filtering rules in its configuration. If a rule is matched, the corresponding action is taken. This can include allowing the packet to pass through, discarding the packet, or modifying certain fields of the packet (such as the source or destination IP address). IP filtering can be used for various purposes in a network, including improving security, optimizing network performance, and enforcing network policies. For security purposes, IP filtering allows administrators to block packets from certain IP addresses or IP ranges that are known to be malicious or unauthorized. It can also be used to allow access only to specific IP addresses or networks, effectively creating a whitelist of allowed communication. In terms of performance optimization, IP filtering can be used to prioritize or throttle traffic based on IP addresses. For example, certain types of traffic may be given higher priority, while others may be limited to prevent congestion or bandwidth abuse. By controlling the flow of packets based on IP addresses, network administrators can ensure that critical applications or services receive the necessary resources. Overall, IP filtering plays a crucial role in network management and security. It provides a means to selectively control the flow of traffic based on IP addresses, allowing network administrators to enforce policies, protect against threats, and optimize network performance.

IP Forwarding Table

An IP forwarding table, also known as a routing table, is a crucial component in computer networking. It is a data structure that is maintained by network routers to determine the next hop for forwarding network packets. Each router in a network maintains its own IP forwarding table, which is dynamically updated based on changes in network topology and routing protocols. The table contains information about the available network paths and the associated metrics, such as hop count or link speed. When a packet arrives at a router, it examines the destination IP address of the packet and consults its IP forwarding table to determine the best path towards the destination. The router looks for a matching entry in the table by performing a longest prefix match on the destination IP address. A longest prefix match means that the router matches the most specific network prefix that covers the destination IP address. The IP forwarding table consists of entries called routes, which define the path to a particular network prefix. Each route in the table includes the destination network prefix, the next hop IP address, and information about the route's metric. The next hop IP address is the IP address of the neighboring router that the packet should be sent to in order to reach the destination. Routing protocols like OSPF or BGP exchange information between routers to update their IP forwarding tables. These protocols use various metrics to determine the optimal path, such as the shortest path or the path with the highest bandwidth. The routers use these metrics to select the best route in the IP forwarding table for packet forwarding. In summary, an IP forwarding table is a data structure used by routers to determine the next hop for forwarding network packets. It contains routes that define the paths to different network prefixes. By consulting the IP forwarding table, routers make informed decisions on packet forwarding based on destination IP addresses and associated metrics.

IP Forwarding

IP Forwarding is a networking function that allows a router to make decisions on where to send network traffic based on the destination IP address. It is a fundamental process in the transmission of data packets across IP networks, enabling efficient and effective routing of information between devices. When a router receives an IP packet, it examines the destination IP address and consults its routing table to determine the appropriate next hop for forwarding the packet. The routing table contains information about known networks and the associated next hops, which may include other routers or directly connected devices.

IP Header Compression

173

IP Header Compression is a technique used in networking to reduce the size of IP headers, which are the overhead information attached to each IP packet. The IP header contains crucial information for routing packets, such as source and destination addresses, protocol information, and other control fields. However, these headers can often be quite large, especially in cases where the network transmission medium has limited bandwidth or high latency. The main purpose of compressing IP headers is to improve the efficiency of IP packet transmission, by reducing the number of bits that need to be transmitted over the network. This can lead to significant benefits in terms of reduced latency, increased throughput, and improved overall network performance. IP Header Compression achieves this by employing various compression techniques to compress the IP header information before transmitting it over the network.

IP Header

An IP Header, also known as an Internet Protocol Header, is a fundamental component of the TCP/IP network protocol suite. It is an essential part of the IP packet structure, providing crucial information for the proper routing, delivery, and interpretation of network data. The IP Header is located at the beginning of an IP packet and consists of a fixed-length structure of 20 bytes, or 160 bits. It contains various fields that carry essential information about the packet's source and destination, the protocol being used, and other necessary parameters for routing and fragmentation. The first field in the IP Header is the Version field, which specifies the version of the IP protocol being used. Currently, the most widely deployed version is IPv4. The Version field helps routers and other network devices determine the format and interpretation of the rest of the header. Next is the Internet Header Length (IHL) field, which indicates the total length of the IP Header in 32-bit words. Since the IP Header is of a fixed length, this field typically has a value of 5, representing 20 bytes. Following the IHL field is the Type of Service (ToS) field, which is used to prioritize packets and apply Quality of Service (QoS) mechanisms. It helps determine the urgency, reliability, and importance of the IP packet during network congestion. The total length field specifies the total length of the IP packet, including the IP Header and the payload data. It allows routers and hosts to process and allocate the appropriate buffer sizes for packet reception. The Identification field is used for packet fragmentation and reassembly. If a packet exceeds the Maximum Transmission Unit (MTU) of a network link, it needs to be fragmented into smaller units. The Identification field helps identify the fragments belonging to the same original packet. Other relevant fields in the IP Header include the Flags field, which contains control bits for fragmentation, and the Time to Live (TTL) field, which limits the lifespan of the packet by decrementing a counter with each hop, preventing packets from circulating endlessly in the network. In summary, the IP Header is a crucial part of the IP protocol, providing essential information for the routing and delivery of network data. Its fields contain important parameters for proper packet interpretation, fragmentation, and routing decisions, ensuring reliable and efficient transmission of data across the internet.

IP Multicast

IP Multicast is a communication protocol utilized in computer networks that enables the transmission of data packets from a single source to multiple recipients simultaneously. Unlike unicast, where data packets are sent one-to-one, multicast allows for the efficient distribution of data to a group of hosts that have expressed interest in a particular data stream. This form of communication is commonly used in applications such as video streaming, online gaming, and audio conferencing. When a sender wishes to transmit multicast data, it assigns a specific IP multicast address to the data stream. This address allows recipients to identify and join the multicast group in order to receive the data. The process of joining a multicast group is facilitated by the Internet Group Management Protocol (IGMP), which is responsible for managing multicast memberships on a local network. IGMP is implemented by hosts to inform routers of their interest in receiving multicast traffic.

IP Routing

IP Routing is the process of forwarding IP packets from one network to another network based on their destination IP address. It is a fundamental function of computer networks, enabling devices to exchange data across different networks, such as the internet. When a device on a network wants to send data to another device on a different network, it uses IP routing to determine the best path for the data to reach its destination. This routing decision is based on the destination IP address of the packet, which is embedded in the packet's header.

IP Security (IPsec)

IP Security (IPsec) is a network protocol suite that provides secure communication over IP networks. It is designed to ensure the confidentiality, integrity, and authenticity of data transmitted between network devices. IPsec operates at the network layer of the OSI model, enabling a secure connection between two hosts or between a host and a network. IPsec employs various security mechanisms, including encryption, authentication, and key management, to protect the IP packets during transit. Encryption transforms the original data into an unreadable format, ensuring that unauthorized individuals cannot understand the information being transmitted. Authentication ensures that the data is not altered or tampered with during transmission, verifying its integrity. Key management involves the secure exchange and management of encryption keys between the communicating entities. IPsec can be used in two different modes: transport mode and tunnel mode. In transport mode, only the payload (data being transmitted) is encrypted, while the header remains intact. This mode is typically used for securing communication between two hosts. In tunnel mode, the entire IP packet, including the header, is encapsulated within a new IP packet and encrypted. This mode is commonly used to establish secure connections between networks, such as virtual private networks (VPNs). IPsec can be implemented in two different protocols: Authentication Header (AH) and Encapsulating Security Payload (ESP). AH provides authentication and integrity protection for IP packets, while ESP provides encryption, authentication, and integrity protection. These protocols can be used individually or in combination, depending on the desired level of security. In summary, IPsec is a network protocol suite that ensures secure communication over IP networks. It utilizes encryption, authentication, and key management to protect the confidentiality, integrity, and authenticity of data transmitted between network devices. IPsec operates at the network layer and can be used in transport mode or tunnel mode, with two different protocols: Authentication Header and Encapsulating Security Payload.

IP Spoofing Detection

IP spoofing detection is a networking technique used to identify and prevent the unauthorized alteration or impersonation of IP addresses within a network. IP spoofing refers to the act of disguising one's identity by altering the source IP address in a packet header to make it appear as if it is originating from a different source. This technique can be used for various malicious purposes, such as launching distributed denial-of-service (DDoS) attacks, gaining unauthorized access to secure systems, or hiding the true source of network traffic. The detection of IP spoofing involves analyzing incoming network traffic to identify and flag packets with forged or misleading source IP addresses. One commonly used method for IP spoofing detection is by comparing the source IP address with the known range of valid IP addresses within the network. If the source IP falls outside of this range or matches with a known spoofed IP address, it is considered suspicious and can be further analyzed or blocked.

IP Spoofing

IP spoofing refers to the act of manipulating the source IP address of a packet to conceal the identity of the true sender. It is a technique commonly used in networking to launch various types of attacks or to bypass security measures. When a packet is sent over a network, it contains both a source IP address and a destination IP address. The source IP address identifies the sender of the packet, while the destination IP address identifies the intended recipient. In IP spoofing, the attacker modifies the source IP address to make it appear as if the packet is originating from a different computer or network.

IP Subnet Calculator

An IP subnet calculator is a tool used in networking to determine the network address, subnet mask, and other relevant information for a given IP address and subnet mask. It assists in the efficient allocation of IP addresses and the partitioning of networks into smaller subnets. The calculator helps network administrators and engineers by simplifying the process of subnetting, which is the practice of dividing a large network into smaller subnetworks. By doing so, it allows for better organization, improved security, and more efficient use of available IP addresses.

175

IP Tables Configuration

IP Tables Configuration refers to the process of setting up and managing rules in the IP tables, which is a user-space utility program that allows network administrators to configure the IP packet filter rules of the Linux kernel firewall implemented as different Netfilter modules. It is a popular choice for securely configuring and controlling network traffic on Linux-based systems. IP tables essentially act as a firewall by filtering network traffic based on predefined rules. These rules can allow, deny, or modify traffic flow based on criteria such as source and destination IP addresses, port numbers, protocol types, and other packet characteristics. The configuration of IP tables involves specifying these rules in a specific order to match and handle network packets efficiently.

IP Tables

IP Tables is a software utility used in computer networking to manage and manipulate the rules of the Linux kernel's Netfilter framework. It serves as a set of commands, or a programming interface, for configuring network packet filter rules in the Linux operating system. Through IP Tables, system administrators can control the flow of network traffic to and from a Linux server, effectively enhancing network security and optimizing network performance. The primary purpose of IP Tables is to filter and manipulate network packets based on various predefined rules. These rules are defined by the administrator and are organized into different chains. Each chain contains a list of rules that determine how packets are handled within a specific context. There are three default built-in chains: INPUT, OUTPUT, and FORWARD. The INPUT chain filters packets addressed to the local system, the OUTPUT chain filters packets originating from the local system, and the FORWARD chain filters packets that are passing through the system from one network interface to another. Each rule within an IP Tables chain consists of several components, including the source and destination IP addresses, port numbers, and protocol type. By configuring these rule components, administrators can selectively allow or deny certain types of network traffic. For example, one might specify a rule that only allows incoming connections to a specific port, while blocking all other incoming connections. IP Tables also supports more advanced rules, such as Network Address Translation (NAT), which allows for the manipulation of IP addresses and ports in network packets. Additionally, IP Tables provides functionality for logging network packets, specifying the action to take when a packet matches a certain rule, and managing complex rule sets using user-defined chains. Furthermore, IP Tables integrates with other networking tools and utilities, enabling administrators to create sophisticated firewall configurations and implement network traffic management policies.

IP Telephony

IP Telephony, also known as Voice over Internet Protocol (VoIP), is a communication technology that allows for the transmission of voice and multimedia content over Internet Protocol (IP) networks. It uses Internet Protocol to convert analog voice signals into digital packets, which are then transmitted over the network to the recipient. IP Telephony is an efficient and cost-effective alternative to traditional telephone services, as it eliminates the need for separate networks for voice and data communication. IP Telephony uses a variety of protocols and algorithms to ensure the reliable and secure delivery of voice data. The Session Initiation Protocol (SIP) is commonly used to establish, modify, and terminate voice sessions between IP phones and endpoints. Real-time Transport Protocol (RTP) is used to transmit the actual voice data between devices. Other protocols, such as H.323 and MGCP (Media Gateway Control Protocol), are also utilized in IP Telephony networks to provide additional functionality and interoperability. One of the main advantages of IP Telephony is its ability to leverage existing IP networks, such as local area networks (LANs) and the Internet, for voice communication. This eliminates the need for separate networks, infrastructure, and wiring for voice communication, resulting in cost savings and simplified network management. Additionally, IP Telephony offers advanced features and functionalities, such as call forwarding, call waiting, voicemail, and video conferencing, which are often more flexible and customizable than traditional telephone services. The use of IP Telephony is widespread in both residential and business environments. In residential settings, consumers can use IP-based applications on their personal computers or dedicated IP phones to make voice calls over the Internet. This allows for cost savings, especially for long-distance or international calls. In business environments, IP Telephony enables organizations to consolidate their voice and data services onto a single network infrastructure, leading to improved efficiency, scalability, and cost-effectiveness. Overall, IP Telephony revolutionizes and transforms the way voice communication is conducted by replacing traditional phone lines with IP networks. It offers numerous benefits, including cost savings, enhanced features, improved scalability, and increased flexibility. As technology continues to advance, IP Telephony is likely to become even more prevalent and integrated into everyday communication.

IP Transit

IP Transit refers to the service that provides network connectivity between internet service providers (ISPs) using the Internet Protocol (IP). It allows ISPs to access and exchange internet traffic with other networks, ensuring seamless communication between different regions and countries. IP Transit is an essential aspect of network infrastructure as it enables data packets to be transmitted across different networks, allowing users to access websites, send emails, make online transactions, and engage in various online activities. It acts as a backbone for ISPs, enabling them to connect to the global internet and serve their customers with reliable and high-speed internet access.

IP Tunneling

IP Tunneling is a technique used in networking to encapsulate one network protocol within another network protocol. It enables the transportation of one type of network protocol over a different type of network. It is also known as IP encapsulation or protocol tunneling. The concept of IP tunneling involves taking a packet from one network protocol, called the inner protocol, and wrapping it within another packet of a different network protocol, called the outer protocol. The outer protocol acts as a carrier or container for the inner protocol. This process allows the inner protocol to traverse a network that only supports the outer protocol.

IPsec VPN

IPsec VPN, short for Internet Protocol Security Virtual Private Network, is a secure network connection that allows users to access private networks over a public network such as the internet. It is commonly used by organizations to establish secure remote connections between two or more locations. IPsec VPN operates by encrypting and authenticating all data that is transmitted over the network, ensuring its confidentiality and integrity. It creates a secure tunnel between the connected devices, preventing unauthorized access or tampering of the transmitted information. The encrypted data is decrypted only at the intended destination, making it unreadable to any potential eavesdroppers or attackers.

IPv4 Vs. IPv6

IPv4 stands for Internet Protocol version 4. It is the fourth version of the Internet Protocol, which is the set of rules that determines how data is sent and received over the internet. IPv4 uses a 32-bit addressing system, which means that it can support approximately 4.3 billion unique IP addresses. However, due to the growing number of devices connected to the internet, the available IPv4 addresses are becoming increasingly scarce. On the other hand, IPv6 stands for Internet Protocol version 6. It is the sixth version of the Internet Protocol and is designed to replace IPv4. IPv6 uses a 128-bit addressing system, which provides an astronomically larger number of unique IP addresses. With IPv6, the total number of addresses available is approximately 340 undecillion, which is a staggering number that can easily accommodate the increasing demand for IP addresses in the future. IPv4 and IPv6 have some key differences that set them apart. One of the main differences is the address format. IPv4 addresses are written in decimal notation, divided into four octets separated by periods (e.g., 192.168.0.1). Meanwhile, IPv6 addresses are written in hexadecimal notation, divided into eight groups of four hexadecimal digits separated by colons (e.g., 2001:0db8:85a3:0000:0000:8a2e:0370:7334). Additionally, IPv6 incorporates several other improvements over IPv4. It includes built-in support for features such as auto-configuration, which simplifies the process of assigning IP addresses to devices. IPv6 also provides enhanced security features, such as IPsec, which helps protect data integrity and confidentiality. Furthermore, IPv6 improves network efficiency by reducing the size of routing tables and minimizing the need for network address translation (NAT). Despite the advantages offered by IPv6, the transition from IPv4 to IPv6 has been relatively slow. This is mainly due to compatibility issues, as many older devices and network infrastructure are still designed to work with IPv4. However, as the depletion of IPv4 addresses becomes more imminent, the adoption of IPv6 is steadily increasing. In summary, IPv4 and IPv6 are different versions of the Internet Protocol that determine how data is transmitted over the internet. IPv4 uses a 32-bit addressing system and currently supports approximately 4.3 billion addresses, while IPv6 uses a 128-bit addressing system and can accommodate an astronomical number of addresses. IPv6 incorporates various improvements over IPv4, including enhanced security, simplified configuration, and improved network efficiency. As the available IPv4 addresses continue to decline, the transition to IPv6 is becoming more essential for the future of networking.

IPv6

IPv6, also known as Internet Protocol version 6, is a network layer protocol that provides an identification and location system for devices on a network. It is the successor to IPv4, which has been the dominant protocol for internet communication since its inception. IPv6 was developed to address the limitations of IPv4 and to meet the growing demands of the internet. One of the main advantages of IPv6 is its expanded addressing capabilities. While IPv4 uses 32-bit addresses, IPv6 uses 128-bit addresses, allowing for a virtually unlimited number of unique addresses. This is especially important as the number of internet-connected devices continues to increase. In addition to expanded addressing, IPv6 also includes several other important features. One of these is improved security. IPv6 includes built-in support for IPsec, a suite of protocols that provides authentication and encryption for network communications. This enhances the privacy and integrity of data transmitted over an IPv6 network. IPv6 also includes support for auto-configuration, which simplifies the process of connecting devices to a network. With IPv6, devices can automatically assign themselves an IPv6 address without the need for manual configuration or the use of DHCP servers. This makes it easier to deploy and manage large-scale networks. Another feature of IPv6 is better support for multicast communication. Multicast allows for the efficient distribution of data to multiple recipients, making it ideal for applications such as streaming media and online gaming. IPv6 includes native support for multicast, improving the scalability and performance of these applications. Overall, IPv6 is an important protocol for the future of networking. With its expanded addressing capabilities, improved security, and support for auto-configuration and multicast, IPv6 is designed to meet the demands of the modern internet and enable the continued growth of connected devices and applications.

ISAKMP (Internet Security Association And Key Management Protocol)

ISAKMP (Internet Security Association and Key Management Protocol) is a protocol used in networking to establish security associations and manage encryption keys between two entities. It operates at the Internet layer and is primarily utilized in virtual private networks (VPNs) to authenticate and negotiate security parameters for the exchange of sensitive information. ISAKMP performs several crucial functions in network security, including: Authentication and Key Exchange: ISAKMP allows two entities, typically a client and a server, to authenticate each other and establish a secure connection. This is achieved through the exchange of keys and the use of digital certificates, ensuring that only authorized parties can access the network. Security Association Establishment: ISAKMP assists in the creation of security associations, which define the security parameters for communications between entities. These parameters include encryption algorithms, authentication methods, and session lifetimes. By establishing a secure SA, ISAKMP ensures that the subsequent data exchange remains protected. Key Management: ISAKMP manages encryption keys used for secure communication within a network. It generates and distributes session keys, which are temporary keys used for a specific communication session. ISAKMP also supports the exchange of long-term keys between entities to enable secure communication beyond a single session. Data Encryption: Once a secure connection is established and a security association is in place, ISAKMP facilitates data encryption to protect the confidentiality and integrity of the transmitted information. It ensures that sensitive data remains hidden and prevents unauthorized access or tampering.

ISDN (Integrated Services Digital Network)

ISDN (Integrated Services Digital Network) is a digital telecommunications network that provides the capability to transmit voice, video, and data simultaneously over the same communication line. It is a set of protocols and standards that allow for the integration of various services, such as phone calls, video conferencing, and internet access, within a single network infrastructure. ISDN was developed to replace traditional analog telephone networks and offer faster, more reliable, and higher quality communication services. It utilizes digital signals instead of analog signals, enabling the transmission of voice and data in a more efficient and secure manner. ISDN networks operate based on the use of circuit-switching technology, whereby a dedicated communication path is established for the duration of a call or session. ISDN consists of two main channels: the B (bearer) channel and the D (delta) channel. The B channel is responsible for carrying the actual data, such as voice or video, while the D channel is used for control signaling. The B channel is further divided into two 64 kbps (kilobits per second) channels, allowing for simultaneous transmission of different types of data. This division supports services like video conferencing, where the audio and video data can be transmitted separately but synchronized at the receiving end. The D channel, on the other hand, operates at a lower speed of 16 kbps and is responsible for managing call setup, termination, and other control functions. ISDN offers several advantages over analog networks, including higher data transfer rates, improved call quality, and faster call setup times. It also provides features like caller ID, call forwarding, conferencing, and simultaneous data transfer, which were not available in traditional analog networks. ISDN can be used in both residential and business environments, offering flexible and scalable communication solutions. In conclusion, ISDN is a digital telecommunications network that enables the simultaneous transmission of voice, video, and data over a single communication line. It utilizes circuit-switching technology and offers faster, more reliable, and higher quality communication services compared to traditional analog networks. With its integration capabilities and advanced features, ISDN continues to be a valuable solution for various communication needs.

ISP Backbone Network

An ISP Backbone Network, also known as an Internet Service Provider Backbone Network, is the central high-speed infrastructure of an Internet Service Provider (ISP) that forms the core of their network. The backbone network is responsible for transmitting and routing data between various points within the ISP's network and connecting them to the wider Internet. As the name suggests, the backbone network serves as the backbone or main channel of communication for an ISP. It is designed to handle a large volume of data traffic and provide high-speed connectivity to ensure fast and reliable Internet access for customers. The backbone network is built using a combination of high-capacity routers, switches, and transmission links such as optical fibers.

ISP Backbone Optimization

An ISP (Internet Service Provider) backbone refers to the core network infrastructure that supports the transmission of data between various locations in the ISP's network. This backbone is responsible for carrying large amounts of data traffic and ensuring its efficient and reliable delivery. ISP backbone optimization is the process of enhancing the performance and efficiency of the backbone network to better handle the increasing traffic demands and provide a better user experience. It involves implementing various techniques and strategies to maximize the utilization of the network resources and minimize bottlenecks and congestion.

ISP Backbone

An ISP backbone, in the context of networking, refers to the primary network infrastructure used by an Internet Service Provider (ISP) to transmit data between different locations and to connect their customers to the broader Internet. It acts as the central backbone or foundation of the ISP's network, enabling the delivery of Internet services to end users. The ISP backbone typically consists of high-capacity routers, switches, and fiber optic links that interconnect various Points of Presence (PoPs) and data centers. These PoPs are strategically placed in different geographic locations to ensure optimal network performance and coverage. The backbone network is designed to handle large volumes of data traffic and provide reliable connectivity with minimal latency and downtime.

ISP (Internet Service Provider)

An Internet Service Provider (ISP) is a company or organization that provides internet access services to individuals and businesses. ISPs connect customers to the internet through various means such as wired or wireless connections. ISPs play a crucial role in enabling individuals and businesses to access and utilize the vast resources offered by the internet. They serve as the bridge between end-users and the global network of interconnected computer networks known as the internet.

ISP Load Balancing

ISP Load Balancing is a networking technique that involves distributing incoming Internet traffic across multiple Internet Service Providers (ISPs). It is used to optimize the utilization of available network resources and ensure a high level of network availability and performance. Load balancing is achieved by directing traffic through multiple ISPs in a way that evenly distributes the workload across the available connections. This can be done through various methods, such as round-robin, weighted round-robin, or dynamic load balancing algorithms.

ISP Peering

ISP peering, short for Internet Service Provider peering, is a network interconnection agreement between different Internet Service Providers (ISPs) to exchange traffic directly between their networks. It allows the ISPs to connect their networks and exchange data without having to rely on third-party networks or transit providers. Peering agreements are typically established between ISPs that have a significant amount of Internet traffic to exchange. By directly connecting their networks, ISPs can improve the efficiency and performance of their networks, as well as reduce costs by bypassing transit providers.

ISP Redundancy

ISP redundancy refers to the practice of having multiple Internet Service Providers (ISPs) in a network infrastructure to ensure a high level of network availability and reliability. It is a crucial aspect of network design that aims to minimize the impact of single points of failure, such as ISP outages or network congestion. In an ISP redundant network setup, multiple ISPs are connected to the network, providing alternate paths for data to travel. This redundancy helps to diversify the network's reliance on a single ISP and avoids a complete loss of connectivity if one ISP fails or experiences connectivity issues. By distributing network traffic across multiple ISPs, the network can achieve better performance, improved uptime, and reduced latency.

ISP Speed Test

A speed test performed by an internet service provider (ISP) is a diagnostic tool used to measure the performance and quality of an internet connection. It provides valuable information about the speed and reliability of the connection, allowing users to assess if their ISP is delivering the expected service level. The ISP speed test measures several key metrics that are important for network performance. These metrics include download speed, upload speed, and latency. Download speed refers to the rate at which data is transferred from a remote server to the user's device, while upload speed measures the rate at which data is transferred from the user's device to a remote server. Latency, commonly referred to as ping, is the time it takes for a data packet to travel from the user's device to a remote server and back. These metrics are expressed in megabits per second (Mbps) or kilobits per second (Kbps). The ISP speed test works by sending a series of data packets between the user's device and a remote server. The time it takes for these packets to travel back and forth is measured, and the results are used to calculate the download speed, upload speed, and latency. This test is usually conducted using a dedicated server that is geographically close to the user's location to ensure accurate results. The results of an ISP speed test can be used to determine if an internet connection is meeting the desired performance requirements. For example, a high download speed is crucial for activities like streaming HD videos or downloading large files. A low latency is important for online gaming or real-time communication applications like video conferencing. By comparing the test results with the ISP's advertised speeds, users can identify if there is any discrepancy and contact their ISP for further assistance and support. Additionally, the ISP speed test can help users troubleshoot network issues by identifying potential bottlenecks, such as outdated modem or router hardware, network congestion, or signal interference. By pinpointing the exact cause of a slow or unreliable internet connection, users can take appropriate steps to resolve the issue and improve their overall network performance. In conclusion, an ISP speed test is a valuable tool that allows users to measure the performance and quality of their internet connection. It provides important metrics such as download speed, upload speed, and latency, which help users assess if their ISP is delivering the expected service level. The results of the speed test can assist with troubleshooting network issues and optimizing internet performance.

ISP Troubleshooting

An ISP (Internet Service Provider) Troubleshooting refers to the process of identifying and resolving issues related to internet connectivity or services provided by an ISP. It involves diagnosing problems that may arise in a network and implementing the necessary steps to fix them. In the context of networking, ISP troubleshooting can encompass various tasks. It typically begins by identifying the specific issue that is causing the disruption in internet connection or services. This can be done through a series of steps, including analyzing network equipment, reviewing network configurations, and inspecting physical connections. The primary goal is to determine the root cause of the problem. Once the problem is identified, the next step in ISP troubleshooting is to implement a solution. This can involve different actions depending on the nature of the issue. It may require reconfiguring network settings, replacing faulty equipment, or contacting the ISP for assistance. The troubleshooting process may also involve the use of specialized tools and software to aid in diagnosing and resolving the issue. Furthermore, ISP troubleshooting may involve collaboration between the ISP and the network administrator or end user. In some cases, the ISP may need to provide support or guidance to resolve more complex problems that are beyond the control of the end user or network administrator. This collaboration is essential for ensuring a swift resolution of the problem. In summary, ISP troubleshooting is the systematic process of identifying and resolving issues related to internet connectivity or services offered by an ISP. It involves diagnosing problems, determining their root cause, and implementing appropriate solutions. By efficiently troubleshooting ISP-related issues, network administrators and end users can ensure a reliable and uninterrupted internet connection.

Identity And Access Management (IAM)

Identity and Access Management (IAM) is a network security framework that ensures the proper authentication, authorization, and management of individuals' identities and their access to various resources within a network. IAM plays a critical role in maintaining the security and privacy of sensitive information by ensuring that only authorized individuals have access to specific network resources. It accomplishes this through a combination of processes, policies, and technologies that work together to enforce access controls and restrict unauthorized access.

In-Service Software Upgrade (ISSU)

In-Service Software Upgrade (ISSU) refers to a process in networking that allows a device or system to upgrade its software while maintaining uninterrupted service and avoiding any impact on the network operations. It enables network administrators to perform software upgrades, patch installations, or bug fixes without having to disrupt or restart the device or system, thus ensuring continuous service availability. ISSU is a crucial feature in networking, particularly in environments where downtime is highly undesirable or costly, such as data centers, telecommunication networks, or critical infrastructure networks. It eliminates the need for planned maintenance windows or scheduled system reboots to update software, reducing service disruptions and enhancing overall network reliability.

Incident Response Plan (IRP)

An Incident Response Plan (IRP) in the context of networking is a formal document that outlines the procedures and actions to be taken when an incident occurs in a network environment. IRPs are designed to help organizations respond quickly and effectively to network incidents, such as security breaches, network outages, or other disruptions. The goal of an IRP is to minimize the impact of the incident on the network and to restore normal operations as soon as possible.

Information Security Management System (ISMS)

An Information Security Management System (ISMS) is a framework that organizations use to manage and protect their sensitive information assets. It encompasses a systematic approach to managing sensitive company information, including the people, processes, and technology systems involved. One key aspect of an ISMS is the identification of information security risks and the implementation of controls to mitigate those risks. This involves conducting risk assessments, which identify potential vulnerabilities and threats that could impact the confidentiality, integrity, or availability of information. Controls are then put in place to reduce or eliminate these risks. The ISMS also includes policies and procedures that guide employees on how to handle sensitive information and respond to security incidents. This ensures that everyone within the organization understands their roles and responsibilities in protecting information assets from unauthorized access or disclosure. Effective communication and training play a crucial role in an ISMS. Employees need to be aware of the importance of information security and their individual responsibilities in maintaining it. Regular training programs help to reinforce best practices and ensure that employees stay up-to-date with the latest threats and vulnerabilities. Another essential component of an ISMS is ongoing monitoring and review. This involves conducting regular audits to assess the effectiveness of controls and identifying areas for improvement. Incident management processes are put in place to respond to security incidents promptly and effectively, minimizing any potential damage. In conclusion, an ISMS provides a comprehensive approach to managing information security within an organization. It involves identifying risks, implementing controls, establishing policies and procedures, and ensuring ongoing monitoring and review. By implementing an ISMS, organizations can better protect their sensitive information assets and minimize the risk of security breaches.

Ingress Filtering

Ingress filtering is a network security measure that involves the examination and filtering of incoming network traffic to prevent malicious or unauthorized data packets from entering an internal network. This type of filtering is commonly implemented at the network perimeter, where data enters the network from external sources such as the internet. The main purpose of ingress filtering is to enforce security policies and protect the internal network from various types of threats, including denial-of-service (DoS) attacks, spoofed IP addresses, and other forms of network-based attacks. By filtering out unwanted or potentially harmful traffic at the network edge, ingress filtering helps to minimize the impact of these attacks and ensure the integrity and availability of the internal network resources. When implementing ingress filtering, network administrators typically configure rules or filters that define the allowed or expected incoming traffic based on predefined criteria, such as source IP addresses, destination ports, and protocols. These filters are applied at the network devices, such as routers or firewalls, that serve as the first line of defense for the network. One of the primary benefits of ingress filtering is its ability to prevent IP address spoofing. By analyzing the source IP addresses of incoming packets, ingress filters can identify and discard packets with forged or illegitimate IP addresses, which are commonly used in various types of network attacks. This helps to prevent attackers from impersonating trusted entities or bypassing security measures by masking their true source IP addresses. In addition to preventing spoofed IP addresses, ingress filtering also helps to mitigate DoS attacks by filtering out excessive or abnormal traffic. This includes filtering traffic with unusually high packet rates, packet sizes, or other anomalous characteristics that may indicate an ongoing DoS attack. By discarding or throttling such traffic, ingress filtering helps to preserve the network's available resources and ensure the normal operation of legitimate network traffic.

Intermediate System To Intermediate System (IS-IS)

The Intermediate System to Intermediate System (IS-IS) is a routing protocol used in computer networking that operates at the OSI network layer. It is designed to efficiently exchange routing information and compute optimal paths between routers in a network. IS-IS is commonly used in large Service Provider networks and is one of the few protocols that can scale effectively to support networks with thousands of routers. IS-IS uses a link-state routing algorithm, which means that each router in the network maintains a database containing information about all the links and routers in the network. This database is then used to compute the shortest path to a destination when forwarding traffic. IS-IS supports both IPv4 and IPv6 addressing and can be used with multiple protocols, such as IP, IPX, and OSI protocols. In IS-IS, routers are classified as either Intermediate Systems (IS) or End Systems (ES). Intermediate Systems are the routers that participate in the IS-IS routing process, while End Systems are the hosts connected to the network. Each router in the network is assigned a unique ID, called a System ID, which is used to identify the router and differentiate it from other routers in the network. IS-IS uses a hierarchical routing model, where routers are organized into areas. An area is a logical grouping of routers that share similar network characteristics. The routers within an area exchange routing information, and routers in different areas exchange summarized routing information to reduce the size of the routing tables and minimize overhead. The backbone area, also known as Level 2, is a special area that connects all the other areas in the network. The IS-IS protocol uses a two-level hierarchy to organize routing information. The Level 1 routing domain consists of routers within an area, while the Level 2 routing domain consists of routers in the backbone area. Level 1 routers are responsible for intra-area routing, while Level 2 routers handle inter-area routing and connect different areas together. In conclusion, IS-IS is a routing protocol that enables efficient exchange of routing information and computation of optimal paths in large networks. It uses a hierarchical routing model and supports both IPv4 and IPv6 addressing. IS-IS is widely used in Service Provider networks and can scale effectively to support networks with thousands of routers.

Internet Control Message Protocol (ICMP)

Internet Control Message Protocol (ICMP) is an integral part of the Internet Protocol (IP) suite and is responsible for facilitating the exchange of error messages and operational information between network devices. It operates at the network layer of the TCP/IP model and is used to report errors, diagnose network issues, and perform network management tasks. ICMP messages are encapsulated within IP packets and are typically generated by network devices such as routers and hosts in response to specific events or requests. These messages are then sent back to the source IP address to provide information about the status or problems encountered during transmission. The main functionalities of ICMP can be categorized into three primary areas: error reporting, network congestion control, and network management. Error reporting is an essential aspect of ICMP, as it allows network devices to communicate and report errors encountered during packet delivery. For example, if a packet is unable to reach its destination due to various reasons, such as network congestion or routing issues, ICMP generates an error message known as an Internet Control Message Protocol Error Message (ICMP error message). This message is then sent back to the source IP address to inform the sender about the encountered error. ICMP error messages include ICMP Destination Unreachable, ICMP Time Exceeded, and ICMP Redirect. ICMP also plays a vital role in network congestion control. When a network is congested and experiences high traffic load, ICMP messages such as ICMP Source Quench are sent to the sender to reduce the transmission rate. This congestion control mechanism can prevent network congestion and optimize traffic flow. Furthermore, ICMP is crucial for network management tasks, as it provides network administrators with valuable information about network performance, configuration errors, or other operational issues. ICMP messages like ICMP Echo Request (Ping) and ICMP Echo Reply are commonly used for network diagnostics, allowing administrators to assess network connectivity and measure round-trip time (RTT) between devices. In conclusion, ICMP is a fundamental protocol within the IP suite that enables network devices to communicate error messages, control network congestion, and assist in network management tasks. Its role in facilitating network troubleshooting and maintaining optimal network performance is essential for the functioning of modern computer networks.

Internet Exchange Point (IXP)

An Internet Exchange Point (IXP) is a physical location where multiple Internet Service Providers (ISPs) and networks connect and exchange Internet traffic. It serves as a point of interconnection for these networks, allowing them to directly exchange data traffic without the need for a third-party network. IXPs play a crucial role in the infrastructure of the Internet by facilitating efficient and cost-effective interconnection between ISPs and networks. By connecting to an IXP, ISPs and networks can improve the performance, reliability, and cost of their Internet connections, as well as reduce their reliance on expensive long-haul links. At an IXP, ISPs and networks connect their routers and switches to a shared Ethernet fabric. This fabric acts as a neutral and transparent platform for data exchange. When two connected networks want to exchange traffic, they establish a direct peering relationship, also known as a bilateral agreement. This agreement allows them to exchange traffic through the IXP without having to pay a transit provider or rely on third-party networks. The benefits of connecting to an

IXP include reduced costs, improved network performance, and increased control over routing. By exchanging traffic directly at the IXP, ISPs and networks can save money on transit fees, which are typically based on the volume of data traffic exchanged. Additionally, direct peering can improve network performance by reducing latency and increasing bandwidth capacity. IXPs also offer increased control over routing, as they allow ISPs and networks to choose their upstream providers and determine the most efficient paths for their traffic. This control enables them to optimize their network infrastructure and improve the quality of service for their customers. In summary, an Internet Exchange Point (IXP) is a physical location where multiple ISPs and networks connect to exchange Internet traffic. By connecting to an IXP, ISPs and networks can reduce costs, improve performance, and have greater control over routing. IXPs are an essential component of the Internet infrastructure and play a vital role in facilitating the efficient and reliable exchange of data traffic between networks.

Internet Group Management Protocol (IGMP)

The Internet Group Management Protocol (IGMP) is a networking protocol used by hosts and adjacent routers on an Internet Protocol (IP) network to report their multicast group memberships to any neighboring routers. It is an integral part of IP multicast, which enables efficient one-to-many or many-to-many communication over a network. IGMP operates at the network layer (Layer 3) of the TCP/IP model and is designed to enable efficient multicasting by keeping track of the hosts interested in receiving multicast packets. It enables hosts to join and leave multicast groups dynamically.

Internet Protocol (IP)

The Internet Protocol (IP) is a networking protocol that provides a set of rules for sending and receiving data over interconnected networks. It forms the foundation of the internet and is responsible for the delivery of packets of information between devices. IP operates at the network layer of the OSI model and uses a unique addressing system to identify each device on a network. Every device connected to a network, whether it be a computer, smartphone, or server, is assigned an IP address that serves as its unique identifier. This address consists of a series of four numbers, known as octets, separated by periods. Each octet can range from 0 to 255, allowing for a total of approximately 4.3 billion possible IP addresses. One of the key features of IP is its ability to route packets of data across multiple networks. When a device wants to send data to another device, it breaks the information into small packets, each containing a portion of the data, along with the IP addresses of the source and destination devices. These packets are then routed through a series of interconnected networks based on the IP addresses, until they reach their intended destination. Another important aspect of IP is its support for different versions, namely IPv4 and IPv6. IPv4 is the most widely used version and employs 32-bit addressing, limiting the number of available IP addresses. In contrast, IPv6 uses 128-bit addressing, providing a significantly larger pool of addresses to accommodate the growing number of devices connected to the internet. IP also includes additional functionality to facilitate reliable and efficient communication between devices. This includes the use of protocols such as Transmission Control Protocol (TCP) and User Datagram Protocol (UDP) to ensure the correct delivery and sequencing of packets. Additionally, IP supports the fragmentation and reassembly of packets, allowing for the transmission of data across networks with varying maximum packet sizes. In conclusion, the Internet Protocol (IP) is a fundamental networking protocol that enables the exchange of data between devices on interconnected networks. It establishes a unique addressing system, routes packets of data across networks, and provides additional functionality to ensure reliable communication.

Internet Protocol Security (IPsec)

Internet Protocol Security (IPsec) is a protocol suite used in networking to provide secure communication over a public network, such as the Internet. It is designed to ensure confidentiality, integrity, and authenticity of data transmitted between network devices by encrypting the data packets and authenticating the communication participants. IPsec offers a range of security services, including access control, data confidentiality, data integrity, data origin authentication, and anti-replay protection. These services are accomplished through a combination of cryptographic algorithms and protocols.

Internet Protocol Version 4 (IPv4)

The Internet Protocol Version 4 (IPv4) is a widely used networking protocol that defines how data packets are sent and received over the internet. It is the fourth version of the Internet Protocol and is currently the most prevalent protocol used for internet communication. IPv4 is designed to provide unique addresses to every device connected to the internet, allowing them to communicate with each other. It uses a 32-bit address space, which means it can support approximately 4.3 billion unique addresses. These addresses are represented in the form of four sets of numbers, separated by periods, such as 192.168.0.1. IPv4 employs a connectionless packet-switched network model, which means that data is split into smaller packets and transmitted independently. Each packet contains the source and destination addresses, as well as other information necessary for routing and error control. These packets are then sent from the source device to the destination device through a series of routers, which forward the packets towards their intended destination. One of the key features of IPv4 is its versatility in addressing and routing. It supports both unicast, multicast, and broadcast communication. Unicast communication involves sending data from one source to a single destination, while multicast communication enables the source to send data to a group of devices. Broadcast communication allows the source to send data to all devices on the network. Additionally, IPv4 also includes protocols for error detection, fragmentation, and reassembly, ensuring the reliable delivery of data packets across networks with varying speeds and conditions. It utilizes checksums to verify the integrity of packets and can fragment large packets into smaller ones to accommodate networks with lower data transmission rates. Although IPv4 has been widely used for several decades, the exponential growth of internet usage has led to the depletion of available IPv4 addresses. To address this issue, IPv6, a newer and more advanced version of the protocol, was developed. However, IPv4 continues to play a crucial role in networking and is still widely supported by hardware and software devices.

Internet Protocol Version 6 (IPv6)

Internet Protocol Version 6 (IPv6) is a network protocol that provides unique IP addresses to devices connected to a network, allowing them to communicate with each other over the internet.IPv6 was introduced as the successor to Internet Protocol Version 4 (IPv4) due to the limited number of available IPv4 addresses. Unlike IPv4, which uses 32-bit addresses and can support approximately 4.3 billion unique IP addresses, IPv6 uses 128-bit addresses and can support a significantly larger number of unique addresses.IPv6 addresses are represented as eight groups of four hexadecimal digits, separated by colons. An example of an IPv6 address is 2001:0db8:85a3:0000:0000:8a2e:0370:7334. Each group of four hexadecimal digits represents 16 bits, resulting in a total of 128 bits.In addition to the larger address space, IPv6 also introduced several other improvements and features. One of the key features of IPv6 is its ability to support auto-configuration, which allows devices to automatically assign themselves an IP address without the need for manual configuration or the use of Dynamic Host Configuration Protocol (DHCP).IPv6 also provides built-in support for security through the implementation of Internet Protocol Security (IPsec). IPsec helps to ensure secure communication by encrypting and authenticating IP packets, protecting them from unauthorized access or modification.Another important feature of IPv6 is its support for multicast communication. Multicast allows a single packet to be sent to multiple destinations simultaneously, reducing network traffic and improving scalability.While IPv6 has been available for many years, its adoption has been relatively slow. This is due to various factors, including the large investment required to upgrade existing networks, lack of compatibility with older devices and software, and the continued availability of IPv4 addresses through the use of Network Address Translation (NAT).However, as the demand for IP addresses continues to grow with the increase in internet-connected devices, the adoption of IPv6 is becoming increasingly important. IPv6 provides a scalable and future-proof solution to the address exhaustion problem faced by IPv4, ensuring the continued growth and functionality of the internet.In conclusion, IPv6 is a network protocol that offers a larger address space, improved security, auto-configuration, and multicast support compared to its predecessor, IPv4. While its adoption has been slow, IPv6 is essential for the continued growth and functionality of the internet in the face of increasing demand for unique IP addresses.

Internet Relay Chat (IRC)

185

Internet Relay Chat (IRC) is a text-based communication protocol that enables users to chat and exchange messages in real-time over the internet. It is designed to allow multiple users to participate in discussions, collaborate, and share information with each other. IRC operates through client-server architecture, where users connect to IRC servers using an IRC client software. The client software allows users to connect to specific IRC servers and join various channels or rooms where conversations take place. IRC utilizes a decentralized network structure, meaning that IRC servers are interconnected, forming a vast network called the IRC network. Users can choose from a wide range of IRC servers available and connect to their preferred server based on factors such as location, server stability, and community preferences. Once connected to an IRC server, users can join different channels or create their own. Channels are like virtual meeting rooms where users can communicate with each other. Each channel has a unique name, typically indicated by the "#" symbol, such as #technology or #music. Users can send text messages to channels or specific users by simply typing their messages and pressing enter. These messages will then be received and displayed to all connected users in the respective channel or user's private message window. Users can also send private messages to specific users by specifying their username. IRC supports various communication features, such as file sharing, voice chat, and even scripting capabilities through add-ons or extensions. However, the basic functionality of IRC remains focused on text-based communication. Overall, IRC provides a platform for real-time collaboration and communication among users from around the world. It has been widely used for various purposes, including community discussions, technical support, online gaming, and social interactions.

Internet Service Provider (ISP) Peering

Internet Service Provider (ISP) Peering refers to the practice of ISPs interconnecting their networks in order to exchange traffic directly with one another rather than routing it through third-party networks. This direct interconnection between ISPs enables the efficient and cost-effective exchange of internet traffic, leading to improved network performance and user experience. ISP peering is typically accomplished through the establishment of physical connections between ISPs' network infrastructures, either at physical Internet Exchange Points (IXPs) or through private peering arrangements. These connections allow ISPs to exchange routing information and route traffic directly between their networks, resulting in reduced latency and increased available bandwidth for their customers. This direct interconnection between ISPs also helps to distribute internet traffic more evenly across networks, reducing congestion and improving overall network reliability. By exchanging traffic directly at peering points, ISPs can avoid the need to traverse multiple intermediate networks, which can introduce bottlenecks and potential points of failure. ISP peering has various benefits for both ISPs and their customers. For ISPs, peering enables them to optimize their network performance by reducing the reliance on costly and congested transit links. This allows ISPs to offer faster and more reliable internet connectivity to their customers. Peering also improves network resiliency as it provides alternative routing paths in case of network outages or congestion. Customers of ISPs that engage in peering also benefit from improved internet connectivity. With direct peering connections, ISPs can provide lower latency for accessing content and services hosted on other peered networks. This translates to faster webpage loading times, smoother video streaming, and better overall online user experience.

Internet Service Provider (ISP)

An Internet Service Provider (ISP) is a company that provides individuals and organizations with access to the Internet. ISPs connect their customers to the Internet through various means, such as dial-up, broadband, or wireless connections. ISPs play a crucial role in the functioning of the Internet. They act as intermediaries between end-users and the rest of the Internet infrastructure. When a user wants to access a website or send an email, their device communicates with the ISP's network to establish a connection. The ISP then routes the data packets to the appropriate destination and enables the user to receive the requested information. ISPs offer a range of services to meet the diverse needs of their customers. These services may include internet access, email accounts, web hosting, domain registration, virtual private networks (VPNs), and more. Some ISPs also provide additional features like parental controls, antivirus software, and online storage options to enhance the user experience and ensure security. ISPs are responsible for maintaining a robust network infrastructure to support a high volume of data traffic. This involves managing routers, switches, servers, and other networking equipment to ensure reliable connectivity and fast data transmission speeds. ISPs also invest in upgrading their infrastructure to keep up with the ever-increasing demands of bandwidth-intensive applications and technologies. In addition to providing connectivity, ISPs typically offer customer support services to address technical issues and assist with account management. They may have support teams available via phone, email, or online chat to troubleshoot internet connection problems, configure network settings, or help with billing inquiries. ISPs are subject to regulations and policies set by governments and industry authorities. These regulations often aim to ensure fair competition, protect consumer privacy, and maintain net neutrality principles. ISPs are also required to comply with legal requests for user information from law enforcement agencies, while also prioritizing the privacy and security of their customers.

Internet Of Things (IoT)

The Internet of Things (IoT) refers to the network of physical devices, vehicles, appliances, and other objects embedded with sensors, software, and connectivity to exchange data and interact with each other through the internet. In a networking context, IoT represents the extension of internet connectivity beyond traditional computing devices to various everyday objects, allowing them to send and receive data. These objects, or "things," are embedded with sensors and communication capabilities that enable them to connect to the internet and interact with other devices or systems, resulting in increased automation, efficiency, and convenience.

Intranet Design

An intranet is a private network that uses internet protocols and technology for the purpose of sharing information, collaborating on projects, and facilitating communication and workflow within an organization. It is a closed network accessible only to the members of the organization, typically using secure login credentials. The design of an intranet involves creating a user-friendly and intuitive interface that allows employees to easily navigate and access the information and resources they need. The design should prioritize simplicity, efficiency, and effective communication, aiming to enhance productivity and streamline processes within the organization.

Intranet Development

Intranet development refers to the process of creating and implementing an internal network that is accessible only within an organization. It involves the design, development, and deployment of a private network infrastructure that enables seamless communication and collaboration among employees, departments, and branches within an organization. The primary objective of intranet development is to establish a secure and reliable platform that facilitates the sharing of information, resources, and services within an organization. It typically involves the setup and configuration of various networking components such as servers, switches, routers, and firewalls to ensure smooth and efficient data transfer. An intranet is typically built using Internet Protocol (IP) based technologies, including TCP/IP for data transmission and HTTP for serving web pages. It can incorporate a wide range of web-based applications and services, such as email, file sharing, document management, discussion boards, and workflow systems, which enable employees to communicate, collaborate, and access information securely. The development process of an intranet includes several key steps. Firstly, the organization needs to define its objectives and requirements for the intranet, such as the desired functionalities, security measures, and scalability. It is important to conduct a thorough analysis of the existing IT infrastructure and evaluate the compatibility and integration requirements of the intranet with the organization's systems and applications. Next, a detailed design plan is created, outlining the network architecture, hardware and software components, security measures, and user interface. The development team then proceeds with the implementation phase, which involves the coding, testing, and integration of the various components. This is followed by the deployment and configuration of the intranet infrastructure, including servers, networking equipment, and security mechanisms. A crucial aspect of intranet development is security. Organizations need to implement robust security measures such as firewalls, access controls, and encryption to protect sensitive and confidential information from unauthorized access, ensuring data privacy and integrity within the intranet environment. Regular monitoring, auditing, and upgrading of the intranet infrastructure are necessary to address potential vulnerabilities and mitigate security risks. In conclusion, intranet development is the process of creating a private internal network that fosters efficient communication, collaboration, and information sharing within an organization. It involves the design, deployment, and maintenance of a secure and reliable network infrastructure that supports a wide range of web-based applications and services.

Intranet Portal Development

An intranet portal is a secure and private website that is deployed within an organization's internal network to provide a centralized platform for communication, collaboration, and access to information. It acts as a gateway or entry point for employees to connect with various resources, tools, and services within the organization. The development of an intranet portal involves the creation and integration of web-based applications, databases, and content management systems to facilitate efficient and organized access to internal resources. It typically includes features such as employee directories, document management, calendars, news and announcements, discussion forums, project management tools, and access to relevant business applications. By utilizing the power of network connectivity and web technologies, an intranet portal enables seamless communication and collaboration among employees across different departments or teams. It acts as a centralized hub where employees can access the latest information, share knowledge and best practices, and collaborate on projects or tasks regardless of their physical location within the organization. Security is a crucial aspect of intranet portal development, as it involves handling sensitive company data and information. Access to the portal is tightly controlled through user authentication and authorization mechanisms, ensuring that only authorized personnel can access specific sections or resources. Measures such as encryption, firewalls, and intrusion detection systems are implemented to protect against unauthorized access and data breaches. Overall, the development of an intranet portal enhances organizational efficiency and productivity by improving communication, streamlining access to information, and fostering collaboration. It serves as a central repository of knowledge and resources, facilitating better decision-making and enabling employees to work more effectively as a cohesive unit.

Intranet Portal

An Intranet Portal is a private website that is accessible only to an organization's internal users, such as employees, partners, or authorized members. It functions as a central gateway or hub that provides access to various resources, tools, and information relevant to the organization and its employees. The primary purpose of an Intranet Portal is to facilitate internal communication and collaboration within an organization, streamlining access to important information and services. It serves as a centralized platform for employees to access company announcements, news, policies, procedures, departmental updates, and other internal communications. The portal often includes features like discussion forums, chat or messaging systems, and company directories, enabling employees to connect, share ideas, and collaborate on projects. In addition to communication and collaboration, an Intranet Portal typically hosts a range of applications and tools to support various business processes and operations. This can include document management systems, project management tools, employee self-service portals, HR systems, training platforms, and more. These applications are often integrated within the portal to provide a seamless user experience and easy access to necessary tools. Security is a critical aspect of an Intranet Portal, as it contains sensitive information that should only be accessible to authorized users. Access to the portal is typically restricted through user authentication, using methods such as usernames, passwords, or other forms of identity verification. This ensures that only authorized individuals can access the portal and its resources, protecting the organization's confidential data and sensitive information. Overall, an Intranet Portal serves as a centralized hub for an organization's internal operations, providing employees with a secure and convenient platform for communication, collaboration, and access to various resources. It helps improve productivity, enhances internal communication and collaboration, and enables efficient access to important information and tools within the organization.

Intranet Security Measures

Intranet security measures refer to a set of protocols, practices, and technologies implemented to safeguard the internal network and the resources contained within it. These measures are designed to protect the confidentiality, integrity, and availability of information shared within the intranet, preventing unauthorized access, data breaches, and other malicious activities. In order to ensure comprehensive security, organizations employ a variety of measures that are typically implemented at different levels within the network infrastructure. These measures include: 1. Access Control: Access control mechanisms are put in place to restrict unauthorized users from accessing sensitive resources within the intranet. This can include employing strong authentication methods such as usernames, passwords, or biometric credentials, as well as implementing role-based access controls to restrict access based on user roles and responsibilities. 2. Firewalls: Firewalls are essential components of intranet security, serving as a barrier between the internal network and the untrusted external network, typically the internet. They monitor and control incoming and outgoing traffic, enforcing predetermined security policies to block malicious traffic and prevent unauthorized access. 3. Intrusion Detection and Prevention Systems (IDPS): IDPS are deployed to detect and prevent any attempts at unauthorized intrusion or malicious activities within the intranet. These systems monitor network traffic and analyze it for signs of suspicious behavior or known attack patterns, triggering alarms or taking proactive measures to prevent potential threats. 4. Encryption: Encryption is used to protect sensitive data transmitted across the intranet by converting it into an unreadable format. This ensures that even if intercepted, the data cannot be easily understood by unauthorized parties. Encryption can be implemented at multiple levels, including data-at-rest and data-in-transit. 5. Security Auditing and Logging: In order to maintain a secure intranet environment, it is crucial to have systems in place that can track and monitor security events. Security auditing and logging mechanisms enable the recording and analysis of security-related incidents, allowing organizations to identify suspicious activities, investigate breaches, and take appropriate actions to strengthen the overall security posture. By implementing these and other security measures, organizations can protect their valuable information, maintain the integrity of their internal network, and mitigate the potential risks associated with unauthorized access or data breaches within the intranet environment.

Intranet Security

An intranet is a private network that is designed to be used exclusively by the members of an organization, such as employees, contractors, or partners. Intranets are often used to facilitate communication, collaboration, and sharing of resources among these members. Intranet security refers to the measures and strategies put in place to protect and secure the information, data, and resources contained within an intranet. It encompasses a wide range of technologies, processes, and policies aimed at mitigating risks, detecting and preventing unauthorized access, and ensuring the confidentiality, integrity, and availability of the information stored and transmitted within the intranet.

Intranet Site

An intranet site is a private network of computers that are connected and accessible only within an organization or a specific work group. It is designed to facilitate internal communication, collaboration, and information sharing among employees or authorized users. Unlike the internet, which is a global network that connects computers and networks from around the world, an intranet is limited to a specific organization or company. It provides a secure and controlled environment where sensitive and confidential information can be shared without the risk of unauthorized access.

Intranet Vs. Extranet

An intranet and an extranet are two distinct types of computer networks that are commonly used in organizations. In the context of networking, an intranet refers to a private network that is limited to a specific organization. It uses the same technology and protocols as the internet but is accessible only to the organization's employees or authorized users. The main purpose of an intranet is to facilitate communication, collaboration, and information sharing within the organization. An intranet is usually built using local area network (LAN) technologies and can include various resources such as file-sharing systems, email services, internal websites, and databases. It is designed to be secure, with access control mechanisms in place to ensure that only authorized individuals can access the network resources. Intranets are often used to disseminate company policies, share important documents, and provide a platform for employees to access relevant information. In contrast, an extranet is a network that extends beyond the boundaries of an organization to include external users such as customers, suppliers, or partners. It allows these external users to access specific resources or services that are shared by the organization. Extranets are typically used for collaboration with external entities, such as sharing product information, conducting transactions, or coordinating business processes. Similar to an intranet, an extranet also utilizes internet technologies and protocols for communication, but with appropriate security measures in place to protect the organization's resources and information. Access to the extranet is usually controlled through user authentication and authorization mechanisms to ensure that only authorized external users can access the shared resources.

Intranet

An intranet can be defined as a private computer network that is used within an organization to facilitate communication, collaboration, and the sharing of information and resources among its members. An intranet operates using the same principles as the internet, but with restrictions on access that limit its use to authorized users within the organization. It allows employees to access and share files, documents, and data, as well as communicate with each other through tools such as email, instant messaging, and forums. The main purpose of an intranet is to provide a secure and centralized platform for employees to access information and resources necessary to perform their jobs effectively. It serves as a central hub where members of the organization can find important company news, policies, procedures, and other relevant information. One of the key features of an intranet is its ability to host internal websites and web-based applications. Using web technologies, organizations can develop and deploy internal websites and tools for various purposes, such as employee portals, project management systems, human resources information systems, and knowledge bases. These web-based applications can be accessed by authorized users from any device with internet connectivity. An intranet also promotes collaboration and teamwork within an organization. It provides employees with tools and platforms to create, edit, and share documents, work on projects together, and contribute to discussions and decision-making processes. This improves communication and information flow within the organization, leading to increased productivity and efficiency. In terms of networking, an intranet is typically implemented using local area network (LAN) technologies. It consists of network infrastructure, such as routers, switches, and servers, that enable the transmission of data and communication between different devices within the organization. Security measures, such as firewalls, access controls, and encryption, are put in place to protect the intranet from unauthorized access and ensure the confidentiality and integrity of the information stored and transmitted on the network.

Intrusion Detection System (IDS)

An Intrusion Detection System (IDS) is a network security technology that monitors network traffic and system activities in order to detect and alert on any unauthorized or malicious activities. IDS works by analyzing network packets and system logs to identify suspicious patterns or known attack signatures. It uses a combination of signature-based and anomaly-based detection methods to identify potential threats and intrusions. The role of an IDS is to provide real-time monitoring and analysis of network traffic to identify activities that may indicate a security breach or compromise. It helps to detect and prevent attacks such as unauthorized access, data breaches, malware infections, and denial of service (DoS) attacks. There are two main types of IDS: network-based IDS (NIDS) and host-based IDS (HIDS). NIDS monitors network traffic by capturing and analyzing packets flowing through network devices such as routers and switches. It can detect network-based attacks by examining packet headers and payloads for any suspicious or malicious activity. NIDS can also detect anomalies in network traffic, such as unusually high volumes of traffic or unusual patterns of communication. HIDS, on the other hand, is installed on individual hosts or servers to monitor and analyze system activities. It looks for any abnormal behavior or anomalies in system logs, file changes, registry modifications, and other system activities. HIDS can detect attacks that target specific hosts, such as malware infections, privilege escalation attempts, or unauthorized access attempts to sensitive files or directories. Both NIDS and HIDS generate alerts or notifications when they detect a potential intrusion or security event. These alerts are sent to a central management console or security operations center (SOC) where security analysts can investigate and respond to the incident. Ultimately, an IDS plays a crucial role in securing networks by providing proactive monitoring and detection of potential security threats. It helps organizations to identify and respond to security incidents in a timely manner, minimizing the impact of attacks and maintaining the integrity and confidentiality of their network resources and data.

Intrusion Detection

In the context of networking, intrusion detection refers to the process of identifying unauthorized access attempts or malicious activities targeting a network or its resources. It involves monitoring network traffic and system events to detect and respond to suspicious or anomalous behavior that may indicate a security breach. Intrusion detection systems (IDS) are deployed within a network infrastructure to analyze network packets, log files, and other network-related data. These systems utilize various techniques to identify potential threats and security vulnerabilities: 1. Signature-based detection: This approach involves comparing network traffic patterns or system events against a database of known attack signatures. If a match is found, an alert is generated to notify system administrators about the potential intrusion. 2. Anomaly-based detection: Anomaly detection techniques establish a baseline of normal network behavior and identify deviations from this baseline. Any deviation that falls outside the normal range is flagged as potentially malicious and triggers an alert. 3. Heuristic-based detection: Heuristic techniques use predefined rules or algorithms to identify suspicious patterns or behaviors that may indicate an intrusion. These rules are designed to capture common attack scenarios or known vulnerabilities. Once an intrusion is detected, appropriate actions can be taken to mitigate the threat and prevent further damage. This may include blocking network traffic from the source IP address, isolating compromised systems, or initiating incident response protocols. Overall, intrusion detection plays a critical role in ensuring network security by proactively monitoring and identifying potential threats. By promptly detecting and responding to unauthorized access attempts or malicious activities, organizations can minimize the impact of security breaches and protect their valuable data and resources.

Intrusion Prevention System (IPS)

An Intrusion Prevention System (IPS) is a network security technology that is designed to detect and prevent malicious activities or attacks on a network. It acts as a line of defense between the internal network and external threats by monitoring network traffic in real-time and taking actions to block or prevent any potentially harmful activities. IPS works by analyzing network traffic patterns and comparing them against a database of known attack signatures or patterns. It uses various techniques such as signature-based detection, anomaly-based detection, and behavior-based detection to identify and block potential threats. Signature-based detection involves comparing network traffic against a database of known attack signatures, while anomaly-based detection looks for deviations from normal network behavior. Behavior-based detection focuses on identifying patterns of behavior that may indicate malicious intent.

Jitter

Jitter is a term commonly used in the context of networking to refer to the variation or inconsistency in the delay of data packets. When transmitting data over a network, the time it takes for a packet of data to travel from one point to another can vary due to various factors such as network congestion, hardware limitations, and network protocols. Jitter is measured as the difference in the delay between when a packet is expected to arrive and when it actually arrives. It is typically expressed in milliseconds (ms) or microseconds (μs). In a network with low jitter, the packets arrive at their intended destination with minimal delay variation, allowing for smooth and consistent data transmission. High levels of jitter can negatively affect network performance and the quality of real-time applications such as voice and video communication. When packets arrive at irregular intervals due to high jitter, it can result in choppy audio or video playback, dropped calls, and overall degraded user experience. Jitter can be caused by several factors, including network congestion, inadequate network infrastructure, packet loss, and variations in network latency. It can also be introduced by the devices used in the network, such as routers and switches, or by issues with the software and protocols used for data transmission. To mitigate the effects of jitter, various techniques can be employed. These include the use of jitter buffers, which temporarily store arriving packets to smooth out the variations in delay before forwarding them to their destination. Quality of Service (QoS) mechanisms can also be implemented to prioritize certain types of traffic, ensuring that latency-sensitive applications receive preferential treatment. In summary, jitter refers to the inconsistency in the delay of data packets during transmission over a network. It can negatively impact the performance of real-time applications and is influenced by factors such as network congestion, hardware limitations, and network protocols. Techniques such as jitter buffers and QoS mechanisms can help mitigate the effects of jitter and improve network performance.

Jumbo Frame

A jumbo frame refers to a type of Ethernet frame that exceeds the standard maximum transmission unit (MTU) size of 1500 bytes. In other words, it allows for the transmission of larger data packets compared to regular frames. The purpose of jumbo frames is to improve network efficiency and reduce overhead by reducing the number of frames that need to be transmitted and processed. By increasing the MTU size, jumbo frames can carry more data in a single frame, thereby reducing the number of headers and trailers required for transmission. This results in a more efficient use of network bandwidth and reduces the overall network latency. Additionally, fewer frames require processing by network devices such as switches and routers, which can further improve network performance.

Key Derivation Function (KDF)

A Key Derivation Function (KDF) is a cryptographic algorithm used in networking to derive one or more secret keys from a master key or a password. It is an essential component in secure communication protocols and key management systems, ensuring the secure generation of derived keys for various purposes. The primary function of a KDF is to derive cryptographic keys that can be used for encryption, authentication, and other security services. It takes as input a base key, typically a shared secret like a master key or a password, and produces one or more derived keys that are computationally unrelated to the input key. These derived keys are used to protect sensitive information and ensure the confidentiality, integrity, and authenticity of network communications. One of the crucial aspects of a KDF is its ability to withstand various cryptographic attacks and ensure the security of the derived keys. It should be resilient against brute-force attacks, preimage attacks, and other known cryptographic vulnerabilities. Additionally, a KDF should possess specific properties like forward secrecy, where the compromise of one derived key does not compromise the security of other derived keys. There are various KDF algorithms used in networking, including PBKDF2 (Password-Based Key Derivation Function 2), HKDF (HMAC-based Extract-and-Expand Key Derivation Function), and KDF1 and KDF2 (Key Derivation Functions specified in ISO/IEC 18033-2). These algorithms employ different techniques to ensure the secure derivation of keys, such as key stretching, which increases the computational cost of deriving the keys to slow down potential attacks. In summary, a Key Derivation Function (KDF) is a cryptographic algorithm used in networking to generate one or more derived keys from a master key or a password. It plays a vital role in securing network communications by providing computationally unrelated keys for encryption, authentication, and other security services. The chosen KDF algorithms should possess the necessary properties to withstand cryptographic attacks and ensure the confidentiality, integrity, and authenticity of network communications.

Keylogger

A keylogger, in the context of networking, is a type of malicious software that is designed to capture and record keystrokes made on a computer or mobile device. The purpose of a keylogger is to covertly monitor a user's activities, specifically the inputs they make through their keyboard, without their consent or knowledge. Keyloggers can be either hardware-based or software-based, with the latter being more common. Software keyloggers are typically installed on a device either manually or through social engineering techniques such as phishing emails or malicious downloads. Once installed, the keylogger runs discreetly in the background, capturing and recording every keystroke made by the user. These captured keystrokes can then be accessed and analyzed by the attacker, who can have access to important confidential information such as login credentials, credit card numbers, and sensitive personal data. This information can be used for various malicious purposes, such as identity theft, financial fraud, or gaining unauthorized access to accounts. Keyloggers can also capture other types of input, such as mouse clicks, clipboard contents, and screenshots, depending on their capabilities. Some keyloggers may even have the ability to record audio or take control of a device's webcam, further compromising the user's privacy. Protecting against keyloggers requires a combination of security practices and tools. It is crucial to regularly update and patch operating systems and applications to prevent vulnerabilities that can be exploited by keyloggers. Employing reliable antivirus and anti-malware software can help detect and remove keyloggers from infected devices. Additionally, developing good browsing habits, such as avoiding suspicious websites and not clicking on unknown links or attachments, can reduce the risk of inadvertently downloading and installing keyloggers. In conclusion, a keylogger is a form of malware that captures and records keystrokes made on a device without the user's consent. It poses a significant threat to the user's privacy and security, as it can gather sensitive information that can be used for criminal activities. Vigilance, consistent patching, and the use of security tools are necessary measures to protect against keyloggers.

Keystroke Logging

A keystroke logging is a method used in networking to capture the keystrokes made by a user on a specific device, such as a computer or mobile device. It involves the recording of every key pressed by the user, including letters, numbers, symbols, and special function keys. This method is often used for monitoring purposes, such as in network security or employee monitoring. It allows network administrators or employers to keep track of the activities performed on a particular device, and can provide valuable information for troubleshooting, forensic analysis, and security audits.

L2F (Layer 2 Forwarding)

L2F (Layer 2 Forwarding) is a network protocol that allows for the secure transmission of data packets between remote networks over the internet. It operates at the data link layer (Layer 2) of the OSI networking model, facilitating the transparent forwarding of frames between different LANs (Local Area Networks). The primary purpose of L2F is to support virtual private networks (VPNs), which enable organizations to connect their geographically dispersed networks securely. By encapsulating data packets from one network within packets from another network, L2F provides a mechanism for securely transmitting data over public networks, such as the internet. It achieves this by establishing a secure tunnel between the source and destination networks.

LAN Cable

A Local Area Network (LAN) cable, also known as an Ethernet cable or network cable, is a physical medium used to connect devices in a LAN. It is typically made up of copper or fiber-optic wires enclosed in a plastic casing, and it carries electrical signals between devices, allowing them to communicate and share information. The primary function of an LAN cable is to transmit data between devices by establishing a wired connection. It serves as a bridge between computers, routers, switches, and other network devices, enabling them to send and receive data packets. The cable connects to the network interface card (NIC) or Ethernet port of each device, providing a reliable and stable means of communication. LAN cables are categorized into different types, based on their construction and performance. The most commonly used types include: 1. Twisted Pair Cable: This type of cable consists of pairs of insulated copper wires twisted together. It is further classified into different categories, such as Cat5, Cat6, and Cat7, with each category offering different levels of bandwidth and transmission speeds. 2. Coaxial Cable: Coaxial cables have a central conductor surrounded by an insulating layer, a metallic shield, and an outer insulating layer. They are commonly used for cable television (CATV) distribution and high-speed internet connections. 3. Fiber-Optic Cable: Fiber-optic cables use thin strands of glass or plastic to transmit data using pulses of light. They offer higher bandwidth and faster transmission speeds compared to copper-based cables, making them ideal for long-distance and high-performance networks. LAN cables are typically terminated with connectors, such as RJ-45 or RJ-11, to ensure proper insertion and connection. These connectors are plugged into Ethernet ports or jacks on devices, establishing a secure and reliable physical connection. In conclusion, LAN cables are essential components in computer networks, providing a physical means of connecting devices. They allow for the transmission of data between devices, facilitating seamless communication and information sharing within a LAN. The specific type of LAN cable used depends on the network requirements and the desired performance level.

LAN (Local Area Network)

A Local Area Network (LAN) is a computer network that connects devices within a limited geographic area such as a home, office, or campus. It allows multiple devices, such as computers, printers, and servers, to communicate and share resources efficiently and securely. A LAN typically consists of interconnected devices, called nodes, which are connected by network cables or wireless connections. These nodes can be computers, laptops, servers, switches, or other network devices. By connecting these devices, a LAN enables data transfer and communication between them. In a LAN, each device is assigned a unique identifier, known as an IP address, which allows it to send and receive data. These IP addresses are typically assigned by a network administrator or through a dynamic IP address allocation system such as DHCP (Dynamic Host Configuration Protocol). The primary purpose of a LAN is to facilitate resource sharing and collaboration among connected devices. For example, users on a LAN can share files, printers, and Internet connections. This allows for more efficient use of resources, cost savings, and increased productivity. LANs can also be used to establish secure connections between devices. Network security measures, such as firewalls and encryption protocols, can be implemented to protect data and prevent unauthorized access to the network. LANs can be connected to other LANs or larger networks, such as wide area networks (WANs), through routers or gateways. This allows for communication between devices on different LANs and enables access to external resources, such as the Internet. Overall, LANs play a crucial role in modern computer networks by providing a localized and efficient means of communication and resource sharing. They are used in various settings, including homes, businesses, educational institutions, and government organizations.

LAN Party

A LAN party is an event where a group of people gather together to play multiplayer video games on a Local Area Network (LAN). It typically involves participants bringing their own computers and connecting them through wired or wireless connections to a central network switch or router. LAN parties are commonly organized by gamers who want to socialize and play games together in a dedicated gaming environment. These events provide an opportunity for gamers to compete against each other, collaborate on team-based games, or simply enjoy a shared gaming experience. During a LAN party, the participants' computers are connected to a central network infrastructure, which enables communication and gameplay between the devices. This network infrastructure often includes a network switch or router that acts as a central hub for data transfer. LAN parties can vary in size, ranging from small gatherings of friends in a home setting to large-scale events in dedicated venues or convention centers. The larger LAN parties may even feature tournaments or competitions with prizes for the winners. In order to participate in a LAN party, each attendee must bring their own computer and the necessary peripherals, such as a monitor, keyboard, and mouse. It is also common for participants to bring their own gaming consoles, controllers, and other gaming accessories. To ensure a smooth gaming experience, LAN parties often require a reliable and fast network connection. This can be achieved through wired connections using Ethernet cables, or wireless connections using Wi-Fi technology. Network administrators typically configure the network settings and enforce certain rules to maintain fair gameplay and prevent cheating. In addition to gaming, LAN parties may include other social activities such as food and drinks, music, and casual conversations. These events provide an opportunity for gamers to connect with like-minded individuals, make new friends, and share their passion for gaming.

LAN Segment

A LAN segment refers to a portion of a Local Area Network (LAN) that is created by dividing the network into smaller, more manageable sections or segments. This division is typically done to improve network performance, security, and scalability. In a LAN, devices such as computers, printers, and servers are connected to a common network infrastructure that allows them to communicate with each other. In a small LAN, all devices are typically connected to a single network switch or hub, forming a single LAN segment. However, as the number of devices and the network traffic increases, it can become more challenging to maintain an efficient and reliable network. By dividing a LAN into segments, network administrators can improve network

194

performance by reducing the amount of network traffic on each segment. This is important because when multiple devices share the same network segment, they must compete for the available bandwidth. By separating devices into smaller segments, network administrators can allocate resources more effectively, ensuring that each segment has sufficient bandwidth for its devices. Moreover, LAN segmentation can enhance the security of a network. By separating devices into different segments, network administrators can implement security measures, such as firewalls or access control lists, to control the flow of traffic between segments. This helps prevent unauthorized access to sensitive data and limits the spread of malware or malicious attacks across the network. LAN segmentation also improves network scalability. As a LAN grows, it can become challenging to add new devices or expand the network infrastructure without causing disruptions or slowdowns. By dividing the LAN into segments, network administrators can easily add new segments or expand existing ones without affecting the entire network, providing greater flexibility for network growth and expansion. In summary, a LAN segment is a logical division of a LAN that helps improve network performance, security, and scalability. By dividing a LAN into smaller segments, network administrators can allocate resources more effectively, implement targeted security measures, and easily expand the network to accommodate future growth.

LAN Speed Optimization Tips

LAN speed optimization refers to the process of improving the data transfer rate and efficiency within a local area network (LAN). It involves the implementation of various techniques and strategies to enhance network performance, reduce latency, and increase throughput. There are several tips that can be applied to optimize LAN speed: 1. Use Quality Ethernet Cables: Ensure that high-quality Ethernet cables are used for the LAN infrastructure. Poor-quality cables can result in signal loss and decreased network performance. 2. Update Network Switches: Regularly update network switches to newer models that support higher data transfer rates. Upgrading switches can help improve overall LAN performance. 3. Implement VLANs: Virtual Local Area Networks (VLANs) can be used to separate network traffic and improve overall network efficiency. By dividing the LAN into logical segments, VLANs help reduce broadcast traffic, increase security, and prioritize network traffic. 4. Upgrade Network Interface Cards (NICs): Updating network interface cards on devices connected to the LAN can significantly boost network speed. Newer NICs support higher data transfer rates and offer improved performance. 5. Optimize Network Settings: Fine-tuning network settings such as MTU (Maximum Transmission Unit), TCP window size, and Jumbo Frames can help optimize LAN speed. Adjusting these settings based on network requirements can enhance network performance. 6. Utilize Link Aggregation: Link aggregation, also known as port trunking, combines multiple physical connections into one logical link. This technique increases overall bandwidth and provides load balancing and redundancy. 7. Enable Flow Control: Flow control mechanisms, such as IEEE 802.3x, can be enabled on network devices to regulate data transmission. By managing the flow of data, flow control helps prevent packet loss and improves network performance. 8. Manage Network Traffic: Prioritize network traffic by implementing Quality of Service (QoS) mechanisms. QoS allows specific applications or types of traffic to be given priority, ensuring critical data is delivered with minimal delay. 9. Monitor Network Performance: Regularly monitor network performance using network monitoring tools. This allows administrators to identify bottlenecks, congestion, or other issues that may affect LAN speed and address them promptly. 10. Keep Network Firmware and Software Up to Date: Update firmware and software on network devices regularly. New firmware releases often include performance improvements and bug fixes that can enhance LAN speed.

LAN Speed Optimization

LAN Speed Optimization refers to the process of maximizing the efficiency and performance of a Local Area Network (LAN). A LAN is a network that connects devices within a limited geographical area, such as a home, office, or campus. The optimization of LAN speed involves implementing various techniques and strategies to improve the data transfer rate, reduce latency, and enhance overall network performance. There are several factors that can impact the speed and performance of a LAN, including network hardware, software configurations, and network traffic. By optimizing these factors, network administrators can ensure smooth and efficient communication between devices connected to the LAN. One common technique used in LAN speed optimization is the use of quality-of-service (QoS) mechanisms. QoS allows for the prioritization of network traffic, ensuring that critical data, such as voice or video streams, receive higher priority and bandwidth compared to less important traffic. This can help prevent network congestion and latency issues, resulting in better overall performance. Another important aspect of LAN speed optimization is the use of proper network cabling and hardware. The use of high-quality Ethernet cables, switches, and routers can significantly improve data transfer rates and reduce packet loss. Additionally, implementing technologies such as Gigabit Ethernet or 10 Gigabit Ethernet can further enhance network speed. LAN speed optimization also involves optimizing network protocols and configurations. For example, enabling jumbo frames, which allow for the transmission of larger packets, can boost network performance. Additionally, adjusting network buffer sizes and TCP/IP settings can help reduce latency and packet loss. Regular network monitoring and maintenance are vital for LAN speed optimization. By monitoring network traffic, administrators can identify bottlenecks and areas that require improvement. Implementing regular maintenance tasks, such as firmware updates and security patches, can also help ensure optimal network performance.

LAN Speed Test

LAN Speed Test is a software tool used in the field of networking to measure the speed and performance of a Local Area Network (LAN). It is specifically designed to test the data transfer rate between computers within a network, allowing network administrators or users to assess the efficiency and reliability of their network connections. The primary purpose of LAN Speed Test is to provide an accurate measurement of the speed at which data can be transmitted between devices in a LAN environment. This measurement is typically expressed in terms of megabits per second (Mbps) or gigabits per second (Gbps) and serves as an indicator of the network's capacity to handle data-intensive tasks such as file transfers, video streaming, online gaming, and other bandwidth-intensive activities.

LAN Switch

A LAN switch, short for local area network switch, is a networking device that operates at the data link layer of the OSI model. It is designed to connect multiple devices within a local area network, allowing them to communicate with each other efficiently and securely. A LAN switch functions by receiving data packets from one device and then forwarding them to their intended destination within the local network. It uses the Media Access Control (MAC) addresses embedded in the packets to determine the appropriate port to send them to. This process of examining the MAC addresses and making forwarding decisions is known as switching. LAN switches provide several advantages over traditional network hubs, which simply broadcast all incoming data to all connected devices. Firstly, switches create dedicated communication links between devices, enabling simultaneous data transfers and reducing congestion on the network. This improves overall network performance and decreases the chances of collisions and packet loss. Another significant advantage of LAN switches is their ability to enhance network security. By operating at the data link layer, switches can filter and isolate traffic based on MAC addresses, effectively creating separate segments within the network. This allows for the implementation of various security measures, such as VLANs (Virtual Local Area Networks) and access control lists, which can restrict unauthorized access and protect sensitive data. Furthermore, LAN switches often support additional features such as Quality of Service (QoS) prioritization, which allows certain types of traffic, such as video or voice data, to be given priority over others. This ensures that time-sensitive or critical applications receive adequate bandwidth and are not affected by lower-priority traffic. In summary, a LAN switch is a crucial component of a local area network, connecting multiple devices and facilitating efficient and secure communication among them. By using MAC addresses to make forwarding decisions, LAN switches improve network performance, reduce collisions, and provide enhanced security features. They play a vital role in managing and optimizing the flow of data within a local network.

LAN Troubleshooting

LAN Troubleshooting refers to the process of identifying, analyzing, and resolving issues or problems that occur in a Local Area Network (LAN). A LAN is a network infrastructure that interconnects devices within a limited geographic area, such as a home, office building, or campus. Troubleshooting is crucial for ensuring the smooth operation of the LAN and

196

maintaining uninterrupted network connectivity. The first step in LAN troubleshooting is to gather information about the reported problem. This involves communicating with network users to understand their specific issues, such as slow internet speeds, intermittent connectivity, or the inability to access network resources. Once the problem is identified, the troubleshooting process begins. Diagnostics tools are commonly used to troubleshoot LAN issues. These tools can help network administrators and technicians identify the root cause of the problem by examining various network parameters, such as network traffic, packet loss, latency, and error rates. Examples of diagnostic tools include network analyzers, ping utilities, and packet capturing software. Common LAN problems include network congestion, faulty cabling, misconfigured network devices, and software conflicts. Troubleshooting these issues often involves a systematic approach, starting from the physical layer and progressing up to the network and application layers. For example, if a LAN connection is not working, the troubleshooting process may involve checking the physical connections, verifying network settings, and ensuring that the appropriate drivers are installed and up to date. LAN troubleshooting also involves addressing security-related concerns. Network breaches, malware infections, and unauthorized access can disrupt the normal functioning of a LAN. Troubleshooting security issues may include conducting security audits, implementing firewalls and intrusion detection systems, and educating network users about safe browsing practices. In conclusion, LAN troubleshooting is a critical aspect of maintaining a functional and secure network infrastructure. By employing systematic diagnostic methods and proper analysis, network administrators can identify and resolve LAN issues in a timely manner, minimizing network downtime and maximizing network performance.

LAN Vs. WLAN

A Local Area Network (LAN) is a network that connects devices in a limited area, such as a home, office, or building. It is typically implemented using wired connections and Ethernet technology. A LAN allows devices, such as computers, printers, and servers, to communicate with each other and share resources, such as files and peripheral devices. A Wireless Local Area Network (WLAN), on the other hand, is a network that connects devices without the need for physical wired connections. It uses wireless technology, such as Wi-Fi (Wireless Fidelity), to transmit data over the airwaves. A WLAN provides the same functionality as a LAN but eliminates the constraints of physical cables.

Latency Measurement Techniques

Latency Measurement Techniques refer to the methods used to measure the delay or latency in a network communication system. Latency is the amount of time it takes for a data packet to travel from its source to its destination, and is a key factor in determining the performance and responsiveness of a network. There are several techniques employed to measure latency in a network. One commonly used technique is the round-trip time (RTT) measurement. RTT is the time it takes for a packet to travel from the source to the destination and back again. It is typically measured by sending a packet from the source to the destination and timing how long it takes for the reply packet to come back. This technique provides an estimate of the latency between the two points.

Latency Measurement Tools

A latency measurement tool, in the context of networking, refers to a software or hardware-based solution that is used to measure and quantify the latency of network connections. Latency, also known as network delay or ping time, is the time it takes for data packets to travel from the source to the destination within a network. This type of tool plays a crucial role in network performance management and troubleshooting, helping network administrators identify and diagnose latency issues. By measuring the latency between various network devices, administrators can gain insights into the responsiveness and overall quality of the network.

Latency Optimization Techniques

Latency optimization techniques refer to a set of strategies and methods employed in networking to reduce the delay or latency in data transmission between communication devices. Latency, also known as network delay, is the time taken for a data packet to travel from its source to its destination. It is typically measured in milliseconds and can significantly impact the performance and responsiveness of network applications. There are various factors that contribute to latency, including the physical distance between devices, network congestion, processing delays, and the capacity of network equipment. To overcome these challenges and minimize latency, network administrators and engineers employ several optimization techniques.

Latency Optimization

Latency optimization refers to the process of reducing the amount of time required for data to travel between a source and a destination in a network. It focuses on minimizing delays and decreasing the overall amount of time it takes for information to reach its intended recipient. Latency, in the context of networking, is the time it takes for a data packet to travel from the sender to the receiver. It is often measured in milliseconds (ms) and can be influenced by various factors such as the distance between devices, network congestion, and the efficiency of network protocols.

Latency Reduction Strategies

Latency reduction strategies refer to the various techniques and approaches used in networking to minimize the delay or time taken for data to travel from its source to its destination. Latency, also known as network delay or lag, is the time it takes for information to be transmitted across a network, and it can have a significant impact on the overall performance and user experience in various networked applications. There are several strategies that can be employed to reduce latency and improve network performance. One such strategy is optimizing network infrastructure, which involves upgrading hardware components such as routers, switches, and cables to ensure faster and more efficient data transmission. By using high-capacity and low-latency equipment, the time taken for data to travel through the network can be significantly reduced. Another strategy for reducing latency is implementing traffic prioritization and Quality of Service (QoS) mechanisms. By classifying and prioritizing network traffic based on its importance or requirements, critical data can be given higher priority, ensuring faster transmission and reduced latency. This can be achieved through techniques such as traffic shaping, packet prioritization, and bandwidth allocation. Network caching is another effective latency reduction strategy. Caching involves storing frequently accessed data or content in a cache, which is a temporary storage area closer to the users. By serving content from the cache instead of retrieving it from the original source every time, latency can be significantly reduced. This is particularly beneficial for static content, such as web pages, images, and videos, which can be cached at various levels within the network infrastructure. In addition to these strategies, minimizing network congestion through effective traffic engineering and load balancing can also help reduce latency. By evenly distributing network traffic across multiple paths and optimizing network utilization, delays due to congestion can be minimized. This can be achieved through techniques like dynamic routing protocols, link aggregation, and intelligent traffic management.

Latency Reduction Tools

Latency Reduction Tools are software or hardware techniques used in the field of networking to minimize the delay or latency in data transmission between network devices. Latency refers to the time it takes for a packet of data to travel from the source to the destination across a network. It is a critical factor in determining the overall performance and user experience in network communications. The need for latency reduction arises due to various reasons. In a network, there can be bottlenecks or congestion points that cause delays in data transmission. Additionally, long distances between the source and destination can introduce significant latency. Latency reduction tools aim to address these issues and improve the efficiency of data transfer. There are several techniques employed by latency reduction tools to minimize the delay in network communications. One common approach is data compression, where the size of the data packets is reduced before transmission. This helps in reducing the time it takes to transmit the data over the network. Another technique is data caching, where frequently accessed data is stored in a cache closer to the user, reducing the need to retrieve the data from the original source. Some latency reduction tools also utilize traffic shaping and prioritization techniques. By managing the flow of data and giving priority to certain types of traffic, such as real-time or time-critical communications, delays can be minimized. Additionally, network optimization algorithms are employed to analyze network traffic patterns and optimize the routing of data packets, reducing the overall latency. In summary, latency reduction tools play a crucial role in improving the performance and responsiveness of network communications. By employing various techniques such as data compression, caching, traffic shaping, and optimization algorithms, these tools aim to minimize the delay or latency in data transmission and enhance the overall user experience.

Latency Test

Latency test in the context of networking refers to the measurement of the delay or the time it takes for data packets to travel from the source to the destination across a network. It is an important metric in evaluating the performance and efficiency of a network. Latency is typically measured in milliseconds and can be affected by various factors such as network congestion, distance between the source and destination, and the quality of the network infrastructure. The lower the latency, the faster the network response time, resulting in a better user experience and smoother data transfer.

Latency Testing Tools

Latency testing tools are software applications or services used in networking to measure the delay or latency of data transmission between two or more network devices. These tools help network administrators and engineers evaluate the performance and efficiency of their network infrastructure by assessing how long it takes for data to travel from a source device to a destination device and back. The main purpose of latency testing tools is to determine the delay or latency experienced by data packets as they traverse a network. Latency refers to the time it takes for data to travel from its source to its destination, and back again, usually measured in milliseconds (ms). In networking, latency is a critical metric because it directly impacts the responsiveness and speed of network applications, services, and overall user experience. Latency testing tools typically work by sending test packets or generating network traffic between two or more devices and measuring the time it takes for the packets to reach their destination and return. These tools provide detailed insights into the latency experienced at different points in the network, helping network administrators identify bottlenecks or areas of improvement. Latency testing tools enable network professionals to analyze and monitor network performance in real-time or over extended periods. They often offer features such as graphical representations of latency measurements, historical data analysis, and alerts for unusual latency spikes. Some advanced tools may also provide additional metrics like jitter (variation in latency), packet loss, and throughput to provide a more comprehensive assessment of network performance. By using latency testing tools, network administrators can proactively identify and resolve latency-related issues, optimize network configurations, or make informed decisions on network upgrades or optimizations. They can also assess the impact of changes in the network environment or troubleshoot latency-related problems in specific applications or services. In conclusion, latency testing tools play a crucial role in evaluating and maintaining optimal network performance by measuring the delay or latency experienced by data packets. These tools enable network administrators to identify and troubleshoot latency issues, optimize network configurations, and ensure a responsive and efficient network infrastructure.

Latency

Latency in the context of networking refers to the time delay that occurs between the moment a data packet is sent from one location to another and the moment it is received at its destination. It is usually measured in milliseconds (ms) and is a crucial factor in determining the overall performance of a network. Latency can be influenced by several factors, including the physical distance between the sender and receiver, the quality and capacity of the network infrastructure, and the level of congestion or network traffic. It is important to note that latency is different from network bandwidth, which refers to the amount of data that can be transmitted within a given time frame.

Layer 2 Tunneling Protocol (L2TP)

The Layer 2 Tunneling Protocol (L2TP) is a networking protocol used to create Virtual Private Networks (VPNs). It allows the creation of secure connections over a public network, such as the internet, by encapsulating data packets within an additional layer of headers. The primary purpose of L2TP is to establish a point-to-point connection between a user's device and a VPN server, enabling the user to access private network resources remotely. L2TP operates at the data link layer (Layer 2) of the OSI model, which is responsible for the reliable transmission of data between adjacent network nodes. By leveraging the existing infrastructure of the internet, L2TP enables users to establish secure connections without the need for dedicated physical connections or expensive leased lines. When a user initiates an L2TP connection, their device acts as an L2TP client and establishes a tunnel with the VPN server. This tunnel is a logical connection that encapsulates the user's data packets and protects them from being intercepted or tampered with by unauthorized parties. L2TP uses the Internet Protocol (IP) as its transport protocol, allowing it to deliver data reliably across networks. Since it operates at the data link layer, L2TP can work with a wide range of network protocols, making it highly versatile. One of the key features of L2TP is its ability to support multiple encryption algorithms, ensuring the confidentiality of data transmitted through the VPN tunnel. It can also authenticate users using various methods, such as passwords, pre-shared keys, or digital certificates. Additionally, L2TP can establish connections through Network Address Translation (NAT) devices, allowing users behind NAT networks to connect to VPN servers. In summary, the Layer 2 Tunneling Protocol (L2TP) is a versatile networking protocol that enables the creation of secure connections over public networks. By encapsulating data packets within an additional layer of headers, L2TP establishes tunnels between users' devices and VPN servers. Through its support for encryption and authentication, L2TP ensures the confidentiality and integrity of data transmitted over VPN connections.

Layer 7 Load Balancing

Layer 7 Load Balancing is a networking technique used to distribute incoming network traffic across multiple servers or resources in order to efficiently manage and balance the workload. It operates at the application layer (Layer 7) of the Open Systems Interconnection (OSI) model which is responsible for managing communication between applications. Layer 7 Load Balancing involves the use of a load balancer, which acts as the intermediary between the client and the server. When a client sends a request, the load balancer receives the request and determines the most suitable server to handle that request based on various factors such as server health, performance, and availability. The load balancer intelligently distributes the requests amongst the servers using different algorithms such as round-robin, least connections, or weighted distribution. This ensures that each server receives an equal or fair share of the incoming traffic, preventing any single server from becoming overwhelmed or overloaded. Layer 7 Load Balancing not only helps in distributing the workload but also provides additional benefits. It improves the overall performance and response time for end users by redirecting requests to servers that are less busy or located in optimal geographical regions. It also enhances the availability and reliability of the application by automatically rerouting requests to another server in case of server failures or downtime. Furthermore, Layer 7 Load Balancing allows for advanced traffic management by analyzing and inspecting the content of the requests. It provides flexibility to direct specific types of requests to specialized servers or resources based on the request's characteristics. For instance, it can redirect video streaming requests to servers with high bandwidth or sensitive transactions to more secure servers. In summary, Layer 7 Load Balancing is a networking technique that distributes incoming network traffic across multiple servers at the application layer, ensuring efficient workload management, improved performance, availability, and content-based traffic routing.

Link Aggregation

Link Aggregation (or EtherChannel, Port Channel, Bonding, Trunking) is a technique used in computer networking to combine multiple physical links into a single logical link. The purpose of link aggregation is to increase the bandwidth, improve fault tolerance, and provide load balancing across the aggregated links. Link aggregation works by grouping multiple physical links between devices, such as switches or routers, into a single logical link that appears as a single higher bandwidth link. This logical link is then treated as a single entity in terms of forwarding traffic and performing network operations.

Link-State Routing

Link-State Routing is a routing algorithm used in computer networks to determine the best path for data transmission. It is based on the idea that each network node has a complete map or "snapshot" of the entire network, including information about the state of all links and nodes. This information is shared among the nodes using a flooding mechanism, allowing each node to calculate the shortest path to any destination within the network. Link-State Routing operates by creating a database that holds information about the network topology, which includes details about the status and availability of all network links. Each network node independently collects this information and updates its own database, which is then used to calculate the shortest path to a destination. The algorithm then selects the best path based on certain metrics, such as the number of hops or link quality.

Load Balancer Algorithm

A load balancer algorithm is a method or technique used in the field of computer networking to distribute incoming network traffic across multiple servers or computing resources to optimize resource utilization, improve reliability, and enhance performance. Load balancing aims to evenly distribute workloads among multiple servers, ensuring that no single server is overwhelmed while others remain idle. This process involves efficiently allocating incoming client requests to various servers based on predefined policies or algorithms.

Load Balancer

A Load Balancer is a networking device or software that evenly distributes incoming network traffic across multiple servers or computer systems to optimize resource utilization, maximize throughput, and ensure high availability of network applications and services. Load balancing technology plays a significant role in managing traffic flow and enhancing the performance of networks. It acts as an intermediary between clients or users and the server infrastructure, efficiently distributing incoming requests in a way that avoids overloading any specific server, thus preventing performance degradation or service disruption. Load balancers enable organizations to scale their applications and systems without experiencing downtime or latency issues.

Load Balancing Algorithm

A Load Balancing Algorithm is a method used in computer networking to efficiently distribute incoming network traffic across multiple servers or resources, in order to optimize the overall performance and avoid overloading any single server. The main goal of load balancing is to ensure that all servers in a network are utilized evenly, preventing any bottlenecks or excessive loads on a specific server. Load balancing algorithms play a crucial role in managing network traffic, especially in high-traffic environments such as data centers or web applications with numerous users. These algorithms use various criteria to determine how to distribute incoming requests among multiple servers, including server capacity, current workload, response time, and availability.

Load Balancing Algorithms Comparison

Load balancing algorithms are used in computer networks to distribute incoming traffic across multiple servers or nodes in order to optimize resource utilization, improve performance, and ensure high availability and fault tolerance. These algorithms play a crucial role in network infrastructure as they determine how requests from clients are distributed among the available resources. There are various load balancing algorithms that can be implemented, each with its own advantages and disadvantages. Round Robin, Weighted Round Robin, Least Connections, and Least Response Time are some of the commonly used algorithms in load balancing. Round Robin is a simple and widely used algorithm that distributes traffic evenly among available resources in a cyclic manner. Each request is sent to the next server in the rotation, ensuring fairness in resource allocation. However, Round Robin does not take into account the current load or capacity of each server, potentially leading to inefficient utilization of resources. Weighted Round Robin is an extension of the Round Robin algorithm, where each server is assigned a weight representing its capacity or capability to handle requests. Servers with higher weights receive a larger proportion of traffic, allowing for better resource allocation. This algorithm is particularly useful when the servers have different capacities. Least Connections is an algorithm that directs each new request to the server with the fewest active connections. By providing equal opportunities to underutilized servers, Least Connections promotes better utilization of resources and prevents overload on heavily loaded servers. However, this algorithm does not consider the processing power or capacity of each server, potentially leading to disproportionate load distribution. Least Response Time is another algorithm that aims to minimize response time by selecting servers with the shortest response time. This algorithm collects response time data from each server and directs requests to the server with the lowest recorded response time. While this approach can significantly improve performance, it requires continuous monitoring and accurate measurement of response times. Overall, load balancing algorithms are essential for maintaining network efficiency, optimizing resource usage, and ensuring high availability of services. The choice of algorithm depends on the specific requirements of the network and the characteristics of the servers involved. Implementing an appropriate load balancing algorithm can contribute to better performance, scalability, and reliability in a networked environment.

Load Balancing Algorithms

Load balancing algorithms refer to the set of techniques used in computer networking to distribute workload among multiple computer systems, network links, CPUs, or other resources. The primary goal of load balancing is to optimize resource utilization, enhance system performance, and ensure high availability of network services. Load balancing algorithms employ various strategies to distribute incoming network traffic across multiple servers or resources, minimizing the chances of any single server or resource becoming overwhelmed. This distribution of work is achieved by considering factors such as server or resource capacity, current and historical workload, response times, and other relevant metrics. By balancing the load evenly, these algorithms prevent any single server or resource from being overloaded, which can lead to degraded performance or even system failure. There are several common load balancing algorithms used in networking, including: 1. Round Robin: This algorithm distributes incoming requests evenly across a group of resources in a cyclic manner. Each resource is sequentially assigned incoming requests in order, ensuring that each resource handles an equal number of requests over time. 2. Least Connections: In this algorithm, incoming requests are directed to the resource or server with the fewest active connections at the time. This ensures that resources with lower current workloads receive more requests, thereby balancing the load across the available resources. 3. Weighted Round Robin: Similar to the Round Robin algorithm, this approach assigns a weight or priority to each resource based on its capacity or processing power. The resources with higher weights receive more requests, enabling better utilization of resources based on their capabilities. 4. IP Hash: This algorithm uses the source IP address of an incoming request to determine which resource or server should handle it. By consistently assigning requests from the same IP address to the same server, it ensures that requests from the same client are always directed to the same resource, enabling session persistence. These load balancing algorithms, among others, play a pivotal role in optimizing resource utilization, enhancing network performance, and ensuring high availability of network services in modern networking environments.

Load Balancing Solutions

Load balancing solutions refer to networking strategies or technologies that distribute incoming network traffic across multiple servers or resources to optimize performance, reliability, and availability. These solutions manage and allocate network requests in a way that balances the workload, enhances efficiency, and prevents any single component from being overwhelmed or becoming a single point of failure. Load balancers act as intermediaries between clients and servers, receiving incoming network traffic and then distributing it across a cluster or pool of servers. They are equipped with intelligent algorithms and mechanisms that analyze factors like server health, current load, and network conditions to make informed decisions about where to direct incoming requests. Load balancing solutions offer several advantages in networking environments. Firstly, they enhance scalability and capacity by allowing organizations to add or remove servers as needed, without impacting the overall performance. This dynamic allocation of resources ensures that network traffic is evenly distributed, preventing any server from being overloaded and maximizing the utilization of available resources. Secondly, load balancing solutions improve the reliability and availability of network services. By distributing traffic across multiple servers, they create redundancy and eliminate the risk of a single point of failure. In the event of a server failure, the load balancer automatically routes traffic to the surviving servers, ensuring uninterrupted service delivery. Additionally, load balancing solutions optimize performance by enabling efficient traffic management. They direct requests to the server that can best handle them based on factors like server response times, geographic location, and the specific workload characteristics. This helps reduce latency, improve response times, and enhance the overall user experience. Load balancing solutions can be implemented using hardware devices or software-based solutions. Hardware load balancers are physical appliances that are placed in front of the server infrastructure and manage traffic at the network layer. Software load balancers, on the other hand, are virtual instances or applications that run on servers and operate at the application layer. In conclusion, load balancing solutions play a crucial role in optimizing network performance, enhancing reliability, and ensuring scalability. By efficiently distributing network traffic across multiple servers, these solutions improve response times, prevent overload, and minimize downtime, ultimately providing a seamless network experience for users.

Load Balancing Strategies

Load balancing strategies in the context of networking refer to the techniques used to distribute network traffic across multiple servers or resources to optimize performance, ensure high availability, and prevent overload. These strategies help to evenly distribute tasks or requests, thereby improving the overall efficiency and reliability of the network. There are several load balancing strategies commonly used in networking: 1. Round Robin: This strategy distributes incoming requests in a cyclic manner, allowing each server to handle an equal number of requests. It is a simple and fair approach that ensures all servers or resources are utilized evenly. 2. Least Connections: Using this strategy, the load balancer directs incoming requests to the server with the fewest active connections. It ensures that the server with the lightest load at any given time handles each new request. 3. IP Hash: In IP hashing, the load balancer calculates a hash value based on the source IP address of the client. This hash value is used to determine which server should handle the request. It ensures that requests from the same client are always directed to the same server, which is useful for maintaining session information or caching. 4. Weighted Round Robin: With weighted round robin, each server is assigned a weight proportional to its processing power or capacity. Servers with higher weights receive more requests, while those with lower weights handle fewer requests. This strategy allows for a more flexible and efficient allocation of resources. 5. Least Response Time: This strategy directs new requests to the server with the shortest response time. It takes into account the current load on each server and selects the one that is likely to provide the fastest response. 6. Destination IP Affinity: Also known as sticky sessions or session persistence, this strategy ensures that requests from the same client are directed to the same server for the duration of a session. It is often used in situations where maintaining state information is crucial, such as in e-commerce applications. These load balancing strategies play a vital role in modern networking, helping to optimize resource allocation, improve scalability, and enhance the overall performance and reliability of networked systems.

Load Balancing Techniques In Cloud

Load balancing techniques in the context of networking refer to the methods and strategies used to evenly distribute incoming network traffic across multiple servers or resources in a cloud environment. The goal of load balancing is to ensure that each server or resource handles a fair share of the network traffic, preventing any individual resource from being overwhelmed and maintaining the overall performance and availability of the network. There are several load balancing techniques commonly employed in cloud networking: 1. Round Robin: This technique distributes incoming traffic sequentially across the available servers or resources. Each request is assigned to the next server/resource in the rotation, ensuring an equal distribution of traffic across all resources. 2. Least Connections: With this technique, incoming traffic is routed to the server/resource with the fewest active connections. This ensures that heavily loaded resources are not overwhelmed and helps to maintain a more balanced distribution of network traffic. 3. Weighted Round Robin: This technique assigns a weight to each server or resource based on its capabilities and performance. Servers/resources with higher weights are assigned more traffic, while those with lower weights receive fewer requests. This allows for a more efficient allocation of network traffic based on the capacity and capabilities of each resource. 4. IP Hash: This technique uses the source IP address of incoming traffic to determine which server/resource should handle the request. By hashing the source IP address, a consistent mapping is created between the IP address and the server/resource, ensuring that subsequent requests from the same IP address are always routed to the same server/resource. This helps to maintain session persistence for clients accessing cloud services. These load balancing techniques play a crucial role in cloud networking by efficiently distributing network traffic across multiple servers or resources, improving overall performance, scalability, and availability of cloud-based services.

Load Balancing Techniques

Load Balancing Techniques in the context of networking refer to the methods and processes used to distribute network traffic across multiple servers or resources. The main objective of load balancing is to optimize resource utilization, maximize throughput, minimize response time, and ensure high availability of services by evenly distributing the workload. One common technique for load balancing is the Round Robin algorithm, which distributes incoming requests to each server in a circular manner. This approach ensures that no single server is overwhelmed with requests while all servers participate in handling the workload. Another method is Weighted Round Robin, where servers are assigned different weights based on their processing capabilities, enabling more powerful servers to handle larger portions of the traffic. This technique allows for greater flexibility and customization in load balancing. An alternative technique is Least Connection, which assigns incoming requests to the server with the fewest active connections. This ensures that the workload is evenly distributed based on the current server capacity, preventing any single server from being overloaded. Least Response Time is a similar approach that directs traffic to the server with the fastest response time, prioritizing efficient resource utilization. Dynamic load balancing techniques involve continuously monitoring server performance and adjusting the load distribution accordingly. One such method is the Least Load method, which takes into account the current server load before making load balancing decisions. By considering both the server's capabilities and current utilization, this technique aims to achieve optimal performance and prevent server overload. Content-aware load balancing is another approach that evaluates the specific content or type of incoming requests and uses this information to determine the most appropriate server to handle the traffic. This technique can distribute requests based on factors such as file type, HTTP headers, or user location, ensuring efficient allocation of resources based on specific requirements. Overall, load balancing techniques are crucial in maintaining network performance, high availability, and scalability. By evenly distributing the workload across multiple servers, these techniques enhance resource utilization, minimize response times, and improve the overall user experience.

Load Balancing

Load balancing is a networking technique that involves distributing incoming network traffic across multiple servers to optimize resource utilization, increase reliability, and improve performance. It aims to evenly distribute the workload across servers, ensuring that no single server becomes overwhelmed while others are underutilized. Load balancing involves the use of a load balancer, which acts as the intermediary between client devices and the server pool. When a client sends a request to access a website, for example, the load balancer receives the request and checks the availability and performance of the servers in the pool. Based on predefined algorithms and configurations, the load balancer then redirects the request to an appropriate server that has the capacity to handle the incoming traffic. One of the key benefits of load balancing is scalability. By distributing the workload across multiple servers, load balancing allows organizations to easily add or remove servers as needed, depending on the amount of incoming traffic. This scalability helps in ensuring that websites or applications can handle a high volume of users without experiencing downtime or performance issues. Another advantage of load balancing is fault tolerance. In the event that a server fails or becomes unavailable, the load balancer automatically routes traffic to other servers in the pool, ensuring that the service remains uninterrupted. This fault tolerance also improves the overall reliability of the network infrastructure, making it more resistant to single points of failure. Load balancing algorithms play a crucial role in determining how the traffic is distributed among the servers. There are several algorithms available, such as round-robin, least connections, weighted round-robin, and IP hash. These algorithms consider factors like server capacity, current load, response times, and geographic proximity when deciding which server should handle a particular request. In conclusion, load balancing is a networking technique that evenly distributes incoming network traffic across multiple servers. It improves resource utilization, enhances reliability, and optimizes performance by preventing any single server from being overwhelmed. With the use of load balancing algorithms, organizations can efficiently manage their network infrastructure to handle high volumes of traffic and provide a seamless user experience.

Local Area Network (LAN)

A Local Area Network (LAN) is a computer network that connects devices within a limited area, such as a building, office, or group of nearby buildings. It allows for the sharing of resources and information between connected devices, such as computers, servers, printers, and storage devices. In a LAN, the devices are typically connected using Ethernet cables or wireless connections. The network is usually owned and managed by a single organization, such as a business or educational institution, and the devices on the network can communicate with each other directly without the need for any external connections.

Local Loop

A local loop, in the context of networking, refers to the physical connection between a subscriber's location and the nearest central office of the telecommunications service provider. It is also commonly known as the "last mile" or "subscriber loop." The local loop is an essential component of a telecommunications network, as it enables the transmission of data, voice, and other communication services between the subscriber and the service provider. It comprises a pair of copper wires, coaxial cables, or fiber optic cables, depending on the technology used in the network. The local loop serves as the final link in the communication chain, connecting the subscriber's premises to the network infrastructure. The length of the local loop can vary, ranging from a few meters to several kilometers, depending on the distance between the subscriber's location and the central office. Traditionally, the local loop was predominantly based on copper wires, commonly known as twisted pairs, which enabled analog voice signals to be transmitted. Copper-based local loops have several limitations, including limited bandwidth and susceptibility to interference and signal loss over long distances. To overcome these limitations, newer technologies such as coaxial cables and fiber optic cables have been widely deployed. Coaxial cables provide higher bandwidth and improved signal quality compared to copper wires, while fiber optic cables offer even greater bandwidth, faster data transmission rates, and immunity to electromagnetic interference. In recent years, the local loop has become a critical component in delivering high-speed internet access to residential and business subscribers. With the proliferation of broadband technologies such as Digital Subscriber Line (DSL), cable internet, and fiber-to-the-home (FTTH), the local loop plays a crucial role in bridging the gap between the service provider's network and the end-user's premises. In conclusion, the local loop is the physical connection that links a subscriber's location to the nearest central office of the telecommunications service provider. It is a vital element in enabling communication services, such as voice, data, and internet access, to be transmitted between the subscriber and the service provider.

Logic Bomb Attack

A logic bomb attack in the context of networking refers to a malicious code or software program that is intentionally inserted into a computer system or network and is designed to execute a particular action when specific conditions are met. Unlike a virus or a worm, which propagate themselves and spread to other systems, a logic bomb typically remains dormant until triggered by a specific event or date. When triggered, a logic bomb can cause a variety of detrimental effects on the network, ranging from data corruption and deletion to system failures and disruptions of network services. The potential damage caused by a logic bomb attack depends on its design and the permissions and access levels of the user who triggered it. The primary objective of a logic bomb attack is to cause disruption, exploit vulnerabilities, or gain unauthorized access to sensitive information. This can have serious consequences for individuals, businesses, and organizations, including financial losses, compromised data privacy, and reputational damage. Logic bombs are often deployed as a hidden part of a legitimate program or software, making them difficult to detect until they are triggered. In many cases, logic bombs are created by insiders with privileged access to the network, such as disgruntled employees or contractors seeking revenge or personal gain. Preventing and mitigating the impact of logic bomb attacks requires a multi-layered approach to network security. This includes implementing robust access controls and permissions management, regularly updating and patching software systems, monitoring network activity for any suspicious behavior, and educating users about the risks of downloading and executing unknown files. Furthermore, organizations should have incident response plans in place to promptly detect, contain, and remediate logic bomb attacks. This involves regularly backing up critical data, implementing intrusion detection systems and firewalls, and conducting regular security audits to identify and eliminate potential vulnerabilities in the network. In conclusion, a logic bomb attack in networking refers to a malicious code or software program that remains dormant until triggered by specific conditions. Its purpose is to cause disruption, gain unauthorized access, or exploit vulnerabilities in a network. Preventing and mitigating the impact of logic bomb attacks requires a comprehensive approach to network security, including strong access controls, regular software updates, monitoring of network activity, and incident response plans.

Logic Bomb

A logic bomb in the context of networking refers to a malicious program or code that is inserted into a computer system or network with the intention of causing disruption or damage. It is a type of cyber-attack that is typically triggered by a specific event or condition, leading to the activation of the bomb and subsequent harmful effects. When a logic bomb is deployed, it remains dormant within the network or system until the predefined conditions are met. These conditions can vary depending on the attacker's objectives, but they are typically related to certain dates, times, or actions taken by users or devices within the network. Once the trigger event occurs, the logic bomb is activated, and it starts executing its malicious code. The purpose of a logic bomb can range from simply causing annoyance or inconvenience to causing serious damage to a network or system. For example, a logic bomb might be programmed to delete important files, corrupt data, disrupt network communication, or even spread to other connected devices, leading to a widespread system failure. The deployment of a logic bomb requires access to the target system or network, often by an insider or someone with malicious intent. Once in the system, the logic bomb can be hidden within legitimate applications, scripts, or files, making it difficult to detect and remove. To protect against logic bombs and other forms of cyber-attacks, network administrators and security professionals implement various security measures. These may include using up-to-date antivirus software, regularly patching and updating system software, restricting access privileges to sensitive areas of the network, and implementing intrusion detection and prevention systems. In conclusion, a logic bomb in the context of networking refers to a malicious program or code that is designed to cause damage or disruption when triggered by specific conditions. It can have serious consequences for a network or system, ranging from data corruption to widespread system failure. Protection against logic bombs requires robust security measures and constant vigilance.

Logical Link Control (LLC)

Logical Link Control (LLC) is a sublayer of the Data Link Layer (Layer 2) in the OSI model of network communication. It is responsible for managing communication between devices on a local area network (LAN). LLC provides a reliable and error-free data transmission service to higher layers of the network stack. LLC operates by establishing a logical connection between two devices, known as the sender and receiver, using a technique called framing. Framing involves breaking data into smaller, manageable chunks called frames. These frames are then transmitted over the network, along with control information such as sequence numbers and error-checking codes. The receiver uses this information to verify the integrity of the received data and to reassemble it in the correct order, if necessary. LLC also handles flow control, which ensures that a sender does not overwhelm a receiver with data. Flow control mechanisms, such as the sliding window protocol, enable the sender to regulate the rate at which frames are transmitted based on the receiver's ability to process them. This prevents data loss and congestion on the network. Another key function of LLC is error detection and correction. It uses mechanisms such as cyclic redundancy check (CRC) to add error-checking codes to each frame. The receiver can then use these codes to identify and discard frames that contain errors. In case of error detection, LLC can request the retransmission of the affected frames to ensure data integrity. In addition, LLC allows for multiplexing and demultiplexing of data from different network protocols, making it possible for multiple protocols to share the same physical network interface. It achieves this through the use of Service Access Points (SAPs), which provide an interface between LLC and higher layers of the network stack. In summary, LLC is responsible for framing, flow control, error detection and correction, as well as multiplexing and demultiplexing of data. It ensures reliable and efficient data transmission between devices on a local area network, making it an essential component of network communication.

Long-Haul Network

A long-haul network, in the context of networking, refers to a wide area network (WAN) infrastructure that connects geographically separated locations over long distances. It is designed to transmit data, voice, and video traffic between different cities, countries, or continents. The primary purpose of a long-haul network is to facilitate communication and data exchange between distant locations efficiently and securely. It accomplishes this by using various technologies and protocols to establish reliable connectivity over long distances, often spanning hundreds or thousands of kilometers.

Long-Term Evolution (LTE)

Long-Term Evolution (LTE) is a wireless communication standard that supports high-speed data services and increased capacity for mobile networks. It is designed to deliver faster, more reliable, and more efficient wireless communication compared to previous generations of technology, such as 3G. LTE offers significant improvements in terms of data transfer rates, network latency, and overall user experience. With LTE, users can enjoy faster download and upload speeds, lower latency for real-time applications, and enhanced voice quality for voice over LTE (VoLTE) services. LTE utilizes a packet-switched network architecture, where data is transmitted in small data packets over the network. This enables efficient data transfer and allows for simultaneous transmission of voice and data services. LTE also employs advanced radio frequency techniques, such as Orthogonal Frequency Division Multiplexing (OFDM) and Multiple Input Multiple Output (MIMO), to enhance network performance and capacity. One of the key features of LTE is its support for seamless handovers between different base stations, also known as "handover optimization." This allows for uninterrupted connectivity while moving between coverage areas, such as when driving or using public transportation. LTE also supports interworking with other wireless technologies, such as 2G and 3G, ensuring backward compatibility and smooth transition for legacy devices and networks. Another important aspect of LTE is its use of advanced network scheduling techniques, such as Quality of Service (QoS) management and traffic prioritization. These techniques ensure that network resources are allocated efficiently, based on the type of service and the specific needs of each user. This helps to guarantee a consistent and reliable user experience, even in high-traffic scenarios. LTE has been widely adopted across the globe, becoming the dominant technology for mobile communication. It enables a wide range of applications and services, including multimedia streaming, online gaming, video conferencing, and Internet of Things (IoT) deployments. As mobile data demands continue to grow, LTE provides a solid foundation for the evolution towards even faster and more advanced technologies, such as 5G.

MAC Address Filtering

MAC address filtering is a security feature used in networking to allow or deny access to a network based on an individual device's MAC (Media Access Control) address. A MAC address is a unique identifier assigned to each network interface card (NIC), which is utilized to communicate over a network. This filtering technique involves creating a list of approved MAC addresses that are permitted to access the network, and denying access to any device whose MAC address is not included in the list. The filtering process occurs at the network's access points, such as routers or wireless access points, which examine the MAC address of incoming devices and compare them against the approved list. MAC address filtering adds an extra layer of security to a network by preventing unauthorized devices from connecting to it. It is commonly used in environments where only specific devices should be granted network access, such as corporate networks, government organizations, or educational institutions. One of the advantages of MAC address filtering is that it offers a simple and straightforward way to control network access. By maintaining an up-to-date list of approved MAC addresses, network administrators have the ability to easily manage which devices are allowed to connect to the network and which are not. However, this method of filtering also has its limitations. MAC addresses can be easily spoofed, meaning that a malicious user can impersonate an approved device by falsifying its MAC address. Additionally, managing a large number of MAC addresses can become cumbersome and time-consuming, particularly in dynamic environments where devices are frequently added or removed. In conclusion, MAC address filtering is a security mechanism used in networking to control access to a network based on the unique MAC addresses of devices. While it provides a simple way to manage network access, it is not foolproof and can be bypassed by determined attackers. Therefore, it is often used in conjunction with other security measures to enhance the overall security of a network.

MAC Address Spoofing Prevention

MAC Address Spoofing Prevention is a defensive mechanism implemented in networking to counteract the unauthorized manipulation of Media Access Control (MAC) addresses. MAC address spoofing refers to the act of forging or altering the MAC address of a network device to deceive other devices or systems on the network. MAC addresses are unique identifiers assigned to each network interface card (NIC) by the manufacturer. They are used to distinguish devices and facilitate communication within a local area network (LAN). In a typical network setup, devices use their MAC addresses to send and receive data packets. However, MAC addresses can be easily changed or falsified by attackers to bypass security controls, gain unauthorized access, or conduct illicit activities. MAC Address Spoofing Prevention techniques aim to detect and prevent the misuse of MAC addresses. One commonly employed approach is port security that restricts the MAC addresses allowed to transmit data on a specific port. By associating a single MAC address with a specific physical port, the network can deny access to any other MAC addresses attempting to use that port. This prevents attackers from impersonating authorized devices or introducing unauthorized hardware. In addition to port security, network administrators can implement MAC address filtering to further mitigate MAC address spoofing risks. This involves creating a whitelist of approved MAC addresses that are allowed to communicate on the network. Any devices attempting to connect with a MAC address not present in the whitelist will be denied access. Furthermore, some advanced network devices and operating systems offer additional security features like MAC address lockdowns or MAC address binding. MAC address lockdowns bind a specific MAC address to a particular port, making it impossible for other devices to connect using a different MAC address on the same port. MAC address binding, on the other hand, associates an IP address with a specific MAC address, ensuring that only a device with a matching MAC address can use the assigned IP address.

MAC Address

A MAC address, short for Media Access Control address, is a unique identifier assigned to a network interface card (NIC) by the manufacturer. It is a hardware address that operates at the data link layer of the OSI model. The MAC address consists of a 48-bit number, typically written as six pairs of hexadecimal digits separated by colons or hyphens. The first half of the MAC address (24 bits) represents the organizationally unique identifier (OUI) assigned to the manufacturer, while the second half (24 bits) is unique to each individual NIC.

MAC Filtering

MAC Filtering is a security feature in computer networks that allows or denies access to network resources based on the Media Access Control (MAC) address of a device. The MAC address is a unique identifier assigned to each network interface controller (NIC) by the manufacturer. When MAC Filtering is enabled on a network device, such as a router or a firewall, it compares the MAC addresses of devices attempting to connect to the network against a list of approved or blocked addresses. If a device's MAC address is not on the approved list, it is denied access to the network resources, effectively preventing unauthorized devices from connecting.

MAC Layer

The MAC layer, also known as the Media Access Control layer, is a critical component of the networking architecture. It is situated in the data link layer of the OSI model and is responsible for providing a means for multiple devices to access and transmit data over a shared communication medium. At its core, the MAC layer defines the rules and procedures necessary for devices to share the available bandwidth fairly and efficiently. It coordinates access to the transmission medium by implementing various access control techniques, such as contention-based or centralized scheduling methods.

MAC Spoofing Detection Methods

MAC Spoofing Detection is a network security measure that aims to identify and prevent the unauthorized manipulation or falsification of Media Access Control (MAC) addresses. MAC addresses are unique identifiers assigned to network devices, such as computers, smartphones, and routers. They play a crucial role in ensuring effective communication among devices within a network. However, MAC addresses can be spoofed, meaning that an attacker can forge or modify the MAC address of a device to gain unauthorized access or conduct malicious activities on the network. There are several methods for detecting MAC spoofing, all of which aim to identify inconsistencies or anomalies in MAC address information. One commonly used method is through monitoring and analyzing network traffic. By examining incoming and outgoing packets, network administrators can identify MAC addresses that do not match expected or previously recorded addresses. This can indicate a potential MAC spoofing attempt. Another method for detecting MAC spoofing is through the use of network access control mechanisms. These mechanisms can restrict network access based on predefined security policies and rules. When a device tries to connect to the network, it must present its MAC address for verification. If the MAC address does not match the one that is expected or authorized for that device, access can be denied. Additionally, some network devices or systems may implement MAC address filtering. This involves creating a list of authorized MAC addresses and only allowing network traffic from devices with addresses on that list. If a device with a different MAC address attempts to access the network, it will be blocked, triggering a potential MAC spoofing detection. In conclusion, MAC spoofing detection methods are essential for maintaining network security and integrity. By continuously monitoring and analyzing network traffic, implementing access control mechanisms, and utilizing MAC address filtering, administrators can identify and prevent unauthorized devices from accessing the network, reducing the risk of potential security breaches.

MAC Spoofing Detection

MAC Spoofing Detection is a process used to identify and prevent unauthorized devices from impersonating legitimate devices on a network by manipulating their Media Access Control (MAC) addresses. MAC addresses are unique identifiers assigned to network devices, such as computers, smartphones, and routers. They are used by the network to identify and communicate with these devices. However, MAC addresses can be easily changed or spoofed, allowing an attacker to mask their true identity and gain unauthorized access to a network. The purpose of MAC Spoofing Detection is to detect and prevent such attacks by implementing various techniques. One common approach is to use MAC address filtering, also known as MAC whitelisting. This involves creating a list of approved MAC addresses and only allowing devices with these addresses to connect to the network. Any device with a spoofed MAC address that is not on the whitelist will be denied access. Another method used for MAC Spoofing Detection is network monitoring. By continuously monitoring the network traffic, unusual MAC address changes or inconsistencies can be detected. For example, if a device suddenly changes its MAC address or uses multiple MAC addresses simultaneously, it can be an indication of MAC address spoofing. In addition, some network security tools can analyze the behavior and characteristics of devices on the network to identify suspicious activities that may indicate MAC spoofing. For example, if a device with a known MAC address suddenly starts sending an unusually high volume of data or accessing restricted resources, it could be a sign of MAC spoofing. Overall, MAC Spoofing Detection is a crucial aspect of network security, as it helps to prevent unauthorized access and protect against various types of attacks. By implementing MAC address filtering, continuous network monitoring, and behavior analysis, organizations can enhance their network security and ensure that only trusted devices are allowed access.

MAC Spoofing Prevention

MAC Spoofing Prevention refers to the measures taken to prevent unauthorized manipulation or impersonation of the Media Access Control (MAC) address in a computer network. MAC spoofing is a technique used by attackers to change or impersonate the MAC address of a networked device, such as a computer, router, or access point. The MAC address is a unique identifier assigned to each network interface controller (NIC) at the manufacturing stage. It is used at the data link layer of the networking protocol stack and is necessary for device identification and communication within a network. MAC spoofing can have malicious intentions. An attacker may change their MAC address to match that of another device on the network in order to bypass security controls that are based on MAC address filtering. By impersonating an authorized device, the attacker can gain unauthorized access to the network and possibly intercept or manipulate network traffic. To prevent MAC spoofing, network administrators can implement various measures: 1. MAC Filtering: Network devices, such as routers or access points, can be configured to only allow network access to specific MAC addresses. This whitelist-based approach ensures that only authorized devices with known MAC addresses can connect to the network. 2. Port Security: Network switches can be configured to limit the number of MAC addresses allowed on a specific port. If an excessive number of MAC addresses are detected, the port can be automatically disabled to prevent unauthorized access. 3. Network Monitoring: Network administrators can use network monitoring tools to detect and identify abnormal or suspicious MAC address activities. Unusual changes or multiple MAC addresses associated with a single port can indicate possible MAC spoofing attempts. 4. Secure Network Protocols: Implementing secure network protocols, such as IEEE 802.1X, can enhance the security of the network by requiring devices to authenticate themselves before gaining access. This prevents unauthorized devices from connecting and reduces the risk of MAC spoofing. By implementing these MAC spoofing prevention measures, network administrators can enhance the overall security of their networks and protect against unauthorized access and potential malicious activities.

MAC Spoofing

MAC Spoofing is a technique used in computer networking to change the Media Access Control (MAC) address of a network interface card (NIC). The MAC address is a unique identifier assigned to each NIC by the manufacturer, and it is used to identify devices on a local network. By spoofing the MAC address, an attacker can impersonate a different device or hide their true identity. MAC Spoofing works by manipulating the network interface at a low level. The MAC address is stored in the hardware of the NIC, and it is typically not modifiable. However, software tools can be used to override the hardware settings and manually set a different MAC address. This allows the attacker to masquerade as a legitimate device or bypass certain security measures that rely on MAC addresses for identification. There are several reasons why someone might engage in MAC Spoofing. One common use case is to bypass MAC address filtering, which is a security measure used by some networks to only allow connections from approved devices. By spoofing a trusted MAC address, an attacker can gain unauthorized access to the network. MAC Spoofing can also be used to evade network monitoring and tracking. By constantly changing the MAC address, it becomes difficult for network administrators and surveillance systems to keep track of a particular device's activities. This can be especially useful for maintaining anonymity or avoiding detection while engaging in malicious activities. It is worth noting that MAC Spoofing is typically employed in local area networks (LANs) rather than wide area networks (WANs), as WANs often use IP addresses for device identification instead of MAC addresses. Additionally, MAC Spoofing is considered a form of network attack and is generally prohibited and illegal without proper authorization. Network administrators can implement various security mechanisms to detect and prevent MAC Spoofing, such as MAC address logging, MAC address filtering, and network intrusion detection systems (NIDS).

MIMO (Multiple-Input Multiple-Output)

MIMO, which stands for Multiple-Input Multiple-Output, is a technique used in networking to improve the data transmission rate and reliability of wireless communication systems. It is a method that takes advantage of multiple antennas at both the transmitter and receiver to achieve higher performance compared to traditional single-antenna systems.In a MIMO system, multiple antennas are used at both ends of the communication link. The transmitter uses multiple antennas to transmit multiple streams of data simultaneously, while the receiver uses multiple antennas to receive and separate these streams of data. By using multiple antennas, MIMO technology can exploit the spatial dimensions of the wireless channel to achieve higher data rates and better reliability.One of the key advantages of MIMO is its ability to mitigate the effects of multipath fading and interference in wireless communication. Multipath fading occurs when signals transmitted from a transmitter reach the receiver through multiple paths due to reflections, diffractions, and other phenomena in the wireless environment. This can lead to signal attenuation and distortion, causing errors in the received data. MIMO addresses this issue by using multiple antennas to transmit and receive multiple copies of the same data over different paths, which increases the chances of correctly receiving the data at the receiver.Another advantage of MIMO is its ability to increase the spectral efficiency of wireless communication systems. Spectral efficiency refers to the amount of data that can be transmitted over a given bandwidth. With MIMO, multiple data streams can be transmitted simultaneously over the same frequency band, effectively increasing the capacity of the wireless channel. This is particularly valuable in scenarios where the available spectral resources are limited.MIMO technology is widely used in various wireless communication standards, such as Wi-Fi (802.11n, 802.11ac), 4G LTE, and 5G. It has become an integral part of modern wireless networks, enabling higher data rates, improved coverage, and better reliability. With the increasing demand for high-speed and reliable wireless connectivity, MIMO will continue to play a crucial role in the development of future wireless communication systems.

MPLS (Multiprotocol Label Switching)

MPLS, or Multiprotocol Label Switching, is a networking technology that is widely used for efficient packet forwarding. It operates at the OSI (Open Systems Interconnection) network layer, specifically layer 2.5, bridging the gap between the data link layer (layer 2) and the network layer (layer 3) of the OSI model. The primary purpose of MPLS is to improve network performance by providing faster and more reliable packet forwarding. It achieves this by assigning labels to packets and using these labels to make routing decisions. These labels are attached to the packet headers at the ingress router and are used by the intermediate routers to forward the packets along the correct path to the egress router and ultimately their destination.

MTU (Maximum Transmission Unit)

The Maximum Transmission Unit (MTU) refers to the maximum size of a datagram or frame that can be transmitted in a network protocol without being fragmented. It represents the largest amount of data that can be sent in a single packet, ensuring efficient and reliable transmission of data. The MTU is a crucial parameter in network communication as it directly affects the performance and efficiency of data transmission. Each network protocol has its own set MTU value, which is determined by factors such as the physical medium used, the network infrastructure, and the protocol itself. When a device wants to send data over a network, it breaks the data into small chunks called packets or frames. These packets are then transmitted from the sender to the recipient, where they are reassembled into the original data. The MTU determines the maximum size of these packets. If the data to be transmitted exceeds the MTU, fragmentation occurs, which means the data is divided into smaller packets to fit within the MTU limit. The recipient must then reconstruct the original data by reassembling the fragmented packets. Fragmentation can impact network performance and increase latency, as it requires extra processing by both the sender and the recipient. Alternatively, if the data to be transmitted is smaller than the MTU, it can still be sent in a single packet. This can improve network efficiency as there is no need for fragmentation or reassembly. The MTU is typically determined during the establishment of a network connection. Each device participating in the network communication must negotiate and agree on a common MTU value to ensure seamless transmission of data. In some cases, routers and network devices can also adjust the MTU on the fly, depending on the network conditions and requirements. In conclusion, the MTU is the maximum size of a packet or frame that can be transmitted without fragmentation in a network protocol. It plays a critical role in ensuring efficient and reliable data transmission, impacting network performance and efficiency.

Malicious Software (Malware)

Malicious Software, commonly known as Malware, refers to any software specifically designed to gain unauthorized access or cause damage to computer systems or networks. It is a significant threat in the field of networking as it can disrupt the normal functioning of networks, compromise sensitive data, and impede the overall productivity of an organization. Malware can take various forms, such as viruses, worms, Trojans, spyware, adware, and ransomware. These malicious programs often infiltrate computer systems and networks through deceptive tactics, such as email attachments, software downloads, or exploiting vulnerabilities in operating systems or applications. Once inside a network, malware can cause numerous harmful effects. Viruses and worms, for example, can replicate themselves and spread across the network, infecting other connected devices and compromising their security. They can also consume network resources, leading to a degradation in performance and subsequent network downtime.

Trojans, on the other hand, masquerade as legitimate software and trick users into executing them. Once activated, they can create backdoors in the network, allowing unauthorized access to cybercriminals. This can lead to the theft of sensitive information, such as login credentials or financial data. Spyware and adware are designed to gather information about users and their online activities. They can track browsing habits, capture keystrokes, and display unwanted advertisements. In addition to invading privacy, these types of malware can also slow down network traffic and compromise overall network security. Ransomware, a particularly devastating type of malware, encrypts files and holds them hostage, demanding a ransom for their release. If not addressed promptly, ransomware can result in irreversible data loss and significant financial damage to an organization. Preventing and mitigating the impact of malware requires the implementation of robust security measures. These include regular software updates, installing reliable antivirus software, employing firewalls, and conducting regular security audits. Additionally, user awareness and education play a vital role in reducing the risks associated with malware attacks.

Malvertising

Malvertising, short for malicious advertising, refers to the practice of using online advertisements containing malicious code or links to infect computer systems or direct users to fraudulent websites. It is a networking security threat that utilizes the trusted and widespread nature of online advertisements to exploit vulnerabilities and compromise the security of internet users. Malvertising is a form of cyberattack where threat actors disguise their malicious activities within legitimate-looking advertisements that appear on various websites, including popular and reputable ones. The attackers take advantage of the ad networks that distribute these advertisements, often bypassing security checks and slipping harmful content into the ad inventory. Upon viewing or clicking on these deceptive ads, users' devices can become compromised, leading to potential data breaches, financial losses, or the installation of malware.

Malware Analysis Tools

A malware analysis tool is a software application or tool that is specifically designed to analyze and investigate different types of malware in the context of networking. It helps in identifying and understanding the behavior, characteristics, and potential threats associated with various malware samples. These tools are crucial in networking as they play a vital role in detecting, combating, and mitigating the risks and damages caused by malware attacks. They assist network administrators, security professionals, and researchers in gaining insights into the workings of malware, allowing them to develop effective countermeasures and enhance network security.

Malware Analysis

Malware analysis is the process of dissecting malicious software to understand its functionality, behavior, and potential impact on network systems. It involves studying the code, behavior, and characteristics of malware to identify its purpose, origins, and potential vulnerabilities in order to develop effective countermeasures and mitigate its risks. In the context of networking, malware analysis focuses on understanding how malicious software can infiltrate, spread, and exploit vulnerabilities within network systems. This analysis enables network administrators and security experts to better comprehend the threats posed by malware and develop strategies to prevent, detect, and respond to these threats.

Malware Detection Tools

Malware detection tools refer to software applications or programs that are specifically designed to detect, identify, and mitigate or eliminate malware threats in a networking environment. Malware, derived from the term "malicious software," encompasses a wide range of harmful software types such as viruses, worms, Trojans, spyware, adware, ransomware, and more. These tools are crucial for network security as they help organizations safeguard their computer systems, electronic data, and digital infrastructure from potential malware attacks. By constantly monitoring and scanning computer networks, these tools can identify and alert administrators about the presence of malware. This allows security teams to take immediate action to prevent further damage and protect sensitive information.

Malware Detection

Malware detection refers to the process of identifying and mitigating malicious software, also known as malware, in a computer network. Malware is a broad term that encompasses various types of harmful software, including viruses, worms, Trojans, ransomware, and spyware. These malicious programs can cause significant harm to network systems, compromising their integrity, confidentiality, and availability. The detection of malware involves identifying and alerting the presence of any suspicious or unauthorized code or behavior within a network. This process requires the implementation of robust security measures, including antivirus software, firewalls, intrusion detection systems (IDS), and other advanced threat detection technologies. These tools work collectively to analyze incoming and outgoing network traffic, scan files and software for known patterns or signatures of malware, and identify any abnormal or suspicious activities.

Malware Prevention Measures

Malware prevention measures refer to a set of actions taken within a networking environment to mitigate the risk of malware attacks and effectively safeguard computer systems and networks from malicious software or code. These measures are implemented to prevent unauthorized access, protect sensitive information, maintain system integrity, and ensure the optimal functioning of networked devices. One key malware prevention measure is the installation and regular update of antivirus and antimalware software. These programs are designed to detect, quarantine, and remove malware from an infected device. Antivirus software scans files and programs, looking for patterns or signatures that match known malware. It also monitors the system in real-time to identify and block suspicious activities. Regular updates are crucial to keep up with the constantly evolving nature of malware and to ensure the software can effectively detect and neutralize new threats. A secure network architecture is another essential malware prevention measure. Network administrators employ various strategies to secure the network infrastructure, including implementing firewalls, intrusion detection and prevention systems (IDPS), and secure access controls. Firewalls act as a barrier between internal and external networks, monitoring and filtering incoming and outgoing network traffic. Similarly, IDPSs detect and block unauthorized access attempts, as well as alert administrators to potential security breaches. Secure access controls, such as strong passwords, multifactor authentication, and network segmentation, help restrict access to authorized users only. Regular software updates and patches are crucial in preventing malware attacks. Developers constantly release updates to fix vulnerabilities and weaknesses that can be exploited by malware. Applying these updates promptly ensures that known vulnerabilities are patched, reducing the risk of malware exploiting them. Network administrators often use automated patch management systems to streamline the process of deploying updates across multiple devices within the network. User education and awareness are also important malware prevention measures. Training employees and network users on safe computing practices, such as being cautious with email attachments, avoiding suspicious downloads, and regularly backing up data, can significantly reduce the likelihood of malware infections. Phishing awareness programs can help users recognize and avoid social engineering techniques used by attackers to deceive and trick individuals into disclosing sensitive information or executing malicious code.

Malware Prevention Software

A malware prevention software refers to a type of security tool or program that is designed to protect computer networks from malicious software, commonly known as malware. This software plays a crucial role in safeguarding the integrity, availability, and confidentiality of network resources by identifying and preventing the installation, execution, or spread of various types of malware. Malware, a combination of the words "malicious" and "software," encompasses a wide range of harmful programs such as viruses, worms, Trojans, ransomware, spyware, adware, and keyloggers. These malicious programs can infiltrate a network through various means, including email attachments, infected websites, malicious downloads, and vulnerabilities in software or operating systems. Malware prevention software employs several strategies to protect network systems from these threats. It typically includes features such as real-time scanning, threat detection, and removal capabilities. Real-time scanning involves constantly monitoring files, processes, and network traffic to identify any suspicious activities or known malware signatures. When a potential threat is detected, the software takes immediate action to quarantine or remove the malicious file to prevent further damage. In addition to real-time scanning, malware prevention software also relies on threat detection techniques such as behavior analysis, signature-based scanning, and heuristic analysis. Behavior analysis involves monitoring the behavior of programs and processes to identify any unusual or malicious activities. Signature-based scanning compares files and processes against a database of known malware signatures, while heuristic analysis uses algorithms to identify potential threats based on their characteristics and behavior patterns. Furthermore, malware prevention software often includes web filtering capabilities to block access to malicious websites or URLs, which are known to distribute malware. It may also incorporate firewall protection to monitor incoming and outgoing network traffic and prevent unauthorized access to network resources. In conclusion, malware prevention software plays a crucial role in protecting computer networks from the ever-evolving and sophisticated threats posed by malware. By employing a range of scanning, detection, and prevention techniques, this software helps to ensure the security and reliability of network systems, minimizing the risk of data breaches, system disruptions, and financial losses.

Malware Prevention

Malware prevention, in the context of networking, refers to the proactive measures taken to protect computer networks and the devices connected to them from malicious software, commonly known as malware. Malware encompasses a wide range of harmful software, including viruses, worms, Trojans, ransomware, spyware, and adware. These malicious programs are designed to exploit vulnerabilities in computer systems, steal sensitive information, disrupt network operations, and cause financial and reputational damage to individuals and organizations. Effective malware prevention involves multiple layers of defense strategies to mitigate the risks associated with malware infections. These strategies include: 1. Antivirus software: Deploying and regularly updating antivirus software on all network devices such as servers, workstations, and mobile devices is crucial in detecting and eliminating known viruses and malware variants. 2. Firewalls: Installing and configuring firewalls at the network perimeter helps monitor and control incoming and outgoing network traffic, preventing unauthorized access and blocking malicious content. 3. Patch management: Keeping operating systems, applications, and firmware up to date with the latest security patches helps fix known vulnerabilities that malware attackers often exploit. 4. User education: Training network users to recognize and avoid suspicious emails, websites, downloads, and removable media can significantly reduce the risk of malware infections caused by social engineering techniques. 5. Network segmentation: Dividing a network into separate segments with different security levels allows for better control and containment of potential malware outbreaks, limiting their impact on the entire network. 6. Access control: Implementing strong authentication mechanisms, such as multi-factor authentication, and restricting access privileges based on the principle of least privilege, helps prevent unauthorized users from gaining access to sensitive network resources. 7. Regular backups: Creating and maintaining up-to-date backups of critical data and systems can minimize the damage caused by malware attacks, allowing for quick recovery without paying ransom or losing important information. By implementing these malware prevention measures, network administrators can significantly reduce the risk of malware infections and protect the integrity, confidentiality, and availability of network resources.

Malware Removal

Malware removal in the context of networking refers to the process of eliminating malicious software or code from a networked system or a group of computers that are connected to each other. Malware, short for malicious software, is any software specifically designed to damage, disrupt, or gain unauthorized access to computer systems or networks. Malware poses significant risks to networking environments as it can compromise the confidentiality, integrity, and availability of data and resources. Common types of malware include viruses, worms, Trojans, ransomware, spyware, adware, and rootkits. These malicious programs can infiltrate a network through various means, such as email attachments, infected websites, removable media, or network vulnerabilities. The process of malware removal involves several steps to ensure the complete eradication of the malicious software and prevent future infections: Detection: The first step in malware removal is detecting the presence of malware within the network. This can be done through various means, such as antivirus scans, network monitoring tools, or behavior analysis. Detection helps in identifying the extent of the infection and the specific malware strains present. Isolation: Once malware is detected, immediate action should be taken to isolate the infected system or systems from the rest of the network. This is done to prevent the malware from spreading further and causing more damage. Isolation can involve disconnecting infected computers from the network, disabling network services, or implementing network segmentation. Remediation: The next step is to remove the malware from the infected systems. This can be done through manual removal techniques or by using specialized malware removal tools. The remediation process may involve deleting infected files, repairing system files, removing malicious registry entries, or restoring from a clean backup. It is essential to ensure that all traces of the malware are completely eliminated to prevent re-infection. Prevention: Once the malware has been removed, proactive measures should be taken to prevent future infections. This includes regular antivirus updates, patch management, network security assessments, user education, and enforcing security policies. Preventive measures help in reducing the risk of future malware infections and maintaining a secure network environment. Overall, malware removal in a networking context is a critical process to protect networked systems from the harmful effects of malicious software. It involves detection, isolation, remediation, and prevention to ensure the integrity and security of the network.

Malware Sandbox

A malware sandbox, in the context of networking, refers to a controlled environment that is used to analyze and detect malware. It is a security mechanism designed to examine potentially malicious programs, files, or websites in a separate and isolated space from the rest of the network, thereby preventing potential harm to the network infrastructure. The purpose of a malware sandbox is to provide a secure environment for analyzing viruses, worms, trojans, ransomware, and other types of malware. This is done by executing the malware in an isolated setting, allowing security researchers to observe its behavior and understand its potential impact without risking the integrity and safety of the network. When a suspicious program or file is encountered, it is introduced to the malware sandbox where it is executed and closely monitored. The sandbox environment typically emulates the underlying architecture and operating system, allowing the malware to run as it would on a real system. However, the sandbox also introduces security measures that restrict and control the malware's access to the network and sensitive resources. By executing the malware in a controlled environment, security professionals can observe its activities, track its behavior, and identify any potential threats it poses. The sandbox provides a safe space to analyze the malware's code, identify its propagation methods, and uncover its malicious intentions. Furthermore, a malware sandbox often includes advanced features that aid in malware analysis, such as behavior analysis, memory inspection, and network traffic monitoring. These capabilities help security researchers gain insights into the malware's characteristics, enabling them to develop effective countermeasures and improve network defenses. In addition to analyzing and detecting malware, a sandbox also plays a vital role in preventing the initial infection and spread of malware within a network. By isolating potentially harmful files and programs, it acts as a barrier, preventing them from interacting with the production environment and accessing critical systems. This allows security teams to proactively detect and mitigate malware threats before they can cause extensive damage.

Malware

A malware, short for malicious software, refers to any software or code that is designed to disrupt, damage, or gain unauthorized access to computer systems, networks, or user devices. Malware can take various forms, such as viruses, worms, Trojans, ransomware, spyware, adware, and botnets. Malware is typically spread through various attack vectors, including email attachments, malicious websites, infected files, removable media, and network vulnerabilities. Once it infiltrates a system or network, malware can execute a range of harmful activities, such as stealing sensitive information, corrupting or deleting files, disrupting network communication, or enabling unauthorized access to the compromised system. Viruses are one common type of malware that can replicate and attach themselves to legitimate programs or files, spreading from one device to another. Worms, on the other hand, can exploit security vulnerabilities to replicate and spread independently across networks, without requiring a host program. Trojans, named after the infamous Trojan horse, disguise themselves as legitimate software or files, tricking users into executing them. Once activated, Trojans can provide unauthorized access to the attacker, allowing them to control the compromised device or steal sensitive information. Ransomware is a particularly insidious type of malware that encrypts the victim's files, holding them hostage until a ransom is paid. Spyware and adware are designed to collect user information without their consent, such as browsing habits or personal data, often for advertising or surveillance purposes. Botnets, on the other hand, are networks of compromised devices, controlled by a central attacker, that can be used collectively to launch coordinated attacks, send spam, or carry out fraudulent activities. Protecting against malware requires a multi-layered approach, including the use of comprehensive antivirus and anti-malware software, regular software updates, strong passwords, system and network monitoring, and user training to recognize and avoid potential threats. Additionally, practicing safe browsing habits, using secure connections, and implementing robust network security measures are crucial to mitigating the risk of malware infections.

Man-In-The-Cloud Attack

A Man-in-the-Cloud (MitC) attack is a type of cyber attack that targets cloud storage services and aims to gain unauthorized access to user data. In this attack, an attacker leverages vulnerabilities in the synchronization process between a user's device and their cloud storage account to gain control over the victim's data stored in the cloud. The attack typically starts with the attacker compromising the victim's device through various means, such as social engineering, phishing, or malware. Once the attacker has control over the device, they exploit the synchronization feature provided by cloud storage services to gain access to the victim's data. In a MitC attack, the attacker manipulates the synchronization tokens used by the cloud storage service to keep track of file changes and updates. By intercepting and altering these tokens, the attacker can trick the cloud service into performing unintended actions, such as syncing malicious files or granting unauthorized access to the attacker. The impact of a successful MitC attack can be severe. The attacker can potentially gain complete access to the victim's cloud storage account, including sensitive files, personal documents, photos, and other confidential information. This can lead to various consequences, such as identity theft, financial loss, or unauthorized disclosure of sensitive information. To mitigate the risk of a MitC attack, it is essential for users to follow best practices for securing their devices and cloud storage accounts. This includes using strong, unique passwords for cloud storage accounts, enabling multi-factor authentication, regularly updating devices and software, and being cautious of phishing attempts or suspicious emails. Cloud service providers also play a crucial role in preventing MitC attacks. They should implement robust security measures, such as strong encryption, access controls, and anomaly detection systems, to detect and prevent unauthorized access attempts. Additionally, providers should educate their users about the risks and provide guidance on how to secure their data in the cloud.

Man-In-The-Middle (MitM) Attack

A Man-in-the-Middle (MitM) attack is a type of cyber attack that occurs when a malicious actor intercepts and relays communication between two parties, without either party being aware of the interception. In the context of networking, a MitM attack typically takes place on a local network or between a client and a server. The attacker positions themselves between the legitimate communication path, allowing them to intercept, modify, or manipulate the data being transmitted.

Managed Switch

A managed switch is a networking device that provides advanced configuration and control capabilities in a local area network (LAN). Unlike unmanaged switches, a managed switch allows network administrators to have more control over the networking infrastructure. With a managed switch, administrators can monitor and manage the switch remotely, adjust configurations, and control network traffic. It offers features such as VLAN (Virtual Local Area Network) support, Quality of Service (QoS) settings, access control lists (ACLs), and SNMP (Simple Network Management Protocol) for network monitoring and diagnostics.

Media Access Control (MAC)

Media Access Control (MAC) is a sublayer of the Data Link Layer in computer networking. It is responsible for controlling and managing access to a shared communication medium by multiple devices connected to a Local Area Network (LAN). In a LAN, multiple devices such as computers, servers, printers, and switches may need to access the network simultaneously. The

MAC sublayer ensures that only one device can transmit data over the medium at any given time, avoiding collisions and ensuring efficient and reliable communication.

Media Converter

A media converter, in the context of networking, is a device that is used to convert the format or signal type of network data between different media types. It is commonly used to connect and integrate different types of network segments that use different types of media, such as copper cables and fiber optic cables. Media converters are typically used in situations where there is a need to extend the distance or connect different types of network segments. For example, if a network uses copper cables but needs to connect to a remote location that can only be reached using fiber optic cables, a media converter can be used to convert the copper signal into a fiber optic signal, and vice versa at the remote location.

Mesh Network

A mesh network is a networking system in which each device in the network serves as a node and is interconnected with every other device. This interconnection creates multiple paths for data to travel, ensuring efficient and reliable communication within the network. In a mesh network, there is no central hub or single point of failure. Instead, each device acts as both a sender and a receiver, relaying data to other devices in the network. This decentralized architecture makes mesh networks highly resilient and self-healing in the event of a node failure or network disruption.

Mesh Router

A mesh router is a networking device that is designed to provide a seamless and reliable Wi-Fi network coverage throughout a large area or space. It consists of multiple interconnected nodes or access points which are strategically placed to create a mesh network. The main purpose of a mesh router is to eliminate Wi-Fi dead zones and ensure that every corner of the area or space has a strong and stable internet connection. Unlike traditional routers, which rely on a single access point to broadcast Wi-Fi signals, a mesh router creates a network of interconnected nodes that work together to provide a unified and consistent network coverage.

Mesh Topology

A mesh topology is a type of network architecture where each node or device in the network is connected to every other node or device. This results in multiple redundant paths and direct point-to-point connections, leading to increased fault tolerance and high reliability. In a mesh network, each device acts as a relay station, passing data from one node to another until it reaches its final destination. This allows for multiple paths to be established between any two devices, preventing a single point of failure. Even if one or multiple nodes fail, the network can dynamically reroute the traffic through alternative paths, ensuring uninterrupted connectivity. A mesh topology can be implemented in two ways: full mesh and partial mesh. In a full mesh network, every device is directly connected to every other device. This results in a large number of connections and is typically used in small networks. In a partial mesh network, only some devices have a direct connection to all other devices, while others are connected to a subset of devices. Partial mesh topologies are more scalable and are commonly used in larger networks. One of the key advantages of a mesh topology is its robustness. Since there are multiple paths available, the network can automatically route around areas of congestion or failure, ensuring continuous data flow. Additionally, mesh networks have the ability to self-heal by finding and reestablishing alternative routes in case of node or link failures. Despite its benefits, implementing a mesh topology can be complex and expensive due to the large number of connections required. It also requires more resources and bandwidth compared to other topologies. However, the increased redundancy and fault tolerance offered by mesh networks make them suitable for critical applications where uninterrupted connectivity is essential.

Mesh Wi-Fi Benefits

Mesh Wi-Fi is a networking system that provides significant benefits over traditional wireless networks. It utilizes a mesh topology, where multiple devices, referred to as nodes or access points, work together to create a seamless and reliable network. One of the primary advantages

217

of mesh Wi-Fi is its ability to extend network coverage throughout a larger area. Traditional routers are limited in terms of range, and as a result, certain areas may experience weak or no signal. In contrast, mesh Wi-Fi uses multiple access points strategically placed throughout the area, ensuring that there are no dead zones and providing a strong and consistent signal throughout the entire network. Another benefit of mesh Wi-Fi is its self-healing capability. In a traditional network, if one access point fails, the entire network may be affected, resulting in downtime and a loss of connectivity. With mesh Wi-Fi, if one access point fails or experiences an issue, the other nodes can seamlessly take over, redistributing the network load and ensuring uninterrupted connectivity for all devices. Mesh Wi-Fi also offers improved network performance. By having multiple access points, the network can handle a higher number of devices simultaneously without experiencing significant slowdowns. This is particularly beneficial in environments with a high number of connected devices, such as homes with multiple smart home devices or offices with numerous employees. Additionally, mesh Wi-Fi systems often come with advanced features, such as seamless roaming. This allows devices to seamlessly switch between access points as users move throughout the network, ensuring that they stay connected without experiencing any disruptions. In summary, mesh Wi-Fi networks provide extended coverage, self-healing capabilities, improved performance, and advanced features like seamless roaming. These benefits make mesh Wi-Fi an ideal choice for homes, businesses, and other environments where a strong, reliable, and scalable network is required.

Mesh Wi-Fi Network Security

A mesh Wi-Fi network is a type of wireless network that consists of multiple access points, or nodes, that are interconnected to create a unified network. This network topology differs from traditional Wi-Fi networks, where a single router serves as the central point of access. In a mesh network, each node acts as both a sender and a receiver, allowing packets of data to hop from one node to another until it reaches its destination. Mesh Wi-Fi networks offer several advantages, including improved coverage, capacity, and reliability. Since each node in the network acts as a potential access point, the range of the network can be extended by simply adding more nodes. This allows for seamless connectivity even in large or complex environments where traditional Wi-Fi networks might struggle to provide coverage. Additionally, mesh networks can dynamically adapt to changing network conditions, automatically routing traffic through the most efficient path or avoiding congested nodes. When it comes to security, mesh Wi-Fi networks employ various measures to protect against unauthorized access and data breaches. One of the key security features is encryption, which ensures that data transmitted over the network is securely encoded and can only be deciphered by authorized devices. The most common encryption protocols used in mesh networks are WPA2 (Wi-Fi Protected Access II) and WPA3, which provide robust security against eavesdropping and unauthorized access. In addition to encryption, mesh networks often implement other security measures such as authentication and access control. These mechanisms help to verify the identity of devices attempting to connect to the network and enforce restrictions on access based on user credentials or other criteria. By implementing strong authentication and access control protocols, mesh Wi-Fi networks can prevent unauthorized users from gaining access to the network or intercepting data.

Mesh Wi-Fi Security

Mesh Wi-Fi security refers to the measures and protocols implemented to protect a mesh Wi-Fi network from unauthorized access and ensure the confidentiality, integrity, and availability of data transmitted within the network. Mesh Wi-Fi, also known as a mesh network, is a type of wireless local area network (WLAN) that uses multiple access points to create a distributed network infrastructure. These access points, or nodes, are interconnected to form a self-healing and self-configuring network that provides seamless Wi-Fi coverage throughout a larger area compared to traditional Wi-Fi networks. One of the main security concerns in mesh Wi-Fi networks is preventing unauthorized access to the network, as a compromised node can lead to unauthorized access to data and devices within the network. To address this, mesh Wi-Fi networks typically employ authentication and encryption mechanisms. Authentication ensures that only authorized devices can join the network, while encryption ensures that data transmitted across the network remains confidential and cannot be intercepted by unauthorized parties.

Mesh Wi-Fi Setup

218

A mesh Wi-Fi setup is a networking solution that uses multiple Wi-Fi access points (APs) to provide seamless, reliable, and high-performance wireless coverage throughout a large area. Instead of relying on a single router to provide Wi-Fi connectivity, a mesh Wi-Fi system consists of multiple APs that work together to form a mesh network. In a traditional Wi-Fi setup, a single router is responsible for transmitting wireless signals and providing internet connectivity to all devices within its range. However, this can lead to various limitations such as dead zones, weak signals, and reduced performance in larger spaces. With a mesh Wi-Fi system, these issues are addressed by distributing the Wi-Fi coverage more evenly throughout the area. The primary component of a mesh Wi-Fi system is the main AP, which is connected to the modem or router that provides the internet connection. This main AP acts as the gateway and manages the network, handling tasks such as assigning IP addresses and routing traffic. Additional APs, also known as satellite nodes or mesh nodes, are strategically placed throughout the area to extend the coverage and form a mesh network. Each AP in a mesh Wi-Fi system communicates with the others to create a seamless network. This communication can occur through wired connections or wireless connections, depending on the specific system. The APs share information about the wireless environment, such as signal strength and network congestion, to ensure optimal performance and to allow devices to seamlessly roam between APs without experiencing disruptions. A key advantage of a mesh Wi-Fi setup is the ability to provide consistent Wi-Fi coverage across a large area. The APs work together to eliminate dead zones and ensure that devices receive strong and reliable signals, regardless of their location within the network. Additionally, the mesh network automatically optimizes itself, adapting to changes in the environment and network conditions to deliver the best possible performance. Overall, a mesh Wi-Fi setup is an effective solution for improving wireless connectivity in environments where a single router is insufficient. It provides seamless coverage, eliminates dead zones, and enhances network performance, making it an ideal choice for homes, offices, and other large spaces.

Mesh Wi-Fi Signal Strength

Mesh Wi-Fi signal strength refers to the measurement of the quality and power of the wireless signal in a mesh network. A mesh network is a type of network architecture that consists of multiple interconnected devices, called nodes, which work together to create a seamless and robust network coverage. In a mesh Wi-Fi network, each node acts as a wireless access point, allowing devices to connect to the network and access the internet. The strength of the signal between these nodes plays a crucial role in determining the overall network performance and user experience. The signal strength is determined by various factors, including the distance between the nodes, the number of obstacles (such as walls or furniture) between them, and the quality of the radio hardware used in the nodes. A strong signal strength ensures a stable and reliable connection, while a weak signal may result in slower speeds, dropped connections, and overall poor network performance. Mesh Wi-Fi systems typically employ various techniques to optimize and improve signal strength. These include: 1. Mesh Routing: Mesh networks use dynamic routing algorithms to automatically determine the best path for data transmission between nodes. This helps to optimize signal strength by redirecting traffic through nodes with stronger signals, minimizing interference and ensuring efficient data transmission. 2. MIMO Technology: Multiple-Input Multiple-Output (MIMO) technology is commonly used in mesh Wi-Fi systems to improve signal quality. MIMO uses multiple antennas to transmit and receive data simultaneously, increasing the capacity and range of the network, and enhancing signal strength. 3. Channel Selection: Mesh Wi-Fi systems intelligently analyze the wireless spectrum and automatically select the least congested channels for data transmission. This helps to optimize signal strength by minimizing interference from neighboring Wi-Fi networks. In summary, mesh Wi-Fi signal strength is a crucial aspect of network performance in a mesh network. It determines the quality and reliability of the wireless connection between nodes, and optimizing signal strength is essential for ensuring a seamless and robust network experience.

Metasploit Framework

Metasploit Framework is a powerful open-source penetration testing tool that is used in the field of computer networking. It is designed to discover vulnerabilities in computer systems and networks by simulating real-world attacks. The framework provides a set of tools and resources that security professionals can use to identify weaknesses in a network's defenses. The Metasploit Framework offers a wide range of exploits, payload generators, scanners, and auxiliary modules that can be used to test the security of networked devices and systems. Exploits are pieces of code or software that take advantage of vulnerabilities in target systems, allowing attackers to gain unauthorized access or control. Payload generators are used to create payloads or malicious code that can be deployed during an attack. Scanners are tools that can be used to identify potential targets and vulnerabilities, while auxiliary modules provide additional functionality and capabilities. Using the Metasploit Framework, security professionals can identify vulnerabilities in a network, assess the level of risk they pose, and develop strategies to mitigate these risks. By simulating real-world attacks, security professionals gain insights into the effectiveness of their defenses and can proactively address any weaknesses or vulnerabilities discovered during the testing process. One of the key benefits of the Metasploit Framework is its modular design, which allows users to customize and extend its capabilities. By leveraging the framework's modules, users can create their own exploits, payload generators, and scanners tailored to their specific needs. This flexibility makes the Metasploit Framework a valuable tool in the field of computer networking and security. In conclusion, the Metasploit Framework is a powerful open-source tool used for penetration testing and vulnerability assessment in computer network environments. It provides a comprehensive set of tools and resources that enable security professionals to identify vulnerabilities, test network defenses, and develop strategies for risk mitigation.

Metasploit

Metasploit is a powerful penetration testing framework that serves as a tool for network security professionals to discover vulnerabilities in computer systems and networks. It provides a wide range of tools and exploits that allow security testers to assess the security posture of a network or system, ultimately identifying potential weaknesses that could be exploited by cyber attackers. The framework consists of various components, including an extensive database of known vulnerabilities, exploit modules, payload generators, and auxiliary modules. These modules can be used in combination to carry out various types of penetration tests, such as remote exploitation, web application testing, and client-side attacks.

Metropolitan Area Network (MAN)

A Metropolitan Area Network (MAN) is a computer network that spans a geographic area larger than a Local Area Network (LAN) but smaller than a Wide Area Network (WAN). It typically covers a city or a metropolitan region, connecting various smaller networks such as LANs, campus networks, or other MANs. MANs are designed to provide high-speed connectivity and data transfer between different locations within the same metropolitan area. A MAN operates by using a combination of wired and wireless technologies to connect multiple devices, such as computers, servers, switches, routers, and other network devices, across a metropolitan area. It utilizes various communication mediums, including fiber optic cables, Ethernet, microwave links, and Wi-Fi, to establish reliable and fast connections between different network nodes. One of the key advantages of a MAN is its ability to cover a larger geographical area while providing faster data transfer rates compared to LANs. This makes it suitable for businesses and organizations that require high-speed connectivity between their different branches or offices within a city or metropolitan region. MANs also offer better scalability, allowing for the addition of more devices and users as the network expands. In terms of network architecture, a MAN can be designed in different topologies such as ring, bus, or star. The choice of topology depends on factors such as network requirements, cost, and available infrastructure. Redundancy measures, such as backup connections or alternate routes, are often implemented to ensure network availability and fault tolerance. Overall, a Metropolitan Area Network serves as an intermediate network between LANs and WANs, offering fast and reliable connectivity over a larger geographical area. It provides a flexible and efficient solution for organizations looking to connect their various locations within a metropolitan region, enabling seamless communication and data sharing between different branches or offices.

Mobile Device Management (MDM)

Mobile Device Management (MDM) refers to the process and tools used by Network Administrators to manage and control mobile devices within an organization. It involves the deployment, monitoring, and securing of mobile devices and the data they access. MDM enables administrators to enforce policies, distribute applications, and provide support to mobile devices from a centralized platform. The primary goal of MDM is to ensure the security and compliance of mobile devices, especially when they are used for business purposes. It allows administrators to configure and control various aspects of mobile devices such as access permissions, encryption, passcodes, and device settings. By managing these elements, MDM helps prevent unauthorized access and protects sensitive data on mobile devices. MDM solutions provide a range of features and functionalities to simplify device management. These include device enrollment, inventory management, remote configuration and monitoring, application management, and policy enforcement. Administrators can remotely configure settings, install or remove applications, and enforce security policies across multiple devices, regardless of their location. Another crucial aspect of MDM is the ability to secure and manage corporate data on mobile devices, as well as separate it from personal data. Containerization technology is often used to isolate business applications and data from personal ones, ensuring that sensitive information remains protected even if the device is lost or stolen. MDM solutions often offer secure content sharing, data backup, and remote wiping capabilities to further enhance data security. In conclusion, Mobile Device Management (MDM) is a critical component of network administration that enables organizations to efficiently manage and secure their mobile devices. It allows administrators to enforce policies, control device settings, and protect sensitive data, ensuring the seamless and secure use of mobile devices within an organization.

Mobile Device Security

Mobile Device Security refers to the measures and protocols put in place to protect the data and information stored on, accessed by, and transmitted through mobile devices within a network. With the proliferation of mobile devices and their increasing use for business purposes, ensuring their security has become crucial to protect sensitive information from unauthorized access, theft, and malicious attacks. The primary objective of mobile device security in a network is to safeguard the confidentiality, integrity, and availability of data. Confidentiality ensures that data is only accessible by authorized individuals or entities, protecting against data breaches and unauthorized access. Integrity ensures that data remains unaltered and trustworthy throughout its lifecycle, preventing tampering or corruption. Availability ensures that mobile devices are functional and accessible to authorized users, preventing service interruption and downtime. Mobile device security encompasses various layers of protection, including physical, network, and application security. Physical security involves measures such as device locks, biometric authentication, and remote wipe capabilities to prevent unauthorized physical access and to erase data in case of loss or theft. Network security focuses on securing mobile devices while connected to a network, using techniques such as VPN (Virtual Private Network) connections, encryption, and firewall protection to protect data during transmission. Application security involves implementing secure coding practices, frequent software updates, and app permissions management to mitigate the risk of exploiting vulnerabilities in mobile applications. Additionally, mobile device security involves user awareness and education to encourage safe browsing habits, avoiding suspicious links or downloads, and using strong and unique passwords. This helps prevent social engineering attacks, phishing attempts, and password breaches. Regular audits, vulnerability assessments, and penetration testing are also essential components of mobile device security, ensuring that any vulnerabilities or weaknesses in the network or mobile devices are identified and addressed promptly. In conclusion, mobile device security is crucial in a networked environment to protect the sensitive data stored, accessed, and transmitted through mobile devices. By implementing robust measures at various layers, including physical, network, and application security, organizations can mitigate the risk of data breaches, unauthorized access, and malicious attacks that could compromise the confidentiality, integrity, and availability of data.

Modem

A modem, short for modulator-demodulator, is a device used in networking to connect a computer or other devices to the internet or to another computer network. It is a hardware device that converts digital information from a computer into analog signals that can be transmitted over a telephone line or a cable connection. Similarly, it also converts analog signals from a telephone line or cable connection into digital information that can be understood by a computer. A modem acts as a bridge between a computer or a local network and the internet or a wide area network (WAN). When a computer wants to send data over the internet or a network, the modem modulates its digital signals into analog signals that are suitable for transmission over the physical medium, such as a telephone line or a coaxial cable. On the receiving end, the modem demodulates the analog signals back into digital signals that can be understood by the recipient's computer or network.

Modulation

Modulation is a key concept in the field of networking, as it refers to the process of manipulating a signal's characteristics to enable it to carry information across a communication channel. It involves altering a carrier wave, typically a high-frequency signal, in order to embed data or information onto it. There are several modulation techniques used in networking, each with its own advantages and applications. These techniques serve different purposes and are employed based on factors such as the bandwidth requirements, distance, and interference present in the communication channel.

Multi-Factor Authentication (MFA)

Multi-Factor Authentication (MFA) is a security mechanism used in computer networks to enhance the protection of user accounts and data by requiring multiple forms of authentication to verify the identity of a user. It is a crucial component in network security as it adds an extra layer of defense against unauthorized access, reducing the risk of malicious activities such as identity theft, data breaches, and unauthorized usage. MFA combines two or more different authentication factors to authenticate a user. These factors can be classified into three categories: knowledge factors, possession factors, and inherence factors. Knowledge factors are something the user knows, such as a password or PIN. Possession factors are something the user possesses, for example, a physical token or a mobile application. Inherence factors are something inherent to the user, like their fingerprint or facial recognition. The process of MFA involves the following steps: when a user attempts to access a system or resource, they are prompted to provide multiple forms of authentication. For example, they may need to enter their username and password (knowledge factor), followed by a unique code generated by an authentication app on their smartphone (possession factor). The system then verifies each authentication factor to ensure they match the stored credentials. If all factors are successfully authenticated, the user is granted access to the network or resource. MFA provides several security benefits compared to traditional single-factor authentication methods. Firstly, it significantly reduces the risk of unauthorized access, as an attacker would need to compromise multiple authentication factors instead of just one. Secondly, it enhances user accountability by linking the authentication process to specific individuals, making it more difficult for malicious activities to be disguised or attributed to someone else. Additionally, MFA protects against various types of attacks, such as brute-force attacks (which attempt to guess a user's credentials) and phishing attacks (which aim to trick users into revealing their login information). In conclusion, Multi-Factor Authentication is a powerful security mechanism that reinforces network security by requiring users to provide multiple forms of authentication. By combining different factors, it effectively verifies the identity of users and reduces the risks associated with unauthorized access and data breaches.

Multi-Layer Security

Multi-Layer Security refers to the approach of implementing multiple layers of security measures within a network infrastructure to protect against various types of cyber threats. Each layer is designed to address specific vulnerabilities and potential attack vectors, creating a comprehensive security framework. The concept of Multi-Layer Security is based on the principle that relying solely on a single security measure is not sufficient to provide adequate protection against the increasingly sophisticated and diverse range of threats faced by modern networks. By employing a combination of different security measures at various network layers, organizations can significantly enhance their defense capabilities.

Multi-Tenant Security

Multi-Tenant Security in the context of networking refers to the measures and protocols implemented to ensure the security and isolation of resources and data within a multi-tenant network environment. In a multi-tenant network, multiple organizations or users share a common infrastructure, such as servers, storage, and networking resources. Each tenant, or organization, operates and manages their own virtual environment within the shared infrastructure. Multi-tenant architectures are commonly used in cloud computing, where cloud service providers offer services to multiple customers on the same physical infrastructure. The primary goal of multi-tenant security is to enforce strict isolation between tenants to prevent unauthorized access or interference. This includes ensuring that each tenant's resources are securely partitioned and that their data remains private and protected from other tenants or external threats. One of the key security measures in a multi-tenant environment is proper network segmentation. This involves creating virtual networks or subnets for each tenant, effectively separating their traffic from others. This segmentation can be achieved through technologies like Virtual LANs (VLANs) or Virtual Private Networks (VPNs), which provide logical isolation between tenants. Additionally, access control mechanisms are crucial for multi-tenant security. Access controls determine who can access specific resources within the environment. This can be enforced through identity and authentication protocols, such as user accounts, role-based access control (RBAC), or access control lists (ACLs), which define granular permissions for each tenant. Data encryption is also vital in a multi-tenant environment to protect sensitive information. Encryption ensures that data remains unreadable to unauthorized parties, even if it is intercepted. Secure communication protocols like SSL/TLS are commonly used to encrypt data in transit, while encrypting storage solutions (e.g., disk encryption) protect data at rest. Furthermore, monitoring and auditing play a crucial role in multi-tenant security. Continuous monitoring and logging of network activities can help detect and mitigate potential security breaches. Auditing processes can provide insights into any security incidents, enabling organizations to take necessary actions and ensure compliance with security standards and regulations.

Multicast

Multicast is a networking process that enables the transmission of data packets from a sender to multiple recipients simultaneously. Unlike unicast, which transmits data to a single recipient, multicast allows a sender to reach multiple receivers within a single transmission. In a multicast scenario, the sender identifies a specific multicast group IP address that recipients can join. These recipients express their interest in receiving data from the sender by joining the multicast group. The sender then sends a single copy of the data packet, which is then received and processed by all the members of the multicast group.

Multihoming

Multihoming refers to the practice of connecting a network or host to multiple network interfaces or service providers in order to increase reliability, performance, or to achieve specific routing goals. It allows a network or host to have multiple paths to reach a destination, providing redundancy and load balancing. By connecting to multiple network interfaces or service providers, a network or host can distribute its traffic across multiple paths, reducing the risk of single points of failure and increasing overall network reliability. If one link or service provider fails, traffic can be automatically rerouted to the available paths, ensuring uninterrupted connectivity. This can be particularly important for critical applications or services that require high availability.

Multipath Routing

Multipath routing is a technique used in computer networks to efficiently distribute traffic across multiple paths or links in order to optimize network performance, enhance reliability, and improve load balancing. It involves the selection and utilization of alternative paths to transmit data packets from a source to a destination. By distributing traffic across multiple paths, multipath routing allows for increased bandwidth utilization and improved fault tolerance. In a traditional network routing scenario, a single path is usually determined for transmitting data packets from source to destination. However, in certain cases, a single path may not be the most efficient or reliable option. This is where multipath routing becomes beneficial. It enables the utilization of multiple paths simultaneously, which can significantly improve network performance and reliability. Multipath routing algorithms typically operate at the network layer of the OSI model and make decisions based on various factors such as link metrics, congestion levels, and network topology. These algorithms aim to distribute traffic evenly across available paths while considering factors like path quality, link capacity, and network congestion. Multipath routing can be implemented using different approaches, such as link-state routing protocols (e.g., OSPF), distance-vector routing protocols (e.g., EIGRP), or application layer load balancing techniques. Each approach has its own advantages and trade-offs. One of the main benefits of multipath routing is that it improves network performance by optimizing bandwidth usage. By distributing traffic across multiple paths, it reduces congestion and minimizes packet loss, resulting in faster and more efficient data transmission. Additionally, multipath routing enhances network reliability by providing redundancy. If one path fails or becomes congested, the traffic can be rerouted through alternative paths, ensuring uninterrupted connectivity. In conclusion, multipath routing is a technique used in networking to distribute traffic across multiple paths or links, optimizing network performance and enhancing reliability. It enables the utilization of alternative paths to transmit data packets and allows for increased bandwidth utilization, improved fault tolerance, and better load balancing. Multipath routing algorithms make decisions based on various factors, and implementation can vary based on the chosen approach. Overall, multipath routing plays a crucial role in efficient and reliable network communication.

NIST Cybersecurity Framework

The NIST Cybersecurity Framework is a set of guidelines, standards, and best practices developed by the National Institute of Standards and Technology (NIST) to help organizations manage and reduce cybersecurity risks. It provides a common language and framework for organizations to assess and improve their ability to prevent, detect, and respond to cyber threats. In the context of networking, the NIST Cybersecurity Framework helps organizations address the unique challenges and vulnerabilities associated with the network infrastructure. It helps organizations develop a comprehensive and structured approach to securing their network assets and protecting sensitive information from unauthorized access.

NVRAM (Non-Volatile RAM)

NVRAM (Non-Volatile RAM) is a type of memory that retains data even when the power is turned off or lost. It stores configuration information and settings that are essential for the operation of networking devices such as routers and switches. NVRAM plays a critical role in networking as it allows devices to retain vital information, such as startup configurations and operating parameters. This memory is non-volatile, meaning that it is not erased when the power is turned off, making it an essential component for the proper functioning of network devices. One of the key features of NVRAM is its ability to store startup configurations. These configurations include information about the device's operating system, network settings, and protocols. When a networking device is powered on, it reads the startup configuration from the NVRAM and applies it to initialize its operating system and network interfaces. This allows the device to be quickly brought back to its desired state after a power outage or a restart. In addition to startup configurations, NVRAM also stores other important settings that are necessary for the operation of networking devices. These settings can include security parameters, such as passwords and access control lists, as well as routing tables, interface configurations, and other device-specific parameters. By storing these settings in non-volatile memory, network devices can maintain their operation even when the power is interrupted or lost. NVRAM typically has a limited capacity compared to other types of memory, such as RAM. Therefore, it is important for network administrators to manage the usage of NVRAM effectively. This can involve optimizing the configuration files stored in NVRAM to reduce their size, regularly backing up and archiving NVRAM content, and ensuring that it is not overloaded with unnecessary or outdated information. In conclusion, NVRAM is a crucial component in networking devices as it stores essential configuration information and settings. Its non-volatile nature allows devices to retain this information even in the event of a power loss. Network administrators must manage NVRAM effectively to ensure the smooth operation of their networking infrastructure.

Networking

Networking is the practice of connecting electronic devices together to share resources and information. It involves the use of physical or wireless connections to enable communication between devices such as computers, routers, and servers. In a networking context, devices are typically connected through a network infrastructure, which includes various components such as cables, switches, routers, and access points. These components work together to facilitate the transmission of data packets between devices. A network can be classified based on its architecture, such as a local area network (LAN), wide area network (WAN), or metropolitan area network (MAN). LANs typically cover a small geographical area, such as a home, office, or campus, and are used to connect devices within a specific location. WANs, on the other hand, span large distances and are used to connect multiple LANs or remote devices together. MANs cover a larger area than LANs but smaller than WANs. Networking protocols play a crucial role in ensuring the smooth flow of data across a network. Protocols define a set of rules and conventions that devices must follow to communicate effectively. Examples of commonly used networking protocols include TCP/IP, Ethernet, and Wi-Fi. Networking allows devices to access shared resources such as files, printers, and internet connections. By establishing connections between devices, users can transfer data, share information, and collaborate more efficiently. Additionally, networking enables the implementation of services such as email, web browsing, and streaming media. Security is a significant concern in networking, as it involves protecting sensitive data from unauthorized access and malicious attacks. Measures such as firewalls, encryption, and authentication protocols are implemented to ensure the confidentiality, integrity, and availability of network resources. Overall, networking plays a crucial role in modern society, facilitating communication, collaboration, and resource sharing. It enables the seamless transfer of data and the creation of complex systems, supporting various applications and services.

Network Access Control (NAC)

Network Access Control (NAC) is a cybersecurity solution that plays a pivotal role in preventing unauthorized access to network resources and ensuring the security and compliance of a network. NAC establishes a framework that allows network administrators to enforce policies and control access to the network based on various factors such as user identity, device type, and security posture. The primary objective of NAC is to provide secure and controlled access to the network by authenticating and authorizing every user and device that attempts to connect. NAC accomplishes this by implementing a set of guidelines that specify the conditions under which a user or device can gain access to the network, restricting access to non-compliant or suspicious systems. By using NAC, organizations can mitigate security risks by ensuring that only authorized personnel and devices are granted access to the network. This helps in preventing potential threats such as unauthorized devices, malware, or rogue users from compromising the network infrastructure. NAC also offers the ability to dynamically respond to security incidents by quarantining or restricting access to devices exhibiting suspicious behavior or failing compliance checks. NAC provides a range of features that contribute to network security, including network visibility, authentication, and endpoint compliance checking. Network visibility enables administrators to have a comprehensive view of the devices and users connected to the network, aiding in identifying potential risks. Authentication ensures that users and devices provide valid credentials to gain access to the network, while endpoint compliance checking ensures that devices meet the organization's security and policy requirements before being allowed to connect. NAC solutions can be implemented using various techniques such as VLAN enforcement, agent-based enforcement, or 802.1X authentication. VLAN enforcement involves segregating different user groups into separate virtual LANs, thereby limiting access only to authorized network segments. Agent-based enforcement requires the installation of specialized software agents on client devices to monitor and enforce access policies. 802.1X authentication utilizes the Extensible Authentication Protocol (EAP) to authenticate users and devices before granting network access. In summary, NAC is a vital component of network security that provides organizations with the means to control and secure access to their networks. By implementing NAC, organizations can enforce policies, authenticate users and devices, and maintain compliance, thereby enhancing overall network security.

Network Adapter

A network adapter, also known as a network interface card (NIC) or network interface controller (NIC), is a hardware component that allows a device to connect to a computer network. It provides the physical interface between the device and the network medium, enabling communication between the device and other devices or resources on the network. The network adapter is responsible for converting data from the device into a format that can be transmitted over the network and vice versa. It handles tasks such as encapsulating data into network packets, adding necessary headers and trailers to the packets, and ensuring that the packets are correctly transmitted and received by the intended recipient. A network adapter typically connects to the computer's motherboard through a peripheral component interconnect (PCI) slot or on newer systems, through a peripheral component interconnect express (PCIe) slot. It can be either integrated into the motherboard or installed as an expansion card. The physical connection to the network is established through an Ethernet cable, which is plugged into the network adapter's Ethernet port. The network adapter operates at the data link layer of the network protocol stack. It implements the protocols and standards necessary for communicating on the network, such as Ethernet, Wi-Fi, or Bluetooth. The adapter has a unique identifier called a media access control (MAC) address, which is used to identify the device on the network. Network adapters can support different network speeds and technologies, such as 10/100/1000Mbps Ethernet or gigabit Wi-Fi. They may also include additional features and capabilities, such as support for virtual LANs (VLANs), jumbo frames, or network offloading. Advanced network adapters may have multiple ports or support for specialized networking protocols. In summary, a network adapter is a vital component in networking as it facilitates the connection between devices and computer networks. It enables devices to send and receive data over the network, translating the data into a format that can be transmitted and ensuring its correct delivery to the intended destination.

Network Address Management

Network Address Management refers to the process of controlling and organizing the allocation of network addresses in a networked environment. It involves the management and administration of IP addresses, which are unique identifiers assigned to each device connected to a network. In a network, devices communicate with each other using IP addresses. These addresses help in identifying the source and destination of data packets, ensuring that they reach the correct device. Network Address Management plays a crucial role in ensuring that IP addresses are assigned efficiently and are available to all devices in a network. The process of Network Address Management typically involves several tasks. This includes the assignment of IP addresses to devices, monitoring their usage, and handling address conflicts. It also encompasses the management of address allocation policies, subnetting, and maintaining a centralized repository of address assignments. One of the key components of Network Address Management is DHCP (Dynamic Host Configuration Protocol). DHCP allows for the automatic allocation and configuration of IP addresses in a network. It dynamically assigns temporary addresses to devices, eliminating the need for manual configuration and reducing the risk of address conflicts. In addition to DHCP, Network Address Management may also involve the use of network address translation (NAT). NAT allows multiple devices in a network to share a single IP address, effectively conserving address space. Effective Network Address Management is essential for maintaining the stability and scalability of a network. It ensures that IP addresses are allocated efficiently, avoiding address exhaustion and optimizing the use of available address ranges. Additionally, it helps in streamlining network operations, simplifying troubleshooting, and enhancing security by enabling proper identification and tracking of devices.

Network Address Translation (NAT)

Network Address Translation (NAT) is a process used in networking to modify IP addresses in network packets as they traverse a router or firewall. The main purpose of NAT is to conserve IP addresses and enable communication between networks with different addressing schemes. NAT operates by replacing the source or destination IP address of a packet with a different IP address. This allows a private network with non-routable IP addresses to share a single public IP address for communication with external networks, such as the internet. When a device from the private network sends a packet to an external network, the router or firewall changes the source IP address of the packet to the public IP address before forwarding it. Similarly, when a packet is received from an external network, the destination IP address is changed to the corresponding private IP address before delivering it to the appropriate device within the private network.

Network Administrator

A Network Administrator is an individual responsible for managing and maintaining computer networks within an organization. They are responsible for ensuring that the network operates efficiently, securely, and reliably to meet the organization's needs and requirements. The Network Administrator's primary duties involve designing, implementing, and supporting the organization's network infrastructure. This includes configuring network devices such as routers, switches, firewalls, and access points. They also oversee the installation and maintenance of network hardware and software, ensuring compatibility, proper functioning, and adherence to industry standards. Additionally, a Network Administrator is responsible for monitoring network performance to identify and resolve any issues that may arise. This involves conducting regular network audits, analyzing network traffic, and troubleshooting network connectivity problems. They also collaborate with other IT teams to diagnose and resolve network-related issues that affect overall system performance. Security is a crucial aspect of a Network Administrator's role. They implement and enforce security measures to protect the organization's network from unauthorized access, viruses, malware, and other potential threats. This includes configuring firewalls, implementing Virtual Private Networks (VPNs), and managing user access and privileges. They also stay up-to-date with the latest security trends and technologies to ensure proactive protection against emerging threats. Network Administrators are responsible for documenting network configurations, changes, and incidents. They maintain accurate network documentation, including network diagrams, IP address assignments, and hardware and software inventories. This documentation ensures effective troubleshooting, facilitates future network upgrades or expansions, and provides reference material for other IT teams and personnel. Effective communication is an essential skill for a Network Administrator. They collaborate with different stakeholders, including IT staff, management, and end-users, to understand their network needs and provide appropriate solutions. They also keep stakeholders informed of network outages, upgrades, and other relevant network-related information, ensuring minimal disruption and maximum productivity. In summary, a Network Administrator is responsible for managing and maintaining an organization's computer network infrastructure. They ensure the network operates efficiently, securely, and reliably by designing and implementing network solutions, monitoring network performance, enforcing security measures, maintaining accurate documentation, and effectively communicating with stakeholders.

Network Analysis Tools

Network analysis tools refer to a collection of software applications and utilities used to conduct comprehensive evaluations and assessments of computer networks. These tools are specifically designed to gather and analyze data related to network traffic, performance, and security, enabling network administrators and engineers to diagnose network issues and optimize network performance.Network analysis tools typically offer a wide range of functionalities that facilitate effective network monitoring, troubleshooting, and planning. These functionalities include:1. Network Traffic Analysis: Network analysis tools allow users to capture and examine network traffic data to identify patterns, diagnose bottlenecks, and detect network anomalies. They utilize packet sniffing techniques to capture and analyze network packets, providing valuable insights into network performance and identifying potential security threats.2. Performance Monitoring: These tools enable real-time monitoring of network performance metrics such as bandwidth utilization, latency, packet loss, and throughput. Administrators can measure and track network performance over time, identify areas of improvement, and take proactive measures to ensure optimal network performance.3. Protocol Analysis: Network analysis tools provide protocol analysis capabilities, allowing administrators to inspect and decipher network protocols and analyze their behavior. This helps in troubleshooting network issues, identifying protocol-specific problems, and optimizing protocol configurations.4. Security Analysis: Network analysis tools help in monitoring and detecting security vulnerabilities, intrusions, and attacks. By analyzing network traffic, these tools can identify suspicious activities, identify potential security breaches, and provide insights into network security risks.5. Network Traffic Forensics: These tools enable the analysis and reconstruction of network traffic for forensic investigations. They can assist in identifying the source and nature of network attacks, collecting evidence, and providing critical information for incident response and legal proceedings.Overall, network analysis tools play a critical role in maintaining and optimizing network performance, ensuring network security, and addressing network issues efficiently. Through their comprehensive functionalities, these tools empower network administrators and engineers to effectively monitor, troubleshoot, and plan network infrastructure, ultimately contributing to the smooth functioning of computer networks.

Network Architecture

Network architecture refers to the design and arrangement of networks, including the physical and logical components, as well as the protocols and technologies used to enable communication and data transfer between devices. In the context of networking, network architecture encompasses various elements that contribute to the overall structure and functionality of a network. It involves determining the layout and organization of devices, such as routers, switches, and servers, as well as the connections and pathways between them. This includes considerations of network topology, which defines how devices are interconnected and how data flows within the network. Network architecture also involves the selection and configuration of protocols and technologies that facilitate communication over the network. This includes choosing the appropriate network protocols, such as TCP/IP, Ethernet, and Wi-Fi, which define the rules and procedures for transmitting data. It also involves configuring network devices with appropriate settings and addressing schemes to ensure proper communication and data transfer. The design of a network architecture also takes into account factors such as scalability, reliability, and security. Scalability refers to the ability of the network to accommodate additional devices and increase its capacity as the network grows. Reliability involves designing the network in such a way that it is highly available and minimizes downtime. Security considerations encompass implementing measures to protect the network from unauthorized access, data breaches, and other potential threats. In summary, network architecture is the blueprint for designing and implementing a network. It encompasses the physical and logical components, as well as the protocols and technologies used to enable communication and data transfer. By carefully designing and configuring the network architecture, organizations can create efficient, reliable, and secure networks that meet their specific requirements.

Network Attached Storage (NAS)

A Network Attached Storage (NAS) refers to a dedicated file storage device that operates on a network, providing centralized data storage and access to multiple users simultaneously. It is designed to provide a convenient and efficient way of storing and sharing files across the network, without relying on a specific computer or server. NAS devices are typically connected to a local area network (LAN) through Ethernet cables or wireless connections. They contain one or more hard drives that are organized into logical volumes, allowing users to store and retrieve files from a shared directory. These devices can be accessed by multiple devices, such as computers, laptops, smartphones, and tablets, regardless of the operating system they are using.

Network Bandwidth Allocation Strategies

Network Bandwidth Allocation Strategies refer to the methods and techniques used to distribute the available bandwidth resources among the different applications, users, or devices connected to a network. Bandwidth allocation is a crucial aspect of network management as it directly impacts the performance and efficiency of the network. There are several strategies commonly employed to allocate network bandwidth effectively: 1. Equal Allocation: This strategy distributes the available bandwidth equally among all the users, applications, or devices connected to the network. Each entity receives an equal share of the bandwidth, regardless of its specific requirements or usage patterns. While this approach ensures fair distribution, it may not be suitable for networks with varying demands. 2. Weighted Allocation: In this strategy, different weights or priorities are assigned to different entities based on their importance or specific requirements. The bandwidth is then allocated proportionally to each entity's weight, allowing higher priority entities to receive a larger share. This approach prioritizes critical applications or users, ensuring their performance is not compromised. 3. Dynamic Allocation: Dynamic allocation strategies monitor the network utilization in real-time and adjust the bandwidth allocation accordingly. It involves dynamically allotting more bandwidth to entities with higher demand and reducing it for those with lower demand. This approach maximizes the overall network efficiency by allowing resources to be utilized optimally based on the current requirements. 4. Traffic-based Allocation: Traffic-based allocation strategies analyze the type, volume, and patterns of network traffic to allocate bandwidth. Different protocols, applications, or services are classified based on their bandwidth needs and importance. High-bandwidth applications, such as video streaming or file downloads, may be allocated more resources compared to low-priority traffic like email or web browsing. 5. Quality of Service (QoS): QoS-based allocation strategies focus on ensuring a certain level of service quality for specific applications or users. Different classes or levels of service are defined, each with its own bandwidth requirements and guarantees. Bandwidth allocation is then performed based on these predefined QoS parameters, giving priority to applications or users that require a higher quality of service. By employing various bandwidth allocation strategies, network administrators can optimize the usage of available bandwidth, enhance performance, and fulfill the diverse requirements of different applications, users, or devices connected to the network.

Network Bandwidth Allocation

Network bandwidth allocation refers to the process of dividing the available network bandwidth among various devices, applications, or users connected to a network. It is a crucial aspect of network management as it determines how much bandwidth is assigned to each entity on the network, ensuring fair and efficient utilization of network resources. Bandwidth allocation is typically implemented by network administrators or through automated algorithms that prioritize and distribute the available bandwidth based on predefined rules or policies. These policies can be based on factors such as the type of traffic, QoS (Quality of Service) requirements, user priorities, or application-specific needs. One common approach to network bandwidth allocation is called dynamic allocation. In this method, the available bandwidth is allocated on-demand, meaning that it is allocated in real-time based on the current network conditions and requirements. For example, during periods of high network traffic, more bandwidth can be allocated to critical applications or users, ensuring that they receive sufficient resources to operate optimally. Another approach is static allocation, where the bandwidth is divided in fixed proportions among various entities. This method is particularly useful when there are predictable traffic patterns or when specific devices or applications require a guaranteed amount of bandwidth at all times. However, it may lead to underutilization of network resources if the allocated bandwidth is not fully utilized by the respective entity. Some common techniques for network bandwidth allocation include traffic shaping, traffic policing, and traffic prioritization. Traffic shaping involves controlling the rate at which data is transmitted, smoothing out bursts of traffic to prevent congestion. Traffic policing involves monitoring and enforcing predefined traffic limits, discarding excess traffic that exceeds these limits. Traffic prioritization assigns different priority levels to different types of traffic, ensuring that high-priority traffic receives preferential treatment in terms of bandwidth allocation. Effective network bandwidth allocation is essential for maintaining a well-functioning network with optimal performance and minimal congestion. It allows for efficient resource utilization, maximizes network throughput, and ensures that critical applications or users receive the necessary bandwidth to operate effectively. By carefully allocating network bandwidth, network administrators can optimize network performance, reduce latency, and provide a satisfactory user experience for all connected devices and users.

Network Bandwidth Management

Network bandwidth management refers to the practice of optimizing and controlling the amount of data that can be transmitted over a network within a given timeframe. It involves implementing techniques and strategies to ensure that network resources are utilized efficiently and effectively. In networking, bandwidth refers to the maximum data transfer rate that a network can support, typically measured in bits per second (bps). It represents the capacity of a network to transmit data. Bandwidth management is necessary because network resources are finite, and it is important to allocate these resources fairly and prioritize critical traffic. Network bandwidth management involves several key processes: Traffic shaping: This process involves controlling the flow of network traffic to optimize bandwidth usage. It allows for the prioritization of certain types of traffic or applications over others. Traffic shaping techniques can help prevent congestion and ensure that critical applications receive sufficient bandwidth. Quality of Service (QoS): QoS is a set of protocols and mechanisms that enable the differentiation and prioritization of network traffic. It allows specific traffic to be classified based on its importance or requirements, ensuring that important traffic receives better service and resources. QoS mechanisms can help optimize bandwidth allocation and provide better network performance. Bandwidth allocation: Bandwidth management involves allocating network bandwidth based on various factors such as application requirements, user priorities, and network policies. By effectively distributing available bandwidth, network administrators can ensure that critical applications or users have sufficient resources while preventing any single user or application from monopolizing the bandwidth. Traffic monitoring and analysis: Network bandwidth management requires constant monitoring and analysis of network traffic. By monitoring traffic patterns and analyzing data usage, network administrators can identify any bottlenecks or bandwidth-intensive activities. This information can be used to make informed decisions about network optimization, such as identifying areas for traffic optimization or potential bandwidth upgrades.

Network Bandwidth Optimization Tools

Network bandwidth optimization tools refer to software or hardware-based solutions that are designed to improve the efficiency and utilization of network resources, particularly the available bandwidth. These tools employ a variety of techniques and algorithms to effectively manage network traffic, reduce congestion, and ensure the optimal usage of bandwidth resources. One of the primary objectives of network bandwidth optimization tools is to minimize bandwidth wastage and increase the overall network performance. These tools aim to identify and prioritize critical network traffic, such as real-time audio or video streaming, while managing less important or non-essential traffic in a way that minimizes their impact on network performance. By doing so, these tools help to maximize the available bandwidth and ensure that it is allocated in the most efficient manner.

Network Bandwidth Optimization

Network bandwidth optimization refers to the process of maximizing the efficiency and utilization of available network bandwidth. It involves implementing various techniques and strategies to reduce network congestion, minimize data transfer delays, and optimize overall network performance. The goal of network bandwidth optimization is to make the most efficient use of the available network resources, ensuring that data is transmitted and received in the most efficient manner possible. By optimizing network bandwidth, organizations can improve the speed and reliability of their network connections, enhance user experience, and reduce costs associated with data transfer and network infrastructure.

Network Bandwidth Testing

Network bandwidth testing refers to the process of measuring the capacity or throughput of a network connection. It involves evaluating the speed and efficiency at which data can be transmitted across a network infrastructure, typically measured in bits per second (bps) or bytes per second (Bps). The primary purpose of network bandwidth testing is to assess the performance and reliability of a network, identify potential bottlenecks, and determine the maximum amount of data that can be transmitted within a given period of time. By measuring the available bandwidth, it becomes possible to optimize network resources, improve data transfer rates, and ensure a smooth and uninterrupted flow of information.

Network Bandwidth

Network bandwidth refers to the maximum amount of data that can be transmitted over a network connection in a given amount of time. It is a measure of the capacity or speed at which data can be transferred between devices or systems within a network. Bandwidth is typically expressed in bits per second (bps) and can vary depending on factors such as network infrastructure, data transmission technology, and network congestion. Higher bandwidth allows for faster data transfer rates, while lower bandwidth can result in slower transfer speeds.

Network Behavior Analysis (NBA)

Network Behavior Analysis (NBA) is a method used in the field of networking to monitor and analyze network traffic and behavior patterns of devices within a network. It focuses on detecting and identifying any anomalies or threats that may exist within the network, such as suspicious activities or unauthorized access attempts. NBA works by collecting and analyzing data packets that flow through the network, using various techniques and algorithms to identify any abnormal behaviors. It involves continuously monitoring network traffic, examining the characteristics of the packets, and comparing them against predefined rules and patterns to determine if they indicate any potential security risks. NBA can be used for both real-time monitoring and retrospective analysis. In real-time monitoring, it actively observes network traffic as it occurs, allowing for immediate detection and response to any threats or abnormalities. Retrospective analysis, on the other hand, involves analyzing historical network data to identify patterns or trends that may indicate potential security issues or breaches that have already occurred. By using NBA, network administrators and security teams can gain valuable insights into the behavior of network devices and users. It enables them to detect and respond to security incidents and threats in a timely manner, reducing the risk of data breaches or unauthorized access to sensitive information. NBA can also help in identifying and mitigating network performance issues. By monitoring network traffic patterns, administrators can identify bottlenecks, overloaded devices, or other issues that may affect network performance and take appropriate actions to optimize network resources. In summary, Network Behavior Analysis (NBA) is a method used in networking to continuously monitor and analyze network traffic and behavior patterns. It enables the detection of anomalies and potential security threats, as well as provides insights into network performance. By leveraging NBA, organizations can strengthen their network security defenses and proactively address any network-related issues.

Network Cabling

Network cabling refers to the physical infrastructure used to connect electronic devices, such as computers, servers, routers, and switches, to form a network. It involves the installation and configuration of cables to establish reliable and efficient connections between devices within a local area network (LAN) or wide area network (WAN). The main purpose of network cabling is to facilitate the transmission of data, voice, and video signals between devices and enable them to communicate and share resources. It serves as the backbone of a network, providing the necessary connectivity for devices to exchange information and access shared resources, such as printers, storage devices, and internet connections.

Network Configuration Best Practices

Network Configuration Best Practices refer to a set of guidelines and recommendations that help optimize the performance, security, and reliability of a computer network. These best practices are aimed at ensuring that the network is properly configured and effectively managed to meet the requirements and demands of the users. Proper network configuration involves various aspects, such as hardware and software settings, network architecture, security measures, and management policies. Implementing best practices in each of these areas helps prevent network bottlenecks, minimize downtime, and reduce the risk of security breaches or unauthorized access.

Network Configuration Management Best Practices

Network Configuration Management Best Practices refer to a set of guidelines and methods implemented in networking systems to ensure efficient and effective management of network configurations. These practices aim to optimize network performance, mitigate risks, and streamline administrative tasks. Effective network configuration management is crucial for maintaining the stability and security of a network, particularly in complex and large-scale environments. By adhering to best practices, network administrators can minimize errors, simplify troubleshooting, and enhance overall network performance.

Network Configuration Management Software

Network Configuration Management Software refers to a tool or application used by network administrators to automate and streamline the management of network configurations within an organization's networking infrastructure. It includes a set of features and functionalities that enable administrators to centrally control and monitor network devices, such as routers, switches, firewalls, and servers. Network configuration management software is designed to simplify the process of configuring, deploying, and maintaining network devices. It allows administrators to define and enforce consistent network policies, apply configuration changes across multiple devices simultaneously, and ensure compliance with industry regulations and best practices.

Network Configuration Management

Network Configuration Management refers to the process of managing and organizing the various configurations and settings of network devices in an efficient and systematic manner. It involves the monitoring, updating, and tracking of network devices such as routers, switches, firewalls, and servers, to ensure that they are properly configured and functioning optimally. The main objective of Network Configuration Management is to maintain a stable and reliable

231

network infrastructure by keeping track of the configuration parameters and changes made to network devices. This includes managing details such as IP addresses, subnet masks, routing tables, access control lists, and numerous other settings that determine the behavior and performance of the network. By implementing Network Configuration Management, organizations can ensure that their network devices are consistent and compliant with the desired network policies and standards. It allows for better control and coordination of network configurations, reducing the risk of errors and inconsistencies that can lead to network outages or security vulnerabilities. The process typically involves the use of specialized software tools that automate the tasks of configuration management. These tools facilitate the management of a large number of network devices by centralizing the configuration data, providing a single interface for managing configurations, and allowing for efficient deployment of configuration changes across multiple devices. Network Configuration Management also encompasses features such as configuration backup and restore, which enable organizations to recover from device failures or roll back to a known working configuration. It may also include the ability to schedule configuration backups and automate the process of applying configuration changes, ensuring that the network remains up-to-date and secure. Overall, Network Configuration Management plays a vital role in ensuring the reliability, stability, and security of network infrastructures. It enables organizations to efficiently manage their network devices, streamline configuration processes, and minimize the risk of network disruptions and vulnerabilities.

Network Configuration Standards

A network configuration standard refers to a set of predefined rules and guidelines that dictate how devices and services should be configured and connected in a computer network. It serves as a framework for organizing and managing network resources, ensuring consistency, security, and interoperability. Network configuration standards are essential as they provide a common basis for network administrators to build and maintain networks. These standards establish a uniform set of configurations, protocols, and policies that all network components must adhere to. By following these standards, organizations can achieve a more efficient and secure network infrastructure.

Network Configuration Tools

A network configuration tool is a software application or program that is used to manage and configure various network settings and components within a computer network. It provides a user-friendly interface to network administrators or IT professionals, allowing them to easily configure and maintain network devices, such as routers, switches, firewalls, and servers. These tools assist in the overall management of the network infrastructure by enabling administrators to perform tasks such as: - Setting up IP addresses and subnet masks for devices - Configuring network protocols and services - Managing network security settings, such as firewalls and access control lists - Monitoring network performance and troubleshooting connectivity issues - Managing network resources and sharing data between devices - Configuring virtual private networks (VPNs) and remote access connections - Implementing quality of service (QoS) settings to prioritize network traffic - Managing network storage and file sharing - Automating network configuration tasks through scripting or templates. By utilizing network configuration tools, administrators can simplify the process of configuring and managing network devices and settings. These tools often offer graphical user interfaces (GUIs) that allow for intuitive navigation and configuration, eliminating the need for complex command-line interfaces. This improves efficiency and reduces the likelihood of human error when making changes to network configurations. In addition, network configuration tools provide centralized management capabilities, allowing administrators to control and monitor multiple network devices from a single interface. This streamlines the configuration and maintenance processes, especially in large-scale networks with hundreds or thousands of devices. Overall, network configuration tools are essential in ensuring the smooth operation and security of computer networks. They simplify the process of managing and configuring network devices, enhancing network performance, and reducing the time and effort required to maintain a stable and secure network infrastructure.

Network Configuration

A network configuration refers to the specific arrangement and settings of devices, protocols, and services that enable communication and data transfer within a network. It involves the

232

configuration of various network components such as routers, switches, firewalls, and network interfaces to ensure efficient and secure communication between devices. Network configurations are typically designed to meet the specific needs of an organization, taking into consideration factors such as the number of devices, the type of network topology, and the desired level of security. The process of configuring a network involves determining the IP address scheme, subnetting, and assigning IP addresses to devices. It also includes setting up routing tables, configuring network protocols, and enabling network services like DHCP (Dynamic Host Configuration Protocol) and DNS (Domain Name System). In a network configuration, routers play a crucial role in determining the path that network traffic takes. They are responsible for forwarding data packets between different networks and ensuring that they reach their intended destination. Routers are configured with routing protocols such as OSPF (Open Shortest Path First) or BGP (Border Gateway Protocol) to exchange routing information and make routing decisions. Switches, on the other hand, are used to connect multiple devices within a network. They are configured with VLANs (Virtual Local Area Networks) to segregate different departments or groups within an organization and provide better network performance and security. Firewalls are implemented to protect the network from unauthorized access and to filter incoming and outgoing network traffic based on specified rules. Network configuration also involves implementing security measures such as encryption and authentication protocols to ensure the confidentiality and integrity of data transmitted over the network. This includes configuring VPN (Virtual Private Network) tunnels, SSL (Secure Sockets Layer) certificates, and access control lists. In conclusion, a network configuration refers to the process of setting up and configuring network devices, protocols, and services to enable effective and secure communication within a network. It encompasses various aspects such as IP addressing, routing, switching, security, and network services. A well-designed and properly configured network is essential for reliable and efficient network communication.

Network Congestion Control

Network congestion control is a crucial mechanism used in computer networks to regulate and manage the flow of data when there is an excess of network traffic. It involves techniques and algorithms that aim to prevent or mitigate network congestion, ensuring efficient data transfer and optimal network performance.In a computer network, congestion occurs when the demand for network resources exceeds its capacity, resulting in delays, packet loss, and degraded network performance. Congestion can occur at various points in the network, such as routers, switches, and links. It can be caused by factors like high network utilization, heavy data traffic, faulty equipment, or inefficient routing algorithms.Network congestion control aims to prevent or alleviate congestion, ensuring that data flows smoothly within the network. It involves the use of various techniques and mechanisms to regulate the flow of data and manage network resources effectively. These techniques can be categorized into two main approaches:1. Open-loop Congestion Control: This approach focuses on preventing congestion before it occurs. It involves techniques such as admission control, where the network accepts or rejects new traffic based on its capacity. Other techniques include traffic shaping and traffic engineering, which aim to regulate the flow of data and optimize network performance.2. Closed-loop Congestion Control: This approach detects congestion after it occurs and takes corrective measures to alleviate it. The most widely used closed-loop congestion control mechanism is Transmission Control Protocol (TCP), which uses techniques like congestion avoidance and congestion control algorithms. TCP monitors network conditions, adjusts its transmission rate, and reacts to packet loss to ensure efficient data transfer.Effective network congestion control relies on a combination of these techniques and mechanisms. It requires monitoring and analyzing network conditions, detecting congestion, and taking appropriate actions to regulate data flow. The goal is to maintain a balance between network capacity and traffic demand, ensuring optimal network performance and minimizing packet loss and delays.In conclusion, network congestion control is an essential aspect of computer networking. It plays a vital role in managing network resources, preventing congestion, and ensuring efficient data transfer. By employing various techniques and mechanisms, network congestion control helps maintain network performance and reliability, even during periods of high traffic demand.

Network Congestion

Network congestion refers to the state of a computer network when the demand for its resources exceeds the capacity to deliver them in a timely manner. It occurs when there is a significant increase in data traffic, resulting in a bottleneck and a decrease in overall network performance. When a network becomes congested, it experiences several issues that can affect its functionality. The most common problem is increased latency, which manifests as a delay in the transmission and reception of data packets. This delay can significantly impact the performance of real-time applications, such as video streaming or voice over IP (VoIP) services, leading to buffering, choppy audio, or dropped calls.

Network Diagram

A network diagram is a graphical representation of a network's structure, connections, and components. It provides a visual depiction of how devices and systems are interconnected, allowing network administrators and engineers to understand and manage the network effectively. Network diagrams are typically used to illustrate the physical or logical layout of a network. They can be simple or complex, depending on the size and complexity of the network being represented. In simpler networks, a diagram may show only the basic components such as routers, switches, and endpoints, while in more complex networks, it may include additional elements like firewalls, load balancers, and servers. The purpose of a network diagram is to provide a clear and concise overview of the network infrastructure. It helps network administrators in many ways, including: 1. Planning and design: Network diagrams are essential tools for planning and designing new networks or making changes to existing ones. They help identify any potential bottlenecks or design flaws and allow for better decision-making during the planning phase. 2. Troubleshooting: When network issues occur, having a network diagram can help identify the root cause of the problem more quickly. It allows administrators to trace the path of network traffic, locate potential points of failure, and determine how devices are interconnected. 3. Documentation: Network diagrams serve as documentation for the network's architecture, configurations, and connections. They can be used as reference materials for future troubleshooting, upgrades, or expansion projects, ensuring that knowledge about the network is preserved and shared. 4. Communication: Network diagrams are an effective way to communicate the network's structure and design to stakeholders, such as management, clients, or vendors. They provide a common language that can facilitate discussions and help non-technical stakeholders understand the network's complexity. In conclusion, a network diagram is a visual representation of a network's structure and connections. It is a valuable tool for planning, troubleshooting, documenting, and communicating information about a network. By providing a clear and concise overview of the network's components and interconnections, it enables effective management and decision-making in network administration and engineering.

Network Discovery Protocol (NDP)

Network Discovery Protocol (NDP) is a communication protocol used in networking to identify and collect information about devices connected within a network. It operates at the network layer of the OSI model and is primarily used in IPv6 networks.NDP serves two main purposes: neighbor discovery and address resolution. Neighbor discovery involves finding and tracking devices within the same network segment, while address resolution deals with mapping network layer addresses to link layer addresses.

Network Discovery Tools

A network discovery tool is a software application or hardware device used in the field of networking to identify and map devices and resources on a network. It enables network administrators to gather information about the devices connected to a network, such as IP addresses, MAC addresses, and open ports, as well as discover network services and protocols. Network discovery tools function by sending requests or probes to devices on a network and analyzing the responses received. These tools typically use various networking protocols, such as ICMP (Internet Control Message Protocol), SNMP (Simple Network Management Protocol), and UPnP (Universal Plug and Play), to gather information and identify devices. They may also employ techniques like ARP (Address Resolution Protocol) scanning and DNS (Domain Name System) enumeration to discover and resolve network resources.

Network Encryption

Network encryption is a security measure used in computer networking to protect data as it is

234

transmitted between devices. It involves the process of converting information into a coded form that can only be deciphered by authorized recipients. This is achieved through the use of cryptographic algorithms and keys that encrypt the data at the source and decrypt it at the destination.The primary goal of network encryption is to ensure the confidentiality, integrity, and authenticity of transmitted data. Confidentiality refers to preventing unauthorized individuals from reading or accessing the information. Integrity ensures that the data remains unaltered during transmission, meaning it was not tampered with or modified in any way. Authenticity verifies the identity of the sender and recipient to prevent impersonation or unauthorized access.Network encryption operates at different layers of the networking stack, including the physical, data link, network, transport, and application layers. At each layer, different encryption techniques and protocols may be used depending on the specific requirements of the network infrastructure and the level of security needed.One widely used encryption protocol is Transport Layer Security (TLS), which operates at the transport layer and provides secure communication over the internet. TLS encrypts data using symmetric encryption, where the same key is used for both encryption and decryption, as well as asymmetric encryption, where different keys are used for encryption and decryption. It also provides mechanisms for authentication and integrity checking, ensuring the reliability and trustworthiness of the transmitted data.In addition to TLS, other encryption techniques like IPsec (Internet Protocol Security) and VPN (Virtual Private Network) are used to secure network communications. IPsec operates at the network layer and encrypts data packets to prevent eavesdropping and unauthorized access. VPN, on the other hand, creates a secure tunnel between two or more devices, encrypting all traffic passing through it.Overall, network encryption plays a crucial role in safeguarding sensitive information and ensuring the secure transmission of data over computer networks. By employing strong encryption algorithms and protocols, organizations can protect their data from unauthorized access, interception, and tampering.Network encryption is an essential component of modern networking, enabling secure communications in various applications such as e-commerce, online banking, and remote access to corporate networks.

Network Engineer

A Network Engineer is a professional who designs, implements, and manages computer networks. They are responsible for maintaining the connectivity and performance of the network infrastructure in an organization, ensuring that data communication between devices is efficient and secure. In their role, Network Engineers analyze network requirements and design solutions that meet the organization's needs. They evaluate network architecture, hardware, and software to determine the most effective configurations. This includes selecting routers, switches, firewalls, and other network devices to create a robust and scalable network infrastructure. Once the network design is established, Network Engineers install and configure the necessary components. They set up IP addresses, allocate network resources, and establish security protocols to protect against unauthorized access or data breaches. They also troubleshoot any connectivity or performance issues that arise, utilizing diagnostic tools to identify and resolve network problems. In addition to their technical expertise, Network Engineers must have a strong understanding of network protocols and standards. They are familiar with TCP/IP, DNS, DHCP, and other networking protocols that enable data transmission across the network. They also stay updated on the latest advancements in networking technologies and regularly upgrade the network infrastructure to improve performance and security. Network Engineers work closely with other IT professionals, such as system administrators, security analysts, and database administrators, to ensure seamless integration and operation of various network-dependent systems. They collaborate with other teams to develop disaster recovery plans, implement network security measures, and optimize network performance to support the organization's overall goals. In summary, a Network Engineer is responsible for designing, implementing, and managing computer networks to ensure efficient and secure data communication. They possess knowledge of network protocols and standards, select and configure network devices, troubleshoot issues, and collaborate with other IT professionals to support the organization's network infrastructure.

Network Hardening

Network Hardening refers to the process of securing a computer network by implementing various measures to protect it from unauthorized access, potential attacks, and other security threats. It involves strengthening the network infrastructure, systems, and devices to reduce vulnerabilities and enhance overall security. There are several key aspects to network hardening. Firstly, access controls are implemented to ensure that only authorized users can access the network. This includes using strong passwords, enforcing multi-factor authentication, and implementing user account management policies. Additionally, network hardening involves configuring firewalls, routers, and switches to restrict access and control incoming and outgoing traffic. Furthermore, network hardening includes regular updates and patches to fix vulnerabilities in operating systems, applications, and network devices. This helps to ensure that known security flaws are addressed and that the network is protected against potential exploits. Network administrators should also monitor network logs and perform regular vulnerability assessments to stay informed about any potential security risks. Another important aspect of network hardening is implementing encryption mechanisms to protect data transmitted over the network. This may involve using secure protocols such as SSL/TLS for websites, encrypting sensitive information stored in databases, and enabling VPNs for secure remote access. Network segmentation is also a crucial part of network hardening. By dividing the network into separate segments or subnets, an additional layer of security is created. This helps to contain potential breaches and limit the impact of an attack on the entire network. In conclusion, network hardening plays a vital role in securing computer networks from unauthorized access, attacks, and other security threats. It involves various measures such as access controls, firewall configuration, regular updates and patches, encryption, and network segmentation. By implementing these measures, network administrators can strengthen the network's security posture and mitigate potential risks.

Network Hub

A network hub is a networking device that serves as a central point for connecting multiple devices in a local area network (LAN). It works at the physical layer of the OSI model and is used to share network resources and facilitate communication between devices. The main purpose of a network hub is to connect multiple devices in a LAN by receiving data packets from one device and broadcasting them to all other devices connected to it. This means that when a device sends data to the network hub, the hub forwards the data to all other devices, regardless of the intended recipient. This is commonly referred to as "broadcasting" or "flooding" the network. As a result, all devices connected to the hub receive the data, and it is up to each device to determine whether the data is intended for it or not. A network hub operates at the physical layer of the OSI model, which means it is responsible for transmitting raw data signals over the network. It uses repeaters to regenerate and strengthen the signal, allowing it to be transmitted over longer distances without degradation. However, hubs do not perform any processing or filtering of the data they receive, as they lack the intelligence of more advanced networking devices like switches or routers. Although network hubs were widely used in the past, modern networking technologies have largely replaced them with more efficient devices, such as switches. Unlike hubs, switches are capable of creating dedicated connections between devices, which enables simultaneous communication between multiple devices without causing congestion or data collisions. This makes switches more suitable for today's high-speed networks, where the simultaneous transmission of data is essential. In summary, a network hub is a basic networking device that connects multiple devices in a LAN by broadcasting data packets to all connected devices. It operates at the physical layer and lacks the intelligence of more advanced networking devices like switches. While hubs have been largely replaced by switches in modern networks, they still have limited use in small or simple networks where cost is a significant factor.

Network Interface Card (NIC)

A Network Interface Card (NIC) is a hardware component that connects a computer or other network-enabled device to a local area network (LAN) or a wide area network (WAN). It provides the physical connection between the device and the network, allowing it to send and receive data packets. The NIC is an essential component in computer networking, as it handles the translation of data between the computer and the network. It converts the digital signals generated by the computer into a format that can be transmitted over the network, and vice versa. The NIC is responsible for modulating and demodulating signals, encoding and decoding data, and applying error detection and correction techniques to ensure reliable data transmission. Physically, a NIC typically comprises a printed circuit board with one or more peripheral component interconnect (PCI) or PCIe slots for connecting to the computer's

236

motherboard. It may also include one or more ports or jacks for connecting to the network cables. Common types of network cables used with NICs include twisted pair cables (such as Ethernet cables) and fiber optic cables. The NIC may also have indicator lights to display the status of the network connection. The NIC communicates with the computer's operating system through device drivers, which are software programs that enable the computer to recognize and use the NIC. These drivers provide the necessary instructions for the operating system to control the NIC's functionality, including setting network parameters, establishing connections, and managing data transfer. NICs are available in various speeds and configurations to accommodate different networking requirements. The speed of a NIC is usually measured in terms of its data transfer rate, which is typically expressed in megabits or gigabits per second. Common types of NICs include Ethernet adapters, wireless network adapters, and fiber optic adapters. In summary, a Network Interface Card (NIC) is a hardware component that enables a computer or network-enabled device to connect to a network. It facilitates the translation of data between the device and the network, ensuring reliable data transmission. The NIC communicates with the computer's operating system through device drivers and is available in various speeds and configurations to meet different networking needs. """"

Network Layer

The network layer is the third layer of the OSI model and is responsible for the transmission of data packets across different networks. It provides services to the transport layer by establishing logical paths for data transfer between source and destination devices. In the context of networking, the network layer handles the addressing and routing of data packets. It encapsulates the transport layer's data into packets, adds the necessary network layer header information such as source and destination IP addresses, and determines the route that the packets will take through the network.

Network Load Balancing (NLB)

Network Load Balancing (NLB) is a networking technique that distributes incoming network traffic across multiple servers in order to optimize performance, increase availability, and enhance reliability. It is commonly used in high-traffic websites, large-scale applications, and data center environments.NLB works by creating a virtual cluster of servers that appear to clients as a single server. The cluster is assigned a single IP address and a unique name, which clients use to access the services provided by the cluster. When a client initiates a connection, NLB evaluates the load and availability of each server in the cluster and dynamically routes the incoming traffic to the server with the lightest load.There are different deployment modes for NLB, including unicast and multicast. In the unicast mode, each server in the cluster shares a common MAC address, which is associated with the virtual IP address. When a server sends a response, it changes the source MAC address of the outgoing packets to its own unique MAC address. In the multicast mode, each server keeps its original MAC address, and a multicast MAC address is used for the virtual IP address. This allows the servers to respond individually while still sharing the virtual IP address.NLB supports various load balancing algorithms to distribute the load among the servers. These algorithms include round-robin, weighted round-robin, least connections, weighted least connections, and affinity-based. Round-robin evenly distributes incoming traffic to each server in a cyclical manner. Weighted round-robin assigns a weight to each server, allowing more traffic to be directed to certain servers based on their capacity. Least connections routes traffic to the server with the fewest active connections. Weighted least connections takes into account the server's capacity when determining the number of active connections. Affinity-based load balancing directs traffic from a specific client to the same server, ensuring session persistence.Overall, NLB plays a crucial role in optimizing network performance and ensuring high availability by evenly distributing network traffic across multiple servers. It helps to prevent server overload, reduces response time for clients, and supports scalability for growing network environments.

Network Load Balancing

Network Load Balancing is a technique used in networking to distribute incoming network traffic across multiple servers or devices to ensure that they operate efficiently and without experiencing overload. This distribution of traffic helps to minimize the risk of any single server becoming overwhelmed and ensures high availability and responsiveness of the network. Load balancing can be accomplished through various methods, including algorithms that determine the distribution of traffic based on factors such as server capacity, current load, or geographic location. The goal is to distribute the workload evenly across multiple servers, preventing any one server from becoming a bottleneck and potentially causing performance issues or downtime.

Network Management Protocol (SNMP)

Network Management Protocol (SNMP) is a widely-used protocol in networking that allows network administrators to manage, monitor, and control network devices in a consistent and organized manner. It is an application layer protocol that is used to collect and organize information about devices on a network, and to modify and control their behavior. SNMP operates through a client/server model, where network devices being managed are referred to as agents, and the management applications are referred to as managers. The agents continuously collect and store information about device performance, status, and configuration, and make this information available to the manager upon request. The manager can then use this information to monitor the network, identify and troubleshoot performance issues, and make necessary changes to optimize network efficiency. SNMP is designed to be vendor-neutral and can be implemented on various devices, including routers, switches, servers, printers, and firewalls. It uses a structured management information base (MIB) to organize and represent information about network devices. The MIB is a hierarchical database that defines the managed objects and their properties. Each managed object is identified by an object identifier (OID) that serves as a unique name for the object in the MIB hierarchy. SNMP uses a set of operations to communicate between the agents and managers. These operations include getting the value of a specific object, setting the value of an object, and receiving notifications or traps from the agents. The manager can send requests to the agent to retrieve specific information, modify settings, or perform other actions. The agent responds to these requests by sending back the requested information or performing the requested action. SNMP can be implemented in different versions, such as SNMPv1, SNMPv2, and SNMPv3. Each version adds enhancements and security features to the protocol. SNMPv3, for example, supports secure authentication and encryption of SNMP messages to ensure the confidentiality and integrity of the information exchanged between agents and managers. In conclusion, SNMP is a vital protocol in network management that provides a standardized way to monitor, control, and manage network devices. It enables efficient network administration, troubleshooting, and optimization, contributing to the overall performance and stability of computer networks.

Network Management System (NMS)

A Network Management System (NMS) refers to a software platform that enables the centralized monitoring, control, and administration of network devices and services. It provides network administrators with a comprehensive view of the entire network infrastructure, allowing them to efficiently manage and troubleshoot network issues. The primary purpose of an NMS is to ensure the smooth operation and optimal performance of computer networks. It achieves this by collecting and analyzing data from network devices such as routers, switches, servers, and firewalls. The collected data includes information on network traffic, bandwidth utilization, device status, and performance metrics. The NMS offers a range of functionalities that aid in network management. It allows administrators to configure network devices remotely, identify and resolve network faults, allocate network resources, and track network performance over time. It also assists in capacity planning by providing insights into network traffic patterns and trends. One of the key features of an NMS is its ability to generate alerts and notifications based on predefined thresholds. Administrators can set thresholds for various parameters such as CPU usage, bandwidth utilization, and error rates. When these thresholds are exceeded, the NMS triggers alerts, allowing administrators to promptly address the issues before they escalate. Another critical aspect of an NMS is its reporting and analysis capabilities. It enables administrators to generate detailed reports on network performance, device health, and security incidents. These reports help in identifying bottlenecks, detecting anomalies, and planning network upgrades or optimizations. Furthermore, an NMS often includes advanced features like network mapping and visualization, which provide an intuitive graphical representation of the network topology. This facilitates better understanding and visualization of network relationships and dependencies. In summary, a Network Management System is an essential tool for efficiently managing and maintaining network infrastructure. It simplifies the administration of

238

complex networks, improves network performance and availability, and enhances network security.

Network Monitoring

Network monitoring refers to the process of continuously observing and analyzing the performance and activity of computer networks. It involves the collection and evaluation of network data to identify and address any issues or anomalies that may arise within the network infrastructure. The primary objective of network monitoring is to ensure the smooth and efficient operation of networks by detecting and resolving problems in a timely manner. It provides network administrators and IT professionals with vital information and insights into the overall health and performance of the network, allowing them to proactively manage and optimize network resources.

Network Node

A network node is a device or a computer that is connected to a computer network. It can be physical hardware or software configured to perform various networking functions and provide services to other devices on the network. Network nodes play a crucial role in the functioning of computer networks as they enable communication between different devices, allow data transfer, and facilitate the sharing of resources. These nodes can range from simple devices like switches and routers to more complex devices like servers and firewalls.

Network Operating System (NOS)

A Network Operating System (NOS) is a specialized operating system designed to manage and coordinate the activities of multiple computers and devices within a network. It provides the necessary software and services for systems to communicate, share resources, and run applications across the network. NOS serves as a middleware between the network protocols and the hardware, enabling network administrators to efficiently manage and control the network infrastructure. It handles the tasks of routing, switching, and managing network connections, ensuring optimal performance and reliability.

Network Packet Analyzer

A Network Packet Analyzer is a tool used by network administrators to capture, analyze, and interpret network traffic. It provides detailed information about the packets flowing through a network, allowing administrators to troubleshoot issues, optimize network performance, and enhance network security. With a Network Packet Analyzer, administrators can gain insights into the communication between different devices on a network. It captures packets of data as they travel across the network, and then decodes and analyzes them to extract useful information. This information includes the source and destination addresses, protocols used, packet size, timestamps, and much more.

Network Performance Metrics

Network performance metrics refer to the quantitative measurements used to assess the efficiency, reliability, and overall performance of a computer network. These metrics are essential for network administrators and engineers to monitor, analyze, and optimize network performance, ensuring that it meets the desired requirements and objectives. One of the primary network performance metrics is bandwidth, which measures the amount of data that can be transmitted over a network in a given time. It is usually expressed in bits per second (bps) and is crucial for determining the network's capacity and how much data can be transmitted at a particular time. A higher bandwidth indicates a faster network and better performance. Latency is another critical network performance metric that measures the delay or time taken for a data packet to travel from the source to the destination. It is usually measured in milliseconds (ms) or microseconds (µs) and is essential for determining the responsiveness and real-time nature of network applications. Lower latency results in faster response times and more efficient communication. Packet loss is a network performance metric that calculates the percentage of data packets lost or not delivered successfully over a network. It occurs due to congestion, hardware failures, or other network issues. Minimizing packet loss is crucial for maintaining data integrity and ensuring reliable communication. Jitter is a metric that measures the variation in the delay of data packets arriving at the destination. It can cause unevenness in real-time applications and affects the quality and reliability of voice and video communication over IP networks. A lower jitter value indicates more consistent packet delivery and better performance. Throughput is a performance metric that refers to the amount of data successfully transmitted over a network in a specific period. It is typically measured in bits per second (bps) and represents the network's overall capacity or efficiency. Higher throughput results in faster data transfer and better network performance. Other important network performance metrics include network availability, which measures the percentage of time a network is operational and accessible, and network utilization, which assesses the extent to which the network resources are being used. These metrics are necessary for identifying potential bottlenecks, optimizing network performance, and ensuring the highest level of network availability and efficiency.

Network Performance Monitoring (NPM)

Network Performance Monitoring (NPM) is a crucial aspect of networking that involves the continuous monitoring and analysis of network traffic and performance metrics. It is designed to ensure the optimal functioning of a network by identifying and resolving performance issues, bottlenecks, and anomalies that can hinder the network's efficiency. NPM utilizes various monitoring tools and techniques to collect and analyze data about network traffic, throughput, latency, packet loss, bandwidth utilization, and other performance indicators. This data is then used to generate insights and reports that help network administrators and engineers optimize the network's performance, troubleshoot problems, and make informed decisions for network maintenance and upgrades. NPM operates by deploying monitoring agents, also known as probes or sensors, across the network infrastructure. These agents passively capture network packets and collect performance data from devices such as routers, switches, firewalls, servers, and endpoints. The collected data is then aggregated and analyzed to provide a comprehensive view of the network's health and performance. The primary goals of NPM are to ensure network availability, reliability, and responsiveness. By monitoring network performance, administrators can proactively identify potential issues, such as bandwidth congestion, network bottlenecks, or security threats, and take preemptive measures to mitigate them. Additionally, NPM helps in capacity planning by providing insights into traffic patterns, peak usage periods, and resource utilization, enabling administrators to optimize network resources and allocate bandwidth effectively. NPM also plays a crucial role in ensuring Service Level Agreements (SLAs) are met. By continuously monitoring and measuring network performance metrics, organizations can validate if their network service providers are meeting the agreed-upon SLAs. This enables organizations to hold their service providers accountable and take necessary actions to improve the quality of service. In conclusion, Network Performance Monitoring is a fundamental practice that helps organizations maintain and optimize their network infrastructure. By monitoring and analyzing network performance metrics, administrators can identify and address issues before they impact the network's availability, reliability, and responsiveness. This leads to improved user experience, increased productivity, and enhanced operational efficiency.

Network Port

A network port, in the context of networking, refers to a virtual communication endpoint that enables data to be sent or received between devices within a computer network. It is a numerical identifier that differentiates various network services and applications running on a host or server. Network ports are governed by the protocols of the Internet Protocol (IP) suite, particularly the Transmission Control Protocol (TCP) and User Datagram Protocol (UDP). Each network port is assigned a unique number, known as the port number, which ranges from 0 to 65,535. This port number, combined with the IP address of the device, forms a socket that allows communication to occur. The source device specifies the port number it wishes to use for a particular service or application, while the destination device listens for incoming data on that specific port. TCP/IP relies on port numbers to establish a connection between devices. TCP uses a three-way handshake to establish a connection, ensuring reliable and ordered data delivery, while UDP provides a connectionless service, ideal for applications that require low latency or real-time communication. Commonly used network ports are standardized and known as well-known ports, such as port 80 for HTTP, port 443 for HTTPS, and port 25 for SMTP. Network ports support a wide range of network services and applications. For instance, port 21 is used for FTP (File Transfer Protocol), port 22 for SSH (Secure Shell), port 53 for DNS (Domain Name System), and port 3389 for Remote Desktop Protocol (RDP). These services enable functionalities like file transfer, secure remote login, domain name resolution, and remote access to computers. In conclusion, a network port is a virtual endpoint that allows communication between devices within a network. It plays a crucial role in TCP/IP communications, utilizing unique port numbers to enable the transmission of data between specific services or applications running on devices within the network.

Network Protocol Analyzer

A Network Protocol Analyzer is a type of software or hardware tool that is used to capture, monitor, and analyze network traffic. It is also commonly known as a packet sniffer or network analyzer. The main purpose of a Network Protocol Analyzer is to provide insights into the functioning of a network and to troubleshoot network issues. By capturing and analyzing network packets, it can help network administrators to identify and resolve problems such as network congestion, unauthorized access, performance issues, and security breaches.

Network Protocol Testing

Network Protocol Testing refers to the process of testing the functionality, reliability, and performance of network protocols. Network protocols are a set of rules and procedures that govern the communication between different devices and systems within a network. These protocols ensure that data is transmitted and received in a consistent and efficient manner. The testing of network protocols is vital to ensure that they are implemented correctly and meet the required standards. This testing includes the verification of various aspects of the protocol, such as its compliance with industry standards, its ability to handle different types and volumes of data, and its resistance to various types of network conditions and failures.

Network Protocol

A network protocol is a set of rules and conventions that dictate how devices in a computer network communicate with each other. It establishes the format and sequence of messages exchanged between devices, as well as the actions to be taken by the devices upon receiving or sending these messages. Network protocols define the procedures and methods for addressing, routing, and delivering data packets from one device to another across a network. They provide a standardized framework for devices to interact and ensure that data can be transmitted and received accurately and efficiently.

Network Redundancy

Network Redundancy is a concept in networking that ensures the availability and reliability of network connections, systems, and components. It is a design strategy that aims to minimize downtime and service disruptions by implementing backup systems and duplicate resources. In the context of networking, redundancy refers to the duplication of critical network components, such as routers, switches, links, and servers. This duplication provides alternative paths for data transmission and ensures that if one component fails, the network can still function smoothly using the backup resources. Network redundancy can be achieved through various techniques and technologies. One common approach is to create redundant links between network devices. This involves connecting network devices with multiple physical or virtual connections, allowing data to flow through alternate paths in the event of a link failure. Redundant links can be established using technologies such as link aggregation, where multiple physical links are combined to create a single logical link with increased bandwidth and fault tolerance. Another method for achieving network redundancy is by using redundant network devices. Instead of relying on a single router or switch, redundant devices are deployed in parallel to create a highly available network infrastructure. These devices operate in an active-active or active-passive mode, where the backup device takes over in case the primary device fails, ensuring seamless network operation. Redundancy can also be implemented at the application layer through the use of redundant servers. By deploying multiple servers and load balancing techniques, network traffic can be distributed across these servers, ensuring high availability and fault tolerance. If one server fails, the load balancer redirects traffic to the remaining functional servers, minimizing service disruption. In addition to hardware redundancy, network redundancy can also be achieved through protocols such as Spanning Tree Protocol (STP) or Rapid Spanning Tree Protocol (RSTP). These protocols enable network devices to detect and prevent loops in the

241

network topology, ensuring a loop-free and redundant network design. They also provide mechanisms for rapid convergence in case of link or device failures, reducing the impact on network performance. Overall, network redundancy is a critical aspect of network design that ensures the continuous operation of networks, even in the face of failures or disruptions. It provides fault tolerance, improves network reliability, and minimizes downtime, consequently enhancing productivity and user experience. By implementing redundancy strategies, network administrators can build robust and resilient networks that meet the demands of modern networking environments.

Network Security Key

A network security key, also known as a Wi-Fi password or a wireless passphrase, is a string of characters used to authenticate and secure access to a wireless network. It plays a crucial role in maintaining the confidentiality, integrity, and availability of network data and resources. In the context of networking, a network security key serves as an encryption key that helps protect wireless communication. When setting up a Wi-Fi network, the network administrator or owner assigns a unique security key to prevent unauthorized access and ensure that only authorized users can connect to the network. The network security key is primarily used in WPA (Wi-Fi Protected Access) and WPA2 (Wi-Fi Protected Access II) security protocols, which are standard security measures adopted by most modern Wi-Fi networks. These protocols use a combination of encryption algorithms, such as TKIP (Temporal Key Integrity Protocol) and AES (Advanced Encryption Standard), to encrypt the data transmitted over the wireless network. When a user tries to connect to a protected Wi-Fi network, they are prompted to enter the network security key. Once the correct security key is entered, the user's device uses it to generate an encryption key that is shared between the device and the access point (wireless router). This encryption key is then used to encrypt and decrypt all data sent between the user's device and the access point, ensuring that the communication remains secure and private. The network security key is typically a combination of alphanumeric characters, including uppercase and lowercase letters, numbers, and special characters. It is recommended to use a strong and complex security key to enhance network security. A strong security key should be at least 8-12 characters long and include a mix of different character types. Overall, the network security key is a fundamental component of securing wireless networks. It acts as a barrier against unauthorized access and protects the confidentiality of sensitive data transmitted over the network. By using a strong security key, network administrators can mitigate the risk of unauthorized intrusion, data breaches, and other security threats.

Network Security Policy

A network security policy is a formal document that outlines the guidelines and procedures for ensuring the security of a network infrastructure. It provides a set of rules and guidelines that define how network resources should be accessed and protected from unauthorized access, as well as how to respond to security incidents. The main objective of a network security policy is to reduce the risk of security breaches, protect sensitive information, and ensure the availability and integrity of network resources. It serves as a framework for implementing various security controls and measures to safeguard the network infrastructure from potential threats, both internal and external. A network security policy typically includes the following components: 1. Access control: It defines the rules and procedures for granting and managing access to the network. This includes authentication mechanisms, password policies, and user privileges. 2. Network device configuration: It outlines the guidelines for configuring network devices such as routers, switches, and firewalls to ensure the security of the network infrastructure. 3. Data protection: It specifies how sensitive data should be handled, transmitted, and stored within the network. This includes encryption, data backup procedures, and data retention policies. 4. Incident response: It outlines the procedures for responding to security incidents, such as unauthorized access attempts, malware infections, or data breaches. This includes incident reporting, investigation, and recovery processes. 5. Network monitoring: It defines the monitoring mechanisms and tools used to detect and respond to network security threats. This may include intrusion detection systems, log monitoring, and vulnerability scanning. 6. Employee awareness and training: It emphasizes the importance of security awareness among employees and provides guidelines for training and educating them about network security best practices. By implementing a network security policy, organizations can establish a secure network infrastructure, mitigate the risk of security breaches, and protect the confidentiality and integrity of their data. It helps create a proactive approach to network security, ensuring that measures are in place to prevent unauthorized access, detect potential threats, and respond effectively to security incidents.

Network Security

Network security is a crucial aspect of networking that encompasses measures and protocols put in place to protect the integrity, confidentiality, and availability of network resources and data. It involves the implementation of various security measures to prevent unauthorized access, unauthorized use, disruption, or modification of network services and information. The primary goal of network security is to establish an effective defense mechanism that safeguards network infrastructure, devices, and data from potential threats such as malware, hackers, viruses, and other malicious activities. This is achieved through the usage of multiple layers of security controls, including firewalls, intrusion detection systems (IDS), virtual private networks (VPNs), network access controls, and encryption techniques. Firewalls serve as a first line of defense by monitoring incoming and outgoing network traffic and applying predefined rules to allow or block specific types of traffic based on their source, destination, or content. This helps in preventing unauthorized access to sensitive information or resources. Intrusion Detection Systems (IDS) are used to monitor network traffic for suspicious or malicious activities. They analyze network packets and compare them against known attack patterns or signatures and generate alerts or take immediate action depending on the severity of the threat detected. Virtual Private Networks (VPNs) create a secure and encrypted connection over a public network, such as the internet, ensuring that data transmitted between two endpoints is protected from eavesdropping or interception. This is particularly useful when employees need to access corporate resources from remote locations. Network access controls enable organizations to define and enforce policies for granting or restricting access to network resources based on user credentials, device types, or network locations. This helps in preventing unauthorized users or devices from gaining access to sensitive information. Encryption is another essential aspect of network security that involves the conversion of data into a secure form to prevent unauthorized access. It ensures that even if data is intercepted, it remains meaningless to unauthorized parties due to the encryption algorithms in place. Overall, network security is a critical component of any networking environment, as it plays a fundamental role in protecting the confidentiality, integrity, and availability of information and network resources. By implementing robust security measures and protocols, organizations can minimize the risks and potential damages associated with network-based attacks and ensure a secure and reliable network infrastructure.

Network Segmentation

Network segmentation is the process of dividing a computer network into smaller, isolated subnetworks, known as segments, to enhance security, optimize performance, and improve network management. Each segment typically consists of a group of interconnected devices, such as computers, servers, printers, and other network resources. The primary objective of network segmentation is to create boundaries between different parts of a network, thus preventing unauthorized access, reducing the impact of potential security breaches, and minimizing the spread of malicious activities. By dividing a network into segments, organizations can implement measures specific to each segment to ensure data confidentiality, integrity, and availability. One of the main benefits of network segmentation is improved security. By separating critical assets or sensitive information from the rest of the network, organizations can restrict access to authorized users only. In the event of a security breach, segmentation limits the lateral movement of attackers, preventing them from easily propagating through the network. Each segment can have its own security controls, such as firewalls, access controls, and intrusion prevention systems, tailored to its specific requirements. Moreover, network segmentation helps optimize performance by reducing network congestion and improving network responsiveness. By isolating different types of traffic or resource-intensive applications into separate segments, organizations can ensure that bandwidth is allocated efficiently and each segment operates at its optimal performance level. This segmentation also enables more effective bandwidth management, as resources can be allocated based on specific segment needs. In addition to security and performance benefits, network segmentation enhances network management and simplifies troubleshooting. With smaller, more manageable segments, network administrators can implement policies, permissions, and configurations on a per-

243

segment basis, allowing for easier network governance and control. Troubleshooting becomes less complex as issues can be isolated to specific segments, reducing the scope of investigation and minimizing disruptions to other parts of the network. In conclusion, network segmentation is a vital practice that offers significant advantages in terms of security, performance, and network management. By dividing a network into smaller segments, organizations can enhance their overall network infrastructure while ensuring the protection and proper management of critical resources and sensitive data.

Network Sniffer

A network sniffer, also known as a packet sniffer or network analyzer, is a tool used in computer networking to capture and analyze network traffic. It works by intercepting and examining data packets that are transmitted over a network, providing insights into the various aspects of network communication and helping to identify and troubleshoot network issues. The primary purpose of a network sniffer is to capture and analyze the data packets flowing across a network. It allows network administrators or analysts to inspect the contents and details of these packets, including the source and destination IP addresses, port numbers, protocols used, and various other network-layer information. By capturing and analyzing these packets, a network sniffer enables users to gain a deep understanding of network behavior, identify performance bottlenecks, detect network anomalies or security threats, and diagnose network problems.

Network Topology Diagram

A Network Topology Diagram is a visual representation of the arrangement or layout of a computer network. It depicts the physical and logical connections between devices, nodes, and components of the network. This diagram provides a clear overview of how the network is structured, showing the interconnections and relationships between different elements. The purpose of a network topology diagram is to aid in understanding the network's architecture and to guide network administrators in managing and troubleshooting the network. It allows them to identify potential bottlenecks, points of failure, or areas that require improvement. Additionally, the diagram can be used as a documentation tool, providing a reference for future network modifications or expansions. In a network topology diagram, the various network components are represented by symbols or icons, with lines indicating the connections between them. The symbols can represent devices such as routers, switches, servers, computers, or even wireless access points. The lines typically represent physical cables, wireless connections, or logical connections. There are several types of network topologies that can be depicted in a diagram, including star, bus, ring, mesh, or hybrid topologies. The choice of topology depends on factors such as the size of the network, the required level of redundancy, and the type of applications running on the network. The diagram should clearly indicate the location of each component and the direction of the connections. It may also include additional details such as IP addresses, subnet masks, or VLAN assignments. Colors or labels can be used to differentiate between different types of connections or network segments. Network topology diagrams are an essential tool for network administrators to plan, design, and maintain complex networks. They provide a visual representation that simplifies the understanding of network configurations and aids in the identification and resolution of network issues. By accurately documenting the network layout, topology diagrams facilitate efficient troubleshooting and ensure the smooth operation of the network. In conclusion, a network topology diagram is a visual representation that depicts the arrangement of devices and connections in a computer network. It serves as a blueprint for network administrators, assisting them in managing, troubleshooting, and documenting the network. With its clear and concise representation, a network topology diagram is a valuable tool for efficient network operation.

Network Topology

A network topology refers to the arrangement and structure of a computer network. It defines how the different devices, such as computers, servers, switches, routers, and other networking devices, are connected and communicate with each other. There are various types of network topologies that can be used, each having its own advantages and disadvantages. These topologies determine the efficiency, reliability, scalability, and performance of the network. The most commonly used network topologies are: 1. Bus Topology: In this topology, all devices are connected to a common transmission medium, known as a bus. The devices share the same communication line and can transmit or receive data at any time. However, if the bus fails, the entire network becomes unusable. 2. Star Topology: In this topology, all devices are connected to a central networking device, such as a hub or a switch. Each device has its own dedicated connection to the central device, allowing for better fault tolerance and scalability. However, if the central device fails, the entire network is affected. 3. Ring Topology: In this topology, the devices are connected in a closed loop, forming a ring. Each device is connected to two neighboring devices, and data is transmitted in a circular manner. This topology has better fault tolerance than a bus topology, as data can flow in both directions. However, if one device fails, the entire network can be disrupted. 4. Mesh Topology: In this topology, each device is connected to every other device in the network. It provides the highest level of redundancy and fault tolerance, as multiple paths can be used for data transmission. However, it requires a large number of connections and can be more expensive to implement. 5. Tree Topology: Also known as a hierarchical topology, it resembles a tree structure, with multiple levels of devices. It combines the characteristics of bus and star topologies, allowing for better scalability and fault tolerance. However, if the central devices at higher levels fail, the lower-level devices are affected. Each network topology has its own advantages and disadvantages, and the choice depends on the specific requirements of the network, such as the number of devices, distance, cost, and desired performance. Ultimately, the network topology determines how efficiently and effectively the network functions, providing connectivity and enabling communication between devices.

Network Traffic Analysis

Network Traffic Analysis refers to the process of monitoring and analyzing the flow of data packets across a computer network. It involves capturing, examining, and interpreting network traffic to gain insights into network performance, security threats, and overall network health. Network traffic analysis plays a crucial role in network management and security as it helps network administrators and cybersecurity professionals in understanding how data is transmitted and received within a network, identifying network anomalies, detecting network intrusions, and optimizing network performance. During the process of network traffic analysis, various data points are collected, including the source and destination IP addresses, port numbers, packet size, protocols used, timestamps, and other relevant information. Tools such as network analyzers, packet sniffers, and intrusion detection systems are commonly used to capture and analyze network traffic. These tools provide valuable insights into network behavior, potential vulnerabilities, and abnormal network patterns. The analysis of network traffic allows network administrators to monitor and manage network bandwidth effectively. By identifying the types of applications and protocols consuming the most bandwidth, network administrators can optimize network resources and allocate bandwidth accordingly. This helps in maintaining a smooth and efficient network operation, ensuring that critical applications and services receive the necessary network resources. In terms of network security, traffic analysis plays a significant role in detecting and mitigating potential threats. By analyzing network traffic patterns and comparing them to known attack signatures, network administrators can identify and block malicious traffic, preventing unauthorized access and data breaches. Additionally, identifying abnormal network behavior such as frequent connection attempts, large data transfers, or other anomalies can provide early warning signs of a security breach, allowing prompt investigation and response. In conclusion, network traffic analysis is a fundamental practice in networking that involves monitoring and analyzing the flow of data packets within a network. It enables network administrators to optimize network performance, detect security threats, and ensure the efficient use of network resources. By gaining insights into network behavior, network traffic analysis helps in improving network management and cybersecurity posture.

Network Tunnelling

Network Tunnelling refers to a technique used in computer networking where a virtual tunnel is created within a physical network infrastructure. This tunnel allows the encapsulation of one network protocol within another, effectively transmitting data packets from one network to another. The encapsulation process involves wrapping the original network protocol within a different protocol, allowing the data to traverse incompatible or restricted networks. The main purpose of network tunneling is to enable communication between two networks that may not directly support the same protocols or have strict security measures in place. By encapsulating the original network protocol within a compatible one, tunneling allows data to be transmitted securely and efficiently across networks that would otherwise be incompatible with each other.

Networking Standards (E.G., IEEE 802.11)

Networking standards, such as IEEE 802.11, are established technical specifications that define the protocols and procedures for the operation, compatibility, and interoperability of computer networks and their connected devices. These standards provide a common framework and set of rules that allow different devices and network components to communicate and work together effectively. In the context of networking, IEEE 802.11 is a widely used standard that pertains specifically to wireless local area networks (WLANs). It defines the protocols and specifications for wireless communication between devices, including data transmission and reception, network access control, and security.

Node

A node in the context of networking refers to a computer or device that is connected to a network. It can be any device that is capable of sending, receiving, or forwarding data packets across the network. Nodes can vary in size and capabilities, ranging from a small personal computer or laptop to a large server or router. Every node in a network has a unique identifier called an IP address, which allows other nodes to locate and communicate with it. These IP addresses are used to route data packets to their intended destination. Nodes can be connected to a network in various ways, such as through wired connections like Ethernet cables or wireless connections like Wi-Fi.

OSI Model

The OSI (Open Systems Interconnection) Model is a conceptual framework that standardizes the functions of a communication system into seven different layers. It was developed by the International Organization for Standardization (ISO) in order to facilitate interoperability and provide a clear understanding of how different networking components interact with each other. The seven layers of the OSI Model are as follows: 1. Physical Layer: This layer is responsible for the transmission and reception of raw unstructured data bits over a physical medium. It defines the electrical, mechanical, and functional aspects of the physical network interface. 2. Data Link Layer: The main function of this layer is to provide error-free transmission of data frames between two adjacent network nodes. It ensures that data packets are delivered without errors and in the correct order. 3. Network Layer: The network layer is responsible for the logical addressing and routing of data packets between different networks. It determines the most efficient path for data transmission and handles addressing and routing protocols. 4. Transport Layer: This layer is responsible for the end-to-end reliable delivery of data between applications running on different hosts. It provides session management and ensures the segmentation and reassembly of data into smaller units. 5. Session Layer: The session layer establishes, manages, and terminates communication sessions between applications. It provides services such as session synchronization, checkpointing, and recovery. 6. Presentation Layer: The presentation layer is responsible for the formatting, encoding, and encryption of data to be transmitted across a network. It ensures that data from the application layer is readable and usable by the receiving application. 7. Application Layer: The application layer is the layer closest to the end user and provides services directly to user applications. It allows communication between applications through protocols such as HTTP, FTP, SMTP, etc. In summary, the OSI Model defines a standard framework for communication systems, allowing different networking components to work together seamlessly. It organizes the functions of a communication system into seven distinct layers, each with its own specific roles and responsibilities.

Open Shortest Path First (OSPF)

Open Shortest Path First (OSPF) is a routing protocol used in computer networks to determine the most efficient path for data packets to traverse from source to destination. It is an interior gateway protocol (IGP) that operates within a single autonomous system (AS), such as a local area network (LAN) or a wide area network (WAN). OSPF is a link-state routing protocol, which means routers exchange information about the state of their links and use this information to construct a map of the network topology. Each router maintains a database known as the link-

246

state database (LSDB), which contains information about all the routers and links within the AS. The LSDB is used to calculate the shortest path to reach a destination using a modified version of Dijkstra's algorithm. Routers in an OSPF network exchange link-state advertisements (LSAs) to inform other routers about their local links. The LSAs include information such as the router's ID, the cost of the link, and the state of the link (up or down). By exchanging LSAs, routers can build a complete picture of the network topology and update their LSDBs accordingly. The OSPF protocol uses several algorithms and mechanisms to ensure reliable and efficient routing. These include: - Area-based routing: OSPF networks are divided into areas, each with its own LSDB. This hierarchical structure reduces the size and complexity of the LSDB and allows for better scalability. - Route summarization: OSPF routers can summarize the routes within an area to reduce the amount of routing information exchanged between areas. - Route redistribution: OSPF can exchange routing information with other routing protocols, such as Border Gateway Protocol (BGP), to enable interdomain routing. Overall, OSPF is a robust and flexible routing protocol that provides fast convergence, load balancing, and support for variable-length subnet masking. It is widely used in enterprise networks and internet service providers (ISPs) to ensure efficient and reliable packet forwarding.

Open Web Application Security Project (OWASP)

The Open Web Application Security Project (OWASP) is an online community and resource center focused on improving the security of web applications. It provides transparent and unbiased information, tools, and methodologies to help organizations and individuals secure their web applications. OWASP operates based on the principles of open-source collaboration, community-driven software development, and knowledge sharing. It aims to raise awareness about the importance of web application security and promote best practices for designing, developing, and operating secure web applications.

Optical Carrier (OC)

An Optical Carrier (OC) refers to a standardized terminology and classification system used in telecommunications networks to categorize and describe the transmission capacity of optical fiber networks. It represents a level of service that defines the bandwidth and speed at which data can be transmitted over an optical network. OC levels are determined by the Synchronous Optical Network (SONET) and Synchronous Digital Hierarchy (SDH) standards, which specify the electrical, optical, and signaling characteristics of the network. These standards ensure interoperability and compatibility among different vendors' equipment and devices. The OC designation is followed by a numerical value that indicates the transmission speed of the network. The higher the numerical value, the greater the bandwidth and capacity of the network. Each OC level represents a specific line rate and total bandwidth capacity, which is measured in megabits per second (Mbps) or gigabits per second (Gbps). For example, OC-1 is the lowest level and has a transmission rate of 51.84 Mbps. It provides the capacity to transmit a single optical signal over a fiber optic cable. As the OC level increases, the bandwidth and capacity also increase. OC-3 has a transmission rate of 155.52 Mbps, while OC-48 has a transmission rate of 2.488 Gbps. OC levels are often used by service providers to offer different tiers of network services to customers. Customers can select the desired OC level based on their specific bandwidth requirements. Higher OC levels are typically employed for high-volume data transmission, such as in data centers, internet service providers, and telecommunications companies. Optical carriers are also used in conjunction with multiplexing techniques to aggregate multiple lower-speed signals into a single higher-speed OC level. This allows for efficient utilization of network resources and enables cost-effective transmission of large volumes of data. In summary, the Optical Carrier (OC) system is a standardized method for categorizing and describing the transmission capacity of optical fiber networks. It ensures compatibility among different network equipment and allows service providers to offer a range of bandwidth options to meet the diverse needs of customers.

POP3 (Post Office Protocol 3)

The Post Office Protocol 3 (POP3) is a standardized communication protocol that enables an email client to retrieve email messages from a remote server over a TCP/IP network. POP3 is commonly used for downloading email messages from a mail server to a local device for offline viewing. POP3 operates on port number 110, and it follows a client-server model where the client connects to the server, authenticates itself, and requests the server to deliver the email messages. Once the client retrieves the messages, the server typically deletes them from its storage unless otherwise instructed by the client. When a client initiates a connection to the POP3 server, it establishes a Transmission Control Protocol (TCP) connection to port 110 on the server. The client then sends a multi-line greeting message to the server, and the server responds with a greeting message along with a status code to acknowledge the connection. The client then proceeds to authenticate itself using a username and password combination. The authentication mechanism in POP3 is basic and unencrypted, which means that the username and password are sent over the network in plaintext. This lack of encryption makes POP3 vulnerable to eavesdropping and interception. However, for secure communication, the POP3 Secure (POP3S) protocol can be used, which employs Secure Sockets Layer/Transport Layer Security (SSL/TLS) encryption. After successful authentication, the client can issue various commands to interact with the server, such as retrieving messages, listing the message headers, deleting messages, and marking messages as read. Each command is sent as a short string, and the server responds with a status code to indicate the success or failure of the operation. POP3 is a stateful protocol, meaning that it keeps track of the state of the client's session with the server. This allows the client to resume interrupted downloads and retrieve only the new messages since the last session. Once the client is finished, it can terminate the session by issuing the QUIT command, which closes the TCP connection and ends the interaction with the server.

Packet Analysis

Packet analysis, in the context of networking, refers to the process of capturing and examining individual data packets that traverse a network. It involves analyzing these packets to gain insights into network performance, troubleshoot issues, and enhance security. During packet analysis, network administrators or security professionals use specialized tools called packet analyzers or network analyzers. These tools intercept and capture packets as they move through the network, allowing for detailed inspection and analysis of their contents. Packet analysis provides valuable information about various aspects of network communication. It helps in identifying network bottlenecks, congestion points, and performance issues by examining packet sequencing and timing. By analyzing network traffic patterns and the protocol headers within packets, administrators can diagnose and resolve network problems, such as high latency or packet loss. Furthermore, packet analysis assists in enhancing network security by detecting and investigating suspicious or malicious activity. Security professionals can examine packet payloads to identify signs of network intrusion, unauthorized access attempts, or data breaches. By inspecting packet headers, they can also identify potential vulnerabilities and ensure the proper implementation of security protocols. In addition to performance optimization and security, packet analysis plays a crucial role in network troubleshooting. When network issues arise, administrators can capture and analyze packets to isolate and identify the root cause of the problem. This may involve examining the contents of specific packets, such as error messages or protocol-specific information, to pinpoint the faulty component or misconfigured setting. In summary, packet analysis is the practice of capturing and analyzing individual data packets to gain insights into network performance, troubleshoot issues, and improve security. By examining packet contents, headers, and timing, administrators can optimize network performance, detect security threats, and resolve network problems effectively.

Packet Analyzer

A Packet Analyzer, also known as a network packet sniffer or a network protocol analyzer, is a software tool used to capture and analyze network traffic. It operates at the packet level, monitoring and inspecting individual data packets as they travel across a network. The primary function of a packet analyzer is to capture packets from a network interface or a specific network segment. It can be configured to capture packets on a local machine or on a remote device. Once the packets are captured, the analyzer provides detailed information about each packet, such as the source and destination IP addresses, the protocols being used, the size of the packet, and any additional network layer information. Packet analyzers allow network administrators and security professionals to examine network traffic for troubleshooting, performance monitoring, and security analysis purposes. By capturing and analyzing packets, they can gain insight into the overall health and performance of the network, identify bottlenecks, and detect any abnormal or malicious activity. Packet analyzers support various filtering and sorting capabilities, enabling users to focus on specific types of traffic or packets of interest. This can help in pinpointing the root cause of network issues or investigating security incidents. Additionally, some packet analyzers offer advanced features like session reconstruction, protocol decoding, and customizable analysis rules, allowing for more detailed and in-depth analysis of network traffic. In the field of network security, packet analyzers play a crucial role in detecting and preventing network attacks. By analyzing packet headers and payloads, security professionals can identify patterns associated with known attack signatures or anomalous behavior, thus helping to identify potential security threats and vulnerabilities. Overall, packet analyzers are an essential tool in the field of networking, providing valuable insights into network traffic for troubleshooting, performance analysis, and security monitoring purposes.

Packet Collision

A packet collision refers to a situation in networking where two or more data packets collide and interfere with each other, resulting in the loss or corruption of the transmitted information. It occurs when multiple devices attempt to send data simultaneously over a shared communication channel, such as a network cable or wireless spectrum. In most network communication protocols, data is divided into smaller units called packets for efficient transmission. Each packet contains a portion of the data along with necessary addressing and control information. When a device wants to transmit data, it checks if the communication channel is free. If so, it starts sending the packet. However, if multiple devices try to send packets at the same time, their signals can interfere with each other, causing a collision. When a packet collision occurs, the overlapping signals create a garbled or corrupted message that is unintelligible to the receiving devices. As a result, the affected packets are discarded, and the transmitting devices must reattempt sending the packets. This process of detecting and recovering from collisions is usually managed by the network protocols and protocols implemented in the network devices, such as Ethernet or Wi-Fi. To prevent packet collisions, different techniques are employed depending on the network technology. One common approach is the use of collision detection and avoidance algorithms. These algorithms allow devices to sense if the communication channel is currently being used by another device, and if so, to wait for a random period before attempting to transmit again. This helps minimize the chances of collisions. Moreover, network switches and routers are often used to segment the network and create dedicated collision domains. By dividing the network into smaller parts, collisions are limited to those occurring within each segment, reducing the overall impact on the network's performance. Additionally, the use of full-duplex communication, where devices can transmit and receive data simultaneously, eliminates the possibility of collisions altogether.

Packet Filtering Firewall

Packet Filtering Firewall is a network security device that examines the traffic flowing through a network and filters or blocks packets based on predetermined rules. It operates at the network layer of the OSI model and uses a set of specific criteria to determine whether to allow or deny the passage of packets between networks. A Packet Filtering Firewall analyzes individual packets of data as they are transmitted across a network. It looks at key fields within the packet, such as source and destination IP addresses, source and destination ports, and protocol type, to make filtering decisions. By comparing these packet attributes to a predefined rule set, the firewall determines whether to forward or discard the packet.

Packet Filtering

Packet filtering, in the context of networking, refers to the process of examining packets of data that are transmitted between devices on a network and selectively allowing or blocking them based on predetermined criteria. This filtering is typically performed by a network device, such as a router or firewall, which analyzes packets as they pass through the device. The purpose of packet filtering is to enhance network security by controlling the flow of data and preventing unauthorized access or malicious activities. It is an essential component of a network's defense mechanism, as it helps in protecting sensitive information and systems from potential threats. Packet filtering is based on the information contained in the packets themselves, primarily the headers. These headers contain important details such as source and destination IP addresses, port numbers, and protocol type. By examining this information, network devices can make decisions regarding the handling of each packet. A packet filtering device typically maintains a set of filtering rules that define what actions should be taken for different types of packets. These rules are established based on network policies and security requirements. They can allow or block packets based on various criteria, including source or destination IP addresses, port numbers, protocol type, or even specific patterns or content within the packet payload. When a packet arrives at a filtering device, it is compared against the established filtering rules in a sequential order. If a rule matches the packet's characteristics, the defined action associated with that rule is applied. This action can be allowing the packet to proceed, dropping or blocking the packet, or forwarding it to another device for further processing. Packet filtering can be applied at different points within a network, depending on the desired level of security and control. It can be implemented at the network perimeter, such as a border router, to filter incoming and outgoing traffic between different networks. It can also be used internally within a network to enforce security policies and control the flow of data between different subnets or network segments. In conclusion, packet filtering is a fundamental technique in network security that involves examining packets of data and making decisions based on pre-established rules. It helps in protecting networks from unauthorized access and malicious activities by selectively allowing or blocking packets based on specific criteria. By implementing packet filtering, organizations can enhance their network security and mitigate potential risks.

Packet Header

A packet header in the context of networking refers to the first section of a data packet that contains essential information needed for the successful transmission of the packet over a network. It is a structured collection of fields that provide instructions and identification for the data packet as it travels from the source to the destination. The packet header typically consists of various fields such as source and destination IP addresses, protocol number, packet length, and other control information. These fields play a crucial role in enabling the network devices to correctly route, process, and deliver the packets to the intended recipients.

Packet Inspection

Packet inspection, also known as deep packet inspection (DPI), is a technique used in computer networking to examine the contents of data packets in order to gain insight and control over network traffic. During the transmission of data over the network, the information is divided into small units called packets. These packets contain both the data being transmitted and metadata, which includes information about the source and destination of the packet. Packet inspection involves analyzing the contents of these packets to extract useful information and apply specific actions based on that information. Packet inspection can be performed at different levels of the networking protocol stack, including the network layer, transport layer, and application layer. At the network layer, packet inspection focuses on basic information like source and destination IP addresses. At the transport layer, it examines transport layer protocols such as TCP (Transmission Control Protocol) and UDP (User Datagram Protocol), and tracks the ports being used. At the application layer, packet inspection delves into the payload of the packets, which may include information related to specific applications or protocols such as HTTP, FTP, or VoIP. By inspecting packets, network administrators and security professionals can gain valuable insights into the network traffic flowing through their systems. It allows them to identify the type of traffic, track its origin, and monitor its behavior. For example, packet inspection can help detect malicious activity, such as attempted intrusion or data exfiltration, by analyzing packet contents for patterns or signatures associated with known attacks. It can also be used for traffic shaping and prioritization purposes, where certain types of traffic can be given higher priority or specific actions can be applied based on the type of content being transmitted.

Packet Loss Analysis

Packet loss analysis is a process in networking that involves the assessment and measurement of the loss of data packets during transmission. It refers to the undesirable occurrence of data packets being discarded or not reaching their intended destination, resulting in a disruption in communication and potential data corruption or loss.This analysis helps network administrators and engineers understand the quality and reliability of the network infrastructure by quantifying the packet loss rate and identifying potential causes. By monitoring and analyzing packet loss, network professionals can diagnose and troubleshoot network issues, optimize network performance, and ensure efficient data transmission.

Packet Loss Prevention Techniques

Packet Loss Prevention Techniques refer to the strategies and measures implemented in networking to minimize or eliminate the loss of packets during transmission. When data is transmitted over a network, it is broken down into smaller units called packets. These packets travel from the source to the destination, passing through various network devices and connections. However, due to network congestion, hardware failures, or other reasons, some packets may fail to reach their intended destination, resulting in packet loss. Packet loss can have a significant impact on network performance, causing issues such as delays, poor audio or video quality, and hindered user experience. Therefore, it is crucial to employ techniques that can prevent or mitigate packet loss and ensure reliable data transmission. One of the commonly used techniques to prevent packet loss is Error Correction. Error Correction algorithms are employed at both the sender and receiver ends to detect and correct errors in the received packets. These algorithms use various error-detection codes such as checksums or cyclic redundancy checks (CRC) to determine if any errors have occurred. If an error is detected, the receiver sends a request to the sender for retransmission of the faulty packet, thus minimizing the impact of packet loss. Another technique is Packet Forwarding or Routing. Routers play a vital role in forwarding packets from the source to the destination. By employing efficient routing algorithms, routers can divert packet traffic away from congested or faulty links, reducing the chances of packet loss. Additionally, routers use various quality-of-service (QoS) mechanisms to prioritize certain types of packets, such as real-time voice or video data, ensuring their timely delivery and minimizing the risk of loss. Network Redundancy is another important technique to prevent packet loss. By introducing redundant or backup network paths, such as multiple physical or logical connections, network administrators can ensure that if one path fails or experiences packet loss, the transmission can automatically switch to an alternative path, thus minimizing the impact on data delivery. Overall, packet loss prevention techniques ensure reliable and efficient data transmission by utilizing error correction, efficient routing, and network redundancy measures. By implementing these techniques, network administrators can optimize network performance, reduce latency, and enhance the overall user experience.

Packet Loss Prevention

Packet loss prevention in the context of networking refers to the implementation of measures and strategies to minimize or eliminate the occurrence of packet loss during data transmission over a network. In a network, data is divided into packets, which are then transmitted from a source to a destination across various network devices and links. Packet loss can occur when one or more of these packets fail to reach the destination due to various reasons such as network congestion, hardware issues, or software errors. Packet loss can have serious implications for network performance and user experience. When packets are lost, the information they contain is missing, resulting in data loss and potential disruptions in communication. This can lead to delays, retransmissions, and reduced throughput, negatively impacting the overall performance of applications and services running on the network.

Packet Loss Rate

Packet Loss Rate in the context of networking refers to the ratio of lost or discarded packets to the total number of packets transmitted. When data is transmitted across a network, it is divided into small units called packets. These packets contain both the data being sent as well as the necessary control information. Packet loss can occur when these packets are not successfully delivered to their destination. The Packet Loss Rate is typically expressed as a percentage and is used as a quantitative measure to assess the quality and reliability of a network. A low packet loss rate indicates a well-functioning and efficient network, while a high packet loss rate suggests network congestion, errors, or other issues that can adversely affect performance.

Packet Loss Recovery

Packet Loss Recovery refers to the process of recovering lost or corrupted packets in a computer network. In networking, data is divided into small units called packets, which are then transmitted over the network. These packets contain important information that needs to be successfully delivered to the destination. However, due to various factors such as network congestion, errors, or faulty hardware, packets can be lost or arrive at the destination in a corrupted state. The main goal of packet loss recovery is to ensure the reliable delivery of data by detecting and recovering lost or corrupted packets. This is achieved through various techniques, including retransmission, error detection and correction, and flow control mechanisms. One of the primary methods used for packet loss recovery is retransmission. When a packet is lost or detected as corrupted, the sender retransmits the packet to the receiver. This process is typically controlled by protocols such as TCP (Transmission Control Protocol) in the case of internet communication. The receiver acknowledges the receipt of each packet, allowing the sender to identify and retransmit any missing or corrupted packets. Error detection and correction techniques are also employed to recover lost or corrupted packets. These techniques involve adding extra bits, called check bits or checksums, to the packets. The receiver uses these check bits to verify the integrity of the received packets. If a packet is found to be corrupted, the receiver can request the sender to retransmit the packet. Flow control mechanisms play a crucial role in minimizing packet loss and ensuring efficient packet recovery. These mechanisms regulate the rate of packet transmission to avoid network congestion and buffer overflows. By controlling the flow of packets, these mechanisms prevent the loss of packets due to network congestion or overwhelmed network devices. Packet loss recovery techniques are essential for maintaining the integrity and reliability of network communications. They help to minimize the impact of packet loss on data transmission, ensuring that the intended information reaches the destination in a timely and correctly ordered manner.

Packet Loss

Packet Loss refers to the phenomenon in networking where packets of data are not successfully delivered from the source to the destination. In a network, data is divided into smaller units called packets, which are then transmitted over the network to reach their intended destination. However, due to various factors, some of these packets may not reach their destination, resulting in packet loss. Packet loss can occur for several reasons, including network congestion, hardware or software failures, and errors in transmission. When a packet is lost, it does not reach its destination and must be retransmitted, causing delays and potentially impacting overall network performance.

Packet Sniffer Tools

A packet sniffer tool, also known as a network analyzer or protocol analyzer, is a software or hardware device that captures and analyzes the network traffic passing through a specific network interface. It captures packets of data as they are transmitted over a network and provides detailed information about the communication between network devices and the protocols being used. This information includes the source and destination IP addresses, MAC addresses, port numbers, packet size, and other network layer details. Packet sniffer tools are commonly used by network administrators, security professionals, and network engineers for various purposes. Some common use cases include: 1. Network troubleshooting and problem resolution: By capturing and analyzing network traffic, administrators can identify and diagnose network issues such as slow performance, connectivity problems, or network congestion. They can also identify problematic devices or misconfigured settings. 2. Network monitoring and performance optimization: Packet sniffers help monitor network performance by providing real-time insights into network utilization, bandwidth usage, and response times. This information can be used to optimize network resources, identify bottlenecks, and improve overall network performance. 3. Security analysis and threat detection: Packet sniffers are valuable tools for network security professionals in detecting and investigating security threats. By analyzing network traffic, they can identify suspicious activity, unauthorized access attempts, malware communication, and other security vulnerabilities. 4. Protocol analysis and troubleshooting: Packet sniffers can dissect and decode network protocols to analyze their behavior and identify issues. They can be used to troubleshoot protocol-specific problems, such as compatibility issues, protocol violations, or incorrect configurations. Packet sniffers can operate in either promiscuous mode or non-promiscuous mode. Promiscuous mode allows the tool to capture and analyze all network traffic on a given interface, including traffic not intended for its host. Non-promiscuous mode only captures traffic specifically addressed to the host being monitored. Overall, packet sniffers are powerful tools for network analysis, troubleshooting, and security. They provide insights into the inner workings of a network, helping administrators maintain network integrity, optimize performance, and protect against potential threats.

Packet Sniffer

A packet sniffer, in the context of networking, refers to a software or hardware device that intercepts and captures data packets flowing through a computer network. It allows network administrators or users with sufficient privileges to monitor and analyze network traffic for various purposes such as troubleshooting, security analysis, or traffic optimization. When a computer sends or receives data over a network, it breaks the information into smaller chunks called packets. Each packet contains a portion of the data, along with header information specifying the source and destination addresses, protocol details, and other related metadata. A packet sniffer captures these packets and makes them available for analysis. Packet sniffers can be both passive and active in nature. Passive sniffers don't interfere with the network traffic and merely capture packets for monitoring purposes. In contrast, active sniffers can modify or inject packets into the network, allowing for actions like packet manipulation or protocol simulation. Packet sniffers can operate at different levels of the networking stack, including the network layer, transport layer, or even application layer. Typically, they are deployed at key points in the network infrastructure, such as switches or routers, or on individual devices themselves. To capture packets, a packet sniffer utilizes a technique known as promiscuous mode or monitor mode. In this mode, the network interface card (NIC) is set to capture all packets passing through the network, rather than just those addressed to the specific device. This enables the packet sniffer to intercept and analyze traffic that would not typically be visible to the device. Once packets are captured, a packet sniffer can provide detailed information about the network traffic. It can reveal the source and destination IP addresses, ports, protocols, and the contents of the data payload. By inspecting packet headers and payloads, network administrators can gain insights into network performance issues, security vulnerabilities, unauthorized access attempts, or other anomalous behaviors. In summary, a packet sniffer is a powerful tool for network analysis and monitoring. By capturing and analyzing network traffic, it helps in troubleshooting network issues, identifying potential security threats, and optimizing network performance.

Packet Sniffing

Packet sniffing is a network monitoring technique used to capture and analyze data packets in a network. It involves intercepting and examining the contents of packets as they are transmitted between devices on a network. When data is transmitted over a network, it is broken down into small units called packets. These packets contain information such as the source and destination IP addresses, as well as the actual data being transmitted. Packet sniffing allows network administrators or attackers to capture and inspect these packets to gain information about the network's traffic and the data being transmitted.

Packet Switched Network

A packet-switched network is a type of telecommunications network that transmits and receives data in the form of small, discrete units called packets. These packets contain both the data being transmitted and control information, such as the source and destination addresses. Unlike circuit-switched networks, which create a dedicated communication path between the sender and receiver for the duration of a conversation, packet-switched networks divide data into packets and send them independently across the network. When a device wants to send data over a packet-switched network, the data is first divided into packets of a fixed size. Each packet is then assigned a header that contains information necessary for routing and reassembling the packets at the destination. The packets are then sent from the source device to the network, where they are individually routed to their respective destinations based on the information in their headers. Packet-switched networks offer several advantages over circuit-switched networks. Firstly, they are more efficient in terms of bandwidth utilization. Since data is divided into packets, networks can accommodate multiple conversations happening simultaneously, making more efficient use of available resources. Additionally, packet-switched networks are more resilient to failures because packets can be rerouted around failed connections, ensuring that data can still reach its destination. Common examples of packet-switched networks include the Internet, where data is divided into packets and sent across numerous routers to reach its intended destination. Other examples include local area networks (LANs) and wide area networks (WANs).

253

Packet Switching Network Architecture

Packet switching is a network architecture that enables the transmission of data across a computer network by breaking it down into small packets. Each packet contains a portion of the original data, along with source and destination addresses, in order to facilitate its routing through the network. Unlike circuit-switched networks, packet switching allows network resources to be shared efficiently among multiple users, making it a more flexible and scalable approach to data transmission. In a packet switching network, the data to be transmitted is divided into fixed-size packets before being sent. Each packet is then independently routed through the network based on its destination address, allowing it to take different paths to reach its destination. This decentralized routing mechanism ensures that packets can be transmitted concurrently, improving overall network efficiency. Packet switching networks employ various protocols to ensure the reliable delivery of data packets. One such protocol is the Internet Protocol (IP), which is used in the global network known as the Internet. IP ensures that each packet is correctly addressed and routed to its destination by adding source and destination IP addresses to the packet header. This allows routers in the network to forward the packet based on the destination address, using routing tables to determine the optimal path. Another important protocol used in packet switching networks is the Transmission Control Protocol (TCP). TCP provides reliable, connection-oriented transmission of data across the network. It ensures that packets are delivered in the correct order, without errors or duplications, by assigning sequence numbers to each packet and using acknowledgments to confirm successful transmission. Overall, packet switching network architecture offers several advantages over other networking approaches. It allows for efficient utilization of network resources, as packets can be transmitted concurrently and routed dynamically. It also provides robustness and fault tolerance, as packets can be rerouted if a network link or node fails. Additionally, packet switching enables the integration of different types of data, including voice and video, into a single network, facilitating multimedia communication.

Packet Switching Vs. Circuit Switching Comparison

Packet switching and circuit switching are two different methods of transmitting data in a network. Packet switching involves breaking the data into smaller units called packets, which are then sent individually over the network. Each packet contains a portion of the data, as well as information about its destination address. These packets take different routes to reach their destination, and they may arrive at different times. Upon arrival, they are reassembled to form the complete message. This method allows for efficient utilization of network resources, as multiple packets can be sent over the same channel simultaneously. It also provides robustness, as if one packet gets lost or delayed, the others can still reach their destination. Packet switching is used in modern networks, including the Internet. Circuit switching, on the other hand, establishes a dedicated path between the sender and receiver before any data transfer takes place. This path, known as a circuit, remains open for the entire duration of the communication. During this time, all data is transmitted along this path. Circuit switching guarantees a constant and uninterrupted connection between the sender and receiver, which makes it suitable for real-time applications such as voice and video calls. However, it may lead to inefficient use of network resources, as the circuit remains open even when there is no data being transmitted. Circuit switching was commonly used in traditional telephone networks.

Packet Switching Vs. Circuit Switching

Packet Switching: Packet switching is a method used in computer networks to transmit data by breaking it into smaller units called packets. Each packet contains a portion of the data along with additional information such as the source and destination addresses. These packets are then sent individually over the network and can take different paths to reach their destination. At the destination, the packets are reassembled in the correct order to recreate the original data. Packet switching offers several advantages in networking. Firstly, it allows multiple packets to be transmitted simultaneously, which improves overall network efficiency. Since each packet can take a different route, packet switching also provides fault tolerance and resilience. If a particular network path is busy or has failed, the packets can be rerouted through alternative paths. Additionally, packet switching allows for different types of data to be transmitted concurrently, such as voice, video, and text, as each packet is labeled with the necessary information. Circuit Switching: Circuit switching is a method used in telecommunication networks to establish a

254

dedicated connection between two devices for the duration of a communication session. Unlike packet switching, circuit switching requires the availability of a continuous path or circuit between the sender and receiver. When a connection is established, a dedicated circuit is allocated exclusively for that communication, regardless of whether data is being transmitted or not. Circuit switching offers predictable and guaranteed bandwidth, as the entire capacity of the circuit is reserved for the communication session. This makes it well-suited for real-time applications such as voice calls, where a consistent and uninterrupted connection is essential. However, it can be less efficient for data transmission, especially for sporadic or bursty communication, as unused circuit capacity cannot be utilized by other communication sessions.

Packet Switching Vs. IP Routing

Packet switching is a networking technology that breaks data into small units called packets. These packets are then individually routed to their destination through the network. Each packet contains a portion of the data being transmitted, along with source and destination addresses. The network infrastructure makes decisions on how to route packets based on the current network conditions. This method of data transmission allows for efficient use of network resources and improved transmission reliability. IP routing, on the other hand, is a specific type of packet switching that uses the Internet Protocol (IP) as the primary protocol for routing packets. IP routing involves the use of routers, which are devices that forward packets between different networks. Routers make routing decisions based on the destination IP address contained in each packet. These decisions are determined by network routing protocols, which provide instructions on how to efficiently route packets through the network.

Packet Switching Vs. Message Switching

Packet switching is a method of transmitting data in a network by breaking it into smaller, discrete units called packets. These packets contain both the data being transmitted and control information, such as the source and destination addresses. When a device sends data over a packet-switched network, the data is divided into packets and each packet is individually addressed. Message switching, on the other hand, is a method of transmitting data in a network by sending complete messages from the source to the destination. Instead of breaking the data into smaller packets, the entire message is sent as a whole. This means that the source device must wait for the entire message to be received by the destination before sending the next message.

Packet Switching Vs. Packet Routing

Packet Switching refers to the method of transmitting data over a network by dividing it into smaller units called packets. Each packet contains the necessary information for routing it through the network, including the source and destination addresses. These packets are then independently routed through the network and reassembled at the destination to reconstruct the original data. Packet Routing, on the other hand, is the process of determining the best path or route for forwarding packets from the source to the destination. It involves the use of routing algorithms that consider various factors such as network congestion, link quality, and distance to efficiently deliver packets. In packet switching, the emphasis is on the division of data into packets and their independent routing across the network. It allows for more efficient resource utilization as different packets can be transmitted simultaneously over the network. This enables better utilization of network capacity and faster data transmission. Packet routing, on the other hand, focuses on finding the most optimal path for each packet to reach its destination. It involves the examination of the packet's destination address and the selection of the next hop along the route based on the available network information. Routing algorithms are employed to make decisions on the best path to minimize delays and maximize network efficiency. Packet switching and packet routing are essential components of modern computer networks. They enable efficient and reliable data transmission by breaking down information into smaller units (packets) and intelligently routing them through the network. This approach allows for robust and scalable communication across diverse network topologies. In summary, packet switching refers to the process of dividing data into smaller units (packets) and independently routing them through the network, while packet routing focuses on determining the best path for forwarding each packet based on network conditions. These techniques work together to ensure efficient and reliable data transmission in computer networks.

Packet Switching

Packet switching is a data transmission method used in computer networks where large amounts of data are divided into smaller packets for transmission across a network. Each packet contains a portion of the original data along with control information, such as the source and destination addresses. In a packet switching network, when data is sent from a source device, it is divided into small packets. These packets are then individually sent across the network to the destination device. As each packet arrives at a network router or switch, it is forwarded to the next hop on its route based on the destination address contained in the packet header. Packet switching offers several advantages over other data transmission methods, such as circuit switching. Firstly, it allows for more efficient use of network resources by dividing data into packets and sending them individually. This means that multiple packets can be transmitted simultaneously on different paths, resulting in faster and more efficient data transmission. Secondly, packet switching networks are more resilient to failures. If a link or node in the network becomes congested or fails, packets can be rerouted on alternative paths, ensuring that data can still be transmitted successfully. This is in contrast to circuit switching, where a single dedicated path is established for the entire duration of the communication. Furthermore, packet switching enables the prioritization of certain types of data, such as voice or video packets in real-time applications. By assigning different levels of priority to packets, network administrators can ensure that time-sensitive data is delivered with minimal delay and that bandwidth is efficiently utilized. In conclusion, packet switching is a data transmission method used in computer networks that divides data into smaller packets for more efficient and resilient transmission. It allows for the simultaneous transmission of multiple packets, rerouting in case of network failures, and prioritization of time-sensitive data.

Packet

A packet refers to a unit of data transmitted over a network. It is a fundamental component of network communication, particularly in packet-switched networks like the Internet. Each packet contains both the data being transmitted and its associated control information. In the context of networking, packets are used to manage and deliver data efficiently and reliably across networks, often traversing multiple devices and networks to reach their destination. They are used to segment data into smaller, manageable units that can be easily transmitted and reassembled at the receiving end. A typical packet consists of a header and a payload. The header contains important information used for routing and delivery, such as the source and destination addresses, sequence numbers, error checking codes, and other control information. The payload, on the other hand, contains the actual data being transmitted, such as a file, an email message, or a web page. When data is transferred across a network, it is broken down into packets at the sender's end. Each packet is independently addressed and can take a different route to reach its destination. This allows for greater flexibility and efficiency in network communication, as packets can utilize different network paths based on current congestion, availability, or other factors. At the receiving end, packets are reassembled based on their sequence numbers and other control information. This process ensures that the original data is reconstructed accurately and delivered to the appropriate destination. Packets are crucial for network reliability and performance, as they enable efficient sharing of network resources, error detection and correction, congestion control, and improved overall network performance. They also allow for different types of data, such as voice, video, and text, to be transmitted simultaneously over the same network infrastructure. In summary, packets are the building blocks of network communication, allowing for the efficient transmission and delivery of data across networks. They contain both the data being transmitted and important control information, ensuring reliable and optimized network communication.

Passive Optical Network (PON)

A Passive Optical Network (PON) is a telecommunications technology that allows multiple users to share a single fiber optic connection. It is a cost-effective and efficient solution for providing high-speed internet access, voice, and video services to residential and business customers. PON is a passive network, meaning that it does not require active electronic components or power in the distribution network. Instead, it uses passive optical splitters to divide the signal from the service provider and distribute it to individual subscribers. This eliminates the need for expensive and complex equipment at each subscriber's location. The key components of a PON

256

include the Optical Line Terminal (OLT) at the service provider's facility, the Optical Network Unit (ONU) or Optical Network Terminal (ONT) at the subscriber's premises, and the passive optical splitters in between. The OLT acts as the central point of control and aggregation, while the ONUs/ONTs serve as the interface between the fiber optic network and the subscriber's devices. One of the main advantages of a PON is its ability to support multiple services over a single fiber optic link. This allows service providers to deliver high-speed internet, voice, and video services simultaneously, optimizing their network resources and reducing costs. PONs also offer symmetric speeds, meaning that the upload and download speeds are the same, providing a more balanced and consistent user experience. PONs are known for their scalability and flexibility. They can easily accommodate new subscribers by adding more ONUs/ONTs and optical splitters without significant network modifications. This makes PONs a cost-effective solution for expanding network coverage and increasing capacity as demand grows. Another advantage of PONs is their inherent security. Since the network is passive and does not require active electronic components, it is less vulnerable to hacking and unauthorized access. Additionally, PONs do not suffer from electromagnetic interference, making them more reliable and less susceptible to environmental disturbances.

Passive Vulnerability Scanning

Passive vulnerability scanning, in the context of networking, refers to the process of identifying security vulnerabilities in a network infrastructure without actively engaging with it. Unlike active scanning, which involves actively probing network devices and systems, passive scanning focuses on the collection and analysis of network data and traffic. Passive vulnerability scanning works by monitoring network traffic and analyzing it for potential vulnerabilities and security weaknesses. It does not generate any network traffic itself or attempt to interact with network devices. Instead, it listens to network communications, captures packets, and analyzes the information contained within them. Passive scanning techniques can be classified into two main categories: network traffic analysis and vulnerability identification. Network traffic analysis involves the monitoring and analysis of network packets, looking for patterns or anomalies that could indicate a security vulnerability. This can include analyzing network protocols, examining header information, and even decrypting encrypted traffic. By analyzing the network traffic, passive scanning can identify potential security vulnerabilities, such as misconfigurations, outdated software versions, or unpatched systems. Vulnerability identification focuses on the detection of known vulnerabilities in network devices and systems. This typically involves comparing network traffic and system data against a database of known vulnerabilities, such as the Common Vulnerabilities and Exposures (CVE) database. Passive scanning tools can automatically match the observed network traffic patterns or system configurations with known vulnerabilities, providing network administrators with information about potential weaknesses in their infrastructure. Passive vulnerability scanning provides several advantages over active scanning methods. Firstly, it is non-intrusive and does not disrupt network operations. This makes it particularly suitable for environments where active scanning may be prohibited or highly regulated, such as in government or financial institutions. Additionally, passive scanning is less likely to trigger security alarms or generate false positives, as it does not interact directly with network devices. However, a potential limitation of passive scanning is that it relies on observing network traffic and system data as it naturally occurs. This means that it may not detect vulnerabilities that are only triggered by specific network interactions or user actions. Moreover, passive scanning is generally less comprehensive than active scanning, as it may not detect vulnerabilities that are not exposed through network communications.

Password Cracking

Password cracking is a process of attempting to gain unauthorized access to user accounts or systems by guessing or recovering passwords. It is a security vulnerability that poses a significant threat to network security. In a networking context, password cracking involves using various techniques and tools to decipher passwords that are used to authenticate and authorize access to networks, computers, and online accounts. The purpose of such cracking attempts can be malicious, where attackers exploit weak or easily guessable passwords to gain unauthorized access to sensitive information or to carry out illegal activities. Password cracking can be categorized into two main types: offline and online cracking. Offline cracking involves analyzing password hashes that are stored in the system or network to determine the plaintext passwords. This is achieved through various methods such as brute-forcing, dictionary attacks,

257

rainbow tables, and various cracking algorithms. Online cracking, on the other hand, involves directly attacking the authentication system by attempting to guess passwords using techniques like brute-forcing, social engineering, or using password cracking software. The consequences of password cracking can be severe. Successful cracking can grant unauthorized access to sensitive data, compromise user accounts, and lead to various forms of cybercrimes such as identity theft, data breaches, or financial fraud. It can also lead to significant financial and reputation damage for organizations. To mitigate the risk of password cracking, strong security measures should be implemented. This includes enforcing the usage of complex and unique passwords, implementing multi-factor authentication, regularly updating and patching systems, and conducting frequent security audits. Organizations should also educate their users about the importance of secure password practices and provide guidelines on creating and managing strong passwords.

Password Policy

A password policy in the context of networking refers to a set of rules and guidelines that define the requirements and restrictions for creating and managing passwords within a network environment. This policy serves as a security measure to protect sensitive information and prevent unauthorized access to network resources. The password policy typically includes various elements such as password complexity, password length, password expiration, password history, and account lockout settings. These requirements help ensure that passwords are strong and not easily guessable, reducing the risk of compromise.

Patch Management

Patch management is a crucial aspect of networking that involves the systematic process of acquiring, testing, and deploying patches or updates to software applications and devices within a network infrastructure. It is essential for maintaining the security, stability, and functionality of computer systems and preventing vulnerabilities and exploits that may be exploited by malicious individuals or malware. Patch management is an ongoing process that is necessary for both individual devices and entire networks.

Payload

A payload, in the context of networking, refers to the data or information that is being transmitted over a network. It is the actual content or message that is being sent from one device to another. When data is sent over a network, it is encapsulated in different layers of a network protocol stack. The payload resides in the upper layer of this protocol stack, typically the application layer. For example, when you send an email, the payload is the actual text of the email along with any attachments. Similarly, when you visit a website, the payload includes the HTML, CSS, and JavaScript files that make up the webpage. The payload is accompanied by various control information and headers as it traverses through the different layers of the network protocol stack. These headers provide important information such as the source and destination addresses, as well as information about the data itself, such as the length or type of the payload. Once the data reaches its destination, the payload is extracted from the headers and processed by the appropriate application or service. For example, an email client will extract the payload of an email and display it to the user, while a web browser will parse the HTML payload and render the webpage. The size and nature of the payload can have an impact on network performance. Larger payloads require more bandwidth and can potentially congest the network, leading to slower transmission speeds. Additionally, certain types of payloads, such as multimedia files or large datasets, may require specialized protocols or optimizations to ensure efficient and reliable delivery.

Peer-To-Peer Network Architecture

Peer-to-Peer (P2P) network architecture is a decentralized distributed network design that allows individual devices in the network, referred to as peers, to act as both clients and servers. In this architecture, there is no central server or hierarchy, as peers have equal rights and capabilities. In a P2P network, each peer can initiate communication and contribute resources such as processing power, storage, or bandwidth to other peers in the network. This allows for efficient utilization of resources and promotes scalability. Peers can join or leave the network dynamically without disrupting the overall network operations.

Peer-To-Peer (P2P) Network

A Peer-to-Peer (P2P) network is a type of network where multiple devices (or peers) are connected and can communicate with each other directly, without the need for a central server or authority. In a P2P network, all devices can act as both clients and servers, meaning they can initiate and accept connections from other devices in the network. The devices in the network are equal peers and have the same capabilities and responsibilities. P2P networks are commonly used for file sharing, where users can directly exchange files with each other without relying on a central server. Instead, each user's device functions as both a client and a server, allowing them to download files from other devices and simultaneously share files with others. One of the advantages of P2P networks is their resilience. Since there is no central server, the network can continue to operate even if individual devices fail or leave the network. The distributed nature of P2P networks also reduces the risk of a single point of failure and makes them more scalable. P2P networks can be either structured or unstructured. In structured P2P networks, devices are organized in a specific structure or hierarchy, such as a distributed hash table (DHT), which allows for efficient searching and retrieval of files. On the other hand, unstructured P2P networks have no specific organization and rely on flooding or random search algorithms to discover files. While P2P networks offer several benefits, they also pose some challenges. Due to the direct communication between devices, P2P networks may be more susceptible to security threats, such as malware or malicious attacks. They also require a certain level of collaboration and cooperation among peers to ensure the network functions properly. In conclusion, a Peer-to-Peer network is a decentralized network where devices can directly communicate and share resources with each other without the need for a central server. P2P networks are commonly used for file sharing and can be either structured or unstructured. While they offer resilience and scalability, they also present security challenges that need to be addressed.

Penetration Testing Report

A penetration testing report, in the context of networking, is a formal document that outlines the findings and recommendations resulting from a systematic evaluation of the security of a computer network or system. This evaluation, commonly known as a penetration test or a pen test, is conducted by a skilled and authorized IT professional with the objective of identifying vulnerabilities or weaknesses that could potentially be exploited by malicious individuals or groups. The purpose of a penetration test is to simulate real-world cyber attacks, allowing organizations to identify potential security risks and take appropriate measures to address them.

Penetration Testing

Penetration Testing, also known as Pen Testing, is a formal evaluation process that assesses the security of a computer network or system. It involves the simulation of real-world attacks to identify vulnerabilities that could potentially be exploited by malicious individuals or groups. During a Penetration Test, a team of ethical hackers, known as penetration testers, attempts to exploit the network or system using various methods and tools. The objective is to identify weaknesses and provide recommendations for strengthening security controls.

Pentest Report

A pentest report in the context of networking is a formal document that summarizes the findings, vulnerabilities, and recommendations identified during a network penetration test. The purpose of a pentest report is to provide an in-depth analysis of the network's security posture and to outline steps that need to be taken to mitigate the identified risks. It serves as a critical communication tool between the penetration testers and the stakeholders of the network, such as the management team, network administrators, and security professionals. The structure of a pentest report typically follows a standardized format, including an executive summary, methodology, findings, and recommendations. The executive summary provides a high-level overview of the pentest, highlighting the most critical vulnerabilities and their potential impact. It helps the stakeholders quickly comprehend the key findings without delving into technical details. The methodology section outlines the approach, tools, and techniques employed during the penetration testing process. It details the scope of the assessment, the steps taken to exploit vulnerabilities, and any limitations encountered. This section helps the stakeholders understand the rigor of the testing process and the credibility of the findings. The findings section is the heart of the pentest report, presenting a comprehensive analysis of the identified vulnerabilities and their severity. It includes detailed descriptions of each vulnerability, along with supporting evidence and technical details. The severity of the vulnerabilities is typically rated using a standardized scoring system, such as the Common Vulnerability Scoring System (CVSS). Finally, the recommendations section provides actionable steps to address the identified vulnerabilities and enhance the network's overall security. These recommendations may include patching vulnerable systems, reconfiguring network devices, enhancing access controls, or implementing additional security measures. Each recommendation should be prioritized based on its severity and potential impact on the network's security. Overall, a pentest report serves as a critical tool for assessing and improving the security posture of a network. It helps the stakeholders understand the existing vulnerabilities, comprehend their potential impact, and guides them in making informed decisions to address these issues effectively.

Pharming

Pharming is a malicious technique in the realm of networking where cybercriminals manipulate the domain name system (DNS) to deceive users and redirect them to fraudulent websites. This method involves compromising the DNS server or the user's device to tamper with the DNS resolution process, leading to unsuspecting users being redirected to an attacker-controlled website instead of the legitimate one they intended to visit. Pharming attacks can be conducted in various ways. One common method is through the use of malware, such as a Trojan horse or a virus, that modifies the DNS settings on the victim's computer. By doing so, the malware is able to redirect the user's requests for a specific website to a fake version of that site hosted by the attacker. The manipulated website is designed to resemble the original, often to deceive users into providing sensitive information like login credentials, credit card details, or personal information. Another approach to pharming involves targeting DNS servers directly. Here, attackers exploit vulnerabilities in the server's software or gain unauthorized access to it, allowing them to alter DNS records. By changing the IP address associated with a particular domain name, the attackers can ensure that any requests to that domain are redirected to their malicious website. This method can affect multiple users simultaneously, making it a potentially lucrative technique for cybercriminals. Pharming poses a significant threat to internet users, as it can be challenging to detect. Unlike phishing attacks, where users might be wary of suspicious emails or links, pharming redirects users to fake websites seamlessly, making it more difficult for them to discern its illegitimacy. Additionally, since the attack occurs at the DNS level, even users who enter the correct website address manually or through bookmarks can be redirected to a fraudulent site. To protect against pharming attacks, users are advised to keep their devices and software up to date with the latest security patches. It is also crucial to use reputable antivirus and anti-malware software to detect and remove any malicious code that may be present. Verifying the legitimacy of website addresses before entering sensitive information is paramount as well. Users should look for secure connections (HTTPS) and check for any obvious inconsistencies or warning signs on the website. Lastly, organizations and ISPs can implement secure DNS resolution protocols, such as DNSSEC, to provide an additional layer of protection against pharming attacks. In conclusion, pharming is a technique employed by cybercriminals to manipulate the DNS system and redirect users to fraudulent websites, often with the goal of stealing sensitive information. It is a significant threat that requires vigilance and preventative measures from both users and organizations alike.

Phishing Kit

A phishing kit, in the context of networking, refers to a set of malicious tools and resources designed to deceive individuals or organizations into providing sensitive information such as personal credentials, financial details, or login credentials for online accounts. These kits are typically created and utilized by cybercriminals for conducting phishing attacks, which are fraudulent attempts to obtain sensitive information through deceptive means. The goal of phishing is to trick the target into thinking they are interacting with a legitimate and trustworthy entity, such as a well-known organization or service provider.

Phishing

Phishing is a deceptive technique used by cybercriminals to obtain sensitive information, such as usernames, passwords, and financial details, by impersonating trustworthy entities through electronic communications. These communications may be in the form of email, instant messages, text messages, or even phone calls, where the attacker poses as a legitimate source, such as a bank, social media platform, or online service provider. The main objective of phishing attacks is to manipulate the target into giving away their confidential information by tricking them into believing that they are interacting with a trusted entity. The attacker typically employs various tactics to deceive the victim, including creating authentic-looking websites, forging emails with official logos and branding, and using social engineering techniques to evoke urgency or fear, thereby coercing the victim to take action without questioning the authenticity of the request. Once the victim falls into the phisher's trap and provides the requested information, the attacker can use it for fraudulent activities, such as unauthorized access to online accounts, identity theft, or financial fraud. Phishing attacks can also serve as a gateway for more sophisticated cybersecurity threats, including malware, ransomware, or advanced persistent threats (APTs), leading to significant financial losses, reputational damage, and compromised data security. To protect against phishing, it is essential to remain vigilant and adopt preventive measures. These include: - Verifying the authenticity of communication by independently visiting the official website or using verified contact information instead of clicking on links or replying directly. - Ignoring or deleting suspicious emails, messages, or calls that request sensitive information or appear unusual. - Keeping software, browsers, and security applications up to date, as they often include protections against known phishing techniques. - Using strong, unique passwords and enabling two-factor authentication (2FA) whenever possible to mitigate the impact of potential credential theft. - Educating oneself and others about phishing techniques and raising awareness about common indicators of fraudulent communication.

Physical Layer

The Physical Layer is the first layer of the OSI model and is responsible for the transmission and reception of unstructured raw data bits over a physical medium. It establishes and manages the physical connection between network devices, ensuring that data can be reliably transmitted across the network. The Physical Layer deals with the electrical, mechanical, and procedural aspects of transmitting data. It defines the physical characteristics of the network, such as voltage levels, signaling rates, and physical connectors. It also defines the type of transmission media used, such as copper wire, fiber-optic cable, or wireless signals. At this layer, data is transmitted in the form of electrical signals, light pulses, or radio waves, depending on the type of transmission medium being used. The Physical Layer translates the digital data received from the Data Link Layer into a form that can be transmitted over the physical medium. The Physical Layer is responsible for encoding and decoding data bits into a format suitable for transmission. It converts the data into a series of 0s and 1s, which are then transformed into physical signals that can be transmitted over the network. This process is known as modulation. To ensure reliable transmission, the Physical Layer also performs tasks such as error detection and correction. It adds additional bits to the transmitted data to detect transmission errors and correct them when possible. Error detection and correction techniques such as parity check and checksums are commonly used at this layer. In addition, the Physical Layer handles the synchronization between sender and receiver devices. It ensures that both ends of the communication are operating at the same speed and are in sync, so that data can be transmitted and received accurately. Overall, the Physical Layer plays a crucial role in establishing the physical connection between network devices and enables the transmission of data across the network. It handles the physical characteristics of the network and ensures that data can be sent and received reliably.

Physical Security

Physical security, in the context of networking, refers to the protection of physical infrastructure, equipment, and resources that support the telecommunications and information technology systems. This encompasses measures taken to safeguard data centers, server rooms, network equipment, and other critical assets from unauthorized access, theft, damage, and environmental hazards. The goal is to prevent physical breaches that could compromise the confidentiality, integrity, and availability of network systems and data.

Ping Flood Attack

A Ping Flood Attack is a type of Denial of Service (DoS) attack that targets a network by overwhelming it with a flood of ICMP echo request packets, also known as ping packets. This attack is designed to consume network resources and make a network or host unable to respond to legitimate requests. In a Ping Flood Attack, the attacker uses a tool or script to send a large number of ping packets to the target network or host. These ping packets are sent at an extremely fast rate, creating a flood of traffic. The goal of the attacker is to exhaust the network's bandwidth, processing power, or other resources, causing a disruption in service. Ping Flood Attacks can be executed in various ways, such as: - Smurf Attack: The attacker spoofs the victim's IP address and sends ping requests to multiple broadcast addresses. The network replies to these requests, flooding the victim's network with a large volume of ping replies. - Ping of Death: The attacker sends oversized ping packets that exceed the maximum allowed size of 65,535 bytes. When the victim's system receives these oversized packets, it may crash or become unresponsive, causing a denial of service. - ICMP Flood: The attacker sends a continuous stream of ping packets to the target system, overwhelming its capacity to process and respond to legitimate network requests. Network administrators can defend against Ping Flood Attacks by implementing various mitigation techniques, such as: - Rate Limiting: Limiting the number of ICMP echo requests allowed per second to prevent an overwhelming flood of ping packets. - Filtering: Using firewall rules to filter and block suspicious or excessive ICMP traffic. - Intrusion Detection Systems (IDS): Implementing IDS tools to detect and alert on Ping Flood Attacks in real-time. In conclusion, a Ping Flood Attack is a malicious activity that inundates a network or host with a large volume of ping packets, leading to a denial of service. It is essential for network administrators to implement appropriate security measures to mitigate the impact of such attacks and ensure the availability and stability of the network.

Ping Of Death

The Ping of Death is a type of attack that targets computer networks, specifically the Internet Protocol (IP) communication protocol. It involves sending an oversized or malformed Internet Control Message Protocol (ICMP) echo request packet, commonly known as a ping packet, to a target host or network device. The objective of the Ping of Death attack is to create a denial of service (DoS) or a distributed denial of service (DDoS) condition by overwhelming the target's network or system resources with these malformed packets. The oversized or malformed ping packet can confuse or crash the target device, leading to system instability, network congestion, or even a complete shutdown.

Ping

Networking is the practice of connecting devices and systems together to facilitate communication and the sharing of resources. In this context, "ping" refers to a utility used to test the reachability and responsiveness of a networked device or host. The ping utility sends small packets of data to a specific IP address or domain name and measures the time it takes for those packets to reach the destination and return back to the sender. It is commonly used to diagnose network connectivity issues and determine if a particular device or host is reachable. When a ping command is initiated, the utility starts by sending an Internet Control Message Protocol (ICMP) Echo Request message to the specified IP address or domain name. The receiving device or host will then generate an ICMP Echo Reply message, indicating that the connection is established and the device is operational. Ping can provide valuable information such as the round-trip time (RTT) between the sender and the recipient, as well as the rate of packet loss. A successful ping with a low RTT indicates that the network connection is stable and responsive. On the other hand, a failed ping or a ping with a high RTT may indicate network congestion, connectivity problems, or a non-responsive device. Ping is an essential tool for network administrators and technicians. It allows them to quickly identify and troubleshoot connectivity issues, determine if a device or host is active, assess network performance, and validate network configurations. Ping can be used to test connections within a local area network (LAN) or across the internet. In summary, ping is a networking utility used to test the reachability and responsiveness of a networked device or host. It sends small packets of data and measures the time it takes for them to travel between the sender and the recipient. Ping is commonly used for network troubleshooting and performance assessment.

Point Of Presence (PoP)

In networking, Point of Presence (PoP) refers to a physical location within a telecommunication network where network service providers interconnect their networks and exchange traffic. It can be a building, a data center, or even a specific site within a larger facility. At a PoP, network service providers set up networking equipment, such as routers, switches, and servers, to enable connectivity and facilitate the transfer of data between different networks. The PoP serves as a key aggregation and distribution point for traffic flowing through the network. The primary purpose of a PoP is to improve network efficiency and reduce latency by establishing direct connections between different networks. By colocating their infrastructure at a PoP, service providers can establish peering relationships and exchange traffic without having to rely on third-party networks or Internet Service Providers (ISPs). This direct interconnection allows for faster and more efficient data transfer, as it minimizes the number of hops and potential bottlenecks in the network. Furthermore, a PoP also plays a crucial role in providing network services to end-users. Internet Service Providers often establish PoPs in strategic locations to ensure better coverage and connection quality for their customers. By having a presence in multiple PoPs, ISPs can distribute their network infrastructure geographically, creating a more robust and reliable network. This distributed architecture helps to minimize the impact of localized network failures and improve overall network performance. In addition to facilitating interconnection and enhancing network performance, PoPs also provide other value-added services. These services may include content caching, content delivery, colocation of servers, and hosting services. By leveraging the infrastructure already present at a PoP, service providers can offer these services to their customers, enhancing the overall network experience. In summary, a Point of Presence (PoP) in networking serves as a physical location where service providers interconnect their networks, exchange traffic, and improve network efficiency. It acts as a key aggregation and distribution point, facilitating direct interconnections between different networks. By colocating infrastructure at PoPs, service providers improve the performance and reliability of their networks while also offering value-added services to end-users.

Point-To-Point Protocol (PPP)

Point-to-Point Protocol (PPP) refers to a networking protocol that facilitates the establishment and management of a direct connection between two devices over a serial interface, such as a modem or serial cable. PPP is primarily utilized to connect a computer (known as the client) to a remote network or server (known as the server) through a Point-to-Point Protocol link. PPP serves as a reliable and efficient communication protocol for transmitting data packets over a serial link. It provides a means to encapsulate and transport multiprotocol datagrams, enabling the transmission of various network-layer protocols. PPP operates at the Data Link Layer of the OSI model, ensuring the successful transfer of data between the source and destination. PPP offers several key features that contribute to its widespread usage in networking environments. These features include authentication, compression, error detection, and dynamic IP address assignment. Authentication involves verifying the identity of the connecting devices, ensuring that only authorized users gain access to the network. Compression minimizes the size of the transmitted data, optimizing bandwidth utilization. Error detection mechanisms allow for the identification and correction of data transmission errors. Dynamic IP address assignment enables the automatic allocation of IP addresses to connected clients, simplifying network configuration. PPP operates through a series of distinct phases to establish and maintain the connection between devices. These phases include the Link Establishment Phase, Authentication Phase, Network Layer Protocol Phase, and Network Control Protocol Phase. During the Link Establishment Phase, the client and server negotiate connection parameters, such as link speed and encapsulation type. The Authentication Phase involves the verification of credentials to ensure a secure connection. In the Network Layer Protocol Phase, the selected network-layer protocol to be used over the PPP link is identified. Finally, the Network Control Protocol Phase facilitates the configuration and management of various network services and options. In summary, PPP serves as a reliable and versatile protocol for establishing a direct connection between two devices over a serial interface. Its features, including authentication, compression, error detection, and dynamic IP address assignment, contribute to its effectiveness in transmitting data over networks. Through a series of well-defined phases, PPP enables the establishment and management of secure and efficient connections in networking environments.

Port Forwarding Methods

Port forwarding is a networking technique used to direct traffic from an external network, such as the internet, to a specific device or service within a private network. It enables incoming connections to traverse through the network's router or gateway and reach the desired destination. The process involves mapping a specific port on the public IP address of the network to a port on the internal IP address of the device or service that needs to receive the incoming traffic. There are three common methods used for port forwarding: virtual server, port triggering, and UPnP. The virtual server method allows a specific port on the external IP address to be forwarded to a specific port on an internal device or service. This method is commonly used for services like web servers, gaming servers, or remote desktop applications. Port triggering, on the other hand, dynamically opens a specific port or ports when a particular outbound connection or application is detected. It ensures that the required ports are only open when needed, enhancing security. Lastly, the UPnP (Universal Plug and Play) method allows certain devices to automatically set up port forwarding rules without any manual configuration. It simplifies the process for non-technical users but may introduce potential security risks.

Port Forwarding Techniques

Port forwarding techniques refer to the methods used in networking to redirect network traffic from a specific port on a network gateway to a specific device or service within a local network. It allows external devices or services to communicate with a specific device or service behind a network gateway by mapping a public IP address and port to a private IP address and port within the local network. There are several types of port forwarding techniques commonly used in networking: 1. Local Port Forwarding: This technique is used to forward traffic from a local port on the client machine to a remote host or service on the server. It creates a secure tunnel between the client and server, allowing the client to access remote resources securely. 2. Remote Port Forwarding: This technique is the opposite of local port forwarding. It forwards traffic from a remote port on the server to a local port on the client. It is often used to expose local network services behind a firewall or NAT configuration to the external network. 3. Dynamic Port Forwarding: This technique is also known as a dynamic SOCKS proxy. It allows a client to establish a secure connection with a remote server and redirect network traffic through the secure tunnel. It is commonly used to bypass firewalls or access resources in restricted networks. 4. UPnP Port Forwarding: Universal Plug and Play (UPnP) is a set of networking protocols that allows devices to discover and communicate with each other on a local network. UPnP port forwarding automatically creates and manages port forwarding rules in supported devices to enable communication with external services. 5. Virtual Server Port Forwarding: This technique is used to map a public IP address and port to a specific device or service within a local network. It is typically configured on a network gateway or router and allows external devices or services to access internal resources by forwarding incoming traffic to the correct destination. In conclusion, port forwarding techniques are essential in networking to enable communication with devices or services behind a network gateway. Local port forwarding, remote port forwarding, dynamic port forwarding, UPnP port forwarding, and virtual server port forwarding are some commonly used techniques to redirect network traffic between different network entities.

Port Forwarding

Port forwarding, in the context of networking, refers to the process of directing incoming network traffic from one IP address and port number combination to another. It is primarily used to allow external devices or users to connect to specific services or applications hosted on a local network. When a device on a local network wants to provide a service or application that can be accessed from outside the network, it needs to have the appropriate ports open and properly forwarded. Ports are like virtual doors that allow different types of network traffic to enter or exit a device. By default, most devices have incoming ports closed for security reasons. Port forwarding enables the device to selectively open specific ports and forward the incoming traffic to another device, such as a server or computer, on the same network. This forwarding process can be set up on the device's router or firewall, which acts as a gateway between the local network and the external network. Port forwarding works by mapping a port on the external IP address (usually provided by the internet service provider) to a specific internal IP address and port number of a device on the local network. When an incoming connection is made to the external IP address and port, the router or firewall identifies the forwarding rule and redirects the traffic to the specified device. This process is commonly used for applications that require remote access or hosting services such as web servers, online gaming servers, remote desktop connections, or video surveillance systems. By configuring the appropriate port forwarding rules, these services can be made accessible to users outside the local network. However, it is important to note that improper configuration of port forwarding can pose security risks. Opening ports and exposing devices to the external network may make them vulnerable to unauthorized access or potential attacks. Therefore, it is recommended to carefully manage and review port forwarding settings to ensure only the necessary and secure connections are allowed.

Port Knocking

Port knocking is a network security technique used to protect computer systems from unauthorized access attempts. It is a method of dynamically opening ports on a firewall by sending a sequence of connection attempts on specific ports in a predetermined order. Only when the correct sequence is received will the firewall open the desired port and allow the connection.The idea of port knocking is based on the concept of "security through obscurity," where the security measure is not openly advertised or visible. In traditional firewall setups, ports are kept open for services that need to be accessible. However, this can make the system vulnerable to various network attacks targeting open ports. Port knocking adds an additional layer of protection by hiding the ports from potential attackers.

Port Mirroring

Port Mirroring is a technique used in networking to duplicate network traffic from one switch port (or multiple switch ports) and send it to another port for analysis and monitoring purposes. This allows network administrators to observe and analyze the traffic passing through a specific switch port without interrupting the normal flow of network traffic. By implementing Port Mirroring, network administrators can gain valuable insights into the operation and performance of their network infrastructure. It enables them to analyze network traffic patterns, detect anomalies, troubleshoot network issues, and ensure the security of the network environment.

Port Scanner

A port scanner is a software application used to identify open ports on a network or a specific host within the network. It allows network administrators or security analysts to assess the security of a network by detecting possible vulnerabilities. Port scanning works by sending network packets to specific ports on a target host and analyzing the responses received. Each network service or application on a host generally runs on a specific port number. By scanning these port numbers, a port scanner can determine if the target host is running a specific service.

Port Scanning Techniques

Port scanning techniques refer to the methods used by network administrators or attackers to identify open ports on a target system or network. Ports are communication endpoints that enable devices on a network to send and receive data. Each port has a specific purpose or service associated with it, such as port 80 for HTTP or port 443 for HTTPS. Port scanning involves sending network packets to specific ports and analyzing the responses received. The goal of port scanning can vary depending on the context. Network administrators may use port scanning techniques to identify potential vulnerabilities or misconfigurations in their network. On the other hand, attackers may perform port scanning to find open ports that can be exploited for unauthorized access, data theft, or other malicious activities. There are several port scanning techniques that can be employed: TCP connect scanning: This technique involves opening a full TCP connection with the target port. If the connection is successfully established, it means the port is open. This method is often used as a standard scanning technique since it provides reliable results, but it can be easily detected by intrusion detection systems. TCP SYN scanning: Also known as "half-open scanning," this technique involves sending a SYN packet to the target port. If a SYN/ACK packet is received in response, it means the port is open. However, instead of completing the handshake and establishing a connection, the attacker sends a RST packet to terminate the connection. This method is more stealthy than TCP connect scanning and harder to detect. UDP scanning: This technique involves sending UDP packets to the target port. If a response is received, it indicates that the port is open. UDP scanning is often slower than TCP scanning since UDP is connectionless and does not provide acknowledgments. Additionally, since UDP does not have a "closed" state, distinguishing between open and filtered (firewalled) ports can be challenging. FIN scanning: This technique involves sending a FIN packet to a target port. If the port is closed, it will respond with a RST packet. If no response is received, it means the port is open or filtered. FIN scanning can be used to bypass certain stateful firewalls that do not monitor and block FIN packets. XMAS scanning: Similar to FIN scanning, XMAS scanning involves sending packets with the FIN, PSH, and URG flags set. Like FIN scanning, it can be used to bypass firewalls that do not handle such packets correctly. Port scanning techniques are valuable for both network administrators and attackers. Network administrators can use these techniques to assess the security of their network, identify potential vulnerabilities, and implement appropriate measures to protect against unauthorized access. Conversely, attackers can exploit open ports to gain unauthorized access, compromise systems, or launch further attacks, emphasizing the importance of implementing proper security measures and regularly scanning for open ports.

Port Scanning Tools

A port scanning tool is a software program or utility that is used to identify open ports on a computer or network device. Open ports are network endpoints that allow communication between different devices and applications over a network. They are essential for the functioning of various services and applications such as email, web browsing, file sharing, and remote access. The main purpose of a port scanning tool is to scan a target device or network and determine which ports are open, closed, or filtered. It achieves this by sending a series of network packets to the target device or network and analyzing the response received. The tool can scan a specific set of ports or a range of ports to identify any potential vulnerabilities or security issues. Port scanning tools are commonly used by network administrators, system administrators, and security professionals to assess the security posture of a network. By identifying open ports, these tools can help in identifying potential entry points for unauthorized access or malicious activities. They can also detect misconfigured or outdated services that may pose a security risk to the network. There are various types of port scanning techniques used by scanning tools, including TCP connect scans, SYN scans, UDP scans, and stealth scans. Each technique has its advantages and disadvantages and may be used depending on the specific requirements and network environment. It is important to note that while port scanning tools serve a legitimate purpose in identifying potential security vulnerabilities, they can also be misused for malicious activities. Unauthorized port scans can be considered intrusive and may violate network security policies or laws. Therefore, their use should be limited to authorized and ethical purposes only, and proper consent should be obtained before conducting any scanning activities.

Port Scanning

Port scanning is a network reconnaissance technique used to discover open ports, services, and protocols on a target system or network. It involves sending a series of network requests to various ports in order to determine which ones are active and responsive. This information can be crucial for both legitimate network administration tasks and malicious activities. The process of port scanning begins by sending a request, or probe, to a specific port on a target system. The probe is basically a communication attempt that can take various forms, such as a basic connection request, a specific network protocol request, or a specially crafted packet designed to trigger a response from a specific service. The goal is to determine whether the target system is listening on that specific port and if any service or protocol is available. Port scanning techniques typically involve the use of specialized tools, such as Nmap, that automate the process and provide various options for scanning different types of ports and protocols. These tools often allow users to specify the type of scan they want to perform, such as a basic TCP connect scan, a SYN scan, or an ACK scan, among others. Each of these scan types has its own advantages and limitations, creating a trade-off between stealthiness, accuracy, and speed. Port scanning can be performed for legitimate purposes, such as network auditing, vulnerability assessment, or troubleshooting. By identifying open ports and services, network administrators can ensure proper security measures are in place, detect potential vulnerabilities, or diagnose network connectivity issues. However, port scanning can also be used for malicious activities, such as identifying potential targets for attacks or exploiting known vulnerabilities in specific services. Attackers can use port scanning to find unprotected or poorly configured systems, which can then be targeted for unauthorized access, data theft, or other nefarious purposes. It is important to note that port scanning itself is not inherently malicious. It is the intent and subsequent actions that determine whether port scanning is used for legitimate or malicious purposes. Nevertheless, port scanning activity is often monitored and may be considered suspicious or potentially harmful, especially when performed against unauthorized systems or in violation of network security policies.

Port Security

Port security is a network security measure implemented to control the access of network devices, such as switches and routers, to specific physical Ethernet ports. It is a means of managing and safeguarding the network infrastructure by determining which devices are allowed to connect to specific ports and restricting unauthorized access. Port security allows network administrators to define and enforce access policies based on the Media Access Control (MAC) addresses of devices. Each device has a unique MAC address, which is a hardware identifier consisting of six pairs of hexadecimal numbers. By associating specific MAC addresses with certain ports, administrators can restrict network access to only authorized devices.

Port Triggering

Port triggering is a network configuration technique that allows specific ports on a router or firewall to be dynamically opened when a specific outbound connection is made. It is commonly used to provide temporary access to services or applications that require incoming connections, such as online gaming or video chat. The process of port triggering involves setting up rules that monitor outbound traffic from a specific device or network. When a connection is made to a designated port on an external server or device, the router or firewall notes the source port and IP address used for the connection. This information is then used to determine which ports should be opened on the router or firewall for incoming traffic. The purpose of port triggering is to enhance security by dynamically opening ports only when necessary. Unlike port forwarding, which permanently opens specific ports, port triggering only opens ports when specific outbound traffic triggers the rule. Once the triggering connection is terminated or a predetermined idle time has elapsed, the opened ports are automatically closed. This minimizes the exposure of unused ports to potential attacks from the internet. To illustrate the process, consider a scenario where a user wants to play an online game that requires incoming connections on port 12345. The user's router has port triggering capabilities, and the necessary rule is configured to open port 12345 when outbound traffic is detected on port 54321. When the user initiates a connection to the online game server, the router notes the source port 54321 and the IP address of the user's device. It then opens port 12345, allowing incoming connections to the user's device for the duration of the gameplay session. Once the gameplay session ends, or after a predetermined period of inactivity, the router automatically closes port 12345, ceasing any incoming connections. In summary, port triggering is a network configuration technique that dynamically opens specific ports on a router or firewall when a specific outbound connection is made. It provides temporary access to services or applications that require incoming connections, enhancing security by minimizing the exposure of unused ports to potential attacks.

Port-Based Authentication

Port-based authentication is a network security mechanism employed to control access to a network based on the physical port or point of network connection. It involves verifying the identity of devices or users connecting to a network by examining certain attributes associated with the network port through which the connection is established. In port-based authentication, a network switch or access point is configured to enforce authentication rules for each port. When a device or user attempts to connect to the network, it is required to provide some form of credential, such as a username and password, digital certificate, or hardware token. The authentication process occurs before any network services are allowed, ensuring that only authorized devices or users gain access to the network. Port-based authentication mechanisms typically leverage protocols such as IEEE 802.1X, which enables the supplicant (the device or user attempting to gain network access) to communicate with an authentication server through the network switch or access point. The authentication server verifies the provided credentials and then informs the switch or access point whether the connection should be granted or denied. If the authentication is successful, the network port is enabled, and the device or user is allowed to access network resources. If the authentication fails, the network port remains disabled, blocking network access. Through port-based authentication, network administrators can enforce access control policies, ensuring that only authorized devices or users can connect to the network. This helps prevent unauthorized access, mitigates security risks, and protects sensitive information. It also allows for more granular control over network resources, as different authentication policies can be applied to different network ports or groups of ports based on the desired security requirements. In summary, port-based authentication is a network security mechanism that controls network access based on the physical port or point of connection. By verifying the identity of devices or users attempting to connect to the network, port-based authentication helps enforce access control policies and ensures the security of network resources.

Power Over Ethernet (PoE)

Power over Ethernet (PoE) is a technology that allows electrical power and data to be transmitted over a single Ethernet cable, typically used for networking devices. It eliminates the need for separate power cables, simplifying installation and reducing costs. PoE delivers power using the same Ethernet cable that carries data signals, allowing devices to function without requiring a nearby power outlet. This technology is commonly used in various networking scenarios, such as IP cameras, VoIP phones, wireless access points, and other Internet of Things (IoT) devices.

Privacy Impact Assessment (PIA)

A Privacy Impact Assessment (PIA) is a formal process that examines the potential risks to privacy associated with the collection, use, and disclosure of personal information in a networking context. This assessment is typically conducted when developing or implementing a new networking system, application, or service. The purpose of a PIA is to identify and address privacy concerns and ensure that individuals' personal information is handled in a privacy-preserving manner. It involves a systematic evaluation of the privacy risks and the implementation of appropriate privacy safeguards to mitigate those risks.

Privacy Policy

A Privacy Policy in the context of networking refers to a formal document that outlines how personal information is collected, used, and shared by a network or an organization. It serves as a legal requirement and a means of building trust with users by informing them about the privacy practices and protocols implemented to protect their personal data. A Privacy Policy typically includes the following key components: 1. Information Collection: The policy should clearly state what types of personal information are collected, such as names, email addresses, or browsing activities. It should also specify whether the information is collected directly from the users or obtained from third parties. 2. Data Usage: The policy should explain how the collected data is used by the network or organization. This may include purposes such as providing personalized services, improving user experience, conducting research, or delivering targeted advertisements. 3. Information Sharing: The policy should outline whether the collected data is shared with third parties, such as advertisers or partners. It should specify the circumstances under which such sharing occurs and provide assurances that appropriate measures are taken to protect user data during the sharing process. 4. Data Protection: The policy should describe the security measures implemented to safeguard users' personal information. This may include encryption techniques, access controls, regularly updated security protocols, and employee training on data protection. 5. User Choices and Rights: The policy should inform users about their rights and choices regarding their personal data. This may include options for opting out of certain data collection or sharing activities, accessing and editing personal information, or deleting their data from the network's database. 6. Legal Compliance: The policy should ensure compliance with applicable laws and regulations regarding privacy and data protection. It should specify the jurisdiction under which it operates and provide information about the network or organization's responsibilities in handling user data. In summary, a Privacy Policy in the context of networking is a formal document that outlines how personal information is collected, used, and shared by a network or organization. It serves to inform users about the privacy practices and protocols implemented and ensures compliance with privacy laws and regulations.

Private IP Address

A private IP address is an IP address that is used within a private network, such as a home or office network. It is not globally unique and cannot be directly accessed from the internet. Private IP addresses are assigned to devices within a private network by a DHCP (Dynamic Host Configuration Protocol) server or can be manually configured. The most commonly used private IP addresses are those within the following ranges: • 10.0.0.0 to 10.255.255.255 (10.0.0.0/8) • 172.16.0.0 to 172.31.255.255 (172.16.0.0/12) • 192.168.0.0 to 192.168.255.255 (192.168.0.0/16) Private IP addresses provide a way to conserve and reuse IP address space. By using private IP addresses within a private network, organizations can avoid wasting public IP addresses, which are limited in number. Private IP addresses can be used by multiple devices within the same network, as long as they are unique within that network. This allows for efficient allocation of IP addresses and simplifies network configuration. Private IP addresses are used for communication within a private network. They are not routable on the internet and cannot be used to directly access resources outside of the private network. In order to access the internet or communicate with devices outside of the private network, network address translation (NAT) is used. NAT allows multiple devices within a private network to share a single public IP address. When a device with a private IP address sends a request to the internet, the NAT translates the private IP address to the public IP address before forwarding the request. Private IP addresses provide a level of security for devices within a private network. Since private IP addresses are not publicly accessible, they are not directly exposed to potential threats from the internet. This helps to protect the devices within the network from unauthorized access or attacks. However, additional security measures, such as firewalls, should still be implemented to ensure the network's overall security.

Privilege Escalation Attack

A privilege escalation attack refers to a type of cybersecurity attack wherein an unauthorized user gains elevated privileges or access rights within a network system or application. The attack involves exploiting vulnerabilities or weaknesses in the system to gain higher levels of access than initially granted or intended by the system administrators. Privilege escalation attacks can occur in various forms, targeting different layers within the network infrastructure. They exploit security loopholes, software bugs, or configuration errors to bypass access controls and gain unauthorized access to sensitive information or perform malicious activities.

Privilege Escalation

Privilege escalation refers to the process of gaining higher levels of access or permissions within a network or system than originally intended or assigned. This occurs when an attacker exploits vulnerabilities or weaknesses in the network's security measures to elevate their privileges beyond what was initially granted. Privilege escalation can be achieved through various methods, such as exploiting software vulnerabilities, misconfigurations, or weaknesses in user permissions. Once an attacker gains initial access to a system, they can exploit these vulnerabilities to gain further control and elevate their privileges. There are two main types of privilege escalation: vertical escalation and horizontal escalation. Vertical escalation involves gaining higher levels of access within the same user account, while horizontal escalation involves obtaining privileges from another user account or system. In network security, privilege escalation can have severe consequences. Attackers who successfully escalate their privileges can access sensitive information, manipulate network settings, install malware or unauthorized software, or perform malicious activities without detection. To prevent privilege escalation attacks, network administrators need to implement robust security measures. This includes keeping systems up to date with the latest patches and security updates, regularly reviewing and adjusting user permissions, and using strong passwords or authentication methods. Network segmentation and least privilege principles are also essential in limiting the impact of privilege escalation. In conclusion, privilege escalation in the context of networking refers to the unauthorized elevation of access or permissions within a network or system. It is a critical security concern that can lead to unauthorized actions, data breaches, and compromise of sensitive information. By implementing strict security measures and staying vigilant against vulnerabilities, organizations can mitigate the risk of privilege escalation attacks.

Proxy Server Configuration

A proxy server acts as an intermediary between client devices (such as computers, smartphones, or tablets) and a destination server. It serves as a gateway for client requests to access resources from the internet. The main function of a proxy server is to provide security, privacy, and performance optimization by caching frequently accessed content. When a client device attempts to access a web page or any other online resource, it sends a request to the proxy server instead of directly connecting to the destination server. The proxy server evaluates the request and forwards it to the appropriate destination server on behalf of the client. The destination server then sends the response back to the proxy server, which in turn relays it to the client.

Proxy Server Software

A Proxy Server Software is a computer program or application that acts as an intermediary between clients and servers within a network. It receives requests from clients seeking resources such as web pages, files, or other services, and forwards those requests to the appropriate servers. The servers then send the requested data back to the proxy server, which subsequently retransmits it to the requesting client. The main purpose of a Proxy Server Software is to enhance network performance, security, and privacy. By caching frequently accessed resources, it reduces the load on servers and improves response times for clients. This caching feature allows the proxy server to store copies of web pages, files, or other resources, and serve them directly to clients without retrieving them from the original server. This optimizes network traffic and improves overall browsing speed. In addition to performance optimization, proxy servers also provide security benefits. They act as a shield between clients and external networks, filtering incoming and outgoing traffic to block malicious content, prevent unauthorized access, and enforce network policies. Proxy Server Software can be configured to restrict access to certain websites, control the types of files that can be downloaded, and monitor user activity for policy enforcement or auditing purposes. Proxy servers also offer privacy advantages by masking the IP address of clients. Instead of directly connecting to a server, clients connect to the proxy server, which then makes the request on their behalf. This obfuscation of client IP addresses helps protect anonymity, prevent tracking, and bypass geographical restrictions or censorship imposed by certain websites or regions. In summary, a Proxy Server Software is a crucial component of network infrastructure that improves performance, enhances security, and ensures privacy. Through caching, filtering, and IP address masking, proxy servers optimize network resources, protect against threats, and provide users with a more efficient and secure browsing experience.

Proxy Server

A proxy server is a network device or application that acts as an intermediary for requests from clients seeking resources from other servers. It operates as a gateway between the client and the destination server, forwarding client requests to the server and then returning the server's responses to the client. By sitting between the client and the server, the proxy server can enhance security, efficiency, and performance in a network environment. It can provide various functionalities and benefits to both clients and servers. One of the primary purposes of a proxy server is to improve network security. It can act as a firewall by filtering and blocking certain requests or by examining the content of requests and responses for potential threats or malicious activities. This helps to protect the internal network from external threats, preventing unauthorized access or attacks. Additionally, a proxy server can enhance privacy by hiding the client's IP address. When a request is forwarded through a proxy server, the server's IP address is exposed to the destination server instead of the client's IP address. This can prevent the destination server from directly identifying and tracking the client, adding an extra layer of anonymity. Furthermore, a proxy server can improve network performance and efficiency through caching. When a client makes a request for a particular resource, the proxy server can store a copy of the requested resource in its local cache. If another client subsequently requests the same resource, the proxy server can retrieve it from its cache instead of forwarding the request to the destination server. This reduces the latency and bandwidth usage associated with repeated requests, resulting in faster response times and optimized network utilization. Proxy servers can also enable content filtering and access control. Administrators can configure proxy servers to restrict access to specific websites, block certain types of content, or enforce usage policies. This allows organizations to manage and control internet access, ensure compliance with regulations, and prevent unauthorized usage. In conclusion, a proxy server acts as an intermediary between clients and servers in a network. It enhances security, privacy, and efficiency by filtering requests, caching resources, improving performance, and enabling content filtering. Overall, proxy servers play a crucial role in network management and optimization.

Public IP Address

A public IP address is a unique numerical label assigned to a device connected to a computer network that uses the Internet Protocol (IP) for communication. It serves as an identifier and location indicator, allowing other devices on the internet to communicate with the device that has been assigned the public IP address. In the context of networking, devices on a network are assigned either public or private IP addresses. A public IP address is globally unique and can be accessed from anywhere on the internet. It distinguishes a device from others and enables direct communication with it. On the other hand, a private IP address is used within a local network and is not directly accessible from the internet. A public IP address consists of a series of numbers separated by periods, such as 203.0.113.66. Internet Service Providers (ISPs) are responsible for assigning public IP addresses to their customers. These addresses are allocated from a pool of IP addresses managed by regional internet registries. Public IP addresses play a crucial role in enabling devices to access the internet. They allow devices to send and receive data packets across the network, ensuring seamless communication. Additionally, public IP addresses facilitate services such as web browsing, email, file sharing, video streaming, and online gaming. With the limited availability of public IP addresses, the industry has transitioned to using Network Address Translation (NAT) to conserve address space. NAT allows multiple devices within a private network to share a single public IP address. It achieves this by mapping the private IP addresses of devices to the public IP address when communicating with external networks. In conclusion, a public IP address is a unique identifier assigned to a device connected to a network that uses the internet protocol. It enables communication between devices on the internet and plays a vital role in accessing various online services.

Public Key Infrastructure (PKI)

A Public Key Infrastructure (PKI) is a framework used in networking that enables secure communication and authentication between different entities in a network. It consists of various components and protocols to ensure the confidentiality, integrity, and authenticity of data transmission. At the heart of PKI is the use of asymmetric cryptography, which involves the use of two distinct cryptographic keys: a public key and a private key. The public key is made available to anyone, while the private key is kept secret by the key owner. PKI operates using a hierarchical structure of Certification Authorities (CAs). CAs are trusted entities responsible for issuing and managing digital certificates. These certificates bind a public key to an entity's identity, verifying its authenticity. When a user wants to establish a secure communication with another entity in the network, they can request a digital certificate from a trusted CA. The CA verifies the identity of the user and signs the certificate using its private key. This process is known as certificate issuance. Once the user receives the digital certificate, they can use it to encrypt their communication using the recipient's public key. The recipient can then decrypt the message using their corresponding private key. This ensures confidentiality, as only the intended recipient possesses the private key to decrypt the message. In addition to confidentiality, PKI also ensures data integrity. Before encrypting a message, the sender can use a digital signature algorithm to create a hash value of the message. This hash, along with the sender's private key, is then encrypted using the sender's private key. The recipient can use the sender's public key to decrypt the hash, and then verify the integrity of the message by comparing the decrypted hash with a newly computed hash of the received message. In conclusion, PKI is a crucial framework in networking that enables secure communication and authentication. It uses asymmetric cryptography and digital certificates issued by trusted CAs to ensure confidentiality, integrity, and authenticity in data transmission.

QoS (Quality Of Service)

Quality of Service (QoS) in the context of networking refers to the ability to manage and prioritize the traffic flow within a network to ensure optimum performance and reliability. It involves implementing various mechanisms and protocols to guarantee a satisfactory level of service delivery and to meet the specific requirements of different types of network traffic. QoS mechanisms are used to control and manage network resources, such as bandwidth, delay,

271

jitter, and packet loss, to ensure that critical applications and services receive the necessary resources while non-critical traffic is given lower priority. QoS prioritizes traffic based on certain criteria, such as application type, service level agreements (SLAs), or user-defined policies.

Quality Of Service (QoS) Policy

Quality of Service (QoS) Policy refers to a set of rules and strategies implemented in networking to prioritize certain types of network traffic over others. It involves the allocation and management of network resources to ensure that critical applications or services receive the necessary bandwidth, latency, and reliability to function effectively. With the increasing demand for diverse applications and services over networks, it becomes crucial to maintain a certain level of performance for different applications. QoS policies help achieve this by allowing network administrators to define and enforce specific parameters or conditions for different classes of traffic. These policies are typically applied at the network edge or within the network infrastructure itself. A QoS policy can include various parameters and techniques to differentiate and prioritize traffic flows. One common approach is through traffic classification, where packets are identified and tagged based on specific characteristics such as the source or destination IP address, protocol type, application, or port number. This allows network devices to prioritize or treat packets differently based on their classification. Another important aspect of QoS policy is traffic shaping and prioritization. This involves regulating and controlling the bandwidth allocation for different traffic types to ensure that critical applications or services receive adequate resources. For example, real-time applications such as voice or video conferencing may require low latency and high bandwidth, while bulk file transfers can tolerate higher latency and lower priority. QoS policies also encompass mechanisms for congestion management and avoidance. When network resources become congested, packets may be dropped or delayed, leading to decreased performance and user experience. To mitigate these issues, QoS policies can include techniques such as traffic queuing, prioritization, and traffic policing to manage congestion and ensure fair allocation of network resources. In summary, a Quality of Service (QoS) Policy is a set of rules and strategies implemented in networking to prioritize and manage network traffic. It involves the allocation and management of network resources to ensure that critical applications or services receive the necessary bandwidth, latency, and reliability to function effectively. QoS policies achieve this through traffic classification, traffic shaping, congestion management, and avoidance techniques.

Quality Of Service (QoS) Settings

Quality of Service (QoS) settings in networking refer to the configuration and management of network resources to efficiently and effectively prioritize certain types of network traffic over others. QoS is a mechanism that allows network administrators to allocate bandwidth, control congestion, minimize latency, and enhance the overall performance of the network. QoS settings can be implemented at different layers of the networking stack, including the application layer, transport layer, network layer, and link layer. At each layer, different QoS techniques and mechanisms are employed to ensure the desired level of service for specific types of traffic.

Quality Of Service (QoS)

The Quality of Service (QoS) refers to the ability of a network to provide different levels of performance to different types of network traffic. It aims to prioritize certain types of traffic and allocate resources accordingly to ensure the desired level of service quality. QoS plays a crucial role in networking as it allows for efficient and effective utilization of network resources, ensuring that critical applications and services receive the necessary bandwidth and minimized latency. This is especially important in today's data-driven world where different types of traffic, such as voice, video, and data, coexist on the same network.

RADIUS Accounting Configuration

RADIUS accounting is a configuration method used in networking to gather and record information about user sessions, including authentication and authorization data, and to generate accounting records for billing, auditing, and monitoring purposes. RADIUS, which stands for Remote Authentication Dial-In User Service, is a protocol widely used in networking environments to provide centralized authentication, authorization, and accounting services.

272

While RADIUS authentication and authorization are crucial for controlling access to network resources, RADIUS accounting offers valuable insights into user activity and resource consumption. The configuration of RADIUS accounting involves setting up the necessary parameters and options on RADIUS clients, servers, and accounting systems. The process typically includes defining the accounting protocol, specifying the server's IP address, configuring ports and authentication methods, and determining accounting attributes to be collected. Once RADIUS accounting is enabled, it starts collecting data about various network activities of users. This includes tracking session start and end times, data transfer amounts, duration of sessions, bandwidth usage, and other relevant information. RADIUS accounting records are generated and sent by RADIUS clients to the accounting server, where they are processed and stored in a suitable format, such as log files or databases. The gathered accounting information can be utilized in several ways. Service providers, for example, can utilize the data for billing purposes, generating usage reports, and managing network resources effectively. Organizations can also leverage RADIUS accounting for auditing and compliance purposes, as it provides a comprehensive record of user activities and network resource utilization. Additionally, network administrators can monitor network performance, identify bottlenecks, and troubleshoot issues by analyzing the accounting information. In conclusion, RADIUS accounting configuration in networking involves defining the necessary parameters and options for collecting and recording user session data. It serves multiple purposes, including billing, auditing, monitoring, and resource management. By enabling RADIUS accounting, organizations can gain valuable insights into user activities and make informed decisions regarding network usage and security.

RADIUS Accounting Server

A RADIUS (Remote Authentication Dial-In User Service) Accounting Server is a component in network infrastructure that is responsible for collecting and storing accounting information for user sessions. It allows network administrators to keep track of various aspects of network usage, such as the duration of user sessions, the amount of data transferred, and other relevant details. When a user initiates a session on a network that utilizes RADIUS authentication, the RADIUS Accounting Server starts tracking the session and collecting accounting data. This data includes information such as the user's username, the time the session started, and the IP address of the user's device. RADIUS Accounting Servers play a crucial role in network management and security. By collecting and storing accounting information, they provide network administrators with valuable insights into network usage patterns and potential security risks. The accounting data collected by the RADIUS Accounting Server can be used for various purposes. It can help monitor and manage network resources by providing information on the amount of data transferred by each user or group of users. This data can be used for capacity planning and optimization of network infrastructure. In addition to resource management, RADIUS accounting data can also be used for auditing and compliance purposes. By keeping track of user sessions and their activities, network administrators can ensure that users are complying with the organization's policies and regulations. RADIUS Accounting Servers are typically part of a larger RADIUS infrastructure, which includes other components such as RADIUS authentication servers and RADIUS clients. The accounting server receives accounting data from RADIUS clients, which are responsible for sending accounting data to the server. In summary, a RADIUS Accounting Server is a critical component in network infrastructure that collects and stores accounting information for user sessions. It helps network administrators manage network resources, ensure compliance with policies and regulations, and monitor network usage patterns.

RADIUS Accounting

RADIUS Accounting is a protocol utilized in computer networking to track and record the usage of network resources by users. It provides a standardized method for collecting and storing information about network access, such as login and logout times, data transfer amounts, and the duration of user sessions. This information is crucial for network administrators in effectively managing and maintaining the network, monitoring user activity, and enforcing security policies. The RADIUS Accounting process begins when a user attempts to access the network through a network access server (NAS), such as a router or a wireless access point. The NAS sends an authentication request to the RADIUS server, which verifies the user's credentials and grants or denies access based on the authentication results. If the user is granted access, the RADIUS

273

server starts the accounting process. During the user's session, the RADIUS server collects accounting data, such as start and stop timestamps, the amount of data transferred, and the type of service used. This data is recorded in accounting requests and periodically sent by the NAS to the RADIUS server for storage and analysis. The RADIUS server stores this information in a centralized database, allowing network administrators to retrieve and generate reports on user activity, which can assist in troubleshooting network issues, enforcing usage policies, and monitoring resource consumption. RADIUS Accounting offers several benefits to network administrators. By keeping track of user sessions and resource usage, it enables network administrators to accurately bill users or departments for the services they utilize. Additionally, it aids in identifying potential security breaches, as unusual patterns of activity or excessive resource consumption can indicate unauthorized access or network abuse. The data collected through RADIUS Accounting can also be used for capacity planning, helping administrators determine if additional resources are needed to accommodate increasing user demand. In conclusion, RADIUS Accounting is a crucial protocol in computer networking that provides standardized tracking and recording of network access and usage. It enables network administrators to effectively manage resources, enforce security policies, and monitor user activity. By maintaining a centralized database of accounting data, RADIUS Accounting offers valuable insights for troubleshooting, billing, security, and capacity planning purposes.

RADIUS Authentication Methods

RADIUS (Remote Authentication Dial In User Service) is a networking protocol that provides centralized authentication, authorization, and accounting management for users connecting to a network service. RADIUS authentication methods refer to the different techniques used to verify the identity of users accessing a network.One popular RADIUS authentication method is PAP (Password Authentication Protocol), which transmits the user's credentials (username and password) in plaintext over the network. While PAP is simple to implement, it is considered insecure because the credentials are easily intercepted and can be decrypted.A more secure RADIUS authentication method is CHAP (Challenge-Handshake Authentication Protocol). In this method, the server challenges the user by sending a random value, and the user responds with a response value calculated using a one-way hash function. The server then verifies the response and grants access if it matches the expected value. CHAP provides better security than PAP because the credentials are not transmitted directly, and the challenge-response mechanism prevents replay attacks.EAP (Extensible Authentication Protocol) is a flexible RADIUS authentication method that supports multiple authentication mechanisms, including methods such as EAP-MD5, EAP-TLS, and PEAP. EAP-MD5 uses a similar challenge-response mechanism to CHAP but has the disadvantage of sending the challenge and response values in plaintext. EAP-TLS, on the other hand, uses digital certificates to authenticate both the client and the server, providing a highly secure method. PEAP (Protected Extensible Authentication Protocol) combines EAP with TLS to create a secure tunnel for sending authentication data.In addition to these methods, RADIUS also supports MS-CHAP (Microsoft Challenge-Handshake Authentication Protocol), which is an extension of CHAP developed by Microsoft. It provides additional security features, such as mutual authentication, but is primarily used in Microsoft environments.In conclusion, RADIUS authentication methods are essential in networking to ensure secure access control. PAP, CHAP, EAP, and MS-CHAP are some of the commonly used methods. While PAP is easy to implement, it lacks security. CHAP offers stronger security through challenge-response authentication. EAP provides flexibility by supporting multiple authentication mechanisms, and MS-CHAP is an extension of CHAP with additional features. Implementing the appropriate RADIUS authentication methods based on the requirements of the network ensures a secure and reliable authentication system.

RADIUS Authentication Protocol

The RADIUS (Remote Authentication Dial-In User Service) authentication protocol is a widely used networking protocol that provides centralized authentication, authorization, and accounting services for users attempting to access a network's resources. RADIUS is commonly used in both wired and wireless networks, allowing for secure and efficient authentication of users. The protocol operates in a client-server model, where the client, often a network access server (NAS), initiates a connection request to the RADIUS server for user authentication. RADIUS enables organizations to manage a single authentication database for multiple network access points, providing a unified and scalable authentication mechanism. When a user tries to access a network resource, such as connecting to a Wi-Fi network or accessing a VPN, the NAS sends the user's credentials to the RADIUS server for verification. The RADIUS server then validates the user's credentials against its database, which can include various user information such as usernames, passwords, and access permissions. The RADIUS server employs a variety of authentication methods, including password-based authentication, digital certificates, and token-based authentication. The server compares the supplied credentials with the stored information and either accepts or rejects the authentication request. If the request is accepted, the server sends an accept message to the NAS, allowing the user access to the requested network resources. In case of rejection, the server sends a reject message, denying access to the user. The RADIUS protocol also supports authorization functionalities, allowing the server to grant or deny access to specific network services based on a user's authentication status. This enables network administrators to control and manage user permissions and resource allocations. Additionally, RADIUS offers accounting capabilities by logging and tracking user authentication attempts and network resource usage, providing important auditing and billing information. Overall, the RADIUS authentication protocol plays a crucial role in network security and user management by providing a standardized and efficient method for authenticating and granting network access. Its versatility and wide adoption make it a fundamental component of modern networking infrastructures.

RADIUS Authentication Server

A RADIUS authentication server, also known as Remote Authentication Dial-In User Service, is a network device or software application that performs user authentication, authorization, and accounting (AAA) for remote access clients. The RADIUS server plays a vital role in network security and is widely used in enterprise environments. The primary function of a RADIUS authentication server is to authenticate the identity of users before granting them access to a network or service. When a user attempts to connect to the network, the RADIUS server verifies the user's credentials, such as username and password, using various authentication methods, including Password Authentication Protocol (PAP), Challenge Handshake Authentication Protocol (CHAP), or Extensible Authentication Protocol (EAP). This process ensures that only authorized users can gain access to the network resources, preventing unauthorized access and protecting sensitive data. In addition to authentication, the RADIUS server also handles authorization tasks. It determines the level of access that authenticated users are granted based on predefined policies and rules. These policies can include restrictions on specific services or resources that a user can access, such as limiting internet access or allowing access only to certain network segments. By controlling user access rights, the RADIUS server helps maintain network security and prevent misuse or unauthorized use of network resources. Another crucial role of the RADIUS authentication server is accounting. It collects and records information about user sessions, including the duration of the session, the amount of data transferred, and other relevant details. This accounting data can be used for various purposes, such as billing, auditing, or tracking user activity. By logging and analyzing user sessions, network administrators can monitor network usage, detect any suspicious behavior, and ensure compliance with security policies. Overall, a RADIUS authentication server is a critical component of network infrastructure, providing secure user authentication, authorization, and accounting services for remote access clients. Its role in verifying user identities, controlling access privileges, and tracking user activity helps ensure the integrity and security of the network.

RADIUS Authentication

RADIUS authentication is a method used in computer networking to validate the identity of network users before granting them access to the network. It stands for Remote Authentication Dial-In User Service, and it is widely used in both wired and wireless networks. At its core, RADIUS authentication relies on a centralized server known as the RADIUS server. When a user tries to access the network, the network access server (NAS) forwards the user's credentials, such as username and password, to the RADIUS server for verification and authentication. The RADIUS server then checks the provided credentials against its own database or an external authentication source, such as Active Directory or LDAP. If the credentials are valid, the RADIUS server sends an authentication success message back to the NAS, allowing the user to access the network. On the other hand, if the credentials are invalid, the server sends an authentication failure message, denying the user access. RADIUS

275

authentication offers several benefits in network management. First, it centralizes user authentication, making it easier for network administrators to manage and control access to the network. Instead of configuring and maintaining user accounts on each network device, all user accounts are stored on the RADIUS server. This significantly simplifies the management process and reduces the risk of security vulnerabilities. Furthermore, RADIUS authentication supports various authentication protocols, including PAP (Password Authentication Protocol), CHAP (Challenge-Handshake Authentication Protocol), and EAP (Extensible Authentication Protocol). This flexibility allows organizations to choose the authentication protocol that best suits their security requirements. In addition to user authentication, RADIUS can also provide authorization and accounting services. Once a user is authenticated, the RADIUS server can enforce specific access policies based on the user's profile. This includes controlling the user's level of access, such as granting different permissions to different user groups. Furthermore, RADIUS can log and record user-related events, creating an audit trail that assists in network administration. This accounting functionality allows organizations to track and analyze network usage, making it useful for billing, reporting, and troubleshooting purposes. In summary, RADIUS authentication is a centralized and flexible method for validating the identity of network users before granting them access. It simplifies network management, supports multiple authentication protocols, and offers authorization and accounting services.

RADIUS (Remote Authentication Dial-In User Service)

RADIUS (Remote Authentication Dial-In User Service) is a networking protocol that provides centralized authentication, authorization, and accounting (AAA) for both dial-up and virtual private network (VPN) connections. It allows network administrators to manage and control access to their networks by verifying the credentials of remote users attempting to connect. RADIUS operates as a client-server model, where the RADIUS server is responsible for authenticating and authorizing user requests, while the RADIUS client handles the actual network access. When a user attempts to connect to the network, the client forwards the user's credentials to the server for verification. Authentication is the process of verifying the identity of the user by comparing the provided credentials, such as username and password, with the ones stored in the RADIUS server's database. If the credentials match, the server grants access to the user; otherwise, access is denied. Authorization comes after successful authentication and determines the user's privileges and permissions within the network. The RADIUS server checks the user's attributes, such as group membership or access level, to determine what resources the user is allowed to access. RADIUS also performs accounting, which involves tracking and logging network usage by the authenticated users. It collects information such as the time of connection, duration, data transferred, and applies this information for billing, auditing, or troubleshooting purposes. One of the main advantages of RADIUS is its ability to centralize user management. Organizations can maintain a single user database on the RADIUS server, eliminating the need for separate authentication mechanisms for each network device. This simplifies administration and enhances security by enforcing consistent access policies across the network. Furthermore, RADIUS supports secure protocols like Transport Layer Security (TLS) to encrypt communication between the client and the server, ensuring the confidentiality and integrity of the credentials being transmitted. In conclusion, RADIUS is a fundamental protocol in networking that enables organizations to authenticate, authorize, and account for remote network access. Its client-server architecture, central user database, and support for secure communication make it an essential tool for managing network access and maintaining security.

RADIUS Server

A RADIUS (Remote Authentication Dial-In User Service) server is a network device or software system that provides centralized authentication, authorization, and accounting (AAA) services for remote network access. It is commonly used in internet service provider (ISP) environments, enterprise networks, and virtual private networks (VPNs). Authentication is the process of verifying the identity of users attempting to access the network resources. RADIUS server acts as a central authentication server, receiving authentication requests from remote clients such as VPN gateways, wireless access points, or dial-up servers. It uses a variety of authentication methods such as username/password, digital certificates, or token-based authentication to validate the identity of the users. Authorization is the process of granting or denying access to specific network resources based on the authenticated user's privileges. RADIUS server plays a

276

crucial role in the authorization process by storing and managing user profile information, including access rights and permission levels. It provides a unified platform to centrally manage and enforce access policies across the network, ensuring secure and controlled access to resources. Accounting is the process of tracking and logging network usage for billing, auditing, and analytical purposes. RADIUS server captures and stores information about user activities, including the duration of their sessions, data transfer volumes, and the specific resources accessed. This data can be used for billing customers based on usage, auditing network usage for compliance purposes, or generating reports to analyze network trends and behavior. One of the key advantages of using a RADIUS server is its ability to centralize and manage user authentication across multiple network devices or systems. This eliminates the need for individual devices to maintain their own user databases and authentication mechanisms, reducing administrative overhead and improving security. Additionally, RADIUS server supports user roaming, allowing users to authenticate from different locations while maintaining a consistent profile and access privileges. In conclusion, a RADIUS server is a vital component in network infrastructure, enabling centralized authentication, authorization, and accounting services for remote network access. It ensures secure and controlled access to network resources, simplifies administration, and provides valuable usage data for billing and analysis.

RARP (Reverse ARP)

RARP (Reverse ARP) is a networking protocol used to map a physical address to an IP address in an Ethernet network. It operates in the opposite direction of the traditional ARP (Address Resolution Protocol), which maps an IP address to a physical address. In an Ethernet network, devices communicate with each other using their physical addresses, also known as MAC addresses. These addresses are unique identifiers assigned to network interface cards (NICs) by the manufacturer. On the other hand, IP addresses are logical addresses used for routing and identifying devices on a network. When a device wants to send data to another device on the same network, it needs to know the physical address of the destination device. This is where ARP comes into play. The sender broadcasts an ARP request packet asking for the physical address of the device with a specific IP address. The device with the matching IP address replies with its physical address, allowing the sender to send the data directly to the destination device. However, there are situations where a device doesn't know its own IP address and needs to obtain it dynamically. That's where RARP comes in. RARP is used by diskless workstations or devices that have lost their IP configuration information. Instead of broadcasting an ARP request to find a physical address, a device broadcasts a RARP request to obtain its IP address. The RARP process involves a RARP server, also known as a BOOTP (Bootstrap Protocol) server, which maintains a database of MAC-to-IP address mappings. When a device sends a RARP request, the RARP server checks its database for a matching MAC address and responds with the associated IP address. RARP allows devices without permanent or known IP addresses to obtain their IP configurations dynamically. It is commonly used in diskless workstations, which rely on network booting to load their operating systems and configurations. RARP has been largely replaced by more efficient and secure protocols such as DHCP (Dynamic Host Configuration Protocol), which provides not only IP address assignment but also other configuration parameters to devices.

Radio Frequency (RF)

Radio Frequency (RF) refers to the range of electromagnetic frequencies that are used for wireless communication in networking. It represents the portion of the electromagnetic spectrum with wavelengths ranging from about 1 millimeter to 100 kilometers. RF signals are commonly used for wireless communication in various applications such as Wi-Fi, Bluetooth, cellular networks, satellite communication, and many other wireless technologies. In networking, RF is crucial for the establishment of wireless connections between devices. It allows data to be transmitted and received wirelessly, enabling devices to communicate without the need for physical cables. This wireless communication capability is especially useful in scenarios where it is difficult or impractical to deploy wired connections, such as in remote areas or mobile environments. RF signals are generated and transmitted by devices called transmitters, which convert electrical signals into electromagnetic waves. These waves propagate through space and are received by another device called a receiver, which converts them back into electrical signals. The receiver then processes the data contained in the signals for further use. One key characteristic of RF signals is their ability to travel through obstacles and over long distances, making them suitable for wide-area coverage. However, they can also be easily attenuated or weakened by various factors such as distance, physical barriers, interference from other signals, and environmental conditions. These factors can affect the quality and reliability of wireless connections. Networking devices that utilize RF for wireless communication, such as routers, access points, and mobile devices, need to support specific RF frequencies and standards to ensure compatibility and interoperability. Each wireless technology operates within a specific frequency range, regulated by governmental entities to avoid interference between different wireless devices and services. In conclusion, Radio Frequency (RF) plays a vital role in wireless networking by enabling devices to communicate wirelessly over specific frequency ranges. It allows for the establishment of wireless connections between devices, providing flexibility, mobility, and wide-area coverage. Understanding RF and its characteristics is essential for ensuring reliable and efficient wireless communication in networking.

Ransomware

Ransomware is a type of malicious software (malware) that restricts access to a computer system or files until a ransom is paid to the attacker. It is primarily spread through phishing emails, malicious downloads, or by exploiting vulnerabilities in software or networks. Once the ransomware infects a system, it encrypts the victim's files or locks the entire system, rendering it inaccessible. The attacker then demands payment, usually in the form of cryptocurrency, in exchange for the decryption key or the release of the system.

Red Team Assessment

A Red Team Assessment is a comprehensive evaluation of an organization's network security measures to identify vulnerabilities and weaknesses that could be exploited by malicious actors. It is conducted by a team of security experts who simulate real-world attack scenarios to test the effectiveness of the network's defense mechanisms. During a Red Team Assessment, the team takes on the role of a potential attacker, using various techniques and methodologies to gain unauthorized access to the network. This can include social engineering, network scanning, vulnerability scanning, password cracking, and exploitation of known vulnerabilities. The primary goal of a Red Team Assessment is to uncover vulnerabilities that may have been overlooked during routine security assessments or penetration testing. The process involves testing the network's susceptibility to different types of attacks and determining the potential impact and consequences of a successful breach. Red Team assessments go beyond traditional vulnerability scanning by adopting a more holistic approach. The team not only focuses on identifying weaknesses in individual components but also assesses the effectiveness of the organization's security policies, procedures, and incident response capabilities. By conducting a Red Team Assessment, organizations can proactively identify and remediate vulnerabilities before they are exploited by real attackers. It helps in uncovering potential weaknesses in security controls, identifying gaps in security architecture, and providing insights into the organization's overall security posture. The results of a Red Team Assessment are typically presented to the organization's management and IT teams, highlighting the vulnerabilities found and providing recommendations for improvement. This allows organizations to enhance their network security defenses and implement necessary changes to mitigate the identified risks. In conclusion, a Red Team Assessment is a critical component of a comprehensive network security strategy. It helps organizations stay ahead of potential threats by simulating real-world attack scenarios and identifying vulnerabilities that may have been otherwise overlooked.

Red Team Exercise

A Red Team Exercise in the context of networking refers to a simulated cyber attack conducted by an external team of experts known as the Red Team, with the objective of identifying vulnerabilities and weaknesses in an organization's network infrastructure and systems. The Red Team operates as an adversarial force, simulating the actions of real attackers to test the organization's security defenses. The primary goal of a Red Team Exercise is to assess the effectiveness of an organization's security measures and incident response capabilities. By conducting a simulated attack, the Red Team aims to identify vulnerabilities that could potentially be exploited by malicious actors. This exercise helps organizations understand their security posture, improve their defenses, and enhance their overall cyber resilience. During a Red Team Exercise, the Red Team utilizes a variety of techniques and tools to mimic real-world attack scenarios. They may attempt to gain unauthorized access to the network, exploit software vulnerabilities, or use social engineering tactics to trick employees into revealing sensitive information. The Red Team may also try to escalate privileges, move laterally within the network, or exfiltrate confidential data to assess the organization's ability to detect and respond to these activities. Throughout the exercise, the Red Team documents their findings, including any vulnerabilities discovered, successful compromise attempts, and the overall impact on the organization's systems and data. They provide a comprehensive report that outlines their methodologies, exploited vulnerabilities, and recommendations for mitigating identified risks. Red Team Exercises are an essential component of proactive cybersecurity strategies, as they allow organizations to identify and address security weaknesses before a real attack occurs. By simulating real-world scenarios, organizations can gain valuable insights into their security posture, improve incident response capabilities, and enhance their overall ability to protect against cyber threats.

Red Team

A Red Team is a group of skilled individuals within an organization who are tasked with simulating real-world cyber-attacks in order to evaluate and improve the security of the organization's network infrastructure. The primary objective of a Red Team exercise is to identify vulnerabilities, weaknesses, and potential loopholes in the network's defenses. By using various techniques and tools available to attackers, Red Team members attempt to breach the network security measures, gain unauthorized access to sensitive data, and exploit any identified weaknesses. Red Team exercises involve a comprehensive and systematic approach, which includes reconnaissance, scanning, enumeration, exploitation, and post-exploitation phases. During the reconnaissance phase, the Red Team gathers information about the target network, its systems, and potential entry points. This information is then used to identify vulnerabilities that can be exploited during the scanning phase. In the enumeration phase, the Red Team performs an in-depth analysis of the target network to gather more detailed information about the systems, services, and users. This information helps the Red Team identify additional vulnerabilities and potential attack vectors. Once vulnerabilities are identified, the exploitation phase begins. Red Team members attempt to exploit the identified vulnerabilities and gain unauthorized access to the network systems. This may involve using social engineering techniques, exploiting software vulnerabilities, or leveraging misconfigurations in the network infrastructure. The post-exploitation phase focuses on maintaining access to the compromised systems, escalating privileges, and gathering additional sensitive information. This phase helps determine what level of damage an attacker could cause and highlights areas where security measures need improvement. In conclusion, a Red Team plays a crucial role in network security by conducting controlled attacks on an organization's infrastructure. Their objective is to identify vulnerabilities and weaknesses that could be exploited by real-world attackers. The insights gained from Red Team exercises are used to enhance the organization's security posture and improve its ability to detect, prevent, and respond to cyber threats.

Redundancy

Redundancy in the context of networking refers to the implementation of backup systems or duplicate components within a network infrastructure to ensure high availability and fault tolerance. It involves the duplication or replication of critical network elements such as routers, switches, links, or servers with the purpose of maintaining network connectivity and minimizing downtime in case of failure. The main objective of redundancy is to enhance network reliability and resilience by providing alternative paths or resources that can be utilized in case of an unexpected event. This can be achieved through the use of redundant hardware, software, or network configurations.

Remote Authentication Dial-In User Service (RADIUS)

Remote Authentication Dial-In User Service (RADIUS) is a networking protocol that provides centralized authentication, authorization, and accounting (AAA) for users who connect to a network remotely. It is commonly used in enterprise networks and internet service providers (ISPs) to manage and secure remote access connections. RADIUS operates as a client-server model, where the RADIUS client (typically a network access server) forwards user authentication requests to a central RADIUS server. The server then validates the user's credentials and returns a response to the client, either granting or denying access. Authentication is the process of verifying the identity of a user or device. With RADIUS, user identities are typically stored in a database, such as a directory service or a database management system. When a user attempts to connect to a network, the RADIUS client sends the user's credentials, such as a username and password, to the RADIUS server for verification. The server compares the credentials against its stored database and determines whether the user is authorized to access the network. Authorization involves determining what level of access a user should have once they are authenticated. RADIUS allows network administrators to assign different access rights to different users or user groups. For example, an administrator may grant full network access to a trusted employee, but limited access to a guest or contractor. Accounting is the process of tracking and recording the usage of network resources by authenticated users. RADIUS maintains a detailed log of the network access sessions, including the duration, data transferred, and other relevant information. This data can be used for auditing, billing, and troubleshooting purposes. One of the key advantages of using RADIUS is its ability to centralize the authentication process. This simplifies the management of user credentials and access policies, as well as provides a consistent authentication experience across all remote access connections. Additionally, RADIUS supports various authentication methods, including password-based authentication, token-based authentication, and certificate-based authentication. In conclusion, RADIUS is a networking protocol that facilitates secure and centralized authentication, authorization, and accounting for remote users. It enables organizations to control and manage remote access connections in a scalable and efficient manner.

Remote Desktop Protocol (RDP)

Remote Desktop Protocol (RDP) is a proprietary protocol developed by Microsoft that enables users to connect and control a remote computer over a network. RDP allows users to access and interact with a desktop or application on a remote machine as if they were physically present at that location. It provides a graphical interface that allows users to remotely control another computer and perform tasks as if they were sitting in front of it.

Reverse DNS Lookup

A reverse DNS lookup is a process used in networking to determine the domain name associated with a given IP address. Instead of finding the IP address associated with a domain name, as done in a regular DNS lookup, a reverse DNS lookup performs the opposite task. When a user provides an IP address, the reverse DNS lookup queries the Domain Name System (DNS) to find the associated domain name. This helps in identifying the owner or provider of the IP address and allows for more meaningful and informative data exchange over the internet.

Reverse Firewall Configuration

A reverse firewall configuration, in the context of networking, refers to a security measure that is implemented to protect a network or system by filtering and controlling incoming traffic. Unlike a traditional firewall, which mainly focuses on protecting against unauthorized outbound traffic, a reverse firewall is specifically designed to safeguard against unauthorized inbound traffic. When a request is made from an external source to access a protected network or system, the reverse firewall examines the request and applies a set of predefined rules to determine if the request is legitimate or poses a security risk. The configuration of the reverse firewall allows only authorized traffic to enter the network or system, while blocking or denying any suspicious or malicious traffic attempting to gain access.

Reverse Firewall

A reverse firewall, in the context of networking, refers to a security measure that protects an internal network or system by controlling and monitoring outbound traffic. Unlike a traditional firewall that primarily focuses on filtering inbound traffic, a reverse firewall specifically focuses on outbound traffic. It functions by inspecting and controlling the flow of data packets originating from an internal network or system and heading towards an external network or system. By analyzing the outbound traffic, a reverse firewall can detect and block any malicious or unauthorized activities attempting to leave the internal network.

Reverse Proxy Server

A reverse proxy server is a network component that receives requests from clients and forwards those requests to one or more servers on behalf of the clients. It acts as an intermediary between the clients and servers, providing various benefits and enhancing the overall network performance and security. When a client sends a request to access a particular resource or service, it is first directed to the reverse proxy server. The reverse proxy server then evaluates the request and determines the most appropriate server to handle the request based on predefined rules and configurations. One of the main benefits of using a reverse proxy server is load balancing. By distributing incoming requests across multiple servers, the reverse proxy server can optimize resource utilization and prevent any single server from getting overwhelmed with traffic. This helps to improve the overall response time and availability of the services. In addition to load balancing, a reverse proxy server can also be used for caching. It stores copies of frequently accessed resources locally, allowing subsequent requests for the same resources to be served faster by the proxy server itself rather than going all the way to the original server. This helps to reduce network latency and improve the overall performance of the system. Furthermore, a reverse proxy server can enhance network security by acting as a buffer between the clients and servers. It can inspect incoming requests, filter out malicious or unauthorized requests, and provide an additional layer of protection against various attacks such as DDoS (Distributed Denial of Service) attacks or Web Application attacks. Overall, a reverse proxy server plays a crucial role in network architectures by providing load balancing, caching, and security features. It helps to optimize resource utilization, improve performance, and protect servers from potential threats.

Reverse Proxy Solutions

Reverse Proxy

A reverse proxy is a network device that sits between clients and servers, acting as an intermediary for client requests. It receives client requests and forwards them to the appropriate server, acting on behalf of the client. A reverse proxy operates at the network-level and provides several benefits for network administrators and organizations. It helps optimize performance by caching static content, reducing the load on origin servers. By serving cached content directly to clients, it minimizes latency and improves response times. Additionally, it can distribute client requests across multiple servers, balancing the traffic load and preventing individual servers from becoming overwhelmed.

Root Certificate

A root certificate, also known as a root CA (Certificate Authority) certificate, is a digital certificate that is at the root of the certificate hierarchy in a public key infrastructure (PKI). It is the most trustworthy and authoritative certificate in the hierarchy, as it is used to validate all other certificates within the network. In the context of networking, the root certificate plays a crucial role in establishing secure communication channels between devices or systems. When a user or application tries to establish a secure connection with a server, the server presents its digital certificate as proof of its identity. This certificate is signed by an intermediate CA, which in turn is signed by a root CA. The root certificate acts as the ultimate authority that vouches for the legitimacy of the intermediate CA, and therefore, the server's certificate. Before trusting any certificates presented by servers, client devices must have the corresponding root certificate installed in their trust store. This trust store is a collection of trusted root certificates provided by operating system vendors or trusted third-party authorities. The client verifies the authenticity and integrity of a server's certificate by validating the certificate chain all the way up to the root certificate. The root certificate serves as a centralized point for managing trust within a network. Certificates issued by the root CA are used to secure various network services, including SSL/TLS encryption, digital signatures, secure email communication, and more. It ensures that only trusted entities or servers can participate in secure communication, preventing potential threats, such as man-in-the-middle attacks or unauthorized access. In summary, the root certificate is a fundamental component of network security that establishes the trustworthiness and authenticity of certificates in a PKI. It ensures the secure transmission of data by verifying and validating the identity of servers or entities involved in communication.

Rootkit Detection

A rootkit is a malicious software that is designed to gain unauthorized access and control over a computer system or network. In the context of networking, rootkit detection refers to the process of identifying and removing rootkits from a network to ensure the security and integrity of the networked systems. A rootkit typically works by hiding its presence and activity from the operating system and other security applications. It uses advanced techniques to manipulate system processes, modify system files, and evade detection by traditional antivirus software and security measures. Once installed, a rootkit can perform various malicious activities, such as stealing sensitive information, modifying system configurations, and even launching other types of malware on the network. To detect rootkits in a network, various methods and tools can be used. These include: 1. Signature-based detection: This method involves comparing the files and processes on the network against a database of known rootkit signatures. If a match is found, it indicates the presence of a rootkit. 2. Behavior-based detection: This approach focuses on identifying abnormal or suspicious behavior exhibited by files or processes on the network. It involves monitoring system activity and looking for patterns that are indicative of rootkit activity. 3. Heuristic detection: This method involves using algorithms and rules to identify potentially malicious behavior and patterns. It is particularly effective against new or unknown rootkits that may not have a signature in the detection database. 4. Memory analysis: Rootkits often reside in the computer's memory to avoid detection. Memory analysis techniques can help identify and analyze suspicious memory areas for the presence of rootkit code. In addition to these detection methods, it is essential to keep network systems and software up to date with the latest security patches and regularly scan for malware. Network administrators should also employ proper security measures, such as firewalls, intrusion detection systems, and access controls, to minimize the risk of rootkit infections.

Rootkit

A rootkit, in the context of networking, refers to a malicious software or program that is designed to gain unauthorized access to a computer system, specifically at the root level, where it has the highest level of control and privileges. It is a set of tools and techniques used by attackers to hide their presence and actions from the system's administrators and security measures. A rootkit typically infects a computer system through various means such as email attachments, software downloads, or exploiting vulnerabilities in the system's operating system or applications. Once installed, the rootkit establishes a persistent presence on the system by modifying critical system files and configurations to ensure its survival, even through system reboots or software updates. One of the main goals of a rootkit is to maintain remote access to the compromised system, which allows the attacker to control and manipulate the system as desired. This control can be used for various malicious activities, including stealing sensitive information, launching further attacks on other systems, or using the compromised system as a launching pad for larger-scale attacks. What makes rootkits particularly dangerous is their ability to remain undetected by most traditional security measures such as antivirus software and intrusion detection systems. They use advanced stealth techniques to hide their presence, including modifying system processes, intercepting system calls, and even replacing legitimate system files or drivers with malicious ones. Overall, rootkits pose a significant threat to network security as they can significantly compromise the integrity, confidentiality, and availability of a computer system. Detecting and removing rootkits can be a challenging task, requiring specialized tools and techniques that go beyond traditional security measures. Regular system updates, using reputable security software, and practicing safe browsing and email habits can help mitigate the risk of rootkit infections.

Router Configuration

A router configuration refers to the process of setting up and customizing the settings of a router device in a computer network. A router is a networking device that forwards data packets between computer networks, playing a crucial role in directing network traffic efficiently. Configuring a router involves various tasks to ensure its optimal performance and secure operation. It typically involves accessing the router's administrative interface, either through a web-based graphical user interface (GUI) or a command-line interface (CLI), and adjusting settings according to the network requirements. The configuration process may vary depending on the router manufacturer and the specific model. Some key aspects of router configuration include: 1. IP addressing: Setting up the IP address of the router itself, as well as defining IP addresses for the various devices connected to the network. This includes configuring static IP addresses or using dynamic IP addressing protocols like DHCP. 2. Routing protocols: Configuring routing protocols that enable the router to determine the best path for forwarding packets between networks. Examples of routing protocols include Border Gateway Protocol (BGP), Open Shortest Path First (OSPF), and Routing Information Protocol (RIP). 3. Network security: Implementing security measures to protect the network from unauthorized access and potential attacks. This includes setting up firewall rules, configuring virtual private networks (VPNs), and enabling encryption protocols like IPsec. 4. Quality of Service (QoS): Configuring QoS settings to prioritize certain types of network traffic over others. This ensures that critical applications, such as voice or video conferencing, receive sufficient bandwidth and low latency. 5. Port forwarding and network address translation (NAT): Defining rules to forward specific ports or protocols to specific devices within the network, allowing external access to services running on those devices. NAT is used to modify network address information in IP packet headers, enabling multiple devices to share a single public IP address. Overall, router configuration plays a vital role in establishing a functional and secure network environment. It allows network administrators to tailor the router's behavior as per the specific needs of their organization, ensuring smooth communication and efficient data transmission.

Router

A router is a networking device that forwards data packets between computer networks. It operates at the third layer, known as the network layer, of the Open Systems Interconnection (OSI) model. The main function of a router is to analyze the destination IP address of each incoming data packet and determine the best path to forward it to its intended destination. When a data packet arrives at a router, it examines the IP header to obtain the destination IP address. The router then consults its routing table, which contains a list of IP addresses and corresponding paths. Based on the information in the routing table, the router selects the most appropriate path for the data packet and forwards it accordingly. The routing table is typically populated through either static routes manually configured by a network administrator or dynamic routing protocols that exchange routing information between routers. Routers use various algorithms and protocols to make routing decisions. For example, one commonly used routing algorithm is the shortest path algorithm, which calculates the shortest path between the source and destination IP addresses based on metrics such as hop count, delay, or bandwidth. Routing protocols, such as Border Gateway Protocol (BGP) and Enhanced Interior Gateway Routing Protocol (EIGRP), enable routers to exchange information about network topology and dynamically update their routing tables. Routers can connect different types of networks, such as Local Area Networks (LANs), Wide Area Networks (WANs), and the Internet. They provide interconnectivity and enable communication between devices on different networks. Additionally, routers can perform Network Address Translation (NAT), which allows multiple devices on a LAN to share a single public IP address. In summary, a router is a crucial networking device that plays a vital role in directing data packets between networks. Its ability to analyze destination IP addresses, consult routing tables, and select the best path for data forwarding makes it an essential component in enabling network communication.

Routing Algorithm

A routing algorithm is a process or method used in networking to determine the optimal path for transmitting data packets from a source to a destination within a network. It helps to establish efficient and reliable communication by selecting the most suitable route based on various factors and constraints. Routing algorithms play a crucial role in managing network traffic and ensuring timely delivery of data packets. They are typically implemented in routers and switches, which act as intermediate devices for forwarding packets between different network segments or nodes. These algorithms make decisions based on information such as network topology, link costs, network congestion, and quality of service requirements. The primary objective of a routing algorithm is to find the shortest or least-cost path between a source and destination. This minimizes delay, reduces network congestion, and optimizes resource utilization. Routing algorithms can be classified into two main categories: distance-vector and link-state algorithms. Distance-vector algorithms compute the distance or cost of reaching other network nodes based

283

on the number of hops or the cumulative cost of traversing multiple hops. Examples of distance-vector routing protocols include Routing Information Protocol (RIP) and Interior Gateway Routing Protocol (IGRP). Link-state algorithms, on the other hand, rely on a complete and up-to-date view of the network topology. Each node in the network maintains a database of the network's state, which includes information about its neighboring nodes and links. By employing algorithms such as Dijkstra's algorithm or the Shortest Path First (SPF) algorithm, link-state routing protocols such as Open Shortest Path First (OSPF) and Intermediate System to Intermediate System (IS-IS) determine the most efficient path based on link costs and other metric factors. To select the best route, routing algorithms consider multiple factors, such as link bandwidth, reliability, delay, and available resources. They also adapt to dynamic network conditions and update routing tables accordingly. This flexibility enables efficient recovery from link failures, load balancing across multiple paths, and adaptation to changes in network topology. In summary, a routing algorithm is a critical component of networking that determines the optimal path for data transmission. By considering various factors and constraints, it ensures efficient and reliable communication within a network. Distance-vector and link-state algorithms are the two main types of routing algorithms that guide the forwarding of data packets through the network.

Routing Information Protocol (RIP)

The Routing Information Protocol (RIP) is a dynamic interior routing protocol used in computer networks to facilitate the exchange of routing information between routers. It is primarily designed for small to medium-sized networks. RIP uses the distance-vector algorithm to determine the best path for data packets to travel from one network to another. Each router participating in RIP maintains a routing table, which contains information about the network destinations and the corresponding metrics (cost or distance) associated with reaching them. When a router detects a change in the network topology, such as a link failure or a new network being added, it updates its routing table and broadcasts the changes to its neighboring routers. RIP sends these updates periodically at intervals of 30 seconds by default. RIP uses hop count as the metric to measure the distance between networks. It counts the number of routers (hops) a packet must traverse to reach a destination network. The maximum hop count allowed in RIP is 15, meaning that RIP is limited to networks within 15 hops of each other. Routers running RIP exchange routing information using User Datagram Protocol (UDP). The standard RIP runs on port number 520 for RIP version 1 and 2. RIP version 1 sends updates as broadcast messages, while version 2 supports both broadcast and multicast transmission. In RIP, a router can use the information received from its neighboring routers to update its routing table. If a better path (lower hop count) is discovered, the router updates its table accordingly. RIP uses split horizon with poison reverse technique to prevent routing loops. One limitation of RIP is its slow convergence time, meaning it takes some time for the routers to adjust their routing tables in response to network changes. This makes RIP less suitable for large or complex networks. Additionally, RIP has a relatively low scalability due to the hop count limitation and the frequent exchange of routing updates.

Routing Protocol Selection

Routing protocol selection is the process of determining the most efficient and reliable method for forwarding network packets within a computer network. It involves evaluating different routing protocols and selecting the one that best meets the network requirements and objectives. A routing protocol is a set of rules and algorithms used by routers to determine the optimal path for forwarding packets across an interconnected network. There are several routing protocols available, each designed to address specific network characteristics, such as scalability, reliability, and convergence time. The selection of a routing protocol depends on various factors, including the size and complexity of the network, network topology, traffic patterns, and the desired level of network performance. Different routing protocols have different strengths and weaknesses, so it is important to consider these factors to choose the most suitable one. The most commonly used routing protocols include: 1. Distance-vector protocols: These protocols determine the best path based on the distance or cost to a destination. Examples of distance-vector protocols include Routing Information Protocol (RIP) and Interior Gateway Routing Protocol (IGRP). 2. Link-state protocols: These protocols build a database of network topology by exchanging information with neighboring routers. They use this information to calculate the shortest path to a destination. Examples of link-state protocols include Open Shortest Path First

(OSPF) and Intermediate System to Intermediate System (IS-IS). 3. Hybrid protocols: These protocols combine characteristics of both distance-vector and link-state protocols. They are designed to provide a balance between scalability and convergence time. An example of a hybrid protocol is Enhanced Interior Gateway Routing Protocol (EIGRP). The selection of a routing protocol involves evaluating the capabilities and limitations of each protocol and considering factors such as network size, network topology, and performance requirements. It is important to select a protocol that can effectively handle the network's current demands and accommodate future growth and changes. In conclusion, routing protocol selection is a critical decision in network design and management. By carefully evaluating the available options and considering the specific requirements of the network, administrators can choose a routing protocol that optimizes network performance and reliability.

Routing Protocol Types

A routing protocol is a set of rules and algorithms that determine how data packets are forwarded or transmitted in a computer network. It enables network devices, such as routers, to communicate with each other, exchange information, and make informed decisions about the best path for data transmission. There are several types of routing protocols, each designed for specific network environments and requirements. The main types are: 1. Interior Gateway Protocols (IGPs): These protocols are used within an autonomous system (AS), which is a network under a single administrative domain. IGPs, such as OSPF (Open Shortest Path First) and EIGRP (Enhanced Interior Gateway Routing Protocol), are responsible for routing within the AS and ensure that data is efficiently transmitted between routers within the same network. 2. Exterior Gateway Protocols (EGPs): EGPs, also known as Border Gateway Protocols (BGPs), are used to exchange routing information between different ASs or autonomous systems. BGP is the most widely used EGP and is crucial for the functioning of the global Internet. It allows routers in different ASs to determine the optimal path for forwarding data between networks. 3. Hybrid Routing Protocols: Hybrid protocols combine features of both IGPs and EGPs. These protocols, such as EIGRP, provide a compromise between the simplicity of IGPs and the scalability of EGPs. Hybrid protocols are often used in medium-sized networks where a combination of interior and exterior routing is required. 4. Distance Vector Protocols: Distance vector protocols, such as Routing Information Protocol (RIP), determine the best path for data transmission based on the distance or number of hops. Each router passes information about its own routes to its neighboring routers, and together they build a routing table. Distance vector protocols are relatively simple but can lead to routing loops and less efficient routing decisions in large networks. 5. Link State Protocols: Link state protocols, such as OSPF, exchange information about the entire network topology with all routers in the network. Each router builds a detailed map of the network, including the available links, their bandwidth, and their priority. Link state protocols are more complex and resource-intensive compared to distance vector protocols but provide more accurate and efficient routing decisions.

Routing Protocol

A routing protocol is a set of rules and algorithms that determine how network devices, such as routers, communicate and exchange information with each other to efficiently and effectively forward data packets from source to destination in a computer network. The primary function of a routing protocol is to enable routers to dynamically learn and maintain information about the network topology and its current state. This information is crucial for routers to make intelligent decisions on the optimal paths to forward data packets towards their destinations.

Routing Table Entries

A routing table is a data structure used in networking to determine the best path for forwarding network traffic. It is an essential component of routers and switches, enabling them to efficiently transmit data packets to their intended destinations. Routing table entries, also known as route entries or routing entries, are individual records within the routing table that contain information about specific network destinations. Each entry includes crucial details such as the destination network address, the next-hop gateway or interface, and the cost or metric associated with the path.

Routing Table Optimization Techniques

285

Routing Table Optimization Techniques refer to a set of strategies implemented in computer networks to improve the efficiency and performance of routing tables. Routing tables play a crucial role in network routing, as they contain information about the available paths for data packets to travel from the source to the destination. These optimization techniques aim to reduce the size of the routing table, minimize the overhead of routing protocol messages, and enhance the speed and accuracy of packet forwarding. One common technique used for routing table optimization is route summarization, also known as route aggregation. It involves combining multiple network prefixes into a single summarized route. This helps to reduce the number of entries in the routing table, thus reducing the memory required to store and process the table. Moreover, route summarization eliminates the need for individual routing entries for every specific network address within a given range, resulting in a more concise table that is easier to manage and maintain. Another optimization technique used is route filtering. It involves filtering out unnecessary or irrelevant routing information from being included in the routing table. By selectively choosing which routes to include and which to discard, route filtering helps to reduce the size of the routing table and prevent unnecessary traffic from being routed. Additionally, route filtering contributes to enhanced security by blocking certain routes that may pose risks or vulnerabilities to the network. Furthermore, route redistribution is a technique used for optimizing routing tables in networks that employ multiple routing protocols. It involves the exchange and integration of routing information between different routing domains or protocols. By translating routing information from one protocol into another, route redistribution enables efficient communication and coordination between different routing algorithms and protocols, thus optimizing the overall routing process and maintaining a coherent and consistent routing table.

Routing Table Optimization

Routing Table Optimization refers to the process of improving the efficiency and performance of routing tables in a computer network. A routing table is a data structure stored in network devices, such as routers, which contains information about the paths and destinations in a network. It helps in determining the next hop or interface to forward network traffic. In a large and complex network, routing tables can become extensive and require frequent updates as network conditions change. This can lead to increased processing time, memory usage, and network latency. Routing Table Optimization aims to minimize these issues by streamlining the routing table entries and operations.

Routing Table Update

A routing table update is a process that occurs in networking when changes are made to the information stored in a router's routing table. The routing table is a key component in routing packets of data across a network, as it contains a list of known network destinations and the next hop to reach them. When a routing table update occurs, it means that the information in the routing table has been modified due to changes in the network topology, network devices, or network policies. These updates can happen for various reasons, such as new network connections being established, existing connections being removed, or changes in network link performance.

Routing Table

A routing table is a data structure maintained by a network device, such as a router, that contains information about the available routes for forwarding network traffic. It is used in network communication to determine the best path for data packets to travel from their source to their destination. The routing table is essentially a set of rules, known as routes, that specify how network packets should be forwarded. Each entry in the routing table includes the destination network address and the next hop, which is the next device that should receive the packet along the path to its destination. The next hop can be another router or the final destination device itself.

SMTP Relay Server

An SMTP relay server, also known as a mail transfer agent (MTA), is a network component that acts as an intermediary for transmitting email messages between different mail servers. It plays a crucial role in the email delivery process by routing emails accurately and efficiently across the internet. SMTP, which stands for Simple Mail Transfer Protocol, is the standard protocol used for sending and receiving emails between mail servers. When a user sends an email, their email client or application connects to their outgoing mail server, also known as the SMTP server. The SMTP server is responsible for relaying the email to the recipient's mail server. Here's how the SMTP relay server facilitates the email transmission process: 1. Sender Initiation: The sender composes an email and addresses it to the intended recipient. They specify their outgoing mail server (SMTP server) and provide the recipient's email address. 2. SMTP Connection: The sender's SMTP server establishes a connection with the recipient's SMTP server by using the recipient's domain name or IP address. This connection is typically secured using SSL/TLS encryption. 3. Email Relay: The sender's SMTP server transmits the email to the recipient's server via the SMTP relay server. The relay server acts as a trusted intermediary, responsible for forwarding the email to the correct destination based on the recipient's domain name or IP address. 4. Relaying Process: The relay server authenticates and authorizes the email transmission, ensuring that it complies with security policies and anti-spam measures. It verifies the sender's identity, checks for any content filtering rules, and scans for potential threats or malicious attachments. 5. Final Delivery: Once the relay server ensures the email's integrity and compliance, it delivers the email to the recipient's mailbox by handing it off to the recipient's SMTP server. The recipient can then retrieve the email using their mail client or webmail interface. In summary, an SMTP relay server acts as a reliable intermediary for transmitting email messages between mail servers, ensuring proper delivery, security, and compliance with various protocols and policies.

SMTP Relay Service

An SMTP Relay Service, also known as a Mail Relay Service, is a networking service that allows the transfer of email messages between different mail servers. It functions as an intermediary to ensure the successful delivery of emails from the sender's mail server to the recipient's mail server. SMTP stands for Simple Mail Transfer Protocol, which is the standard protocol used for sending and receiving emails on the internet. When an email is sent, it is typically relayed through a series of mail servers before reaching its final destination. Each of these mail servers acts as a relay, forwarding the email to the next server in the chain until it reaches the recipient's mail server. An SMTP Relay Service plays a crucial role in this process by ensuring that emails are properly relayed and delivered. It accomplishes this by authenticating the sender's mail server, allowing it to send emails on behalf of the sender's domain. This helps prevent unauthorized users from using the service for spamming or phishing purposes. The service also performs various checks and optimizations to enhance the delivery of emails. It verifies the integrity of the sender's email address, scans the email content for any potential issues (such as malware or suspicious attachments), and performs anti-spam checks to identify and filter out unsolicited or unwanted emails. In addition to relaying emails, an SMTP Relay Service also provides additional features and functionalities. It can queue emails during periods of high traffic or server downtime, allowing for later delivery when the server becomes available. It can also provide email tracking and reporting capabilities, allowing senders to monitor the status and delivery of their emails. Overall, an SMTP Relay Service acts as a critical component in the smooth and secure transfer of emails across different mail servers. It ensures that emails are relayed efficiently, protected from spam and malware, and delivered to the intended recipients without any issues.

SMTP Relay

An SMTP relay is a network device or software application that receives and transmits email messages over a network. Its primary purpose is to act as an intermediary between the sender's email server and the recipient's email server, facilitating the delivery of emails across different networks or domains. When a user wants to send an email, their email client (such as Microsoft Outlook or Gmail) connects to their email server using the SMTP (Simple Mail Transfer Protocol) protocol. The email server responsible for sending the email is often referred to as the "SMTP client". However, in some cases, the SMTP client might not be able to deliver the email directly to the recipient's email server. This can happen for various reasons, such as the recipient's email server being offline or the sender's email server being blocked by the recipient's email server. In such situations, the SMTP relay comes into play. The sender's SMTP client relays the email to the SMTP relay, which then takes the responsibility of delivering the email to the recipient's email server. The SMTP relay acts as a temporary storage and forwarding device for emails. It receives emails from the sender's SMTP client and verifies that they are correctly formatted and addressed. If everything is in order, the SMTP relay establishes a connection with the recipient's email server using SMTP and transmits the email to the server for further processing and delivery to the recipient's mailbox. SMTP relays are commonly used in large-scale email systems or organizations that send a high volume of emails. They can be implemented as dedicated hardware devices or as software applications running on specialized servers. In some cases, an organization might use a third-party SMTP relay service provided by an email service provider to handle the email delivery process. In conclusion, an SMTP relay plays a crucial role in ensuring the successful delivery of emails across different networks or domains. By acting as an intermediary between the sender's email server and the recipient's email server, it helps overcome potential obstacles and ensures that emails reach their intended recipients.

SMTP Server Configuration

SMTP Server Configuration refers to the process of setting up a Simple Mail Transfer Protocol (SMTP) server for sending and receiving email messages over a network. SMTP is a standard protocol used for the transmission of email between mail servers, allowing users to send and receive messages across different email systems. An SMTP server acts as a mail transfer agent, responsible for routing email messages from the sender to the recipient's mail server. It uses a client-server architecture, where the client is the email client application used by the sender, and the server is the SMTP server that handles the message transfer.

SMTP Server Security Configuration

A secure SMTP (Simple Mail Transfer Protocol) server configuration refers to the implementation of measures and controls to protect the server from unauthorized access, prevent abuse, and ensure the confidentiality, integrity, and availability of email communication. To enhance the security of an SMTP server, several configuration settings and best practices can be followed: Firstly, secure authentication mechanisms should be implemented to verify the identity of users accessing the server. This can include requiring strong passwords, enforcing password complexity rules, and implementing multi-factor authentication. Additionally, the use of encrypted protocols, such as Transport Layer Security (TLS), can help protect the authentication process and ensure the confidentiality of user credentials. Secondly, access controls should be configured to restrict connections to the SMTP server. This can involve setting up firewall rules to allow only trusted IP addresses or networks to connect to the server. By limiting access to authorized entities, the risk of unauthorized users gaining control of the server and potentially abusing it for spamming or sending malicious emails can be mitigated. Thirdly, proper email filtering and content scanning should be implemented to detect and block spam, malware, and phishing attempts. This can be achieved by employing reputable antivirus and antispam software, as well as regularly updating the filters and rules to stay protected against evolving threats. Furthermore, logging and monitoring mechanisms should be enabled to track and record any suspicious activities or unauthorized access attempts. By reviewing logs and analyzing network traffic, administrators can quickly identify potential security breaches and take necessary actions to mitigate them. Lastly, regular patching and updates should be performed to keep the SMTP server software and operating system up-to-date with the latest security patches. Unpatched vulnerabilities in software can be exploited by attackers to gain unauthorized access or disrupt the server's operation. In conclusion, a secure SMTP server configuration involves implementing authentication mechanisms, access controls, email filtering, logging and monitoring, and regular updates to protect against unauthorized access, abuse, and ensure the secure transmission of emails.

SMTP Server Security

An SMTP server, also known as a Simple Mail Transfer Protocol server, is a computerized application that serves as the centralized hub for sending and receiving emails within a network. It is designed to handle the transmission of messages from one email client to another, ensuring their proper delivery through a series of predefined protocols. In the context of networking, SMTP server security refers to the measures taken to protect the server and the data it handles from unauthorized access, misuse, and potential threats. This includes implementing various security mechanisms to prevent data breaches, unauthorized email relaying, and other malicious activities.

SMTP Server Troubleshooting

SMTP Server Troubleshooting is the process of identifying and resolving issues related to the Simple Mail Transfer Protocol (SMTP) server, which is responsible for sending and receiving emails in a networked environment. The SMTP server is a critical component of email communication, as it plays a crucial role in ensuring the successful delivery of messages between email clients. However, various factors can cause problems with the SMTP server, resulting in email delivery failures or other issues. When troubleshooting SMTP server problems, several steps can be followed to diagnose and resolve the issues: 1. Verify Server Configuration: The first step is to check the SMTP server configuration settings to ensure they are correctly set up. This includes verifying the server address, port number, authentication requirements, and any other relevant settings. 2. Check Connectivity: Next, it is essential to confirm that the SMTP server is accessible and can be reached from the network. This can be done by pinging the server or using other network diagnostic tools to test the connection. 3. Review Logs: Examining the log files of the SMTP server can provide valuable insights into the root cause of the problem. The logs may contain error messages, connection attempts, or other information that can help identify the issue. 4. Test Email Delivery: Sending test emails to and from the SMTP server can help determine if the problem lies with the server itself or with the email client or recipient server. By analyzing the results of these tests, it becomes easier to narrow down the potential causes. 5. Check Firewall and Antivirus Settings: Sometimes, firewalls or antivirus software can block the SMTP server's communication. Verifying the settings of these security measures and temporarily disabling them for testing purposes can help determine if they are causing the issue. 6. Consult Documentation and Online Resources: In case the previous steps do not resolve the problem, referring to the SMTP server's documentation or searching online resources for known issues and their solutions can provide additional guidance. By following these steps and systematically analyzing the SMTP server's configuration, connectivity, logs, and other factors, network administrators can effectively troubleshoot and resolve SMTP server problems to ensure smooth email communication within the networked environment.

SMTP Server

A Simple Mail Transfer Protocol (SMTP) Server is a computer program or software that allows for the sending and receiving of electronic mail (email) over a network. It is a vital component of the email infrastructure and plays a significant role in the overall process of email communication. SMTP is a set of rules and conventions that define how email messages should be transmitted and delivered across networks. The SMTP server acts as an intermediary between the sender's email client and the recipient's email server, facilitating the transfer of email messages from one point to another.

SMTP (Simple Mail Transfer Protocol)

SMTP (Simple Mail Transfer Protocol) is a widely used network protocol specifically designed for the reliable transmission of email messages between computers and servers. It establishes a set of rules and procedures for how email messages should be sent and received over a network, ensuring that they are delivered to the correct destination and in the correct format. SMTP operates on the application layer of the TCP/IP protocol stack, which means it utilizes the services provided by lower-level protocols such as TCP (Transmission Control Protocol) to establish a connection between the sending and receiving mail servers. This connection allows for the transfer of email messages in a reliable and orderly manner. When an email is sent using SMTP, it follows a series of steps to ensure its successful delivery. First, the sending server establishes a TCP connection with the receiving server on port 25, which is the default port for SMTP communication. This connection is usually made using the Simple Mail Transfer Protocol (SMTP) service that runs on the receiving server. Once the connection is established, the sending server initiates the email transfer by issuing commands to the receiving server. The SMTP commands are simple text-based instructions that indicate the sender's identity, the recipient's address, and the content of the email message. These commands include HELO (or EHLO), MAIL FROM, RCPT TO, DATA, and QUIT, among others. Each command is followed by a response code from the receiving server, indicating whether the command was recognized and executed successfully. SMTP ensures the reliable delivery of email messages by employing various mechanisms such as error detection, retransmission, and acknowledgment. If an error occurs during the email transfer, SMTP can retransmit the message or notify the sender of the failure. This ensures that email messages are not lost or corrupted during transmission. In addition to its role in email transmission, SMTP also allows for email delivery between different mail servers. When an email message is sent from one domain to another, SMTP enables the transfer of the message from the sender's mail server to the recipient's mail server, regardless of their physical location. In conclusion, SMTP is a vital protocol in computer networking that facilitates the transfer of email messages between computers and servers. It provides a reliable and standardized method for sending and receiving email, ensuring that messages are delivered accurately and efficiently.

SMTP Troubleshooting

The Simple Mail Transfer Protocol (SMTP) is a protocol used for the transfer of electronic mail (email) between computer systems in a network. It is an application layer protocol that relies on the underlying Transmission Control Protocol (TCP) to provide reliable communication. SMTP troubleshooting involves the process of identifying and resolving issues that may occur during the transmission of emails using the SMTP protocol. These issues can cause delays, failures, or other problems in delivering email messages. There are several common problems that can occur during SMTP communication, including: 1. Connection issues: This can include problems with establishing a connection to the mail server or maintaining a stable connection. It can be caused by network connectivity issues, firewall settings, or problems with the mail server itself. 2. Authentication issues: SMTP servers may require authentication before allowing email transmission. Troubleshooting may involve identifying and resolving issues with incorrect or expired credentials, or problems with the authentication server. 3. Server configuration issues: Misconfiguration of the mail server can lead to issues with SMTP communication. This can include incorrect settings for domains, mail routing, or security settings. Troubleshooting may involve reviewing and correcting these configuration settings. 4. DNS issues: SMTP relies on the Domain Name System (DNS) to resolve domain names to IP addresses. Problems with DNS can cause delays or failures in delivering email messages. Troubleshooting may involve checking DNS settings, resolving DNS issues, or using alternative DNS servers. 5. Spam filtering issues: Some email servers have spam filters in place that may incorrectly classify legitimate emails as spam. Troubleshooting may involve checking spam filter settings, whitelisting email addresses, or working with the recipient's IT team to resolve filtering issues. In order to troubleshoot SMTP issues, it is important to gather as much information as possible about the problem. This can include reviewing server logs, checking network connectivity, testing SMTP settings, and contacting the relevant IT teams or service providers for assistance. By following a systematic troubleshooting process and addressing each possible issue step by step, it is possible to identify and resolve SMTP problems, ensuring reliable email communication within a network.

SQL Injection Attack

SQL Injection Attack is a security vulnerability that occurs when an attacker manipulates the input data in a web application's SQL query, with the intention of bypassing the application's security measures and accessing or manipulating the underlying database. This type of attack takes advantage of a lack of proper input validation and sanitization mechanisms implemented by the web application. By injecting malicious SQL code into user inputs, the attacker can execute arbitrary SQL queries, potentially gaining unauthorized access to sensitive information, altering or deleting data, or even taking control of the entire database system.

SQL Injection Exploit

An SQL Injection is a type of cyber attack that targets websites and applications using a vulnerable Structured Query Language (SQL) database. It is a technique where an attacker inserts malicious SQL code into a database query, manipulating the behavior of the application and potentially gaining unauthorized access to sensitive information.SQL Injection attacks take advantage of input fields on a website or application that do not properly validate or sanitize user input. These input fields are often used to construct SQL queries that interact with a database.

By inserting malicious SQL statements into these input fields, an attacker can bypass authentication mechanisms, retrieve, modify, or delete data, and potentially gain full control over the database.The impact of an SQL Injection attack can be severe. It can lead to data breaches, unauthorized access to sensitive information, loss of trust from customers, and legal consequences for the organization. Attackers can extract usernames, passwords, credit card numbers, or any other data stored in the database.To prevent SQL Injection attacks, it is crucial to implement proper input validation and sanitization techniques. This includes validating user input against expected formats, using parameterized queries or prepared statements instead of dynamic SQL, and enforcing principle of least privilege by granting minimal privileges to database users.Additionally, regularly updating and patching the software and frameworks used in an application can help protect against known vulnerabilities that attackers may exploit. Application developers should also follow secure coding practices, such as encoding user input, avoiding the use of concatenated SQL strings, and implementing security mechanisms like firewalls and intrusion detection systems.

SQL Injection

SQL Injection is a type of cyber attack that targets web applications running on a backend database management system (DBMS) through the exploitation of vulnerable input fields. It involves the insertion of malicious SQL code into a query, allowing the attacker to manipulate or retrieve unauthorized data from the database. This attack takes advantage of the fact that many web applications dynamically generate SQL queries by concatenating user input with the query string. If proper input validation and sanitization measures are not implemented, an attacker can insert specially crafted input that alters the intended functionality of the query. The consequences of a successful SQL Injection attack can be severe. The attacker may be able to bypass authentication mechanisms, gain unauthorized access to sensitive data, modify or delete data, or even take control of the entire web application. Furthermore, SQL Injection attacks can be difficult to detect and mitigate, making them a significant concern for network security professionals. To prevent SQL Injection attacks, several best practices should be followed. First, the use of parameterized queries or prepared statements can help eliminate the risk of SQL Injection by separating user input from the query logic. This approach ensures that the input is treated as data rather than executable code. Additionally, input validation and sanitization techniques should be employed to filter out any malicious input or escape special characters. Employing the principle of least privilege, where database accounts only have the necessary permissions, can limit the damage an attacker can cause if they manage to exploit a vulnerability. In conclusion, SQL Injection poses a significant threat to the security of web applications and databases. By exploiting vulnerabilities in input validation and sanitization, attackers can gain unauthorized access to sensitive information or manipulate database operations. Network security professionals must implement proper mitigation techniques, such as using parameterized queries and input validation, to protect against SQL Injection attacks.

SSH (Secure Shell)

SSH (Secure Shell) is a cryptographic network protocol that provides a secure method of accessing and managing remote devices over an unsecured network. It allows users to securely log in to a remote system or server and perform various tasks such as executing commands, transferring files, and managing network services. SSH works by establishing an encrypted connection between the client (the user's device) and the server (the remote device). This encryption ensures that all data transferred between the client and the server is protected from unauthorized access or tampering. One of the key features of SSH is the use of public-key cryptography to authenticate the client and the server. This involves the generation of a key pair consisting of a public key and a private key. The public key is placed on the server, while the private key remains with the client. When a connection is established, the client uses its private key to encrypt a challenge sent by the server. The server then verifies the client's identity by decrypting the challenge with the client's public key. This authentication process ensures that only authorized clients can access the server. In addition to authentication, SSH also provides secure data transfer and integrity checks. All data transferred between the client and the server is encrypted using a symmetric encryption algorithm. This encryption prevents eavesdropping and protects the confidentiality of the data. SSH also employs hash functions to verify the integrity of the data. Hash values are calculated on both ends of the connection, and if they do not match, it indicates that the data was tampered with in transit. SSH supports various protocols and allows for the secure execution of remote commands, remote administration of systems, and file transfers. It is commonly used by system administrators, network engineers, and developers to remotely manage devices, troubleshoot issues, and securely transfer files between systems. In summary, SSH is a cryptographic network protocol that provides secure access and management of remote devices. It ensures confidentiality, data integrity, and authentication through encryption, hash functions, and public-key cryptography. SSH is a vital tool for secure remote administration and file transfers in networking environments.

SSL Certificate

An SSL (Secure Sockets Layer) certificate is a digital certificate that is used to establish a secure and encrypted connection between a client and a server over a network. It serves as a proof of identity and protects sensitive information transmitted between the client and the server. When a client connects to a server using HTTPS (HTTP over SSL/TLS), the server presents its SSL certificate to the client. The client checks the validity and authenticity of the certificate to ensure the server's identity. If the certificate is trustworthy and matches the server's identity, a secure and encrypted connection is established.

SSL Pinning

SSL pinning, also known as certificate pinning, is a security measure implemented at the networking level to enhance the trust and integrity of secure connections. It involves associating a specific SSL/TLS certificate or a public key with a particular server or domain, effectively "pinning" the connection to that entity. When SSL pinning is enabled, the client device or application verifies the server's identity by comparing the presented SSL certificate or public key with the pre-established trusted certificate or public key. This process helps prevent man-in-the-middle attacks by ensuring that the client only accepts connections with the specified server or domain.

SSL (Secure Sockets Layer)

SSL (Secure Sockets Layer) is a cryptographic protocol that provides secure communication over a computer network. It is designed to establish a secure connection between a client and a server, ensuring the confidentiality, integrity, and authenticity of data transmissions. SSL operates at the transport layer of the network protocol stack and is widely used in applications such as web browsing, email, instant messaging, and virtual private networks (VPNs). It enables users to securely exchange sensitive information, such as login credentials, credit card details, and personal data, over insecure networks. When a client initiates a connection request to a server, SSL is used to establish a secure session between them. The SSL handshake process involves several steps: 1. Client Hello: The client sends a hello message to the server, specifying the supported SSL/TLS versions, encryption algorithms, and other parameters. 2. Server Hello: The server receives the client hello message and responds with a server hello message, selecting the SSL/TLS version, encryption algorithm, and other parameters that will be used for the secure session. 3. Certificate Exchange: The server sends its digital certificate to the client to authenticate its identity. The certificate contains the server's public key, which will be used for encryption. 4. Key Exchange: The client generates a random pre-master secret and encrypts it using the server's public key. The server decrypts the pre-master secret using its private key and both the client and server use this shared secret to derive symmetric session keys for encryption and decryption. 5. Authentication and Session Establishment: The client verifies the server's digital certificate to ensure its authenticity. The server may also request client authentication if required. Once the authentication is successful, the SSL session is established, and secure data transmission can begin. During the SSL session, data is encrypted before being transmitted, ensuring that it remains confidential and cannot be intercepted or tampered with by unauthorized parties. SSL also provides mechanisms for verifying the integrity of data to detect any changes that may have occurred during transmission. In conclusion, SSL is a fundamental security protocol that enables secure communication between clients and servers over a network. It establishes a secure session and ensures the confidentiality, integrity, and authenticity of data transmissions, protecting sensitive information from unauthorized access or manipulation.

SSL/TLS Protocols

The SSL/TLS protocols are secure communication protocols that provide encryption, authentication, and integrity protection for data transmitted over a network. SSL (Secure Sockets Layer) and TLS (Transport Layer Security) are cryptographic protocols that are used to establish secure connections between clients and servers in a network environment. These protocols ensure that data transmitted between the client and server is protected against eavesdropping, tampering, and forgery.

SSL/TLS (Secure Sockets Layer/Transport Layer Security)

SSL/TLS, which stands for Secure Sockets Layer/Transport Layer Security, is a cryptographic protocol designed to provide secure communication over a computer network. It is commonly used to ensure the confidentiality, integrity, and authenticity of data transmitted between a client (such as a web browser) and a server. The SSL/TLS protocol works by establishing an encrypted connection between the client and server, ensuring that any data transmitted between the two parties is protected from eavesdropping or tampering. This is achieved through the use of cryptographic algorithms, such as symmetric encryption, asymmetric encryption, and message integrity checks. When a client connects to a server using SSL/TLS, the protocol initiates a handshake process to establish the secure connection. This includes the exchange of cryptographic keys and the negotiation of encryption algorithms and protocols. Once the handshake is completed, the client and server can exchange data in a secure manner. An important feature of SSL/TLS is its ability to authenticate the server to the client, ensuring that the client is communicating with the intended server and not an imposter. This is typically done through the use of digital certificates, which are issued by trusted third-party entities known as Certificate Authorities (CAs). The digital certificate contains the server's public key and is used to verify the server's identity. In addition to server authentication, SSL/TLS also supports client authentication, where the client presents a digital certificate to the server to prove its identity. This can be useful in scenarios where the server needs to ensure that only authorized clients can access its resources. SSL/TLS is widely used in various network protocols, such as HTTPS (HTTP over SSL/TLS), SMTPS (SMTP over SSL/TLS), and FTPS (FTP over SSL/TLS). It provides a crucial layer of security to ensure the protection of sensitive data transmitted over the network.

Scalable Networking

Scalable networking refers to the ability of a network to efficiently handle a growing number of users, devices, and data traffic without compromising performance or functionality. It ensures that the network infrastructure can accommodate increased demands and provides an optimal user experience even as the network expands. In a rapidly evolving digital landscape, where the number of connected devices and data consumption continue to rise, scalable networking is crucial. It allows organizations to meet the demands of a dynamic and expanding network environment, facilitating seamless connectivity, efficient data transfer, and reliable access to resources. By implementing scalable networking solutions, businesses can scale their operations without experiencing network bottlenecks or performance degradation. There are several key components to consider when designing a scalable network infrastructure. Firstly, network capacity should be easily expandable to accommodate increased user connections and data traffic. This can be achieved through the use of scalable network architectures like hierarchical or modular designs, which allow for the addition of new equipment and resources without disrupting the entire network. Secondly, scalability in terms of network bandwidth is essential. Bandwidth determines the amount of data that can be transmitted over the network at any given time. To ensure scalability, networks should be designed with sufficient bandwidth capacity to handle increasing data flows. This can be achieved through the use of technologies like link aggregation, load balancing, and high-speed network links. Lastly, infrastructure components such as switches, routers, and servers should be scalable, allowing for the addition or removal of devices as needed. Scalable networking also encompasses the ability to dynamically allocate resources based on demand, ensuring optimal utilization and efficient network operation. In summary, scalable networking refers to the design and implementation of network architectures and infrastructure that can easily adapt and grow to accommodate increasing user, device, and data demands. It plays a critical role in enabling organizations to expand their network capabilities without sacrificing performance or reliability.

Secure Socket Layer (SSL)

Secure Socket Layer (SSL) is a cryptographic protocol that provides secure communication over a computer network. It ensures the confidentiality, integrity, and authenticity of transmitted data between two endpoints, typically a client and a server. SSL operates in the transport layer of the Open Systems Interconnection (OSI) model, allowing applications to establish secure and encrypted connections. SSL uses a combination of symmetric and asymmetric encryption techniques to secure the data transmission. When a client wants to establish an SSL connection with a server, it initiates a handshake process. During this process, the client and server negotiate various parameters, including the encryption algorithm, session keys, and digital certificates. Once the handshaking is complete, SSL uses symmetric encryption to encrypt the data transmitted over the network. This means that both the client and server share the same session key for encrypting and decrypting the data. The symmetric encryption ensures that the data remains confidential and protected from unauthorized access. In addition to encryption, SSL also provides integrity and authenticity checks. It uses cryptographic hashes and digital signatures to verify the integrity of the transmitted data. This ensures that the data received by the recipient is the same as the data sent by the sender. The digital certificates, issued by trusted certificate authorities (CAs), play a crucial role in verifying the authenticity of the server. SSL has become an industry standard for securing sensitive data over the internet. It is commonly used for securing web browsing, email communication, online banking, and e-commerce transactions. The widespread adoption of SSL has led to its successor, Transport Layer Security (TLS), which is an improved and more secure version of the protocol.

Secure Sockets Layer Virtual Private Network (SSL VPN)

A Secure Sockets Layer Virtual Private Network (SSL VPN) is a secure method of accessing a private network remotely over the public Internet or other insecure networks. It utilizes the encryption capabilities of the SSL/TLS protocol to establish a secure connection between the remote user's device and the network's resources. SSL VPNs provide a secure channel for transmitting data by encrypting the information exchanged between the remote user and the network. This encryption ensures that the data remains confidential and protected from unauthorized access during transmission. Additionally, SSL VPNs authenticate the remote user's identity to ensure that only authorized individuals can access the network's resources.

Security Assertion Markup Language (SAML)

Security Assertion Markup Language (SAML) is an XML-based open standard protocol that enables the exchange of authentication and authorization data between an identity provider (IDP) and a service provider (SP) in a network environment. SAML is primarily used for single sign-on (SSO) authentication scenarios, where a user can access multiple applications and services using a single set of credentials. It provides a standardized framework for securely transmitting user identity and attribute information across different domains, allowing users to authenticate once and access multiple resources without having to re-enter their credentials.

Security Assessment

A security assessment in the context of networking refers to the evaluation and analysis of the security posture of a network infrastructure. It involves the identification of potential vulnerabilities, risks, and threats that could compromise the confidentiality, integrity, and availability of network resources and data. During a security assessment, various techniques and tools are used to assess the effectiveness of security controls and mechanisms implemented within the network. This includes examining network configurations, reviewing security policies and procedures, performing vulnerability scans, and conducting penetration testing. The primary objective of a security assessment is to identify weaknesses and gaps in the network's defense systems, and to propose appropriate measures to mitigate the identified risks. This process helps organizations to proactively address vulnerabilities before they can be exploited by malicious actors. One key aspect of a security assessment is the identification and assessment of network vulnerabilities. This involves the examination of potential entry points or vulnerabilities in the network infrastructure, such as unpatched software, misconfigured devices, weak passwords, or outdated firmware. By identifying these vulnerabilities, organizations can take necessary steps to patch or remediate them, reducing the risk of successful attacks. Another important aspect of a security assessment is evaluating the effectiveness of security controls and mechanisms. This includes examining firewall configurations, intrusion detection systems, access controls, and encryption protocols. By assessing the effectiveness of these controls, organizations can identify any weaknesses or potential gaps in their security infrastructure, and implement appropriate measures to strengthen them. Additionally, a security assessment involves reviewing security policies and procedures to ensure they align with industry best practices and regulatory requirements. This ensures that organizations have defined guidelines and procedures in place to prevent, detect, and respond to security incidents effectively. By conducting regular security assessments, organizations can proactively identify and address potential security risks, minimize the likelihood of successful attacks, and protect their network infrastructure and valuable data from unauthorized access, modification, or disclosure.

Security Breach

A security breach, in the context of networking, refers to the unauthorized access, disclosure, or modification of confidential or sensitive information. It can also involve the disruption or alteration of networks, systems, or services, leading to potential harm or damage to an organization or individual. Security breaches can occur due to various factors, including software vulnerabilities, weak or compromised passwords, social engineering attacks, malware infections, insider threats, or inadequate security measures. When a breach occurs, it can result in severe consequences, such as financial loss, reputational damage, legal implications, and potential harm to individuals or businesses.

Security Incident Response Team (SIRT)

A Security Incident Response Team (SIRT) is a specialized group within an organization responsible for handling and responding to security incidents in the context of networking. When it comes to network security, incidents such as unauthorized access, data breaches, malware infections, and network outages can have severe consequences for an organization's operations, reputation, and customer trust. To effectively respond to these incidents in a timely manner, a dedicated team with the necessary expertise and resources is essential. The primary role of a SIRT is to detect, analyze, contain, and mitigate security incidents within a network environment. They act as the first line of defense when an incident occurs and are responsible for coordinating the response efforts to minimize the impact and restore normal operations as quickly as possible. SIRTs typically consist of highly skilled individuals from various disciplines, including network administrators, security analysts, forensic experts, and incident response coordinators. Together, they form a cohesive unit that can effectively manage incident response activities. The key responsibilities of a SIRT include: 1. Incident Detection: The SIRT monitors network activities and systems for potential security breaches, employing various tools and techniques for early detection of security incidents. 2. Incident Analysis: Once an incident is detected, the SIRT conducts a thorough analysis to determine the source, impact, and methodology used in the attack. They gather and analyze relevant data, such as log files, network traffic, and system configurations, to gain a comprehensive understanding of the incident. 3. Incident Containment: After analyzing the incident, the SIRT takes immediate actions to contain and limit its spread. This may involve isolating affected systems, blocking network access, or shutting down compromised services to prevent further damage. 4. Incident Mitigation: The SIRT works intelligently to mitigate the impact of the incident, ensuring that affected systems are repaired, restored, and hardened against future attacks. They also provide guidance and recommendations to prevent similar incidents from occurring in the future. 5. Incident Communication: Effective communication is crucial during an incident response. The SIRT is responsible for notifying relevant stakeholders, including management, legal teams, and authorities, about the incident, its impact, and the steps being taken to address it. Overall, a Security Incident Response Team plays a critical role in maintaining the security and integrity of a network environment. Their expertise, coordination, and swift actions are essential to effectively respond to incidents and minimize the potential damages that can result from security breaches.

Security Incident

A security incident in the context of networking refers to an unauthorized event or activity that compromises the integrity, confidentiality, or availability of computer networks, systems, or data. It can include a wide range of incidents such as unauthorized access attempts, data breaches, malware infections, network disruptions, or other malicious activities. These incidents can have severe consequences, including financial losses, reputation damage, legal implications, and the compromise of sensitive or valuable information. Detecting and responding to security incidents is crucial to mitigate the potential impact and prevent further damage.

Security Information And Event Management (SIEM)

Security Information and Event Management (SIEM) is a comprehensive networking solution designed to provide real-time visibility into security incidents and threats within a network environment. SIEM combines the capabilities of security information management (SIM) and security event management (SEM) into a unified system, allowing for proactive monitoring, analysis, and response to security events across the network. The primary purpose of SIEM is to collect, aggregate, and correlate log data from various sources, such as network devices, servers, applications, and security systems, to detect and investigate potential security incidents. By centralizing log data, SIEM enables network administrators and security teams to gain a holistic view of the network activities and identify any patterns or anomalies that may indicate a security breach or malicious activity. With SIEM, organizations can set up real-time alerts and automated response mechanisms based on predefined security policies and rules. This proactive approach helps organizations mitigate risks and reduce the impact of potential security threats. SIEM also enables organizations to generate detailed reports and audit logs for compliance purposes, allowing them to demonstrate adherence to regulatory requirements and industry standards. Moreover, SIEM solutions provide advanced analytics capabilities, such as behavioral profiling, anomaly detection, and threat intelligence integration, to enhance the detection and response capabilities. These analytics help identify abnormal user behavior, potentially compromised systems, and emerging threats in real-time, enabling quick and effective incident response. In addition to security monitoring and incident response, SIEM also plays a crucial role in network management and operations. By analyzing log data and identifying areas of improvement, SIEM can help optimize network performance, identify operational inefficiencies, and streamline security processes. This holistic approach to network security and management enables organizations to achieve a better overall security posture and operational efficiency.

Security Onion

Security Onion is an open-source network security monitoring and log management solution designed for identifying and analyzing potential security threats in computer networks. It is designed to assist network administrators and security analysts in detecting and responding to malicious activities by providing a centralized platform for collecting and analyzing network traffic data, intrusion detection events, and system logs.

Security Patch

A security patch is a software update that is designed to fix vulnerabilities or address weaknesses in a computer network's security system. It is an essential component of network security management, as it helps in preventing unauthorized access, data breaches, and other potential security threats. Security patches are typically developed by software developers or vendors to address known security vulnerabilities or weaknesses that have been identified in their software or network systems. These vulnerabilities can be exploited by hackers or malicious actors to gain unauthorized access, steal sensitive data, or disrupt network operations.

Security Token Authentication (STA)

Security Token Authentication (STA) is a method used in networking to provide secure access to resources, systems, or applications. It is a two-factor authentication process that combines something a user knows, such as a password, with something a user possesses, such as a physical token or a smartphone application. STA works by requiring users to enter their login credentials, which typically consist of a username and password. Once these credentials are verified, the authentication system generates a unique token that is tied to the user's session. This token is then sent to the user's device, either through a physical token device or a mobile application. When the user attempts to access a resource, system, or application, they are prompted to enter this token, which acts as a second layer of authentication. This process ensures that even if a user's password is compromised, unauthorized access is prevented without possession of the physical token or access to the user's mobile device. Security Token Authentication offers several advantages over traditional username/password authentication methods. Firstly, it provides an additional layer of security by requiring a physical token or access to a mobile device in addition to the password. This makes it much more difficult for an attacker to gain unauthorized access even if they manage to obtain a user's password. Furthermore, STA can be used to provide time-based authentication, where the token expires after a certain period. This enhances security by ensuring that even if a token is stolen or lost, it becomes useless after the predetermined time limit. Additionally, STA can provide accountability and traceability as each token is unique and tied to a specific user session. This allows network administrators to track and monitor user activities, which is particularly useful in situations where compliance with security or regulatory standards is necessary.

Security Token Service (STS)

A Security Token Service (STS) is a component in networking that is responsible for issuing security tokens to users, which can then be used for authentication and authorization purposes. It acts as a trusted third party that validates the identity of users and provides them with tokens that can be used to access various resources. When a user tries to access a protected resource, they first need to authenticate themselves to the STS. This can be done through various authentication methods such as username/password, multifactor authentication, or integration with external authentication providers. Once the user is authenticated, the STS issues a security token that represents the user's identity. The security token contains information about the user's identity, such as their username and any relevant attributes or claims. It is digitally signed by the STS to ensure its authenticity and integrity. The token also includes a validity period, after which it expires and cannot be used for authentication anymore. When the user presents the security token to a resource provider, such as a web application or a service, the provider can verify the token's authenticity by validating the digital signature. It can also extract the user's identity and any associated claims or attributes from the token to make authorization decisions. The use of STS provides several advantages in networking. It allows for centralized authentication and authorization, reducing the need for each resource provider to maintain its own user database or authentication system. It also enables single sign-on (SSO) capabilities, where users only need to authenticate once to gain access to multiple resources or applications. Furthermore, STS supports federated identity, allowing users from different organizations or domains to access shared resources using their own identity providers. This enables seamless collaboration and integration across organizational boundaries.

Security Token

A security token in the context of networking is a form of authentication that is used to prove a user's identity when accessing a network. It is a digital credential that is typically issued by a trusted authority, such as a network administrator or a certificate authority. The security token is usually in the form of a physical device, such as a smart card or a USB token, or it may be a software-based token that is stored on a mobile device or computer. The token is used in conjunction with a username and password to provide an additional layer of security for network access.

Server Cluster

A server cluster is a group of interconnected computers that work together to provide high availability and scalability for networked services. In a server cluster, multiple servers are connected through a network and operated as a single system to distribute and manage tasks efficiently. The primary goal of a server cluster is to ensure uninterrupted service availability and handle increased workload demands by distributing the processing load across multiple servers. Server clusters are commonly used in large-scale networks where high availability and reliability are critical. By distributing the workload across multiple servers, server clusters can achieve fault tolerance and eliminate single points of failure. If one server fails or becomes overloaded, another server in the cluster can take over and continue providing services, without disrupting the overall functionality of the network.

Server Configuration

Server configuration refers to the process of setting up and adjusting the settings and parameters of a server system to optimize its performance and ensure its proper functioning within a networked environment. It involves a series of tasks and decisions that are made to tailor the server to meet the specific requirements and needs of the network. During server configuration, various aspects of the server are considered and adjusted, including hardware, software, and network settings. Hardware configuration involves determining the appropriate hardware components and their settings, such as processors, memory, storage devices, and network interface cards. Software configuration involves installing and configuring the operating system, applications, and services that will run on the server. Network configuration involves setting up network connections, IP addresses, domain names, and other network-specific settings. The purpose of server configuration is to optimize the server's performance, reliability, security, and efficiency. By fine-tuning the server settings, administrators can ensure that the server operates at its best capacity and provides the required services to clients and users. It also allows for the customization of the server to meet the specific needs of the network, such as load balancing, resource allocation, and security measures. Effective server configuration requires a thorough understanding of the server hardware and software components, as well as the network infrastructure and requirements. Administrators must consider factors such as the expected workload, the number of users, the types of applications and services running on the server, and the network traffic and security needs. This information is used to determine the appropriate server settings, including memory allocation, disk space, processor utilization, and network bandwidth. Regular maintenance and monitoring of the server configuration are also necessary to ensure its ongoing performance and security. It is important to regularly update the server software and apply patches and security updates to address vulnerabilities and prevent unauthorized access. Monitoring tools and techniques are used to track server performance, identify bottlenecks or issues, and make necessary adjustments to optimize performance. In conclusion, server configuration is a critical task in networking that involves setting up and adjusting the settings and parameters of a server system to optimize its performance and ensure its proper functioning within a networked environment. It encompasses hardware, software, and network settings and aims to customize the server to meet the specific requirements and needs of the network.

Server Farm Architecture

Server Farm Architecture refers to a network infrastructure designed to efficiently handle and distribute data processing and storage tasks across multiple servers. It involves the interconnected setup of numerous servers that work together to provide high availability, scalability, and reliability for the desired applications or services. Server farms are commonly used by organizations that require large computing power and storage capacity to meet the demands of their clients or internal users. These farms act as a centralized hub for processing and storing data, ensuring continuous availability and quick response times. The architecture of a server farm typically consists of multiple layers, each serving a specific purpose in the data processing workflow. At the front-end, load balancers distribute incoming traffic across different servers, ensuring a balanced workload and preventing any single server from becoming overwhelmed. Load balancers also assist in handling failover situations by redirecting traffic to healthy servers in the event of a server failure. Behind the load balancers, multiple application servers handle the actual processing of incoming requests. These servers are designed to operate in parallel, allowing for efficient utilization of computing resources and reducing response time for the end users. They may be clustered together to provide additional redundancy and fault tolerance. Server farms also include database servers that store and manage the organization's data. These servers are responsible for handling data queries, updates, and storage. High-performance storage systems such as Network-Attached Storage (NAS) or Storage Area Networks (SAN) are often integrated into the farm architecture to ensure fast and reliable data access. Finally, server farms are supported by a robust network infrastructure that allows for seamless communication between the various components. This includes high-speed switches and routers, as well as redundant network links to prevent single points of failure and ensure continuous connectivity. By implementing a server farm architecture, organizations can benefit from increased reliability, scalability, and performance. The distributed nature of the architecture allows for efficient resource utilization and can accommodate rapid growth in demand without compromising service quality. Additionally, the redundant and fault-tolerant design helps ensure continuous availability, minimizing downtime and maximizing user satisfaction. Overall, server farm architecture plays a crucial role in meeting the ever-growing demands of modern computing environments, providing a robust and scalable foundation for delivering various services and applications.

Server Farm

A server farm is a network of interconnected servers that are used to provide computational resources, storage capacity, and networking capabilities to support various applications and services. It is a centralized facility that houses multiple servers and associated networking infrastructure, designed to handle high volumes of data and provide efficient and reliable access to resources. In a server farm, the servers are typically organized in racks or cabinets, with each server dedicated to specific tasks or applications. These servers can range from high-performance machines with large processing power to specialized servers optimized for storage or networking capabilities. The servers are connected through a network infrastructure that enables communication and data transfer between the servers and other devices in the network. Server farms are commonly used by organizations that require a large-scale and reliable computing environment. They are particularly useful in situations where the demand for computational resources is high, such as data centers, cloud service providers, and large enterprises with heavy reliance on IT infrastructure. By deploying multiple servers in a server farm, organizations can achieve several key benefits. First, a server farm enables load balancing, where incoming requests and data are distributed across multiple servers, ensuring that no single server is overloaded. This helps to improve the performance and availability of applications and services by avoiding bottlenecks and maximizing resource utilization. Second, server farms provide high scalability, allowing organizations to easily add or remove servers as needed to accommodate changes in demand. This flexibility is crucial in dynamic environments where computing requirements can vary significantly over time. Finally, server farms offer fault tolerance and redundancy. With multiple servers in a farm, organizations can implement backup and failover mechanisms to ensure uninterrupted operation in case of hardware failures or other issues. This helps to minimize downtime and ensure reliable access to resources and services. In summary, a server farm is a network of interconnected servers that provides computational resources, storage capacity, and networking capabilities. It enables load balancing, scalability, fault tolerance, and redundancy, making it an essential component of modern network infrastructure for organizations requiring high-performance and reliable computing environments.

Server Hardware Management

Server hardware management refers to the process of monitoring, maintaining, and optimizing the physical components of a server system in a networked environment. It involves overseeing the hardware infrastructure, such as servers, storage devices, network equipment, and peripheral devices, to ensure their smooth operation and efficient resource utilization. This management process encompasses various tasks, including server provisioning, configuration, troubleshooting, and performance tuning. It requires expertise in hardware installation, maintenance, and repair to ensure seamless data transmission, secure data storage, and reliable server performance.

Server Hardware

A server hardware refers to the physical components of a computer that are specifically designed to be used in a server environment. It includes various hardware components such as the motherboard, central processing unit (CPU), memory modules, storage devices, network interface cards (NIC), and power supplies. The motherboard is the main circuit board of the server hardware, which houses and connects all the other components. It provides slots and connectors for attaching the CPU, memory modules, storage devices, and other expansion cards. The CPU, also known as the server's processor, is responsible for executing instructions and performing calculations. It is a crucial component that determines the speed and efficiency of the server. Memory modules, often referred to as RAM (random access memory), provide temporary storage for the server to hold data that is frequently accessed. The amount and type of memory installed in a server can greatly impact its performance and ability to handle multiple tasks simultaneously. Storage devices, such as hard disk drives (HDD) and solid-state drives (SSD), are used to store and retrieve data. Servers typically have multiple storage devices to accommodate the large amounts of data they handle. Network interface cards (NIC) enable the

299

server to connect to a network, allowing it to communicate with other devices and access resources across the network. Power supplies are responsible for providing the necessary electrical power to the server hardware. They convert the incoming electrical power from the wall outlet to the appropriate voltages required by the server components. In addition, servers often have redundant power supplies to ensure uninterrupted operation in case of a power failure. Server hardware is designed to be more reliable, durable, and resource-efficient than regular desktop computer hardware. They are built to handle heavy workloads, provide high availability, and support the demands of a networked environment. The selection and configuration of server hardware depend on factors such as the intended use, required performance, scalability, and budget constraints.

Server Management

Server management refers to the process of overseeing and controlling the activities of one or more servers in a network environment. It involves the monitoring, administration, and maintenance of servers to ensure their optimal performance, availability, and security. The responsibilities of server management include configuring, installing, and deploying servers, as well as managing user access permissions, software updates, and server resources. It also involves monitoring server performance, troubleshooting technical issues, and implementing security measures to protect against unauthorized access and data breaches.

Server Monitoring Tools

Server monitoring tools are software applications that allow network administrators to monitor and manage the performance, availability, and security of servers in a network environment. These tools provide real-time insights and alerts, enabling administrators to proactively identify and address issues, prevent downtime, optimize resource utilization, and ensure the overall health and efficiency of the server infrastructure. The primary objective of server monitoring tools is to monitor key metrics and parameters of servers such as CPU usage, memory utilization, disk space, network traffic, response time, and service availability. By continuously monitoring these critical aspects, administrators can detect anomalies, identify bottlenecks, and take necessary actions to prevent performance degradation or server failures.

Server Rack

A server rack is a physical structure used to house and organize networking equipment, such as servers, switches, routers, and other network devices. It provides a consolidated and secure space for these devices to be mounted and connected. The server rack is designed with specific features to optimize the networking infrastructure's performance, accessibility, and scalability. It typically consists of a metal frame that can accommodate multiple devices, allowing them to be stacked vertically or horizontally.

Server

A server is a computer or system that manages network resources, services, and requests from clients. It is designed to provide functionality and accessibility to users or clients connected to a network. Servers perform various tasks, such as storing and managing data, hosting websites or applications, managing user authentication and authorization, and handling network communications. Servers play a critical role in networking as they facilitate the sharing of resources and information within a network. They act as a central hub where multiple clients can connect and access the shared resources. These resources can include files, databases, software applications, printers, and more. One of the primary functions of a server is to provide data storage and management. It acts as a repository for files and data that can be accessed and shared by multiple users or clients. Servers can be configured to provide different types of storage, including file storage, database storage, or even cloud storage. Another important role of servers is hosting websites or applications. Web servers, for example, store and serve website files to users who request them through a web browser. They handle HTTP requests and deliver the requested web pages or files to the client's device. Similarly, application servers host and manage software applications, enabling users to access and use them remotely. Servers also handle user authentication and authorization, ensuring that only authorized users can access specific resources or services. They manage user accounts, passwords, and permissions, controlling who can access what within the network. This helps in maintaining data security and preventing unauthorized access to sensitive information. Furthermore, servers are responsible for handling network communications. They facilitate the transmission of data between clients, allowing them to communicate and exchange information. Servers utilize various protocols and technologies to ensure reliable and secure data transmission, such as TCP/IP, SMTP, FTP, and more. In summary, a server is a crucial component of computer networking, providing resources, services, and connectivity to clients or users within a network. It performs tasks like data storage, hosting websites or applications, managing authentication and authorization, and handling network communications.

Session Fixation Attack

A session fixation attack is a type of security vulnerability in computer networking that allows an attacker to hijack a user's session by manipulating session identifiers. In this attack, the attacker forces a victim to use a specific session identifier, which they have control over, by tricking the victim into authenticating with it. Once the victim's session is established using the attacker's chosen identifier, the attacker can then take over the session and impersonate the victim. The session identifier is a unique token or string of characters that is generated by the server and assigned to each user upon authentication. It is used by the server to identify and track the user's session during their interaction with the application or website. By manipulating the session identifier, an attacker can bypass authentication mechanisms and gain unauthorized access to the victim's account or privileged functionalities. The session fixation attack typically follows a specific sequence of steps. First, the attacker identifies a vulnerable application or website that uses session identifiers. They then generate a valid session identifier and trick the victim into clicking on a specially crafted link that directs them to the targeted application or website. Upon clicking the link, the victim's browser sends the session identifier to the server, establishing the session. At this point, the attacker can either use the established session themselves or wait for the victim to log in with their legitimate credentials. Once the victim logs in, the attacker now has control over the session and can carry out malicious activities. To defend against session fixation attacks, developers and administrators can employ several countermeasures. One common approach is to regenerate the session identifier upon successful authentication or periodically throughout the session. This prevents attackers from fixing a session identifier before the victim logs in or continually using a fixed identifier. Additionally, enforcing the use of secure and unique session identifiers, storing them securely, and protecting the session management mechanism from vulnerabilities can also help mitigate the risks associated with session fixation.

Session Hijacking

Session Hijacking, also known as session stealing or cookie hijacking, is a malicious technique that involves the unauthorized seizure of an active network session. During a networking session, such as a user's interaction with a website or an online service, a session is established. This session assigns the user a unique identifier, typically in the form of a session ID or a session cookie. This identifier is used to recognize and validate the user's identity throughout their session. An attacker exploiting session hijacking aims to gain control over this session identifier, allowing them to impersonate the legitimate user and perform unauthorized actions on their behalf. This can lead to severe consequences, including unauthorized access to sensitive information, manipulation of user data, or even complete account takeover. There are various techniques through which session hijacking can occur. One common method is known as session sniffing, where an attacker intercepts and analyzes network traffic to obtain the session identifier. This can be done through eavesdropping on the network or by compromising an insecure communication channel. Furthermore, session hijacking can be facilitated through the exploitation of vulnerabilities in the protocols or software systems used for session management. Weak encryption methods, poorly implemented authentication mechanisms, or predictable session IDs make it easier for attackers to hijack sessions. To prevent session hijacking, various countermeasures can be implemented. These include utilizing secure communication channels, such as Transport Layer Security (TLS), to encrypt the session data. Implementing strong and unpredictable session IDs, regularly rotating them, and using secure HTTP-only cookies help mitigate the risk of session hijacking. In conclusion, session hijacking is a detrimental attack in which an unauthorized individual seizes control over an active network session. It exploits vulnerabilities in session management systems to gain unauthorized access to user accounts or sensitive information. Implementing robust security measures can help protect against session hijacking and enhance the overall security of network communications.

Shadow IT

Shadow IT refers to the use of technology, systems, software, or applications that are used within an organization without the knowledge, approval, or control of the IT department or any other governing body. It encompasses any technology that is being used by employees or departments without authorization, supervision, or adherence to established policies and procedures. Shadow IT can manifest in various ways, such as employees using personal devices and applications for work-related tasks, adopting cloud services or online platforms without IT involvement, or using unauthorized software or tools to fulfill business needs. It often arises due to the need for agility, productivity, or convenience, as employees seek quick and efficient solutions to their technology requirements.

Shellcode

Shellcode in the context of networking refers to a small piece of code that is injected into a vulnerable system or network device, typically as part of an exploit or attack. This code is written specifically to take advantage of a specific vulnerability or weakness in the target system, and its primary purpose is to execute malicious actions or commands. The goal of shellcode is to provide an attacker with unauthorized control over the target system or device. Once the shellcode is successfully injected and executed, it can open a backdoor or command shell, allowing the attacker to remotely access and control the compromised system. This unauthorized control can then be used to launch further attacks, steal sensitive information, or disrupt network services.

Simple Network Management Protocol (SNMP)

Simple Network Management Protocol (SNMP) is a standard protocol used for managing and monitoring network devices on a computer network. It provides a set of rules and guidelines for collecting and organizing information about network devices, and allows network administrators to remotely manage and monitor these devices. SNMP is an application layer protocol that operates over the Internet Protocol (IP). The main goal of SNMP is to enable network administrators to monitor and control network devices from a central location. It allows administrators to gather important information about the status and performance of network devices, such as routers, switches, servers, and printers. SNMP achieves this by defining a standardized set of messages and data structures that network devices can use to communicate with a network management system (NMS). SNMP is based on a client-server model, where a network management system acts as the SNMP manager, and network devices act as SNMP agents. The SNMP manager sends requests to the SNMP agents to collect information, and the agents respond with the requested data. The manager can also send commands to the agents to modify their configuration or behavior. SNMP operates through a hierarchical structure known as the Management Information Base (MIB). The MIB is a collection of managed objects, each identified by a unique object identifier (OID). Each managed object represents a specific attribute or parameter of a network device, such as the device's interface status, CPU utilization, or network traffic statistics. SNMP uses a simple and lightweight message format for communication between the manager and the agents. The messages are typically transmitted over UDP/IP, making SNMP efficient and suitable for use in large-scale networks. The protocol supports various types of operations, such as retrieving information (GET), setting values (SET), and generating event notifications (TRAP) when certain conditions occur. In summary, SNMP is a standard protocol that enables network administrators to monitor and manage network devices. It provides a standardized framework for communication between a central network management system and network devices, allowing administrators to gather information about device status and performance, and control their configuration remotely.

Simple Network Time Protocol (SNTP)

Simple Network Time Protocol (SNTP) is a protocol used in computer networks to synchronize the time between various devices. It is an extension of the Network Time Protocol (NTP) that simplifies its functionality while maintaining basic time synchronization capabilities. SNTP is

302

commonly used in environments where precise time synchronization is not required, such as in small networks or by devices with limited processing power. SNTP operates by exchanging time synchronization messages between a client and a server. The client requests a time update from the server by sending a query message, and the server responds with a time stamp indicating the current time. The client can then adjust its own system time based on the received timestamp. The time synchronization messages are small in size and utilize UDP (User Datagram Protocol) as the underlying transport protocol, making them lightweight and efficient. Unlike NTP, SNTP lacks certain advanced features and mechanisms that are designed to ensure highly accurate time synchronization. It does not implement the full NTP's complex algorithms for error estimation and correction. Additionally, SNTP does not support peer-to-peer synchronization or high-precision time measurements. However, these simplifications result in reduced processing and memory requirements, making SNTP suitable for resource-constrained devices or networks that do not demand precise time synchronization. SNTP can operate in both client-server and broadcast modes. In client-server mode, a client initiates time synchronization requests with a server. The server responds to these requests and provides the client with the current time. In broadcast mode, a time server broadcasts time synchronization messages to all devices on the network, and the devices adjust their system time accordingly. This mode is useful in scenarios where simultaneous synchronization of multiple devices is required. In summary, SNTP is a simplified version of NTP used for basic time synchronization in computer networks. It offers a lightweight and efficient solution, suitable for devices with limited resources or environments where precise time synchronization is not critical.

Site-To-Site VPN

A Site-to-Site VPN, also known as a router-to-router VPN, is a secure connection established between two or more geographically separate private networks over a public network, typically the internet. It provides a secure and encrypted communication channel between the connected networks, allowing data to be transmitted securely and privately. The Site-to-Site VPN utilizes various protocols and encryption methods to ensure confidentiality, integrity, and availability of the transmitted data. The most commonly used protocols for establishing a Site-to-Site VPN are IPsec (Internet Protocol Security) and SSL/TLS (Secure Sockets Layer/Transport Layer Security). IPsec is widely used for securing network layer communications. It operates at the network layer of the OSI model, providing encryption, authentication, and integrity checking. IPsec uses two main protocols: the Authentication Header (AH) and the Encapsulating Security Payload (ESP). AH provides integrity and authentication services, while ESP adds encryption services. SSL/TLS, on the other hand, operates at the application layer of the OSI model and is mainly used for securing web-based applications. It utilizes public key encryption to establish a secure connection between the participating networks. SSL/TLS VPNs are often used for remote access and client-to-site VPN configurations. To establish a Site-to-Site VPN, each participating network must have a compatible VPN gateway or router. These devices establish a secure tunnel over the public network, allowing the connected networks to communicate securely. The VPN gateways handle the encryption and decryption of the data, ensuring its confidentiality and integrity. Site-to-Site VPNs are commonly used by businesses with multiple locations, allowing them to connect their branch offices or remote sites securely and privately. This enables seamless and secure communication between the different networks, improving collaboration, data sharing, and resource access.

Social Engineering Toolkit (SET)

The Social Engineering Toolkit (SET) is a network security tool that facilitates the testing of networks and systems against social engineering attacks. Social engineering is a method used by attackers to manipulate and deceive individuals into disclosing sensitive information or performing actions that could compromise the security of a network or system. SET provides a framework for conducting social engineering campaigns and allows security professionals to simulate various social engineering scenarios to identify and address vulnerabilities. It is designed to be easy to use and does not require extensive technical knowledge.

Social Engineering

Social engineering refers to the manipulation or deceiving of individuals in order to gain unauthorized access to sensitive information or to influence their behavior for personal gain. It involves exploiting human psychology, trust, and vulnerabilities rather than relying on technical flaws or vulnerabilities in computer systems. In the context of networking, social engineering can occur through various methods such as phishing, impersonation, and pretexting. Phishing involves sending fraudulent emails or messages that appear to be from a reputable source, tricking the recipient into revealing confidential information or performing certain actions. Impersonation occurs when an attacker pretends to be someone else, such as a trusted colleague or IT support personnel, to manipulate individuals into providing sensitive information or granting unauthorized access. Pretexting involves creating a false scenario or pretext to deceive individuals into disclosing information or performing actions that can compromise network security. One common form of social engineering in networking is known as "shoulder surfing." This occurs when an attacker discreetly observes a person entering passwords or sensitive information, either by physically standing close enough to see their screen or by using hidden cameras or other surveillance techniques. The attacker can then use this information to gain unauthorized access to the network or steal sensitive data. Social engineering attacks can have severe consequences for network security. Attackers can gain unauthorized access to sensitive data, compromise network infrastructure, or even manipulate individuals to perform actions that can lead to financial loss or other damages. Therefore, it is crucial for organizations to implement robust security measures, such as employee training on recognizing and responding to social engineering attacks, enforcing strong password policies, and implementing multi-factor authentication.

Software-Defined Networking (SDN)

Software-Defined Networking (SDN) is an architectural approach to networking that separates the control plane from the data plane, allowing for centralized control and programmability of the network. In traditional networking, the control plane and data plane are typically integrated into the same networking device, such as a router or switch. This integration limits the flexibility and agility of the network, making it difficult to adapt to changing traffic patterns and requirements. With SDN, the control plane is abstracted from the underlying hardware and implemented in software, running on a central controller. The controller acts as the brain of the network, directing and managing the forwarding decisions made by the data plane devices. By separating the control plane from the data plane, SDN enables network administrators to define and control network behavior through software applications and policies, rather than relying on the configuration and capabilities of individual network devices.

Software-Defined Wide Area Network (SD-WAN)

Software-Defined Wide Area Network (SD-WAN) is a networking technology that allows organizations to build and manage their wide area network infrastructures using software-defined principles. Unlike traditional wide area networks, which typically rely on expensive and complex hardware, SD-WAN leverages virtualization and cloud-based technologies to simplify network management and increase its flexibility and agility. With SD-WAN, organizations can configure and control their wide area networks through a centralized software controller, eliminating the need for manual configuration of individual network devices. This centralization enables organizations to automate network provisioning and management tasks, reducing the time and effort required to deploy, monitor, and troubleshoot their networks. SD-WAN provides several key benefits to organizations. First and foremost, it improves network performance by dynamically routing traffic across multiple network paths, optimizing the use of available bandwidth and minimizing latency. This is achieved by using intelligent traffic routing algorithms that analyze network conditions in real-time and make routing decisions based on performance metrics such as packet loss, latency, and available bandwidth. Another significant advantage of SD-WAN is its ability to enhance network security. It allows organizations to easily implement and enforce security policies across their wide area networks, ensuring consistent and centralized security management. SD-WAN also provides advanced encryption and authentication mechanisms to protect data transmitted over the network, safeguarding against cyber threats and unauthorized access. Furthermore, SD-WAN simplifies network management by providing a single interface for monitoring and configuring the entire wide area network. This centralized management greatly reduces the complexity and administrative burden associated with managing a large-scale network infrastructure. It also enables organizations to scale their networks more efficiently and effectively, as new branch sites can be easily integrated into the network architecture without extensive manual configuration. In conclusion, SD-WAN is a software-defined networking technology that revolutionizes wide area network management. By providing centralized control, dynamic traffic routing, enhanced security, and simplified management, SD-WAN offers organizations greater flexibility, agility, and efficiency in building and managing their wide area network infrastructures.

Spanning Tree Protocol (STP)

The Spanning Tree Protocol (STP) is a network protocol that helps prevent loops in Ethernet networks. It is used to ensure that there is only one active path between any two network devices to avoid data collisions and improve network performance. STP works by selecting a single bridge in the network to be the root bridge, which becomes the reference point for all other bridges in the network. Each bridge calculates its own cost to reach the root bridge based on the link speed. The bridge with the lowest cost to reach the root bridge becomes the designated bridge for that network segment. STP operates in a loop prevention fashion by blocking any redundant paths that could result in loops. It does this by forwarding traffic only through the designated bridges, while blocking traffic on the non-designated bridges. This ensures that there is a single active path between any two devices in the network. If a network segment loses its connection to the root bridge, STP will automatically recalculate the spanning tree in order to reestablish connectivity. This ensures that the network can quickly adapt to changes in the network topology and maintain network availability. In larger networks, STP alone may not provide sufficient performance. In these cases, enhancements such as Rapid Spanning Tree Protocol (RSTP) or Multiple Spanning Tree Protocol (MSTP) may be used to provide faster convergence and load balancing capabilities. In conclusion, the Spanning Tree Protocol (STP) is a network protocol that prevents loops in Ethernet networks by selecting a root bridge and designating paths between bridges. It ensures that there is a single active path between any two network devices, improving network performance and preventing data collisions.

Spear Phishing

Spear phishing is a form of cyber attack that targets a specific individual or organization. It is a type of phishing attack that is more personalized and targeted, making it more difficult to detect and defend against. In a spear phishing attack, the attacker typically gathers information about the target, such as their name, position, and any other relevant details. This information is then used to craft a highly convincing and tailored email or message that appears to be from a trusted source, such as a coworker or supervisor. The goal of spear phishing is to trick the target into taking a specific action, such as clicking on a malicious link or opening a malicious attachment. Once the target falls for the deception, their computer or network can be compromised, allowing the attacker to gain unauthorized access or steal sensitive information. Unlike traditional phishing attacks that cast a wide net and target multiple individuals or organizations, spear phishing is highly targeted and focused. The attacker takes the time to research and understand their target, increasing the likelihood of success. Spear phishing attacks often exploit the trust and familiarity between individuals within an organization. By impersonating someone the target knows, such as a colleague or superior, the attacker is able to lower the target's guard and increase the chances of a successful attack. To protect against spear phishing attacks, organizations should implement strong security measures, such as email filters and antivirus software, to detect and block suspicious emails or messages. Employees should also be trained to recognize the signs of a spear phishing attack and to verify the authenticity of any unusual or unexpected requests.

Spectrum Analyzer

A spectrum analyzer in the context of networking refers to a device or software tool used to analyze and monitor the frequency spectrum of signals in a network. It provides valuable insights into the different frequencies present in the network, their strength, and any potential interference or anomalies. By capturing and analyzing the frequency spectrum, a spectrum analyzer helps network administrators and engineers to optimize network performance, troubleshoot issues, and ensure efficient utilization of the available frequency spectrum.

Spoofed Email

Spoofed Email is a deceptive practice in networking where the sender of an email falsifies the information contained in the email header to make it appear as if it originated from a different source. It is a form of email fraud often used for malicious purposes such as phishing, spreading malware, or conducting scams. When an email is spoofed, the header information, including the sender's email address and sometimes even the domain name, is manipulated to mislead the recipient into believing that the email is legitimate and trustworthy. Typically, the recipient sees a familiar or reputable email address in the "From" field, which gives the appearance of the email being sent by someone they know or a trusted organization. By disguising the origin of the email, spoofers attempt to gain the recipient's trust and increase the likelihood of their malicious intentions being fulfilled. They may try to trick the recipient into revealing confidential information, such as passwords, credit card details, or personal data, by directing them to fraudulent websites or convincing them to download malicious attachments. Spoofed emails can also be used to distribute malware or propagate computer viruses by persuading recipients to open infected files or click on malicious links. Spoofing emails is possible due to weaknesses in the Simple Mail Transfer Protocol (SMTP), which is the standard protocol used for sending emails across the internet. The lack of robust authentication mechanisms within SMTP allows senders to easily forge email headers without being detected. Additionally, spoofers often take advantage of open mail relays or compromised email servers to further disguise the true source of their emails. Protecting against spoofed emails requires a multi-layered approach. Implementing advanced email authentication methods such as Domain-based Message Authentication, Reporting, and Conformance (DMARC), Sender Policy Framework (SPF), and DomainKeys Identified Mail (DKIM) can help verify the authenticity of incoming emails and reduce the risk of accepting spoofed messages. Organizations should also educate their users about the risks associated with suspicious emails, encouraging them to be cautious when clicking on links, opening attachments, or providing sensitive information.

Spoofing

Spoofing refers to the act of falsifying or impersonating information in order to deceive or trick network devices or users. It involves manipulating certain aspects of data packets, such as the source IP address, MAC address, or even the entire headers, to mislead or bypass security measures or gain unauthorized access. Spoofing attacks exploit vulnerabilities in the network or system, often resulting in various malicious activities. One common type of spoofing is IP spoofing, where an attacker alters the source IP address of a packet to make it appear as if it is coming from a different source. This can be used to bypass IP-based authentication or to redirect traffic to a different destination. By falsifying the IP address, the attacker can disguise their identity and make it difficult to trace the origin of the attack. This technique is often employed in distributed denial-of-service (DDoS) attacks, where multiple spoofed IP addresses are used to overwhelm a target system or network. ARP spoofing, or ARP poisoning, is another form of spoofing that targets the Address Resolution Protocol (ARP) in a local network. In this attack, the attacker sends falsified ARP messages to associate their own MAC address with the IP address of another legitimate device. By doing so, the attacker can intercept and redirect network traffic meant for the legitimate device. This can enable various malicious activities, such as eavesdropping on sensitive information, conducting man-in-the-middle attacks, or even injecting malicious code into the intercepted traffic. DNS spoofing is yet another type of spoofing attack that targets the Domain Name System (DNS). By falsifying DNS responses, an attacker can redirect users to malicious websites or intercept their communications. For example, an attacker can spoof a DNS response to associate a legitimate domain name with their own malicious IP address, tricking users into unknowingly visiting a fraudulent website that appears identical to the legitimate one. This technique is often used in phishing attacks to steal sensitive information, such as login credentials or financial details.

Stateless Firewall

A stateless firewall is a network security device that filters incoming and outgoing network traffic based on predetermined rules without maintaining any information about the state or history of the network connections. It operates at the network level (Layer 3) of the OSI model and examines each packet individually, making decisions based on factors such as source and destination IP addresses, ports, and protocols. Stateless firewalls are commonly used to enforce security policies and protect network assets from unauthorized access or malicious activities. When a packet arrives at a stateless firewall, it analyzes its header information and compares it against the configured rules. The firewall evaluates each rule sequentially and either permits or denies the packet based on a match. If a packet matches a rule that permits it, the firewall allows it to pass through to its destination. Conversely, if a packet matches a rule that denies it, the firewall drops the packet and prevents it from reaching its intended destination. One characteristic of a stateless firewall is that it does not maintain or track any state information about network connections. This means that it does not remember any previous packets or establish any kind of session information. As a result, every incoming packet is treated independently, and the firewall makes a decision solely based on the individual packet's header information at that moment. Stateless firewalls are therefore not aware of the larger context of the network communication or whether a packet is part of an established connection. This can limit the capabilities of a stateless firewall when it comes to handling certain types of attacks or more complex security requirements. However, stateless firewalls offer several advantages in terms of performance and simplicity. By not tracking connection state or maintaining session information, they have a reduced processing overhead and can handle high-speed network traffic more efficiently. They are also easier to configure and manage since they do not require as much memory or computational resources compared to stateful firewalls. Additionally, stateless firewalls are often used in conjunction with other security mechanisms, such as intrusion detection and prevention systems, to provide layered protection and enhance overall network security.

Static Routing

A static routing is a method of network routing, where network administrators manually configure the routes in a router's routing table. This manual configuration defines the paths that the router will use to forward data packets across a network. In static routing, the routing table is set up using a fixed set of predetermined routes. Each route consists of a destination network address and the next-hop address, which specifies the next router or interface that a packet should be sent to in order to reach its destination. The routes are manually configured by the network administrator, typically using a command-line interface or a graphical user interface provided by the router's operating system.

Storage Area Network (SAN)

A Storage Area Network (SAN) is a high-speed network that connects multiple storage devices to a centralized storage resource. It is a dedicated network that provides block-level access to data storage devices such as disk arrays, tape libraries, and optical drives. SANs are designed to meet the increasing demands of storage and data management in modern computing environments. They offer a scalable and flexible storage infrastructure, allowing organizations to store and manage large amounts of data efficiently. SANs use Fibre Channel (FC) or Ethernet protocols to connect storage devices to servers. Fibre Channel is the traditional choice for SANs, offering high-performance and low latency connections. Ethernet-based SANs, also known as iSCSI (Internet Small Computer System Interface), use TCP/IP to transmit data over standard Ethernet connections, providing a cost-effective solution for smaller organizations or remote locations. One of the key advantages of SANs is their ability to centralize storage resources. By connecting multiple storage devices to a single SAN, organizations can consolidate their storage infrastructure and simplify management tasks. This allows for better utilization of storage capacity and improves data accessibility and availability. Furthermore, SANs provide advanced features such as data replication, snapshots, and backup and recovery capabilities. These features enable organizations to implement reliable and robust data protection strategies, ensuring the continuity of business operations. SANs also support various storage technologies, including RAID (Redundant Array of Independent Disks), which improves performance and provides fault tolerance. In addition, SANs can be extended over long distances using specialized equipment, allowing organizations to implement disaster recovery and data replication strategies between geographically dispersed locations. In summary, a Storage Area Network is a dedicated network that connects multiple storage devices to a centralized storage resource. It offers block-level access to storage, supports advanced data management features, and provides scalability, reliability, and performance for storage-intensive applications.

Subnet Design Guidelines

Subnet Design Guidelines refers to the set of best practices and principles used in networking to efficiently allocate and manage IP addresses within a network. In the context of networking, an IP address is a unique identifier assigned to each device connected to a network, allowing them to communicate with one another. However, the number of available IP addresses is limited, and subnetting is used to divide them into smaller, more manageable groups. The primary objective of subnet design guidelines is to optimize address allocation and enhance network performance. This involves considering various factors such as network size, growth projections, and administrative boundaries. One key guideline is to allocate IP addresses based on the needs of the network. This includes considering the number of devices that will require an IP address, as well as any future expansion plans. By accurately estimating the number of required IP addresses, subnet design can ensure efficient utilization and avoid address scarcity or wastage. Another important consideration is the logical organization of subnets. This involves grouping devices that frequently communicate with one another into the same subnet. Devices within the same subnet can directly communicate without the need for routing through other subnets, resulting in faster communication and reduced network congestion. Subnet design guidelines also emphasize the need for scalability. This involves planning for future growth by reserving sufficient address space for additional networks or subnets. Additionally, it is recommended to implement variable-length subnet masking (VLSM), allowing for more flexible allocation of IP addresses based on the size requirements of each subnet. Proper documentation and labeling of subnets is essential for effective network management. This includes maintaining a detailed record of the allocated IP address ranges, associated subnets, and their respective purposes. Clear labeling ensures easy identification and simplifies troubleshooting in case of any issues within the network. In conclusion, subnet design guidelines play a crucial role in optimizing IP address allocation and network performance. By considering factors such as network size, growth projections, logical organization, scalability, and documentation, these guidelines help create a well-structured and efficient network environment.

Subnet Design

Subnet Design refers to the process of dividing a large network into smaller subnetworks or subnets. This division is based on the concept of subnetting, which helps optimize network performance, improve security, and simplify network management. In networking, an IP address is used to identify devices on a network. It consists of two parts: the network portion and the host portion. The network portion identifies the network to which a device belongs, while the host portion identifies the specific device within that network. Subnetting allows for efficient utilization of IP addresses by further dividing the network portion into subnets. When designing a subnet, several factors need to be considered. One important factor is the number of devices in a network and the expected growth rate. By dividing the network into subnets, the number of available IP addresses can be increased, avoiding IP address exhaustion and ensuring scalability. Another factor to consider is network performance. By dividing a large network into smaller subnets, network traffic can be localized, reducing congestion and improving overall performance. Subnetting also allows for the implementation of network policies and traffic prioritization at a more granular level, enhancing network efficiency. Security is also enhanced through subnet design. By creating separate subnets for different departments or user groups, network administrators can implement strict access controls and firewall rules between subnets. This isolates sensitive data and resources, reducing the risk of unauthorized access or data breaches. Subnet design greatly simplifies network management. With smaller subnets, it becomes easier to troubleshoot and isolate network issues because the scope of the problem is more confined. Network administrators can apply changes, updates, and configurations to subnets without affecting the entire network, streamlining maintenance tasks and reducing network downtime.

Subnet Mask Calculator

A subnet mask calculator is a tool used in network planning and configuration to determine the range of IP addresses that can exist within a particular network. It is a numerical value that consists of four sets of numbers, each ranging from 0 to 255, and is expressed in the form of four octets separated by periods. The subnet mask plays a crucial role in dividing IP addresses into logical networks or subnets. It helps to differentiate between the network part and the host part of an IP address. The network part represents the identifier for the specific network, while the host part identifies individual devices within that network. To comprehend the subnet mask calculation, it is essential to understand the binary representation of IP addresses. Each octet in the subnet mask can be converted into an 8-bit binary number, with each bit indicating its significance in relation to network and host portions. A value of 1 in a bit position represents the network part, while 0 represents the host part. The subnet mask calculator determines the network size based on the total number of bits set to 1 in the subnet mask. By counting the number of bits set to 1, it is possible to calculate the number of networks that can be created and the number of hosts that can exist within each network. For example, a subnet mask of 255.255.255.0 (represented in binary as 11111111.11111111.11111111.00000000) signifies a network size of 256 hosts (2^8). When applied to an IP address, this subnet mask allows for the creation of 256 subnets, each having a maximum of 256 host IP addresses. Using a subnet mask calculator removes the need for manual calculations, allowing network administrators to quickly determine the available range of IP addresses within a given subnet. It aids in efficient network design, allocation of IP addresses, and configuration of network devices, ensuring optimal utilization of resources and enhanced network performance. In conclusion, a subnet mask calculator is a valuable tool in networking that simplifies the process of determining the network range and enables efficient IP address allocation. By providing a clear distinction between the network and host portions, it aids in effective network planning and configuration.

Subnet Mask

A subnet mask is a 32-bit number used in networking to divide an IP address into network and host portions. It is a binary pattern that specifies which bits in the IP address represent the network and host parts. In simpler terms, a subnet mask helps determine the boundaries of a network and allows devices to communicate within that defined network. The subnet mask consists of four sets of numbers separated by periods. Each set represents 8 bits, resulting in a total of 32 bits. The bits that are set to 1 in the subnet mask indicate the network portion, while the bits set to 0 represent the host portion. For example, a subnet mask of 255.255.255.0 means that the first 24 bits (or three sets of 8 bits) represent the network, and the remaining 8 bits are for the hosts within that network. When a device receives an IP address, it also receives a subnet mask that corresponds to the network it belongs to. By comparing the IP address with the subnet mask, the device can determine whether a destination IP address is on the same network or a different network. If the destination IP address is on a different network, the device will send the packet to the default gateway, which acts as the bridge between different networks. Subnet masks are crucial for the proper functioning of IP networks. They allow network administrators to efficiently allocate IP address space by dividing it into smaller subnets. Subnetting helps organizations optimize their network resources by ensuring that devices are grouped together based on their geographic location, department, or any other logical criteria. Additionally, subnet masks aid in the secure isolation of different networks, as they prevent devices on one network from directly accessing devices on another network without passing through a router or gateway.

Subnet Masking

Subnet masking is a technique used in computer networking to divide an IP network into smaller subnetworks called subnets. It involves modifying the default subnet mask of an IP address to create these subnets. The subnet mask is a 32-bit value that consists of a series of binary 1s followed by a series of binary 0s, and it determines the network and host portions of an IP address. When a packet is sent over a network, the destination IP address is checked against the subnet mask to determine whether the destination is on the same subnet as the sender. If they are not on the same subnet, the packet is routed to the appropriate router or gateway that can forward it to the correct subnet.

Subnetting Calculator

A subnetting calculator is a tool used in computer networking to divide a larger network into smaller subnetworks called subnets. It helps in optimizing network performance and managing IP addresses efficiently. Subnetting is the process of splitting a network into multiple smaller networks known as subnets. Each subnet contains a range of IP addresses that can be assigned to devices within that particular subnet. This division allows for better organization, improved security, and more efficient use of network resources. A subnetting calculator automates the subnetting process, making it easier and faster for network administrators to design and implement their networks. By entering the network address and the desired number of subnets or hosts per subnet, the calculator determines the subnet mask and provides a summary of the resulting subnets. The subnetting calculator performs a series of mathematical operations to determine the subnet mask and other relevant parameters. It takes into account the binary representation of the IP address and uses boolean operations to calculate the necessary subnet information. These calculations involve converting the IP address and subnet mask into binary form, performing bitwise logical operations, and converting the results back into decimal form for human-readable output. The subnetting calculator displays the results in a clear and concise manner, providing information such as the subnet ID, subnet broadcast address, network address range, and number of assignable IP addresses. This information is essential for configuring routers, switches, and other networking devices. Using a subnetting calculator helps network administrators efficiently allocate IP addresses to devices within their networks. It ensures that each device has a unique IP address and prevents address conflicts. Additionally, subnetting enables network segmentation, allowing for the implementation of different security policies, traffic control, and better overall network performance. In conclusion, a subnetting calculator is a valuable tool for network administrators to plan, design, and implement their networks effectively. It simplifies the subnetting process, automates complex calculations, and provides essential information for network configuration.

Subnetting Practice

Subnetting is a process in computer networking that involves dividing a single network into smaller subnetworks, or subnets. This division is done to optimize network performance, improve security, and streamline network management. When a network is subnetted, it is divided into multiple subnetworks, each with its own unique IP address range. This allows for more efficient use of IP addresses and better resource allocation within the network. The process of subnetting involves two main components: subnet masks and IP addressing. A subnet mask is a 32-bit number that separates the network and host portions of an IP address. It determines the size of the subnet and the number of available IP addresses within each subnet. There are different types of subnetting, such as classful subnetting and classless subnetting. Classful subnetting is based on the early IP addressing scheme, where IP addresses were divided into classes (A, B, C) based on the size of the network. Classful subnetting uses fixed subnet masks, which limits flexibility in subnet design. In contrast, classless subnetting, also known as Variable Length Subnet Masking (VLSM), allows for more flexibility in subnet design. With VLSM, subnet masks can have varying lengths, allowing for more precise allocation of IP addresses to subnets. Subnetting is a fundamental concept in IP networking and is commonly used in large networks to improve efficiency and manageability. It enables network administrators to divide a network into logical segments, each with its own addressing scheme and routing configuration. Overall, subnetting is an essential technique in computer networking that brings numerous benefits, such as improved network performance, enhanced security, and simplified network management.

Subnetting Techniques

Subnetting techniques refer to the process of dividing a large network into smaller subnetworks, known as subnets. This technique enhances network efficiency by enabling better management of IP addresses and improving network security. Subnetting involves creating subnets within a network by borrowing bits from the host portion of an IP address, resulting in a subnet mask. This mask divides the IP address into network and host portions, allowing for the allocation of IP addresses to individual subnets. There are several subnetting techniques that network administrators utilize to efficiently allocate IP addresses and manage networks: 1. Fixed Subnetting: In fixed subnetting, a fixed number of hosts are assigned to each subnet. This technique simplifies network management but may lead to inefficient use of IP addresses if the number of hosts in each subnet varies. 2. Variable Length Subnet Masking (VLSM): VLSM allows for the creation of subnets with different subnet mask lengths. This technique maximizes the efficient use of IP address space by assigning smaller subnets to areas with a higher concentration of hosts and larger subnets to areas with fewer hosts. 3. Supernetting: Supernetting or route summarization combines multiple smaller networks into a single larger network, reducing the number of routing table entries. This technique reduces the size of routing tables, improves network performance, and simplifies network management. 4. Subnet Zero and Subnet Broadcast: Subnet zero refers to the use of the first subnet, which was previously

310

reserved. Subnet broadcast refers to the use of the last IP address in a subnet for broadcasting purposes. Both techniques have their advantages and disadvantages and are subject to specific networking requirements and protocols. By employing subnetting techniques, network administrators can optimize network resources, efficiently manage IP addresses, improve network performance and security, and simplify network management.

Subnetting

Subnetting is a network addressing technique used in computer networks to partition a single IP address space into multiple smaller subnetworks, called subnets. It involves dividing a network into smaller, more manageable parts to improve efficiency and security. The main purpose of subnetting is to break down a large network into smaller subnets, each with its own subnet address and subnet mask, to efficiently utilize the available IP address space and optimize network performance. This allows for efficient allocation of IP addresses to devices within each subnet and facilitates easier management and troubleshooting of network-related issues. Subnetting is particularly useful in large networks with a significant number of devices. By dividing the network into smaller subnets, the broadcast traffic is reduced, which improves the overall network performance. Additionally, subnetting enhances network security by isolating different departments or sections of a network. It allows for the implementation of access control measures, such as firewall rules or Virtual Local Area Networks (VLANs), to restrict unauthorized access and enhance network security. The process of subnetting involves separating the host portion of an IP address from the network portion. This is done by creating a subnet mask, which is a 32-bit number that distinguishes the network portion and the host portion of an IP address. The subnet mask contains a series of 1s representing the network portion, followed by a series of 0s representing the host portion. By using bitwise operations with the IP address and the subnet mask, the network address and host address of a device can be determined. In summary, subnetting is a vital technique in computer networking that enables the division of a large network into smaller subnets. It improves network efficiency, optimizes IP address allocation, enhances network security, and aids in efficient management and troubleshooting of network-related issues.

Switch Fabric

Switch Fabric, in the context of networking, refers to the underlying hardware and software technologies that enable the internal communication and data transfer within a switching device or a network switch. It provides the necessary infrastructure for the efficient and seamless transmission of data packets between different network interfaces or ports. The switch fabric acts as a central processing unit for the switch, managing the incoming and outgoing data traffic and ensuring its proper routing. It consists of multiple components, such as high-speed interconnects, crossbar switches, and buffers, that collectively work together to handle the data forwarding and switching operations.

Switch Port Configuration

Switch port configuration refers to the process of setting up and modifying the settings of a switch port in a computer network. A switch port is a physical interface on a network switch that allows devices to connect to the network. The configuration of a switch port involves various parameters and settings that determine how the port operates and functions within the network. Switch port configuration is an essential aspect of network management as it allows administrators to control the behavior and functionality of individual switch ports. By configuring switch ports, administrators can enable or disable specific features, define security settings, allocate bandwidth, and establish communication parameters for connected devices. Some of the key elements that can be configured on a switch port include: • VLANs (Virtual Local Area Networks): Switch ports can be assigned to specific VLANs to segment network traffic and improve network performance and security. • Trunking: In a network with multiple switches, trunking allows for the aggregation of multiple ports into a single logical link, increasing bandwidth and providing redundancy. • Port Security: Switch ports can be configured to prevent unauthorized access by using features such as MAC address filtering, limiting the number of connected devices, or enabling dynamic port security. • Quality of Service (QoS): Configuring QoS on switch ports allows for prioritization of specific types of network traffic, ensuring that critical applications or services receive sufficient bandwidth and low latency. • Link Aggregation:

311

By configuring link aggregation, multiple physical links between switches or devices can be combined to create a single logical link, increasing bandwidth and providing link redundancy. In addition to these parameters, switch ports can be configured to enable various protocols and features such as Spanning Tree Protocol (STP), port mirroring, Power over Ethernet (PoE), and many others. In summary, switch port configuration involves the setup and customization of various settings and parameters on a switch port to control its behavior, functionality, and interaction within a network.

Switch Port Management Software

Switch Port Management Software is a network management tool that enables users to efficiently and effectively manage the ports on network switches. It provides a centralized platform for configuring, monitoring, and troubleshooting switch ports, ensuring optimal network performance and security. In a computer network, switches play a crucial role in connecting devices and facilitating communication between them. Each switch contains a number of ports that connect to various devices such as computers, servers, printers, and other networking equipment. Managing these ports individually can be a time-consuming and error-prone task, especially in large networks with a high number of devices. Switch Port Management Software simplifies the management of switch ports by offering a comprehensive set of features and functionalities. It allows network administrators to remotely configure and monitor switch ports from a central location. This eliminates the need to physically access each switch for configuration changes, saving time and effort. The software provides a user-friendly interface that displays detailed information about each switch port, including its status, speed, duplex mode, VLAN membership, and other relevant parameters. Administrators can easily identify and troubleshoot port-related issues, such as congestion, errors, or improper configurations, by analyzing the real-time data provided by the software. Furthermore, Switch Port Management Software enables administrators to enforce security policies by controlling access to switch ports. They can define access control lists, VLANs, and other security measures to restrict unauthorized access and secure the network. The software also allows for the centralized management of link aggregation, spanning tree protocols, and other advanced networking features. In summary, Switch Port Management Software is a valuable tool for network administrators in managing and optimizing switch ports. It simplifies the configuration, monitoring, and troubleshooting of switch ports, enhancing network performance, security, and efficiency.

Switch Port Management

Switch Port Management is the process of administering and controlling the ports on a network switch. A network switch, also known as a multiport bridge, is a device that connects multiple network segments together and directs data packets from one port to another. Each port on a switch is a connection point for devices, such as computers, printers, and servers, which enables communication within a local area network (LAN). In a networking environment, switch port management involves configuring and monitoring the ports on a switch to ensure optimal performance, security, and efficiency. This includes tasks such as assigning ports to specific VLANs (Virtual Local Area Networks), enabling or disabling ports, adjusting port settings, and monitoring port traffic. The primary objective of switch port management is to control the flow of network traffic and provide secure and efficient communication between devices. By configuring the ports correctly, network administrators can segment traffic into different VLANs to improve network security and performance. They can also prioritize certain types of traffic, such as voice or video data, by configuring Quality of Service (QoS) settings on ports. Switch port management also involves monitoring the ports for any abnormalities or bottlenecks. Administrators can use various network monitoring tools to monitor port traffic, detect and troubleshoot network issues, and ensure that each port is operating at an optimal level. In addition to configuration and monitoring, switch port management often includes implementing security measures. This can involve setting up access control lists (ACLs) to control which devices are allowed to connect to specific ports, implementing port security features to prevent unauthorized devices from connecting, and configuring port mirroring to capture and analyze network traffic for security purposes. In summary, switch port management is a critical aspect of network administration that involves configuring, monitoring, and securing the ports on a network switch. By effectively managing switch ports, network administrators can ensure efficient traffic flow, improve network performance and security, and troubleshoot any issues that may arise.

Switch Port Security Measures

Switch port security measures are a set of techniques and configurations implemented on network switches to secure the physical ports and prevent unauthorized access to the network. These measures ensure that only authorized devices and users are allowed to connect to the network through the switch ports while blocking any unauthorized or malicious attempts. One of the main techniques used in switch port security is MAC address filtering. This technique restricts access to the switch ports based on the MAC addresses of the devices trying to connect. Network administrators can configure the switch to only allow specific MAC addresses or a range of MAC addresses to communicate through each port, effectively denying access to any other devices. This helps prevent unauthorized devices from connecting to the network and gaining access to sensitive data or resources. Another important measure is port security, which allows administrators to limit the number of MAC addresses that can be learned on a port. This prevents attackers from connecting multiple devices to a single port, a technique commonly known as MAC flooding or port hopping. By defining the maximum number of MAC addresses allowed per port, administrators can ensure that only one authorized device is connected, thereby reducing the risk of network attacks. Furthermore, switch port security also includes features such as disabling unused ports, enabling port status monitoring, and implementing port security violation modes. By disabling unused ports, network administrators eliminate potential entry points for unauthorized devices. Port status monitoring allows the detection of any changes in the connected devices, providing alerts and notifications when new devices are connected. Various violation modes, such as shutdown, restrict, or protect, allow administrators to choose how the switch should respond when a violation of the port security policies occurs. In conclusion, switch port security measures are crucial for ensuring the integrity and security of a network. They help prevent unauthorized access, protect against network attacks, and reduce the risks associated with malicious activities. By implementing MAC address filtering, port security, and other related configurations, network administrators can effectively control and manage the connections made through switch ports, thereby creating a more secure networking environment.

Switch Port Security Tools

Switch port security tools are a set of networking features and functionalities that help ensure the security and integrity of switch ports within a network infrastructure. These tools are designed to prevent unauthorized access, detect and mitigate security threats, and enforce network policies at the switch port level. Switch port security tools include various mechanisms and techniques that allow network administrators to control and monitor the traffic and devices connected to individual switch ports. One of the key functionalities is the ability to define and enforce access control lists (ACLs) at the switch port level. ACLs define the rules and conditions for allowing or denying traffic based on various criteria such as source and destination IP addresses, protocols, and port numbers. These tools also provide the capability to configure and manage port security features such as MAC address filtering and port security lockdown. MAC address filtering allows administrators to specify a whitelist or blacklist of MAC addresses that are allowed or denied access to a specific switch port. This helps prevent unauthorized devices from connecting to the network and restricts access to only authorized devices. Port security lockdown imposes restrictions on a switch port once a certain number of MAC addresses have been detected. This can help prevent the unauthorized connection of switches or hubs to a port and mitigate the risk of network attacks such as MAC flooding or VLAN hopping. In addition to access control and port security features, switch port security tools also offer functionalities for monitoring and detection. These include features such as port scanning, packet sniffing, and traffic analysis. These tools allow administrators to identify and monitor network traffic, detect anomalies, and investigate potential security breaches or violations. Overall, switch port security tools are essential components of network security infrastructure. They provide the means to enforce access control, prevent unauthorized access, and ensure the integrity and confidentiality of network communications at the switch port level.

Switch Port Security

Switch Port Security is a feature in networking that ensures the security and integrity of connections in a network by restricting unauthorized access to switch ports. It is implemented on network switches to prevent unauthorized devices from connecting to the network and to protect

313

against various security threats, such as unauthorized data access, network disruptions, and potential attacks. With switch port security, administrators can define and enforce specific security policies for individual switch ports, thereby allowing only authorized devices to connect to the network. This is achieved by configuring the switch to limit the number and type of devices that can connect to a particular port. By doing so, switch port security ensures that only approved devices, such as computers, servers, and network appliances, can establish a connection, while denying access to any unapproved or unauthorized devices.

Switch

A switch, in the context of computer networking, is a device that connects multiple devices, such as computers, printers, and servers, within a local area network (LAN). It operates at the data link layer of the OSI model and is responsible for the efficient transmission of data packets between connected devices. Switches are used to create a network infrastructure that allows devices to communicate with each other over a LAN. Unlike hubs, which simply receive incoming data and broadcast it to all connected devices, a switch intelligently directs data packets only to the specific device for which the data is intended.

Switching Hub

A switching hub, also known as a network switch, is a networking device used to connect multiple devices within a local area network (LAN). It operates at the data link layer of the OSI model, providing the functionality to forward data packets between devices based on their MAC addresses. A switching hub acts as a central communication point for devices within a LAN, enabling them to share resources and communicate with each other. Unlike a hub, which broadcasts incoming data packets to all connected devices, a switching hub intelligently examines the destination MAC address of each packet and forwards it only to the device it is intended for, reducing unnecessary network traffic and improving overall efficiency.

Switching Techniques

Switching Techniques refer to the methods and mechanisms used in networking to enable the efficient and reliable transfer of data packets between network devices. It involves the process of connecting multiple network segments to facilitate communication and data transmission. There are primarily three types of switching techniques commonly used in computer networks: circuit-switching, message-switching, and packet-switching. Each technique has its own characteristics and advantages, catering to specific network requirements. Circuit-switching is an older switching technique that creates a dedicated communication path between two devices for the entire duration of a conversation. It establishes a physical connection by reserving bandwidth and ensuring a continuous flow of data. This method is commonly used in traditional telephone networks and offers guaranteed and reliable transmission. However, it is less flexible and inefficient for data networks due to the constant reservation of resources. Message-switching, on the other hand, breaks up data into small messages or packets, which are then transmitted independently across the network. Each packet is individually routed based on the destination address and can take different paths to reach the destination. This technique eliminates the need for continuous reservation of resources, making it more efficient compared to circuit-switching. However, it suffers from delays and congestion as packets can be delayed or lost along the way. Packet-switching is the most widely used switching technique in modern computer networks. It divides data into small packets and sends them independently across the network. Each packet contains the necessary information for proper routing and reassembly at the destination. This technique offers high efficiency and robustness, as packets can take different routes and be reassembled in the correct order at the destination. It also allows for the simultaneous transmission of multiple packets. Packet-switching is widely used in Ethernet, IP, and other commonly used network protocols. In conclusion, switching techniques play a crucial role in networking by providing efficient and reliable data transmission. Circuit-switching guarantees dedicated connections, message-switching breaks data into packets for independent transmission, and packet-switching divides data into packets for optimal routing and reassembly. Understanding these techniques helps network administrators design and implement networks that meet specific requirements.

TCP Congestion Control

TCP congestion control is a mechanism implemented in networking to manage and regulate the flow of data between a sender and a receiver in order to prevent network congestion. It ensures that the amount of data being transmitted does not exceed the capacity of the network and avoids overloading the network resources, such as routers and links. When a sender wants to transmit data to a receiver using TCP (Transmission Control Protocol), it needs to consider the network conditions before sending data. TCP congestion control uses a combination of techniques to achieve this, aiming to maintain a balance between efficiency and fairness in data transmission. The primary objective of TCP congestion control is to detect and actively respond to congestion in the network. It uses a feedback mechanism that relies on the acknowledgment (ACK) packets sent by the receiver to determine the state of the network. The sender adjusts its transmission rate based on the feedback received from the receiver, allowing it to adapt to the current network conditions. One of the key techniques employed in TCP congestion control is called "Additive Increase, Multiplicative Decrease" (AIMD). In this approach, the sender increases its transmission rate by a small amount when ACK packets are received successfully. However, if congestion is detected, the sender reduces its transmission rate by a larger percentage. This process continues as the sender dynamically adjusts its transmission rate to find an optimal point that avoids congestion. TCP congestion control also utilizes another technique called "Slow Start" to initially establish the appropriate transmission rate. When a new connection is established or the network is underutilized, the sender starts by sending a small number of packets. If the receiver successfully acknowledges all the data, the sender gradually increases the transmission rate until congestion is detected. In conclusion, TCP congestion control plays a crucial role in maintaining network stability and preventing congestion. By dynamically adjusting the transmission rate based on network feedback, it helps ensure efficient and fair data transmission between senders and receivers.

TCP Handshake

The TCP handshake is a three-step process that establishes a reliable connection between two computers over a TCP/IP network. It is a fundamental part of the TCP protocol and is commonly used in applications such as web browsing, email, and file transfer. The TCP handshake begins when one computer, known as the client, initiates a connection to another computer, known as the server. The handshake process ensures that both computers are ready to send and receive data, establishes the initial sequence numbers for data transmission, and confirms the successful establishment of the connection before any data transfer begins. The first step of the TCP handshake is the SYN (synchronize) packet. The client sends a SYN packet to the server to initiate the connection. This packet includes a random sequence number that the server will use to confirm the connection. The SYN packet also includes other TCP control flags and options, such as window size and maximum segment size, which help optimize the subsequent data transfer. In the second step, the server receives the SYN packet and sends back a SYN-ACK (synchronize-acknowledge) packet. This packet acknowledges the receipt of the client's SYN packet and includes its own sequence number. The server also includes TCP control flags and options in the SYN-ACK packet to communicate additional information to the client. The third and final step of the TCP handshake is the ACK (acknowledge) packet. Upon receiving the SYN-ACK packet, the client sends an ACK packet back to the server. This packet acknowledges the server's sequence number and confirms the establishment of the connection. The ACK packet may also include additional TCP control flags and options, such as window size updates. Once the TCP handshake is complete, both computers are synchronized and ready to exchange data. By establishing a reliable connection, the TCP handshake ensures that data is transmitted successfully and in order, and that any potential issues or errors are detected and addressed.

TCP/IP Header

The TCP/IP header refers to the information that is added to the beginning of a data packet when it is sent over a TCP/IP network. It contains various fields that provide essential information for the transmission and the handling of the packet. The TCP/IP header typically consists of several fields, including the source and destination IP addresses, protocol information, and error checking codes. These fields are used by the network devices to properly route the packet to its destination and to ensure data integrity throughout the transmission.

TCP/IP Networking Protocols

315

TCP/IP Networking Protocols are a set of rules and protocols that govern the communication and data transmission between devices connected to a network. TCP/IP stands for Transmission Control Protocol/Internet Protocol, and it is the most widely used networking protocol suite in the world. TCP (Transmission Control Protocol) is responsible for breaking data into packets, ensuring the reliable delivery of packets, and reassembling them at the destination. It provides a connection-oriented communication model, where a connection is established between the sender and receiver before data transmission can occur. TCP manages the flow control, error detection, and congestion control mechanisms, making sure that data is transmitted accurately and efficiently. IP (Internet Protocol) is responsible for the addressing and routing of packets across the network. It assigns unique IP addresses to devices connected to the network, enabling them to send and receive data. IP uses a connectionless communication model, where packets are transmitted independently and may take different routes to reach the destination. IP determines the best path for packets using routing protocols and manages the fragmentation and reassembly of packets if necessary. Together, TCP and IP form the foundation of the internet and are the backbone of modern networking. TCP/IP protocols provide a standardized way for devices to communicate with each other over different networks, regardless of the underlying hardware or operating systems. They enable data to be transmitted reliably and efficiently across large and complex networks, such as the internet. In addition to TCP and IP, the TCP/IP suite includes other important protocols, such as UDP (User Datagram Protocol), ICMP (Internet Control Message Protocol), and DNS (Domain Name System). These protocols handle specific tasks, such as real-time data transmission, network diagnostics, and translating domain names into IP addresses. Overall, TCP/IP Networking Protocols play a crucial role in enabling devices to communicate and exchange data over networks. They provide the necessary mechanisms for reliable and efficient data transmission, making the internet and other networks reliable and accessible.

TCP/IP Networking

TCP/IP networking is a set of protocols used for establishing and maintaining communication over networks. TCP/IP stands for Transmission Control Protocol/Internet Protocol and is the underlying technology that allows devices to connect and communicate with one another on the internet. The TCP/IP suite consists of several protocols that work together to ensure reliable and robust communication. The Transmission Control Protocol (TCP) is responsible for breaking down data into smaller packets, establishing a reliable connection between devices, and managing the reliable delivery of data. The Internet Protocol (IP) is responsible for addressing and routing the packets across networks, ensuring that they reach their intended destination. TCP/IP networking operates at the network layer of the OSI model, which is the layer responsible for managing the logical addressing and routing of data. It provides a standardized and scalable solution for connecting devices across different networks, allowing them to communicate seamlessly. One of the key features of TCP/IP networking is its ability to handle both local area networks (LANs) and wide area networks (WANs). This makes it highly versatile and suitable for a range of networking scenarios, from small office networks to global internet communications. Another important aspect of TCP/IP networking is its support for various network services and applications. It provides protocols like the Internet Protocol (IP), Address Resolution Protocol (ARP), Internet Control Message Protocol (ICMP), and Internet Group Management Protocol (IGMP), among others, which enable functions such as addressing, error detection, and multicasting. TCP/IP networking also includes protocols for specific applications, such as the Hypertext Transfer Protocol (HTTP) for web browsing, File Transfer Protocol (FTP) for file sharing, and Simple Mail Transfer Protocol (SMTP) for email communication. These application protocols, built on top of the TCP/IP suite, allow for the efficient and secure exchange of data and information. In conclusion, TCP/IP networking is a comprehensive suite of protocols that enable the establishment and maintenance of communication between devices on networks. It provides the foundation for internet connectivity and supports a wide range of network services and applications.

TCP/IP Stack

The TCP/IP stack, also known as the Internet Protocol Suite, is a set of protocols used for communication between devices on a network. It provides a standardized framework for transmitting data over the internet and is the foundation upon which the internet operates. At its core, the TCP/IP stack is composed of four main layers: the Network Interface Layer, Internet

Layer, Transport Layer, and Application Layer. Each layer has a specific role and contributes to the overall functionality of the protocol suite. The Network Interface Layer, also referred to as the Link Layer, is responsible for the physical transmission of data between devices. It handles tasks such as addressing, framing, and error detection, ensuring that data is transmitted reliably across the network. The Internet Layer, also known as the IP Layer, is responsible for packet forwarding and routing. It addresses the issue of connecting multiple networks together and allows for the routing of packets from source to destination. The Internet Protocol (IP) is the primary protocol used in this layer, assigning unique IP addresses to devices and facilitating the delivery of packets across networks. The Transport Layer is responsible for end-to-end communication and ensures reliable data delivery between applications. The Transmission Control Protocol (TCP) is the main protocol used in this layer, providing features such as flow control, congestion control, and error recovery. It establishes a connection between the sender and receiver, breaks data into manageable chunks called segments, and ensures that all segments are received correctly and in order on the other end. The Application Layer is the topmost layer of the TCP/IP stack and contains various protocols and applications that enable network services for end-users. Examples of protocols in this layer include Hypertext Transfer Protocol (HTTP), File Transfer Protocol (FTP), and Simple Mail Transfer Protocol (SMTP). These protocols allow users to access web pages, transfer files, and send emails, among other functionalities. In summary, the TCP/IP stack is a suite of protocols that provides a standardized framework for communication on the internet. It encompasses four layers, each with its own specific functions and protocols, working together to enable reliable data transmission and network services.

TCP/IP (Transmission Control Protocol/Internet Protocol)

TCP/IP (Transmission Control Protocol/Internet Protocol) is the foundational protocol suite used for communication in computer networks. It provides a set of rules and standards that enable devices to communicate and exchange data over the internet or any other network. TCP/IP consists of two main protocols: TCP (Transmission Control Protocol) is responsible for establishing and maintaining connections between devices on a network. It ensures reliable and ordered delivery of data by dividing it into smaller packets, which are then transmitted and reassembled at the receiving end. TCP guarantees that all packets arrive at their destination without errors and in the correct order. IP (Internet Protocol) is in charge of addressing and routing data packets across networks. It assigns a unique IP address to each connected device, allowing them to send and receive data. IP is responsible for the logical organization of devices on a network and directs packets to their intended recipients, even if they are located in different parts of the world. TCP/IP provides a reliable and efficient communication mechanism by incorporating other protocols and services. For example, the Internet Control Message Protocol (ICMP) helps diagnose and report errors in the network, while the Domain Name System (DNS) translates human-readable domain names into IP addresses. Additionally, TCP/IP supports protocols for email transmission (SMTP), file transfer (FTP), and web browsing (HTTP). Overall, TCP/IP serves as the foundation for internet communication, connecting millions of devices worldwide. Its modular and extensible nature has allowed it to evolve and adapt to changes in networking technology over the years. Despite the emergence of alternative network protocols, TCP/IP remains the dominant protocol suite for both local and global networks. Its versatility, reliability, and wide compatibility make it an essential component of modern networking.

TCP/IP Troubleshooting Tips

TCP/IP troubleshooting refers to the process of identifying and resolving issues related to the Transmission Control Protocol/Internet Protocol (TCP/IP). TCP/IP is a set of protocols that define how data packets are transmitted over the internet. When troubleshooting TCP/IP, network administrators must diagnose and address problems that may arise in the communication between devices on a network. There are several common issues that can occur with TCP/IP networks, including: 1. Connectivity problems: This can include issues with establishing a connection between devices, such as a failure to establish a TCP connection or an inability to resolve domain names to IP addresses. 2. Performance issues: Slow network speeds or high latency can indicate problems with TCP/IP, such as packet loss or congestion on the network. 3. Security issues: TCP/IP networks can be vulnerable to various security threats, such as unauthorized access or data breaches. Troubleshooting involves identifying and resolving these security issues to ensure a secure network environment. When troubleshooting

TCP/IP, network administrators can use several techniques: 1. Ping: The Ping command can be used to test network connectivity by sending ICMP echo requests to a specific IP address or hostname. It helps identify issues with network connectivity, such as a device being offline or a firewall blocking communications. 2. Traceroute: Traceroute is a command that shows the route and the time taken by packets to reach a specific destination. It helps identify connectivity problems and can pinpoint where the issue is occurring. 3. IP Configuration: Checking the IP configuration of devices can help identify issues such as duplicate IP addresses or incorrect subnet masks. Ensuring that devices are correctly configured can resolve connectivity problems. 4. Firewall and Security Settings: Reviewing firewall rules and security settings can help identify and resolve security-related issues. Ensuring that the appropriate ports are open and secure configurations are in place can enhance network security. In conclusion, TCP/IP troubleshooting involves diagnosing and resolving issues related to the TCP/IP protocol suite. By using various techniques such as Ping, Traceroute, IP configuration checks, and reviewing firewall and security settings, network administrators can identify and address problems in TCP/IP networks, ensuring reliable and secure communication between devices.

TCP/IP Troubleshooting

TCP/IP Troubleshooting refers to the process of identifying and resolving issues related to the TCP/IP protocol suite in a computer network. The TCP/IP protocol suite is the foundation of modern networking and is used to connect devices and facilitate communication over the internet. When troubleshooting TCP/IP issues, the aim is to diagnose and resolve problems that may occur at various layers of the TCP/IP protocol stack, including the Network Interface layer, Internet layer, Transport layer, and Application layer. Common issues that may arise include network connectivity problems, slow or intermittent network performance, and incorrect or incomplete data transmission. The troubleshooting process typically begins with gathering information about the problem, such as the symptoms, network topology, and configurations of relevant devices. This may involve using various tools, such as ping, traceroute, and netstat, to gather data and perform tests. Once the information is collected, the next step is to analyze the data and narrow down the possible causes of the issue. This may involve examining network packets, reviewing log files, and consulting network diagrams. Through this analysis, the troubleshooter can identify potential misconfigurations, network congestion, faulty hardware, or software incompatibilities. Once the potential causes are identified, the troubleshooter can then proceed with implementing corrective actions to resolve the issue. This may involve reconfiguring network settings, updating firmware or software, replacing faulty hardware components, or adjusting network traffic management policies. After the corrective actions are implemented, it is essential to verify the effectiveness of the solutions by testing and monitoring the network. This helps ensure that the issue has been successfully resolved and that the network is functioning as expected. In conclusion, TCP/IP troubleshooting is a systematic approach to diagnose and resolve issues related to the TCP/IP protocol suite in a computer network. It involves gathering information, analyzing data, identifying potential causes, implementing corrective actions, and verifying the effectiveness of the solutions. By following this process, network administrators can effectively maintain and troubleshoot TCP/IP networks.

TCP/IP Utilities

TCP/IP utilities are a set of tools used in networking to troubleshoot and manage network connections and communication. TCP/IP, which stands for Transmission Control Protocol/Internet Protocol, is the standard communication protocol used for the internet and most local area networks (LANs). These utilities allow network administrators and users to diagnose and solve problems related to network connectivity, data transmission, and network configuration. They provide a range of functionalities, including network scanning, packet capturing, network analysis, and network monitoring. Some commonly used TCP/IP utilities include: - Ping: This utility is used to test the reachability of a network device or host and to measure the round-trip time for packets sent from the source to the destination. - Traceroute: Traceroute is used to trace the route that packets take from the source to the destination. It shows the IP addresses of all the intermediate hops and the round-trip time for each hop. - Netstat: Netstat displays active network connections, open ports, and listening ports on a local machine. It provides information about the status of the TCP/IP stack, including established connections and socket states. - Nslookup: Nslookup is a command-line tool used to query the Domain Name System (DNS) to retrieve information about domain names, IP addresses, and other related data. - Wireshark: Wireshark is a powerful network protocol analyzer used to capture and analyze network traffic in real-time. It can be used to troubleshoot network issues, detect network intrusions, and monitor network performance. In addition to these utilities, there are many others available that serve specific purposes, such as DHCP server/client utilities, SMTP mail server utilities, and FTP client/server utilities. These tools provide network administrators with the necessary means to manage and maintain a functioning network infrastructure.

TCP/IP

The Transmission Control Protocol/Internet Protocol (TCP/IP) is a suite of communication protocols that are used to connect devices on the internet and other computer networks. TCP/IP provides a reliable and efficient way to transmit data packets between devices, ensuring that the packets are delivered intact and in the correct order. TCP/IP is divided into two main protocols: the Transmission Control Protocol (TCP) and the Internet Protocol (IP). These protocols work together to enable communication between devices and enable data transmission over the internet. TCP is responsible for breaking data into packets, numbering them for identification, and ensuring that they are delivered to their destination. It establishes a connection between the sender and receiver and provides error checking and flow control mechanisms to ensure the reliable delivery of data. TCP also manages congestion control to avoid overwhelming the network with excessive traffic. IP is responsible for addressing and routing packets across the network. It assigns unique IP addresses to devices and uses these addresses to determine the correct destination for the packets. IP also handles fragmentation, which allows data to be divided into smaller packets that can be transmitted more efficiently. It ensures that packets are sent to the correct destination by using routers to forward packets between different networks. TCP/IP is a widely used protocol suite that forms the foundation of the internet. It allows devices to communicate over networks of different types and sizes, enabling the exchange of information and services. It abstracts the underlying network infrastructure, providing a common language that allows different devices and operating systems to communicate seamlessly. In conclusion, TCP/IP is a suite of communication protocols that enable reliable and efficient data transmission over the internet and computer networks. It consists of TCP, which handles data delivery and reliability, and IP, which handles addressing and routing. TCP/IP is essential for connecting devices and enabling communication on the internet.

TFTP (Trivial File Transfer Protocol)

TFTP (Trivial File Transfer Protocol) is a simple protocol used for transferring files between computers on a network. It is primarily used in environments where reliable and advanced features of other file transfer protocols, such as FTP (File Transfer Protocol), are not necessary. TFTP operates on top of the User Datagram Protocol (UDP) and is implemented with a client-server architecture. The TFTP client initiates the file transfer by sending a request to the TFTP server. The server then responds to the client's request based on the type of operation requested, which can be either a read (RRQ) or write (WRQ) operation. When a client requests to read a file from the server, the server responds with the requested file's contents in data packets. Each data packet typically contains a fixed-sized block of data and a block number. The client acknowledges the receipt of each data packet by sending an acknowledgment (ACK) packet with the corresponding block number. This process continues until the entire file has been transferred. On the other hand, when a client requests to write a file to the server, the server sends an acknowledgment (ACK) packet indicating that it is ready to receive the file. The client then sends the file's content in data packets to the server, along with a block number for each packet. The server acknowledges the receipt of each data packet by sending an ACK packet with the corresponding block number. This process continues until the entire file has been transferred. TFTP has a few key characteristics that differentiate it from other file transfer protocols. Firstly, TFTP does not support authentication or user identification, meaning that anyone with access to the TFTP server can read or write files. Secondly, TFTP does not provide any mechanisms for error recovery or retransmission of lost packets. This makes TFTP less reliable than protocols like FTP, but also more lightweight and simpler to implement. In conclusion, TFTP is a basic protocol for transferring files over a network. While it lacks advanced features and reliability mechanisms found in other file transfer protocols, TFTP's simplicity and lightweight nature make it suitable for certain low-stakes and resource-constrained environments.

319

Telecommunications

Telecommunications in the context of networking refers to the transmission of information over a distance using electronic means. It involves the use of various technologies and devices to enable communication between individuals, organizations, and systems. The main goal of telecommunications in networking is to establish a reliable and efficient means of transmitting data, voice, and video signals. This enables the exchange of information, the sharing of resources, and the implementation of various applications and services.

Telnet

Telnet is a client-server protocol used in networking that allows a user to establish a remote connection to a host or server. It enables the user to access and interact with the remote system as if they were physically present at the location where the system is hosted. The Telnet protocol operates on the application layer of the TCP/IP networking model and uses the Transmission Control Protocol (TCP) to establish and manage the connection. It provides a virtual terminal interface, which means that the user can perform various operations on the remote system, such as executing commands, accessing files, and running applications. When a user initiates a Telnet session, the Telnet client application establishes a connection with the Telnet server application running on the remote system. The client sends commands and input to the server, and the server responds with output, allowing the user to remotely control the system. One of the key features of Telnet is its ability to transmit the user's keystrokes and receive the server's responses in plaintext, making it easy to understand and interpret the communication between the client and server. However, this lack of encryption makes Telnet vulnerable to potential security risks, as sensitive information can be intercepted and viewed by unauthorized parties. While Telnet was widely used in the early days of networking, its popularity has decreased with the advent of more secure protocols like SSH (Secure Shell). SSH provides encrypted communication and enhanced security measures, making it a preferred choice for remote access to systems. In conclusion, Telnet is a client-server protocol that allows users to establish remote connections to systems over a network. It provides a virtual terminal interface and operates on the application layer of the TCP/IP networking model. However, its lack of encryption makes it less secure compared to alternatives like SSH.

Threat Actor

A threat actor refers to any individual, group, or entity that poses a threat to the security and integrity of computer networks and systems. These actors are involved in cyberattacks and malicious activities, such as stealing sensitive information, disrupting network operations, or causing financial losses. Threat actors can exist in various forms, ranging from amateur hackers to organized crime syndicates and even state-sponsored groups. They have diverse motives for their activities, including financial gain, political agendas, espionage, or simply causing chaos and disruption. Threat actors employ a wide range of techniques and tools to exploit vulnerabilities in networks and systems. These can include malware, social engineering, phishing attacks, denial-of-service (DoS) attacks, and zero-day exploits. They often target weaknesses in network infrastructure, operating systems, applications, and human behavior to gain unauthorized access or compromise sensitive data. Once a threat actor gains access to a network, they may engage in various nefarious activities. These can include exfiltrating sensitive data, installing backdoors or remote access tools, escalating privileges, or using the compromised network as a launching pad for further attacks. To combat threat actors, organizations employ various security measures and practices. These can include implementing strong access controls, regularly updating security patches, educating employees about potential risks and best practices, monitoring network traffic for suspicious activities, and implementing intrusion detection and prevention systems. However, threat actors constantly evolve their tactics and techniques, making it challenging for organizations to keep up with the ever-changing cybersecurity landscape. As a result, organizations must maintain a proactive approach to cybersecurity, staying informed about emerging threats, and continually updating their defense mechanisms. In conclusion, threat actors are individuals or groups with malicious intent who seek to compromise computer networks and systems for personal gain or other motives. Understanding their tactics and staying prepared with robust cybersecurity measures is essential for organizations to protect their networks and sensitive data.

Threat Intelligence Feed

A Threat Intelligence Feed in the context of networking refers to a source of timely and relevant information about threats that have the potential to compromise the security of network systems. It is a service that provides up-to-date intelligence on various types of cyber threats, such as malware, phishing attacks, data breaches, and network vulnerabilities. Threat intelligence feeds are typically delivered in a structured format and are used by organizations to enhance their security posture. These feeds are collected and curated by security experts and researchers who analyze and monitor various sources for the latest threat information.

Threat Intelligence

Threat Intelligence in the context of networking refers to the collection, analysis, and use of information about potential cyber threats. This information is gathered from various sources and is focused on identifying, understanding, and mitigating security risks to networks, systems, and data. The objective of threat intelligence is to proactively anticipate and respond to emerging threats, vulnerabilities, and attacks in order to prevent or minimize damages to network infrastructure and resources. It enables organizations to stay one step ahead of cybercriminals by gaining insights into their tactics, techniques, and procedures.

Token Ring

A Token Ring is a type of local area network (LAN) technology that uses a token-passing protocol to control access to the network. It is a networking standard defined by the IEEE 802.5 standard. In a Token Ring network, data is transmitted in a ring-like topology, where each device is connected to two neighbors, forming a logical ring. The physical connection is typically made using twisted-pair or fiber-optic cables. The ring topology ensures that every device has an equal opportunity to transmit data, as data travels in a sequential manner around the ring. In order to transmit data, a device must first possess a token, which is a special frame that circulates around the network. When a device has the token, it has the right to transmit data. The token-passing protocol ensures that only one device can transmit at a time, preventing collisions and ensuring orderly transmission of data. When a device wants to transmit data, it waits until it receives the token. Once it has the token, it attaches its data to the token and sends it around the network. Other devices in the network inspect the token as it passes by, checking if it contains data for them. If a device receives the token and finds that it has data to transmit, it removes the data from the token and attaches its own data. The token continues circulating until it reaches the intended recipient, who removes the data and releases the token back into the network. Token Ring networks typically operate at speeds of 4 or 16 Mbps, although faster versions have been developed. They provide a deterministic access method, meaning that the order of transmission is predictable and can be controlled. This makes Token Ring networks suitable for applications that require guaranteed bandwidth and low latency. However, Token Ring networks have become less commonly used in favor of Ethernet networks, which offer higher speeds and easier implementation. Token Ring networks require additional hardware, such as a token passing mechanism, which can increase complexity and cost. Additionally, Ethernet has evolved to support similar determinism through technologies like Quality of Service (QoS).

Topology

A network topology refers to the arrangement or layout of devices and their connections in a computer network. It defines how devices such as computers, servers, switches, and routers are interconnected and how data flows between them. In networking, various types of topologies are used to establish connections and organize networks based on their structure and requirements. These topologies include: 1. Bus Topology: In a bus topology, all devices are connected to a central cable called the "bus." Data is transmitted in both directions along the bus, and all devices receive the transmitted data. However, if the bus cable fails, the entire network becomes unreachable. 2. Star Topology: The star topology features a central device, such as a switch or hub, with all other devices connected directly to it. Each device has a dedicated connection to the central device. This topology provides high reliability as the failure of one device does not affect the rest of the network. 3. Ring Topology: The ring topology connects devices in a circular manner, where each device is connected to exactly two neighboring devices. Data circulates around the ring in one direction, and each device receives the data and forwards it to the next device. In case a device or a link breaks, the entire network can be affected. 4. Mesh Topology: Mesh topology establishes a direct connection between every device in the network. This results in high reliability and fault tolerance, as data can be rerouted through multiple pathways if a device or link fails. Mesh topologies can be full mesh (every device connects to every other device) or partial mesh (some devices have limited direct connections). 5. Tree Topology: Tree topology combines multiple star topologies into a hierarchical structure. It consists of a root node, from which multiple child nodes branch out. This arrangement allows for scalable and manageable networks, but if the root node fails, the entire network may become unreachable. These topologies can be used individually or in combination to create complex network architectures based on the needs of an organization or the type of network required. Network topologies play a crucial role in determining factors such as scalability, performance, fault tolerance, and ease of management in a computer network.

Tor Network

The Tor Network, also known as The Onion Router, is a decentralized network composed of thousands of volunteer-operated servers, or nodes, that allows users to browse the internet anonymously. Founded in the early 2000s, Tor was originally developed by the United States Naval Research Laboratory with the goal of protecting online communications and championing internet privacy. At its core, the Tor Network functions by routing internet traffic through a series of encrypted connections, or relays, provided by its volunteer nodes. When a user accesses the internet through Tor, their connection is bounced through multiple relays before reaching its destination. Each relay only knows the IP address of the relay before it and the IP address of the relay it is going to, ensuring that neither the user's IP address nor their actual location can be easily traced. Tor's layered encryption approach, known as onion routing, is a fundamental aspect of its security. When a user sends a request through the Tor Network, each relay decrypts a layer of encryption, uncovering where the traffic should be sent next. This process continues until the final relay, known as the exit node, decrypts the final layer and sends the request to its intended destination. By encrypting the original request multiple times, Tor ensures that no single relay knows both the source and destination of the user's traffic, adding a layer of anonymity.

Traceroute

Traceroute is a network diagnostic tool used to track the route that packets take from one host to another over an IP network. It provides useful information about the network path between the source and destination devices, including the number of hops, latency, and the IP addresses of intermediate routers along the way. When a traceroute command is issued from a source device, it sends a series of packets to the destination device with increasing Time-To-Live (TTL) values. Each packet's TTL is set to a specific value, starting from 1 and incrementing by 1 for each subsequent packet. The TTL field in an IP packet denotes the number of network hops (routers) the packet can traverse before it is discarded. As the initial packet reaches the first hop (router) on the network, the TTL expires, and the router sends back an ICMP Time Exceeded message to the source. This message contains the IP address of the router. By obtaining this information, the traceroute utility can identify the first hop in the network path. The process is then repeated for subsequent packets, increasing the TTL each time, until the destination device is reached. Traceroute displays the results in a tabular format, listing the IP addresses of each router encountered along the route, as well as the round-trip time (RTT) for each hop. The RTT represents the time taken for a packet to travel from the source to the specific router and back. This information allows network administrators to identify network performance issues, troubleshoot connectivity problems, and pinpoint areas of congestion or latency. Traceroute can also provide insights into the network topology by revealing the number of hops required to reach a destination. This can be useful for analyzing network efficiency and identifying potential bottlenecks. Additionally, traceroute can be used to determine if a packet is taking an unexpected or inefficient route, which may indicate routing misconfigurations or network failures. In summary, traceroute is a valuable network diagnostic tool that helps identify the path packets take between devices on an IP network. By analyzing the results, network administrators can gain insights into network performance, troubleshoot connectivity issues, and optimize their network infrastructure.

Traffic Shaping

Traffic shaping is a networking technique used to manage and control the flow of data packets within a network. It is implemented by network administrators to prioritize and allocate network resources effectively, ensuring that bandwidth is utilized optimally and network performance is maximized. By regulating the transmission of data packets, traffic shaping helps to maintain network stability and prevent congestion, allowing for smooth and efficient data transmission. In a network, data is transmitted in the form of packets, and these packets can have varying sizes and priorities. Traffic shaping allows administrators to set rules and policies to determine the handling of different types of packets. This can involve prioritizing certain types of traffic over others or limiting the bandwidth for specific applications or users. By classifying and regulating packets based on their characteristics, traffic shaping enables administrators to shape the traffic according to specific requirements or policies defined for the network. There are several benefits to implementing traffic shaping in a network. One major advantage is the ability to manage congestion effectively. By controlling the rate at which data packets are transmitted, administrators can prevent the network from becoming overloaded and ensure that mission-critical applications receive the necessary bandwidth to function properly. Additionally, traffic shaping allows for the allocation of resources based on priority, which can be especially important in networks that handle real-time applications such as voice or video communication. Another advantage of traffic shaping is the ability to ensure fairness in bandwidth allocation. By setting policies that limit the bandwidth for specific applications or users, administrators can prevent a single user or application from monopolizing the available bandwidth, ensuring that all users have a fair share of network resources. This helps to prevent individual connections from negatively impacting overall network performance, providing a more equitable and consistent user experience. In conclusion, traffic shaping plays a crucial role in managing network traffic by controlling the flow of data packets. By implementing traffic shaping techniques, administrators can prioritize and allocate network resources effectively, manage congestion, and ensure fairness in bandwidth allocation. By regulating the transmission of data packets, traffic shaping helps to optimize network performance and maintain a stable and efficient network environment.

Transmission Control Protocol (TCP)

The Transmission Control Protocol (TCP) is a core protocol in the Internet protocol suite. It is responsible for establishing and maintaining reliable communication between devices over an IP network. TCP operates at the transport layer and provides a connection-oriented, point-to-point communication service. TCP works by breaking the data into smaller segments called packets, which are then sent over the network. It uses a combination of sequence numbers, acknowledgments, and timeout mechanisms to ensure the reliable delivery of data. Each packet is assigned a unique sequence number to maintain the order of transmission and detect any missing or duplicate packets. When a TCP connection is established between two devices, a three-way handshake process is initiated. During this process, the sending and receiving devices exchange control messages called SYN (synchronize) and ACK (acknowledge). This handshake ensures that both devices are ready and willing to establish a connection. Once the connection is established, TCP provides a reliable and ordered data stream. It acknowledges the successful receipt of packets and requests retransmission of any missing or corrupted packets. It also performs flow control to prevent overwhelming the receiving device with more data than it can handle. TCP guarantees the delivery of data in the same order as it was sent and provides mechanisms to handle congestion and network errors. It handles lost packets by retransmitting them and adjusts the transmission rate based on network conditions. TCP also supports multiplexing, allowing multiple applications or processes to use a single TCP connection simultaneously. In summary, TCP is a fundamental protocol for reliable and ordered communication over IP networks. It ensures the delivery of data in the correct order, handles congestion and errors, and provides mechanisms for flow control and multiplexing. TCP forms the foundation of many internet applications, such as web browsing, email, and file transfer.

Transmission Control Protocol/Internet Protocol (TCP/IP)

The Transmission Control Protocol/Internet Protocol (TCP/IP) is a suite of networking protocols that allows computers to communicate with each other over the internet or other interconnected networks. TCP/IP provides a reliable and standardized method for data transmission, addressing, and routing in computer networks. It is the foundation of the modern internet and is widely used in various network applications. TCP/IP is composed of two main protocols: the Transmission Control Protocol (TCP) and the Internet Protocol (IP). These protocols work together to enable the reliable and efficient transmission of data packets between devices. TCP is responsible for breaking data into packets, establishing connections between devices, and ensuring that packets are delivered in the correct order. It provides a reliable and error-free communication channel by implementing mechanisms such as flow control, congestion control, and error detection. TCP guarantees that data packets are delivered intact and in the same order they were sent. IP, on the other hand, is responsible for addressing and routing packets across networks. It assigns a unique IP address to each device connected to the network, allowing them to be identified and located. IP determines the best path for data packets to travel from the source device to the destination device, considering factors such as network congestion and availability. It is a connectionless protocol, meaning that each packet is treated independently and can take a different route to reach its destination. Together, TCP and IP provide a robust and scalable networking solution that allows for the reliable transmission of data across networks of varying sizes and topologies. TCP/IP has become the de facto standard for internet communication and is used by numerous applications, including web browsing, email, file transfer, and streaming. It enables devices from different manufacturers and operating systems to communicate seamlessly, fostering the global connectivity that defines the modern digital age. TCP/IP has undergone several revisions and improvements over the years, with the current version being IPv6, which provides a larger address space and improved security features compared to its predecessor, IPv4. However, both versions of IP remain compatible within the TCP/IP suite, ensuring interoperability across different network environments.

Transmission Medium

A transmission medium, in the context of networking, refers to the physical medium or channel through which data is transmitted from one network device to another. It provides the pathway for data communication between devices and plays a crucial role in the overall performance and efficiency of a network. The transmission medium can be wired or wireless, with each having its own advantages and limitations. Wired transmission mediums use physical cables or wires to transmit data signals, while wireless transmission mediums use electromagnetic waves to transmit data without the need for physical connections. Common examples of wired transmission mediums include twisted pair cables, coaxial cables, and fiber-optic cables. Twisted pair cables, such as Ethernet cables, are widely used for local area network (LAN) connections due to their cost-effectiveness and ease of installation. Coaxial cables are commonly used for cable television and broadband internet connections, offering higher bandwidth capabilities than twisted pair cables. Fiber-optic cables, on the other hand, use light signals to transmit data, providing high-speed and long-distance communication with minimal signal degradation. Wireless transmission mediums utilize various frequencies of electromagnetic waves to transmit data signals through the air. Some popular wireless transmission mediums include Wi-Fi, Bluetooth, and cellular networks. Wi-Fi enables wireless connectivity within a limited range, making it suitable for local area networks. Bluetooth is a short-range wireless technology commonly used for connecting peripheral devices to computers or mobile devices. Cellular networks, such as 3G, 4G, and 5G, provide wireless communication over long distances, enabling mobile connectivity and internet access. The choice of transmission medium depends on several factors, including the distance of communication, required bandwidth, cost, and environmental considerations. Wired transmission mediums typically offer higher bandwidth and better security compared to wireless mediums, but they require physical connections and are limited by cable length. Wireless transmission mediums provide greater mobility and flexibility but may suffer from signal interference and slower speeds in certain environments. In many cases, a combination of both wired and wireless transmission mediums is used to create a robust and reliable network infrastructure.

Transport Layer Security (TLS)

Transport Layer Security (TLS) is a cryptographic protocol designed to ensure secure communication over a network, particularly the internet. It operates at the Transport Layer of the OSI model, providing end-to-end secure communication between two applications. TLS provides authentication, confidentiality, and integrity, making it possible for two parties to securely exchange information without the risk of eavesdropping, tampering, or unauthorized access. It uses a combination of symmetric and asymmetric encryption algorithms to achieve its security goals. The main features of TLS include: 1. Encryption: TLS uses encryption algorithms to protect the confidentiality of the data being transmitted. It encrypts the data using a symmetric encryption algorithm, and the encryption key is exchanged securely using asymmetric encryption. 2. Authentication: TLS supports mutual authentication, allowing both the client and the server to verify each other's identities. This is done using digital certificates, which are issued by trusted third-party Certificate Authorities (CAs). The certificates contain the public key of the entity and are used to establish a secure connection. 3. Integrity: TLS provides mechanisms to ensure that the data transmitted between the client and the server has not been tampered with during transit. This is achieved using message authentication codes (MACs), which are computed using cryptographic hash functions. 4. Perfect Forward Secrecy: TLS supports perfect forward secrecy, which means that even if the long-term private key used for encryption is compromised, previously intercepted encrypted communications cannot be decrypted. 5. Negotiation: TLS supports negotiation of encryption algorithms and protocols during the handshake process. This allows clients and servers to select the most secure algorithm and protocol that both parties support. TLS operates using a combination of protocols and algorithms, including the Handshake Protocol, the Record Protocol, and various encryption and hash functions. It has evolved over time, with newer versions addressing vulnerabilities and improving security. In conclusion, Transport Layer Security (TLS) is a cryptographic protocol that provides secure communication over a network. It ensures confidentiality, integrity, and authentication, allowing two applications to securely exchange information. TLS is an essential component of secure internet communication, protecting sensitive data from unauthorized access, tampering, and eavesdropping.

Transport Layer

The Transport Layer is one of the layers in the network protocol stack that is responsible for providing reliable and efficient communication between hosts or endpoints on a network. Its main function is to establish end-to-end connectivity and ensure the reliable delivery of data between applications running on different devices or systems. It does this by breaking data into smaller units called segments, which are then transmitted over the network and reassembled at the receiving end. The Transport Layer also handles any necessary error correction and flow control mechanisms to ensure that data is transmitted accurately and without overwhelming the receiving device or network. It provides a variety of protocols and services to meet different application requirements and network conditions. One of the key protocols of the Transport Layer is the Transmission Control Protocol (TCP), which provides a connection-oriented, reliable communication service. TCP establishes a virtual connection between two endpoints and guarantees the delivery of data by using acknowledgments, retransmissions, and other mechanisms to recover lost or corrupted segments. Another major protocol of the Transport Layer is the User Datagram Protocol (UDP), which provides a connectionless, unreliable communication service. UDP is faster and more lightweight than TCP but does not provide the same level of reliability, as it does not include error detection or retransmission mechanisms. In addition to TCP and UDP, the Transport Layer also includes other protocols and services such as the Stream Control Transmission Protocol (SCTP), which provides reliable, connection-oriented transport with support for multi-homing and multi-streaming. Overall, the Transport Layer plays a crucial role in network communication by ensuring that data is correctly and efficiently transmitted between applications running on different hosts or endpoints. Its protocols and services facilitate reliable end-to-end connectivity and support the diverse requirements of various applications and network environments.

Tunneling

Tunneling is a networking technique that allows the encapsulation of one network protocol within another network protocol. It involves taking data packets from one network and encapsulating them within the data packets of another network. This process allows data to be transmitted securely over an insecure network or to traverse networks that are not directly connected. Tunneling works by creating a tunnel between two endpoints using a tunneling protocol. This protocol sets up the rules and procedures for the encapsulation and transmission of data packets. The encapsulated packets from the source network are then transmitted over the destination network, appearing as if they originated from that network. Tunneling is commonly used in virtual private networks (VPNs) to create secure connections over the internet. It provides a way for remote users to securely access a private network, such as a company's intranet, by encapsulating their data within the internet protocol (IP) packets. This creates a secure tunnel for the data to travel through, protecting it from interception and unauthorized access. Tunneling can also be used to connect networks that use different protocols. For example, if two networks are using different routing protocols, tunneling can be used to encapsulate the routing protocol packets within IP packets, allowing the networks to communicate with each other. This enables interoperability between different network protocols and helps overcome compatibility issues. Another use case for tunneling is in IPv6 transition mechanisms. As the world transitions from IPv4 to IPv6, tunneling protocols are used to encapsulate IPv6 packets within IPv4 packets, allowing them to be transmitted over IPv4 networks. This enables communication between devices using different IP versions and helps facilitate the transition to the newer IPv6 protocol.

Two-Factor Authentication (2FA)

Two-Factor Authentication (2FA) is a security measure used in networking to enhance the authentication process for user access to various systems and services. It adds an extra layer of security to the traditional username-password authentication method by requiring users to provide additional proof of identity. 2FA requires users to provide two different types of credentials to verify their identity. These typically fall into three categories: something the user knows, something the user possesses, or something the user is. The first factor is usually a username and password combination, which the user knows. The second factor can be something that the user possesses, such as a mobile device or a hardware token, or something that the user is, such as a fingerprint or facial recognition. This combination of factors makes it more difficult for unauthorized individuals to gain access to systems and services, even if they manage to obtain the user's password. It adds an extra layer of protection by requiring an additional piece of information or physical presence that is unique to the user. When a user attempts to log in to a system or service that uses 2FA, they first enter their username and password. Once these credentials are verified, the system prompts them to provide the second factor of authentication. This could be a unique code generated by an authentication app on their mobile device, a one-time password sent via SMS, or a fingerprint scan. 2FA significantly reduces the risk of unauthorized access as it requires potential attackers to bypass multiple layers of security. Even if a hacker manages to obtain a user's password, they would still need access to the second factor, which adds an extra barrier for malicious activities. In conclusion, Two-Factor Authentication (2FA) is an additional security measure used in networking that requires users to provide two different types of credentials to verify their identity. It adds an extra layer of protection by requiring an additional piece of information or physical presence that is unique to the user, making it more difficult for unauthorized individuals to gain access to systems and services.

UDP Flood

UDP Flood is a form of DDoS (Distributed Denial of Service) attack that targets network devices and servers by overwhelming them with a high volume of User Datagram Protocol (UDP) packets. UDP Flood attacks exploit the stateless nature of the UDP protocol, flooding the victim's network infrastructure with UDP packets that consume significant resources and disrupt normal network operations. In a UDP Flood attack, the attacker typically sends a large number of UDP packets to flood the victim's network. Since UDP is connectionless and stateless, the victim's devices or servers do not require any prior communication or verification before accepting the packets. This makes it relatively easy for an attacker to initiate a UDP Flood attack by simply sending UDP packets with a spoofed source IP address. The main goal of a UDP Flood attack is to consume the available network bandwidth, CPU resources, and other system resources of the victim's network infrastructure. This results in a high volume of incoming UDP packets that the victim's devices or servers are unable to handle, leading to a denial of service situation. As a result, legitimate users are unable to access the network services provided by the victim's devices or servers. UDP Flood attacks are particularly effective against network devices and servers that rely heavily on UDP-based protocols, such as DNS (Domain Name System) servers and VoIP (Voice over IP) systems. Since UDP does not provide any built-in mechanisms for verifying the authenticity or integrity of the received packets, it is challenging for the victim's devices or servers to differentiate between legitimate and malicious UDP packets. To mitigate UDP Flood attacks, various techniques can be implemented, such as traffic filtering, rate limiting, and anomaly detection. Network administrators can apply packet filtering rules to identify and drop incoming UDP packets that exhibit abnormal characteristics. Additionally, rate limiting mechanisms can be employed to restrict the number of UDP packets that can be accepted from a single source IP address. Intrusion detection and prevention systems can also be deployed to identify and block UDP Flood attacks in real-time.

UDP Header Fields

UDP (User Datagram Protocol) is a transport layer protocol that is commonly used for providing a connectionless and unreliable communication service between hosts on a network. Unlike TCP (Transmission Control Protocol), UDP does not guarantee the delivery of packets or provide mechanisms for retransmission or flow control. Instead, it manages to provide a minimal overhead while allowing for faster transmission speeds. The UDP header consists of four main fields: the source port, the destination port, the length, and the checksum. These fields are used to ensure the successful transmission and reception of UDP datagrams. The source port field is 16 bits in size and identifies the port number on the sender's host from which the UDP packet originates. This allows the recipient to know which application or process sent the datagram. The destination port field, also 16 bits in size, specifies the port number on the receiver's host that the UDP packet is intended for. It enables the recipient to direct the datagram to the appropriate application or process. The length field, also 16 bits in size, indicates the total length of the UDP packet (including the header and data) in bytes. It provides the receiver with the necessary information to extract the complete datagram from the network. The checksum field is 16 bits in size and is used to ensure data integrity during transmission. It is calculated over the entire UDP packet (header and data) and inserted by the sender. The recipient verifies the checksum to detect any errors introduced during transmission. However, unlike TCP, UDP does not request retransmissions for corrupted or lost packets. In addition to these core fields, the UDP header may also include additional optional fields, such as the source and destination IP addresses, but these are not mandatory. The minimum size of a UDP header is 8 bytes, with an additional 4 bytes if the optional fields are present. Overall, the UDP header fields play a crucial role in the successful transmission and reception of UDP datagrams. They provide information for identifying the source and destination ports, ensuring the integrity of the data, and determining the length of the packet. While UDP sacrifices reliability for speed and simplicity, its use cases, such as real-time streaming and gaming, make it a valuable protocol in networking applications.

UDP Header

A UDP header, also known as User Datagram Protocol header, is a fundamental component of the UDP protocol used in computer networking. UDP is a connectionless transport layer protocol that provides a simple and lightweight mechanism for sending and receiving datagrams over an IP network. The UDP header is an integral part of the UDP protocol and is attached to each UDP packet. The UDP header consists of several fields that provide essential information for the proper delivery of the packet. The fields contained within the UDP header include: Source Port: This field specifies the port number of the sender, allowing the recipient to identify the application or process that sent the datagram. Destination Port: This field signifies the port number of the receiver, enabling the recipient to direct the datagram to the appropriate application or process. Length: The length field indicates the total length of the UDP header and the UDP data in bytes. This value allows the recipient to determine the size of the entire UDP datagram. Checksum: The checksum field is used for error detection to ensure the integrity of the UDP header and data. The value of this field is computed based on the contents of the UDP packet and is then compared by the receiver to the computed checksum value to detect any transmission errors. The UDP header is relatively simple compared to other transport layer protocols such as TCP. It does not provide reliability or flow control mechanisms like TCP does, making UDP a connectionless and unreliable protocol. However, UDP is often preferred in scenarios where speed and low overhead are prioritized over reliability, such as real-time streaming applications or DNS queries. In summary, the UDP header is a crucial component of the UDP protocol, allowing for the efficient transmission of datagrams over IP networks. By including important information such as source and destination port numbers, length, and checksum, the UDP header enables the successful and accurate delivery of UDP packets.

UDP Protocol

The User Datagram Protocol (UDP) is a communication protocol used in computer networks. It is a simple, connectionless, and unreliable transport layer protocol. UDP operates on the Internet Protocol (IP) layer and is designed for scenarios where speed and efficiency are prioritized over data reliability. Unlike the Transmission Control Protocol (TCP), which provides a reliable and ordered delivery of data, UDP does not guarantee the delivery of packets or the sequential order of packet arrival.

UDP (User Datagram Protocol)

The User Datagram Protocol (UDP) is a connectionless and unreliable transport protocol that operates at the transport layer of the Internet Protocol Suite. It provides a simple and straightforward method for sending and receiving datagrams between devices on a network. Unlike the Transmission Control Protocol (TCP), which ensures reliable and ordered delivery of data by establishing a connection and implementing mechanisms for flow control and error recovery, UDP offers minimal overhead and does not provide any guarantee for reliable delivery or order of arrival.

UDP Vs. ICMP

UDP (User Datagram Protocol) and ICMP (Internet Control Message Protocol) are two different protocols used in computer networking. UDP is a simple transport layer protocol that operates in conjunction with IP (Internet Protocol) to provide a connectionless, unreliable, and lightweight communication service. It is often used for applications that require fast transmission of data, such as online gaming, streaming media, and VoIP (Voice over IP). UDP does not provide error-checking or reliability mechanisms, making it faster and more efficient than TCP (Transmission Control Protocol) but also less reliable. UDP datagrams are sent without establishing a connection and may be lost, duplicated, or arrive out of order at the receiving end. ICMP, on the other hand, is a network layer protocol used for network management and diagnostic purposes. It is mainly used by network devices, such as routers and switches, to communicate error messages and provide feedback about the network status. ICMP messages are encapsulated within IP packets and sent to the source of the original IP packet. Some common uses of ICMP include ping, traceroute, and network error reporting. ICMP messages include information about network congestion, unreachable destinations, time exceeded, and echo requests/replies.

UDP Vs. IP Comparison

UDP (User Datagram Protocol) and IP (Internet Protocol) are both foundational protocols used in networking. They are part of the TCP/IP protocol suite and contribute to the overall functionality of the internet. While UDP and IP are related, they serve different purposes and have distinct characteristics. IP is responsible for addressing and routing packets across networks. It provides a logical framework that allows data to be transmitted from one device to another. IP is connectionless, meaning it does not establish a dedicated path for data transmission. Instead, it breaks data into packets and adds addressing information to each packet, allowing routers to forward them to their destination. IP operates at the network layer (Layer 3) of the OSI model and provides a best-effort delivery service, where packets may arrive out of order, be duplicated, or even lost. UDP, on the other hand, is a transport layer protocol that works on top of IP. It provides a lightweight, low-overhead communication mechanism for applications. Unlike the Transmission Control Protocol (TCP), UDP does not ensure reliable and ordered delivery of data. Instead, it offers a connectionless service, similar to IP. UDP is often used in scenarios where low latency and speed are prioritized over reliability, such as real-time communication applications (e.g., voice and video streaming). With UDP, data is divided into small units called datagrams, and each datagram contains the necessary addressing information. UDP does not provide error checking or retransmission mechanisms, so any error or loss in transmission must be handled at the application layer.

UDP Vs. IP

UDP (User Datagram Protocol) and IP (Internet Protocol) are two important protocols used in networking. IP is a protocol responsible for addressing and routing network packets across the internet. It is the foundation of the internet and provides the logical addressing scheme for all devices connected to a network. IP ensures that packets are delivered to the correct destination

328

by using unique IP addresses assigned to each device. It also handles fragmentation of data if the packets exceed the maximum transmission unit (MTU) size of the network. UDP, on the other hand, is a transport layer protocol built on top of IP. It provides a simple and lightweight way to transmit data between devices in a network. Unlike TCP (Transmission Control Protocol), UDP does not establish a connection before sending data. It is a connectionless protocol that offers best-effort delivery, meaning it does not guarantee the delivery of packets nor does it provide acknowledgment or retransmission of lost packets. UDP is commonly used for real-time applications where speed and low latency are crucial, such as video streaming, online gaming, or VoIP (Voice over IP). Its lack of reliability makes it suitable for scenarios where occasional packet loss is acceptable, and retransmission would introduce unwanted delays. IP, on the other hand, is an essential protocol used throughout the internet to ensure the correct delivery of packets across networks. It is responsible for addressing and routing packets, while UDP is a protocol that operates on top of IP and provides a lightweight method for transmitting data without reliability guarantees. Both protocols play crucial roles in enabling communication in computer networks.

UDP Vs. TCP Comparison

UDP, or User Datagram Protocol, and TCP, or Transmission Control Protocol, are both network protocols used to transmit data across the Internet. They are part of the Internet Protocol Suite, which defines the rules and standards for communication between devices on a network. Both UDP and TCP provide reliable communication, but they operate in different ways and have different characteristics. TCP is a connection-oriented protocol, which means it establishes a connection between the sender and receiver before transmitting data. It ensures that all data packets are delivered in order and without errors. TCP provides a reliable and ordered delivery of data, and it guarantees that the data will be received as sent. TCP also includes mechanisms for flow control, congestion control, and error correction, making it suitable for applications that require a high level of reliability, such as web browsing, email, and file transfer. On the other hand, UDP is a connectionless protocol, which means it does not establish a connection before transmitting data. It is a simple and lightweight protocol that does not provide any guarantees about the order or delivery of data packets. UDP is faster and more efficient than TCP because it does not have the overhead of establishing and maintaining a connection. It is commonly used for streaming media, real-time communication, and online gaming, where a small delay is acceptable and a few lost packets are not critical.

UDP Vs. TCP

UDP, which stands for User Datagram Protocol, is a connectionless transport layer protocol in computer networking. It is one of the core protocols of the internet protocol suite and is widely used in applications that require efficient, low-latency, and loss-tolerant communication. Unlike TCP, UDP does not provide reliable data delivery or congestion control mechanisms. Instead, it focuses on simplicity, minimal overhead, and fast transmission. UDP operates by encapsulating data into packets, also known as datagrams, which are then sent from a source to a destination over an IP network. Each packet contains not only the data but also the source and destination port numbers, checksum, and other necessary information for proper routing and error detection. However, UDP does not establish a connection before transmitting data, nor does it guarantee that the packets will reach their destination in the correct order or at all. Consequently, UDP is often used for applications that prioritize speed and efficiency over data integrity and reliability. TCP, short for Transmission Control Protocol, is a connection-oriented transport layer protocol used for reliable, ordered, and error-checked delivery of data packets over an IP network. It is the most widely used transport protocol on the internet and is built on top of the IP protocol. TCP provides a reliable and efficient data stream between two applications through features such as flow control, congestion control, and error recovery. TCP operates by establishing a connection between a client and a server before transmitting any data. This connection is achieved through a three-way handshake, where the client and server exchange control messages to synchronize sequence numbers and negotiate connection parameters. Once the connection is established, TCP ensures that data is delivered to the destination in the correct order by implementing sequencing and acknowledgment mechanisms. It also provides flow control to prevent overwhelming the receiving device and congestion control to manage network congestion effectively.

329

Unicast

Unicast is a type of communication in computer networking where a message from a single sender is delivered to a specific recipient or a group of recipients separately. It is a one-to-one form of communication, in contrast to multicast or broadcast that involve one-to-many or one-to-all transmissions, respectively. In a unicast communication, the sender transmits a message to a unique IP address of a destination device, which could be an individual computer or a network-enabled device such as a printer or a server. The network infrastructure then routes the message to the specific recipient based on the destination IP address. This routing is typically achieved through the use of routing protocols and switches that follow a predetermined network path to deliver the message. Unicast communication is commonly used in various networking applications. For instance, when a user sends an email or visits a website, the data is typically sent using unicast transmission to the intended recipient's IP address. Similarly, when downloading a file from a server, the server sends the file through unicast to the client's IP address. One of the main advantages of unicast communication is its efficiency in delivering messages to a specific destination. Since the message is only sent to the intended recipient, unnecessary network traffic is minimized compared to multicast or broadcast communications. This targeted delivery also allows for greater privacy and security since the message is not visible to other devices on the network. However, unicast communication can pose scalability challenges in certain scenarios. When a large number of devices need to receive the same message, separate unicast transmissions are required for each recipient. This can result in increased network congestion and resource utilization. In such cases, multicast or broadcast communication may be more suitable.

Unified Security Management (USM)

Unified Security Management (USM) refers to a comprehensive approach to network security that integrates various security technologies into a centralized management platform. It encompasses the monitoring, detection, prevention, and response to security threats and incidents, allowing organizations to gain better visibility and control over their network infrastructure. USM combines multiple security capabilities into a single solution, providing a holistic view of the network's security posture and simplifying the management of security processes. It typically includes features such as log management and analysis, intrusion detection and prevention, asset discovery, vulnerability assessment, and threat intelligence. The central management platform in a USM solution serves as a centralized repository for security events and logs generated by different security devices and systems deployed within the network. It collects, aggregates, and correlates data from various sources, helping security teams identify patterns, detect anomalies, and prioritize threats. With USM, organizations can proactively identify and respond to security incidents in real-time. The solution leverages threat intelligence feeds, security analytics, and machine learning algorithms to rapidly detect and mitigate known and unknown threats. It provides security teams with actionable insights, enabling them to make informed decisions and take corrective measures to protect the network. Additionally, USM enables organizations to assess their network's vulnerabilities and identify potential risks. It conducts regular scans and assessments to uncover weaknesses in the network infrastructure, systems, and applications. This helps in prioritizing security remediation efforts and reducing the attack surface. USM also improves regulatory compliance by providing tools and reports that assist in meeting industry-specific security standards and regulations. The centralized management platform offers configurable dashboards, alerts, and reports that help organizations demonstrate compliance and support audit requirements. In summary, Unified Security Management offers an integrated and centralized approach to network security, allowing organizations to effectively monitor, detect, prevent, and respond to security threats. It provides enhanced visibility, control, and automation, enabling security teams to efficiently protect their networks from a wide range of cyber threats.

Unified Threat Management (UTM)

Unified Threat Management (UTM) refers to a comprehensive network security solution that combines various security features into a single device or platform. It integrates multiple security functions, such as firewall, intrusion detection and prevention, virtual private network (VPN), antivirus, antispam, content filtering, and more. UTM is designed to protect networks from various types of threats and attacks that can target an organization's digital assets and sensitive

330

information. A UTM device acts as a gateway between an organization's internal network and the external world, monitoring and controlling all incoming and outgoing traffic. It provides a central point of control for managing and securing network traffic, making it easier to enforce security policies and protect against emerging threats. By consolidating multiple security functions into a single device, UTM simplifies network management and reduces the complexity of deploying and maintaining different security solutions.

VLAN Configuration

A VLAN, or Virtual Local Area Network, is a method of creating multiple virtual networks within a physical network infrastructure. It allows users to logically group devices together, regardless of their physical location, into separate broadcast domains. VLANs can be configured to provide security, manageability, and scalability to networks. VLANs are typically implemented at the switch level by assigning ports to different VLANs. Each VLAN operates as if it were a separate network, with its own IP addresses, subnet masks, and network configurations. Devices within the same VLAN can communicate with each other as if they were connected to the same physical LAN, while devices in different VLANs require routing to communicate.

VLAN Implementation

VLAN implementation refers to the process of creating and configuring virtual local area networks (VLANs) within a network infrastructure. VLANs are used to segment a network into logical, isolated groups, allowing for improved network performance, security, and manageability. By implementing VLANs, network administrators can enhance the overall functionality and organization of their network. VLANs enable the division of a physical network into multiple virtual networks, which can span across multiple switches and subnets. This segmentation allows for more efficient bandwidth utilization and improves scalability.

VLAN Management

VLAN Management refers to the process of creating, configuring, and organizing Virtual Local Area Networks (VLANs) within a networking environment. VLANs are used to logically segment a physical network into multiple virtual networks, allowing for improved network efficiency, security, and organization. In a VLAN-based network, devices that are part of the same VLAN can communicate with each other as if they were connected to the same physical network, even if they are geographically dispersed. VLANs are often used to group devices based on department, function, or security requirements, providing a way to separate traffic and apply different policies or settings to each VLAN. VLAN Management involves several key tasks. Firstly, VLAN creation involves defining the VLAN on the network switches and assigning a VLAN ID. This ID is used to tag the network packets belonging to that VLAN, allowing the switches to identify and forward them accordingly. VLANs can be created based on different criteria, such as port-based VLANs, where devices connected to specific switch ports are assigned to a particular VLAN, or MAC-based VLANs, where devices with specific MAC addresses are assigned to a VLAN. Once VLANs are created, VLAN configuration involves assigning devices to the appropriate VLANs. This can be done manually by configuring the network switches or automatically using protocols like the VLAN Membership Policy Server (VMPS). VLAN configuration also includes defining inter-VLAN routing, which enables communication between VLANs and the outside network. VLAN Management also includes monitoring and troubleshooting VLANs. This involves monitoring VLAN utilization, performance, and security, and taking necessary actions to optimize or resolve issues. VLAN management tools and protocols, such as VLAN Trunking Protocol (VTP), can help simplify VLAN administration by automatically propagating VLAN configuration changes across network switches.

VLAN Tagging Configuration

VLAN Tagging Configuration refers to the process of assigning a Virtual Local Area Network (VLAN) identifier or tag to network packets. VLANs are used to logically segment a network, allowing for better management and security by grouping devices into different broadcast domains. VLAN tagging creates separate virtual networks within a physical network infrastructure. In a VLAN tagging configuration, each network packet is assigned a VLAN tag that identifies the specific VLAN it belongs to. This tag is inserted into the packet's header by the sending device and is used by switches and routers to ensure the packet is correctly handled within the network. VLAN tags contain a numerical identifier between 1 and 4094, which allows for the creation of a large number of unique VLANs. VLAN tagging can be implemented in two main ways: Port-based VLAN tagging and Protocol-based VLAN tagging. In Port-based VLAN tagging, individual physical ports on a network switch are configured to belong to a specific VLAN. Any packets received or sent through these ports are automatically assigned the corresponding VLAN tag. In Protocol-based VLAN tagging, network protocols such as IEEE 802.1Q are used to identify and tag VLAN packets. This method allows for more flexibility as VLAN tags can be assigned based on protocols used in the packet. To configure VLAN tagging, there are several steps involved. First, the VLANs need to be created on switches or routers that support VLAN tagging. Next, the network ports need to be assigned to their respective VLANs. This can be done by configuring the switch or router with the necessary VLAN IDs and associating them with specific ports. Finally, the VLAN tagging mode needs to be enabled on the devices and interfaces that will be involved in VLAN tagging. VLAN tagging has numerous benefits in networking. It allows for the segmentation of a network into smaller independent broadcast domains, reducing network congestion and improving security. VLAN tagging also enables the implementation of Quality of Service (QoS) policies, allowing for better prioritization of network traffic. It simplifies network management by facilitating the isolation and control of network resources. Additionally, VLAN tagging enables the creation of virtual networks that span multiple physical locations, allowing for better scalability and flexibility in network design and deployment.

VLAN Tagging Methods Comparison

VLAN tagging is a method used in computer networking to identify and separate network traffic into different virtual LANs (VLANs). VLANs are virtual networks created within a physical network infrastructure, allowing the segmentation of traffic for improved security, scalability, and network management. There are three common VLAN tagging methods that are used in networking: ISL (Inter-Switch Link), 802.1Q, and VLAN Tagging Protocol. These methods differ in the way they add and manage VLAN tags in network packets. The ISL VLAN tagging method was developed by Cisco and is proprietary to their devices. It encapsulates entire Ethernet frames with an ISL header, adding a VLAN tag to the packet. This header contains information about the VLAN ID and other related data. While ISL tagging can be used between Cisco switches, it is not compatible with non-Cisco devices. ISL is an older method and has been largely replaced by the 802.1Q standard. The 802.1Q VLAN tagging method is an industry-standard defined by the IEEE. It inserts a VLAN tag into the Ethernet frame, leaving the original Ethernet header intact. This tag contains information about the VLAN ID, allowing switches and routers to identify and forward the packet to the correct VLAN. Unlike ISL, 802.1Q tagging is widely supported by various networking devices from different vendors. It allows for interoperability and enables the creation of VLANs across multiple switches from different vendors. The VLAN Tagging Protocol (VTP) is a Cisco proprietary protocol that simplifies the management of VLANs within a network. It allows for the automatic propagation of VLAN information across switches, reducing the administrative overhead of manually configuring VLANs on each device. VTP operates by sending VLAN information in special VTP messages, which are encapsulated within ISL or 802.1Q tagged frames.

VLAN Tagging Methods

VLAN Tagging is a method used in computer networking to identify and separate different virtual local area networks (VLANs) within a larger physical network infrastructure. It involves assigning a specific tag or label to each network packet, which allows for the segregation and routing of traffic to different VLANs based on these tags. There are primarily two methods of VLAN Tagging: VLAN Tagging with Ethernet Frames, and VLAN Tagging with Trunk Links. VLAN Tagging with Ethernet Frames is the most commonly used method. In this method, a small amount of additional information is added to the Ethernet frame to indicate the VLAN to which the packet belongs. This additional information is known as the VLAN Tag or VLAN ID. The VLAN Tag is inserted into the Ethernet frame header by the source device and read by the receiving devices to determine the VLAN to which the packet belongs. The VLAN Tag consists of a 12-bit VLAN ID field, which allows for the identification of up to 4096 unique VLANs. VLAN Tagging with Trunk Links is used when multiple VLANs need to be transported over a single

332

physical link. In this method, a special type of Ethernet frame known as a Trunk Frame is used. The Trunk Frame is capable of carrying multiple VLANs by encapsulating individual VLAN-tagged frames within it. The Trunk Frame contains a header with information about the VLANs encapsulated within it, allowing the receiving devices to separate and route the VLAN traffic accordingly. The Trunk Frame uses a different VLAN Tag format than the VLAN Tagging with Ethernet Frames method, with a 4-byte VLAN Tag that includes a 12-bit VLAN ID field, along with additional fields for priority and other flags.

VLAN Tagging

VLAN Tagging refers to the process of marking network frames or packets with a unique identifier known as a VLAN tag. This tag enables network switches to identify and handle these packets appropriately based on their VLAN membership. In a VLAN (Virtual Local Area Network) setup, a network switch is divided into multiple logical or virtual switches, each representing a distinct VLAN. By assigning VLAN tags to network packets, devices within a VLAN can communicate with each other as if they were connected to the same physical LAN, even if they are physically separate. When a device sends a network packet, the sending device attaches a VLAN tag to the packet header before transmitting it onto the network. This VLAN tag contains information about the VLAN the packet belongs to, such as the VLAN ID. Upon receiving a tagged packet, network switches examine the VLAN tag and use the information to determine the appropriate VLAN to forward the packet to. This allows switches to control the flow of traffic between VLANs, ensuring that network packets are isolated and delivered to the correct destinations. VLAN tagging is particularly useful in scenarios where multiple VLANs coexist on a single physical network infrastructure. It enables network administrators to segregate network traffic, improve network performance, and increase security by preventing unauthorized access to sensitive data. There are two main methods of VLAN tagging: IEEE 802.1Q and ISL (Inter-Switch Link). IEEE 802.1Q is the most common and widely supported method in modern networking equipment. It inserts a VLAN tag into the Ethernet frame header, whereas ISL encapsulates the entire Ethernet frame and adds a header identifying the VLAN. In conclusion, VLAN tagging facilitates the efficient utilization of network infrastructure by allowing multiple VLANs to coexist and communicate over a single physical network. It provides network administrators with the ability to customize and control network traffic flow, improving network security, performance, and scalability.

VLAN Trunking Protocol (VTP)

VLAN Trunking Protocol (VTP) is a network protocol used in computer networking to manage and synchronize VLAN configurations within a domain. It enables the automatic propagation of VLAN information across switches in a network, reducing the need for manual configuration on each individual switch. VTP operates by designating one switch in the network as the VTP server, which stores and manages the VLAN database. This server distributes VLAN information to other switches in the domain, known as VTP clients, through periodic advertisements. The VTP server also handles any changes or additions to the VLAN configuration, ensuring consistency across the network. When a switch receives a VTP advertisement, it compares the received VLAN database with its own. If the received database has a higher revision number, indicating a more recent update, the switch updates its VLAN configuration to match the received one. This allows for automatic VLAN propagation and synchronization throughout the network. VTP supports three different modes: server, client, and transparent. The VTP server is responsible for managing the VLAN database and distributing updates to clients. VTP clients receive and apply VLAN changes from the server, but they cannot make any changes themselves. Transparent mode switches do not participate in VTP updates but can still forward VTP advertisements to other switches. This mode is useful for separating VTP domains or interoperating with switches from different VTP domains. It is essential to carefully configure VTP in a network, as misconfiguration can lead to unexpected changes or loss of VLAN information. It is recommended to always use VTP version 3, which provides increased security and better control over VLAN propagation. Furthermore, ensuring that the correct VTP mode is set on each switch is crucial to maintaining the desired VLAN configuration.

VLAN Trunking

VLAN trunking refers to the process of allowing multiple VLANs to be transmitted over a single link between switches or routers, enabling the efficient utilization of network resources and improving network flexibility and scalability.In networking, a VLAN (Virtual Local Area Network) is a logical grouping of devices that are located on different physical LAN segments but communicate as if they were on the same LAN. VLANs provide administrators with the ability to logically segment a network, enhance security, and optimize network performance.Trunking, on the other hand, is the technique used to carry traffic from multiple VLANs through a single network link. It involves using a standard Ethernet connection to transport VLAN-tagged frames. A trunk link is a point-to-point connection between two switches or a switch and a router, allowing the transmission of multiple VLANs.VLAN trunking operates on the basis of a tagging system. When traffic passes through a trunk link, each frame is encapsulated with a VLAN tag that contains information about the VLAN to which it belongs. This tagging allows switches or routers to differentiate between different VLANs and correctly route and forward the traffic to the appropriate destination.The two most commonly used protocols for VLAN trunking are IEEE 802.1Q and ISL (Inter-Switch Link). IEEE 802.1Q is the industry standard that defines how VLAN tags are assigned, managed, and transported. ISL, on the other hand, is a proprietary protocol developed by Cisco Systems. While IEEE 802.1Q is more widely supported, ISL is primarily used in Cisco environments.VLAN trunking provides several benefits to network administrators. It helps optimize network performance by reducing the number of physical connections required to support multiple VLANs. It also simplifies network management by allowing VLAN configurations to be centralized and applied to multiple switches using VLAN trunking protocols. This flexibility enables administrators to add, remove, or modify VLANs without having to reconfigure every switch individually.In summary, VLAN trunking is a network technique that enables the transmission of multiple VLANs over a single network link. By encapsulating frames with VLAN tags and using VLAN trunking protocols, network administrators can efficiently manage and optimize their networks, leading to increased scalability and flexibility.

VLAN (Virtual Local Area Network)

VPN Encryption

A VPN (Virtual Private Network) encryption refers to the process of securing data that is transmitted over a VPN connection by converting it into a format that is indecipherable to unauthorized parties. Encryption is an essential aspect of VPN technology as it provides privacy, confidentiality, and integrity to the data exchange between devices connected to the network.In the context of networking, VPN encryption uses different cryptographic algorithms and keys to transform plaintext data into ciphertext, ensuring that the information remains confidential and secure during transmission. The encryption process involves manipulating the original data using a mathematical function, which can only be reversed with the appropriate decryption key.

VPN Protocols

A VPN (Virtual Private Network) protocol is a set of rules or procedures that govern the secure transmission of data between devices over a public network, such as the Internet. It establishes a secure, encrypted connection, creating a virtual tunnel that enables users to send and receive data privately and securely. There are several VPN protocols available, each with its own advantages and limitations. The choice of protocol depends on factors such as security requirements, network infrastructure, and performance needs.

VPN Security Protocols

A VPN (Virtual Private Network) is a secure connection that allows users to access a private network over a public network such as the internet. It enables users to send and receive data as if they were directly connected to the private network, even if they are physically located elsewhere. VPN security protocols refer to the methods and technologies used to ensure the confidentiality, integrity, and authenticity of the data transmitted over a VPN. These protocols provide the necessary encryption and authentication mechanisms to protect sensitive information from unauthorized access or tampering.

VPN Tunnel Protocols

A Virtual Private Network (VPN) tunnel protocol refers to the set of rules and procedures used to create and maintain secure connections between two or more networks over a public network such as the internet. These protocols ensure the confidentiality, integrity, and authenticity of the data transmitted between the network endpoints. There are several commonly used VPN tunnel protocols, each with its own characteristics and advantages: 1. Point-to-Point Tunneling Protocol (PPTP): PPTP is one of the oldest and most widely supported VPN tunnel protocols. It is relatively easy to configure and provides good performance. However, its security is considered weak compared to newer protocols. 2. Layer 2 Tunneling Protocol (L2TP): L2TP combines the best features of PPTP and Cisco's Layer 2 Forwarding (L2F) protocol. It provides a more secure tunnel by using encryption and authentication, making it suitable for remote access VPNs. 3. Internet Protocol Security (IPsec): IPsec is a suite of protocols that provides a robust and highly secure VPN tunnel. It operates at the network layer and can be used in various configurations, such as Transport Mode (only encrypting the data payload) or Tunnel Mode (encrypting the entire IP packet). 4. Secure Socket Tunneling Protocol (SSTP): SSTP is a proprietary VPN tunnel protocol developed by Microsoft. It uses the SSL/TLS protocol for encryption and can be used on Windows systems. SSTP is known for its compatibility and ease of use. 5. OpenVPN: OpenVPN is an open-source VPN tunnel protocol that uses the OpenSSL library for encryption. It is highly configurable, supports various authentication methods, and can operate on multiple platforms. Each VPN tunnel protocol has its own strengths and weaknesses, and the choice of protocol depends on the specific requirements of the network and the level of security needed. The selection of the right protocol is crucial in ensuring the privacy and security of data transmitted over the VPN tunnel.

VPN Tunnel Security Measures

A VPN (Virtual Private Network) tunnel is a secure connection between a user's device and a private network over the internet. It ensures the confidentiality, integrity, and availability of data transmitted between the user and the network. To achieve this, several security measures are implemented within the VPN tunnel. Firstly, encryption is a fundamental security measure in a VPN tunnel. It transforms data into an unreadable format during transmission, making it unintelligible to unauthorized users. Encryption algorithms, such as AES (Advanced Encryption Standard), are commonly used to protect sensitive information from being intercepted or accessed by attackers. Secondly, authentication plays a critical role in VPN tunnel security. It verifies the identity of both the user and the network before the establishment of the tunnel. This ensures that only authorized users can access the private network, preventing unauthorized access from potential attackers. Common authentication methods include passwords, digital certificates, and two-factor authentication. Thirdly, VPN tunnels employ secure key exchange mechanisms to establish a secure channel between the user and the private network. This enables the generation of unique session keys that are used for encryption and decryption of data. Key exchange protocols, such as Diffie-Hellman, facilitate the secure exchange of these session keys, protecting them from interception or tampering. Additionally, VPN tunnels often utilize tunneling protocols, such as IPsec (Internet Protocol Security), to encapsulate and protect data packets during transmission. These protocols establish a secure path through the internet, preventing data from being intercepted or modified. Tunneling protocols also provide additional security features, such as data integrity checks and anti-replay mechanisms, to ensure the integrity and consistency of data. In conclusion, VPN tunnel security measures encompass encryption, authentication, secure key exchange, and tunneling protocols. Collectively, these measures safeguard the confidentiality, integrity, and availability of data transmitted between a user's device and a private network, providing a secure and trusted connection over the internet.

VPN Tunnel Security

A VPN (Virtual Private Network) tunnel is a secure, encrypted connection established over a public network, most commonly the Internet. It allows users to securely access private networks and resources remotely, while ensuring the confidentiality and integrity of the data transmitted between the user's device and the network. The primary purpose of a VPN tunnel is to create a secure communication path between two endpoints, typically a user device and a corporate network, by encapsulating the data in a protective layer. This layer, known as an encrypted tunnel, shields the information from unauthorized access or interception while it traverses the untrusted public network. When a VPN connection is established, the user's device first authenticates with the VPN server using specific credentials. Once authenticated, the server creates a secure tunnel between the device and itself, encrypting the data packets before they

335

are sent over the public network. The encryption of the data packets ensures that even if intercepted, the information within them cannot be understood or tampered with by unauthorized parties. The encrypted packets are decrypted at the VPN server and forwarded to the destination network, effectively extending the user's private network securely over the public network. The security of a VPN tunnel relies on various mechanisms and protocols, including encryption algorithms, authentication protocols, and key exchange methods. Common encryption protocols used in VPN tunnels include IPSec (Internet Protocol Security) and SSL/TLS (Secure Sockets Layer/Transport Layer Security). Another important aspect of VPN tunnel security is the use of VPN gateways or firewalls, which act as intermediaries between the user devices and the destination network. These gateways provide additional layers of security by filtering and inspecting the incoming and outgoing traffic, preventing unauthorized access and potential threats. In summary, a VPN tunnel is a secure and encrypted connection that enables users to access private networks over the public Internet. It ensures the confidentiality and integrity of the data transmitted by encapsulating it in an encrypted tunnel, thereby protecting it from unauthorized access and interception.

VPN Tunneling Methods

VPN tunneling methods are techniques used in networking to establish secure and encrypted connections between two or more devices across a public or untrusted network, such as the internet. These methods create a virtual tunnel through which data can be transmitted securely, ensuring the confidentiality, integrity, and authenticity of the transmitted information. One commonly used VPN tunneling method is Secure Socket Tunneling Protocol (SSTP). SSTP is a protocol that allows the use of Point-to-Point Protocol (PPP) over Secure Sockets Layer (SSL) or Transport Layer Security (TLS) channels. This method utilizes the SSL/TLS encryption to securely encapsulate PPP frames, providing a secure tunnel for data transmission. SSTP is widely supported by various operating systems, including Windows, which makes it a popular choice for VPN connections. Another widely used VPN tunneling method is Layer 2 Tunneling Protocol (L2TP). L2TP combines the best features of two other protocols, namely Point-to-Point Tunneling Protocol (PPTP) and Layer 2 Forwarding (L2F). L2TP creates a tunnel and encapsulates the data using the PPP protocol, providing authentication, encryption, and data integrity. L2TP can operate over various protocols, such as IPsec, which enhances the security of the VPN connection. Internet Protocol Security (IPsec) is another VPN tunneling method that provides a robust and secure solution for data transmission. IPsec operates at the network layer, providing network-level encryption, authentication, and data integrity. It uses two main protocols: Authentication Header (AH) and Encapsulating Security Payload (ESP). AH provides authentication and integrity checking of the IP packets, while ESP provides the encryption and confidentiality of the data. IPsec can be implemented in different modes, such as tunnel mode and transport mode, depending on the desired level of security. Overall, VPN tunneling methods play a crucial role in ensuring secure and private communication over public networks. These methods establish a secure tunnel through which data can be transmitted, protecting it from unauthorized access, tampering, and interception. Whether it's SSTP, L2TP, IPsec, or other tunneling methods, they all contribute to enhancing the security and privacy of network communications.

VPN Tunneling

VPN tunneling is a technique used in networking to establish a secure and encrypted connection between two or more devices over an untrusted network, such as the internet. It allows for data transmission that is protected from potential eavesdropping, tampering, or interception by unauthorized entities. When a VPN tunnel is created, it serves as a virtual "pipe" that encapsulates the original data packets within an outer layer of encryption. This encapsulation process, also known as encapsulating security payload (ESP), hides the inner data from anyone who might try to intercept or access it. The encrypted data packets are then transmitted from one end of the tunnel to the other, ensuring confidentiality and integrity of the information being transmitted.

VPN (Virtual Private Network)

A VPN (Virtual Private Network) is a secure and private network connection that allows users to access and transmit data over a public network as if they were directly connected to a private network. It creates a virtual encrypted tunnel between the user's device and the destination network, ensuring that data remains secure and protected from unauthorized access. When a user connects to a VPN, their device establishes a secure and encrypted connection to a VPN server. All the data transmitted between the user's device and the VPN server is encrypted, making it virtually impossible for anyone to intercept or decipher the information. This encryption ensures the confidentiality and integrity of the data, protecting it from hackers, eavesdroppers, and other malicious actors. One of the primary purposes of a VPN is to enable users to securely access resources on a private network over a public network, such as the internet. By connecting to a VPN server located on the private network, users can access resources such as files, applications, and printers as if they were physically present on the same network. This is especially useful for remote workers who need to access sensitive corporate resources from outside the office or for individuals who want to access geographically restricted content. In addition to enhancing security and privacy, VPNs also provide anonymity. By masking the IP address of the user's device and replacing it with the IP address of the VPN server, VPNs make it difficult for websites, online services, and advertisers to track the user's online activities and location. This anonymity adds another layer of privacy protection and allows users to browse the internet with greater freedom and anonymity. In conclusion, a VPN is a network technology that creates a secure and private connection over a public network. It encrypts data, enables remote access to private resources, enhances security, privacy, and anonymity. VPNs have become essential tools for individuals and organizations that prioritize data protection, confidentiality, and secure access to resources.

Virtual LAN (VLAN)

A Virtual LAN (VLAN) is a logical grouping of devices in a computer network, where these devices are not limited by their physical location or connection. VLANs are used to create multiple broadcast domains within a single network infrastructure, allowing network administrators to efficiently manage and control network traffic. By creating VLANs, network administrators can segment their network into smaller, distinct groups, regardless of the devices' physical locations or the type of network connection they use. Each VLAN behaves as if it is a separate network, even though the devices may physically connect to the same switch or network infrastructure.

Virtual Network

A virtual network is a software-defined network (SDN) that allows multiple virtual machines (VMs) or virtual servers to communicate with each other and with the physical network infrastructure. It is a flexible and scalable solution that provides isolation, security, and control over network traffic within a cloud computing environment. In a virtual network, the network infrastructure is abstracted from the physical hardware and is created and managed using virtualization technologies. By decoupling the network from the physical infrastructure, virtual networks provide a high degree of flexibility and agility. Administrators can easily create, modify, and delete virtual networks without the need for physical changes to cables or switches. Virtual networks rely on virtual switches, which are software-based switches that direct network traffic between virtual machines. These virtual switches operate at the data link layer of the network stack and provide connectivity between VMs within the same virtual network. They also connect the virtual network to the physical network infrastructure, enabling communication between virtual and physical resources. Virtual networks offer several advantages. First, they provide isolation between different virtual networks, allowing for the segregation of traffic and resources. This isolation enhances security by preventing unauthorized access to sensitive data. Second, virtual networks improve scalability by allowing the addition of new virtual machines or virtual servers without the need for additional physical hardware. This enables organizations to quickly respond to changing business needs and increase their computing capacity as required. Additionally, virtual networks enable administrators to implement network policies and controls at a granular level. By defining rules and configurations, they can manage network traffic and prioritize certain types of data. This level of control enhances performance and ensures that critical applications receive the necessary bandwidth and resources. In conclusion, a virtual network is a software-defined network that provides a flexible, scalable, and secure environment for virtual machines and virtual servers to communicate with each other and with the physical network infrastructure. By abstracting the network from physical hardware, virtual networks enable organizations to efficiently manage their network resources and adapt to changing

337

business needs.

Virtual Private Network (VPN)

A Virtual Private Network (VPN) is a secure and private network that allows users to connect to a remote network over the internet. It enables users to send and receive data across shared or public networks as if their computing devices were directly connected to the private network. A VPN creates a secure, encrypted tunnel between a user's device and the remote network, ensuring the confidentiality and integrity of transmitted data. By establishing this connection, VPNs provide users with a secure way to access resources on the remote network, such as files, printers, and applications, as if they were physically present in the same location.

Virtual Router Redundancy Protocol (VRRP)

Virtual Router Redundancy Protocol (VRRP) is a network routing protocol that provides redundancy for the default gateway or router in a local area network (LAN). It allows multiple routers to work together as a single virtual router, ensuring high availability and seamless network connectivity in the event of a failure or maintenance of any individual router. VRRP operates by electing a virtual router master, which acts as the primary gateway for all the hosts in the LAN. The other routers in the network are designated as backup routers. The virtual router master is responsible for sending and receiving network traffic, while the backup routers remain in a standby mode, monitoring the virtual router master's availability. If the master fails, one of the backup routers automatically takes over as the new master, ensuring uninterrupted network connectivity.

Virus Signature Database

A virus signature database, in the context of networking, refers to a collection of unique patterns or characteristics that can be used to identify known viruses or malware. These patterns are collected from various sources, such as virus samples, and are stored in a database that is regularly updated to stay current with the latest threats. When a network or computer system is equipped with an antivirus software, it compares files, programs, or network traffic against the virus signature database to determine if any matches are found. If a match is detected, the antivirus software takes appropriate action, such as quarantining or deleting the infected file, preventing the virus from spreading further.

Virus Signature

A virus signature refers to a distinct pattern or characteristic that is unique to a specific type of computer virus. In the context of networking, it is a crucial component in the identification and detection of viruses. When a virus infects a computer, it leaves behind traces of its presence. These traces can be in the form of patterns, code snippets, or behaviors. Security software, such as antivirus programs, use virus signatures to identify these traces and differentiate them from legitimate files or processes.

Virus

A virus in the context of networking refers to a malicious software program that can replicate itself and spread from one computer to another through a network. It is designed to damage, disrupt, or gain unauthorized access to a computer system, often without the knowledge or consent of the user. Viruses can enter a network in various ways, such as through email attachments, infected websites, or file downloads. Once inside the network, the virus can quickly spread to other connected devices, infecting them as well. This ability to replicate and spread makes viruses a significant threat to network security. Once a virus infects a computer system, it can carry out a range of harmful activities. Some viruses are designed to delete or corrupt files, leading to a loss of data. Others may slow down the computer's performance or cause it to crash. Additionally, viruses can create backdoors or security vulnerabilities, allowing unauthorized users to gain access to sensitive information. Network administrators employ various measures to protect their networks from viruses. These measures include installing antivirus software that can detect and remove known viruses, regularly updating software and operating systems to patch security vulnerabilities, and implementing firewalls to monitor and control network traffic. However, viruses continue to evolve, and new strains are constantly being created. This ongoing cat-and-mouse game between virus creators and network administrators necessitates constant vigilance and proactive measures to secure networked systems.

VoIP Phone

VoIP Phone, also known as Voice over Internet Protocol Phone, is a network device that allows users to make telephone calls over the internet instead of traditional analog telephone lines. It converts voice signals into digital packets and transmits them over the internet to a VoIP service provider or directly to another VoIP phone. VoIP Phone uses the Internet Protocol (IP) technology to enable voice communication, leveraging the same infrastructure that is used to transmit data over computer networks. It replaces the need for separate networks for voice and data, providing a more cost-effective and efficient solution for businesses and individuals.

VoIP (Voice Over Internet Protocol)

VoIP (Voice over Internet Protocol) is a networking technology that enables the transmission of voice communications and multimedia sessions over IP networks, such as the internet. It converts analog voice signals into digital data packets, which are then transmitted over the network using IP (Internet Protocol). In traditional telephony systems, voice signals are transmitted over circuit-switched networks, where a dedicated circuit is established for the duration of the call. However, VoIP uses packet-switched networks, where data is divided into small packets and transmitted independently to the destination. This allows voice data to share the network infrastructure with other types of data, such as video and text. One of the key advantages of VoIP is cost savings. By utilizing the existing internet infrastructure, organizations can avoid the costs associated with maintaining separate voice and data networks. Additionally, long-distance and international calls can be significantly cheaper compared to traditional phone services since they are transmitted over the internet rather than traditional telephone lines. Another benefit of VoIP is its flexibility and scalability. VoIP can be easily integrated with other communication systems, such as email, instant messaging, and video conferencing, to create a unified communication platform. It also allows for easy expansion and addition of new lines without the need for physical infrastructure changes. VoIP also offers a range of advanced features and functionalities that are not available with traditional phone systems. These include call forwarding, voicemail, caller ID, call recording, and conference calling. Calls can be made and received using a variety of devices, including computers, smartphones, and IP phones. However, there are some challenges and considerations related to VoIP. Quality of service (QoS) can be affected by factors such as network congestion, latency, and packet loss. Security is another concern, as voice data transmitted over the internet can be vulnerable to eavesdropping and unauthorized access. In conclusion, VoIP is a networking technology that allows for the transmission of voice communications over IP networks. It offers cost savings, flexibility, and a range of advanced features compared to traditional phone systems. However, it also presents challenges related to quality of service and security.

Voice Over IP (VoIP)

Voice over IP (VoIP) refers to a technology that allows the transmission of voice communications over internet protocol (IP) networks. It enables individuals or businesses to make voice calls over the internet instead of using traditional telephone lines. VoIP converts analog audio signals into digital data packets, which are then transmitted over IP networks. These data packets are routed over the internet or any other IP-based network, allowing users to connect and communicate with each other. One of the primary advantages of VoIP is cost savings. Traditional phone services can be expensive, especially for long-distance or international calls. With VoIP, calls are typically cheaper or even free, as they use the existing internet connection instead of separate phone lines. This is particularly beneficial for businesses that make frequent international calls or have multiple branch offices. Another advantage of VoIP is flexibility and mobility. Users can make and receive calls from any device that has an internet connection, such as smartphones, tablets, laptops, or desktop computers. This allows for greater flexibility in terms of where and when calls can be made. VoIP also supports features like call forwarding, voicemail, and conference calling, enhancing communication capabilities. VoIP offers scalability, as it can easily accommodate a growing number of users or locations without significant infrastructure changes. Unlike traditional phone systems that require physical

339

lines and hardware, VoIP relies on the internet and can handle increased call volume and additional users by leveraging existing network resources. However, there are some challenges with VoIP. Since it relies on an internet connection, call quality can be affected by factors such as network congestion or bandwidth limitations. It also requires a stable and reliable internet connection to ensure uninterrupted communication. In conclusion, VoIP is a technology that enables voice communications over IP networks, offering cost savings, flexibility, and scalability. It has become a popular choice for individuals and businesses looking for efficient and cost-effective communication solutions.

Vulnerability Assessment Report

A vulnerability assessment report in the context of networking is a formal written document that provides a systematic overview and analysis of identified vulnerabilities within a network system. This report aims to evaluate the security posture of the network infrastructure, identify potential weaknesses or loopholes in the network, and recommend appropriate remedial actions to mitigate or eliminate the identified vulnerabilities.

Vulnerability Assessment

A vulnerability assessment in the context of networking refers to the process of identifying and evaluating potential weaknesses or vulnerabilities in a network infrastructure. This assessment is typically carried out to determine the overall security posture of the network and to identify any potential entry points that could be exploited by malicious actors. The primary objective of a vulnerability assessment is to proactively identify any weaknesses before they are exploited, enabling organizations to take appropriate measures to mitigate the identified vulnerabilities. The assessment process involves a systematic review of the network's security controls, configurations, and architecture, with a focus on identifying any areas that may be susceptible to unauthorized access, data breaches, or other security incidents. During a vulnerability assessment, various techniques are utilized to identify vulnerabilities, including automated scanning tools, manual inspection of network configurations, and analysis of network logs. These techniques help uncover potential security gaps such as outdated software versions, misconfigured devices, weak passwords, unpatched systems, or other flaws that could be exploited. Once vulnerabilities are identified, they are typically classified based on their severity and potential impact on the network. This classification helps prioritize remediation efforts, with critical vulnerabilities requiring immediate attention and low-severity vulnerabilities being addressed in a more systematic manner. In addition to identifying vulnerabilities, a vulnerability assessment often involves providing recommendations and mitigations to address the identified weaknesses. These recommendations may include implementing security patches, updating software versions, strengthening access controls, segmenting the network, or other measures to enhance the overall security posture of the network. Regular vulnerability assessments are considered an essential component of an organization's overall security strategy. By regularly assessing network vulnerabilities, organizations can stay ahead of potential threats, protect sensitive data, and minimize the likelihood of successful cyberattacks.

Vulnerability Scanner

A vulnerability scanner is a network security tool that is designed to identify potential vulnerabilities in a computer system or network. It is used to assess the security posture of the system by analyzing the system's configuration and identifying any weaknesses that could be exploited by attackers. The vulnerability scanner scans the target system or network by sending out various probes, tests, and requests to identify any weak points that could be exploited. It examines a wide range of factors including configuration settings, open ports, services running, installed software, and even weak passwords. By doing so, it helps administrators and security professionals to quickly identify and prioritize the potential vulnerabilities that need to be addressed.

WAN Connection

A Wide Area Network (WAN) connection is a networking technology that allows computers and devices to connect and communicate over a large geographical area. Unlike Local Area Networks (LANs), which are typically confined to a small geographic area like an office building or campus, WANs connect multiple LANs across long distances, often spanning cities, countries, or even continents. WAN connections utilize various networking technologies and protocols to enable communication between different networks. These technologies include dedicated leased lines, such as T1 or T3 lines, which provide a direct connection between two locations; Virtual Private Networks (VPNs), which use encryption to securely connect remote locations over the internet; and public networks like the internet itself, which can be used to establish connections between geographically separated networks.

WAN Deployment Considerations

WAN Deployment Considerations refer to the critical factors that need to be taken into account when planning and implementing a Wide Area Network (WAN) in a networking environment. A WAN is a geographically dispersed network that connects multiple local area networks (LANs) across a wide area, such as different offices or campuses. When deploying a WAN, careful consideration must be given to several key aspects to ensure optimal performance, scalability, and reliability of the network. These considerations include: 1. Bandwidth Requirements: Assessing the amount of bandwidth required to support the anticipated traffic is crucial. This involves understanding the types and volume of data being transmitted, as well as accounting for future growth and peak usage periods. 2. Network Topology: Planning the network topology involves determining the most appropriate architecture for connecting different locations, such as using point-to-point, hub-and-spoke, or mesh configurations. Factors such as latency, cost, and ease of management should be considered. 3. Network Redundancy: Implementing redundancy mechanisms is essential to ensure high availability and fault tolerance in the WAN. Redundant links, devices, and failover mechanisms like Spanning Tree Protocol (STP) or Virtual Router Redundancy Protocol (VRRP) can minimize downtime in case of link failure or equipment malfunctions. 4. Security Considerations: Protecting transmitted data is critical in a WAN environment that spans over a wide area. Measures like encryption, VPN tunnels, firewalls, and intrusion detection systems need to be strategically deployed to safeguard sensitive information from unauthorized access. 5. Quality of Service (QoS): QoS mechanisms enable prioritization of network traffic to ensure critical applications and services receive the required level of performance. Configuring QoS policies based on specific criteria such as latency, bandwidth, and packet loss can help optimize WAN performance and guarantee service level agreements. 6. Scalability: The network design should allow for future growth and scalability. This involves provisioning adequate network resources, such as IP address ranges, routing protocols, and hardware capabilities, to support additional sites, increased traffic, and expanding infrastructure requirements. By carefully considering these factors, organizations can plan and deploy a well-designed WAN that meets their specific needs, ensuring efficient communication, collaboration, and data exchange across a wide area network.

WAN Deployment

WAN Deployment refers to the process of implementing and configuring Wide Area Network (WAN) infrastructure within an organization, allowing for the centralized communication and sharing of data between multiple locations or branch offices. It involves the setup and management of networking equipment, such as routers and switches, along with the configuration of network protocols and security measures. During WAN deployment, the network administrator or IT team works to establish connectivity between various sites and ensure seamless communication across the WAN. This may include the installation of physical communication links, such as leased lines or fiber optic cables, as well as the configuration of virtual connections using technologies like MPLS (Multiprotocol Label Switching), VPN (Virtual Private Network), or SD-WAN (Software-Defined Wide Area Network). The primary goals of WAN deployment are to enable efficient and reliable data exchange, improve collaboration between geographically dispersed teams, and support access to shared resources and applications. It allows organizations to create a unified network infrastructure that connects their different locations, enabling employees to work together effectively irrespective of their physical location. During the WAN deployment process, various factors are taken into consideration, such as bandwidth requirements, network latency, security requirements, and scalability. The network administrator ensures that the WAN architecture is designed to handle the anticipated traffic volume and provides appropriate Quality of Service (QoS) mechanisms to prioritize critical network traffic. In addition, WAN deployment involves implementing appropriate security measures to protect the organization's data and resources. This may include the use of firewalls,

341

intrusion detection and prevention systems, encryption technologies, and secure authentication mechanisms to safeguard sensitive information transmitted over the WAN. Overall, WAN deployment is a critical task in building a reliable and efficient network infrastructure that connects multiple sites or remote locations. It requires careful planning, configuration, and ongoing management to ensure optimal network performance and secure data transmission across the WAN.

WAN Gateway

A WAN gateway, also known as a wide area network gateway, is a networking device or software that connects a local area network (LAN) to a wide area network (WAN). It acts as an intermediary between the LAN and the WAN, facilitating communication and data transfer between the two networks. The primary function of a WAN gateway is to enable connectivity between different networks across geographically dispersed locations. It serves as the entry and exit point for data packets traveling between the LAN and the WAN. The gateway ensures that the data packets are properly routed and encrypted, providing secure and efficient transmission over the WAN.

WAN Optimization Solutions

WAN optimization solutions refer to a set of techniques and technologies used to improve the performance and efficiency of Wide Area Networks (WANs). A WAN is a network that spans over a large geographic area, connecting multiple local area networks (LANs) and enabling data transmission between different locations. With the growth of cloud computing, remote work, and distributed offices, WANs have become a critical infrastructure for connecting users, applications, and data across multiple locations. However, WANs often face challenges such as high latency, limited bandwidth, and packet loss, which can degrade network performance and user experience. WAN optimization solutions aim to address these challenges and optimize the utilization and performance of the WAN. These solutions typically employ various techniques, including compression, protocol optimization, caching, and traffic management, to reduce data transfer times, minimize bandwidth utilization, and enhance application response times. Compression techniques involve the reduction of data size before transmission by eliminating redundant or repetitive data patterns. This helps to decrease the amount of data that needs to be transmitted over the WAN, thereby reducing bandwidth utilization and improving overall network performance. Protocol optimization involves the modification and improvement of network protocols used for data transmission over the WAN. By optimizing these protocols, WAN optimization solutions can reduce the transmission overhead, minimize latency, and enhance the efficiency of data transfer. Caching is another important technique used in WAN optimization solutions. It involves storing frequently accessed data at remote locations, allowing users to retrieve the data locally rather than sending multiple requests over the WAN. This helps to reduce latency and improve application response times for users. Traffic management techniques are used to prioritize and control network traffic flows over the WAN. By prioritizing critical applications and allocating available bandwidth appropriately, WAN optimization solutions can ensure that the most important data receives the necessary network resources, improving overall network performance and user experience.

WAN Optimization

WAN Optimization refers to the process of improving the performance, efficiency, and reliability of Wide Area Network (WAN) connections by reducing the amount of data transmitted over the network and optimizing the flow of traffic between different locations. WANs are used to connect geographically distributed sites, such as branch offices, data centers, and cloud resources, over long distances. However, WAN connections can suffer from latency, packet loss, and limited bandwidth, leading to slow application performance and user frustration. WAN Optimization aims to address these challenges and enhance the overall network experience.

WAN Redundancy Solutions

WAN redundancy solutions refer to the various methods and technologies implemented in a network to ensure continuous connectivity between multiple Wide Area Network (WAN) links. These solutions are designed to provide fault tolerance and avoid network downtime by automatically redirecting traffic to an alternative link in the event of a link failure or congestion. One common WAN redundancy solution is link aggregation, which involves combining multiple WAN links into a single logical link. This can be achieved using technologies such as Link Aggregation Control Protocol (LACP) or Port Channel. By aggregating the bandwidth of multiple links, organizations can achieve higher throughput and increased network availability. If one link fails, traffic is automatically redirected to the remaining active links, preventing service disruption.

WAN Redundancy

WAN redundancy refers to the implementation of backup or alternative connectivity solutions in a wide area network (WAN) to ensure continuous network availability and minimize downtime. It involves the use of redundant links, devices, or network paths to provide failover capabilities and maintain network connectivity even in the event of a failure or disruption in the primary network connection. The primary purpose of WAN redundancy is to enhance network reliability and resiliency by creating a backup mechanism that can seamlessly take over in case of a failure in the primary network connection. This redundancy can be achieved through various techniques, such as redundant links, load balancing, and software-defined networking (SDN) technologies. Redundant links in a WAN setup involve the use of multiple physical or virtual connections between network devices, such as routers or switches, to ensure network continuity. These links can be configured in an active-passive or active-active mode, depending on the specific requirements and capabilities of the network infrastructure. In an active-passive setup, one link serves as the primary path, while the other remains idle until the primary link fails. When a failure occurs, the backup link automatically takes over to maintain network connectivity. In an active-active setup, both links are utilized simultaneously, distributing network traffic across them for load balancing and fault tolerance. Load balancing is another approach to WAN redundancy, which involves distributing network traffic across multiple links or paths to optimize performance and provide fault tolerance. This technique can be implemented using dedicated load balancer devices or by leveraging SDN technologies. Load balancing ensures that no single link is overwhelmed with traffic, thereby minimizing the risk of congestion or bottleneck issues. In case of link failure, the load balancer can automatically reroute traffic to the remaining functioning links, ensuring continuous network connectivity. SDN technologies, such as software-defined wide area networking (SD-WAN), play a significant role in achieving WAN redundancy. SD-WAN allows the network administrator to dynamically manage and allocate network resources, including multiple WAN connections, based on the real-time demands and conditions of the network. It enables intelligent path selection, load balancing, and failover mechanisms, ensuring uninterrupted network communication even when one or more links experience issues or failures.

WAN (Wide Area Network)

Wide Area Network (WAN) refers to a computer network that spans a large geographical area and connects multiple local area networks (LANs) or other WANs together. It extends over a wide range of distance, often across cities, countries, or even continents, utilizing various telecommunication technologies such as leased lines, satellites, or Internet connections. WANs are typically established and operated by telecommunications companies or Internet service providers to facilitate the efficient exchange of data and communication between different locations. They are crucial for organizations, businesses, and institutions that need to connect their remote offices, data centers, or branch locations in different geographical areas. WANs employ various networking technologies and protocols to ensure reliable and secure transmission of data across different networks. Common examples include Asynchronous Transfer Mode (ATM), Frame Relay, Multi-Protocol Label Switching (MPLS), and Internet Protocol (IP). These technologies enable the efficient routing and switching of data packets between different locations, ensuring that information reaches its intended destination effectively. One of the primary advantages of WANs is the ability to connect multiple LANs together, allowing organizations to share resources, data, and applications across different locations. This facilitates collaboration and improves efficiency, as employees in different offices can access shared files, databases, or software applications in real-time. WANs also provide a high degree of scalability, as they can accommodate the expansion of networks to additional locations without significant infrastructure changes. This flexibility is crucial for organizations with plans for growth or those that need to adapt to changing business needs and requirements.

However, WANs are subject to various challenges and considerations. The performance of a WAN depends on various factors such as bandwidth, latency, and network congestion, which can affect the speed and reliability of data transmission. Security is also a critical concern, as WANs are exposed to potential threats from external sources. It is essential to implement proper security measures, such as firewalls, encryption, and virtual private networks (VPNs), to safeguard data transmitted over a WAN. In conclusion, a Wide Area Network (WAN) is a network infrastructure that connects multiple LANs or other WANs over a large geographical area. It enables the exchange of data and communication between different locations, facilitating collaboration and resource sharing. WANs employ various technologies and protocols to ensure reliable and secure data transmission, while scalability allows for network expansion. Nevertheless, performance, latency, and security considerations are crucial for optimal WAN operation.

WPA3 Security Protocol

WPA3, short for Wi-Fi Protected Access 3, is a security protocol designed for wireless networks to enhance the privacy and protection of user data. It is an improvement over its predecessor, WPA2, and addresses several vulnerabilities found in previous Wi-Fi security standards. WPA3 provides stronger encryption and authentication mechanisms to safeguard wireless communications between devices connected to a network. It employs the use of the Simultaneous Authentication of Equals (SAE) protocol, also known as Dragonfly Key Exchange, which offers improved security against offline dictionary attacks.

WPA3 (Wi-Fi Protected Access 3)

WPA3 (Wi-Fi Protected Access 3) is the latest version of a security protocol designed to protect wireless networks. It is an enhancement of the previous WPA2 standard and offers improved security features to ensure the confidentiality and integrity of data being transmitted over Wi-Fi connections. The primary goal of WPA3 is to provide stronger protection against various security vulnerabilities and attacks that can compromise the confidentiality and privacy of wireless network communications. It achieves this through the implementation of a number of advanced security mechanisms. One of the key security enhancements in WPA3 is the use of Simultaneous Authentication of Equals (SAE). This protocol replaces the Pre-Shared Key (PSK) mechanism used in WPA2, which was susceptible to offline dictionary and brute-force attacks. SAE uses a stronger and more secure key exchange method, making it significantly more difficult for attackers to crack the network password and gain unauthorized access. Another important feature of WPA3 is the introduction of Opportunistic Wireless Encryption (OWE). OWE allows for encrypted Wi-Fi connections even when a network does not require a password. This is particularly useful in public Wi-Fi hotspots, where users may connect to networks without passwords, leaving their data vulnerable to interception. OWE ensures that all data transmitted over such networks is protected from eavesdropping. Furthermore, WPA3 also offers improved protection against brute-force attacks through the implementation of resistance to offline cracking. It randomizes the encryption keys used in each Wi-Fi session, making it much more challenging for an attacker to determine the key even if they manage to intercept the data. Overall, WPA3 brings significant improvements in terms of security for Wi-Fi networks. Its stronger key exchange mechanism, provision for encrypted connections on open networks, and resistance to offline cracking all contribute to a more secure Wi-Fi experience. As a result, network administrators and users can have greater confidence in the privacy and confidentiality of their data when using Wi-Fi networks protected by WPA3.

WPA3-Enterprise (802.1X/EAP)

WPA3-Enterprise is a security protocol designed to enhance the level of protection for enterprise Wi-Fi networks. It is a part of the IEEE 802.11i standard, also known as Wi-Fi Protected Access 3 (WPA3). WPA3-Enterprise is based on the 802.1X/EAP (Extensible Authentication Protocol) framework, which provides secure authentication and key management for client devices attempting to connect to a Wi-Fi network. This protocol is specifically designed for use in large-scale deployments, such as corporate, educational, and government networks. The key feature of WPA3-Enterprise is the use of individualized data encryption, also known as Opportunistic Wireless Encryption (OWE). With OWE, each client is assigned a unique encryption key, which significantly improves the overall security of the network. This prevents unauthorized access and eavesdropping by ensuring that each client's data is encrypted and cannot be deciphered by other devices on the network. In addition to individualized data encryption, WPA3-Enterprise also provides robust authentication mechanisms. It supports a wide range of EAP methods, such as EAP-TLS, EAP-TTLS, and PEAP, which allow for secure authentication of client devices. This ensures that only authorized users are able to connect to the Wi-Fi network, guarding against potential attacks from unauthorized individuals. Furthermore, WPA3-Enterprise incorporates advanced security features, such as forward secrecy, which ensures that even if a client's authentication credentials are compromised, previously transmitted data remains secure. It also includes protections against brute force attacks and dictionary-based password guessing, making it highly resilient against unauthorized access attempts. Overall, WPA3-Enterprise provides an industry-standard security solution for enterprise Wi-Fi networks. With its individualized data encryption, robust authentication mechanisms, and advanced security features, it offers a high level of protection against various types of attacks, making it suitable for use in demanding network environments.

WPA3-Enterprise Setup

WPA3-Enterprise Setup is a networking protocol that provides enhanced security for wireless networks in an organizational setting. It is an extension of the previous security protocol, WPA2-Enterprise, and offers more robust protection against various security threats. WPA3-Enterprise Setup involves the implementation of a centralized authentication server, known as a Remote Authentication Dial-In User Service (RADIUS), which is responsible for authenticating and authorizing client devices attempting to connect to the wireless network. The RADIUS server uses the Extensible Authentication Protocol (EAP) to establish a secure connection with the client device and verify its identity.

WPA3-Personal Security

WPA3-Personal Security is a networking protocol that provides enhanced security for wireless networks. It is the latest iteration of the Wi-Fi Protected Access (WPA) standard and offers stronger protection against unauthorized access to Wi-Fi networks compared to its predecessor, WPA2. WPA3-Personal Security improves upon WPA2 by implementing several new security features. One of the major enhancements is the introduction of Simultaneous Authentication of Equals (SAE), also known as Dragonfly Key Exchange. SAE replaces the Pre-Shared Key (PSK) approach used in WPA2, making it more resistant to offline dictionary-based attacks. SAE also supports forward secrecy, which means that even if an attacker obtains the cryptographic secrets of a past session, they cannot use it to decrypt the communications of future sessions. In addition to SAE, WPA3-Personal Security offers another significant security feature called Opportunistic Wireless Encryption (OWE). OWE ensures that even when a Wi-Fi network does not use a password or a pre-shared key, all communications between devices are still encrypted. This prevents attackers from eavesdropping on the data transmitted over the network, providing an extra layer of protection for users. Furthermore, WPA3-Personal Security strengthens the security of network passwords by requiring the use of stronger, more complex passwords. It introduces a password-based key derivation function called Dragonfly Pseudorandom Function (DRF) to make brute-force attacks more challenging for attackers. Overall, WPA3-Personal Security offers significant improvements in the security of wireless networks. Its implementation of SAE, OWE, and stronger password requirements make it more resilient against various types of attacks, including offline dictionary-based attacks and eavesdropping. By adopting WPA3-Personal Security, network administrators can ensure that their wireless networks are better protected against unauthorized access and data interception.

WPA3-Personal Setup

WPA3-Personal Setup is a security protocol designed for wireless networks to provide a high level of protection for personal users. It is an enhanced version of the previous security standard, WPA2-Personal, and offers stronger encryption and authentication mechanisms. WPA3-Personal Setup utilizes the Simultaneous Authentication of Equals (SAE) protocol, also known as Dragonfly, which replaces the Pre-Shared Key (PSK) used in WPA2. SAE eliminates the vulnerabilities associated with PSKs, such as dictionary attacks and offline cracking of passwords. With SAE, users can establish a secure connection without the need to share a password directly with the access point. The key features of WPA3-Personal Setup include forward secrecy, resistance to offline dictionary attacks, and protection against brute-force attacks. Forward secrecy ensures that even if an attacker captures the encrypted traffic, they cannot decrypt it later, ensuring the confidentiality of data. The resistance to offline dictionary attacks is achieved by using a different encryption key for each authentication attempt, making it difficult for attackers to guess the password through a trial-and-error approach. Additionally, WPA3-Personal Setup includes protections against brute-force attacks, where an attacker tries to guess the password by systematically trying all possible combinations. Another important aspect of WPA3-Personal Setup is the introduction of Wi-Fi Protected Setup (WPS) 3.0, which simplifies the process of connecting devices to a network securely. WPS 3.0 uses a push-button or PIN-based mechanism to establish a secure connection, ensuring that only authorized devices can join the network. In conclusion, WPA3-Personal Setup enhances the security of wireless networks by providing stronger encryption, authentication, and protection against various types of attacks. It addresses the weaknesses of previous security standards and offers improved privacy and confidentiality for personal users.

WPA3-Personal

WPA3-Personal is a security protocol designed for Wi-Fi networks to ensure the confidentiality, integrity, and authentication of wireless communications. It is the latest iteration of the Wi-Fi Protected Access (WPA) standard, succeeding WPA2-Personal. With the increasing number of Wi-Fi enabled devices and the growing need for secure connections, WPA3-Personal addresses several vulnerabilities present in its predecessor to offer stronger protection against unauthorized access and attacks. One of the key features of WPA3-Personal is the use of Simultaneous Authentication of Equals (SAE), also known as Dragonfly Key Exchange. This new protocol replaces the pre-shared key (PSK) method used in WPA2-Personal, enhancing security against offline dictionary attacks. SAE enables users to establish a secure connection without the need for a complex password, while still maintaining the same level of protection. Another significant improvement in WPA3-Personal is the introduction of forward secrecy. In WPA2-Personal, if someone discovers the Wi-Fi network's password, they can potentially decrypt all the past and future network traffic. However, WPA3-Personal prevents this by ensuring that even if the password is compromised, older network traffic cannot be decrypted. Furthermore, WPA3-Personal enhances the protection of Wi-Fi networks by securing unauthenticated network traffic. In WPA2-Personal, unencrypted data can be intercepted, making it susceptible to eavesdropping. WPA3-Personal addresses this issue by encrypting all communication, even if the device is not yet authenticated onto the network. In summary, WPA3-Personal is a security protocol that uses Simultaneous Authentication of Equals, forward secrecy, and encryption of unauthenticated traffic to provide stronger protection for Wi-Fi networks. By implementing these improvements, WPA3-Personal ensures the confidentiality, integrity, and authentication of wireless communications, safeguarding users from unauthorized access and attacks.

WPA3-SAE Security

WPA3-SAE Security, also known as Wi-Fi Protected Access 3 - Simultaneous Authentication of Equals Security, is a network security protocol designed to enhance the security of Wi-Fi connections. It is the successor of WPA2, the previous standard for securing Wi-Fi networks. WPA3-SAE Security introduces several key improvements over its predecessor. One of the main enhancements is the use of the Simultaneous Authentication of Equals (SAE) handshake method, which replaces the Pre-Shared Key (PSK) used in WPA2. SAE is a more secure and reliable authentication method that provides protection against various attack vectors, such as offline dictionary attacks.

WPA3-SAE (Simultaneous Authentication Of Equals)

WPA3-SAE (Simultaneous Authentication of Equals) is a security protocol designed for wireless networks. It is an upgrade to the WPA2 (Wi-Fi Protected Access 2) protocol that provides enhanced security measures to protect data transmission and authentication processes. WPA3-SAE addresses the vulnerabilities and weaknesses present in the WPA2 protocol, making it more resistant to attacks. It introduces several key features, including forward secrecy, strengthened handshake process, and protection against dictionary and brute-force attacks. One of the main security improvements in WPA3-SAE is the use of the Simultaneous Authentication of Equals method for the password-based authentication. This method replaces the Pre-Shared Key (PSK) approach used in WPA2, which is vulnerable to offline dictionary attacks. The Simultaneous Authentication of Equals method relies on the Dragonfly key exchange protocol, which is based on elliptic curve cryptography. It provides stronger protection against password guessing attacks by preventing an attacker from using an offline dictionary of precomputed hashes to guess the password. With WPA3-SAE, the authentication process requires both the client device and the access point to prove their knowledge of the password without actually transmitting it over the network. This ensures that even if an attacker intercepts the authentication process, they cannot gather enough information to guess the password. Furthermore, WPA3-SAE introduces the Dragonfly Handshake, a more secure method for establishing a secure connection between the client and the access point. It strengthens the handshake process by combining the password-based authentication with a Diffie-Hellman key exchange and a nonce. This prevents replay attacks and provides forward secrecy, meaning that if the long-term secret key is compromised in the future, it cannot be used to decrypt past communications. In summary, WPA3-SAE is a security protocol that enhances the protection of wireless networks by incorporating the Simultaneous Authentication of Equals method. It addresses the vulnerabilities of the previous WPA2 protocol, providing stronger authentication and data transmission security, thereby safeguarding sensitive information exchanged over wireless networks.

Web Application Firewall (WAF)

A Web Application Firewall (WAF) is a security solution implemented at the application layer of a network that helps protect web applications from a variety of attacks and vulnerabilities. It monitors and filters HTTP and HTTPS traffic to and from a web application, analyzing it for suspicious or malicious activity. A WAF acts as a reverse proxy, sitting between the web application and the client, inspecting each request and response for potential threats. It applies a set of predefined security rules to identify and block known attack patterns, such as SQL injection, cross-site scripting (XSS), cross-site request forgery (CSRF), and more.

Web Application Scanner

A web application scanner is a tool used in the context of networking to identify and analyze vulnerabilities present in web applications. It is designed to assess the security of a web application by scanning its components, such as URLs, forms, cookies, headers, and parameters, to detect potential security flaws that could be exploited by attackers. Web application scanners work by simulating various attack scenarios, such as SQL injection, cross-site scripting (XSS), and remote file inclusion, to uncover vulnerabilities that may exist in the targeted web application. They automate the process of detecting and reporting these vulnerabilities, making it easier for security professionals to identify and mitigate the risks associated with them.

Web Application Vulnerability Scanner

A Web Application Vulnerability Scanner is a tool used in networking to assess the security of web applications. It is designed to identify vulnerabilities and weaknesses within the application, allowing network administrators and security teams to patch them proactively. The scanner works by simulating attacks on the web application and searching for common vulnerabilities, such as SQL injection, cross-site scripting (XSS), and cross-site request forgery (CSRF). It crawls through the pages of the application, scanning both the input fields and output responses for any potential security flaws. The scanner performs various tests to exploit security weaknesses and vulnerabilities. It checks for input validation vulnerabilities, where the application fails to properly validate user inputs, allowing attackers to inject malicious code. It also looks for insecure session management practices, insecure direct object references, and poor error handling that may reveal sensitive information. Once vulnerabilities are identified, the scanner provides a detailed report highlighting the security flaws found, including information about the affected pages, the severity of the vulnerability, and recommended mitigation steps. The report enables security teams to prioritize their efforts and take appropriate action to mitigate the identified risks. Web Application Vulnerability Scanners are essential tools in the networking industry as web applications are often targeted by attackers due to their public-facing nature. By regularly scanning web applications, vulnerabilities can be discovered and patched

347

before they can be exploited, minimizing the risk of unauthorized access, data breaches, and other security incidents. In conclusion, a Web Application Vulnerability Scanner is a crucial tool that helps network administrators and security teams identify and address security weaknesses in web applications. By using this tool, organizations can enhance the security of their networks and protect sensitive information from potential cyber threats.

Whitelist And Blacklist

A whitelist and a blacklist are terms commonly used in the context of networking to describe two different approaches for controlling access to network resources. Both mechanisms are used to specify which users, devices, or IP addresses are allowed or denied access to a network or specific resources within that network. A whitelist is a list of entities that are granted access to the network or resources based on predefined criteria. In other words, it is a list of trusted or approved entities. When a whitelist is implemented, only the entities included in the list are allowed access, while all others are denied by default. This approach focuses on granting access to known and trusted entities and is often used to enhance the security and integrity of a network. Whitelists are commonly used in scenarios where maximum control and security are crucial, such as in corporate networks or sensitive systems. A blacklist, on the other hand, is a list of entities that are explicitly denied access to the network or resources. It is a list of untrusted or blocked entities. When a blacklist is implemented, all entities not included in the list are granted access, while the ones on the list are denied. This approach is generally used to restrict access to known malicious or unauthorized entities. Blacklists are commonly employed in scenarios where the intention is to protect the network or resources from specific malicious or undesirable entities, such as known hackers or compromised IP addresses.

Whitelist

A whitelist, in the context of networking, refers to a list of trusted entities or sources that are granted permission to access a certain network or system. It acts as a security measure that ensures only authorized entities are allowed access, while blocking or restricting all others. Typically, a whitelist is implemented at the application layer or within a network firewall. When a network or system receives a request for access, it checks the source of the request against the whitelist. If the source is found on the whitelist, the request is granted and the entity is allowed to access the network or system. On the other hand, if the source is not present on the whitelist, the request is denied and the entity is barred from accessing the network or system. Using a whitelist approach provides several advantages for network security. Firstly, it reduces the attack surface by only allowing known and trusted entities to connect to the network or system. This helps prevent unauthorized access and potential malicious activities. Secondly, it enables administrators to have more control over network traffic and user access rights. By carefully curating the whitelist, administrators can specify the exact entities that are allowed to connect, thereby minimizing the risk of security breaches. Additionally, a whitelist can be used to block specific entities or sources that are known to be malicious or pose a threat. This allows administrators to create a barrier against known threats, enhancing the overall security of the network or system. Furthermore, a whitelist can prevent unauthorized access to specific resources or services within a network, ensuring that only those with proper permissions can access sensitive information. In conclusion, a whitelist is a crucial security mechanism in networking that grants access permissions only to known and trusted entities while blocking or restricting unauthorized sources. By leveraging a whitelist, organizations can strengthen their network security and protect their systems from potential threats and unauthorized access.

Wi-Fi Direct

Wi-Fi Direct is a wireless networking technology that enables two or more devices to establish a direct connection with each other without the need for a traditional Wi-Fi access point or router. It allows devices to communicate and share data directly, creating a peer-to-peer network. Unlike traditional Wi-Fi networks that require an access point, Wi-Fi Direct operates by using a device as a group owner, also known as the access point. This group owner advertises its presence and allows other devices within its range to join the network. Once connected, devices can communicate with each other, share files, stream media, or even mirror their screens.

Wi-Fi Extender

A Wi-Fi extender is a device used to expand the coverage area of an existing Wi-Fi network. It is typically used in cases where the existing Wi-Fi signal is weak or does not reach certain areas of a home or office. The Wi-Fi extender works by receiving the existing Wi-Fi signal from a router or access point and then retransmitting it to extend the coverage area. It essentially acts as a bridge between the router and devices that are located in areas with poor Wi-Fi signal.

Wi-Fi Frequency Bands

Wi-Fi frequency bands refer to the range of frequencies that are used to transmit and receive wireless signals for Wi-Fi networks. Wi-Fi operates in two main frequency bands: 2.4 GHz and 5 GHz. These frequency bands provide different advantages and trade-offs in terms of coverage, capacity, and interference. The 2.4 GHz frequency band is the most commonly used Wi-Fi band. It offers a wide coverage area and better penetration through walls and other obstacles. However, because it is a commonly used frequency band for various devices such as cordless phones, baby monitors, and Bluetooth devices, it is prone to interference, which can degrade the performance of Wi-Fi networks operating in this band. Additionally, the 2.4 GHz band has a limited number of available channels, leading to congestion in densely populated areas where multiple Wi-Fi networks are present. The 5 GHz frequency band, on the other hand, provides higher data transfer speeds and is less susceptible to interference compared to the 2.4 GHz band. It offers a greater number of non-overlapping channels, which reduces congestion and allows for more simultaneous connections. However, the 5 GHz band has a shorter range and may have difficulty penetrating walls and other obstacles, resulting in decreased coverage area. Devices operating in the 5 GHz band also require more power, which can impact battery life on mobile devices. In modern Wi-Fi networks, dual-band routers are often used to mitigate the limitations of each frequency band. These routers broadcast separate Wi-Fi networks on both 2.4 GHz and 5 GHz bands, allowing devices to connect to the most appropriate band based on their capabilities and proximity to the router. This ensures optimal performance and coverage for Wi-Fi users. In conclusion, Wi-Fi frequency bands play a crucial role in determining the performance, coverage, and interference levels of Wi-Fi networks. The 2.4 GHz band offers wider coverage but is more prone to interference, while the 5 GHz band provides higher speeds but has a shorter range. Dual-band routers are commonly used to leverage the advantages of both bands and provide optimal Wi-Fi experience for users.

Wi-Fi Hotspot Security Measures

Wi-Fi hotspot security measures refer to the steps and protocols implemented to ensure the protection and privacy of users connected to a public Wi-Fi network. These measures are essential as public Wi-Fi networks are often targeted by cybercriminals who attempt to steal sensitive information or compromise the security of connected devices. There are several key security measures that can be implemented to enhance the security of Wi-Fi hotspots. One such measure is the use of encryption protocols, such as WPA2 (Wi-Fi Protected Access 2), which helps secure the data transmitted between the user's device and the Wi-Fi access point. Encryption scrambles the data, making it unreadable to unauthorized individuals. Additionally, the use of a secure password for accessing the Wi-Fi network adds an extra layer of protection. Another important security measure is the implementation of a firewall. This network security device monitors and filters incoming and outgoing network traffic, preventing unauthorized access and blocking potential threats. Firewalls can be hardware or software-based and are designed to detect and block malicious activities. Network segmentation is another security measure that helps protect hotspot users. By dividing the network into smaller, isolated segments, it becomes more difficult for cybercriminals to gain unauthorized access to sensitive information or exploit vulnerabilities. This measure helps contain any potential breaches, preventing them from spreading to other parts of the network. Regular monitoring and updating of network infrastructure and devices is also crucial. This includes keeping Wi-Fi access points and routers up to date with the latest firmware and security patches. By regularly monitoring for any vulnerabilities or potential security risks, organizations can proactively address and mitigate these threats before they can be exploited. In addition to these technical security measures, user awareness and education play a vital role in Wi-Fi hotspot security. Users should be educated about the risks associated with using public Wi-Fi networks and encouraged to take necessary precautions, such as avoiding sensitive transactions or accessing confidential information while connected to a public hotspot.

Wi-Fi Hotspot Security

Wi-Fi Hotspot Security refers to the protective measures taken to secure a Wi-Fi hotspot network from unauthorized access and potential security threats. A Wi-Fi hotspot is a public or private location that provides wireless internet access to users through a wireless local area network (WLAN). It allows users to connect their devices, such as smartphones, tablets, or laptops, to the internet wirelessly. However, due to the open nature of Wi-Fi networks, they are susceptible to various security risks, including eavesdropping, data theft, and unauthorized access. To ensure the security of a Wi-Fi hotspot, several security measures need to be implemented. One such measure is the use of encryption protocols, such as Wi-Fi Protected Access (WPA) or WPA2. These protocols encrypt the data transmitted between the user's device and the hotspot, making it difficult for attackers to intercept and decipher the data. Another important security measure is the use of strong passwords or passphrases for hotspot authentication. This helps prevent unauthorized users from gaining access to the network. It is recommended to use a combination of upper and lowercase letters, numbers, and special characters to create a strong password. Additionally, network isolation techniques, such as virtual local area networks (VLANs), can be employed to separate different types of network traffic and prevent unauthorized access to sensitive data. Firewalls and intrusion detection/prevention systems can also be used to monitor and block malicious traffic. Regular software updates and patches are crucial in maintaining Wi-Fi hotspot security. Manufacturers often release updates to fix known security vulnerabilities and improve the security of their devices. It is important to regularly update the firmware of hotspot routers and devices connected to the network. In conclusion, Wi-Fi hotspot security involves implementing various measures, such as encryption, strong authentication, network isolation, and regular updates, to protect the network and the data transmitted over it. By following these security practices, both hotspot providers and users can mitigate potential security risks and ensure the privacy and integrity of their data.

Wi-Fi Hotspot

A Wi-Fi hotspot is a wireless access point that allows devices to connect to the internet. It provides internet connectivity by creating a localized wireless network using Wi-Fi technology. This type of network is commonly found in places such as cafes, hotels, airports, and public spaces where multiple users may need to connect their devices to the internet simultaneously. A Wi-Fi hotspot enables these users to access the internet without the need for physical cables or wired connections.

Wi-Fi Infrastructure

Wi-Fi Infrastructure refers to the network of components and devices that enable wireless communication and internet connectivity using the Wi-Fi technology. It consists of various components such as routers, access points, antennas, and other network devices that work together to create a wireless network. In a Wi-Fi infrastructure, the router acts as the central hub that connects to the internet and manages the network. It is responsible for receiving and transmitting data packets between devices on the Wi-Fi network and the internet. The router may also provide additional features such as firewall and network address translation (NAT) to enhance network security. Access points (APs) are devices that enable wireless connectivity for devices within their range. They act as the points of access to the Wi-Fi network and allow devices such as smartphones, laptops, and tablets to connect wirelessly. APs are typically connected to the router or a switch through Ethernet cables. Antennas play a crucial role in the Wi-Fi infrastructure by transmitting and receiving wireless signals. They help extend the coverage range and improve the signal strength of the Wi-Fi network. Depending on the requirements, different types of antennas, such as omni-directional and directional antennas, can be used. Other network devices, such as switches and repeaters, may also be included in the Wi-Fi infrastructure to extend the network connectivity and improve performance. Switches help connect multiple access points and devices together, while repeaters amplify and retransmit the wireless signals to extend coverage range. Wi-Fi infrastructure relies on the Wi-Fi technology, which utilizes the IEEE 802.11 standard to define the specifications for wireless communication. The standard specifies various protocols and frequencies for wireless transmission, allowing devices to communicate and transmit data over the airwaves. Overall, Wi-Fi infrastructure forms the foundation of wireless networks, providing seamless and reliable internet connectivity to a wide range of devices. It enables flexible and convenient access to the internet, allowing users to connect and communicate wirelessly from various locations within the network coverage area.

Wi-Fi Network Design

Wi-Fi network design refers to the process of planning and implementing a wireless local area network (WLAN) infrastructure that allows devices to connect and communicate through wireless signals. It involves determining the layout and configuration of access points (APs) and other networking components to ensure optimal coverage, capacity, and performance. The design of a Wi-Fi network involves several key considerations. One of the primary factors is coverage, which refers to the range and reach of the wireless signal. The goal is to provide reliable connectivity throughout the desired area, such as a home, office, or public space. This requires strategically placing APs to minimize dead zones and signal interference, considering factors like building layout, materials, and obstructions. Capacity is another important consideration in Wi-Fi network design. This relates to the ability of the network to handle multiple devices simultaneously without significant degradation in performance. The design must account for the number of expected connected devices, their data and usage patterns, and the required bandwidth. It may involve distributing APs strategically to balance the load and prevent congestion. Performance optimization is a critical aspect of Wi-Fi network design. This includes ensuring high data rates, low latency, minimal packet loss, and good signal strength. Factors like channel selection, radio frequency (RF) interference, and network security measures can impact performance. The design must address these issues by utilizing proper RF channel assignment, selecting appropriate antennas, and implementing strong network security protocols. In addition to coverage, capacity, and performance, Wi-Fi network design also considers scalability and manageability. A well-designed network should be able to scale as the number of users and devices increase over time. It should also be easy to manage, troubleshoot, and update. This may involve utilizing centralized management software, implementing VLANs or virtual networks, and regularly monitoring and analyzing network performance.

Wi-Fi Range Extender

A Wi-Fi range extender, also known as a wireless repeater or an amplifier, is a networking device used to expand the coverage area of an existing wireless network. It acts as a bridge between the wireless router and the devices that are connected to it, improving the signal strength and extending the range of the Wi-Fi network. A Wi-Fi range extender works by receiving the wireless signal from the router and then re-broadcasting it to areas where the signal is weak or non-existent. It effectively amplifies the signal, allowing devices that are located further away from the router to connect to the network and access the internet.

Wi-Fi (Wireless Fidelity)

Wi-Fi, short for Wireless Fidelity, is a wireless networking technology that allows devices to connect to the internet or other networks without the need for physical wires or cables. It provides a convenient and efficient way for devices such as computers, smartphones, tablets, and IoT devices to communicate and exchange data over a local area network (LAN). Wi-Fi operates on radio frequency signals, typically within the 2.4 gigahertz (GHz) or 5 GHz bands. It uses a wireless access point, such as a router, as a central hub to transmit and receive data between devices. The access point acts as a bridge between the wireless devices and the wired network, allowing them to communicate with each other and gain access to the internet or other network resources. When a device wants to connect to a Wi-Fi network, it scans the available networks in the vicinity and displays a list of options. The user can then select the desired network and enter a password, if required, to establish a secure connection. Once connected, the device can send and receive data to and from the network, enabling internet access, file sharing, streaming media, and other online activities. Wi-Fi networks can be either public or private. Public Wi-Fi networks are commonly found in places such as coffee shops, airports, hotels, and libraries, where users can connect for free or for a fee. Private Wi-Fi networks, on the other hand, are typically set up in homes or businesses and require a password for access, providing a more secure connection. Wi-Fi technology supports various standards, such as 802.11b, 802.11g, 802.11n, and the latest 802.11ac or Wi-Fi 5. These standards define the capabilities and performance of the Wi-Fi network, including the maximum data transfer rates,

351

range, and number of devices that can be connected simultaneously. In summary, Wi-Fi is a wireless networking technology that enables devices to connect to the internet or other networks without the need for physical cables. It uses radio frequency signals and a wireless access point to transmit and receive data between devices. Wi-Fi networks can be public or private, and the technology supports different standards to provide varying levels of performance and capabilities.

Wide Area Network (WAN)

A Wide Area Network (WAN) is a type of computer network that spans a large geographical area, typically connecting multiple local area networks (LANs) together. It provides a means for computers, devices, and users in different locations to communicate with each other and share resources. WANs are designed to facilitate long-distance communication and can cover areas ranging from a few miles to thousands of miles. They utilize various technologies, such as leased lines, satellite links, or dedicated connections provided by Internet Service Providers (ISPs), to establish connectivity between different sites or offices.

Wireless Access Point (WAP)

A Wireless Access Point (WAP) is a network device that allows wireless devices to connect to a wired network. It acts as a bridge between wireless devices, such as laptops, smartphones, and tablets, and the wired network infrastructure. WAPs are essential components of modern enterprise networks and home wireless networks. They enable wireless communication by providing a connection point for wireless devices to access a network's resources and services. Additionally, WAPs facilitate the integration of wireless and wired networks, allowing seamless communication between devices regardless of their connectivity method.

Wireless Fidelity (Wi-Fi)

Wireless Fidelity, commonly known as Wi-Fi, is a technology that enables electronic devices to connect with each other and access the internet without the need for traditional wired connections. It allows users to create local area networks (LANs) wirelessly, providing them with the ability to share resources and communicate with other devices within the network. Wi-Fi operates by using radio waves to transmit data between devices. These radio waves are sent and received by wireless routers or access points, which act as the central hub for the wireless network. Devices such as laptops, smartphones, tablets, and even smart home devices can connect to the Wi-Fi network, allowing users to access the internet and various online services. The Wi-Fi standard is based on the IEEE 802.11 family of protocols, which specify the rules for wireless communication. These protocols define various aspects of the Wi-Fi network, including the frequency bands used, the data transfer rates, and the security mechanisms employed to protect the network from unauthorized access. Wi-Fi networks can operate in different frequency bands, such as 2.4 GHz and 5 GHz. The 2.4 GHz band provides a wider coverage area but can be more prone to interference from other devices and appliances. On the other hand, the 5 GHz band offers faster data transfer speeds and is less crowded, but has a shorter range. To connect to a Wi-Fi network, a device needs to have a wireless network interface, such as a Wi-Fi adapter. When within range of a wireless router or access point, the device can search for available networks and, once connected, obtain an IP address to communicate with other devices on the network and access the internet. Wi-Fi networks can be secured using various authentication and encryption methods to prevent unauthorized access. Common security protocols include WEP, WPA, and WPA2, which use passwords or digital certificates to authenticate users and encrypt data transmitted over the network.

Wireless Intrusion Detection System (WIDS)

A Wireless Intrusion Detection System (WIDS) is a network security technology that is specifically designed to detect unauthorized and malicious activity within a wireless network. It acts as a surveillance system that monitors and analyzes network traffic and wireless access points, looking for signs of intrusions or attacks. WIDS helps to protect the integrity and confidentiality of data transmitted over a wireless network by identifying and responding to potential threats. WIDS works by continuously monitoring the wireless network for any deviations from normal behavior or patterns. It analyzes network traffic, including data packets

352

and control messages, and compares them against predefined rules and patterns of known threats. If an anomaly or suspicious activity is detected, WIDS generates an alert or notification to network administrators, allowing them to investigate and take appropriate action to mitigate the threat.

Wireless Intrusion Prevention System (WIPS)

A Wireless Intrusion Prevention System (WIPS) is a network security technology that helps protect wireless networks from unauthorized access and potential threats. WIPS is designed to monitor and analyze wireless network traffic and identify any suspicious or malicious activity. It aims to prevent unauthorized devices or users from accessing the network and to detect and handle any attempted intrusion or attack. By continuously monitoring the wireless network, a WIPS can detect and respond to a wide range of security issues, including rogue access points, unauthorized devices, denial-of-service attacks, and man-in-the-middle attacks. It provides real-time visibility into the wireless environment and helps identify potential vulnerabilities and weaknesses in the network's security infrastructure. A WIPS typically consists of sensors or access points strategically placed throughout the wireless network infrastructure. These sensors continuously scan the airwaves and collect data about nearby devices and network traffic. They analyze this data using various techniques, such as signature-based detection, behavior analysis, and anomaly detection, to identify any potential security threats. Once a potential threat is detected, the WIPS can take proactive measures to mitigate the risk. It can automatically block unauthorized devices or users from accessing the network, send alerts to network administrators, or take other protective actions to prevent any further damage or compromise to the network's security. Some of the key features of a WIPS include intrusion detection, intrusion prevention, rogue access point detection, wireless traffic analysis, and compliance monitoring. These features help organizations ensure the integrity, confidentiality, and availability of their wireless networks and protect sensitive data from unauthorized access. In conclusion, a Wireless Intrusion Prevention System is a crucial component of a comprehensive network security strategy, particularly for organizations with wireless networks. It provides proactive protection against unauthorized access, detects and responds to security threats, and helps maintain the security and integrity of wireless networks.

Wireless LAN Controller (WLC)

A Wireless LAN Controller (WLC) is a centralized network device that manages and controls multiple access points (APs) in a wireless local area network (WLAN). It provides a centralized and unified management platform for configuration, monitoring, and troubleshooting of the wireless network infrastructure. The primary function of a WLC is to act as a mediator between the APs and the network infrastructure. It enables efficient coordination and management of multiple APs to ensure seamless roaming and connectivity for wireless clients. The WLC controls the power levels, channel assignments, and other radio parameters of the APs, optimizing the performance and coverage of the WLAN. One of the key advantages of using a WLC is its ability to enforce security policies and authentication mechanisms across the entire WLAN. It supports various authentication methods such as WPA2-Enterprise, 802.1X, and captive portal-based login, allowing organizations to enforce strict access controls and protect sensitive data. The WLC also includes intrusion detection and prevention mechanisms to safeguard the wireless network against unauthorized access and attacks. In addition to security, a WLC offers advanced features to enhance the overall performance and user experience of the WLAN. It supports load balancing and band steering, which distribute the client traffic evenly across APs and ensure optimal utilization of the available network resources. The WLC also provides quality of service (QoS) capabilities, allowing network administrators to prioritize and manage different types of traffic based on their importance and requirements. Furthermore, a WLC enables centralized configuration and firmware management for the APs. Network administrators can easily deploy and update the APs' settings and firmware from a single point, reducing the complexity and time required for manual configuration. The WLC also provides real-time monitoring and reporting, enabling administrators to gain insights into the performance, utilization, and health of the wireless network.

Wireless Mesh Network

A wireless mesh network is a type of network architecture that utilizes multiple interconnected devices, known as nodes or access points, to provide wireless communication and coverage over a large area. Each node in the network acts as a relay, forwarding data packets to neighboring nodes. Unlike traditional wireless networks, which rely on a central access point or router to connect devices, a wireless mesh network does not have a single point of failure. This decentralized architecture allows for greater flexibility, scalability, and reliability. In a wireless mesh network, each node communicates directly with its neighboring nodes, forming a self-configuring and self-healing network. If one node fails or becomes unreachable, the network automatically reroutes traffic through alternative nodes, ensuring continuous connectivity. Mesh networks can be implemented using different wireless technologies, such as Wi-Fi, Bluetooth, or Zigbee. They can be used to provide wireless internet access in remote or rural areas, extend coverage in large buildings or campuses, or create resilient networks for disaster management. One of the main advantages of wireless mesh networks is their ability to extend network coverage without the need for additional wiring. Nodes can be easily deployed and connected wirelessly, reducing installation costs and time. Another benefit is the increased capacity and performance. By distributing the network traffic across multiple nodes, mesh networks can handle higher data volumes and support more simultaneous connections. However, there are also some challenges associated with wireless mesh networks. As each node acts as a relay, the overall network capacity decreases as more nodes are added. The distance between nodes and the quality of wireless links can also affect performance. In conclusion, a wireless mesh network is a decentralized network architecture that uses interconnected nodes to provide wireless communication and coverage over a large area. It offers increased flexibility, scalability, and reliability compared to traditional wireless networks, but also presents challenges related to network capacity and link quality.

Wireless Network Adapter

A wireless network adapter, also known as a wireless network card or WLAN adapter, is a hardware device that allows a computer or other electronic device to connect and communicate with a wireless network. It facilitates the transmission and reception of wireless signals, enabling the device to wirelessly access the internet or other network resources. The wireless network adapter serves as the interface between the computer or electronic device and the wireless network. It converts the data and signals from the device into radio waves, which are then transmitted over the air to the wireless router or access point. Similarly, it receives the radio waves from the wireless router or access point and converts them back into data and signals that can be understood by the device. Wireless network adapters use various wireless communication standards, such as Wi-Fi (802.11 standards), to establish a connection with the wireless network. They come in different form factors, including internal cards that are installed within the device's casing, external USB adapters that can be plugged into a USB port, and mini PCIe cards that are commonly used in laptops and tablets. Some wireless network adapters support multiple wireless standards and frequencies, providing compatibility with different types of wireless networks. They can be configured to connect to networks operating in the 2.4 GHz or 5 GHz frequency bands, depending on the capabilities of the adapter and the network. Wireless network adapters are essential for devices that do not have built-in wireless capabilities, such as desktop computers or older laptops. They can also be used to upgrade the wireless capabilities of devices that have outdated or slower wireless adapters. Furthermore, external wireless network adapters can be used to add wireless connectivity to devices that only have wired network interfaces. In summary, a wireless network adapter is a hardware device that enables a computer or electronic device to connect to and communicate with a wireless network. It acts as the intermediary between the device and the wireless network, converting data and signals into radio waves for wireless transmission and reception.

Wireless Network Security

Wireless Network Security refers to the measures and protocols implemented to protect wireless networks, their data, and the devices connected to them from unauthorized access, as well as from various security threats and attacks. It involves the implementation of encryption algorithms, authentication mechanisms, and security policies to safeguard the confidentiality, integrity, and availability of wireless network resources. Wireless networks utilize radio waves to transmit data between devices, making them vulnerable to eavesdropping and unauthorized access. Wireless network security addresses these vulnerabilities through various security mechanisms such as encryption and authentication. Encryption involves encoding the data transmitted over the wireless network, making it unreadable to unauthorized individuals. Authentication ensures that only authorized users and devices can access the network resources by verifying their identity using credentials, such as login credentials or digital certificates. Types of wireless network security include: - WEP (Wired Equivalent Privacy): An older and less secure security protocol that provides basic encryption for wireless networks. - WPA (Wi-Fi Protected Access): A security protocol that enhances the security of wireless networks by using stronger encryption algorithms and more robust authentication mechanisms than WEP. - WPA2 (Wi-Fi Protected Access 2): The most widely used security protocol for wireless networks, which utilizes the Advanced Encryption Standard (AES) encryption algorithm and provides stronger security compared to its predecessors. - WPA3 (Wi-Fi Protected Access 3): The latest generation of wireless network security protocols, offering enhanced encryption and authentication capabilities to protect against emerging security threats. In addition to encryption and authentication, wireless network security also involves the implementation of security policies and best practices. This includes regularly updating firmware and security patches on wireless devices, disabling unused network services, restricting access to network resources based on user roles and privileges, and monitoring network traffic for suspicious activities. Overall, wireless network security is crucial in ensuring the protection of sensitive information, maintaining network integrity, and preventing unauthorized access and cyberattacks on wireless networks.

Wireless Router

A wireless router is a networking device that allows multiple devices to connect to a local area network (LAN) and share a single internet connection wirelessly. It serves as a central hub capable of transmitting data between devices within the network and manages the flow of data traffic between the devices and the internet. The primary function of a wireless router is to enable wireless communication between devices such as computers, smartphones, tablets, and other compatible devices. It acts as a bridge between the devices and the internet service provider (ISP). Through a wireless router, devices can connect to the internet without the need for physical cables, offering flexibility and mobility for users.

Wireless Security

Wireless security, in the context of networking, refers to a set of measures and protocols implemented to protect wireless networks and the devices connected to them from unauthorized access, data theft, and other security threats. With the increasing use of wireless networks, such as Wi-Fi, Bluetooth, and cellular networks, it has become essential to ensure the confidentiality, integrity, and availability of the data transmitted over these networks. Wireless security aims to address the unique challenges and vulnerabilities associated with wireless communication and provide a secure environment for users. One of the primary concerns in wireless security is preventing unauthorized access to the network. This is typically achieved through authentication mechanisms, such as passwords, digital certificates, or biometric identification, which verify the identity of individuals or devices attempting to connect to the network. Access control lists and firewalls are also commonly used to restrict access to specific devices or networks based on predefined policies. Data confidentiality is another critical aspect of wireless security. Encryption techniques, such as WPA2 (Wi-Fi Protected Access 2) and AES (Advanced Encryption Standard), are used to encrypt the data transmitted over wireless networks, making it indecipherable to unauthorized users. Encryption algorithms ensure that even if data is intercepted, it remains unreadable without the proper decryption keys. Integrity ensures that the data remains unchanged during transmission. Hash functions and message authentication codes (MACs) are utilized to verify the integrity of the data, allowing the recipient to detect any modifications or tampering attempts. Additionally, secure protocols like HTTPS (Hypertext Transfer Protocol Secure) ensure the integrity of web-based communications over wireless networks. Wireless security also includes measures to protect against denial-of-service (DoS) attacks, where an attacker overloads the network or a device with excessive traffic, making it difficult for legitimate users to connect or access network resources. Intrusion detection systems (IDS) and intrusion prevention systems (IPS) are deployed to monitor and prevent such attacks, flagging and blocking suspicious network activities. In summary, wireless security encompasses a range of techniques and protocols designed to safeguard wireless networks, devices, and the transmitted data from unauthorized access, interception, tampering, and other security threats. By implementing robust security measures, organizations and individuals can ensure the confidentiality, integrity, and availability of their wireless network resources.

Zero Configuration Networking (Zeroconf)

Zero Configuration Networking (Zeroconf) refers to a set of protocols and techniques that allow devices to automatically discover and connect to each other on a local network without the need for manual configuration or the presence of a centralized server. Zeroconf provides a simplified process for networking devices, eliminating the need for users to manually assign IP addresses or configure DNS settings. It operates on the principle of "plug and play," enabling devices to seamlessly connect and communicate with each other without any user intervention. Zeroconf consists of various protocols that work together to facilitate zero configuration networking. These protocols include: 1. Address Assignment: Zeroconf uses the Zeroconf Addressing Protocol (ZAP), which dynamically assigns unique IP addresses to devices on a network. With ZAP, devices can automatically obtain an IP address without requiring DHCP (Dynamic Host Configuration Protocol) servers. 2. Service Discovery: Zeroconf employs the Multicast DNS (mDNS) protocol for service discovery. Using mDNS, devices can discover other devices and services available on the network by sending and responding to multicast DNS queries. This allows applications and services to be located on the network without the need for a dedicated directory server. 3. Naming Resolution: Zeroconf uses the DNS Service Discovery (DNS-SD) protocol for resolving domain names to IP addresses when traditional DNS servers are not available. DNS-SD enables devices to discover and resolve the IP addresses associated with specific services or devices on the local network. By combining these protocols, Zeroconf simplifies the networking process, enabling devices to seamlessly connect and communicate with each other. It eliminates the need for manual configuration or the presence of a centralized infrastructure, making it ideal for use in ad hoc networks, peer-to-peer setups, home networks, and small office environments. In conclusion, Zero Configuration Networking (Zeroconf) is a set of protocols and techniques that facilitate automatic device discovery and connectivity on a local network, without the need for manual configuration or the presence of a centralized server. It simplifies the networking process, allowing devices to seamlessly connect and communicate with each other using dynamically assigned IP addresses and service discovery mechanisms.

Zero-Day Attack Vector

A zero-day attack vector refers to a type of network attack that exploits unpatched vulnerabilities in software or hardware before the developers or vendors are even aware of them. It is called "zero-day" because it takes place on the same day that the vulnerability is discovered, leaving no time for the developers to create and distribute a fix or patch. These attacks target unknown vulnerabilities, which means that they can bypass existing security measures and go undetected for an extended period of time. This allows hackers to gain unauthorized access to a system, steal sensitive data, install malware or ransomware, or carry out other malicious activities.

Zero-Day Exploit

A zero-day exploit refers to a type of cybersecurity vulnerability or attack that takes advantage of a previously unknown software flaw. The term "zero-day" is derived from the fact that developers and users have zero days to prepare for or defend against these attacks since the flaw is undiscovered until it is exploited. This lack of awareness and preparation makes zero-day exploits particularly dangerous and difficult to prevent or mitigate. In the context of networking, zero-day exploits can target various network devices, protocols, or services. For example, an attacker may discover a vulnerability in a widely-used networking protocol such as TCP/IP or DNS and exploit it to gain unauthorized access, disrupt services, or steal sensitive information. The exploit may take advantage of flaws in the protocol implementation, unauthorized features, or design weaknesses. Network administrators and cybersecurity professionals rely on vulnerability assessment tools and regular software updates to detect and patch known vulnerabilities. However, zero-day exploits pose a significant challenge as there is no prior knowledge or available fix at the time of discovery. This means that even organizations with well-developed security measures can fall victim to these attacks. Zero-day exploits are often used by skilled and well-resourced hackers, such as state-sponsored actors or sophisticated cybercriminals, to gain a strategic advantage and infiltrate targeted systems without detection. The attacking party typically seeks to exploit the vulnerability silently, allowing them to maintain persistence, establish control, or exfiltrate valuable data. Once a zero-day exploit is discovered, the responsible party, which can be a security researcher, the affected vendor, or a third party, will typically work to develop and release a patch or mitigation strategy as quickly as possible. Additionally, network administrators and system owners should update their software and maintain strong monitoring and incident response capabilities to detect and respond to any potential zero-day exploits.

Zero-Day Vulnerability

A zero-day vulnerability, in the context of networking, refers to a software vulnerability that is unknown to the software vendor or developers. It is called "zero-day" because there are zero days or time available for the developers to fix the vulnerability before it is exploited by attackers. This means that the vulnerability is unexpected and unpatched, leaving the affected software or system exposed to potential attacks. These vulnerabilities can be found in various networking components such as routers, switches, firewalls, and even in network operating systems. Exploiting a zero-day vulnerability in a network can result in unauthorized access to sensitive data, the compromise of network security, or the disruption of services. Zero-day vulnerabilities are highly sought after by cybercriminals, as they provide an advantage for launching targeted attacks against organizations. The attackers may use methods like spear phishing, social engineering, or malware to gain access to a network and exploit the vulnerability. Once they have exploited the vulnerability, they can install additional malware, steal data, create backdoors, or even take control of the entire network. The discovery and exploitation of zero-day vulnerabilities can have severe consequences for organizations, as their networks become vulnerable to attacks that cannot be easily detected or prevented. These vulnerabilities are typically sold on the black market or kept secret by organized hacker groups, making them difficult to defend against. Additionally, the lack of available patches or fixes from software vendors makes it challenging for organizations to protect themselves against these vulnerabilities. To mitigate the risks associated with zero-day vulnerabilities, organizations should implement proactive network security measures. This includes regularly updating and patching software and network devices, monitoring network traffic for suspicious activities, and employing intrusion detection and prevention systems. Implementing strong access controls, user authentication, and network segmentation can also help minimize the potential impact of a zero-day vulnerability. In summary, a zero-day vulnerability in networking refers to an undisclosed software vulnerability that is unknown to the software vendor. It poses a significant risk to the security and functionality of network systems, as it can be exploited by attackers before any patches or fixes are available. Organizations should prioritize proactive security measures to protect their networks from potential zero-day attacks.

Zombie Computer

A zombie computer, also known as a zombie or bot, refers to a device that has been compromised by malicious software or malware, allowing it to be controlled remotely by an attacker. In the context of networking, a zombie computer is a device that has been infected with malware and is used to carry out unauthorized activities without the knowledge or consent of the device owner. These infected devices typically include personal computers, laptops, servers, and even IoT devices such as routers, cameras, and smart appliances. Once a device becomes infected, it becomes part of a botnet, which is a network of compromised devices controlled by a command-and-control (C&C) server. Once a computer becomes a zombie, it can be used to launch various types of attacks, such as distributed denial-of-service (DDoS) attacks, spam campaigns, or participate in other illegal activities, all while remaining disguised and seemingly innocent to its owner. The zombie computer essentially becomes a puppet, carrying out instructions from the attacker or botmaster. The security risks associated with zombie computers are numerous. First and foremost, they can be used to launch large-scale attacks that can cripple websites and online services. These attacks can result in financial losses, reputational damage, and disruption of critical services. Moreover, zombie computers can be used to spread malware, steal sensitive information, or engage in fraudulent activities, such as phishing. Protecting against zombie computers requires a multi-layered approach to security. It is crucial for individuals and organizations to regularly update their software and operating systems, as many infections occur due to outdated or unpatched vulnerabilities. Installing and maintaining reputable antivirus and anti-malware software is also essential, as they can help detect and remove malicious software. Furthermore, it is important to exercise caution when downloading files or clicking on links from unknown sources, as these can often be vehicles for malware.

Implementing strong passwords and utilizing two-factor authentication can also help prevent unauthorized access to devices. Additionally, network administrators should monitor network traffic for any suspicious activity and employ firewalls and intrusion detection systems to identify and block potential threats. In conclusion, a zombie computer is a device that has been infected with malware and can be controlled remotely by an attacker. These compromised devices are part of a botnet and can be used to carry out malicious activities without the knowledge or consent of the device owner. Protecting against zombie computers requires a combination of proactive security measures, regular software updates, and user vigilance in order to mitigate the risks associated with these threats.